LINDLEY J. STILES
Professor of Education for Interdisciplinary Studies
Northwestern University
ADVISORY EDITOR TO DODD, MEAD & COMPANY

CRITICISM, CONFLICT,
and CHANGE

Readings in American Education

i

CRITICISM, and

Readings in

DODD, MEAD & COMPANY

Edited by

EMANUEL HURWITZ, Jr.

College of Education
University of Illinois at Chicago Circle

and

ROBERT MAIDMENT

Formerly School of Education, Northwestern University

CONFLICT, CHANGE

American Education

New York   1970

EDITOR'S INTRODUCTION

The title of this book, *Criticism, Conflict, and Change*, aptly identifies the state of education today—at all levels. Controversy has become a way of life for schools, colleges, and universities. To learn to live with the crosscurrents of criticism and conflict while making the right kinds of changes, in the right ways, is the challenge confronting citizens as well as professionals who are responsible for the educational enterprise.

The task of charting the future course for education is complicated by the social tensions that generate in a pluralistic society, such as ours, as we search for ways to give everyone a piece of the educational action. It is frustrating because traditional and cherished practices are being discredited while workable alternatives are yet to be discovered. It is difficult because the roots of emerging patterns are multidisciplinary in character. They stem from organizational theory and research in various branches of the behavioral sciences as well as from the refined practice in such diverse applied fields as law, economics, political science, engineering, business management, public health, social administration, and religion as well as education itself. In addition, new communications and data processing technologies are changing learning, teaching, counseling, and administrative processes.

The function of a text and resource book is to assimilate and organize as much as possible of the available pertinent theory, research, and successful practice for quick and easy study. This book accomplishes this mission with admirable effectiveness. It is interdisciplinary in its scholarship, qualitative in the content selected, objective with respect to competing ideas, and timely in terms of the help provided. In addition, the authors have given the presentation an organization that highlights divergent theory and evidence against a background of the critical dimensions of the educational dilemma. Their own analysis of each dimension guides the reader through a logical consideration of the whole.

The editors of this book are dynamic scholars who are pointing the way to educational change today. Dr. Emanuel Hurwitz, Jr., has taught at the secondary and university levels and is now an active administrator in higher education. His wide study of the literature of education and other fields plus his own background in writing have added strength to the editorial partnership. Dr. Robert Maidment, the senior editor, who

v

is primarily responsible for the conception of this book, has had a wide range of experience in elementary, secondary, and higher education, in both teaching and administration, and is presently on assignment with the institutional management unit of one of the nation's leading management consultant firms. He has held a John Hay Fellowship and served as a consultant to schools throughout the nation. Together these two scholars have produced a book that will be useful to everyone concerned about the future of education in the United States, particularly to young people who are looking ahead to ascertain how they may help to bring about the kind of change that is needed to match the times.

LINDLEY J. STILES

PREFACE

This reader was nearly self-organized. The three-word title, *Criticism, Conflict, and Change,* describes most recent contributions to educational literature. Again, based upon these writings, the seven sections, or "dimensions," formed natural groupings of content emphasis. Finally, the contributions were qualitatively self-selecting. The editors simply blended the efforts. The resulting mosaic, we believe, is highly representative of the interdisciplinary forces and factors which characterize the educational enterprise.

Certain characteristics of this reader warrant specific mention:

1. *The Use of Primary Sources.* The political, social, and legal dimensions, for example, include selections from case studies, field reports, and court decisions.
2. *The Use of Criticism and Conflict as Energizing Elements.* The arbitrary juxtaposition of selections expressing divergent viewpoints enables involvement in controversy.
3. *The Inclusion of Readings by Spokesmen External to the Establishment.* Many selections were written by articulate academicians working outside the educational arena.
4. *The Insistence upon High-Quality Selections.* Not only do the contributors have something to say, they say it well.
5. *The Emphasis upon the Nature of Change.* The entire contents reflect emerging patterns in American education.

The editors gratefully acknowledge the contributors' willingness to permit reprinting and, in some cases, a shortening of their material. Our initial effort produced a reader too ponderous for a one-volume publication. To those contributors whose writings were sacrificed, know that the choices were difficult. Finally, a note of appreciation to Mrs. Genia Graves, Managing Editor of the College Department, and her staff who helped shape and refine the scope of this reader.

EMANUEL HURWITZ, JR.
ROBERT MAIDMENT

CONTENTS

Section Seven
THE TEACHER—EDUCATION DIMENSION   444

THE CRITICAL DIMENSION

The selections in this volume were grouped for convenience and emphasis. The strain of thought within each dimension is not always pure. The contributors to this initial section have written critically about educational issues. Hopefully, their efforts will encourage the reader to explore further and wrestle with some of the basic dilemmas which have consistently beleaguered Americans.

Shakespeare's tale, "full of sound and fury signifying nothing," is uncharacteristic of the American's growing concern over public support of his schools. He is becoming increasingly involved with the intricacies of schooling. The apathetic disposition so frequently noted only a decade ago has crystallized into a posture of enlightenment, enthusiasm, and in some sectors, an energy bordering on militancy.

Such ageless questions as what constitutes an educated man or what are the priorities for education seem to persist. Do educational goals really change? If so, are they currently in need of revision? Our schools have departed dramatically from the 3 R's of Recitation, Rote memory, and Regurgitation. This volume suggests that Americans are deeply enmeshed in the era of the 3 C's—Criticism, Conflict, and Change. This section and those following reflect these three characteristics quite emphatically.

Perceptive, lucid views on the nature of educational processes are needed. Perhaps a "philosophic mindedness," described by Philip G. Smith in *Reflective Thinking* as "a comprehensiveness of thought, penetration in thinking, and flexibility of thinking," is an initial response to the seemingly hopeless plight of our urban schools and the currently prevailing unrest regarding the educational enterprise. Only a short decade ago tradition, textbooks, and teachers colleges were prominent forces influencing the design of American education. Today, parental expectations, various civil rights groups and militants—both teachers and learners—are dominant influences. These demands require thoughtful responses.

American education has not been in clear focus, nor have its critics frequently provided the needed clarity. The criticism, however, is welcomed. Borrowing David Harum's aphorism, "all dogs need fleas," one can assert that all educational systems need critics. The verbal slings and arrows often promote intro-

1

spection and accelerate change. But, change for its own sake? Administrative tinkering? Bandwagon addiction? The critical pieces included in this section do provide options. The reader is again invited to dissect and discuss those issues which evoke criticism, conflict, and change.

The problems persist; the solutions await. Unfortunately, we have been inclined to put bandaids on compound fractures to effect educational cures. The crucial issue of the seventies is very likely to be the education of American youth. Our very survival as a nation may well depend upon imaginative and courageous approaches to quality education for all learners.

1

If a nation expects to be ignorant and free, in a state of civilization, it expects what never was and never will be.

THOMAS JEFFERSON

R. Freeman Butts

SEARCH FOR FREEDOM—
THE STORY OF AMERICAN EDUCATION

The story of American education needs constant retelling. It is a story that few of us know well enough. Yet, education directly involves more than one-half of all Americans and indirectly affects the lives, welfare, security, and freedom of everyone. Students, teachers, and other citizens cannot afford to ignore it.

Fortunately, most Americans have faith in education and believe that educated young people are better equipped to "get ahead" in the world than uneducated ones are. However, the really important reason for believing in the value of education is that it can be the foundation of freedom. In the first place, a truly democratic society must rest upon the knowledge, intelligence, and wisdom of all the people. Without the proper kind of education available to everyone, a free society cannot long endure. Therefore, all people must have the kind of education that will fit them for freedom as responsible citizens.

In the second place, without the proper kind of education, the individual will not be able to develop his own powers as a person. He will not

From R. Freeman Butts, "Search for Freedom—The Story of American Education," *NEA Journal*, March, 1960, pp. 33–48. Reprinted by permission of the author.

be able to give direction to his own action and thought as he may wish. He will not be able to decide wisely for himself what he should do or think.

Freedom from arbitrary restraint, from compulsion, or from tyranny is essential for the free man, but that alone is not enough. If each person is to achieve the genuine freedom of self-direction and self-fulfillment, he must have an education befitting a free man.

Now, what kind of education will best develop the free citizen and the free person? This is the persistent question that runs through the story of American education. It has been answered in different ways at different times in our history. It is still being debated vigorously, and sometimes angrily, today.

This question is so important that every American—and above all, every student and teacher—should make it his business to learn all he can about it. The first requirement is a knowledge of the history of American education. Here are some of the fundamental questions that mark the high lights of the story:

1. What kind of schools and colleges will promote maximum freedom in society?

● To what extent should a free society encourage public schools in contrast to private schools?

● Is freedom better served by religious schools or by secular schools?

● Is a free society better served by local control or by central control of schools?

● Should a free society maintain common schools and colleges open equally to all, or should it divide students into separate schools and colleges according to their race, religion, social class, prospective vocation, or intellectual ability?

2. What kind of educational program will promote maximum freedom for all individuals?

● Should schools and colleges stress practical training or purely intellectual studies?

● Should schools and colleges offer students preparation for many vocations or for just a few?

● Should educational methods stress learning by direct experience or by reading books?

● Should a liberal education be designed for the few or for the many?

If we can understand some of the major answers given to these questions during our history, we shall be on the way to understanding the central idea of American education.

I. Education Under Colonial Rule *(1600 to 1770's)*

For nearly 175 years, the source of governmental authority for the American colonies was the crown and parliament of England. The colonists were, however, ruled locally by legislative assemblies or by individual proprietors or by royal governors who received their authority from the English government in London.

This authority included jurisdiction over education. From the very beginning of American history, education was a function of government. It continued to be so after the states were independent.

The various colonies, however, handled educational matters differently. In the New England colonies, the governing bodies not only exerted general authority over education but also established, supported, and directly administered their own schools.

For example, the colonial legislature of Massachusetts passed a law founding Harvard College in 1636; in the following years it took hundreds of actions concerning the college. In the 1630's, the governments of several towns in New England established schools under their direct jurisdiction and supervision.

In 1642 the colonial legislature of Massachusetts passed a general educational law applying to all parts of the colony. It required all parents to see that their children were taught to read, learn the major laws, know the catechism, and learn a trade. It authorized and required the town officials to see that parents obeyed the law and to levy fines upon those parents who disobeyed.

In 1647 the Massachusetts legislature passed a second law, this time requiring all towns of fifty or more families to appoint a teacher and permitting the towns to pay him out of public taxes if the people so voted. Such a teacher was to teach reading and writing. (We would call him an elementary-school teacher.) Furthermore, the law of 1647 required towns of one hundred or more families to appoint a teacher of Latin grammar. (We would call him a secondary-school teacher.)

The New England version of state authority in education came to this: The colonial government could require parents to have their children educated; the central government of the colony could require local towns to appoint teachers (establish schools); public funds could be raised by taxation to pay the teachers; and public teachers were subject to direct supervision and control by governmental authorities (either the town meeting as a whole or the selectmen or the education committee).

In the Southern colonies the colonial governments had the same legal authority to legislate on educational matters, but they did not pass laws requiring *all* children to be educated. They rather assumed, as in England, that any parent who could afford to educate his own children should do so by making individual arrangements with a private tutor or by sending them to a private school.

The Southern legislatures, however, did pass laws requiring that poor children and orphaned children be apprenticed to a trade and taught the rudiments of reading and religion by their masters.

The governmental attention in the South was directed mainly at lower-class underprivileged children who had no parents or whose parents could not care for them. Even so, the parish or county governments sometimes legislated on educational matters through their boards of vestrymen or magistrates.

Some efforts were even made in the colonial legislatures of Maryland, South Carolina, and Virginia to establish colony-wide systems of public schools. These were unsuccessful, not because there was no governmental authority for education, but because the people at that time did not believe they were necessary.

In the Middle Colonies the same governmental authority was used by the Dutch to establish public schools in New Netherland and by the Quakers in Pennsylvania. But a more tolerant policy toward religion had attracted several different religious denominations to these colonies.

Each group wanted its own religious principles taught in its own school. It was consequently more difficult to teach a single religious outlook in a public school open to children of different faiths than it had been in New England where most people were Congregationalists or in the South where most people were Anglicans.

In the eighteenth century the colonial governments began to permit the different religious groups to establish their own schools in which they could teach their own religious doctrines and their own languages (whether German, Dutch, French, or Swedish). In this way the state gave to religious and charitable bodies the right to conduct schools.

In like manner the colonial governments began to grant charters to small groups of businessmen or landowners. An educational charter gave these groups the right to incorporate as a board of trustees. They could then buy land, build buildings, appoint teachers, and generally manage a school.

Some of these corporate schools came to be known as "academies." One of the most famous was the Philadelphia Academy founded in 1751 by Benjamin Franklin. Others were the Newark Academy in Delaware, the Washington Academy in New Jersey, and the Dummer Academy and Phillips Academy in Massachusetts.

These incorporated academies made education attractive and available to children of middle-class merchants who could afford the tuition. At first it was unclear whether these denominational schools and incorporated academies were public or private schools, but eventually they came to be known as "private" schools in American terminology.

Other private schools were run by individual teachers as profit-making, business enterprises. In the seacoast cities of the eighteenth century these private teachers began to give young people direct preparation for jobs in commerce and trade. In general, the private-school teacher accepted or rejected students as he pleased. He charged what fees he could get, and he managed his affairs as he saw fit—so long as he had enough students to stay in business.

By contrast, the "public" school in the eighteenth century was a non-profit school under the supervision of a governmental agency or a cor-

porate board of control. The parents had the right to send their children
to it; the governing body set the fees and employed the teacher. Hence a
"public" school was not run for the teacher's private profit.

The standards of curriculum were established and the achievement of
pupils evaluated by the board of control, whether governmental or corporate. Later on, the corporate school came to be known as a "private"
school, because it was not operated directly by a governmental board.

In the seventeenth century the "public" or town schools of Massachusetts, Connecticut, and New Hampshire taught the doctrines of a
specific religion, that is, Congregational Calvinism. This was so because
the Congregational church was established by the law of the legislature
in those colonies.

This practice, known as "an establishment of religion," was common
throughout Europe in the sixteenth and seventeenth centuries. The laws
of the state required all people to accept the doctrines and rituals of the
established church and authorized punishment for those who objected.
The law levied taxes on everyone to support the ministers of the established church or churches. The Church of England, for example, was the
established church in several of the Southern colonies; therefore, orthodox Anglicanism was taught in their schools.

But in the course of the eighteenth century, the idea of religious freedom gained great headway in the American colonies. This meant that
such minority religious groups as Quakers, Presbyterians, Baptists,
Dutch Reformed, Lutherans, Methodists, Mennonites, and others gained
freedom to worship as they pleased. As a result, such groups did not wish
to send their children to town schools where their children would be
obliged to accept a religion in which they did not believe. The established churches would not at first consent to the removal of their religion
from the public schools.

The solution in the eighteenth century was to permit the minority
religious groups to establish their own schools. This meant that private
religious schools could operate alongside the public schools. Although
the public schools were weakened, this arrangement contributed to
freedom at a time when the majority religious groups insisted that the
public schools teach *their* religion and *only* their religion.

A few voices began to argue that if public schools did *not* teach a sectarian religion then all children could attend them freely. This was argued by William Smith in Pennsylvania, by William Livingston in New
York, and by Thomas Jefferson in Virginia.

But the time was not yet ripe for such a solution. Although it was a gain
for freedom to permit people to pursue their own way in religion and
education, most people were not yet convinced that *others* should have
the same freedoms *they* had. Nor were they convinced that an education
separated from specific religious doctrines was desirable. The search
for freedom continued.

Meanwhile, as people moved out of the New England towns and cities into the unsettled lands of the country, they could no longer send their children long distances back to the town schools. They therefore began to set up their own local schools. This was the origin of the "district" school.

Representing the ultimate in local control, the district system reflected a decline in central state control of schools as the eighteenth century came to a close. This system had the advantage that it kept the schools close to the people, but it had the disadvantage that some districts ran low-quality schools or none at all. Local control was no guarantee that the quality of schools would be uniformly high.

At the end of colonial rule, common schools in which children of different religions or races learned together were still the exception. It was generally felt that schools should perpetuate the religious or cultural beliefs of the sponsoring agency. Some groups did go so far as to try to set up schools for Indians. Few but Quakers tried to do so for Negroes.

Seldom was it argued in colonial times that the aim of education was to empower every individual to make the most of himself as a person. The first system of education set up in America served to maintain the class distinctions imported from Europe.

Children of poor, lower-class parents had no education at all or were bound out as apprentices to learn a trade. Children of upper-class parents (public officials, clergymen, wealthy landowners) were expected to have an education appropriate to their station in life. The New England colonies broke this pattern somewhat when they required the towns to provide a minimum amount of education for *all* children.

Not all children actually received an education, but the principle was established that a commonwealth must rest upon an educated citizenry even if the education amounted only to bare literacy. Added to this was the Protestant belief that all adherents to the true faith should be able to read the Bible for themselves so that they could know the grounds and reasons for their faith. In any case, the New England town schools went a long way in seeing that a large number of their children received some education. This was the first step toward an education for freedom.

Learning to read, write, recite the catechism, and possibly do some arithmetic was the essence of a beginning or elementary education. In the earliest days, school books were rare and materials were scarce. A common device for teaching reading was a hornbook, a piece of wood with the alphabet and Lord's Prayer on it. The child could carry this around with him until he had learned everything on it.

Somewhat later in the seventeenth century, books began to be used; the most famous was *The New England Primer*. This consisted of the alphabet, simple syllables, words, sentences, and stories, all of a religious and moral character. A child may have spent two or three years obtaining this kind of elementary education. Taking the thirteen colonies as a whole, probably only one child in ten went to school at all.

What we would call secondary education was offered in Latin grammar schools. The immediate reason for stress on Latin was that Harvard College required it for admission because the main bodies of knowledge throughout Europe since the days of the Roman Republic and the Roman Empire had been written in Latin.

Even though the common languages of the people (vernaculars) were being used more widely by the sixteenth and seventeenth centuries, it was still the custom for an educated person to know Latin—and some Greek, if possible.

So the Latin grammar school was designed to prepare sons of the privileged classes for college in order that they might eventually enter one of the "higher" professions, such as the ministry, law, medicine, teaching, or simply that of "gentleman." Relatively few in the total population were expected to attain these callings in life. Most were expected to be tradesmen, farmers, workers, mechanics, or servants. For these an elementary education was considered sufficient—or even more than necessary.

In the course of the eighteenth century, however, cities and towns grew rapidly in size, trade and commerce increased, immigration rose, and goods and services were much more in demand than in the seventeenth century.

The cry was heard that the old classical Latin education was no longer appropriate for preparing young people to engage in these new important occupations of making goods, distributing them, and selling them. Education, some said, should become more practical, not solely intellectual or literary.

Two types of intermediate or secondary schools tried to meet this need. Some were "English" schools, so called because they were taught in English rather than in Latin. The instructors tried to offer whatever studies the young people desired, for example, English language; French, German, Spanish, Italian (languages useful for trade); mathematics (useful for navigation and surveying); commercial arithmetic and bookkeeping (useful in business); geography, history, and drawing (useful for leisure).

In the early decades of the eighteenth century these private-venture schools responded to the needs of the growing middle classes (merchants and tradesmen). They gave an education directly aimed at occupations other than the learned professions, and they catered to girls as well as to boys.

A second type of practical school was the academy, which was usually residential and often under the auspices of a religious denomination or a nonsectarian board of control. The curriculum of these schools, at least as proposed by Benjamin Franklin, was likely to be much broader than that of the Latin grammar school. It might include geography, history, science, modern languages, and the arts and music, as well as the classical languages and mathematics.

Both of these types of schools contributed to freedom by increasing the range of occupations for which they gave preparation. In this way an increasing number of young people from all social classes could gain a larger measure of self-direction and improve their position in society. Both types of schools were frowned upon by the classicists, but the academy survived the opposition because it met the needs of the middle classes. It eventually drove the Latin grammar school out of existence.

In general, then, the colonial period saw gains for freedom in the growth of representative government, the spread of religious freedom, and the rise of energetic middle classes of free men in town and country alike. Education tried to respond to these social movements as well as to a growing liberalism in thought and belief.

At the beginning of the colonial period, orthodoxies in theology, philosophy, and politics dominated the schools. Children were looked upon as sinful creatures who could be ruled only by harsh discipline, fear, and unrelenting obedience. By the end of the period, a growing liberalism meant that, here and there, children and adults alike were treated more humanely and less brutally. Human dignity and respect for persons were safer than they had been.

During most of the colonial period, education for developing a free person moved slowly and haltingly. For the most part, education at all levels was concerned as much with moral training as with intellectual training. If anything, the moral was considered more important and closely bound up with orthodox religion. Teachers were expected to conform in their beliefs to the dictates of whatever group controlled the schools. It was seldom argued that the teacher had a claim to freedom of teaching as an essential characteristic of a free society, a claim to deal freely with ideas even though they might be distasteful to the immediate managers of the school.

The notion that education had a clear responsibility for enabling each individual to develop himself to the utmost was beginning to be stated but was not yet widely accepted. Building schools for a colonial society prior to the Revolutionary War was a dress rehearsal for freedom, not the main performance.

II. A Century of Republican Education* *(1770's to 1870's)*

From the 1770's to the 1870's, Americans planned, built, changed, argued, and fought over the kinds of free institutions that should replace colonial rule. One of these institutions was education. As they set up and operated a republican form of government dedicated to equality, de-

---

° *The terms* republican *and* democratic *are used in their general sense in this feature and do not refer to political parties.*

mocracy, and freedom, they found that they needed an educational system appropriate to such a government.

In many different ways they said that if a republican government—or society—were to prosper and endure, then the people who elected the government, held office, made laws, enforced laws, and consented to be ruled must be educated as responsible citizens.

James Madison, father of the Constitution and author of the Bill of Rights, put it this way:

A popular Government, without popular information, or the means of acquiring it, is but a Prologue to a Farce or Tragedy; or, perhaps both. Knowledge will forever govern ignorance; and a people who mean to be their own Governors must arm themselves with the power which knowledge gives.

But this was not easy to do. The people who had won the Revolutionary War—these so-called Americans—were not really Americans, at least *not yet*. They were English, Scottish, French, German, Dutch, Swedish, and a good many more. And they were soon to be Irish, Italian, Hungarian, Polish, and Russian as well. They spoke different languages and they had different customs. Some had no tradition of self-government and others were fiercely proud or jealous of rule by others.

When it was finally decided that they should all learn the same language and the same principles of republican government, how was this to be done?

The answer was that it could best be done by a common school, taught in English, to which all the children of all the people could go together and learn how to live together and govern themselves.

But some people were poorer and some richer; some had good manners and others were coarse and rude. Should *all* these people really be educated?

Yes, they must be—if free government is to endure.

Well, but who is to pay for the poor ones?

Everyone must pay for all. If there are weak spots anywhere, the whole community of freedom is weakened. So the common schools must be supported by taxes paid by all.

All right, but who is to control these schools?

The only institution of a free society which serves everyone equally and is controlled by everyone is the government. So the government should control the common schools. And to keep the schools close to the people, the state and local governments, rather than the national government, should control the schools.

But won't the schools be subject to political and partisan prejudice?

Well, they might be, so we must create something genuinely new, something that will give all the people their say but keep the schools free of narrow, partisan politics. This can be done by a series of local boards of education subject to but separate from the executive, legislative, and judicial branches of government.

These school boards, often elected directly by the people, could constitute a kind of "fourth branch of government." They would exert direct control over local education under the general authority set up by the state governments and subject to the guarantees of equality and freedom laid down in the United States Constitution and applying to all Americans.

So far so good, but what about religious education? Don't all these Americans with different religions have freedom to run their own schools under the First Amendment of the Constitution and under their state constitutions?

Yes, indeed, they do. But each American will have to decide for himself whether the education that supports a free society should be conducted in separate schools in which religion provides the fundamental framework for all studies or in common schools devoted primarily to the whole range of free institutions in America. If they decide the first way, the children will be divided into separate schools for their entire education and this division will be along religious lines. If the second way, the children will attend the same public school together for their common education and only be separated for their religious education, which can be conducted as may be desired by the home or by the church or by the synagogue.

In the century of republican education, most Americans chose the common school, controlled and supported in common, and embracing a nonsectarian religious outlook.

Their primary concern was to design a universal, free, public school that would promote free institutions and free citizenship. For the first one hundred years of the Republic, the need for creating the common bonds and loyalties of a free community was paramount.

Less attention was given to the claims of diversity and difference as the essence of freedom for individuals. This came later when the Union had been established, made secure against internal opposition, defended against outside invaders, and preserved despite a war between the states themselves.

The republican ideal of the first century of nationhood gave the following answers regarding the control of education:

A free society required public elementary schools to provide the basic information, literacy, and moral teachings required by every free man. For most Americans the term "free man" was limited to white men, until the Civil War legally introduced Negroes to citizenship. Private elementary schools continued to exist but they were declining in numbers and in importance by the 1870's.

Under the effective and determined leadership of an extraordinary galaxy of "public-school men," the idea of universal common schooling was widely accepted in the new United States during the first half of the nineteenth century. Outstanding among these were Horace Mann and James G. Carter in Massachusetts, Henry Barnard in Connecticut, Calvin Stowe in Ohio, Caleb Mills in Indiana, John D. Pierce in Michigan, Ninian Edwards in Illinois, Calvin Wiley in North Carolina, and Charles F. Mercer in Virginia. These men and others made speeches before thousands of people; wrote hundreds of pamphlets, articles, and reports; organized scores of groups and societies to agitate for common schools; and held dozens of positions in state governments or school systems.

They argued that the payment of tuition for schooling was unfair to children of poor parents, who could not pay for an education. They argued that the older forms of public support, like land grants from the federal Land Ordinances of 1785 and 1787, would not support schools on the vast scale now necessary.

They argued that the term "free school" should no longer mean a school in which only the poor children were given free education and all others paid tuition.

They argued that class distinctions could be lessened only when a "free school" meant that *all* children were given a free education together and when the entire school system was supported by taxes levied upon everyone.

Aiding their efforts were the newly formed labor unions, which demanded that the public schools provide universal education.

The states gradually accepted this idea of a free public school. The state legislatures passed laws *permitting* local school districts to tax themselves for such schools; they sometimes gave state funds to *encourage* local districts to tax themselves; and they finally *required* all local districts to tax themselves and establish public schools.

By these means, the local freedom of districts to ignore schooling for their children gave way to the larger freedom to be gained by a total population enlightened by education of all. Local control by districts was gradually limited by requirements set by state constitutions, state legislatures, state boards of education, and state superintendents of schools. It was decided that a free society would be better served if education were planned by the central authority of the states rather than left wholly to the completely decentralized control of local school boards. This was not done without bitter conflict, for many believed that state, as opposed to local, control would be undemocratic and destroy freedom.

But in the 1820's, 1830's, and 1840's it was decided that a state government, responsive to public control, could serve freedom as well as, if not better than, the hundreds of local school districts could do. If a local district were left free to provide a poor education or no education at all for its children, those children would be deprived of their birthright to an education that would prepare them for free citizenship. Thereby, the state's own freedom would be endangered.

A smaller freedom must be limited in the interests of a greater freedom. And to guarantee the larger freedom, the state must exert its authority to see to it not only that schools were available to all but that all children actually attended school. Massachusetts led the way by passing its compulsory attendance law in 1852.

The solution was a genuinely creative one. Authority for providing education was defined in state constitutions and in state laws. State authority for education was carried out by state superintendents of schools responsible to a state board of education, elected by the people or appointed by the governor. New York State created the office of state superintendent of schools in 1812. Massachusetts established a state board of education in 1837 with Horace Mann as secretary, and Connecticut did likewise in 1839 with Henry Barnard as secretary. Other states followed.

These state agencies could then set minimum standards for all the schools of the state. Meanwhile, the direct management of schools would be left in the hands of locally elected school boards, local superintendents, and locally appointed teachers. Local management served the cause of flexibility, diversity, and freedom.

This arrangement was designed to assure that schools would serve the whole *public* and would be controlled by the *public* through special boards of education, not through the regular agencies of the state or local governments. This is why in America we use the term "public schools," not simply "state schools" or "government schools," as they are often called in those countries that have centralized systems of education.

Since the United States Constitution had not mentioned education as a function of the federal government, the free states after the Revolution reclaimed the authority over education that had been the prerogative of the colonial legislatures.

But the United States Constitution and the state constitutions *did* proclaim freedom of religion and separation of church and state as one of the essentials of republican government. That is, neither the federal government nor state governments could interfere in the affairs of churches or use public funds to support them. Therefore, the states could not give public money to schools under the control of churches.

But what about religious instruction in the common public schools? It was soon evident that if common schools taught the doctrines of a particular church they would violate the freedom of conscience of all those who did not agree.

Could the common schools find a common religious outlook and teach that? Many Protestants thought so. They tried to find the common religious doctrines of Christianity and they found them in the Bible. If the schools would teach only the nonsectarian principles of Christianity as contained in the Bible, they argued, all sects would be satisfied. This might have been the case if America had remained exclusively Protestant.

But immigration had brought increased numbers of Roman Catholics and Jews. Besides, many Americans had never officially belonged to any church. Catholics charged that the so-called "nonsectarian" schools were really Protestant in character and that they were therefore sectarian. So Catholics established their own schools and many demanded a share in the public tax funds to support them. Most Protestants and Jews opposed the giving of public money to parochial schools.

Most states finally decided to prohibit any sectarian control over common schools and to prohibit use of public money for private schools under sectarian control. Especially bitter struggles between Protestants and Catholics were decided for the time being by legislation in New York in 1842 and by constitutional amendment in Massachusetts in 1855. Nearly every state had a similar struggle and enacted similar laws.

By the end of the first century of republican education, the general decision was that a free society was better served if the majority of children went to common, nonsectarian schools than if they went to separate, sectarian religious schools. This made it possible for the United States to build a universal system of free elementary schools sooner than any other country in the world.

The line of argument went like this: Nonsectarianism would provide a greater measure of national unity than could be achieved when each sectarian group shepherded its own children into its own schools. The range of communication among children would be restricted if each group continued to run its own schools differently in religion and language from others. Separate schools would create and perpetuate divisions among the people—thus narrowing their outlooks and reducing free interchange of ideas. Free common schools would more certainly serve the cause of free institutions.

At the end of the first century of the Republic, secondary schools, however, were still largely in private and religious hands. This fact did not seem undesirable to most Americans of that particular period.

The private academies provided considerable opportunity to those who could afford some education beyond the essentials. Likewise, most of the 200 colleges were under private and religious control. This, too, seemed reasonable to the majority of Americans at that time: Elementary education for all at public expense would be sufficient to guarantee the basic security of a republican government; advanced education for *leadership* in the state and in the professions could then be obtained privately by those who could afford it.

A few spokesmen, however, began to argue that a free society needed "free" secondary and higher institutions as well as free elementary schools. The public high school, for example, appeared as early as 1821 in Boston. The idea spread rapidly, but the public high schools did not dominate the secondary-school field till the late nineteenth century.

Despite the advocates of free and equal education for all, the era of republican education tried to get along with common schools at the elementary level, but with secondary and higher institutions divided along denominational lines. In general, while the elementary schools served everyone, the academies and colleges and universities catered to the wealthier and upper social classes rather than to the ordinary people.

The major failure to achieve the reformers' goal of a common universal school was the system of segregated schools for Negroes, which appeared occasionally in the North as well as generally in the South. In fact, it was the Roberts case in the Massachusetts Supreme Court in 1849 which set forth the principle that separate schools for Negroes were permissible so long as their facilities were equal to those of the white schools. Charles Sumner's argument that separate schools violated the equal rights of Negroes was rejected by the court, but, even so, Massachusetts and other Northern states moved soon thereafter to abolish their segregated schools by law.

Turning now to the kind and quality of education achieved in the first century of the Republic, we find the main elements of the common-school curriculum continued to be reading, writing, and arithmetic. These three R's were supposed to give the elements of literacy and the intellectual tools necessary for acquiring the knowledge and "popular information" of which Madison spoke.

But, said the school reformers, the citizen of the new Republic needed more than this—much more. He needed a knowledge of history and geography to instill feelings of patriotism, loyalty, and national pride. He needed moral teachings to instill habits of "republican" character. And he needed some practical studies, like bookkeeping or manual training, so that he could get and keep a job.

The common school was designed to do more than give intellectual training. It was to provide citizenship training, character education, and a means by which every child might advance up the economic and social scale as far as his talents would carry him.

By providing such equal opportunity, the common school would protect free institutions. It would promote progress and prosperity; it would reduce poverty and prevent crime. This was a big order to hand to the schools, but the optimism, energy, and faith of the times all prodded the schools to try to do their share—sometimes more than their share—in making the American dream come true.

The "new" school had to have new methods as well as new subjects. Such school reformers as Joseph Neef and Horace Mann argued that the customary strict discipline, corporal punishment, and slavish memorizing of textbooks were not good enough to carry the burden the school must carry. They therefore argued for the enthusiasm, excitement, interest, and eager learning that could come with a more humane and sympathetic attitude toward children.

Of course, the conservatives charged that the reformers would spoil the children if they spared the rod, but the reformers persisted despite the opposition.

The main trouble was that the teachers were not trained to deal with small children constructively. Would the liberal-arts colleges provide this training? Some proposals were made—at Amherst, at Brown, at Michigan, and elsewhere—that they should do so, but the colleges were not interested. So, entirely new institutions called normal schools were created to give their whole attention to the training of elementary-school teachers.

The first of these were founded as private normal schools in the 1820's by Samuel R. Hall at Concord, Vermont, and by James G. Carter at Lexington, Massachusetts. The first state normal school was opened in 1839 at Lexington, and the idea eventually spread throughout the country.

The normal schools taught young people of high-school age how to teach the elementary-school subjects. Compared with the better colleges of the day, their quality was low, but they made possible the rapid building of the common school systems in the several states. They raised school teaching above the level of incidental apprenticeship and began the process of making it a profession, narrow though the training was in the beginning. If the colleges of liberal arts had been as much interested in school teaching as they were in law, medicine, or other professions, the quality and status of the elementary-school teacher might have been higher much sooner than they were.

The curriculum of the secondary schools also began to respond to the political and economic progress of the times. The academies, replacing the Latin grammar schools, taught a wider range of subjects. Thus, students began to have some freedom of choice of studies. And some academies opened their doors to girls, a notable victory for freedom. By the 1870's some 6000 academies dotted the educational landscape.

But the common-school reformers felt that the private academies could never do the job that needed to be done. They therefore argued that free public high schools should be created to provide a practical education for those boys and girls who would not or could not go on to college.

Offering a practical nonclassical curriculum to youth who could live at home while attending secondary school, the public high school was destined to become ever more popular after the Civil War. It added to the range of vocations for which the schools prepared and in this way opened up possibilities of self-improvement through careers that had never before been within reach of the majority of youth.

III. Nearly a Century of Democratic Education *(1870's to 1960's)*

Whereas the republican ideal had been to provide *some* education for a few, the democratic goal was to provide *as much education as possible for all.* The keynote of the century of democratic education was "more education for more people." It had its drawbacks, its setbacks, and its ups and downs, but nothing seemed able to stop for long the surge to education as the essence of the search for freedom.

The march to the schools came faster, the lines stretched longer, and the students grew older as the second century of the Republic moved from the 1870's to the 1960's. By 1900 the great majority of children aged six to thirteen were in elementary schools; by 1960 over ninety-nine per cent were in attendance. Universal elementary schooling for all children had been won.

More remarkable, however, was the march to the secondary schools. By 1900 about ten per cent of children aged fourteen to seventeen were actually in school; in 1930 more than fifty per cent attended; and by 1960 nearly ninety per cent were attending. This comes close to universal secondary education, something not dreamed of by the republican leaders of the first century of nationhood.

In 1760 the average colonist may have had two to three years of schooling; by 1960 the average American had ten to eleven years of schooling. And the end has not been reached. The average years of schooling will probably go to twelve or even to fourteen within a decade or two.

Still more remarkable was the stepped-up tempo of the march to college. In 1910 about five per cent of all youth aged eighteen to twenty-one were attending college; by 1960 nearly forty per cent of all such youth were attending institutions beyond high school. Millions more were attending adult-education classes and courses of instruction being offered by business, industry, labor, the armed services, churches, and voluntary agencies. And education by television and other automatic devices had scarcely begun. The potentials were staggering.

How did all this happen and why? The story is complicated, but a few elements are clear. Republican education may have been sufficient for a society marked by a relatively small population scattered over large areas of rich land and relying mainly upon farming and trading for subsistence. But in a society that relied on science and technology, the situation was radically different.

Not only did the leaders, scholars, experts, and professional men need more and better education, but also the kind of education that *everyone* needed grew steadily greater in quantity and higher in quality. For *this* kind of industrial society, a democratic education would be necessary if freedom were to be maintained.

A society based on steam power, electric power, or nuclear power can be managed and controlled by relatively few people. Technical power leads to political and economic power. To prevent autocratic, dictatorial use of political and economic power by a few, everyone must have an education devoted to freedom. There is no other satisfactory way to limit political or economic power.

So it became increasingly clear that the opportunity to acquire an expanded and extended education must be made available to *all*, to the poor as well as to the rich, to the slow student as well as to the bright, to the South and West as well as to the North and East, to girls as well as to boys, to Negroes as well as to whites, to immigrants as well as to native-born, to Catholic and Jew as well as to Protestant and nonchurchgoer.

The century of democratic education took the doctrines of the common school and applied them almost completely to the secondary school and in part to the college. Equality of opportunity stood alongside freedom as the prime goals of education.

Let us see what happened to the organization and control of education in the age of democratic education:

The nineteenth-century solution to the problem of public and private schools came to this: A system of public institutions ranging from primary school to university, open for everyone as long as his abilities justify, is the best guarantor of a free society based upon equality of opportunity. Private institutions are free to operate alongside the public institutions, but these should be supported voluntarily and should not be given public funds.

In the 1870's a series of court cases (especially the Kalamazoo case in Michigan) agreed that the people of the states could establish and support public high schools with tax funds if they so desired. Thereupon the public high-school movement spread rapidly, and the private academy shrank in importance. Furthermore, all states passed compulsory attendance laws requiring attendance to at least age sixteen. Provision of public secondary schools thereupon became an *obligation* of the states, not just a voluntary matter for the local districts to decide.

Children were permitted to attend properly approved nonpublic schools as a way of meeting state attendance laws. This principle was affirmed by the United States Supreme Court in the Oregon case of 1925 (*Pierce v. Society of Sisters*).

States had the right to supervise, inspect, and set minimum standards for *all* schools and to require children to attend *some* school, but the state could not compel students to attend public schools if their parents preferred private schools. Freedom to have a say in the education of their children was a constitutional right of parents under the Fourteenth Amendment. Besides, private schools were valuable property which could not be destroyed by action of the state without due process of law.

By 1930 the preference of most Americans for public schools was clear; only about nine per cent of children attended nonpublic schools. The public policy hammered out in the nineteenth century was also clear: Public funds should not be used to support private schools. Beginning in the 1930's, however, the clamor began to rise again that the private schools should be given some public aid. Campaigns to get parents to send their children to private schools began to show results.

Today more than sixteen per cent of children are in nonpublic schools, a gain so spectacular that the American people have to face up to certain questions more directly than at any time since the 1830's: Shall we encourage private schools as well as public schools with public money? Is the present balance among public and private schools about right? If not, should we favor private or public schools?

Through the years, much of the controversy over public and private schools has been basically sectarian. Today more than ninety per cent of children attending nonpublic schools are enrolled in parochial schools conducted by the Roman Catholic Church. A whole series of laws and court cases in the nineteenth century decided that religious freedom and separation of church and state meant that the states could not give tax money to support private education. But from 1930 onward, exceptions began to be made.

The Cochran case in 1930 permitted Louisiana to spend tax funds to give free textbooks to children in private as well as public schools; the Everson case in 1947 permitted New Jersey to provide bus transportation for parochial-school pupils; in 1948 the School Lunch Act gave federal money to parochial schools even though state funds could not be so used. Advocates of parochial schools were now arguing that public funds should be used to pay for auxiliary services that benefited the child but were not direct aid to the school as such.

In recent decades, the arguments for diverting public funds to private schools have changed. It is now argued that the states should aid all parents to send their children to the kind of school they wish. This would not aid *schools;* it would aid parents to exercise their freedom of educational choice. So if parents want their children to go to religious schools, they should receive their fair share of tax funds. If they want their children to go to all-white schools, they should receive tax funds to help them do this. Obviously, the whole idea of a common school is now under severe attack.

What the American people will decide in the years to come is in doubt. In fact, the whole idea inherited from republican days that a free society rests upon a common school system maintained and controlled by the free government is in peril.

"Freedom" may come to mean that parents can divide up among themselves the public funds which had originally been designed to support a free educational system which in turn was designed to perpetuate the free society itself. Does freedom of choice for parents mean that the state is obligated to support and pay for that choice?

Such questions as these came to focus sharply in the problem of central and local control. If some towns or regions in a state could not or would not provide good schools for their children, should the children suffer, or should the state try to equalize the burden by giving financial aid to those towns? The answer turned out to be clear: Equalize the burden in fairness to the children.

Most states use tax money, raised all over the state, to support schools in all parts of the state wherever and whenever local property taxes did not provide enough money to operate good schools. Central control in state hands seemed desirable for the purpose.

But what about the federal government? Will the same answer be given? If some *states* cannot or will not provide good schools for their children, should the federal government try to equalize the burden by giving financial aid to the states? If all states try hard, and still some states cannot provide acceptable educational opportunity for all children, should the federal government step in and help out? By and large, the answer thus far has been no; a qualified no, but still no.

To be sure, the Land Ordinances of 1785 and 1787 and other grants gave millions of acres of land to the states for education; the Morrill Act of 1862 helped establish land-grant colleges; the Smith-Lever Act of 1914 supported agricultural and home-economics instruction; the Smith-Hughes Act of 1917 aided vocational education in high schools.

Emergency aid was given in the 1930's and the National Youth Administration and Civilian Conservation Corps helped youth in the depression; a bill was passed to provide aid for federally impacted school districts; the G. I. Bill of Rights helped millions of veterans of World War II and the war in Korea to get an education; and the National Defense Education Act of 1958 gave loans to students and supported specific programs in foreign-language training, science, guidance, and audio-visual methods.

But up to the present, the idea of federal-state partnership in public-school support has not been squarely faced by the federal government. For nearly a hundred years a whole series of bills had been introduced in Congress to achieve this purpose. Beginning with the Hoar bill, Perce bill, and Burnside bill of the 1870's and the several Blair bills in the 1880's, Republicans were the chief advocates of federal aid, but Democrats of the South were afraid that the federal government was trying to punish them and impose Northern ideas upon them.

In the decade between 1950 and 1960 it was the liberal Democrats from the North and West who tried to achieve federal aid, but were thwarted by economy-minded Republicans and by some Southern Democrats who feared federal imposition of integrated schools upon the South. Throughout the century many Roman Catholic leaders opposed federal aid unless it would help parochial as well as public schools.

The race issue, the religious issue, and the economy issue successfully blocked federal aid for decades. After the close of the Civil War, it was touch and go for a while whether federal action would result in equal educational opportunity for Negroes in the South.

The Fourteenth Amendment (1866) guaranteed "equal protection of the laws" to all citizens, but the federal education bills failed and the Civil Rights Act of 1875 was declared unconstitutional. The Southern states proceeded to set up segregated school systems, one system for Negroes and one for whites. The United States Supreme Court decision in *Plessy v. Ferguson* (1896) was taken to mean that separate school systems were permissible provided they had equal facilities.

In the 1940's a whole series of court cases began the process of gaining access for Negroes to the public institutions of the South—first to the universities and then to the schools. The historic decisions headed by the Brown case of May 17, 1954, reversed the "separate but equal" doctrine of Plessy and declared that segregated schools were inherently unequal even if each had "equal" amounts of money spent on it.

In the following years, case after case was taken to court to require boards of education to admit Negroes to the public schools, on an unsegregated basis.

Violence, often instigated by outside agitators, broke out in Clinton, Tennessee, and a number of other places; and federal troops were called to Little Rock, Arkansas, when the governor interfered with a federal court order to integrate the schools. Gradually, however, desegregation spread through the border states and by 1960 was being faced in the "Deep South."

Some Southern governors and legislatures tried to prevent integration by legal devices. Laws were passed to close the public schools, to give public money to parents so they could send their children to segregated private schools, and even to abolish the public-school system itself.

These actions posed the most serious threat to the ideals of both republican and democratic education it was possible to pose. Does a state have the right to abolish its "fourth branch of government"? What *is* essential to a "republican form of government" (as guaranteed in the United States Constitution) if public education is not? Could the principles of a free society withstand this onslaught safely?

If the demands for private religious education and the demands for private segregated education were joined by economy demands for reducing public-school budgets, the result could be a repudiation of the public-school idea itself and a return to the "voluntary" principle of the sixteenth and seventeenth centuries in Europe: Let those have an education who can pay for it; let education be fully private. Or, alternatively: Let us divide up the public moneys among competing racial and religious groups so they can set up their own private schools; let us have many free *private* educational systems.

In either of these cases, the central idea of American education would disappear. An unlimited role for free private enterprise in education would take the place of a limited role for free public enterprise. The freedom of segmented voluntary groups to work at cross purposes would replace the freedom of the people as a whole to work through a system of public schools. The 1960's will doubtless see the struggles heightened. How will the search for freedom come out?

Just as the keynote to *quantity* in education for the century of democratic education has been "more education for more people," so the keynote to *quality* in education has been "better education for all." Each decade had its reformers who demanded better education than the schools were then offering, but there has been little agreement concerning what is "better."

Different reformers have demanded different measures at different times. As the times changed, the schools were behind the times for different reasons. Nowhere else in the world have so many people been so much concerned about education so much of the time—and almost never has everyone been satisfied.

No sooner had the elementary schools been established to start six-year-olds on the road to formal schooling than reformers began to argue that we ought to have a pre-school school called the kindergarten. So, borrowing ideas from Friedrich Froebel in Europe, we began to attach kindergartens to the public schools, beginning in the 1870's. The idea was to help children of four to six years learn by directed play activities.

By 1960 most American cities had kindergartens, and some of them had even established nursery schools for two-to-four-year-olds.

The elementary school itself was subject to recurring reforms. No sooner did it make headway in teaching the three R's to every child than someone, outside the schools or in, would urge it to broaden its curriculum: Add drawing and the arts; add geography and history; add nature study; hygiene and physical training; manual training; domestic science. And these all seemed reasonable.

The famous Swiss educator, Pestalozzi, had said so; Edward A. Sheldon, founder of the Oswego (New York) Normal School, said so; Francis W. Parker, superintendent of schools in Quincy, Massachusetts, said so. And so said a host of others, including such diverse characters as the presidents of Harvard (Charles W. Eliot) and of Columbia (Nicholas Murray Butler), publicists like Joseph Mayer Rice, social workers like Jane Addams and Lilian Wald, reformers like Jacob Riis and Walter Hines Page.

Social reformers, humanitarians, and philanthropists, especially in the cities of the 1890's, were indignant about the endless memory work that marked most schools. Schools, they said, were far too intellectualistic— they dealt almost exclusively with words and numbers that did not mean very much to the children. They felt that schools should be alive, interesting, exciting, practical, and useful.

This seemed fair enough. John Dewey took up the ideas in his experimental school at the University of Chicago, and Teachers College at Columbia University applied them in its experimental Lincoln School.

Eventually "progressive" schools mushroomed on the landscape, and "progressive" ideas became popular in the 1920's and 1930's. Chief among the spokesmen after John Dewey was William H. Kilpatrick at Teachers College, Columbia University.

All sorts of plans were devised to loosen up the formal curriculum and give it life and vitality—units, projects, activities, excursions and visits, handicrafts, gardens, laboratories, audio-visual aids, and much else— anything to overcome the slavish drill on the textbook or notebook. There was little doubt that the general quality of learning for most children was raised as the school added vitality and zest to the learning process.

But in the 1940's and 1950's a new set of "reformers" began to charge that the schools were too soft. Schools, they said, were just letting children play and not teaching them anything. Elementary schools were exhorted to return to the three R's and stiffen up discipline and concentrate on intellectual studies.

Many of the criticisms were overdrawn and unfair, but many had some truth in them. Progressive methods *had* been carried to an extreme by a few spokesmen and by a few teachers who assumed that all children learned better by "direct" experiences, by visits, or by physical activities than they did by reading or writing. A general tightening of school methods was evident by 1960.

Sputnik and Russian education strengthened the critics' hands. But how long would it be before "loosening" and flexibility in the curriculum would again be necessary and a new wave of progressive reform to overcome excessive academic formalism be desirable?

Meanwhile, the controversy over religion in the public schools continued. By the beginning of the twentieth century, most public schools had not only dropped sectarian religious teaching but also much of the nonsectarian religious instruction they had attempted in the early nineteenth century. In other words, although the public schools dealt with moral and spiritual values, they no longer tried to deal with religion at all; they were secular. But after World War II the demand arose again that the public schools restore some kind of religious instruction.

Some Protestants proposed that the Bible be read without comment by the teacher, but Catholics and Jews opposed this as really sectarian. It was proposed that students be given time off from regular classes to receive sectarian instruction from their own religious teachers (released time).

In 1948 the United States Supreme Court in the McCollum decision said that released-time religious instruction could not be given inside public-school buildings, but in 1952 (Zorach decision) the Supreme Court said it could be done outside schools if the public teachers did not coerce or persuade students to go to the religious classes. Neither of these decisions has satisfied many people. Some educators have proposed that public schools avoid religious instruction as such but undertake factual study about religion right along with the study of other regular school subjects, but most religious groups have been cool to this proposal. The formula for honoring religious diversity while still promoting social unity through common schools had not been satisfactorily found.

Reform movements stirred through secondary as well as elementary schools. Most revolutionary reform was the very idea of a secondary school which would accept students of the whole range of ability and try to give all a course of study suited to their abilities and their possible vocations in life.

Most other countries divide children at age eleven or twelve, send a few to academic (college-preparatory) schools, others to vocational schools, and the majority directly to work. The American high school, however, has tried to be a comprehensive school, one in which students from all walks of life would study and work and play together. This meant that many new subjects and courses have been added periodically to the high-school curriculum.

The resulting number of elective studies has worried the colleges. As early as 1893 the National Education Association tried to encourage a standardized high-school curriculum. Noteworthy were the efforts of the Committee of Ten (1893) and the Committee on College Entrance Requirements (1899).

These "reforms" stressed those academic studies which should be required for college entrance; namely, four units in foreign language, two in mathematics, two in English, one in history, and one in science. (The relative inattention to science is at least sixty years old.) It was assumed that such studies would be good for all students whether they were headed for college or not. This was fair enough at a time when seventy-five per cent of high-school graduates were going on to college.

But after 1900 the pressures of enrollment on the high schools grew stronger. By 1918 an NEA Committee formulated *The Seven Cardinal Principles of Secondary Education*, in which preparation for college was definitely less important than it had been twenty years before. Now, the high school's aims were to give attention to health, command of the fundamental processes, worthy home membership, vocational preparation, citizenship, leisure-time activities, and ethical character.

This note continued to be emphasized in the 1930's and 1940's. By 1950 about thirty per cent of high-school graduates were going to college. Preparation for college had actually become a minor function of the high schools.

However, a new wave of reaction (or was it reform?) began to criticize secondary schools for permitting low academic standards, for not stimulating youth to rigorous study, for letting youth take so-called "easy" courses instead of working hard at the regular academic subjects. The success of Russian space flights and the threat of falling behind in the armament race raised fears that American high schools were not doing their jobs.

Many of the critics did not know what they were talking about, but some did. There was little doubt that many high schools could do a better job for college-bound youth than they were doing. Some high-school educators were still assuming that only a small minority of high-school graduates were headed for college. They had not noticed that by 1960 many more high-school students were expecting to go to college.

It might not be long until we would be back where we were in 1900 with seventy-five per cent of high-school graduates bound for college, but with this vast difference: In 1900 only ten per cent of youth were in high school; today ninety per cent are there.

The potential enrollments called for a drastic new look at the secondary school, at both the junior-high and senior-high levels. The first thing the schools did was to give more attention to the academic subjects, especially to the foreign languages, science, and mathematics. The time was ripe, however, for a complete overhauling of the junior-high school, which was just about fifty years old and born in a very different age from that of the 1960's.

Undoubtedly the pressure of high-school graduates upon college doors would lead to even further drastic expansion of junior colleges and other two-year institutions. They too were just about half a century old and, in some ways, the epitome of the democratic movement in American education.

It was being estimated that by the decades following 1970 all students with an IQ of one hundred or over would be finishing at least a two-year college. If this proved to be true, standards of admission to some colleges would go up and in others they were bound to go down.

The question was whether all this educational activity could measure up to the intellectual and moral demands of a free society in the modern world. If individuals used the vast resources of American higher education simply to further their own interests, this was one kind of small freedom all right, but in the long run would it serve the cause of the free society? How to enable American education to serve the cause of the larger freedoms was the paramount question. The answer to this question cannot be rigged. The fate of the nation rides upon it.

At the heart of the answer to the fateful question is the scholarship, the wisdom, the vitality and the freedom of American teachers. If teachers are weak, timorous, or poorly trained, the American idea of education has little chance of success. If powerful or selfish groups demand that teachers conform to *their* ways of thinking or to *their* beliefs, education will be a narrow little thing. And our history here is not too reassuring.

Orthodoxy of belief in colonial days was a prime requirement for teaching. Oaths of loyalty to the crown and to the doctrines of the church were familiar trappings of colonial rule. The American Revolution in its turn demanded that teachers be faithful to the Revolution rather than to the crown; and, similarly, Congress exacted loyalty oaths to the Union in the Reconstruction Period after the Civil War.

Conformity of economic belief, faith in private business enterprise, and opposition to any radical movements were expected of teachers in the nineteenth century. State laws required special loyalty oaths from teachers as early as the 1920's, and as late as 1958 the National Defense Education Act required such oaths from students applying for federal loans.

After World Wars I and II, thirty states passed laws requiring teachers to sign special loyalty oaths. Other laws (notably the Feinberg law of 1949 in New York State) were passed to hunt down and dismiss teachers suspected of belonging to subversive organizations. Many patriotic or-ganizations served as self-appointed censors of school textbooks and complained about outspoken teachers.

The frantic search for communist teachers and others suspected vaguely of "leftist" leaning was fired up by McCarthyism and the wave of legislative investigations that swept the country in the early 1950's.

As a result, a cloud of timidity, suspicion, and fear settled down upon the schools and colleges in what the *New York Times* called "a subtle, creeping paralysis of freedom of thought." Classroom teachers and school administrators tended to avoid acts or ideas that might "cause any trouble" or arouse any criticism.

This general atmosphere of caution and anxiety affecting millions of students did infinitely more damage to the cause of freedom in education than the handful of communist teachers could possibly do. Fortunately, the most active "Red hunts" have now passed, but their revival is an ever-present danger, especially if teachers and students are fearful or are indifferent to the importance of freedom in education.

The first defenses of freedom in education are strong professional or-ganizations of teachers like the American Association of University Professors and the National Education Association. If they do their jobs, they will insist upon high-quality training for teachers, upon fearless and competent scholarship in the classroom, and upon freedom to seek the truth in research and in the publication of findings. They will defend those qualified teachers who come under attack.

The ultimate defenses of freedom in education, however, are the people themselves who will realize that education's main function is to free the minds of the younger generation and to equip them as free citizens and free persons.

The schools and colleges must therefore generate a spirit of intel-lectual, political, and personal freedom throughout the land. To do this, they must in turn have a genuine measure of self-government resting upon the competent scholarship of the teachers.

The most distinctive mark of a free society is that it specifically delegates to its educational institutions the task of constant study and criticism of the free society itself. No other kind of society dares to permit such a thing. No other kind of society prevents its government from endangering the liberties of the people and at the same time entrusts the government with the obligation to guarantee the rights of the people against attack by powerful groups or individuals in the community.

Just as a free government guarantees the freedom of the press, of association, of religion, and of trial by jury, so must a free government guarantee the freedom of teaching and learning.

A free society knows that its surest foundation rests upon the liberal education of the people—a liberal education available freely and equally to all, beginning with the earliest stages of the elementary school, extending to the highest reaches of the university, and limited only by considerations of talent.

As the fourth century of American history reaches its mid-point and as the second century of the American Republic draws to a close, the search for freedom in American education has just well begun. That is why the story of American education must continue to be, in the future even more than in the past, the unflagging search for freedom.

2

The teacher must keep alive that spark of wonder, to prevent it from becoming blasé from over-excitement, wooden from routine, fossilized through dogmatic instruction, or dissipated through random exercise upon trivial things.

JOHN DEWEY
How We Think

John W. Gardner

"VERSATILITY" AND "MORAL DECAY AND RENEWAL"

Versatility

Educating for Renewal. We are beginning to understand how to educate for renewal but we must deepen that understanding. If we in-

From John W. Gardner, *Self Renewal: The Individual and the Innovative Society* (New York: Harper and Row, 1964), Chapters 3 and 12, pp. 21–26, 115–127. Copyright © 1963, 1964 by John W. Gardner. Reprinted by permission of Harper and Row, publishers.

doctrinate the young person in an elaborate set of fixed beliefs, we are ensuring his early obsolescence. The alternative is to develop skills, attitudes, habits of mind and the kinds of knowledge and understanding that will be the instruments of continuous change and growth on the part of the young person. Then we will have fashioned *a system that provides for its own continuous renewal.*

This suggests a standard in terms of which we may judge the effectiveness of all education—and so judged, much education today is monumentally ineffective. All too often we are giving our young people cut flowers when we should be teaching them to grow their own plants. We are stuffing their heads with the products of earlier innovation rather than teaching them to innovate. We think of the mind as a storehouse to be filled when we should be thinking of it as an instrument to be used.

Of course, our schools cannot be wholly preoccupied with education for innovation; they are concerned with continuity as well as change. There are continuities in the human condition, continuities in our own tradition and lessons to be learned from the past. When young people learn what and who they are it helps them to think about what they wish to become—as individuals and as a people. At the higher levels of education they must be given the opportunity to examine critically the shared purposes of their society—a major element in continuity—and to subject these purposes to the reappraisal that gives them vitality and relevance. In every area in which creative thought or action may occur, the individual builds on the heritage of earlier work. It is true that excessive preoccupation with that heritage may diminish his creativity. And it is true that his mode of building on his heritage may be to rebel from it. Still it is his starting point.

But the educational system has always been *relatively* successful in dealing with continuity. The pressing need today is to educate for an accelerating rate of change. Some observers have feared that the need would lead the schools into frantic pursuit of the latest fads, but it has had the opposite effect. Change is so swift that the "latest thing" today may be old-fashioned by the time young people enter adulthood. So they must be taught in such a way that they can learn for themselves the new things of tomorrow. And that leads us back to fundamentals.

We are moving away from teaching things that readily become outmoded, and toward things that will have the greatest long-term effect on the young person's capacity to understand and perform. Increasing emphasis is being given to instruction in methods of analysis and modes of attack on problems. In many subjects this means more attention to basic principles, less to applications of immediate "practical" use. In all subjects it means teaching habits of mind that will be useful in new situations—curiosity, open-mindedness, objectivity, respect for evidence and the capacity to think critically.

Generalists and Specialists. Education for renewal is to a considerable degree education for versatility. And that fact brings us face-to-face with a well-worn controversy: should we be training specialists or generalists? Though many educators respond with vehement confidence, the question poses extremely complex issues.

Specialization is a universal feature of biological functioning, observable in the cell structure of any complex organism, in insect societies and in human social organization. In human societies, division of labor is older than recorded history and has flourished wherever urban civilization has existed.

Specialization involves selective emphasis on certain functions and the dropping of other functions. The human organism is capable of an unimaginably broad range of behavioral variations. Out of this vast range, any individual can develop only a small fraction of the total. All learning is specialization in the sense that it involves reinforcement of some responses rather than others. Nothing illustrates the process better than language learning. The infant has the capacity to understand and to produce a vast variety of speech sounds. Out of this variety he will come to recognize and to utter chiefly those sounds present in his own language—a fraction of the total—and will, as an adult, have considerable difficulty in recognizing and uttering sounds not in his own language. Thus we are all specialists despite ourselves. And so it has always been.

In short, specialization is biologically, socially and intellectually necessary. The highest reaches of education will always involve learning one thing in great depth. The great artist or scientist often achieves the heights of performance through intensive cultivation of a narrow sector of his potentialities.

Clearly, then, we cannot do away with specialization, nor would we wish to. But in the modern world it has extended far beyond anything we knew in the past. And, unfortunately, there are many tasks that can be effectively performed only by men and women who have retained some capacity to function as generalists—leadership and management, certain kinds of innovation, communication and teaching and many of the responsibilities of child-rearing and of citizenship. Furthermore, the extremely specialized man may lose the adaptability so essential in a changing world. He may be unable to reorient himself when technological changes make his specialty obsolete.

Note that it is not a question of doing away with the specialist. It is a question of retaining some capacity to function as a generalist, and the capacity to shift to new specialties as circumstances require.

All social hierarchies involve a kind of specialization, and this too results in losses as well as gains. Subordinates who are deprived of the opportunity to make certain kinds of decisions may lose the capacity to make those decisions. An ironic consequence of such hierarchical specialization is that the individual higher in the scale may lose more in functional capacity than those below him. No one is more helpless than the boss without his accustomed aides. A slave-owning class may experience a deterioration in capacity that is damaging to its own survival. This process has interesting parallels in insect societies. Among certain slaveholding formicine ants, many normal capacities (nest making, care of young, even the capacity to feed themselves) have literally disappeared, leaving only a hypertrophied "military" or slave-making competence.

In human societies there is no reason whatever why the specialist should not retain the capacity to function as a generalist. Whether he actually does so depends partly on his motivation, partly on the manner in which he was educated and partly on the nature of the organization or society in which his abilities mature.

Frontier societies and organizations in early stages of development tend to be simple, fluid and uncompartmentalized, and this puts great pressure on the individual to be functionally generalized. Thus we most commonly encounter the "universal man" in young and relatively unstructured societies or early in an "era." (Recall the versatility of our Founding Fathers.)

In later stages, societies and organizations develop a complex division of labor, high specialization and a great deal of compartmentalization —all of which press the individual to specialize. Every student of organization can comment on the possible hazards of such compartmentalization. To the extent that it diminishes the versatility of the individual it lessens the capacity of the organization to renew itself. If individuals are rigidly specialized and unprepared for change, the human cost of change will be high and the society will resist it stubbornly. But if they are flexible and capable of learning new ways, the human cost of readjustment will be low and there will be little resistance to it. In short, in a world of change the versatile individual is a priceless asset.

The farsighted administrator can and does take action to prevent excessive compartmentalization. He reorganizes to break down calcified organizational lines. He shifts personnel (perhaps even establishes a system of rotation) to eliminate unnecessary specialization and to broaden perspectives. He redefines jobs to break them out of rigid categories.

A free society cannot be rearranged in any such summary fashion, and in the long run perhaps the most effective means of achieving comparable results is through the educational system. Education can lay a broad and firm base for a lifetime of learning and growth. The individual who begins with such a broad base will always have some capacity to function as a generalist, no matter how deeply he chooses to specialize. Education at its best will develop the individual's inner resources to the point where he can learn (and will *want* to learn) on his own. It will equip him to cope with unforeseen challenges and to survive as a versatile individual in an unpredictable world. Individuals so educated will keep the society itself flexible, adaptive and innovative.

Moral Decay and Renewal

The Consensus in a Free Society. It should be apparent why anyone concerned for the continuous renewal of a society must be concerned for the renewal of that society's values and beliefs. Societies are renewed—if they are renewed at all—by people who believe in something, care about something, stand for something. What about our own values and beliefs?

We might begin by asking whether we have in this country any consensus with respect to values. Many discouraged Americans say that we do not. There are others who assert that we *should not* have such a consensus. The latter are usually persons deeply committed to the freedom of the individual, deeply loyal to pluralism and diversity as a way of life. They dread even the hint of an official philosophy or morality, and fear that to seek any common ground in our values will ultimately diminish diversity.

The first thing to be said is that in any society which functions effectively some measure of consensus *does* exist. Without it the society would simply fly to pieces. No set of laws could prevent chaos in a society that lacked rough agreement on certain moral assumptions.

No system of social arrangements, no matter how cleverly devised, no matter how democratic in character, is adequate to preserve freedom unless it is undergirded by certain habits and attitudes which are shared by members of the society. The claims of society and the claims of the individual will always be in potential conflict. Individual freedom cannot stand against the powerful pressures that are brought against it unless it is supported by deep-rooted habits of thinking and acting. If young people have been suckled on the legends of free men, if they have seen their fathers and grandfathers act in defense of freedom, if tradition instructs them in how free men conduct themselves, the chances of freedom are relatively good. Men and women so instructed will "augur misgovernment at a distance, and snuff the approach of tyranny in every tainted breeze."

But freedom must be supported by more than habits and attitudes. Habits and attitudes can be changed. In the modern world there is a continuous clatter from the breaking of old habits; it is one of the characteristic sounds of our time. The idea of freedom, if it is to have durability, must be rooted in man's philosophical and religious views. It is not enough to believe that freedom is a comfortable attribute of one's tradition and way of life. One must also believe that it is a right and necessary attribute. This is another way of saying that allegiance to freedom must grow naturally out of one's moral and ethical values.

Our society has always had a measure of consensus with respect to such values and, whatever the critics may say, we have it still. However fragmented our value system may seem, we do in fact agree on certain truths, share certain aims and acknowledge the validity of certain rules. Measured against the whole panorama of human experience as reported by historians and anthropologists, the dominant values in our society represent a moderately narrow range. What looks like disagreement turns out in the broader perspective to be a haggling over details.

Our agreement in these matters is not in any way incompatible with the ideal of diversity. It is of the very essence of our consensus that it is free and rational. It invites criticism and is subject to varied interpretations. It experiences continuing modification and growth. It is free, unforced and fluid.

Everyone does not have to agree in order for the consensus to be effective. It is only necessary that there be rough agreement among a substantial proportion of those men and women whose intelligence, vigor, awareness and sense of responsibility mark them as shapers of the community purpose.

For anyone interested in innovation the consensus is especially important. If a society enjoys a reasonable measure of consensus, it can indulge in very extensive innovation without losing its coherence and distinctive style. Without the durability supplied by the American consensus, our fondness for innovation and diversity would commit us to chaos and disorder.

In a pluralistic society the consensus must necessarily be at what one might call a middle level of values. Obviously it cannot deal with the surface trivialities of manners and daily customs; neither can it sound the depths. It can deal with fairly fundamental values governing man's behavior and with concepts such as freedom and justice. But those values float over still-deeper reaches of philosophic and religious beliefs. They gain their strength from man's deepest views concerning his own nature. When we reach these depths, however, we are in the presence of matters which concern the individual so profoundly that he must not be asked to compromise them.

To force consensus in the depths of belief would be intolerable. To remain preoccupied with the whitecaps on the surface would be meaningless. So a pluralistic society wisely seeks to establish its consensus in the middle depths.

At that level, in our own case, one finds the ideals of freedom, equality of opportunity, the conception of the worth and dignity of the individual, the idea of justice, the dream of brotherhood. The fact that we are not always faithful to these shared values does not indicate confusion nor a failure of the consensus. *We know the values to which we are being unfaithful.* One might ask, "What difference does it make that we agree on our values if we aren't faithful to them?" The answer is that if one is concerned about therapy, it always makes a difference what the patient is suffering from. This society is suffering not from confusion but from infidelity.

To Point a Moral. In the first half of the twentieth century a large number of people came to believe that the intelligent thing to do was to maintain a "scientific" neutrality or agnosticism with respect to values. Here we must be careful not to blame scientists for views that were often pressed most vigorously by individuals with only a smattering of science. It is true that natural and social scientists have found that a neutrality with respect to certain values is essential to their work. For example, the question of whether the theory of evolution was good or bad in a moral sense could only impede scientists in answering the question that really interested them: whether it was true or false.

But the notion that neutrality with respect to all values can be extended to all of life is an absurdity. Those who share the notion have never succeeded in acting in their personal lives as though they were wholly agnostic with respect to values. They continue to be morally indignant when someone cheats them and morally outraged when someone slanders them. But though they do not act like moral agnostics in matters affecting their personal interest, they have often done so in matters affecting the community at large. They seem to believe that they should remain neutral in any public discussion of moral values.

This reluctance of some moderns to deal with moral values is intensified by the concept of moral relativity. Dispassionate investigation reveals that our own moral precepts have shifted with the years, and that other societies have other moral precepts. Thus there has arisen the idea that all moral judgments are relative to the context in which the judgments are made. Social scientists have achieved this perspective at the cost of great struggle, and we need not begrudge them the legitimate benefits thereof. But we are entitled to express concern when increasing numbers of people accept it as justification for a sort of moral *laissez faire*—a notion that if one simply tolerates all sorts of values and permits them to come into conflict with one another, something good will come of it. In this view it is not necessary—or perhaps even seemly—to work for the things one believes in, because somehow the competition among values will work the whole thing out. In fact one doesn't even need to believe in any particular values: one simply maintains the position of an interested observer.

To reduce this position to absurdity, imagine the attitude spread to the entire population. Then no one would believe in anything, and everyone would be an observer watching the competition. But there would be nothing for the observers to observe because no one would have any values.

A more elusive difficulty facing this and the immediately preceding generation has been the negativism with respect to moral seriousness that reached its peak early in this century and still affects many educated men and women. Our generation grew up, and our parents grew up, at a time when the leading lights of the intellectual world—artists, writers, scientists, scholars—were waging a knock-down-and-drag-out fight to free themselves of the stifling conventionality of the nineteenth century. These rebels themselves were often intensely moral, indeed striving for a higher morality than they could find in the conventionalities of the day. They believed that there was a fatal element of hypocrisy in all contemporary expressions of idealism, and they came to suspect all sermons and all the well-worn words that express moral values.

At first, pricking the balloons of conventional morality was a rather adventurous exercise for courageous individuals. But it soon became a game that all could play, and almost all did play, with less and less imagination, more and more empty imitativeness.

There is no question that the rigidities of Victorian convention were an obstacle to the creative urges of the twentieth century. But that battle is over, and those who continue to rush into the fray as though the enemy were still formidable are beginning to seem a bit ridiculous. It is understandable, to be sure. Men have never been able to resist an extravagant waste of energy in refighting old battles and combating foes long since vanquished. But the more we indulge ourselves in that direction the less likely we are to gird ourselves for real and present battles. We are no longer inhibited by the rigidities of nineteenth-century morality. Zealous wreckers have torn that house down. The question is not one of further pulverizing the fragments but of asking what we intend to do to protect ourselves from the elements.

This alters radically the direction from which we must seek a moral initiative. Once it was the skeptic, the critic of the *status quo,* who had to make a great effort. Today the skeptic *is* the *status quo.* The one who must make the effort is the man who seeks to create a new moral order. Under these circumstances the individual who, out of sheer habit, applies ridicule to any and all expressions of moral earnestness is as old-fashioned as rumble seats and bathtub gin.

Many moderns would rather walk barefoot over hot coals than utter an outright expression of moral concern. They have to say it obliquely, mix it with skepticism or humor, or smother it with pessimism. But embarrassment about the expression of moral seriousness is a disease of people far gone in affectation and oversophistication. Unaffected people will regard it as normal to consult their deepest values and to exhibit an allegiance to those values. And they will expect those values to influence their behavior, within the limits of human fallibility. They will not think it odd or embarrassing to talk about them.

It is a mistake, of course, to equate moral seriousness with dogmatism, solemnity or conformism. Socrates, who was as earnest as a man could be about matters of moral import was far from dogmatic, rarely solemn, and often disrespectful of the "respectable" ideas of his day.

It would be inaccurate to suggest that a serious and clearheaded concern for moral renewal will bring us out onto some sunny upland beyond the troubles that have plagued man since the beginning. Moral seriousness does not resolve complex problems; it only impels us to face the problems rather than run away. Clearheadedness does not slay dragons; it only spares us the indignity of fighting paper dragons while the real ones are breathing down our necks. But those are not trivial advantages.

The Drying Reservoir. Jacques Barzun tells of the little old lady who complained that "the modern thunderstorm no longer clears the air." It is an attitude of mind that is not confined to little old ladies nor to meteorological subjects. Listen to these melancholy lines:

> To whom can I speak today?
> The gentle man has perished
> The violent man has access to everybody.
>
> To whom can I speak today?
> The iniquity that smites the land
> It has no end.
>
> To whom can I speak today?
> There are no righteous men
> The earth is surrendered to criminals.

The writer's abhorrence of the present and his nostalgia for an older, gentler, more righteous time strikes us as very modern. But the poem was not written by a twentieth-century malcontent. It was written by a man contemplating suicide some four thousand years ago in the time of Egypt's Middle Kingdom.

It is an abiding characteristic of man to believe that the old virtues are disappearing, the old values disintegrating, the old, good, stern ways no longer honored. Many people today seem to think that our values, our morality as a people, our devotion to virtue and justice resemble a reservoir that was filled long ago (vaguely, about the time of our grandfathers) and has been seeping away ever since. But our grandfathers thought that the reservoir had been filled by *their* grandfathers and had been seeping away ever since. And their grandfathers thought the same. Why isn't the reservoir empty?

The answer is that the moral order undergoes regeneration as well as decay. Joseph Campbell has written:

> Only birth can conquer death. . . . Within the soul, within the body social, there must be—if we are to experience long survival—a continuous "recurrence of birth" to nullify the unremitting recurrences of death.

Nowhere is this more true than in the realm of values. Men are always corrupting the old symbols, drifting away from the old truths. Give us a clean, clear, fresh idea or ideal, and we can promise within one generation to render it positively moldy. We smother our values in ritual and encrust them with social observances that rapidly become meaningless. But while some are losing their faith, others are achieving new spiritual insights; while some are growing slack and hypocritical in the moral dimension of their lives, others are bringing a new meaning and vitality to moral striving.

Everyone does not play an equally important role in the re-creation and reshaping of values. But a far greater proportion of the populace than one might think has some share in the process. Amiel said: "Every life is a profession of faith, and exercises an inevitable and silent propaganda. As far as lies in its power, it tends to transform the universe and humanity into its own image. [Every man's] conduct is an unspoken sermon that is forever preaching to others."

Young people do not assimilate the values of their group by learning the words (truth, justice, etc.) and their definitions. They learn attitudes, habits and ways of judging. They learn these in intensely personal transactions with their immediate family or associates. They learn them in the routines and crises of living, but they also learn them through songs, stories, drama and games. They do not learn ethical principles; they emulate ethical (or unethical) people. They do not analyze or list the attributes they wish to develop; they identify with people who seem to them to have these attributes. That is why young people need models, both in their imaginative life and in their environment, models of what man at his best can be.

There is a saying popular among intellectuals today that a society utterly secure in its beliefs never talks about them and that a society which constantly reiterates its beliefs is losing its conviction. Perhaps this was true in stable and relatively homogeneous pre-modern societies. It has not been true for *any* modern society. The modern society necessarily talks about its beliefs, argues about them, celebrates them, dramatizes them.

Helping each generation to rediscover the meaning of liberty, justice —"the words on the monuments"—is a perennial task for any society. Each generation is presented with victories that it did not win for itself. A generation that has fought for freedom may pass that freedom on to the next generation. But it cannot pass on the intense personal knowledge of what it takes in courage and endurance to win freedom.

In some cases, young people find that the moral precepts their parents have to offer are no longer relevant in a rapidly changing world. And they often find that in moral matters the precepts their parents utter are contradicted by the behavior their parents exhibit. This is confusing, but not catastrophic. Those writers who imagine that it destroys all possibility of youthful moral striving are wrong. The first task of renewal in the moral sphere is *always* the difficult confrontation of ideal and reality, precept and practice; and young people are very well fitted to

accomplish that confrontation. Their freshness of vision and rebelliousness of mood make them highly effective in stripping the encrustations
of hypocrisy from cherished ideals.

One of the most difficult problems we face is to make it possible for
young people to participate in the great tasks of their time. They have
found a few constructive outlets recently, notably the Peace Corps, but
on the whole such opportunities are rare in a complex technological
society. Alexander might conquer half the known world in his early
twenties, and nineteenth-century New England lads might be sailing
captains in their late teens, but our age lays enormous stress on long
training and experience. We have designed our society in such a way
that most possibilities open to the adolescent today are either bookish
or frivolous. And all too often when we do seek to evoke his moral
strivings the best we can do is to invite him to stand sentinel over a
drying reservoir! What an incredibly dull task for the restless minds and
willing hearts of young people! It is hardly surprising that many young
people think of the moral order as something invented by parents, deans
and commencement speakers for the sole purpose of boring the young.

The notion of the drying reservoir is particularly inappropriate because it suggests that the problem is to preserve something that can
never be added to. In this way it induces defensiveness and ignores all
possibility of creativity. Men thinking in terms of the almost empty
reservoir will be much too preoccupied with preservation to build
creatively for an unknown future.

Instead of giving young people the impression that their task is to
stand a dreary watch over the ancient values, we should be telling them
the grim but bracing truth that it is their task to re-create those values
continuously in their own behavior, facing the dilemmas and catastro-
phes of their own time. Instead of implying that the ideals we cherish are
safely embalmed in the memory of old battles and ancestral deeds we
should be telling them that each generation refights the crucial battles
and either brings new vitality to the ideals or allows them to decay.

In short, the nurturing of values that maintain society's moral tone—
or allow that moral tone to slacken—is going on every day, for good or
ill. It is not the dull exercise in ancestral piety that some adults make it
seem. It goes on in the dust and clamor of the market place, the daily
press, the classroom and the playground, the urban apartment and the
suburban ranch house, and it communicates itself more vividly through
what men do than through what they say. The moral order is not something static, it is not something enshrined in historic documents, or
stowed away like the family silver, or lodged in the minds of pious and
somewhat elderly moralists. It is an attribute of a functioning social
system. As such it is a living, changing thing, liable to decay and dis-
integration as well as to revitalizing and reinforcement, and never any
better than the generation that holds it in trust.

Men and women who understand this truth and accept its implications will be well fitted to renew the moral order—and to renew their society as well. They will understand that the tasks of renewal are endless. They will understand that their society is not like a machine that is created at some point in time and then maintained with a minimum of effort; a society is being continuously re-created, for good or ill, by its members. This will strike some as a burdensome responsibility, but it will summon others to greatness.

3

I say we had best look our times and lands searchingly in the face, like a physician diagnosing some deep disease. Never was there, perhaps, more hollowness at heart than at present, and here in the United States. Genuine belief seems to have left us. The underlying principles of the States are not honestly believ'd in (for all this hectic glow, and these melodramatic screamings), nor is humanity itself believ'd in. What penetrating eye does not everywhere see through the mask.

WALT WHITMAN
1871

Herbert A. Thelen
PREDICAMENT AND PROMISE

Let's begin with the School Burning Theory of Education. The 'thirties were a period of much experimentation in schools, and, after reading a number of accounts of the most significant experiments, I formulated this theory, which I now gladly present to the world.

Imagine a perfectly terrible school. The morale of the faculty is scraping bottom; the students are cliquish and many of them don't even speak to each other; the building is an old barn in a muddy field—an affront to any self-respecting white horse; the citizens are apathetic, depressed, and bored. Now comes Rudolph the Brand-new Schoolman with an Idea: school is part of life, and life just doesn't have to be that way.

From Herbert Thelen, "Predicament and Promise," *Education and the Human Quest* (New York: Harper and Row, 1960), pp. 4–15. Copyright © 1960 by Herbert Thelen. Reprinted by permission of Harper and Row, Publishers.

So, over a period of years, things happen. Somehow time is found in the biology course to plan and plant a garden and lawn; in English and social studies, to survey and report the school's plight in an exciting skit to the townsfolk; in homeroom to clean up the classrooms and make plans for their rehabilitation. Parents are invited to help, and work weekends are inaugurated. The men citizens and high school students work side by side on Saturday morning, doing carpentry and landscaping, painting and construction. The town ladies provide the lunch, and, in the afternoon, the Men's League plays baseball with (or is it against?) the Boy's League. The teachers join in adult activities in town, and lose no opportunity to "involve" citizens. Several committees of students, teachers, and citizens are formed: for developing and equipping the library, modernizing the science laboratories, getting audio-visual equipment, organizing car pools to bring students from outlying districts in to school.

The students, with so many activities to challenge them, develop a club program and an active social life. The student's theater group becomes the talk of the state, and goes on tours. The budding scientists participate in science fairs, and bring home prizes. A student government is formed, and its officers sit on various boards and committees with the townspeople. Election to office in the government is a prize much sought after. The student government quickly converts bullies and terrors from the grammar school into true believers. Through the student government, an employment service helps students into part-time jobs set up by the delighted merchants, farmers, and businessmen. "Give a boy a job" becomes a slogan (the girls learn tatting, I guess). By the end of seven years, juvenile delinquency has all but disappeared.

The parents, infected by the clear-cut purposive ambition of their children, draft some of the teachers to put on courses for adults in the evenings. The beauty of the refurbished school, and its charming auditorium make the town a stopping place for dramatic and musical artists on tour. The town swells with pride, Rudolph the Brand-new Schoolman develops a most distinguished fringe of gray around the temples. And nobody can think of anything further to want.

Many of the original teachers have now left, regretfully, to take important jobs in which they can spread the gospel further. Brilliant new teachers, the pick of their graduating classes, are easy to recruit. They come into a handsome building full of well-mannered students, and these teachers happily re-introduce the old talk-type social studies, the descriptive classification-type biology, the formalized abstract algebra (with workbook), and the grammatically precise book reports on foreign authors—read in translation, of course. The specter of academic achievement rides high in the saddle. The faculty meetings begin to peter out because nobody seems to have anything to talk about. The student clubs lose their zip as the need for their productions disappears. The honor roll is introduced, and a sizable number of flunking students is discovered. The school board budgets $3,825.63 cents each year to cover windows broken during the summer. Vandalism begins to appear in nasty little ways around the school. The students form secret organizations to exclude each other. A tough police captain is elected on his promise to "really lay down the law." The students no longer linger after school; they disperse silently with the last bell at 3 o'clock. Attendance in the adult courses dwindles, and it has been several years since a new course was introduced. Somehow it seems to Rudolph the Brand-new Schoolman—who has developed a paunch—that the "good" families have moved away; and the students in school now certainly aren't up to those he used to get.

The golden age has passed.

The only thing to do now is set fire to the school, plow up the gardens, retire Rudolph, and start over. Except that this should have been done right after "And nobody can think of anything further to want."

The difference between Rudolph's school before and after its golden period is the institutionalization (ossification) of attitudes, procedures, and status hierarchies that will be very difficult to change. Hence the Persian wisdom of shattering to bits and remolding nearer to the heart's desire.

But we are not Persians. I am not sure that even if we were we would burn down our schools. Assuming that we wish to improve them, it seems to me that there are four approaches available. One approach is to bear down more heavily: to make stronger demands and enforce them by means of drastic threats and punishments. This approach in effect argues that when bureaucracy fails the solution is more bureaucracy. In line with this approach is the across-the-board demand that all high school graduates must take an additional year of math, English or science; that achievement will be defined by performance on tests constructed by anonymous experts who do not know the students, do not know what was taught in their class, and do not know the aspects of education valued by the community; that government money will be used to develop counseling for talented children but may not be spent on other children; that all high school physics teachers should teach the same specific materials in the same sequence and with the same activities. All these efforts are potentially valuable, but when they are applied without taking into account the pertinent facts about the students, teachers, and community, they amount in fact to direct impositions "justified" only by the pressure behind their enforcement.

The second approach is tinkering. This can be distinguished from experimentation by the absence of any thought-out theory. This approach assumes that if we are dissatisfied with what we are doing then we should try anything else that sounds plausible and that does not require any significant change in attitude, insight, or administrative arrangements. In line with this approach are most present experiments with ability grouping, closed-circuit TV, team teaching, and "group dynamics" techniques. All these innovations would be valuable if useful things were learned from them, such as how to define "ability" so that better ways can be developed to teach different kinds of students; what sorts of visual and auditory communications are most effective for defined communication requirements; what ways can be employed by teachers working with the same students to complement each other's resources; how to divide responsibility for learning activities among adults and children; what particular emotional and social conditions lead to interactions among students that stimulate different sorts of learning or readiness to learn.

The third approach is experimentation, which is tinkering with something in mind beyond "let's see what will happen." In line with this approach are the very good efforts one finds occasionally to set up a special class for students who are not getting much out of other classes; to make use of new technical aids in the "language laboratory"; to study the use of role-playing as an aid to emergent awareness of attitudes in social studies; to develop better ways of reporting grades to parents. On a larger scale there was the eight-year study of thirty progressive high schools, most of whose major findings have been ignored (e.g., that success in college depends on quality of high school experience *regardless* of the particular subject matter in courses the students took); and the New York activity study, which demonstrated the superiority of teacher-class planning and cooperative determination of goals. The U.S. Office of Education began in 1956 a highly commendable program for research. During its first three years, 234 projects were approved from universities and state educational agencies. Of these, 61 deal with mentally retarded children; 29 with special abilities of students, 26 with staffing problems, 15 with retention of students in school; 14 with school organization and administration. The remaining 89 cover the widest possible range. Most of these studies involve thought-out experiments, and should contribute to the body of educational knowledge.

The fourth approach is through education of everyone concerned (whether they know it or like it) with the enterprise of education. It would involve teachers studying and formulating the basic discipline of the field of knowledge they teach; administrators and counselors studying the bases for deciding which particular children should be assigned to which teachers; community agencies studying the over-all range of education-relevant experiences of students in the community and then trying to decide which kinds of experiences could best be supervised in schools, in families, in clubs, and in work situations.

This fourth approach is the concern here, and we shall see that it is not so much an "approach" as a part of the way of life that must be developed in the school and community. In the remainder of this paper I

shall consider in general terms some of the obstacles to making education a significant part of the human quest; some issues that we shall have
to come to terms with; the nature of the ideas we seek; and finally, the
design for the inquiry undertaken in this book.

Obstacles

The greatest obstacle to improvement of education is the nature
of modern society itself. A great many changes, beginning roughly with
World War I, have occurred in our way of life and I think that to understand the problem of improving education we had better be aware of
some of these changes. What I am about to say applies not only to schools
but to churches, universities, labor unions, governments, industries, and
school boards.

Ever since World War I, which ushered in the present era of industrial
and technological expansion, we have become increasingly fascinated
with our new and useful machines, gadgets, and toys. The Protestant
ethic has always approved of enhancement of the standard of living, and
the dazzling success of technology has taught us increasingly to ask how
to do it rather than why to do it. The great debate about national purposes
and policies has ground to a halt, shot down in part by such slogans as
"maintain the American way of life." Life has become engineering:
engineering of more goods, greater wealth, more power—yes, by heaven,
even "better" human relations. We have assumed, when we thought
about it at all, that these changes could be justified by good reasons and
what we and Rudolph the Brand-new Schoolman did not allow ourselves
to realize was that technological procedures, like the Sorcerer's Appren-
tice, had taken over and *that their own activities had become their own
justification.* Now that other nations are able to compete with us on our
own grounds of technological know-how we have become fearful; our
dependency on procedures is no longer safe. We tell ourselves that
their technology is in the service of bad ends (ideology). But this raises
the uncomfortable question of what are our ends, then, that are so much
better? And it is as we and Rudolph pose this question that we become
aware of the fact we are no longer sure, and that we have substituted the
organization and the procedures for the Human Quest after the "cultivation of the mind, feelings, and manners."

But in the meanwhile, what has been going on in education?

In one sense, the progressive movement in education began at the
same time and for some of the same reasons as the explosion of industrialization during the 'twenties, for both were reactions against the formalism of the 'nineties, and both found their chance to grow during the
chaos following World War I. Progressivism, as practiced, tended to be
a reaction against stifling traditional procedures in schools; and it also,
I suspect, nourished itself on the post-World War I social attitudes of

"teacher has gone, let's kick the house down." (It also brought in some good things, too, which have caught hold in the primary grades, safely remote from adult life.) The difference between the new industrial and educational movements, however, was the difference between the lion and the ant. The industrial lion changed the world and most of its way of life, whereas the ant barely kicked up a local fuss. By the mid-forties the good ideas about building education on the child's own efforts to make choices and test their consequences were clearly on the way out, partly because they had not been understood well enough to attain validity, and partly because of a curious alliance between two oddly mated bedfellows: academic tradition and industrial bureaucracy. The common attitude and value that allied these two powerful forces was the assumption that their procedures were their own justification. At the present time, these strange partners have snuggled together most cozily because each has invented for itself a rationale which, like some exotic perfume, increases the desire of the other. The industrialists are trying to show that industrial expansion is the way to free the human spirit, develop universal democracy, and make peace permanent; whereas the educators are beating the drums for bright creative people with sound scientific training and minds disciplined for industry. Industry looks to liberal education to give substance to its rationalizations, and education looks to industry for its goals.

Issues

We must seek a different kind of education: an education that takes persons into account, that seeks, fosters, and builds on the universal human quest; an education that believes man should be master, not slave, to his own inventions; an education guided by unattainable values, creating its own procedures from insights which reflect detailed knowledge of boys and girls, communities, and worlds without number. In short—an education.

No one decision will be important in this reconstruction, but the cumulative force of many, many decisions guided by a consistent point of view about education will, in the long run, add up.

By "consistent point of view" I mean a thought-out and intelligent position with respect to a number of basic issues. Four of these issues, with which we in our own times must come to terms, are:

Issue I.   The education of a child is contributed to by the school, the family, the peer group, his contacts with events and people in the community. Should we not know or care what the contribution is to a child's education of various types of experiences, in and out of school? Is the net result of conflicting values and assumptions of the different parts of the community breeding confusion and doubt, or furthering self-mastery and wisdom in the child? And what part of the educational job belongs to the school (and why do you think so) and what part to other agencies? And who is to help the "other agencies" do their part properly?—or do they need help? Is education the responsibility of the total community or only of the school and possibly the family?

Issue II. Most statements of objectives of education reduce to two goals, which reflect the biological and the social nature of man. Thus a typical statement is that we want maximum self-realization of human, individual potentialities and we want the development of an enlightened citizenry capable of maintaining a society adapted to its times. Are these two separate objectives, as implied in the hog-wild "child-centered" school of the early 'thirties on the one hand and the talent-oriented "manpower technician" schools of the late 'fifties and early 'sixties on the other hand? If both these objectives have to be listed because gaining one does not insure gaining the other—a position I find most distasteful—then how is the balance to be found? And by what means can the two concerns be integrated within one individual? While we are on this issue, we may also ask: What balance do we seek between individuality and conformity?—and between intellectual and social-emotional development as the aims of education?

Issue III. How are we to regard the "funded capital of human experience," the accumulated knowledge of mankind? Is there a permanent core of true knowledge that must be passed on to each generation or is there only a body of provisional truth whose meaning must be rediscovered and re-interpreted by every learner for himself? Or, as the philosopher would put it, is truth absolute or is it relative to situations? The first position led to the "transmission belt" system of education: lecture, recitation, examination; the second position led to the "activity" plan in education: teacher-pupil planning, action, and evaluation. Are either or both right? Is there some third possibility that makes better sense? If so, what?

Issue IV. The imagination of the civilized world has been captured by the concept, pioneered but not perfected in America, of "equal educational opportunity for all." What does this mean? Does it mean, for example, equal opportunity to learn a particular body of knowledge set by the school—regardless of its meaningfulness to students having different capabilities and need? Or does it mean opportunity to learn whatever each child needs to learn in order to profit from his particular capabilities? Does it mean that every child in every state should have the same amount of money spent on him? Assuming that some teachers are better than others, who should get the best ones—the child who learns most readily or the one who learns least readily? What about the "culturally deprived" child, whose "background" has built-in resistance to learning; or the emotionally disturbed child, whose preoccupations keep him from listening; or the physiologically precocious or immature child, whose biological needs are out of step with the social possibilities for those of his age—what does equal opportunity mean here?

Design for Inquiry

I do not believe that any amount of tinkering will give us the solution we so desperately need to the four philosophical issues described above. And what we need is in any case not just tinkering but a drastic overhauling. Our present limited research-based theories, blooming so profusely in college textbooks, are useful, but we need something in addition: namely, broad general theories and propositions that tell us what the human being is like, why knowledge developed and what it is for, how the school and community influence each other, and so on. The sort of general theory we need takes in a lot of territory; it makes sense for all educational situations. It is also believable; it snuggles down where we live and resonates with our reflected-upon experience. It makes sense even though it cannot be demonstrated by scientific data alone, though neither will it be disproved. Believable general, useful, and handy theories and suppositions serve their purpose like generals and then gradually fade away through incorporation in more general, believable and useful theories.

To invest any general theory with belief is to take a risk; to believe a theory hard enough to act on its suppositions calls for commitments to ideas—not to the idea of an idea but to ideas as representations, inadequate though they may be, of the real world.

So what do we want to know?

Item. We want to know in the most fundamental terms we can what a living, breathing, feeling, and thinking human being is about. We especially want to know what happens when he is confronted with stress, for education is supposed to change people, and to do this it makes demands on them. Moreover if any learning is to result, the demands have to be ones to which the human being does not know for sure how to respond; and hence the stress. We want to know what tendencies in the human being we can count on to help us educate him and we want to see if we can use this knowledge the better to capitalize on these tendencies. We want to know whether inquiry and critical thinking serve a useful purpose for human beings; if so, where did they come from and how can they be strengthened?

Item. We also want to know about knowledge. Educators place great store by knowledge; It is obviously a Good Thing. Is it like money in the bank? Is it power? a bag of tools? a key? a set of filled pigeonholes? an end in itself (like ice cream)? insurance? Is it something to use to distinguish between the educated (good guys) and the uneducated (bad guys)? We also want to know two further things about knowledge: What light does the way knowledge was gained in the first place throw on how it can be learned by others later? And, in view of the arguments between "science" and the "humanities" we want to know what sort of importance each kind of knowledge has.

Item. We want to know what education has to do with society. What does the educational system have to do with the system of government, of economics, of politics? It is all very well to say that education is for the purpose of maintaining our nation or developing a world order, but what does that mean? Does it mean that every individual must be made literate, wise, loyal and conforming? What are the facts about the age-old conflict between the "individual" and "society" or between the adolescent surrounded by social and emotional pressures and the demands of the school that he learn to think?

We want to know what the talk about community-school relationships means. Is a school a cultural island, separated from the community mainland by the same kind of thing that separates fantasy from real life? Does the school lead or follow the community or both? We hear a lot about the need to "involve" citizens in school problems. Who, how, why? Is it just to keep them quiet? or to manipulate them into contributing more money? Is school supposed to "induct youth into the community"? What does that mean? In primitive tribes this is done with teaching by the wise men followed by the celebration of the rites of puberty; how do we do it? What would it mean to have an educative community, with educational responsibilities divided up? Can the school do the job alone? Or is the school only one part of a community-wide educational system which exists in fact whether the school board knows it or not? Can you distinguish education from welfare? And the kind of welfare that goes on in schools from the presumed other kinds that go on elsewhere?

Our inquiry into these matters might begin with a look at Man, Knowledge, and Society simply to understand the nature of the materials education deals with. This examination should reveal to us "factors," processes, and tendencies that represent the realities most pertinent for education; and the values which these tendencies imply as the actual purposes of human effort. These kinds of ideas together set limits and suggest opportunities for educational activity.

Our next step might be to construct the basic suppositions of an educational theory. Such ideas lie in the field where scientific theory and philosophy interpenetrate. They might help to identify generalized and significant tendencies which we believe do exist in America today. We might consider how each of these tendencies might be harnessed to the job of educating children, and we might proceed rather speculatively (and certainly tentatively) to spell out in some detail exactly how this harnessing might be done in the school.

The first general tendency we could propose is the quest for autonomy and captaincy of self, and we could show how this provides the basis for a type of learning experience which we might call "Personal Inquiry." Personal inquiry is driven by strong needs of individuals, and the educational requirement is to place the learner in a carefully chosen environment in which he can discover the insights he needs to behave more "intelligently."

The next general tendency we might propose is the development of the social order, and we could show how this tendency in groups can be used to develop motivation for all sorts of learning. The type of learning experience based on this tendency is labeled "Group Investigation." Group investigation capitalizes on the fact that when people are confined in a room they begin to interact, and the group that emerges must develop a system of controls and supporting attitudes and values of such a kind that the interactions maintain rather than destroy the group. The educational requirement is to guide the group in such a way that its culture and values are oriented to inquiry and to learning appropriate to the school subject or field of knowledge.

The third general tendency is to take action in order to improve the relationships between persons and groups on the one hand and their social and natural environments on the other. The type of learning experience based on this tendency has been dubbed "Reflective Action." With reference to children and youth, reflective action capitalizes on the very strong need, presently thwarted, for an adult-recognized "place" in the functioning of the community. The educational requirement is to help youth become educated through their own voluntary efforts to assume responsible roles in the school and larger community.

I could show how these various tendencies toward the values of autonomy, predictability, and two-way adaptation—scrambled, mixed up, and mutually interfering in today's classrooms—can be used to educate the child. They will, however, not accomplish the whole job of education, and the missing part has to do with those learnings that call for repetition and practice rather than insight. However much we may succeed in making education an experience of inquiry, there will always be an irreducible core of learnings that cannot be developed simply through insight. Some part of the three R's, for instance, must be learned through drill because there is no way in which intelligence can produce the right answer.

Finally, I might tackle the question of how the sort of schools I have been pointing to can be developed, and here we might try to apply our own principles to the action strategy so sorely needed right now in many communities.

4

*The object of the common school system is to give
every child a free, straight, solid pathway by which he
can walk directly up from the ignorance of an infant
to a knowledge of the primary duties of a man, and
can acquire a power and an invincible will to discharge them.*

HORACE MANN
1837

Sterling M. McMurrin
WHAT TASKS FOR THE SCHOOLS?

Among the large problems that are always with us, none is more
persistent, more pervasive, or more basic than the problem of means and
ends—of insuring that our methods, techniques, and instruments are
adequate to the ends we seek, that the ends are relevant to our abilities
and, above all, not dominated and determined by our means. In a society
that feeds on a rapidly advancing and sophisticated technology, the
failure to have clear and forceful purposes and viable ends could be
disastrous. We could become the creators of a technological order in
which our ends would be defined and established by the instruments
that were fashioned to serve us rather than by considerations of human
value, an order in which the things that matter most would be at the
mercy of the things that matter least.

Nowhere is the problem of means and ends more crucial than in education. Confronted by quite remarkable technical possibilities, we are
failing to come to grips with the problem of aims and purposes and to
define adequately the proper function of the schools—their specialized
role in relation to the educative processes of the whole society and their
immediate task in the education of the child. Certainly without clear
purposes—large and small, direct and indirect—the schools cannot successfully plot their course amid the present revolution of numbers,
dollars, and computers. Most revolutions are lost because their aims are
ambiguous and ill-conceived. We cannot afford to lose the revolution in
education by being overwhelmed by the new technology because we
cannot match it with intelligent and resolute purpose.

Because education is a function of the society and its culture, its purposes are determined by them, by the character of the social institutions
and by the values of the culture. In the United States or in any other

From Sterling M. McMurrin, "What Tasks for the Schools?" *Saturday Review*, January
14, 1967, pp. 40–43 (a special issue produced in cooperation with the Committee for Economic Development). Reprinted by permission of the *Saturday Review*.

democratic society, the purposes of education are multiple and complex. The schools, traditionally overconservative in their ways, must cultivate the capacity to change when the conditions of society call for something different or when educational research and technology demand the use of new methods.

The elementary function of education is the perpetuation of the culture. Education is an almost instinctive conservative force that secures whatever is of worth in the social structure and in the substance of the culture. The schools are subtle, sensitive, and highly effective instruments of indoctrination by which every generation gathers up the achievements of the past, employs them in the pursuit of its own ends, and communicates them to future generations.

Our society is marked by scientific intelligence, social conscience, and an acute historical consciousness; it possesses a remarkable capacity for invention and change. Since for us change is inevitable, unless we move forward with resolution our society is in danger of retrogression and our culture in danger of decline. We cannot live simply by the conservation and perpetuation of the past; we must be critical and creative.

The proper function of schools, therefore, is to be the chief agents of progress, whether it is the advancement of knowledge, improvement in the arts, technology, or the social conscience, in institutional organization and administration, or in the attainment of those large visions of the future which are the prime movers of history. For the schools, colleges, and universities provide the most effective means for the achievement of the intellectual skill, knowledge, understanding, and appreciation necessary to the analysis, judgment, and decision without which there can be no genuine progress. We depend upon them to stimulate that freshness of ways, attitudes, and ideas which alone can bring vitality and high achievement to a culture. Achieving an effective relationship between the conservative and creative functions of education is a difficult and unceasing task. Out of the dialectic of conservation and creation issue most of the basic tensions that develop between the schools and their communities.

"Education" refers to society as the totality of socio-economic-political arrangements. It refers, as well, to both the fabric and substance of the culture, its value structure, and its creative process. But in a democratic society the purposes and energies of education must be centered primarily upon the individual, upon the cultivation of his talents and abilities, both for his vocational preparation and the melioration and adornment of his life. And education for the individual means the securing of those conditions which are essential to an authentic individualism.

Deeply imbedded in the political faith of the American people is the belief that whatever contributes importantly to the life of the individual —whatever disciplines his mind, nourishes his values, refines his sensitivities, and prepares him for a productive vocation—contributes also to the solidarity of the society; and that it also brings strength and vitality to the culture and adds to it that authenticity and integrity of spirit without which no civilization can hope to endure. So the purposes of education must be sought across the total spectrum of human interest, experience, and value. The task of education seen in this context is nothing less than the achievement and preservation of a genuinely free society in which men are authentic persons who are masters of the forces which shape their world.

In the past, educators have invested excessively in the development of educational *methods*. There has been too little concern for the *substance* of education and a minimum of interest in its purposes. With the new curriculum reforms the question of substance is gradually gaining the attention which it deserves; but the purposes are still neglected and confused. The all-too-common domination of educational thought by the interest in methodology has meant that method has often been the major determinant of substance and purpose. Our schools would have been much stronger today and would now more effectively perform their function if we had brought the problems of method and substance and purpose into a more honest and effective relationship.

This does not mean that the methods of instruction can be treated indifferently. The discussion of the purpose of the schools, for instance, cannot ignore the developments in educational technology which must now become major factors in our educational planning. This would be an untenable and disastrous separation of means and ends and could lead to gross distortions in the whole structure of education—and, eventually, the destruction of the humane values that we seek through the schools. But the proper ends of education can be realized only if they are placed within the grasp of the schools, where the educational program is designed to conform to the immediate and proximate ends that our methods and expertness are capable of achieving. In view of the great promise of educational technology that it may make new things possible, we should refine our goals and be prepared to move in new directions of learning.

The central tasks of the school are the dissemination of knowledge, the cultivation of the intellect, and induction into the uses of reason. We expect the schools to do many things: to discipline the moral life by sharpening the powers of discernment, making the moral conscience more sensitive and increasing the sense of civic responsibility; to nurture the esthetic life by cultivating artistic appreciation and creativity; to strengthen the spiritual life by refining the sense of worth and value and investing life with meaning and purpose. But unless a school concentrates its purposes first upon knowledge and reason, it will not contribute importantly to these things; rather, it will confuse its purpose, dissipate its energies, and utterly fail in its responsibility.

This does not mean that the educational process should be subordinated to the simple communication of information. The quest for knowledge means far more than this. It entails the full development of the intellectual capacities of the individual, a development that is quite impossible in any other context. It is here that the mind achieves its powers of sensory perception and discrimination; here the individual learns to distinguish the meaningful from the meaningless and gains respect for evidence and for logical discourse. Here he cultivates his powers of intellectual insight, analysis, and generalization, his capacity to discern the universal in the particular, and his comprehension of cause and effect, of order and structure, and his understanding of the nature of theory and the relation of theory to practice. And most important, it is here in the actual pursuit of knowledge that even a child finds the joys of knowing and the virtue of intellectual honesty and develops the passion for truth.

There are, in effect, three primary functions of instruction, which are defined by the immediate task of the schools: the cognitive, the affective, and the conative functions.

The cognitive function of instruction is directed to the achievement and communication of knowledge, both the factual knowledge of the sciences and the formal relationships of logic and mathematics—knowledge as both specific data and generalized structure. It is discipline in the ways of knowing, involving perception, the inductive, deductive, and intuitive processes, and the techniques of analysis and generalization. It involves both the immediate grasp of sensory objects and the abstractive processes by which the intellect constructs its ideas and fashions its ideals.

The affective function of instruction pertains to the practical life—to the emotions, the passions, the disposition, the motives, the moral and esthetic sensibilities, the capacity for feeling, concern, attachment or detachment, sympathy, empathy, and appreciation.

The conative function involves overt behavior—struggling, striving, impulse, commitment, desire, decision, action, and the power of will.

I am not proposing a return to the theory of mental faculties that was long ago abandoned as a gross distortion of the complex character of the human mind and its behavior. But to see these basic categories in the description of the mental functions is to see the intricate and difficult structure of education and to sense the enormity of its task. Most of our work and most of our success has been with the cognitive function of instruction, which is admittedly primary. We know more about cognition and our tools and techniques are best adapted to its task. We are only beginning to move effectively in research into the regions of the affective and conative functions, and we have a long way to go before we will be on firm ground. Here especially there is need for openness, creativeness, and innovation in the substance and methods of education and in the preparation of teachers. The affective and conative facets of education, though less primary, are not less important. But they are more difficult to understand, assess, and negotiate. When we face the challenge of the new technology—how to employ for proper educational ends such instruments as television, teaching machines, or computer systems— our decisions must be made in the light of the total impact of instruction upon knowledge and the rational intellect but not violating the claims of the emotions and volition.

We should recognize here another useful distinction in the total structure of the educational process, what may be called simply verbal-conceptual education as compared with nonverbal-nonconceptual education. In occidental culture especially, our preoccupation with knowledge, reason, and abstraction has produced assumptions, methods, and habits of education that are directed primarily to the construction and communication of ideas and complex conceptualized structures that are highly dependent upon language and language skills. The educated person is one who can deal successfully in a kind of conceptual coinage, whose achievements are especially in the ability to use words and mathematical or logical symbols effectively and to reason discursively in the formation, examination, and exchange of ideas.

I would not depreciate the worth of this dominant element of our education. It is the chief foundation stone of our culture. Upon it depend our philosophic thought, our science and technology, and much more that is precious and basic to the whole structure of our civilization. But we must ask whether in immersing ourselves so exclusively in this cognitive function of education—in education for verbal-conceptual abilities—we have not severely neglected other important and sometimes simpler facets of personality and life—the esthetic pleasures, for instance, that accrue from sharpening the instruments of sensory perception, or the intrinsic values in the appreciation of poetry and art which are available to those whose education has cultivated their intuitive powers and refined their capacities for sympathy and feeling. Or consider the whole area of what we commonly and somewhat loosely call the inner life. This is crucially important territory about which we know little and do less. We cannot assume that because we have been so eminently successful in building a high civilization on the foundations of philosophy and theoretical science we are justified in our failure to explore fully the large possibilities that are open to us to augment and strengthen our cultural achievement.

It is a simple matter to theorize on what is appropriate or inappropriate to social institutions, but it is quite another thing to shape those institutions in practice to conform to the ideal concepts which we construct of them. The schools in fact are subject to countless divergent and conflicting pressures. Their problems are set for them by the real forces of society, and any serious educational planning must respect those forces. Certainly one of the central issues confronting us today is the question of whether the schools should serve other social functions than education as traditionally conceived—the question, for instance, of the limits of their custodial responsibilities, of their obligations to become recreation or community centers, or, far more important, of whether they should be employed as instruments of social policy, as in the enforcement of civil rights laws.

It would be more accurate, of course, to ask not whether these should be school functions, since in various ways they already are well established, but rather to what degree these should be school functions. For among the important causes of the schools' failure to achieve their educational goals is the habit of society of imposing obligations upon them which are foreign to their character, for which they may not be well equipped, and which have little or no relevance to the central purpose of education. More and more the schools are expected to share the tasks of the home in rearing the child, to assume a larger responsibility for the social life of youth, to take on social work which properly belongs to other public agencies, to accept responsibility for delinquency, to bear the blame for every moral deficiency of the individual or the society. The large failures of society in matters of civil rights and race relations, for instance, as expressed especially in the employment, income, and housing patterns of the great cities, have placed an enormous burden upon education. The schools are expected to effectively pursue the proper ends of education and at the same time solve problems of segregation and racial discrimination for which they may be in no way responsible and for which there are no solutions short of a complete and total effort by all agencies and segments of community life.

This is not to suggest that the schools can or should avoid the social tasks that are clearly a part of the educational enterprise and for which they can mobilize effective resources. They have obvious organizational advantages and professional competencies for mounting difficult social problems. But when society fails to recognize the limits that are proper in such matters, it seriously endangers the quality of future intellectual attainment.

The determination of the purposes and ends proper to education is the chief task of the philosophy of education, a discipline which in recent decades has fallen into serious confusion from which it is only now beginning to recover. For some time the philosophy of education has often been reduced to a more or less standard format in which educational policies and procedures are allegedly, by virtue of appropriate intellectual contortions and logical distortions, deduced from premises established in metaphysics, the theory of knowledge, or theory of value. This kind of argument has produced much confusion and not a little dogmatism. Certainly the basic considerations of education have relevance to the nature of reality, the nature of knowledge, and especially to value theory and specific value concepts. But such central issues in the philosophy of education as the purposes of education must be decided not so much by deduction from abstract speculative theses as by such practical considerations as the threat of cultural decline, the establishment of social justice, the national security, the need for strengthening the economy and for satisfying its manpower demands, the aspiration of individuals toward artistic expression, their vocational and professional interests, their anxieties and frustrations, and their demand for autonomy and freedom.

The nation faces a future that is fraught with difficulties and uncertainties. Threatened from without by enemies of overwhelming strength and affected within by the subtle yet powerful forces that issue from the clash of economic interest, the processes of urbanization and industrialization, racial tensions, and political struggle, and endangered by irrationalism, bigotry, and growing personal and social anxieties, it needs as never before the full development of its intellectual capabilities. This means nothing less than achieving the maximum possible education for every individual—education in the requisite knowledge and skills for vocation and profession, and education in that humane knowledge and wisdom that frees the mind from the bondage of ignorance and the spirit from hopelessness and fear. Only a full commitment of our intellectual, moral, and spiritual resources will bring to the culture the vital energy essential to greatness in the years ahead. And only an educational effort that far exceeds our past accomplishments will preserve the distinctive personal quality of life that must always be the mark of a free people.

5

You cannot make children learn music or anything else without to some degree converting them into willless adults. You fashion them into accepters of the status quo—a good thing for a society that needs obedient sitters at dreary desks, standers in shops, mechanical catchers of the 8:30 suburban train— a society, in short, that is carried on the shabby shoulders of the scared little man—the scared-to-death conformist.

A. S. NEILL
Summerhill

Paul Goodman

THE PRESENT MOMENT IN PROGRESSIVE EDUCATION

I

The program of progressive education always anticipates the crucial social problems that everybody will be concerned with a generation later, when it is too late for the paradisal solutions of progressive educators. This is in the nature of the case. Essentially, progressive education is nothing but the attempt to naturalize, to humanize, each new social and technical development that is making traditional education irrelevant. It is not a reform of education, but a reconstruction in terms of the new era. If society would *once* adopt this reconstruction, we could at last catch up with ourselves and grow naturally into the future. But equally in the nature of the case, society rejects, half-accepts, bastardizes the necessary changes; and so we are continually stuck with "unfinished revolutions," as I called them in *Growing Up Absurd*. Then occur the vast social problems that *could* have been avoided—that indeed the older progressive education had specifically addressed—but it is too late. And progressive educators stoically ask, What is the case *now?*

During the current incredible expansion of increasingly unnatural schooling, and increasing alienation of the young, it is useful to trace the course of progressive education in this century, from John Dewey to the American version of A. S. Neill.

II

The recent attacks on Deweyan progressive education, by the Rickovers and Max Raffertys, have really been outrageous—one gets impatient. Historically, the intent of Dewey was exactly the opposite of what the critics say. Progressive education appeared in this country in the intellectual, moral, and social crisis of the development of big centralized industrialism after the Civil War. It was the first thoroughgoing modern analysis of the crucial modern problem of every advanced country in the world: how to cope with high industrialism and scientific technology which are strange to people; how to restore competence to people who are becoming ignorant; how to live in the rapidly growing cities so that they will not be mere urban sprawl; how to have a free society in mass conditions; how to make the high industrial system good for something, rather than a machine running for its own sake.

That is, progressive education was the correct solution of a real problem that Rickover is concerned with, the backwardness of people in a scientific world. To put it more accurately, if progressive education had been generally adopted, we should not be so estranged and ignorant today.

The thought of John Dewey was part of a similar tendency in architecture, the functionalism of Louis Sullivan and Frank Lloyd Wright, that was trying to invent an urbanism and an esthetic suited to machine-production and yet human; and it went with the engineering orientation of the economic and moral theory of Veblen. These thinkers wanted to train, teach—perhaps accustom is the best word—the new generation to the actualities of industrial and technical life, working practically with the machinery, learning by doing. People could then be at home in the modern world, and possibly become free.

At-homeness had also a political aspect. Dewey was distressed by both the robber-baron plutocracy and the bossed mass-democracy; and he was too wise to espouse Veblen's technocracy, engineer's values. Dewey put a good deal of faith in industrial democracy, overestimating the labor movement—he did not foresee the bureaucratization of the unions. As a pragmatist he probably expected that the skilled would become initiators in management and production; he did not foresee that labor demands would diminish to wages and working conditions.

But the school, he felt, could combine all the necessary elements: practical learning of science and technology, democratic community, spontaneous feeling liberated by artistic appreciation, freedom to fantasize, and animal expression freed from the parson's morality and the schoolmaster's ruler. This constituted the whole of Deweyan progressive education. There would be spontaneous interest (including animal impulse), harmonized by art-working; this spontaneity would be controlled by the hard pragmatism of doing and making the doing actually work; and thus the young democratic community would learn the modern world and also have the will to change it. Progressive education was a theory of continual scientific experiment and orderly, nonviolent social revolution.

As was inevitable, this theory was entirely perverted when it began to be applied, either in private schools or in the public system. The conservatives and the businessmen cried out, and the program was toned down. The practical training and community democracy, whose purpose was to live scientifically and change society, was changed into "socially useful" subjects and a psychology of "belonging." In our schools, driver-training survives as the type of the "useful." (By now, I suspect, Dewey would have been urging us to curtail the number of cars.) Social-dancing was the type of the "belonging." The Americans had no intention of broadening the scientific base and taking technological expertness and control out of the hands of the top managers and their technicians. And democratic community became astoundingly interpreted as conformity, instead of being the matrix of social experiment and political change.

III

Curiously, just in the past few years, simultaneous with the attack on "Dewey," his ideas have been getting most prestigious official endorsement (though they are not attributed to Dewey). In the great post-Sputnik cry to increase the scientific and technical pool, the critics of "Dewey" call for strict lessons and draconian grading and weeding-out (plus bribes), to find the élite group. (Dr. Conant says that the "academically talented" are 15% and these, selected by national tests, will be at home *for* us in the modern technical world as its creative spirits.) However, there is an exactly contrary theory, propounded by the teachers of science, e.g. the consensus of the Woods Hole Conference of the National Science Foundation, reported in Professor Bruner's *The Processes of Education*. This theory counsels practical learning by doing, entirely rejects competition and grading, and encourages fantasy and guesswork. There is no point, it claims, in learning the "answers," for very soon there will be different answers. Rather, what must be taught are the underlying ideas of scientific thought, continuous with the substance of the youngster's feelings and experience. In short, the theory is Deweyan progressive education.

To be sure, Professor Bruner and his associates do not go on to espouse democratic community. But I am afraid they will eventually find that also this is essential, for it is impossible to do creative work of any kind when the goals are pre-determined by outsiders and cannot be criticized and altered by the minds that have to do the work, even if they are youngsters. (Dewey's principle is, simply, that good teaching is that which leads the student to want to learn something more.)

The compromise of the National Science Foundation on this point is rather comical. "Physical laws are not asserted; they are, it is hoped, discovered by the student"; "there is a desire to allow each student to experience some of the excitement that scientific pursuits afford"—I am quoting from the NSF's *Science Course Improvement Projects*. That is, the student is to make a leap of discovery to—what is already known, in a course precharted by the Ph.D.'s at M.I.T. Far from being elating, such a process must be profoundly disappointing; my guess is that the "discovery" will be greeted not by a cheer but by a razz. The excitement of discovery is reduced to the animation of puzzle-solving. I doubt that puzzle-solving is what creative thought is about, though it is certainly what many Ph.D.'s are about.

IV

Authentic progressive education, meantime, has moved into new territory altogether, how to cope with the over-centralized organization and Organization Men of our society, including the top-down direction of science by the National Science Foundation. The new progressive theory is "Summerhill."

The American Summerhill movement is modeling itself on A. S. Neill's school in England, but with significant deviations—so that Neill does not want his name associated with some of the offshoots.

Like Dewey, Neill stressed free animal expression, learning by doing, and *very* democratic community processes (one person one vote, enfranchising small children!). But he also asserted a principle that to Dewey did not seem important, the freedom to choose to go to class or stay away altogether. A child at Summerhill can just hang around; he'll go to class when he damned well feels like it—and some children, coming from compulsory schools, don't damned well feel like it for eight or nine months. But after a while, as the curiosity in the soul revives—and since their friends go—they give it a try.

It is no accident, as I am trying to show, that it is just *this* departure in progressive education that is catching on in America, whereas most of the surviving Deweyan schools are little better than the good suburban schools that imitated them. The advance-guard problem is that the compulsory school system, like the whole of our economy, politics, and standard of living, has become a lockstep. It is no longer designed for the maximum growth and future practical utility of the children into a changing world, but is inept social engineering for extrinsic goals, pitifully short-range. Even when it is benevolent, it is in the bureaucratic death-grip of a uniformity of conception, from the universities down, that cannot possibly suit the multitude of dispositions and conditions. Yet 100% of the children are supposed to remain for at least 12 years in one kind of box; and of course those who attend private Deweyan schools are being aimed for 4 to 8 years more. Thus, if we are going to experiment with real universal education that educates, we have to start by getting rid of compulsory schooling altogether.

V

One American variant of Summerhill has developed in a couple of years in an unforeseen direction. Like Summerhill this school is not urban, but, unlike Summerhill, it is not residential. Many of the children come from a nearby colony of artists, some of them of international fame. The artist parents, and other parents, come into the school as part-time teachers, of music, painting, building, dancing.

Being strong-minded, they, and the regular teachers, soon fell out with the headmaster, the founder, who had been a Summerhill teacher; they stripped him of important prerogatives and he resigned. Inevitably other parents had to join in the discussions and decisions, on real and difficult issues. The result seems to have been the formation of a peculiar kind of extended family, unified by educating the children, and incorporating a few professional teachers. But meantime, imitated from Neill, there is the democratic council, in which the children have a very loud voice and an equal vote, and this gives them an institutional means to communicate with, and get back at, their parents. It is stormy and factional. Some parents have pulled out and teachers have quit. Yet, inadvertently, there is developing a brilliant solution to crucial problems of American life: how can children grow up in live contact with many adults; how can those who do the work run the show; how to transcend a rigid professionalism that is wasteful of human resources.

At present one of the teachers at this school is preparing to try out a little Summerhill school in a slum area in New York.

Another Summerhill variant has taken a different course: to use the school almost directly as social action. To overcome the artificial stratification of modern society, it brings together not only Negroes and whites but delinquents and the well-behaved. Naturally this gets the school into trouble with its surroundings. It has had to flee from the South to the North, and it is in trouble again in the North.

Such a combination of education and direct social action is springing up on all sides. The so-called Northern Student Movement is a group of college-students who take a year off from college to tutor urban underprivileged kids referred by the public schools; but the NSM has now declared as its policy *not* to restrict itself to the curriculum and aims of the school system. The Student Non-Violent Coordinating Committee has gone down to the deep South, primarily to help in the voter-registration of disenfranchised Negroes, but also to try out little colleges for adolescents, with 5 graduate-students teaching 25 teenagers a curriculum relevant to their economic and political advancement. Accompanying the numerous school-boycotts there have sprung up "Freedom" schools that started as one-day propaganda demonstrations but have been lively enough to warrant continuing.

In my opinion, the highly official Peace Corps has the same underlying educational significance. At present it is rigidly selective and supercollegiate; indeed it is, by and large, an operation for upper-middle class youth and well-paid professors and administrators: it costs $15,000 to get one youngster in the field for a year. Nevertheless, the whole conception is unthinkable except as dissatisfaction with orthodox schooling and with the status-careers that that schooling leads to.

VI

The future—if we survive and have a future, which is touch and go—will certainly be more leisurely. If that leisure is not to be completely inane and piggishly affluent, there must be a community and civic culture. There must be more employment in human services and less in the production of hardware gadgets; more citizenly initiative and less regimentation; and in many spheres, decentralization of control and administration. For these purposes, the top-down dictated national plans and educational methods that are now the fad are quite irrelevant. And on the contrary, it is precisely the society of free choice, lively engagement, and social action of Summerhill and American Summerhill that are relevant and practical.

Thus just as with Dewey, the new advance of progressive education is a good index of what the real situation is. And no doubt society will again seek to abuse this program which it needs but is afraid of.

6

Not only is American education under fire; the practice of criticizing our schools is well on its way to becoming a national pastime.
MARY ANNE RAYWILD
The Ax-Grinders

H. G. Rickover
A NATIONAL SCHOLASTIC STANDARD

It has long been evident to me that the absence of a standard handicaps American education. Our schools and the diplomas they award have always been qualitatively of the most amazing diversity. This was perhaps unavoidable in earlier times when Americans were still engaged in subduing a wilderness. Different parts of the country were then at different stages of development, and education, of course, reflects the state of culture. It was bound to be better in the long-settled communities along the Atlantic seaboard than in pioneer country. But today we are one nation technologically and culturally; we should be one nation in education as well. Our children's educational needs are the same whether they go to school in California or Maine, in Illinois or Alabama.

Everywhere, and at all times, a country's level of culture and technology sets the requirements for education. Of this, the men who direct

From H. G. Rickover, "A National Scholastic Standard" (mimeographed), pp. 1–22. Copyright 1967 by H. G. Rickover. Reprinted by permission of the author.

our public school system seem to be but dimly aware. They subscribe to a philosophy of education, an ideology, which is at odds with reality. They recognize neither the educational needs of children in today's world, nor the reality of their diverse native endowments which necessarily determine what each can accomplish educationally. Nor do they have a clear concept of the basic purpose of a tax-supported public school system.

Schools do not exist in a vacuum. Nor are they set up to serve as laboratories for testing newfangled ideas dreamed up by theoretical educationists. They are established to supplement home, church, and community as educators of the young. Their primary task is intellectual education, a task no other agency *can* do. It matters not how well they serve children in other ways. They will have failed their purpose if they do not transmit to them the knowledge, and develop in them the intellectual skills that children must acquire if they are to become contributing members of their society.

How well then does American public education perform its primary task? Do our young people acquire at school the knowledge they need to understand our complex modern world, the intellectual skills they need to qualify for the kind of work that is available? Have they received the best preparation—commensurate with their ability and industry— for the responsibilities of adult life?

To meet these responsibilities they must have adequate knowledge in the areas of language, mathematics, science, government, history, and geography. Success in adult life—as an individual, a breadwinner, a citizen—is closely linked to the amount of education one acquires at school in these areas of basic knowledge. Have our children learned as much, *have their minds been stretched as far as would have been the case had they gone to school in some other culturally and technically advanced country?*

The world is now so small, so competitive. The economic and political position of nations is bound, in the long run, to reflect so accurately the quality of their people that what is achieved in foreign school systems can no longer be disregarded by us. There is a sort of international Plimsoll mark in education that sets a standard below which it is unsafe to let public education fall.

My work gives me a unique opportunity to judge the products of our schools. Over the last two decades, I have interviewed several thousand top graduates of the Naval Academy and of our best colleges who wished to enter the nuclear program as designers and builders or as operators of atomic-powered ships. I look for bright, well-educated young men with initiative and the ability to think for themselves. I find, though nearly all the applicants have excellent minds, disturbingly few qualify educationally. I constantly come up against the results of poor education; I see how much talent is wasted, how little progress has been made in education, despite the vast amount of thought and money we have expended in recent years. I find that technically the young men are better trained now, but their general education remains inadequate. The schools are letting us down at a time when the nation has urgent need of the *developed* intellectual resources of all the people.

Ours is the most complicated technical society in history. We live in a democracy, hence under the most difficult kind of political system, since it requires so much of each citizen. We need better educated people to manage our society, better educated citizens to assure that it will be well governed.

In the military, we are used to comparing ourselves with other countries, for we know it would be dangerous to let anyone get ahead of us. After extensively investigating school systems in other advanced countries, I must regretfully say that our competitive position in education vis-à-vis these countries is unsatisfactory. There are many reasons why our schools are less effective educators of the young than schools elsewhere, and I have spoken and written of them at length. Underlying them all and perpetuating them is our commitment to standardless comprehensive schooling.

Five years ago, I testified on English education before the House Appropriations Committee. The late Chairman Clarence Cannon asked by what means I thought Congress might help speed educational progress. My reply was: By establishing a National Standards Committee, and I outlined what kind of committee I thought it should be and what specific functions it should perform. In the preface he wrote to the published hearings, Mr. Cannon expressed the hope that they would "stimulate a national debate on the question of whether there shall be set up an agency of some kind to provide permissive national standards."

It should be said first of all that we are the only civilized country where public education operates without a national academic standard, where neither the names of educational institutions, nor their curricula, nor their diplomas or degrees represent a definitive and known standard of intellectual accomplishment. In Europe—the only area we need to be concerned with since the Europeans (including the Russians) are our only true competitors in public education—it is taken for granted that children must be tested against an objective standard before they are promoted. Otherwise, there might be gaps in knowledge, or repetition of subjects already studied, or children might embark on new programs before they are ready for them.

Educators and public alike are agreed that study programs must be carefully planned and that they must lead to a variety of educational goals, reflecting the variety of learning ability and of vocational objectives of their pupils. They are agreed that for efficient progress, programs must be sequential, each year building on what has been learned in the preceding one, each phase of schooling articulating closely with the one below and above it—as from primary to secondary and from the several secondary schools to vocational-professional schools, building upon the general education received at the secondary level. None of this would be possible if there were no national scholastic standard. Because *all* European schools concentrate on intellectual education, there are transfer possibilities all along the line for anyone who suddenly develops talents he had not previously shown, *provided* he is willing to make the effort to catch up with programs at a higher level.

Next to the greater length of the European as compared to the American school year, it is this close articulation in European public education that makes it possible for European children—*all* of them, bright, average, and slow—to reach any level of scholastic achievement at a much earlier age than ours. It also accounts for the fact that geographic inequalities due to different rates of economic progress in different parts of the country are not as pronounced there, and transfer from the schools of one locality to those of another is easier.

Though our children would greatly benefit from a national scholastic standard, the prospects are not good that we shall be able to obtain it for them. Theory and practice in American public education are strongly opposed to testing children against objective standards.

There is a school of thought which considers tests irrelevant to the process of becoming educated. But this, as one of England's university examiners aptly remarked, would be true only if one felt it "to be sufficient to expose the pupil to learning and undesirable to discover if there are any results." Many schoolmen object to achievement tests because some children would fail and this might injure their psyche. But in life, all of us are constantly tested against objective standards of performance; all of us at some time or another will fail a test. Would it not be better to let children discover at school what their abilities and limitations are, thus giving them experience in coming to terms with the truth about themselves *before* they have to face the demands of the adult world? Fewer young people would then need to be counseled by "career doctors."

I am inclined to think the main reason why our schoolmen oppose a national academic standard is that it contravenes the "Freudian" or "Social" ethic to which most of them are committed—an ethic which deprecates *individual* responsibility for what one makes of his life, and places responsibility on *society*. Those who accept this ethic tend to look upon education as a "right" possessed in equal measure by each child; in other words, a right with no conditions attached to it. It is not enough that there be *equal educational opportunity*; what is demanded is the right to higher education and to degrees *without* giving proof of qualification. Removing the price tag from higher education has had the curious effect in this country of transforming education into a sort of "consumer good" which a democratic society is expected to hand out equally—"fair shares for all."

At present the American people have no yardstick with which to assess the performance of the schools for which they tax themselves so heavily. A national scholastic standard would give them such a yardstick, but the educational establishment will not even tolerate a permissive standard. We therefore have no way of finding out what, concretely, our children have learned at any given age and ability level, or how this compares with achievements in other school systems.

Such feeble attempts as we have made to evaluate our schools have been warded off by raising the bugaboo of federal control of the curriculum. Comparison with education in other advanced countries is rejected on the grounds that all foreign school systems—including the Russian!—are "aristocratic." We alone, it seems, have "democratic" education. Consequently, so it is said, the objectives of American education, the educational needs it serves, are so unique that what is accomplished elsewhere can be of no interest to us. Consider this statement made by an influential educator before a committee of the United States Senate: "Good teaching of reading beyond the fundamentals," he said, "is one thing in a society where a person is being prepared to read and instantaneously believe government propaganda, and it is an entirely different thing in a society where a person may be expected to enjoy the privilege of reading a free press."

I have thought and thought, but I can't get the sense of it. Does he mean it is more important to be able to read in Russia than here? Or does he mean the opposite? Does he really mean that *how* you teach children to read depends upon *what* they are going to read when they grow up?

One is always tempted to see in this or that defect the root cause of mediocre school performance. My own feeling is that most of the inadequacies of American education can be traced back to misconception of what "democratic education" really is. The schoolmen are passionately committed to the dogma that, to be democratic, education must not only be free but comprehensive as well. I would say that it must be both free *and of high quality*. It must provide public schooling that is as good as the costly private schooling available to children whose parents can pay the fees.

As I see it, the reason we and every other advanced country support expensive systems of public education is that we are determined that no child shall be denied schooling because he cannot pay for it. We socialize the cost of education to equalize opportunity.

Educational inequalities resulting from differences in wealth can be eliminated by shifting the financial burden of educating children from parent to taxpayer. *"Inabiltiy to pay" school fees is a removable bar to educational advancement*. There remain then the inequalities of ability and drive that are inborn. Society cannot play God and create children that are identical in mental capacity. Society cannot eliminate educational inequalities resulting from differences in aptitude—*"inability to learn" is an irremovable bar to educational advancement.* Many a poor child is gifted, many a rich child is stupid; either child may be industrious or lazy. The best that society—any society—can do is to make certain that the educational levels a child attains are determined *solely* by his own giftedness or stupidity, industriousness or laziness.

It matters not whether fees are charged or schooling is free, an educational system that takes no account of differences in learning capacity will give neither the bright nor the slow, nor even the average child the education his capacities warrant. When you eliminate "ability to pay" as a criterion for educational advancement you get democratic education; when you eliminate "ability to learn" you get noneducation.

Differences in learning ability, already evident when children enter school, increase year by year, as more difficult subject matter is studied. By about age 11 to 12 *the gap in mental* age in any representative group of children will then be six and one half years overall; three years if the top and bottom two percent of the intelligence range are absent. The *gap in achievement levels* will be greater still; it may be eight years. Studies in geography, history, English composition, literary knowledge, science, arithmetic reasoning, etc., have shown that in every high school grade "the complete range of elementary school achievement is present." Indeed, it *must* be present in a *comprehensive* high school since a substantial segment of the school population is intellectually incapable of advancing beyond the elementary level. Half our children, let it be remembered, are *by definition* below average, they are below 100 I.Q.

Comprehensive schooling in the primary grades is common to every system of public education. Experience has shown that *all* normal children, if properly instructed, *can* master the elementary subjects, though at different rates of speed. So long as the program is the same for all, differences in the *pace* at which children progress can be accommodated. But when mental inequalities affect not merely the speed of learning but its very substance, comprehensive schooling no longer makes sense *in terms of what children need.* They need to be challenged, to stretch their minds, to absorb the maximum amount of knowledge consistent with their endowments. Experience has shown that if they are to have this kind of education, they must separate at the end of elementary school, as indeed they do abroad. On the Continent, especially, there is an adequate choice in types of secondary schools to fit the abilities and goals of bright, average, and below average children.

In this country, comprehensive schooling continues to the end of public education. Abroad, it is discontinued when the point has been reached where subjects which bright children are able to absorb with relative ease have become extremely difficult for average children, and are incomprehensible for those at the bottom of the ability scale who are still struggling with the elementary subjects everybody else has long since mastered. Preoccupied with the comprehensive dogma and the impossible goal of "higher education for all," the educational establishment in this country has failed to develop programs for different levels of ability that are as well thought out, as efficiently organized as the system of secondary schools in Europe.

We have the most expensive public education in the world, yet nowhere can a bright child obtain the excellent academic secondary schooling that European *lycées* and *Gymnasia* provide—usually at no cost or, if a nominal fee is charged, at no cost to those who cannot pay. In these day schools, which are to be found in every town of 10,000 or so, students are carried by age 18 to 19 to a baccalaureate that is fully the equivalent of the B.A. of a first-rate American college, with only the student's "major" missing. No European child is barred by poverty from attaining this educational goal; not a few American children are so barred, for even in a nominally free state university, the cost of room and board may be beyond his financial resources.

Nowhere in our expensive school system can the average child find the excellent secondary schooling below baccalaureate level that is to be found in Europe. Upon the general education that is received in these secondary schools, there is built a network of vocational programs producing competent artisans, technicians of every kind, librarians, nurses, and a great variety of semiprofessionals.

All of Europe has a shortage of unskilled labor and imports large numbers of foreigners; we have a surplus of unskilled labor and a shortage of every kind of skilled technicians and professionals. We go abroad seeking to lure such people with high salaries, a practice which is deplored by countries that have invested much public money in the education of their talented youth and resent this "brain drain."

Nowhere in our expensive school system can you find the equivalent of the "common" school which in Europe provides the absolute minimum of education, the rock bottom below which no one falls who is not hopelessly retarded, since attendance during the period of compulsory education is virtually universal. We still have a serious illiteracy problem. In all of the advanced European countries every normal person is literate and numerate and this has been so for some generations. Speaking of the European "common" school, a prominent French educator, diplomat, and scholar recently said that "a vast amount of experience and understanding," the "imagination and inventiveness" of many great educators had been invested in building it into a school that turns out "youngsters with a real comprehension of their destiny and environment," youngsters who in their early teens already are "equipped with a sense of freedom and a command of verbal expression and communication for which adolescents of other areas may well envy them."

A great deal of nonsense is put forth in support of the dogma that to be democratic, education must be comprehensive, such as that it has never been *proved* that learning proceeds faster in an intellectually homogeneous group, or that it is an *enriching experience* for all if bright, average, and below average children study together, or that it is a *democratic duty* for bright children to be present so that they might act as a sort of "yeast" that will cause the overall level of a heterogeneous class to rise. One senses something of a feeling that nature is "undemocratic" in its distribution of talent and that the school should counteract this. What else but a basic hostility to very bright children can explain the curious American custom of classifying them in the category "exceptional," together with the subnormal, the blind, the deaf, and all others whose distinction from the "norm" is an inborn *defect*?

I am sure educators are kindly people, well-disposed toward the children in their care. Yet, when I read their disquisitions and observe their actions, I cannot help but feel that they sacrifice good education to questionable dogma. In their educational philosophy, social and political objectives appealing to the adult community sometimes take precedence over the need of the school child to be given the best possible chance of becoming an educated person. Does this not "use" the child for purposes not his own? I should like to see the Kantian imperative applied to children, as most of us agree it should apply to adults. He said: "Every man is to be respected as an absolute end in himself; and it is a crime against the dignity that belongs to him as a human being, *to use him as a mere means for some external purpose.*"

One of our most eminent educators says that we are unalterably committed to "a common core of general education which will unite in one cultural pattern the future carpenter, factory worker, bishop, lawyer, doctor, sales manager, professor, and garage mechanic." One wonders whether we are committed to this objective because great educators and scholars, upon mature consideration, and after observing educational experience in many other countries, have come to the conclusion that such comprehensive schooling is the best means to educe or bring out our children's innate mental capacities. Is it not rather a Utopian dream of grown-ups, this vision of children from every conceivable background, bound for every imaginable vocation, all growing up in "democratic togetherness"? A dream that carries us back to the one-room schoolhouse and so to a simpler life when people were friendlier and communities more democratic than today. Those who promise that comprehensive schooling will continue forever, appeal to emotions that run deep in the American character.

Nostalgia for our pioneer past at times assails 20th century Americans, though not to the point of voluntarily relinquishing the sophisticated gadgets that make life pleasant and comfortable. These gadgets are products of a society quite unlike the one where everybody attended the

Little Red Schoolhouse. It is a society where differences between people are much greater than in preindustrial America.

People now differ more in what interests them and in the kind of entertainment they seek. The difference has little to do with money. Cost does not explain why only a tiny minority read the *New York Times* or the *Atlantic Monthly* while multitudes enjoy the comics. People now differ more in the kind of work they do. They differ more educationally. Some of the most vitally important work in our technically advanced society can be done only by persons who must be much more intelligent than most others and who have absorbed a far more intellectually demanding education than the majority of children are able or willing to pursue.

What our children need is not "common core" education leading to a single cultural pattern but diverse schooling suitable to their diverse talents and objectives. A genuinely "democratic" school system should encourage all kinds of individuals to run on all kinds of tracks. Slow teenagers need very intensive instruction in the fundamentals of education; bright ones should be getting into calculus, foreign languages, science, etc.; average ones should be encouraged to absorb as much of true secondary education as possible.

Practical necessity has forced the educational establishment to introduce some diversity into the comprehensive school. This has led to a uniquely American kind of secondary schooling in which there is a "common core" program, supplemented by "electives" chosen by the students. The common core program provides the "Education for *All* American Youth" that the schoolmen demand. Of necessity, it must be devoid of all intellectual content, so that all children may attend it together. It is a mishmash of courses in simple skills with which European schools do not concern themselves; they leave it to the home and to the experiences of life itself to provide young people with this sort of "life adjustment education." The electives are intended to provide diversified education. By leaving the choice to boys and girls, the schools abdicate their responsibility to guide the intellectual development of our youth.

The best compromise so far devised between the dogma of the schoolmen and the educational needs of the children is the multiple-track comprehensive school. Its drawback is that the school must be very large—instead of the several hundred pupils of European secondary schools, ours may have several thousand. This is not good for young people. Even college students resent having to obtain their education in gigantic "knowledge factories." Their sense of being "cheated" by the adult world is at the bottom of most of the student revolts on campuses across the nation. And the students are right. *Educational gigantism has no justification in terms of the needs of students.* Its *only* justification, whether in high school or in college, is the comprehensive dogma to which the adult world subscribes.

Though growing in number, multiple-track schools are still under attack as "undemocratic." Many schoolmen prefer to cope with the diversity of human intelligence by easing educational advancement of the less able. We have gone a long way toward automatic promotion and the granting of diplomas that are little more than certificates of attendance. Witness the following remarks of the superintendent of a large city school system: "Regardless of the variation of high school courses and the range of scholastic achievement . . . straight thinking and democratically minded school administrators have long since adopted the idea of the same diploma for all." He notes with approval, that high school diplomas no longer carry "the name of the course in which the student went through school."

I can see nothing "democratic" in promoting a child before he has mastered a prescribed course. He will only *seem* to move up the educational ladder. In reality he will be standing still on the same rung. Nor is there anything "democratic" in granting diplomas that meet no recognized standard. By not setting standards, we have brought our so-called higher education down to what Dr. Robert B. Davis of Syracuse University so aptly terms "creeping lowest denominatorism." All our diplomas and degrees have suffered the fate of paper money that is not backed by gold bullion. They have no *intrinsic* value. Their value can be ascertained only by checking on the institution that has issued them and the study course for which they were granted.

The process of down-leveling must somehow be stopped. This is what my proposal for a National Standards Committee is intended to do. Let me describe what I have in mind.

I suggested to the Congress that it be a small committee, composed of men of national stature and eminence—trustworthy, intelligent, scholarly, and devoted to the ideal of an American education second to none. The committee would have two tasks:

The first would be purely informational; it would act as an educational watchtower announcing danger when it saw it approaching. The members would keep under continuous scrutiny, and periodically report on the state of American education. Does it meet the needs of our times? Is it scholastically as good as education in countries at similar levels of culture and technology with whom we compete economically, politically, or militarily? How do American children compare in academic knowledge with children in Europe or Russia, say at age 12, or 16, or 18; taking, of course, into consideration different ability levels?

The committee's second task would be to formulate a national scholastic standard on the basis of its findings; a standard which would make us internationally competitive and would also respond to our specific domestic needs. The committee would do this by means of examinations set at different ability levels. No one would have to take them, but those who passed would receive national accreditation. The committee would in no way interfere with established institutions now granting diplomas or degrees. It would simply set up a higher standard, offer it to anyone who wished to meet it, and certify those who had successfully done so.

Neither the committee's informational nor its standard setting function would represent a radical departure from established practice. Many federal agencies collect and distribute information. We need a disinterested agency to tell us the unvarnished truth about the true state of American education. The committee would help prevent complacency and illusions of superiority, and thus save us from such painful shocks as Sputnik and other evidence of Russian scientific proficiency have given us in the past few years. There is precedent, too, for the committee's setting of permissive national standards. We have something very like it in the 1965 Water Pollution Act.

Under this legislation the federal government is authorized—*if so requested by a state*—to research and develop new methods of pollution control and to award grants-in-aid to localities and states wishing to use these federally established methods. We have here a national standard very much like the scholastic standard of the proposed committee, in that it is not *imposed* but merely *offered as a service* on a take it or leave it basis.

Let me interject a word here as to what I mean by the word "standard." It has, as you know, a number of different connotations. I use it in the sense that comes first to mind: a specific requirement or level of excellence deemed worthy of esteem or reward. Not a *law*, enforceable in the courts. Falling below standard does not put one in jail. Nor a *conventional rule* imposed by society. Failure to meet the standard does not get one socially ostracized. No one *has to* live up to the standard. It is simply an *optional criterion* for determining the value of an act or accomplishment. For those who accept the standard it becomes the yardstick by which the worth of these acts or accomplishments is determined.

Water pollution and mediocre education have this in common: they are problems that cannot be solved by local and state authorities *alone*, but require some assistance from the federal government. Population growth and technology threaten us with a severe water shortage unless we devise better means to preserve the quality of our water resources so that they may be used over and over again. Pollution abatement has therefore become a national problem, and we accept a new kind of federal aid, just as we accept federal aid for clean air and for automobile safety. I believe improvement of the quality of American education is at least as pressing as the need for an assured supply of clean water, pure air, or safe automobiles. Education is now the indispensable medium for survival and progress. Education is so basic to the quality of our national life that by steering it in the right direction we can change America's future; we can make it secure. To steer it right we need a new kind of federal aid—the kind of aid that the proposed National Standards Committee would offer.

I hope I may convince you that it would be entirely proper and exceedingly useful for us to have such an agency. Let me make it crystal clear that nothing in my proposal would violate the constitutional separation of powers between federal and state governments, nor go counter to our tradition of control of schools by the local community. I envisage the rendering of a *service*, not *regulation* in any way, shape, or manner. The proposed committee would not *usurp* the functions of any existing institution.

Its job would be to draw up national examinations going deeply into a candidate's true knowledge and intellectual caliber—not IBM graded multiple choice tests. I suggested to the Appropriations Committee that we might model them on the English national examinations which offer tests in many subjects. Students choose the subject and the level at which they wish to be examined. This is marked on their certificate which will list their so-called "passes."

Our committee might provide one set of examinations at the level appropriate for a high school graduate who aspires to enter a first-rate college; another set of examinations at the level of students who may wish to prepare for a semiprofessional or technician's job not requiring a bachelor degree but still requiring a good secondary schooling. Still another for graduates of various types of colleges, especially those bound for the teaching profession. I stress again that no one would need to take these examinations; but those who did pass them successfully would obtain national certification; perhaps the notation National Scholar stamped on their regular diplomas or degrees. The seal would clearly indicate what the holder had achieved.

There are many occasions when it is important to know what educational level a person has reached. Admissions officers of higher educational institutions or prospective employers have a valid reason for wanting to know what exactly are the qualifications of an applicant. Think how much time and money would be saved if his diploma or degree indicated this clearly! Everywhere abroad it is taken for granted that diplomas and degrees conform to a specific standard—a standard known to everyone. Setting the standard is not regarded as government intrusion or tyranny but as a welcome service to students, their parents, and the taxpayers who bear the cost of public education.

Everyone benefits when there is a standard. At one stroke it does away with misleading educational labels so that any layman has the means of judging whether a school or college is doing its job properly. By offering the reward of a certified diploma to our children, many who now drift through school would be encouraged to aspire to higher academic goals. You can't expect children to study hard subjects such as mathematics, science, and languages when next door others are effortlessly accumulating equal credits by easy life-adjustment courses in "Family Life." It surely isn't "undemocratic" to reward those who exert themselves with a diploma that takes note of their accomplishments. This is what certification by a National Standards Committee would do.

There is no question in my mind that a large sector of the American people wants better education. Public interest has grown tremendously. Every time I speak or write on education I receive a large number of letters.

What strikes me in these letters is the sense of individual helplessness they reveal. Individually, my correspondents have long known that education must be drastically reformed but they don't know how to induce the school system to act. The very size of our nation alienates public agencies from the individual and accounts for much of the political apathy for which the people are frequently castigated. Yet all too often they can find no one in public office to supply the leadership that is needed to carry out their wishes. Especially when this requires tackling, on the local and on the national level, so powerful a lobby as our educational establishment. People like myself can try to bring the truth to the public so that it may be able to reach a consensus—and this I believe has now been accomplished. Enough people want school reform to warrant public action.

The Spanish philosopher Ortega y Gasset once wrote a book on the thesis—to quote him—that "the most radical division it is possible to make of humanity is that which splits it into two classes of creatures: those who make great demands on themselves, piling up difficulties and duties; and those who demand nothing special of themselves, but for whom to live is to be every moment what they already are." I read this as a young man and it impressed me deeply. And all my life I have unconsciously judged people and institutions by whether or not they set themselves a standard; whether they measure themselves against a criterion that requires effort because they deem it worthy of effort.

Let us in education as in everything else heed Jefferson's advice, to "dream of an aristocracy of achievement arising out of a democracy of opportunity."

7

Education in this country has steadily improved since the systematic study of the science of education was started about 1890. No doubt it will continue to improve at about the same speed, and schools in the year

*2000 will be somewhat better than they are today. The
question is, could they be better than that?*
                    J. LLOYD TRUMP
                    DORSEY BAYNHAM
                    Focus on Change

Douglas W. Hunt
THE PREMISE OF CHANGE

Change is nothing new in American education. Schools were
organized shortly after the first settlers arrived, and, although these were
European in orientation, they soon reflected the conditions and needs of
the colonists. With the establishment of the Boston Latin School in 1635
and Harvard College a year later, the New England settlement, then but
15 years old, demonstrated the early importance that it attached to education. Although extremely limited, the first schools did train the leaders
and clergy so necessary if the New England colonies were to be self
governing.

These schools and the others which followed were pragmatic, meeting
the needs of the times with the best tools available. That is still our goal
—the times have changed—the store of knowledge greatly expanded—
the immediacy more keenly felt.

In addition to schools reflecting the needs of the society, a second
dimension was added with the early determination that education
through high school should be available, and later required, for all. This
is a proud accomplishment of American education—looked upon with
admiration by many other nations. Our greatness has often been attributed—in part—to this broad foundation of practical education which all
Americans possess.

Today, however, this is no longer enough. A third dimension has become of prime importance—and this is quality. We have won the battle
of quantity—so necessary in a democracy—now we must be concerned
with refinement if that same democracy is to prosper and continue the
advance.

All of these efforts have involved change—a breaking of old patterns
and traditions. We have demonstrated that we can teach all boys and
girls to be productive members of our complex society; we are now concerned with how best to teach these same students so that they will be
even more effective—the shift is from quantity to quality, lock steps will
still be broken, change will still be necessary, a challenge remains.

From Douglas W. Hunt, "The Premise of Change," The National Association of Secondary School Principals *Bulletin*, Vol. 47, May, 1963, pp. 1–3. Copyright 1963 by the Association. Reprinted by permission of the Association.

This need is widely recognized; few leaders advocate the *status quo*, most seek quality, yet there is much debate over the depth of change. We might classify this roughly into three groups. The first suggests quality by *subtraction*, reducing the number of students in our schools and allowing only the more talented to proceed into high school and on to college. There is little doubt that by removing the lower 25 to 50 per cent of the students and eliminating lower level courses, we could easily attain a higher quality of education for those who remain, but this would be a retreat—and repugnant to most of us in the democracy. A second avenue, advocated by many educators and critics alike, involves *addition* —more schools, more teachers, more materials, longer school days, year-around schools; all under closer supervision and governed by more regulations. They suggest more courses, more counselors, more stringent graduation requirements, and, of course, more money. Still a third group sees the need for close examination of what we are doing—careful stock taking and evaluation and only then—the introduction of *basic change* in the institutional arrangements for education, in instructional methods, and in the organization of the curriculum. This group questions, and unlike the other two, it does not have the answers—it suspects that they are not easy—or even universal. They are concerned that the rationale for what is done in the schools is better understood. At present they are still questioning ways that have become traditional and experimenting in searching better answers. This job has just begun but these ideas, some call them innovations, are emerging:

1. *Individual differences* can be recognized and educational programs tailored to meet them.

2. *Time* can be used more effectively, there is nothing sacred about the 45- or 50-minute period.

3. *Human talents* can be utilized more efficiently—30 students and one teacher is not always the best arrangement.

4. *The curriculum* can be organized effectively in many different ways.

5. *Technology* offers much promise for education, both in terms of instruction and administration.

6. *Physical facilities* can be more fully utilized to facilitate the educational process. The school building should reflect the instructional program.

The concepts and ideas of this third group involve the greatest potential change—and for that reason require thorough study and critical evaluation.

Few of us will agree with all of the projects or findings of the staff utilization studies, out of which many of these programs have grown. Nevertheless, we must recognize that while all change does not signify progress, progress is not possible without change. If nothing more—and

I rather suspect that they have done far more—they have raised questions and sought answers—their work suggests change and offers much promise for the future. It still remains, however, for each school system to determine the most effective ways for its teachers to teach and students to learn; this must be the premise of change.

8

Where division of labor exists in a society, equality of treatment is a philosophical issue. There can never be assurance of complete equality unless all people are doing the same thing. Obviously this is not possible in a complex society. Because this condition exists, all persons, as well as all groups, tend to alter their relative status with regard to others to their own advantage. Hence, there is always jockeying for position and status among all the segments of the society. Those who are on top are trying to stay there, those beneath are pressing to rise.

DAN W. DODSON

Christopher Jencks
THE PUBLIC SCHOOLS ARE FAILING

Americans are justifiably proud of their public schools, which have turned a nation of semiliterate farmers and immigrants into the world's most competent people in less than a century. But in one important area, the urban slums where some 30 million Americans now live, the public schools have been doing a terrible job. They prepare almost none of their students for college, and this means that almost none will be able to get a good job or live a comfortable life. More than half the students in these schools are made so miserable that they drop out at the first legal opportunity, filled with despair and rebellion against society.

Many educators claim that these students come from such wretched homes that the schools cannot do much to educate them. Yet while slum children are clearly difficult to educate, experiments have repeatedly shown that with the right kind of school the job can be done. Many educators admit this, and say that all they need is more money. Yet, the harsh fact is that money alone won't do the trick. The schools in Harlem

From Christopher Jencks, "The Public Schools Are Failing," *Saturday Evening Post*, April 23, 1968, pp. 14, 18. Reprinted by permission of the author.

spend almost twice as much per pupil as those in Milwaukee, and the results are nothing like twice as impressive.

Why haven't the people who run our big-city schools been able to find solutions to their problems? The reason, I think, is that effective remedies would require basic changes in the character of the public-school system itself. After several years of studying the problem, I have concluded that we cannot hope to establish good schools in the slums so long as we cling to the tradition of direct public management of public schools. What we need in the slums are privately managed schools, financed and ultimately controlled by the taxpayer. To those who have always assumed that private schools are for the rich, this will seem a startling idea, but it shouldn't be.

Public management means public accountability—not just for long-term educational results but for every penny, every minute and every word of every educator on the public payroll. In such a system the fate of a school's alumni inevitably seems less important than avoiding overt conflict and "staying out of trouble." If nobody is found with his hand in the till, if no "subversives" are alleged to be in the classrooms, if no serious discipline problems arise, if no unfavorable news stories appear, if taxes don't have to be raised, public officials seem to feel that all is well.

The public schools' obsessive fear of "trouble" leads to an incredible proliferation of restrictive regulations. The working assumption of those in charge seems to be that everyone in the system is incompetent, irresponsible and potentially dishonest. Everyone is therefore told to follow detailed procedures laid down by someone "higher up" and is held accountable for his conformity to the rules. State legislators assume that if local school boards are left to their own devices they will hire incompetents, so the legislature imposes elaborate (and largely irrelevant) state certification requirements for teachers. The school board assumes that the superintendent is likely to steal (or at least squander) public funds, and insists on reviewing even trivial expenditures. The superintendent assumes the principals have questionable judgment, and insists on prior approval of their budgets, personnel, curriculum and even teaching materials. The principals, in turn, assume that teachers are inherently self-indulgent, and give them little control over the school or even over their own syllabi. Some principals go so far as to install intercom systems with which they can monitor classes. The teachers are also infected by the pervasive deference to authority and tradition, and try to impose it on their pupils by placing innumerable restrictions on social and academic behavior. Everywhere there is an atmosphere of suspicion more appropriate to a prison.

These problems are not, of course, unique to the slums. They are found to some extent in every publicly managed school system, be it urban, suburban, small town or rural. Why have the results been so much worse in schools serving the poor? The answer is that poor children are harder to educate. Educators who deal mainly with slum children have every reason to fear trouble and failure. They are therefore less willing to innovate, more anxious to hide behind rules and precedents, more conditioned to saying "No."

In such a system the only way to get along is to go along with those over you. The student tries to dope out what the teacher wants and to provide it; in effect, the student becomes a con man. (Usually all the teacher wants is a reasonable amount of quiet in class and docility about doing assignments.) The teacher, in turn, tries to figure out what the principal wants. (In most cases, filing grades and attendance records promptly, and avoiding complaints count more than whether the children learn anything.) The principals, in turn, try to keep the central administration happy (and the superintendent tries to keep the school board happy) by not sticking their necks out and by damping down conflicts before they get into the newspapers.

Innovation from the bottom up is obviously impossible and unthinkable in such a system. But even innovation from the top down is difficult. If, for example, the school board tries raising salaries in order to attract more enterprising teachers, it must still assign them to the same old schools, where they are still treated like filing clerks. The more imaginative and dedicated usually leave after a year or two for other schools—sometimes suburban, sometimes private—which treat them better. If the principal tells veteran teachers he wants them to revamp the curriculum, they immediately begin looking to him—not to their students—for clues about what kinds of changes to propose. In the unlikely event that a teacher tells his students to "think for themselves," the students automatically interpret this as another frustration in their efforts to "give teach what he wants."

I know no cure for this kind of sickness. In private organizations it leads either to bankruptcy or to the creation of cartels to protect the diseased institution from healthy competitors. The choice is the same in the public sector, but cartels are easier to establish. Public schools, for example, have a monopoly on educational opportunities for the poor. Prosperous families can send their children to private schools or move to suburbs, where the schools are less rigidly bureaucratic and have more faith in their pupils. The poor are stuck with whatever the city fathers and school board see fit to provide.

It seems to me that this lack of choice is at the heart of our educational problems. If so, the solution is to create a variety of competing schools, both publicly and privately managed, and then give poor families a chance to choose among them. To some this will sound "un-American"—an attack on the "common school" and the "democratic" character of public control. But to me the present monolithic system of urban education, controlled by a remote central administration neither responsive nor responsible to individual parents, is what seems "un-American." If we Americans are as alarmed as we say about "creeping socialism," if we really believe in "pluralism" and "private initiative," then we should apply our principles to urban education as well as to business. This does not mean reducing public financial support for big-city schools. Nor does it mean abandoning the principle of public responsibility and overall control. It does mean that on a day-to-day basis we should rely much more heavily on private management, judging its adequacy on the basis of long-term results.

How might this be done? Two possibilities deserve a trial. The first is tuition grants for needy parents who want to take their children out of the public schools and send them to approved private ones. The federal antipoverty program has already begun to do this for a few hundred high-school students through its "Upward Bound" program. This effort should be expanded and extended to include not only the posh boarding schools now involved but all sorts of private schools, old and new, elementary and secondary.

The second possibility is for public agencies to begin contracting with private groups to manage schools. Some school boards already use this approach to preschool education, and on the whole it has worked smoothly. The Federal Government has also turned to private groups to manage its Job Corps camps, and while there have been problems the overall record is impressive.

Used in combination, large-scale scholarship programs and private management contracts would unleash an enormous amount of energy and talent which is now untapped.

Universities could run schools serving the poor. If the University of California can manage the Atomic Energy Commission installation at Los Alamos, surely it could manage schools in Watts, under contract with either the Los Angeles school board or the Los Angeles anti-poverty program.

Private corporations could go into the education business, either on a profit or nonprofit basis. If I.B.M. can manage a Job Corps camp for the poverty program, it might well run a Harlem elementary school better than the present public-school bureaucracy does.

Groups of like-minded teachers who find themselves frustrated by the existing school system could band together and set up new kinds of schools. By giving teachers a free hand to do things that excite them, teacher-initiated schools might attract and retain a much better staff than the present system does.

Parents, neighborhood antipoverty boards and other agencies could set up their own schools in competition with, or under contract to, the school board. The result might be a restoration of truly local control, which has long been a dead letter in the slums.

Today all a public school has to do to stay in business is keep from falling or burning down. If dissatisfied parents could send their children to many different kinds of publicly financed schools, however, and if unpopular schools' budgets were cut when enrollment fell, the days of the time-servers would be numbered. Such a competitive system would do far more than present budgetary nit-picking to ensure that the taxpayers' money was being well spent.

Private management would also be a way of getting away from the neighborhood school, which has always been a major obstacle to innovation. Recent debate over neighborhood schools has been between white parents who don't want Negroes in their children's classrooms and civil-rights groups which want to end *de facto* segregation. In this debate almost everyone has assumed that, race aside, neighborhood schools would be desirable. Yet both pedagogically and administratively the neighborhood system has serious defects. A neighborhood school is expected to serve everyone who happens to live near it; such a school must seek a lowest common denominator which offends nobody. This is a formula for pedagogic disaster. All good education offends some people, and imaginative educators need to be able to tell some parents to take their children elsewhere. The neighborhood school cannot do this, and as a result it can do very little at all.

The great virtue of a privately managed school is that it need not make everyone happy. So long as it satisfies enough people to keep its classes full, it is free to go its own way. Those who don't like what it is doing can turn to another school with a different philosophy. (In heavily populated slums there can be a number of competing schools within walking distance of most homes. In cities with decent public transportation, the choice can be even wider.)

Given real freedom and real choice, big cities could accommodate all kinds of minority tastes and needs which are now ignored. At certain stages of their lives, for example, some children need to attend a school solely for boys or solely for girls. This option, now usually available only to rich families, should be open to all. Similarly, some children need schools which are extremely permissive. Other children go through stages in which they require strict discipline. The present system mixes both kinds of children in a single public school which follows a middle-of-the-road policy. But if scholarships were widely available, or if private groups could get contracts to manage publicly financed schools, we could make both kinds of opportunity available to everyone. Without this kind of diversity education can never achieve real excellence.

"But," you may say, "private management would make schools less democratic. Some would become bastions of privilege while others would get only poor students." This might indeed happen if public officials let it. But tax subsidies could easily be restricted to those private schools which took a cross-section of the population. One must also remember that in the big urban centers where most Americans now live, even public management has also led to racial and economic segregation. Indeed there is some evidence that public management is more likely to lead in this direction than private management. Many private schools try to mix rich and poor by offering scholarships for needy students; few suburban schools would admit slum children even if their way were paid.

Privately managed schools might have still another advantage over the present public system. They would probably be able to get more adequate financial support. Public management has produced a system of budget-making which is almost certain to perpetuate poverty. Boards of education first decide how much they can afford to spend, based largely on what they spent last year and to a lesser extent on what nearby school districts spent. Then they try to buy as much education as they can on this budget, adequate or not. If they relied on contracts with private groups, however, they might well approach the problem more ambitiously. They might begin by setting forth in broad outline what the children for whom they are responsible need to learn and become. Then they would ask private groups to submit proposals for doing the job. The initial bids would undoubtedly cost far more than most boards of education now think they can afford. Still, a few contracts could be let, simply to see if private groups would deliver on their promises. If it turned out that by spending enough in the private sector school boards could bring slum children up to the same level of competence as suburbanites, the demand that they do so might become irresistible.

THE SOCIAL DIMENSION

Modern society is a massive conglomerate of interlocking and interacting systems. Each of these single systems operates and develops within the shadow and influence of the others. In relation to any single system of society, all of the others constitute its environment. Any maladjustment between a system and its environment produces crisis. Thus, just as environmental factors influence change or even destroy a biological system, so do forces in society similarly affect a social system. Since the environment of the educational system is society, the system accepts its ultimate values, aims, and priorities from society. Controversy surrounding these values, aims, and priorities constitutes the social dimension of education. The social dimension is ensured of a vital character because of the dynamic nature of society. As forces within society influence changes in values, these changing values impinge upon the educational system, requiring substantial adjustments and adaptation.

The present crisis in education stems from a serious disjunction between the educational system and its environment. Society has undergone drastic changes in the past two decades to the extent that it has outstripped the ability of the educational system to respond. There is great need for the educational system to leap ahead in its adaptation to changing conditions. If a greater lag develops between the changes in environment and the response of the educational system, the total disruption of that system and its environment, society, could easily result.

The national belief that education offers an equal opportunity for all citizens is at variance with the local demands for the best possible education. This disparity is manifest in a comparison between the cities and the suburbs. The people of the suburbs see an equality of opportunity and have excellent, if not the best possible, education available. In the cities a large proportion of the citizens experience inequality of opportunity and are becoming increasingly aware of the lack of excellence in the quality of education afforded them. The added factors of social class, race, and economic status combine to put further strain on the educational system.

Past adherence to the dictum that "all are equal but some are more equal than others" has ignored misery, spawned conflict, sparked conflagration, and brought ominous rumblings of violent change in society. Such a concept is no longer acceptable. The less equal are demanding to be heard. In accord with this demand all but the last two of the following readings are directed at criticism, conflict, and change in two related areas: the problems of education in the big cities, and the state of education in the black community. These and the causes underlying student unrest discussed in the final two selections are the most immediate and important factors currently influencing the educational system and its environment.

1

Now if I were a teacher . . . dealing with Negro children . . . I would try to teach them . . . that those streets, those houses, those dangers, those agonies by which they are surrounded are criminal. . . . I would teach [the Negro child] that he doesn't have to be bound by the expediencies of any given Administration, any given policy, any given time—that he has the right and the necessity to examine everything.
                                                    JAMES BALDWIN

James Baldwin
A TALK TO TEACHERS

Let's begin by saying that we are living through a very dangerous time. Everyone in this room is in one way or another aware of that. We are in a revolutionary situation, no matter how unpopular that word has become in this country. The society in which we live is desperately menaced, not by Khrushchev, but from within. So any citizen of this country who figures himself as responsible—and particularly those of you who deal with the minds and hearts of young people—must be prepared to "go for broke." Or to put it another way, you must understand that in the attempt to correct so many generations of bad faith and cruelty, when it is operating not only in the classroom but in society, you will meet the most fantastic, the most brutal, and the most determined resistance. There is no point in pretending that this won't happen.

Now, since I am talking to schoolteachers and I am not a teacher myself, and in some ways am fairly easily intimidated, I beg you to let me leave that and go back to what I think to be the entire purpose of education in the first place. It would seem to me that when a child is born, if I'm the child's parent, it is my obligation and my high duty to civilize

From James Baldwin, "A Talk to Teachers," *Saturday Review*, December 21, 1963, pp. 42–44, 60. Reprinted by permission of the author and publisher.

that child. Man is a social animal. He cannot exist without a society. A society, in turn, depends on certain things which everyone within that society takes for granted. Now, the crucial paradox which confronts us here is that the whole process of education occurs within a social framework and is designed to perpetuate the aims of society. Thus, for example, the boys and girls who were born during the era of the Third Reich, when educated to the purposes of the Third Reich, became barbarians. The paradox of education is precisely this—that as one begins to become conscious one begins to examine the society in which he is being educated. The purpose of education, finally, is to create in a person the ability to look at the world for himself, to make his own decisions, to say to himself this is black or this is white, to decide for himself whether there is a God in heaven or not. To ask questions of the universe, and then learn to live with those questions, is the way he achieves his own identity. But no society is really anxious to have that kind of person around. What societies really, ideally, want is a citizenry which will simply obey the rules of society. If a society succeeds in this, that society is about to perish. The obligation of anyone who thinks of himself as responsible is to examine society and try to change it and to fight it—at no matter what risk. This is the only hope society has. This is the only way societies change.

Now, if what I have tried to sketch has any validity, it becomes thoroughly clear, at least to me, that any Negro who is born in this country and undergoes the American educational system runs the risk of becoming schizophrenic. On the one hand he is born in the shadow of the stars and stripes and he is assured it represents a nation which has never lost a war. He pledges allegiance to that flag which guarantees "liberty and justice for all." He is part of a country in which anyone can become President, and so forth. But on the other hand he is also assured by his country and his countrymen that he has never contributed anything to civilization—that his past is nothing more than a record of humiliations gladly endured. He is assured by the republic that he, his father, his mother, and his ancestors were happy, shiftless, watermelon-eating darkies who loved Mr. Charlie and Miss Ann, that the value he has as a black man is proven by one thing only—his devotion to white people. If you think I am exaggerating, examine the myths which proliferate in this country about Negroes.

Now all this enters the child's consciousness much sooner than we as adults would like to think it does. As adults, we are easily fooled because we are so anxious to be fooled. But children are very different. Children, not yet aware that it is dangerous to look too deeply at anything, look at everything, look at each other, and draw their own conclusions. They don't have the vocabulary to express what they see, and we, their elders, know how to intimidate them very easily and very soon. But a black child, looking at the world around him, though he cannot know quite what to make of it, is aware that there is a reason why his mother works so hard, why his father is always on edge. He is aware that there is some reason why, if he sits down in the front of the bus, his father or mother slaps him and drags him to the back of the bus. He is aware that there is some terrible weight on his parents' shoulders which menaces him. And it isn't long—in fact it begins when he is in school—before he discovers the shape of his oppression.

Let us say that the child is seven years old and I am his father, and I decide to take him to the zoo, or to Madison Square Garden, or to the U.N. Building, or to any of the tremendous monuments we find all over New York. We get into a bus and we go from where I live on 131st Street and Seventh Avenue downtown through the park and we get into New York City, which is not Harlem. Now, where the boy lives—even if it is a housing project—is in an undesirable neighborhood. If he lives in one of those housing projects of which everyone in New York is so proud, he has at the front door, if not closer, the pimps, the whores, the junkies—in a word, the danger of life in the ghetto. And the child knows this, though he doesn't know why.

I still remember my first sight of New York. It was really another city when I was born—where I was born. We looked down over the Park Avenue streetcar tracks. It was Park Avenue, but I didn't know what Park Avenue meant *downtown*. The Park Avenue I grew up on, which is still standing, is dark and dirty. No one would dream of opening a Tiffany's on that Park Avenue, and when you go downtown you discover that you are literally in the white world. It is rich—or at least it looks rich. It is clean —because they collect garbage downtown. There are doormen. People walk about as though they owned where they were—and indeed they do. And it's a great shock. It's very hard to relate yourself to this. You don't know what it means. You know—you know instinctively—that none of this is for you. You know this before you are told. And who is it for and who is paying for it? And why isn't it for you?

Later on when you become a grocery boy or messenger and you try to enter one of those buildings a man says, "Go to the back door." Still later, if you happen by some odd chance to have a friend in one of those build-ings, the man says, "Where's your package?" Now this by no means is the core of the matter. What I'm trying to get at is that by this time the Negro child has had, effectively, all the doors of opportunity slammed in his face, and there are very few things he can do about it. He can more or less accept it with an absolutely inarticulate and dangerous rage inside— all the more dangerous because it is never expressed. It is precisely those silent people whom white people see every day of their lives—I mean your porter and your maid, who never say anything more than "Yes Sir" and "No Ma'am." They will tell you it's raining if that is what you want to hear, and they will tell you the sun is shining if *that* is what you want to hear. They really hate you—really hate you because in their eyes (and they're right) you stand between them and life. I want to come back to that in a moment. It is the most sinister of the facts, I think, which we now face.

There is something else the Negro child can do, too. Every street boy —and I was a street boy, so I know—looking at the society which has produced him, looking at the standards of that society which are not honored by anybody, looking at your churches and the government and the politicians, understands that this structure is operated for someone else's benefit—not for his. And there's no room in it for him. If he is really cunning, really ruthless, really strong—and many of us are—he becomes a kind of criminal. He becomes a kind of criminal because that's the only way he can live. Harlem and every ghetto in this city—every ghetto in this country—is full of people who live outside the law. They wouldn't dream of calling a policeman. They wouldn't, for a moment, listen to any of those professions of which we are so proud on the Fourth of July. They have turned away from this country forever and totally. They live by their wits and really long to see the day when the entire structure comes down.

The point of all this is that black men were brought here as a source of cheap labor. They were indispensable to the economy. In order to justify the fact that men were treated as though they were animals, the white republic had to brainwash itself into believing that they were, indeed, animals and *deserved* to be treated like animals. Therefore it is almost impossible for any Negro child to discover anything about his actual history. The reason is that this "animal," once he suspects his own worth, once he starts believing that he is a man, has begun to attack the entire power structure. This is why America has spent such a long time keeping the Negro in his place. What I am trying to suggest to you is that it was not an accident, it was not an act of God, it was not done by well-meaning people muddling into something which they didn't understand. It was a deliberate policy hammered into place in order to make money from black flesh. And now, in 1963, because we have never faced this fact, we are in intolerable trouble.

The Reconstruction, as I read the evidence, was a bargain between the North and South to this effect: "We've liberated them from the land— and delivered them to the bosses." When we left Mississippi to come North we did not come to freedom. We came to the bottom of the labor market, and we are still there. Even the Depression of the 1930s failed to make a dent in Negroes' relationship to white workers in the labor unions. Even today, so brainwashed is this republic that people seriously ask in what they suppose to be good faith, "What does the Negro want?" I've heard a great many asinine questions in my life, but that is perhaps the most asinine and perhaps the most insulting. But the point here is that people who ask that question, thinking that they ask it in good faith, are really the victims of this conspiracy to make Negroes believe they are less than human.

In order for me to live, I decided very early that some mistake had been made somewhere. I was not a "nigger" even though you called me one. But if I was a "nigger" in your eyes, there was something about *you* —there was something *you* needed. I had to realize when I was very young that I was none of those things I was told I was. I was not, for example, happy. I never touched a watermelon for all kinds of reasons. I had been invented by white people, and I knew enough about life by this time to understand that whatever you invent, whatever you project, is you! So where we are now is that a whole country of people believe I'm a "nigger," and I *don't*, and the battle's on! Because if I am not what I've been told I am, then it means that *you're* not what you thought *you* were *either!* And that is the crisis.

It is not really a "Negro revolution" that is upsetting this country. What is upsetting the country is a sense of its own identity. If, for example, one managed to change the curriculum in all the schools so that Negroes learned more about themselves and their real contributions to this culture, you would be liberating not only Negroes, you'd be liberating white people who know nothing about their own history. And the reason is that if you are compelled to lie about one aspect of anybody's history, you must lie about it all. If you have to lie about my real role here, if you have to pretend that I hoed all that cotton just because I loved you, then you have done something to yourself. You are mad.

Now let's go back a minute. I talked earlier about those silent people— the porter and the maid—who, as I said, don't look up at the sky if you ask them if it is raining, but look into your face. My ancestors and I were very well trained. We understood very early that this was not a Christian nation. It didn't matter what you said or how often you went to church. My father and my mother and my grandfather and my grandmother knew that Christians didn't act this way. It was as simple as that. And if that was so there was no point in dealing with white people in terms of their own moral professions, for they were not going to honor them. What one did was to turn away, smiling all the time, and tell white people what they wanted to hear. But people always accuse you of reckless talk when you say this.

All this means that there are in this country tremendous reservoirs of bitterness which have never been able to find an outlet, but may find an outlet soon. It means that well-meaning white liberals place themselves in great danger when they try to deal with Negroes as though they were missionaries. It means, in brief, that a great price is demanded to liberate all those silent people so that they can breathe for the first time and *tell* you what they think of you. And a price is demanded to liberate all those white children—some of them near forty—who have never grown up, and who never will grow up, because they have no sense of their identity.

What passes for identity in America is a series of myths about one's heroic ancestors. It's astounding to me, for example, that so many people really appear to believe that the country was founded by a band of heroes who wanted to be free. That happens not to be true. What happened was that some people left Europe because they couldn't stay there any longer and had to go someplace else to make it. That's all. They were hungry, they were poor, they were convicts. Those who were making it in England, for example, did not get on the Mayflower. That's how the country was settled. Not by Gary Cooper. Yet we have a whole race of people, a whole republic, who believe the myths to the point where even today they select political representatives, as far as I can tell by how closely they resemble Gary Cooper. Now this is dangerously infantile, and it shows in every level of national life. When I was living in Europe, for example, one of the worst revelations to me was the way Americans walked around Europe buying this and buying that and insulting every-body—not even out of malice, just because they didn't know any better. Well, that is the way they have always treated me. They weren't cruel, they just didn't know you were alive. They didn't know you had any feelings.

What I am trying to suggest here is that in the doing of all this for 100 years or more, it is the American white man who has long since lost his grip on reality. In some peculiar way, having created this myth about Negroes, and the myth about his own history, he created myths about the world so that, for example, he was astounded that some people could prefer Castro, astounded that there are people in the world who don't go into hiding when they hear the word "Communism," astounded that Communism is one of the realities of the twentieth century which we will not overcome by pretending that it does not exist. The political level in this country now, on the part of people who should know better, is abysmal.

The Bible says somewhere that where there is no vision the people perish. I don't think anyone can doubt that in this country today we are menaced—intolerably menaced—by a lack of vision.

It is inconceivable that a sovereign people should continue as we do so abjectly, to say, "I can't do anything about it. It's the government." The government is the creation of the people. It is responsible to the people. And the people are responsible for it. No American has the right to allow the present government to say, when Negro children are being bombed and hosed and shot and beaten all over the deep South, that there is nothing we can do about it. There must have been a day in this country's life when the bombing of four children in Sunday School would have created a public uproar and endangered the life of a Governor Wallace. It happened here and there was no public uproar.

I began by saying that one of the paradoxes of education was that precisely at the point when you begin to develop a conscience, you must find yourself at war with your society. It is your responsibility to change society if you think of yourself as an educated person. And on the basis of the evidence—the moral and political evidence—one is compelled to say that this is a backward society. Now if I were a teacher in this school, or any Negro school, and I was dealing with Negro children, who were in my care only a few hours of every day and would then return to their homes and to the streets, children who have an apprehension of their future which with every hour grows grimmer and darker, I would try to teach them—I would try to make them know—that those streets, those houses, those dangers, those agonies by which they are surrounded, are criminal. I would try to make each child know that these things are the results of a criminal conspiracy to destroy him. I would teach him that if he intends to get to be a man, he must at once decide that he is stronger than this conspiracy and that he must never make his peace with it. And that one of his weapons for refusing to make his peace with it and for destroying it depends on what he decides he is worth. I would teach him that there are currently very few standards in this country which are worth a man's respect. That it is up to him to begin to change these standards for the sake of the life and the health of the country. I would suggest to him that the popular culture—as represented, for example, on television and in comic books and in movies—is based on fantasies created by very ill people, and he must be aware that these are fantasies that have nothing to do with reality. I would teach him that the press he reads is not as free as it says it is—and that he can do something about that, too. I would try to make him know that just as American history is longer, larger, more various, more beautiful, and more terrible than anything anyone has ever said about it, so is the world larger, more daring, more beautiful and more terrible, but principally larger—and that it belongs to him. I would teach him that he doesn't have to be bound by the expediencies of any given Administration, any given policy, any given time—that he has the right and the necessity to examine everything. I would try to show him that one has not learned anything about Castro when one says, "He is a Communist." This is a way of not learning something about Castro, something about Cuba, something, in fact, about the world. I would suggest to him that he is living, at the moment, in an enormous province. America is not the world and if America is going to become a nation, she must find a way—and this child must help her to find a way—to use the tremendous potential and tremendous energy which this child represents. If this country does not find a way to use that energy, it will be destroyed by that energy.

2

The middle-class American would like to see the urban slums cleaned out and Great Cities built; but he also shows a strong preference for "living among his own kind." . . . The really great problems for urban development in the last third of the century will be to resolve certain basic value conflicts, to overcome some outmoded ideas, and to experiment with new institutional arrangements to achieve agreed-upon social goals.

HARVEY S. PERLOFF
Daedalus, Summer, 1967

Samuel Tenenbaum

THE TEACHER, THE MIDDLE CLASS, THE LOWER CLASS

I live on the West Side of Manhattan in a rather solid middle-class house with doorman and all. My neighbors have been complaining for a long time that the neighborhood has been running down. But the building I live in has held like a bastion, a strong fifteen-story fortress. My neighbors felt safe and protected once within its high walls, until a hotel on the opposite side of the street began to be used by the city relief agency to house indigent families. The hotel, a great affair, once magnificent, in bygone days probably catered to people of substance. This is the way, I suppose, of an American city. It represents the great human flow and ebb, the tidal waves of a dynamic culture that pushes people and fortunes around endlessly.

But this is not really my story. I meant to speak of how these lower-class people affected us, the middle-class people in our house; and what I myself learned in terms of my own feelings as a teacher. If I am a little roundabout, forgive me.

First of all, in what seemed almost overnight (and in actuality was not more than a month), this once great hotel was seething with life and ferment and energy. This comparatively quiet block took on all the aspects of a slum block and some of the aspects of a perpetual carnival. Hordes of children, like milling cattle, cluttered the once empty street; children of all ages, from one year to—well, they looked like eighteen and twenty. Boys and girls mixed in packs, and it was difficult to think of them as

From Samuel Tenenbaum, "The Teacher, the Middle Class, the Lower Class," *Phi Delta Kappan*, November, 1963, pp. 82–86. Reprinted by permission of the publisher.

single, individual children. They shouted, they screamed, they pushed, they fought. In the midst of play, they would suddenly get into individual fights and collective fights. Violence, aggression, play, and friendliness seemed all mixed up. Every wall on the block was used, either to play ball on or to throw things on. The streets became cluttered with debris, especially broken glass. Where they got all the glass to break is beyond me. The area around this hotel became one vast accumulation of litter. Also, it was quite common for children to throw things from the windows at passersby. The parents apparently did not object, for I never saw a parent reprimand a child for this. The children resembled an uncontrolled, undisciplined herd, doing what they wished, with neither mother nor father in sight to curb, admonish, or chastise. In fact, when these lower-class children moved in, some of the motherly women in our building occasionally attempted to discipline a child, invariably with frightening results. A cluster of febrile humanity arose like spontaneous combustion to repel the invader, and these well-intentioned women felt lucky if they escaped unharmed. Such incidents only increased my neighbors' sense of helplessness and fear. In the end, my middle-class neighbors, through painful experience, learned to look on aloofly and distantly as children of six and seven smoked and young boys and girls openly engaged in physical contact. Attracted by such scenes, almost glued to them, these neighbors of mine expressed by bodily demeanor and by speech their shock and disapproval.

The parents of the children themselves acted strangely. In all states of undress, they hung out of windows, while below mixed adult groups, and groups including children, congregated, drinking beer, joshing, pushing each other about and carrying on in a merry and boisterous way through all hours of the night.

The tenants of our building, guarded more carefully than ever by doormen, made it a point never to loiter outside (which seemed to them a confession of idleness and lack of industry). They were in the habit of going in and out of the building with scarcely anyone seeing or hearing them; they were quiet, inconspicuous, and rarely communicated with neighbors, even though they may have lived together for a quarter of a century.

In contrast, the welfare families lived outside, on the street, conspicuously, loudly, openly. Their social life centered almost exclusively around those who happened to live in the same building. That did not mean it was a serene kind of neighborliness. We never knew when a fist fight or some loud fracas would start and it was not unusual for the occupants of our building to be awakened by a horrible commotion—even the firing of bullets—at 2 or 3 o'clock in the morning. Some of my neighbors were infuriated by such behavior and indignantly called the police, demanding that something be done immediately.

There was one type of behavior, however, that affected my neighbors beyond all others. I cannot say that they liked to see children smoking or engaged in open sex play; it violated their sense of morality. But they could somehow stand that. What they couldn't stand, what frightened them, was the violent, hostile way in which lower-class families found their amusement. An almost palpable atmosphere of aggression and violence hovered over the street. The children would attack an automobile —literally attack it as locusts attack a field—climb on top of it, get inside, and by combined, co-operative effort shake and tug until they left it a wreck. The older men would strip the tires from a car and sell them. A three-wheeled delivery bicycle from a local merchant provided a special holiday. The children gathered from nowhere and everywhere, piled on the delivery bicycle, and drove it up and down the street loaded down with humanity. When they made no dent in the vehicle by this misuse, in disgust they poked at it and pushed it in an effort to make it come apart. I have never seen young people work so assiduously as they did riding, pushing, and shaking the cart. They didn't give up until it was completely destroyed. I have seen children, several of whom could not have been more than seven or eight years old, at this job of destruction past 10 p.m.; and they all appeared to be having the merriest time. Even their innocent, friendly play was violent. Suddenly, strong, tall, gangling adolescent boys would dash pell-mell down the street, like stampeding cattle, shrieking and screaming, pushing, shoving, mauling each other.

Of course, this hotel where they lived was not meant for families with many children. Since it was enormous in size, at least fifteen stories high, it probably represented the most concentrated slum of all times, greater than could possibly prevail in Harlem. You might say as I did: "What can you expect? Children have to play. Here they are growing up without a mother, or a mother who never seems to make her presence felt, like animals, without love or warmth, pushing out for some sort of life on the street. Are not these unfortunate children more sinned against than sinning?"

So I spoke to my neighbors. Yet I knew that was not the whole truth. Nearby, within a few blocks, were two magnificent parks: Riverside Drive and Central Park. There they could have green fields and space and freedom. Yet none made a move to play there. Although I believe I understand many other facets of their conduct, this aspect remains a mystery I cannot fathom.

Broadly, this gives you some notion of what happened to a quiet, respectable block when invaded by the lower classes. What happened to my neighbors? First there was general, immediate, universal consternation and some took direct action. Posthaste some moved out; they wouldn't live, they said, with such trash. A second group remained. This group didn't mind the shenanigans, the broken glass, the commotion, but they experienced an awful fear of personal attack. Many of them became so frightened by the invaders that they stayed home at night. The sense of physical peril was probably the most frightening and demoralizing aspect of the situation, though I never heard of anyone being molested or attacked. There was a great deal of damage to parked cars, and we soon learned to avoid that side of the street. It was peculiar to see the gaping empty spaces near the hotel curb, when all around were cars choking for an inch of space.

After the first shock had passed, the tenants of our building took action. The middle class is not without power, which it exercises in its own way (generally of course polite, proper, and without violence). A committee got up a petition and collected signatures asking that a policeman be stationed on our street twenty-four hours a day. A tenant with political connections began to put them to work. I hear that the matter has reached the mayor himself, and that the welfare agency plans to remove families with children from the hotel since, after the petition, the Powers-That-Be agreed that it is an improper place for them.

But these lower-class people are still across the street and the fear remains. Even worse, my middle-class neighbors are convinced that these new people are trash, some monstrous excretion of mankind, a lower order of animal, apart from the human species. So long as such attitudes persist, these unfortunate newcomers—poverty-stricken, ignorant, addicted to vice, drink, violence, and brutality—will never be understood in terms of what causes such living: their bleak, helpless, and hopeless state, their lack of identity and purpose. My middle-class neighbors will piously continue to stay aloof, judging them; and this judgmental attitude itself makes the gulf wider. It is inconceivable that our middle-class house will ever join in friendship or good will to these lower-class invaders.

What I was witnessing had enormous meaning for me as a student of education and as one who teaches future teachers. I thought I knew the problem of the lower-class student; it is all explained in the textbook. Like other instructors, I have discussed the problem in polite, academic terms. But this experience made me see clearly and vividly, as nothing else has, how farfetched and remote is our present school system for these children—in philosophy, methodology, approach, values, and meaning.

In contrast to the lower-class children, how preciously kept is each child in our house; how carefully clothed; how carefully guarded; how often admonished by parents, grandparents, relatives, and friends. In the elevator, the icy tone of the father to his seven-year-old son: "Is that hat glued on to your head, John?" How quickly and politely that hat comes off. How often are they shown pride and love. "My son is the valedictorian of his class. He plans to go to Harvard, get his Ph.D., and teach chemistry." Even our doorman, hard and brusque and violent with lower-class children, takes on a different tone and manner with the building children; to them he is gentle and tender and protective. The children themselves for the most part are loving and lovable. As they imbibe attention and love, as these qualities are poured into them, they have them to give out. If at times the children become rambunctious, the doorman finds it sufficient to threaten them with parental disclosure and they fall in line. There is no discipline problem. From infancy on, they experience discipline.

These children have pride and are conscious of family position. Even if you are a stranger, they will inform you that their father, a lawyer, is involved in some famous current trial; or he has been called to Washington on an important mission; or that their father or grandfather owns this well-known establishment or business. And they tell you with equal pride what they themselves plan to be; and they act as if they have already achieved it and have a right to all the honors thereof.

On school holidays our building takes on a festive air as the children come home from out-of-town schools and colleges. You see a little boy with a ramrod figure sporting a magnificent uniform; he attends a military academy. Parents take special pride in introducing children all around. For these holidays parents have a well-planned schedule— theaters, lunches downtown, visiting and inter-visiting, parties that their children give and parties that they go to. The building is full of young people coming and going; it is really most pleasant and exciting.

Yes, the children in this middle-class building are solicitously nurtured. Just as the parents seem to have purpose and direction for themselves, so the children seem also to have imbibed purpose and direction. Some of them, still in elementary school, speak of college and careers. Coming home in the afternoon, they hold their books tightly and neatly; for it is obvious that for them books represent important and powerful tools for the future.

What a stark contrast are these children on the opposite side of the street! These children seem to have no purpose, no objective; they seem to live for the moment, and the big objective is to make this moment pass away as amusingly and excitingly as possible. And no matter what, they seem a lot more bored and idle than the middle-class children. They hang around, in gangs or small groups, and in boredom they poke at one another or get into mischief; they are ready for any or everything, but mostly nothing happens and there they are, hanging around in idleness.

Even when playing near the house, the children in our building go to the parks already referred to, and they participate in organized games, or if not, they telephone to a friend or friends to meet and play together. In contrast, the children on the opposite street have many of the characteristics of neglected alley cats, growing up in a fierce, hostile jungle. The children from the two sides of the street never mix. Since the invasion of this new element, the children in our building are more closely supervised than ever; they are so apart in thinking and feeling that functionally they are like two different species.

As I saw these two groups first-hand, I understood how easily middle-class children fit conventional school systems; how almost from infancy they have been trained for the role of a good, conforming member of this institution; and how easily and naturally their middle-class teachers would respond with understanding and affection.

Also, I could see how wrong, how incongruous and meaningless this school was for lower-class children; how their very being was an irritant to it, and it to them; how ill-prepared they were for the demands of the school; how what they were and how they lived would elicit from their middle-class teachers scorn, resentment, rejection, hostility, and—worst of all—how these children would create in their teachers fear, a physical, sickening fear, as thirty or forty of them crowded together in one room hour after hour, day after day. This was the most demoralizing feature of all. For once fear sets in, you can no longer understand, appreciate, or help; what you want is distance, separation, safety; or if this is impossible, you want the backing of superior strength or a counter fear; and one cannot educate or help another human being through force or fear.

As I thought of what was happening to my block, I was astonished to realize how in nearly all respects our teachers respond to lower-class children just as my house neighbors do. They cannot understand their idleness, their purposelessness, their lack of ambition. They regard such traits as some congenital evil. Like my neighbors, they are indignant and shocked by their sexual frankness, and are astonished and chagrined by parental indifference to children's progress in school. When parents do come to school they may even side with the child against the teacher. Like my neighbors, teachers remain in a perpetual state of fear of these children, at their acting out, their defiance of discipline, their destructiveness and vandalism. "Look at what they did!" a teacher will say, pointing to a desk ripped open or shattered panes of glass, speaking as if some holy altar had been violated. Looking at these lower-class children distantly, unapprovingly, and judgmentally, as my neighbors did, many teachers feel trapped, frightened, helpless. Like my neighbors, when a child gets into trouble with the law, they often take a smug satisfaction in the tragedy, as if their original judgment had been vindicated. "I knew he would come to a bad end." Middle-class virtue is written all over them.

A good case can be and has been made that the only purpose of our educational system is to inculcate middle-class values, to create a middle-class person; and its purpose is not at all to transmit knowledge and subject matter. If this is true, and I am beginning to feel that it is, the main task of our schools, to repeat, is to train children in the proprieties, the conventions, the manners, the sexual restraints, the respect for private property of the middle class; and also to promote such middle-class virtues as hard work, sportsmanship, and ambition—especially ambition.

The aim becomes to create a gentleman, a person striving for high achievement, so that he can attain the middle-class ideal: money, fame, a lavish house in the suburbs, public honors, etc.

I now perceive more clearly why lower-class children are such problems in school, why they do so poorly, why they are so alien to this institution, why they stand out like sore thumbs. Bluntly put, they don't fit in at all with what the schools and teachers demand, want, and expect.

I now understand why even bright lower-class children do not do nearly as well in school as middle-class children of equal and even lower ability; why bright lower-class children drop out of school even when intellectually capable of doing the work. They never feel part of the institution, their school is not theirs, their team is not theirs, their classmates are not theirs.

Just as the children in my building did not mix with the children on the hotel side of the block, so they do not mix in school. But here in school middle-class children are on home ground; it is *their* school, *their* teachers, *their* clubs, *their* team, *their* classmates. Parents of lower-class children also feel strange and remote from the institution, frightened by its conventions. Sometimes a lower-class child, through the influence of some good, loving, middle-class person, generally a teacher, begins to aspire to middle-class status. The parents, instead of reinforcing middle-class values, may resent these new feelings in the child and fear that he is being alienated from them; they will try to keep the child in his own class. I know a fine and able student who applied for a scholarship and was accepted by a prestige college. Her father, a laborer, was incensed at the whole idea. We were turning his daughter's head. A good girl should get a job, come home, help her mother, and get married. When he was told that college and marriage are not incompatible, he showed every doubt that the two go together. Then he took another tack. Deep study in college, he said, affects the head, and his daughter had fragile health; he didn't want her to become rattle-brained. Finally, he trotted out his last argument: he wasn't going to have his daughter gallivanting off and mixing with those snobs and good-for-nothings. The father won out.

It also happens, undoubtedly with greater frequency in America than in any other major culture, that a lower-class child does break out of his group to enter the middle class. A play, "The Corn Is Green," deals with this theme. It is the true account of a Welsh boy whose teacher, Miss Cooke, out of dedication and devotion, held the youth steadfast in his studies. After many trials, the young man passed his examinations and won an Oxford scholarship. The son of a nursemaid and a seaman, he became an eminent playwright, actor, and director, and, incidentally, the author of "The Corn Is Green."

It sometimes happens that a member of the middle class will flunk out of his class also, although this is quite rare, as a review of your own experience will indicate. Middle-class parents will go to any extreme to save their children for middle-class status. How would an eminent and respected professional person regard his son who worked as a janitor or as a laborer, although the young man might be quite happy with his work and the work right for him? Middle-class parents attempt all kinds of shenanigans to keep their offspring in their class. We all know of the student who fails at a good university, whereupon the parents find a mediocre school where he can obtain the degree. The parents rejoice, for the boy is now a college graduate; he has achieved middle-class status and need not disgrace the family.

I am beginning to feel that if we want to help lower-class children we will have to reorient our thinking and philosophy. We will have to adopt fundamental reforms, radical and crucial in nature, so that the school as an institution will be more nearly in conformity with the cultural and behavioral patterns of this class. I am beginning to think that it might be best if we would enlist in this task the more able and brighter lower-class members, with the hope that they will be better able to cope with the lower-class child. Little good can come to any child when a teacher relates to him with fear and condemnation.

What has long been a national fetish, almost religious in fervor, is the effort to shape all children, regardless of their state or condition, in the middle-class mold. It would appear that the chief end of man is to glorify the middle class. When teachers fail at this task, they regard themselves and the school as failures. I believe that until now we have done a remarkable job in converting this "melting pot" material into a sort of middle-class stew, although frequently of questionable taste and quality.

I raise this question: Should all people strive to become middle-class? Hasn't our middle-class culture produced a society with more than its share of tensions, anxieties, neuroses, and psychoses? How many souls have been blighted, twisted, and distorted by its impossible demands! Middle-class culture, it is true, stresses ambition and achievement, but does it not leave altogether too many of us feeling and thinking of ourselves as failures, even when we have striven mightily and have done our best? And how many, after high achievement, still feel discontented, unhappy, striving ever higher? For there is no end goal to achievement; the goal is almost by definition unattainable. As a clinical psychologist who has seen men and women in travail, I can only say that I have nothing but sympathy for the middle-class child; the demands made on him by parents and his sub-culture are often unbearable. I think of him as frequently caught in a vortex, the victim of uncontrollable forces, so strong that they may destroy him.

In our sanctimonious way, we have assumed that this, our middle-class culture, represents the best of all possible worlds. We have never examined lower-class culture with the view of asking: Is there perhaps something in another way of life to alleviate our own sickness? Like my

house neighbors, we have regarded every deviation with moral condemnation. Even if all these feelings about middle-class values are right,
even if we should continue to force lower-class children into middle-
class molds, shouldn't we recognize that for some children this can never
be achieved? It isn't for them, as a duck isn't for running a race with a
rabbit. In this world isn't there a need and an honorable place for car-
penters, plumbers, and, yes, laborers? Aren't we doing infinite harm to
children by our insistence that they be something they cannot be, and
then making them feel like failures because they have not achieved what
they cannot achieve? Wouldn't it be better if we found out what they *can*
be, and then set about changing our schools so that we can help them, not
to become middle-class, but to become the best selves they are capable
of becoming?

3

*The schools of the city did not, of course, create their
problems. But rather than helping solve them, they
have made them worse.... Where they should be
forces of neighborhood integration and cohesion, they
have become sources of division and conflict. Not all
city schools are prisons; not all offer substandard programs; yet it is clearly the old and the decayed that
characterize the city....*

PETER SCHRAG
Village School Downtown

Jonathan Kozol
WHERE GHETTO SCHOOLS FAIL

There has been so much recent talk of progress in the areas of
curriculum innovation and textbook revision that few people outside the
field of teaching understand how bad most of our elementary school
materials still are. In isolated suburban school districts children play ingenious Monopoly games revised to impart an immediate and first-
person understanding of economic problems in the colonial period. In
private schools, kindergarten children begin to learn about numbers
with brightly colored sticks known as cuisenaire rods, and second-grade

From Jonathan Kozol, *Death at an Early Age* (Boston: Houghton Mifflin Co., 1968).
Reprinted by permission of the publisher. ("Where Ghetto Schools Fail," as reprinted
here, appeared as an article in *Atlantic Monthly*, October, 1967, pp. 107–110.)

children are introduced to mathematics through the ingenuity of a package of odd-shaped figures known as Attribute Games. But in the majority of schools in Roxbury and Harlem and dozens of other slum districts stretching west across the country, teaching techniques, textbooks, and other teaching aids are hopelessly antique, largely obsolete, and often insulting or psychologically oppressive for many thousands of Negro and other minority schoolchildren.

I once made a check of all books in my fourth-grade classroom. Of the slightly more than six hundred books, almost one quarter had been published prior to the bombing of Hiroshima; 60 percent were either ten years old or older. Of thirty-two different book series standing in rows within the cupboard, only six were published as recently as five years ago, and seven series were twenty to thirty-five years old. These figures put into perspective some of the lofty considerations and expensive research projects sponsored by even the best of the curriculum development organizations, for they suggest that educational progress and innovation are reaching chiefly the children of rich people rather than the children of the urban poor.

Obsolescence, however, was not the only problem in our textbooks. Direct and indirect forms of dicrimination were another. The geography book given to my pupils, first published eighteen years ago and only modestly updated since, traced a cross-country journey in which there was not one mention, hint, or image of a dark-skinned face. The chapter on the South described an idyllic landscape in the heart of Dixie: pastoral home of hardworking white citizens, contented white children, and untroubled white adults.

While the history book mentioned Negroes—in its discussion of slavery and the Civil War—the tone of these sections was ambiguous. "Men treasure freedom above all else," the narrative conceded at one point, but it also pointed out that slavery was not an altogether dreadful institution: "Most Southern people treated their slaves kindly," it related, and then quoted a stereotyped plantation owner as saying: "Our slaves have good homes and plenty to eat. When they are sick, we take care of them. . . ."

While the author favored emancipation, he found it necessary to grant to arguments on the other side a patriotic legitimacy: "No one can truly say, 'The North was right' or 'The Southern cause was better.' Remember, each side fought for the ideals it believed in. For in Our America all of us have the right to our beliefs."

When my class had progressed to the cotton chapter in our geography book, I decided to alter the scheduled reading. Since I was required to make use of the textbook, and since its use, I believed, was certain to be damaging, I decided to supply the class with extra material in the form of a mimeographed sheet. I did not propose to tell the children any tales about lynchings, beatings, or the Ku Klux Klan. I merely wanted to add to the study of cotton-growing some information about the connection between the discovery of Eli Whitney's cotton gin and the greater growth of slavery.

I had to submit this material to my immediate superior in the school, a lady whom I will call the Reading Teacher. The Reading Teacher was a well-intentioned woman who had spent several years in ghetto class-rooms, but who, like many other teachers, had some curiously ambiv-alent attitudes toward the children she was teaching. I recall the moment after I had handed her that sheet of paper. Looking over the page, she agreed with me immediately that it was accurate. Nobody, she said, was going to quibble with the idea that cotton, the cotton gin, and slavery were all intertwined. But it was the question of the "advisability of any mention of slavery to the children at this time," which, she said, she was presently turning over in her mind. "Would it," she asked me frankly, "truly serve the advantage of the children at this stage to confuse and complicate the study of simple geography with socioeconomic factors?" Why expose the children, she was asking essentially, to unpleasant facts about their heritage?

Then, with an expression of the most honest and intense affection for the children in the class, she added: "I don't want these children to have to think back on this year later on and to remember that we were the ones who told them they were Negro." This remark seemed to take one step further the attitude of the textbook writers. Behind the statement lay the unspoken assumption that to be Negro was a shameful condition. The longer this knowledge could be kept from the innocent young, the better off they would be.

After the journey across America, the class was to study the life of the desert Arab. Before we began, the Reading Teacher urged upon me a book which she said she had used with her own classes for a great many years. It was not the same book the children had. She told me she pre-ferred it, but that it was too old to be in regular use.

I took the book home that night and opened it up to a section on the Arabs:

> The Bedouin father is tall and straight. He wears a robe that falls to his ankles and his bare feet are shod in sandals of camel's leather. . . . Behind the Bedouin father walk his wife and his children. . . .
>
> These people are fine looking. Their black eyes are bright and in-telligent. Their features are much like our own, and, although their skin is brown, they belong to the white race, as we do. It is scorching desert sun that has tanned the skin of the Arabs to such a dark brown color.

Turning to a section on Europe, I read the following description:

> Two Swiss children live in a farmhouse on the edge of town. . . .
> These children are handsome. Their eyes are blue. Their hair is
> golden yellow. Their white skins are clear, and their cheeks are as
> red as ripe, red apples.

Curious after this to see how the African Negroes would be treated, I
turned to a section on the Congo Valley:

> The black people who live on this great continent of Africa were
> afraid of the first white men who came to explore their land. They
> ran and hid from them in the dark jungle. They shot poisoned arrows
> from behind the thick bushes. They were savage and uncivilized. . . .
> Yumbo and Minko are a black boy and a black girl who live in this
> jungle village. Their skins are of so dark a color that they look almost
> black. Their noses are large and flat. Their lips are thick. Their eyes
> are black and shining, and their hair is so curly that it seems like
> wool. They are Negroes and belong to the black race.

Perhaps without being conscious of it, the Reading Teacher had her
own way of telling the children what it meant to be Negro.

Not all books used in a school system, merely by the law of averages,
are going to be consistently and blatantly poor. A large number of the
books we had in Boston were only mildly distorted or else devastatingly
bad only in one part. One such book, not used in my school but at the
junior high level, was entitled *Our World Today*. Right and wrong, good
and bad alternate in this book from sentence to sentence and from page
to page:

> The people of the British Isles are, like our own, a mixed people.
> Their ancestors were the sturdy races of northern Europe, such as
> Celts, Angles, Saxons, Danes and Normans, whose energy and abil-
> ities still appear in their descendants. With such a splendid inher-
> itance what could be more natural than that the British should
> explore and settle many parts of the world and in time build up the
> world's greatest colonial empire? . . .
> The people of South Africa have one of the most democratic gov-
> ernments now in existence in any country. . . .
> Africa needs more capitalists. . . . White managers are needed . . .
> to show the Negroes how to work and to manage their planta-
> tions. . . .
> In our study of the nations of the world, we should try to under-
> stand the people and their problems from their point of view. We
> ought to have a sympathetic attitude towards them, rather than con-
> demn them through ignorance because they do not happen always
> to have our ways. . . .
> The Negro is very quick to imitate and follow the white man's way
> of living and dressing. . . .

The white man may remain for short periods and direct the work, but he cannot . . . do the work himself. He must depend on the natives to do the work. . . .

The white men who have entered Africa are teaching the natives how to live. . . .

Sooner or later, books like these will be put to pasture. Either that, or they will be carefully doctored and rewritten. But the problem they represent is not going to be resolved in any important way by their removal or revision. Too many teachers admire and depend on such textbooks and prefer to teach from them. The attitudes of these teachers are likely to remain long after the books have been replaced.

Plenty of good books are available, of course, that give an honest picture of the lives of black Americans. The tutorial programs in Boston have been using them, and so have many of the more enlightened private schools. In the public schools of this city, however, it is difficult to make use of books that depart from the prescribed curriculum. When I made a tentative effort to introduce such materials into my classroom, I encountered firm resistance.

Earlier in the year I had brought to school a book of poetry by the Negro author Langston Hughes. I had not used it in the classroom, but it did at least make its way onto a display board in the auditorium as part of an exhibit on important American Negroes, set up to pay lip service to "Negro History Week."

To put a book by a Negro poet on display is one thing. To open the book and attempt to read something from it is quite another. In the last weeks of the spring I discovered the difference when I began to read a few of the poems to the children in my class. It was during a period in which I also was reading them some poems of John Crowe Ransom, Robert Frost, and W. B. Yeats.

Hughes, I have come to learn, holds an extraordinary appeal for many children. I knew this from some earlier experiences in other classes, and I remembered, in particular, the reaction of a group of young teen-agers in a junior high the first time I ever had brought his work into a public school. On the book's cover, the children could see the picture of the dark-skinned author, and they did not fail to comment. Their comments concentrated on that single, obvious, overriding fact:

"Look—that man's colored."

The same reaction was evident here, too, among my fourth-grade students: the same gratification and the same very vivid sense of recognition. It seemed a revelation to them that a man could have black skin and be a famous author.

Of all the poems of Langston Hughes that we read, the one the children liked the best was a poem entitled "Ballad of the Landlord." The reason, I think, that this piece of writing had so much meaning for them was not only that it seemed moving in an obvious and immediate human way, but also that it *found* its emotion in something ordinary. It is a poem which allows both heroism and pathos to poor people, sees strength in awkwardness, and attributes to a poor person standing on the stoop of his slum house every bit as much significance as William Wordsworth saw in daffodils, waterfalls, and clouds. At the request of the children, I mimeographed some copies of that poem, and although nobody in the classroom was asked to do this, several of the children took it home and memorized it on their own. I did not assign it for memory, because I do not think that memorizing a poem has any special value. Some of the children just came in and asked if they could recite it. Before long, almost every child in the room had asked to have a turn.

One day a week later, shortly before lunchtime, I was standing in front of my class playing a record of French children's songs I had brought in. A message-signal on the wall began to buzz. I left the room and hurried to the principal's office. A white man whom I had never seen before was sitting by her desk. This man, bristling and clearly hostile to me, as was the principal, instantly attacked me for having read to my class and distributed at their wish the poem entitled "Ballad of the Landlord." It turned out that he was the father of one of the few white boys in the class. He was also a police officer.

The mimeograph of the poem, in my handwriting, was waved before my eyes. The principal demanded to know what right I had to allow such a poem—not in the official course of study—to be read and memorized by children. I said I had not asked anyone to memorize it, but that I would defend the poem and its use on the basis that it was a good poem. The principal became incensed with my answer and blurted out that she did not consider it a work of art.

The parent was angry as well, it turned out, about a book having to do with the United Nations. I had brought a book to class, one of sixty or more volumes, that told about the UN and its Human Rights Commission. The man, I believe, had mistaken "human rights" for "civil rights" and was consequently in a patriotic rage. The principal, in fairness, made the point that she did not think there was anything wrong with the United Nations, although in the report later filed on the matter, she denied this, and said, instead, "I then spoke and said that I felt there was no need for this material in the classroom." The principal's report went on to say that she assured the parent, after I had left the room, that "there was not another teacher in the district who would have used this poem or any material like it. I assured him that his children would be very safe from such incidents."

I returned to my class, as requested, and a little before two o'clock the principal called me back to tell me I was fired. She forbade me to say good-bye to the children in the class or to indicate in any way that I was leaving. She said that I was to close up my records, leave the school, and report to School Department headquarters the next morning.

The next day an official who had charge of my case at the School Department took a much harder line on curriculum innovation than I had ever heard before. No literature, she said, which is not in the course of study could *ever* be read by a Boston teacher without permission of someone higher up. She said further that no poem by any Negro author could be considered permissible if it involved suffering. I asked her whether there would be many good poems left to read by such a standard. Wouldn't it rule out almost all great Negro literature? Her answer evaded the issue. No poetry that described suffering was felt to be suitable. The only Negro poetry that could be read in the Boston schools, she indicated, must fit a certain kind of standard. The kind of poem she meant, she said by way of example, might be a poem that "accentuates the positive" or "describes nature" or "tells of something hopeful."

The same official went on a few minutes later to tell me that any complaint from a parent meant automatic dismissal. "You're out," she said. "You cannot teach in the Boston schools again. If you want to teach, why don't you try a private school someday?"

Other Boston officials backed up these assertions in statements released during the following hectic days. The deputy superintendent, who wielded considerable authority over these matters, pointed out that although Langston Hughes "has written much beautiful poetry, we cannot give directives to the teacher to use literature written in native dialects." She explained: "We are trying to break the speech patterns of these children, trying to get them to speak properly. This poem does not present correct grammatical expression and would just entrench the speech patterns we want to break."

A couple of weeks later, winding up an investigation into the matter, School Committee member Thomas Eisenstadt concluded that school officials had handled things correctly. Explaining in his statement that teachers are dismissed frequently when found lacking in either "training, personality or character," he went on to say that "Mr. Kozol, or anyone else who lacks the personal discipline to abide by rules and regulations, as we all must in our civilized society, is obviously unsuited for the highly responsible profession of teaching."

In thinking back upon my year within the Boston system, I am often reminded of a kind of sad-keyed epilogue that the Reading Teacher used to bring forward sometimes at the end of a discussion: "Things are changing," she used to say with feeling; "I am changing too—but everything cannot happen just like that."

Perhaps by the time another generation comes around a certain modest number of these things will have begun to be corrected. But if I were the parent of a Negro child, I know that I would not willingly accept a calendar of improvements scaled so slowly. The anger of the mother whose child's years in elementary school have been squandered may seem inexplicable to a person like the Reading Teacher. To that mother, it is the complacency and hypocrisy of a society that could sustain and foster so many thousands of people like the Reading Teacher that seem extraordinary. The comfortable people who don't know and don't see the ghettos deliberate in their committee rooms. Meanwhile, the children whose lives their decisions are either going to save or ruin are expected to sit quietly, fold their hands patiently, recite their lessons, draw their margins, bite their tongues, swallow their dignities, and smile and wait.

4

Public education in a [racially homogenous] setting is socially unrealistic, blocks the attainment of the goals of democratic education, and is wasteful of manpower and talent, whether this situation occurs by law or by fact.
UNITED STATES COMMISSION ON CIVIL RIGHTS

Robert Schwartz, Thomas Pettigrew, and Marshall Smith

DESEGREGATION: ASSESSING THE ALTERNATIVES

Collapse of Consensus

There has been a collapse of consensus among liberal whites and militant Negroes about how to desegregate the nation's schools.

Some don't believe in integrated education any more. Some now claim it can't work.

Many young Negroes have given up hope of ever achieving racial integration and demand community control over all-Negro schools in the ghetto. White liberals find themselves split on the issue—much as they have been over the Vietnam War. There is virtual unanimity among liberals for moral as well as educational reasons that racially integrated schooling is desirable and must remain an ultimate objective. But there is sharp and often acrimonious debate over short-term policy decisions—with the educator typically caught in the crossfire.

One outspoken portion of the white liberal community is combining forces with white extremists who never accepted the goal of integration. Joining this fold are the most strident separatists among Black Power advocates, and together this strange coalition is trying to breathe new life

From Robert Schwartz, Thomas Pettigrew, and Marshall Smith, "Desegregation: Assessing the Alternatives," *Nation's Schools*, March, 1968, pp. 61–66, 117. Reprinted by permission of the publisher.

into the "separate-but-equal" doctrine that the Supreme Court thought it had effectively laid to rest in 1954. While continuing to profess school integration as the ideal solution, these liberals are now repeating many of the contentions of such symbols of segregation as George Wallace and Louise Day Hicks, whom they were roundly castigating only a few short years ago: White Americans simply will not accept interracial schools; integration is demographically impossible to achieve anyway; integration is the pipedream of unrealistic "do-gooders" and intellectuals, and Negroes are happier and can get a fine education in truly first-rate ghetto schools. Old programs no longer identify the players in today's racial drama.

Long-range educational decisions, however, cannot be made on the basis of ideological contentions.

The future directions of our nation's schools are too crucial to be determined by the domestic aberrations of war and short-run expediencies. Educators must responsibly fashion a design for the rest of this century out of the best information we have available and all of the alternatives as we can perceive them. Today's educational thinking raises three broad policies as future alternatives: 1) compensatory education, 2) decentralization and community control, and 3) desegregation and integration.

Alternative I: Compensatory Education

Conventional explanations of why disadvantaged pupils don't do as well as advantaged pupils are being contradicted by mounting research evidence.

In 1906 Bernard Shaw wrote in the preface to *The Doctor's Dilemma:*

> Or, to take another common instance, comparisons which are really comparisons between two social classes with different standards of nutrition and education are palmed off as comparisons between the results of a certain medical treatment and its neglect. Thus, it is easy to prove that the wearing of tall hats and the carrying of umbrellas enlarges the chest, prolongs life, and confers comparative immunity from disease; for the statistics show that the classes which use these articles are bigger, healthier, and live longer than the class which never dreams of possessing such things.

For many years Americans had a stock answer to explain the differences in achievement level between advantaged and disadvantaged groups. It was clear that the advantaged had access to better facilities, curriculum and teachers. And that this access "caused" the differences in achievement levels also seemed "obvious." It is frightening to realize that in the face of mounting evidence contradicting this "answer," the reaction of many educators, policy makers, and journalists has not been to reject their beliefs but to advocate them more than ever, to call for "taller hats" and "larger umbrellas" for the ghetto.

Such a reaction has promoted increased ESEA Title I support for compensatory education leading to new materials, more adults in the classroom, and team teaching in the context of the "neighborhood ghetto school." There is little question but that the funding of massive compensatory programs for the ghetto dweller would be a simpler political solution than integration *if* compensatory programs really worked, *if* these schools did overcome the educational achievement deficits that the "disadvantaged" child brings to school with him.

The sad fact is, however, that segregated compensatory programs have not succeeded. If there exists such a program in a ghetto school that has enabled students to approach and *sustain* grade level achievements, it has not been rigorously evaluated and publicly reported. This unhappy truth is extensively documented in Chapter Four of the U. S. Civil Rights Commission's Report, "Racial Isolation in the Public Schools", in which results of major compensatory efforts from a number of cities are reported in detail. More recently the evaluation of the heralded More Effective Schools program in New York City by the Center for Urban Education produced familiar results.

Such results are not easily swallowed by those who have long assessed the quality of education in terms of dollar inputs. The discovery that pupil achievement levels are apparently insensitive to changes in traditional inputs (teachers excluded) hasn't been and shouldn't be blindly accepted. Those who disagree with this conclusion generally argue that either the compensatory programs have not been in effect long enough for improvement to be seen or that the programs have not been adequately funded. And in criticism of the evidence offered by the U.S. Office of Education's Equality of Educational Opportunity report (the Coleman Report) supporting the conclusion of little or no independent effect of traditional inputs, these same persons contend that even if the report's measures were adequate, the existing differences in school resources between schools is so small that it is impossible to estimate the relationship between school resources and achievement. Because the pupil-teacher ratio is so similar across the country, for example, we have no way of estimating the effect of reducing it from 25/1 to 6/1 at the elementary level.

It is impossible to offer absolutely conclusive evidence refuting any of these points. Critics will always claim that we must wait even longer to see the results, spend even more money, and provide more teachers per classroom. The burden of proof, however, is on these "true believers."

Actually, the most difficult fact for true believers to accept is that there is little positive effect in simply increasing the teacher-pupil ratio. Although the tutorial goal of Mark Hopkins at one end of a log and a single student at the other end is recognized as impractical, it, or conditions approximating it, is considered to guarantee success. But consider the economic and practical implications of supplying one qualified teacher for every six disadvantaged students as defined by ESEA Title I eligibility. David K. Cohen estimates the initial costs in teacher training, salaries and classroom construction to be approximately $20 billion. He further estimates that the annual salary expenditures on teachers of poor children would increase from about $1.7 billion to about $8.6 billion, or from 8 per cent to 43 per cent of the total instructional expenditures for *all* children. This line of reasoning assumes, of course, that enough qualified candidates could be found and trained, and that they can be persuaded to work in ghetto rather than suburban schools. It also assumes that the political will can be mustered to reallocate national priorities to the point where current ESEA expenditures are dramatically increased. And even if such a program were realized, there is little indication that it would be successful in truly equalizing public educational opportunity.

Reliance upon the mechanical solution of increasing the teacher-pupil ratio has been criticized on theoretical as well as empirical grounds. Perhaps the most familiar criticism of this approach is that smaller classes are of no help if the teachers are too inflexible to adjust in teaching styles and instructional strategies. This notion gained indirect support from the findings of the Coleman Report and from the recently published British survey, *Children and Their Primary Schools*, commonly called the Plowden Report. In both reports, rough measures of the quality of the teachers in a school are strongly associated with the achievement of the students. The association is independent of the social class of the individual student and the student body and of the level of other school attributes. The relationship is much stronger for minority group students than for majority (white) students, and it appears to be accumulative in that it increases over the years from first to twelfth grade. Apparently, competent teachers are successful no matter what the class size.

The problem with such findings is that they lead to few direct policy implications. And though long-term policy directed toward recruitment of "smarter" teachers (more pay, better working conditions, and so forth) might eventually produce a solution for the ghetto, what about the next 10 years? Certainly increased attention to approaches for improving the quality of teaching seems to be called for and at the expense, if necessary, of standard hardware improvements.

Alternative II: Decentralization

Decentralization means different things to educators and state legislatures and proponents of Black Power, who seek black control of black schools.

A second alternative now being proposed for the ills of urban education is decentralization and community control. Since decentralization is in some danger of becoming another fashionable educational catchword, we should point out that the term means at least two distinctly different things to different groups of people. For educators, decentralization seems largely to be an organizational concept: It is a device for dealing with the administrative rigidity and bureaucratic inertia that inevitably characterize most large formal organizations. The movement to decentralize the New York City school system, for example, certainly predates the Black Power movement. New York reorganized its local school boards in 1961 in an attempt to let some air into the system, and, in 1965, 31 district superintendents were appointed to have jurisdiction over these local units. Although both moves were in part motivated by the desire to bring the schools closer to the people, there was no substantial transfer of power from the board's central headquarters at 110 Livingston Street to the districts.

In the past year or two, administrative decentralization has been talked about, and in some cases implemented, in more and more of our major cities. The Chicago school system, for example, has been divided into three large districts each of which is under the semiautonomous jurisdiction of an associate superintendent. In Washington a panel of outside consultants led by Prof. A. Harry Passow of Teachers College has recommended the reorganization of the school system into eight decentralized units; and in Philadelphia, Los Angeles, and Boston various decentralization plans have been put forward. But there is an increasing gap between the decentralization schemes recommended by schoolmen and the demands of militant black leaders. This gap is best illustrated by the reception accorded the report of the Mayor's Advisory Panel on Decentralization of the New York City Schools.

Although this is not the place to go into the details of the Bundy Plan, it is worth noting that in the act leading to the creation of the advisory panel, the state legislature requested the creation of "educational policy units" that would:

> . . . afford members of the community an opportunity to take a more active and meaningful role in the development of educational policy related to the diverse needs and aspirations of the community.

The premise underlying this request is that:

> Increased community awareness and participation in the educational process is essential to the furtherance of educational innovation and excellence in the public school system within the city of New York.

It seems likely that the state legislature was led to think of decentralization in terms of increased community participation in educational policymaking because of the demands stemming from certain ghetto communities. One obvious source of these demands was the experience of parents and community leaders at East Harlem's Intermediate School 201 in the summer and fall of 1966. A less obvious, but probably more significant source, was the participation of many ghetto residents in various antipoverty programs. We are thinking here especially of the ill-fated community action program, which in its initial phase promised the "maximum feasible participation of the poor." But whatever the sources of the legislature's insistence on increased community participation in policymaking, the point worth noting is that the advisory panel's recommendation of "a community school system" has achieved the improbable success of provoking the board of education, the supervisors' association, and the teachers' union to close ranks in opposition to it.

The relationship between decentralization and community control, on the one hand, and Negro American achievement, on the other hand, is undoubtedly more complex than advocates appear to assume. If the decentralization plan carves out ghetto districts and separates them from "white" districts, racial segregation of schools may be institutionalized for generations to come. The result of such further educational ghetto-ization cannot be definitively predicted, of course, but present data would point in the direction of lower achievement and aspirations of future Negro students. But this need not be the case. New York City, or any other American city, *can* be decentralized in such a way as to further desegregation—though by itself, of course, decentralization cannot complete the task.

Black Power proponents brush aside such considerations. They are convinced that black community control alone can improve ghetto schools, instill racial pride, and elevate achievement. All of these contentions, however, are ideological assumptions, not demonstrated truths. Unlike the hard data which supports the efficacy of racially integrated schools, these critical assumptions are held to be true by fiat. To be sure, community and parental involvement as well as racial pride are values to be sought as ends in themselves. But their positive causal connections with achievement and later attainments are not as yet demonstrated. Like ardent supporters of ghetto compensation, Black Power advocates have the burden of proof for their sweeping assumptions.

Alternative III: Racial Desegregation

Who knows if racial integration will work or fail? So far, it could be argued, no one does because it is largely a strategy that has never been tried.

Critics of racial integration, white and black, often claim that it is a bankrupt strategy that failed; actually, it is largely a strategy that has never been tried. To the extent it has been attained in schools, it has typically succeeded in three key realms: the academic achievement of Negro children, the racial attitudes and preferences of white children, and the racial attitudes and preferences of Negro children. Each of these consequences merits attention.

The Coleman data, as analyzed and reported in chapter three of the Civil Rights Commission's *Racial Isolation of Public Schools* monograph, support with a large sample what limited research in individual school districts from White Plains to Berkeley has indicated repeatedly: Negro American children as a group evince and sustain substantially greater academic achievement if they are members of predominantly white classrooms. This effect is especially strong if the child begins his interracial education in the first three grades. And the achievement of white children in such classrooms is not lowered when contrasted with that of comparable white children in all-white classrooms.

Not all desegregation, of course, leads to superior Negro achievement.

Interracial schools, like uniracial ones, can be good, bad or indifferent, since the mere racial mix of students is no magic guarantee of learning as some integrationist ideologists imply. But desegregation is the prerequisite of the ideal condition—the true cross-racial acceptance of integration. In other words, a *desegregated* school is merely an institution with an interracial student body, usually mostly white; it implies nothing about the quality of the interracial interaction. By contrast, an integrated school is a desegregated one with numerous cross-racial friendships and little or no racial tension. The Commission on Civil Rights, in closer examination of the Coleman data, discovered that the chief academic benefits of interracial education occurred primarily in the genuinely integrated schools.

Some researchers regard the improved learning of integrated Negro youngsters as a total result of social class and not race. That is, most Negro schools are comprised primarily of lower class children, while most white schools are comprised primarily of middle class children. Considerable research, including the Coleman Report, shows the vast importance for achievement of attending a school with a middle class milieu. Thus, these researchers conclude that it is actually the typically higher social class backgrounds, and not the race, of his new classmates that raises the integrated Negro child's test scores. There is no doubt that this social class effect is central to the process, but our interpretation of the relevant data to date is that there is also a racial benefit for achievement. In any event, this debate between researchers is strictly academic for the educational policy maker. With the most generous definition, only about one-fourth of Negro America is middle class. Consequently, the only way the vast majority of Negro students can attend schools with a dominant middle class milieu is through racial desegregation.

While important, high achievement test scores are surely not the only goal of education. Indeed, many integrationists argue for biracial schools solely in terms of the nonacademic benefits of diverse contacts. Preparation for the interracial world of the future, they insist, demands interracial schools today for both white and Negro youth.

Both the Coleman and Commission Reports speak to this issue, too.

The Coleman Report shows that white students who attend public schools with Negroes are the least likely to prefer all-white classrooms and all white "close friends"; and this effect, too, is strongest among those who begin their interracial schooling in the early grades. Consistent with these results are data from Louisville, Kentucky, on Negro pupils. In an open choice situation, Negro children are likely to select mostly-white high schools only if they are currently attending mostly white junior high schools. In short, integration leads to a preference among both white and Negro children for integration, while segregation promotes further segregation.

A Civil Rights Commission survey of urban adults in the North and West discussed in its report suggests that these trends continue into adulthood. Negro adults who themselves attended desegregated schools as children tend to be more eager to have their children attend such schools and do in fact more often send their children to such schools than comparable Negro adults who attended only segregated schools as children. They are typically making more money and more frequently in white-collar occupations than previously segregated Negroes of comparable origins. Similarly, white adults who experienced as children integrated schooling differ from comparable whites in their greater willingness to reside in an interracial neighborhood; to have their children attend interracial schools, and to have Negro friends. The cumulative nature of integration, then, is not limited to just the school career, but also tends to span generations for both whites and Negroes.

Those who consider only test scores in urging bigger and better ghetto schools might well think deeply about these racial attitude and preference data. Even if it were somehow possible to generate first-rate academic performance in ghetto schools, would not such institutions and their all-white counterparts be still producing yet another generation of racially bigoted Americans who regard racial separation as desirable and right? Children educated in racially separate schools naturally come to see the world through "race-colored" glasses.

Integrated schooling is not something paternalistically provided "for Negroes." Nor, for that matter, is it something "for whites." It is in a real sense an educational alternative necessary to the ultimate solution of the nation's most serious domestic problem. Integrated schools, then, are "for America."

Are These Alternatives Mutually Exclusive?

The solutions offered for helping segregated schools—decentralization, reduced pupil ratios—make even more sense for helping desegregated schools.

We have discussed the major ideas in education today related to race relations as if they were alternatives, as if you had to choose one to the exclusion of the others. We did this because we feel it accurately reflects the typical context in which they are discussed. In particular, compensatory education, decentralization and community control are often presented as substitutes for racial desegregation. We reject such thinking. Our reading of the evidence to date leads to the belief that to the degree these ideas have merit they have still more merit in interracial schools. Thus, compensatory programs in integrated schools have frequently attained lasting success, in contrast to the typical failure of similar compensatory programs in virtually all-Negro settings.

We believe that there is a case to be made for decentralization and more community participation in the running of the schools, just as there is a strong argument for compensatory education, but only as these policies *accompany* the drive for integration rather than substitute for it. There is no question that school systems in large cities are overly bureaucratic and inflexible, and that they should become more responsive to local needs. We support the notion of strengthening the authority of school principals and their faculties, and we share the hope that increased participation by parents in the life of the school will have a salutary effect on the motivation of the children.

But if these ideas make sense for segregated schools, they should make even more sense for integrated ones. Similarly, if teaching technics are developed in compensatory programs to capitalize on reduced pupil ratios, these technics should prove effective in an integrated setting. Integration *by itself* is not going to be enough to close the achievement gap. If experiments in decentralization prove to have a positive impact on achievement, these findings should influence our planning for *all* schools.

Is Racial Integration Possible?

Once the Vietnam War ends, federal funds available for school construction could serve as a powerful incentive for metropolitan cooperation in education.

But why make the case for integrated schools, ask members of the new segregationist coalition, if it is impossible to achieve? Even if it is demonstrably by far the most effective approach around which others revolve, is it not foolish and naive to pursue an unattainable goal?

Those who wish to abandon school desegregation "prove" its impossibility by pointing to the racial demography of our cities: Four of five Negro Americans who live in metropolitan areas reside in central cities, while half of metropolitan white Americans now reside in suburbs. Emphasizing New York City and Washington D.C. as urban prototypes, they conclude that school integration is simply never going to be achieved. So why not "educate children where they are" and replicate in our schools the racial and social class homogeneity of housing patterns?

We are aware of these facts of racial demography; and we do agree with the unstated premise in this reasoning that housing patterns of racial separation will not erode rapidly enough to be of any real significance to the schools. But after careful study of this issue, we firmly believe the conclusion to be correct only if, once again, one is willing to make a number of critical assumptions about the future. The pattern of black central cities and white suburban rings makes future school integration impossible only if one: ignores the majority of American cities that are not likely ever to resemble either New York or Washington; assumes that Negro ghettos will not extend into suburbs (as Chicago's westside ghetto will soon expand into Oak Park); assumes that the single site model of so-called "neighborhood" schools will dominate future school plans despite its uneconomic features; assumes that the overwhelmingly white parochial systems in key central cities will not cooperate more and more with public systems; assumes that virtually all school district and municipal boundaries will stay frozen.

In evaluating these crucial assumptions, the reader should keep in mind another demographic reality never mentioned by the apostles of separatism: Virtually the same percentages of Negro and white Americans reside in the nation's 212 metropolitan areas—roughly two-thirds of each group. In other words, Negroes comprise the same one-ninth proportion of metropolitan America as they do for the nation at large. As soon as we grasp this important fact, the question of racial numbers acquires a different dimension. Even metropolitan Washington D.C. has many more white than Negro school children, and this racial ratio has not radically changed in recent years.

But is metropolitan *cooperation* (consolidation is not required) truly possible? Were it necessary solely as a device to integrate schools, we would admit that it is, perhaps, utopian. Yet the forces pushing metropolitanism are far deeper. Duplication of services throughout the multiple municipalities of our typical metropolis are grossly expensive and wasteful, and the intensifying pressures on local budgets are generating cross-boundary cooperation in many realms. Two large southern cities— Miami, Dade County, and Nashville, Davidson County—have gone the full route and consolidated their metropolitan areas.

When metropolitan cooperation for racial integration occurs *without* financial incentives, we regard it as an important precedent. Thus, we deem the modest Rochester, Hartford, and Boston experiments as significant forerunners, even though the transporting of small numbers of Negro children to already-existing, overwhelmingly white suburban schools is not an ultimate solution.

Once the Vietnam War draws to a close and federal funds are again available for new domestic initiatives, major support for school construction will almost certainly become a reality. But how will it be spent? It could be spent largely by central cities to build fine new facilities deep in the ghetto—and thereby institutionalize school segregation into the next century. Or it could be used for metropolitan complexes drawing from large and heterogeneous attendance areas. Such school construction funds could be restricted to voluntary, suburban-central city consortia and thus become a powerful incentive for metropolitan cooperation in education. Unlikely? Well, similar federal programs for metropolitan cooperation in other realms have been operating successfully for some years.

Well planned metropolitan complexes spanning all grade levels and convenient to mass transit arteries would provide ideal settings for compensatory efforts, decentralization, and community involvement. Economies of scale would allow truly massive programs of compensation to take place under conditions of social class as well as racial integration. Pie-slice attendance areas would effectively set up decentralized districts without sealing in homogeneous districts by race and class. And though the size of these multiple-school complexes is often cited as antithetical to local participation, numerous educational innovations have been suggested to counter this: parental school boards for the complex with everything but taxing power; smaller individual schools than are now economically possible for "neighborhood" schools; centralized athletic, theatrical, library, medical and other facilities so superb that adults would wish to employ the complex as a community center. Quality takes on a new dimension in these terms.

School integration, then, *is* possible, but we must plan and strive for it if it is to be achieved. Platitudes about school integration being an ideal and ultimate goal are worthless, however, if by our actions we delay or obstruct the process indefinitely. No one claims that attaining school integration will be easy. Yet if the effort is judged impossible before it is made, the prejudgment becomes a self-fulfilling prophecy.

5

A decentralized school system and simplistic desegregation are political palliatives and educational nonsense.

JOHN R. EVERETT
Atlantic, December, 1968

Art Buchwald
WAYWARD BUSING

We walked into the office of a New York newspaper the other day and found a Negro friend of ours completely downcast.

"What's the matter?" we asked him.

"I just moved to a nice section of the Bronx," he said, "into a lovely house on a nice street with grass and flowers and trees. The neighbors gave me no trouble—as a matter of fact, they were very nice to me. The kids were happy as could be. It cost me $3,000 a year more, but I didn't care. It was worth it."

"What happened?" we asked.

"Now they want to put my kids to school in Harlem."

"That doesn't sound right."

"They figured my kids should be with underprivileged kids so they'll know what it's like. But I told them my kids know what it's like in an underprivileged school and we'd like to try an overprivileged school for a while."

"What did they say?"

"They said I should have stayed in Harlem if I wanted my kids to go to a good school. I can't expect them to go to a good school if I'm going to live in a good neighborhood. That wouldn't make sense."

"They have a point, you know," we said. "If everyone who lived in a good neighborhood sent their kids to a good school, whom would you send to the bad schools?"

"But I don't know why I have to live in a bad neighborhood to send my kids to a good school."

"Because the schools in a bad neighborhood are bad, and you wouldn't want to send them to a bad school, would you?"

"That's why I moved in the first place," he said.

"Well, you should have thought about it before you moved. Just because you live in a good neighborhood is no reason why you should send your kids to a good school."

"It's not as simple as that. I have a friend who lives in a bad neighborhood, but, because of the busing, the authorities decided to make it a good school. They fixed it all up and brought in some first-rate teachers. Then they bused his kids to a good neighborhood which had a lousy school. He complained he wanted his kids to go to the good school in the bad neighborhood, but they told him his kids had to be bused to the lousy school in the good neighborhood, so the kids from the good neighborhood would have a good school to go to in the lousy neighborhood."

"Well," we said, "if that's true, why wouldn't your kids be able to go to a good school in a lousy neighborhood?"

"Because the school they want to send my kids to is a lousy school in a lousy neighborhood. Besides, how are my kids going to meet any kids from the good neighborhood if they go to the lousy school?"

"Maybe on the bus?" we suggested.

"I don't think so. I believe there is only one solution. I think I'll move back to Harlem and send the kids to private school."

6

From the jungle of American cities to the jungle of Africa, education is expected to create order out of chaos. The schools, while operating in the enclaves of the urban slums, are asked to wipe out the ignorance, poverty, and violence that are undermining the schools themselves.

FRED M. HECHINGER

Harold Howe, II
THE TIME IS NOW

Considering the authority that education officials have at our command to correct racial injustice in our schools, I feel that we have accomplished very little so far. While we have gone on urging moderation, sweet reason, and bigger and better panel discussions, the schools throughout the nation remain almost as segregated today as they were in 1954, when the Supreme Court decided that racially segregated education was illegal.

The small progress that the South has made toward desegregation has been offset by increasing *de facto* segregation in cities of the North. Since 1954, an entire sub-generation of Negro and white youngsters who started first grade in that year has now graduated from high school, most without any classroom experience with the other race. The facts today are that a Negro youngster in an American elementary school has,

From Harold Howe, II, "The Time is Now," *Saturday Review,* July 16, 1966, pp. 57–58. Copyright Saturday Review, Inc., 1966. Reprinted by permission of the author and publisher.

on the national average, not much more than 15 per cent of his classmates from the majority white group; in the Southern states the figure is
nearer to 5 per cent; white high school students can expect to have nine
out of ten of their classmates from their own white group. The picture
does not inspire calm satisfaction.

Moderation has a great deal to be said for it, of course, especially by
the moderates. I am reminded of the prayer that St. Augustine addressed
to heaven when he was a young man. "Oh Lord," he said, "make me
chaste. But not yet."

Our words have urged the nation to desegregate its schools. But our
reluctance to act has said even more loudly, "not yet." Somehow we
seem to have been lulled into a blind faith in gradualism, a mindless
confidence that some morning, some year, a suddenly transformed electorate will spontaneously and joyously decide that this is the day to integrate America.

Well, it's not going to happen. The majority of American whites display no likelihood of becoming enthusiastic about school desegregation
and the changes it demands in the immediate future. The law of this land
nevertheless beckons every one of us, calling on us to recognize that de-
segregating the schools is our legal responsibility, that it will not be easy
work, and that it is futile to expect the years to erode those passions that
today make the processes of desegregation unpopular. Gradualism—no
matter what we call it—has failed, and I think it is fair to say that those
who continue to espouse it are fooling themselves and in many ways,
failing our nation.

It seems to me time for school officials to form a third front for racial
equality in the United States.

At one end of the civil rights movement today we have the gradualists,
both white and Negro, a polite and sometimes sluggish team, deeply re-
spectful of the public and sometimes given to assuring each other that it
is possible to make an omelette without breaking eggs. At the other end
are the activists, both the nonviolent demonstrators and those weary and
desperate Americans who have come to feel that violence is the only
way to get anything done.

The failure of the gradualists would seem at bottom to be fear, fear of
rocking a boat which, no matter how leaky, appears at least to be floating
somewhere. The failure of the activists is that while they know in general terms what they want to achieve, and are willing to pay a heavy price
to obtain it, they have neither the position in society nor the professional's knowledge of the means and importance of advancing racial
equality within the framework of law.

School officials have both position and knowledge. Those of us professionally engaged in education are charged with setting educational
policy within our respective jurisdictions, and we are familiar with a

variety of methods that can be used to advance school desegregation. What we have often lacked is a productive commitment.

I say *productive* because for all our recognition of the importance of school desegregation to our society, the fact remains that we have not achieved much of it. I say *commitment* because achieving desegregation does not require fury or breastbeating; it does require something much more important: the recognition that school desegregation must be accomplished, and the determination to do it.

The fact is that no matter how hard we try, we will not be able to keep things quiet. A revolution is brewing under our feet, and it is largely up to the schools to determine whether the energies of that revolution can be converted into a new and vigorous source of American progress, or whether their explosion will rip this nation into two societies. We simply cannot wait until dramatic action becomes safe, for at this point it is much less dangerous to make a mistake than to do nothing.

Feeding that revolution is a major shift in American folkways. Today approximately two of every three adult Negroes living in the North were born and raised in the South. This move has necessarily had a major impact—often a bewildering impact—on the individual. In some ways, the life he left in the South was less segregated than it is in the North. The Negro child born in the South was, to be sure, raised on the notion that he would always occupy a subservient position, but it was nevertheless a subservient position within a white society.

The young northern Negro of today's city lives in a black society. He has few points of contact with whites, and those few—when you reflect on them—are revealing. He is likely to encounter a white teacher, a white policeman, and a white merchant. He can pass his entire adolescence without having to deal with the white world outside the ghetto, and his ideas of that world are based on three types: the teacher, often a symbol of boredom and irrelevance; the policeman, a symbol of authority, if not of repression; and the merchant, often a symbol of white cunning.

And so the young Negro setting forth from the ghetto to confront this white world expects it is going to misunderstand him and oppress him, and too often he finds evidence to justify his fears. It is no wonder that, if he has any spunk and imagination, he rejects the fatalism of his father and decides that it is the part of a man to change this sorry mess he inherited. And if it takes violence to change it—well, that's what it takes.

It is this young Negro who must be convinced that the United States is his home, not his prison, and that it is a country worth fighting for, not a cage to be fought out of. It may already be too late to change his mind. But it is not too late to provide his younger brothers and sisters with a healthier belief, nor too late to protect white children from the destructive stereotypes that most white adults inherited from their own segregated education.

The broad position we must all assume on this matter comprises two parallel and equally important policies. One cannot work without the other. The first is to make the schools of the central city such good schools that they attract people rather than repel them. The second is to use every possible device to include within each school a cross section of the social and economic backgrounds of the metropolis. A student should meet America in his school—not a segregated segment of it. The concept of racial balance may be impractical except as an ideal in a city with more Negroes than whites and a continuing white exodus. But keeping our eyes on that ideal can help us to do practical things now to slow the exodus and provide equal educational opportunity.

Some very practical things are now underway at the instigation of state and local officials acting on their own to make equal educational opportunity a reality—sometimes in the face of community opposition, but sometimes hand-in-hand with community determination to eradicate a century-old injustice.

The Denver school board, for example, has authorized double sessions at one of its high schools in order to cut class size and reduce pupil-teacher ratios to a point where teachers can use new instructional techniques to best advantage. A special pilot program of compensatory education was provided for, and the administrative staff was instructed to draft plans to bus enough Negro student-volunteers to other schools to achieve better racial balance at a school that was in danger of becoming all-Negro.

Summer programs in Little Rock are fully integrated as to staff and students and are being conducted in formerly all-white schools. Portland, Oregon's program of saturation services for inner city schools aims at producing an education program so good that it will reverse the flight of middle-class whites from racially balanced schools in fringe areas.

The St. Paul school system is considering a plan to combine a rapid-transit system with a cluster of four or five 300-acre educational parks that would bring youngsters from the ghetto, from other city schools, and from parochial and suburban schools into central locations for classes ranging from nursery school through junior college.

In describing the St. Paul plan, School Superintendent Donald Dunnan admitted that the educational park may not be the entire answer to school desegregation. "But," he said, "it is the kind of step that's needed. Everybody has been saying, 'Let's do something.' We are."

And that is the point—to do something.

But let us agree on this: that in terms of the magnitude of the task, none of these approaches—not the special arrangements made by the schools nor the programs sponsored by the federal government—is a perfect instrument for doing the job they are supposed to complete. Yet that is precisely why educators who know both the uses and the limitations of these ideas must act on them, for we must supply in courage and in action what our plans lack in ingenuity. There is no such thing as the perfect way to achieve school desegregation. There is no magic key that will unlock all the doors that private prejudice and public pressure have placed in the way of equal opportunity in education. We must simply bore ahead with the tools we have, and it won't be pleasant, and it won't be quiet, and it would be much nicer if someone else would share the work.

But the job is there to do, and if any of us entered education with the idea that it would be a soft touch, this is as good a time as any to concede that we made a big mistake. There is lots of conversation about local control of the schools; if we really believe in it we must make it work.

We are in the midst of a struggle for excellent education for every American youngster, and we must use every likely tool we can devise. Local school administrators must consider such means as redrawing school district boundaries, and consolidating with neighboring districts for educational purposes, even though political boundaries may remain unchanged. We cannot wait for mayors and city councils to do the work they hired us to do. And sometimes we must do work they don't want us to do.

There is no point in waiting for real estate salesmen to get the message from on high and ease our job by selling homes to anyone who wants them. There is no point in our waiting for American corporations to start hiring Negro men as readily as they do light-skinned, well-dressed Negro women. Neither American home salesmen nor American personnel managers have ever insisted that they have a major responsibility for building American democracy. They have never pretended to do anything but their jobs.

American schoolmen, however, have quite properly taken a large share of the credit for establishing national unity and freedom of opportunity. Our predecessors in the classroom helped 20,000,000 European immigrants become Americans, and we haven't stopped bragging about it yet. If we are to retain that pride in our tradition, I think we must recognize that the great achievements of the past are not only a legacy, but also a heavy burden. If we want to wear the laurels, we must also carry the load.

The load we must carry is that of irritating a fair percentage of our white constituents, of embarrassing some governors and mayors, of alarming some newspaper publishers, and of enraging suburban taxpayers who in proportion to their means are not paying as much for their good schools as paupers in the cities are paying for their bad ones.

And all this means that, finally and most grievously, we must run the risk of being invited to resign. Unless all of us are willing to put our jobs and our integrity on the line, we should admit that American educators are no longer prepared to be the prime movers in American education.

7

*Out of the people, the buildings, the commerce, there
grew up a city; an awkward, lumbering giant, with
limitless powers for good or evil—waiting to be instructed.*

LINDLEY J. STILES

Joseph Alsop

NO MORE NONSENSE ABOUT GHETTO EDUCATION!

It is time to stop talking nonsense about Negro education. It is
time to start dealing with the hard, cruel facts of the problem of the
ghetto schools, which is in turn the very core of the race problem in the
United States. Above all it is time to cease repeating, "End *de facto*
segregation!" as though this virtuous incantation were a magic spell.
For school desegregation must always be a central and essential goal;
but sad experience has proved that desegregation is very far from being
an instant remedy.

For any practical-minded man, who holds that putting an end to racial
injustice is the highest and most urgent task of this country at this time,
the foregoing are the only possible comments on Judge James Skelly
Wright's much-publicized decision concerning the District of Columbia's schools. The school system of the capital is sordid and shameful,
and Judge Wright's moral indignation is only too well founded. Yet
this decision can even be described as wicked; for it is always wicked
to hold out false hopes and offer fake panaceas to those in desperate need
of hope and help. And that, in essence, is precisely what Judge Wright's
decision has done to the people of Washington—a city which has
gradually become no more than a gigantic Negro ghetto thinly concealed
behind a pompous white federal façade.

In justice to Judge Wright, it must be said at once that his evident good
intentions were by no means the only good features of his decision. His
condemnation of the discriminatory "track system" was fully justified.
His comparison between the District's school expenditure—near to the
lowest per pupil of any big city in this country—and the District's police
expenditure—the nation's highest *per capita*—was both pointed and
valuable. It was useful to emphasize, too, that per-pupil outlays in the

From Joseph Alsop, "No More Nonsense About Ghetto Education," *The New Republic*,
July 22, 1967, pp. 18–23. Reprinted by permission of the author and publisher.

District's few remaining white and quasi-white schools exceed the outlays in the deep ghetto schools by over a third. But it must be noted also, in this connection, that Judge Wright was here unknowingly putting his finger on one of the greatest deficiencies in the extremely deficient Coleman report (which seems to have influenced him greatly). For the Coleman report, as Samuel Bowles and Henry M. Levin have noted in an important paper, never tested its conclusions about "equal" education by exploring the widespread existence of differential, per pupil outlays *within* school districts, as here in Washington.

But all this sinks into insignificance, as compared with the main thrust of Judge Wright's decision, which was to put forward more desegregation as the solution for the ghetto school problem in Washington, and presumably, as the solution in all the other American big cities where the same problem is festering and growing more inflamed with every passing year. In Washington, to begin with, serious school desegregation is such an obvious impossibility that it is plain silly to talk about it. Officially, any school that is more than half Negro is defined as segregated. But in the District of Columbia, the primary and elementary schools are 93 percent Negro, and even the high schools are pushing up toward 90 percent. Therefore, total, forcible homogenization of the entire school system would still leave Washington with overwhelmingly segregated schools. Indeed, this kind of forcible homogenization would quite certainly result in even greater segregation; for the predictable consequence would be an increase in the Negro percentage in the primary and elementary schools from 93 percent to 98 or 99 percent.

Unprepared desegregation in a grossly underfinanced school system has in fact been one of the two main causes of this city's transformation into an urban super-ghetto—a kind of near-Watts on a metropolitan scale. Since the war, every one of the great urban centers above the Mason-Dixon line has received countless thousands of Negro immigrants from the South. From this cause alone, Washington's Negro population has grown very greatly; but Negro immigration has been only one aspect of the two-sided demographic movement that has now produced a city two-thirds Negro and one-third white. The other aspect, equally important, has been white emigration to the affluent suburbs. And the crucial role of the schools in this white emigration can in turn be clearly seen, if you merely look at those who have fled and those who have stayed behind. Those who have stayed behind number close to 250,000; yet this white population of about a quarter of a million includes only 13,000 children of school age! Of the District's 13,000 white children of school age, furthermore, rather more than 5,000 attend parochial or other private schools. The conclusion is inescapable that Washington's remaining white population is almost exclusively composed of (a) old people, (b) single people, (c) couples without children of school age, and (d) couples who can afford to send their children to parochial or private schools or who live in the few neighborhoods where the schools are still mainly white. No such demographic result as that shown above could conceivably have been produced in the normal course of events. It means, beyond question, that just about every white couple outside the above-listed categories has moved to the suburbs, at least as soon as it came time to send the children to school.

The available statistics are grossly inadequate, but enough is known to show that precisely the same kind of two-sided demographic movement is tending to produce much the same sort of result in a good many other American urban centers. Washington, which has been treated as an exceptional case, is merely an *advanced* case. The best figures I have got thus far are for last year. Taking the percentages of Negro children in the primary and elementary schools as the gauge, one can then show how far six other major cities have traveled to date, along the road that has made the nation's capital into a concealed super-ghetto. Here is the picture:

Baltimore, schools 64 percent Negro, equals Washington in 1954–55.

Chicago, schools 56 percent Negro, equals Washington in 1952–53.

Cleveland, schools 53 percent Negro, equals Washington in 1951–52.

Detroit, schools 57 percent Negro, equals Washington in 1953–54.

Philadelphia, schools 60 percent Negro, nearly equals Washington in 1954–55.

St. Louis, schools 64 percent Negro, equals Washington in 1954–55.

Two fundamental problems are revealed by these figures. The first is what may be called the progressive ghettoization of a whole series of America's great urban conglomerations. In the fairly near future, this phenomenon can too easily produce social and economic consequences that hardly bear thinking about. Ghetto city centers, from which even commerce, banking and industry will have fled to the fatly affluent white suburbs, are not an attractive prospect, either for the wretched ghetto-denizens, or for anyone else. But this is not the problem to which I have been trying to address myself. I have been trying to show, rather, that in almost all cases, the practical result of *unprepared* desegregation is *an enlarged ghetto with a greater number of segregated schools than there were in the first instance.* This has in truth been the experience in every major Northern city known to me. Furthermore, it has been the experience in a good many cases in which the ugly influence of racial prejudice can be effectively ruled out. In the first flush of civil rights enthusiasm, for example, the parents of a liberal-Jewish neighborhood in Brooklyn voted all but unanimously to pair their school with a nearby ghetto school. The New York Board of Education promised special support (which took the ludicrously inadequate form of a general patch-up of the school buildings). PS 7 and PS 8 were then merged, wholly on the motion of the white parents. But within a very short time, two segregated schools had come into being where there had been one before. The pairing caused school quality to go to Hell in a hack; and the white parents, seeing their children's education in jeopardy, either sent them to private schools or moved to the suburbs. And these were the very same parents, mind you, who had sponsored the pairing.

When the Burden Becomes Too Much

This is only one item of evidence—there is a mass of it, for instance, in the supporting studies behind the Watts report—to show that school quality is a far more important factor than racial feeling, in this white flight from desegregated schools that has made such a mockery of the good intentions of people like Judge Wright. When a middle-class school receives a massive infusion of children of extremely deprived background—whether Puerto Rican, or Mexican-American, or Appalachian white, or Negro—there are only two possible results. Either the added burden of the disadvantaged, educationally retarded children becomes too much for the teaching staff, whereupon school quality promptly and shockingly deteriorates and middle-class emigration quickly begins. Or the local school authorities take all the special measures that are needed to maintain school quality, in which case—thus far an almost unheard-of case—there is an excellent chance that most of the emigration can be averted.

Nor is this the end of the grim story. If we are honest with ourselves, the overwhelming majority of the children of the ghettos are going to be educated exclusively in ghetto schools; and this is going to go on happening for many years to come, no matter how much poulticing and patching and court-ordering we may do. Free busing can and should be offered. Gerrymandered white school districts can and should be condemned (while due preparation is also made to maintain school quality). More integrated housing patterns can and should be promoted by every means possible. But these measures (strengthened, if you please, by every other measure you may happen to fancy) can never do more than fray the fringes of the ghetto school problem in cities with school populations 50 percent Negro and above. It is scandalous—it is indeed a bitter indictment of the large group in the American intellectual community that has concerned itself with the matter—that so few have been willing to face the distasteful, inescapable truth, which has been glaringly visible for years. The truth is that whatever else we may do, the problem of the ghetto schools must be mainly solved *inside the ghetto schools*, at any rate for a long time to come.

The Unique Non-Remedy

As an example of the scandal, consider the recent Civil Rights Commission report on "Racial Isolation in the Public Schools." It shows that America's schools are just about as segregated as they ever were, despite all the court orders that have been issued since 1954, and all the attempts, more or less sincere, to comply with those court orders. It says nothing of the white emigration that has played such a huge role in making a nonsense of the court orders. Using evidence chosen with suspicious selectivity (and misusing it gravely at that, if the Philadelphia data are any guide), the report further seeks to discredit school improvement inside the ghettos. By implication, it takes the shocking though fashionable liberal educators' view once so bitterly but accurately summarized by Floyd McKissick in this journal's pages, that if you "put Negro with Negro, you get stupidity." And having established school desegregation as the unique remedy, the report finally proposes busing on a massive scale as the best means to secure desegregation. Yet the report is datelined Washington, where no amount of busing would make the school system anything but segregated—short of a constitutional amendment permitting forcible imposition of wholly different living and schooling patterns in the District, Maryland and Virginia. Are we then to conclude that more than 90,000 Negro schoolchildren in Washington are to be forever condemned to defeat and despair? Or are we to conclude that this report, like so many other very similar documents, is the product of the kind of self-serving reasoning that must too often be expected, alas, from virtuous academics with a personal vested interest in a badly researched theory?

The answer is, of course, that it is not only viciously heartless and socially disastrous, but also wholly needless, to accept the viewpoint of the Civil Rights Commission and Judge Wright. There is something arrogant, there is even something disgusting, in this strange view that ghetto children can never be rescued, can never be educated, unless they are subjected to the benign classroom influence of white middle-class children. Ghetto children have all the potential of any other children; but in their background of poverty and deprivation, they have a heavy handicap. What is needed, therefore, is to overcome the handicap, by those special measures I have already mentioned as useful and needful to prepare for school desegregation, wherever desegregation is feasible. This means taking a series of steps of the most ABC simplicity. First, the children's school experience must begin early, at least in prekindergarten. For the inability to speak common English, which afflicts so many children of the ghettos, can only be overcome by catching them very young. Second, they must be taught in small classes—not more than 15 in pre-kindergarten and kindergarten, and not more than 22 or so in grades one through six. Otherwise, *teaching* will cease and keeping order will become the sole aim. For ghetto children mainly come from homes wholly unoriented to learning and to books. Gaining and holding their learning-attention (which is the right way to maintain sound discipline) is therefore the most difficult feat for every teacher in every ghetto school. And only reduced classes permit good, average teachers to accomplish this feat. Third, a certain number of backup teachers are needed—one extra for each three or four classes—so that when Billy and Sally, Victor and Jane begin to fall behind, these laggards can be promptly gathered into still smaller classes, for more concentrated work until they catch up again. Fourth, all the obvious extras in the way of remedial reading, health care, psychiatric care, etc., also have to be provided. These are, in fact, the principal features of the More Effective Schools program, that has been under way in New York City for three years. One wonders why this program was not chosen for study by the authors of the Civil Rights Commisssion's report. Perhaps the answer is that in the More Effective Schools, all children have shown a very great average improvement, and those children who have begun in pre-kindergarten and continued on from there are actually performing, on average, *at grade level or above.* If this program had been chosen for analysis, it would have sadly undermined the thesis of the authors of the Civil Rights Commission report; but it is nonetheless quite wonderful news, which should be published in Mao-style Big Character Posters in the corridors of every university where educational theorists flourish.

That it should be news at all, is a considerable showup of the ways of thinking and working and dealing with facts of all too many American white liberal intellectuals. In this instance, it goes without saying that properly prepared school desegregation is the ideal solution of the educational problem of America's Negro minority. It goes without saying, too, that wherever desegregation can be successfully accomplished, the moral and social duty to accomplish it must never be dodged or ducked, even if the needed preparations for successful desegregation are difficult, time-consuming and costly. But a good many of our liberal intellectuals never appear to have heard the rule, *"Le mieux est l'ennemi du bien"*; it never appears to occur to them, in fact, that exclusive pursuit of the ideal solution can prevent the practical solution; and few of them seem to have bothered to do the tedious homework, on urban demographic patterns, for instance, that would have shown them how far the ideal solution is out of reach for most ghetto children at present. Their performance would be less unadmirable, I must add, if they had been content to urge their ideal solution, despite its unreality for all but a small minority of ghetto children. But they have not been content. A good many of the liberal educators and sociologists have done everything possible to discredit and to block the practical solution of the educational problem of our Negro minority, which is radical school improvement inside the ghetto. These people seem to have taken the attitude, in fact, that if they could not get desegregation, nothing else would do—and to hell with the millions of Negro children who have little hope of entering integrated schools!

Quality on the Cheap

This has been a main reason, one suspects, for the extraordinary belatedness and extreme paucity of the serious attempts to help these children, and for the almost universal failure to defend and support those attempts when they have been made. In New York in 1957, for instance, the Demonstration School Project produced excellent results at the high school level, at a cost of about $200 per pupil above the normal outlay. Whereupon the New York Board of Education, by an automatic reflex, tried to get the same results at about one-third the extra cost, in the Higher Horizons program, which was a flat bust. But did anyone protest the debasement of the Demonstration School Project into Higher Horizons? Almost no one did; and meanwhile a chorus of progressive educators has ever since been heard, proclaiming that Higher Horizons' wholly predictable failure was final proof of the uselessness of improved education in ghetto schools. In the same fashion, the More Effective Schools program, which has an extra per-pupil cost of about $430 a year, is beginning to be nibbled to death by the economy-ducks on the Board of Education; but no one has sprung to its defense except this writer and, far more importantly, the United Federation of Teachers, whose leaders largely devised the program. And this program, launched in 1964–65, is literally the first to produce clear test results showing that ghetto children can be given a fully adequate education in ghetto schools. For when the testers say that the children who were caught young enough by the More Effective Schools are performing, on average, *at grade level and above,* they merely mean that these children are performing just as well as white middle-class children. And this is the first case of complete victory over that terrible educational lag that is the curse of America's Negro minority.

For economic and social reasons, because of injustice and discrimination, above all, because of the circumstances in which this heedless, ruthless society condemns them to live, Negro children normally enter the first grade considerably behind white children; and worse still, they generally fall further and further behind, the longer they stay in school. On average, those who stay through high school are by then three and a half years below grade level, which means that the *average Negro high school graduate only has a slightly better than eighth grade education.* "Stay through high school" is in fact the right phrase, rather than "go through high school." Since the average is at the level of eighth-grade-plus, it is not surprising that the military draft tests have revealed a shockingly high proportion of functional illiterates, even among Negro high-school graduates. Add the two-thirds and more of Negro boys and girls who drop out before finishing high school, and you have a frightening result.

Briefly, 400,000-plus eighteen-year-old Negroes are annually injected into this country's socio-economic bloodstream; but of these 400,000-plus, hardly 10 percent have the true equivalent of a normal white middle-class high school education—which means no more than an ordinary *blue-collar education!* In other words, we annually add to the American body politic no less than 360,000 Negroes of both sexes who are wholly unequipped to get or hold any job in which grossly deficient schooling is a handicap—and that means, more and more with every passing year, just about any job at all! If a malevolent and astute racist were asked to design a system guaranteed to prevent Negro achievement, to promote bitterness, frustration and violence, to perpetuate and even to intensify discrimination, this is the system that he would surely come up with. To reform this system, any outlay, any sacrifice, any effort, however great and however painful, is not merely a moral imperative; it is also a political and social imperative of the most pressing and urgent character. And the system is not going to be reformed, alas, by more desegregation orders.

What Will It All Cost?

The outlays for adequate reform will be enormous indeed, when and if we make up our minds to pursue desegregation by all means possible, but also, and above all at this stage, to insure quality education in the ghetto schools that are beyond practical reach of early desegregation. The job can only be done by the federal government, for the cities and states are already overstrained; and it will cost billions—how many billions, no one has figured out, but certainly quite a number.

There are two points to make in this connection. First of all, anyone who discovered a reasonably reliable cancer cure, and then withheld it because of its expense, would be treated as a monster. And in effect, we are talking, here, about a social-political-economic cancer that is approaching the terminal state. Secondly, however, the proof by the More Effective Schools that improved schools really can cure the cancer is by no means a proof that the MES program is the ideal cure. There may be other, better, perhaps cheaper ways to get comparable results. Since what is required is positive discrimination—by which I mean very much heavier investment per pupil in ghetto and other deprived neighborhoods—it is obvious that the discrimination should be no greater than is absolutely necessary. (In New York there is aleady resentment of the MES program, even within the ghettos, among parents of children whose neighborhood schools have not been included in the program—and since there are only 21 More Effective Schools, and expansion of the program has been halted by the duck-nibblers, that means, potentially, resentment by something like nine-tenths of the ghetto parents in New York.) Thus a systematic and unbiased effort should be inaugurated, to see whether comparable results can be attained in more economical ways. Such an effort should center in New York City, for the test-background of MES, though so brief, is unique and therefore essential for comparative purposes. Instead of unsystematic nibbling, such as the Board of Education has now begun, expansion of the MES program should clearly be resumed. A follow-on program should equally clearly be adopted, in particular in the relevant junior high schools. Otherwise

many of the MES children will experience the kind of disheartening setback on entering jungle-junior-high, that the Head Start children have
experienced when they have entered unimproved primary schools. But
these supportive measures should also be combined with experiments to
discover whether altering this or that expensive feature—using one backup teacher for every four classes, instead of one for every three as at
present, for example—will produce satisfactory results.

The only point on which there should be no compromise is the schoolchildren performing *at grade level*. And if even larger investments are
shown to be required—for example, in recreational and para-education
activities after normal school hours, in the schools of the very most
tragic neighborhoods—then there should be no nasty nonsense about
this being "too expensive," to quote the mole-sighted new chairman of
the New York Board of Education, Albert Giardino. When you are talking
about cancer cures, "too expensive" is an impermissible phrase. And of
course, in this systematic experimental effort, due attention should also
be given to the other efforts of school improvement much more recently
launched under Title I of the Education Act, which will surely be remembered as the greatest domestic achievement of the Johnson Administration. If one or another of these show, when the tests have all been
made, that there is another, cheaper or better way to get the ghetto children to perform *at grade level*, that will be the system to back whole-
heartedly.

In this business, there are only three rules. First, face the facts as they
are, and deal with them as they are. Second, spend no more than is
needed for the children to perform, on average, at grade level; for this
is the outside limit of positive discrimination that other people are likely
to tolerate. But, third, invest until it hurts cruelly, if need be, so that the
average performance of the children of the ghettos reaches grade level
or above; for there is no other cure for the cancer that threatens American
urban life.

I am not so foolish as to suppose that the hoary, furtive vice of racial
prejudice can be abruptly overcome by this long-range cure, any more
than I suppose that *prepared* school desegregation can do more than
greatly soften the effects of racial prejudice. But I submit, the white
people of goodwill in America, and above all our well-intended liberal
intellectuals, have been almost inconceivably unrealistic, flabbly-
minded and lazy about learning the facts concerning this cardinal Amer-
can problem. Take a minority differentiated by skin color. Tolerate a
national school system that gives nine-tenths of this minority an education very widely inferior to the normal education of blue collar workers,
let alone persons of higher achievement. How, then, can you expect or
hope for an end to discrimination and racial prejudice?

Or if you want the other side of the medal, look at the few areas in
American life, in which prejudice and discrimination have been, if not

absolutely banished, at least minimized in recent years to the point where there is no grave problem. Too few people recall that in the lifetimes of a good many of us, Marian Anderson and Joe Lewis were, in some sense, nine day wonders as well as precursors. And too few people are even aware that real integration of the armed services only began in the line in Korea. (I can still remember AWOL Negro soldiers from the segregated logistical units, and even from the unhappy 24th Regiment, coming up to the hottest parts of the line—one or two, or three or four, or even 10 or 12 a day—to ask whether there was any place for them in battalions in combat; and I remember, too, how they were warmly welcomed, though the battalion commanders always knew they were AWOL, simply because the line was stretched so thin in those first months of the war!) Yet in the arts—not just jazz, but all the arts and throughout show business—and sports and the armed services, discrimination has now been so largely overcome. And what has so largely overcome discrimination in these tragically few departments of our national life? Brilliant Negro achievements is the answer. And what has permitted this achievement in these special areas? Again, the answer is the relative easiness of achievement in these few areas, despite deficient schooling, for those with aptitude and ambition and courage.

Moral Cart Before the Practical Horse

Once again, I am not so foolish as to suppose that high achievement in every area of national life would be immediately guaranteed, even if every one of the 400,000-plus Negroes who become 18 each year were assured of a first-rate high school education, with the university to follow, of course, for the abler boys and girls. Prejudice is an ugly reality. The tentacles of custom, born of prejudice, are also ugly realities. Yet those same tentacles had the armed forces in their grip less than two decades ago, and had the world of sports in their grip hardly more than three decades ago. And what has lopped off the tentacles? Negro achievement, and nothing but Negro achievement. For no amount of enforced desegregation would have ended discrimination in the hard-bitten army and harder-bitten professional sports teams, if Negroes had not pegged even, and often much better than even, with their white fellow soldiers and fellow athletes. Yet in most areas of our national life, conspicuous Negro achievement is all but impossible, simply because so few American Negroes as yet receive normally decent schooling. Give them the needed education. At the outset, it may be, only seven in 20 will break through the barriers of prejudice and custom. But those few will surely inspire the next generation to say, "If *they* could do it, *we* can do it." And by the same token, white prejudice will surely be eroded, in every area where Negroes are enabled to achieve highly.

The truth is that in our approach to almost every aspect of the race problem—whether segregation, or discrimination, or Negro poverty, or whatever it may be—we have persistently been placing the moral cart before the practical horse. Education is the key to the whole problem, because education leads to jobs; jobs lead to achievement; and achievement reduces discrimination. That is the common-sense formula, which puts the horse ahead of the cart. And if we do not get the moral cart moving at long last—if we cannot provide good education and decent jobs for our Negro fellow citizens, and if these first steps do not begin to erode discrimination and open ever wider doors of opportunity—then this country can too soon become a place in which none will wish to live, who still care much about the things that America is supposed to stand for.

Some may say: "But if many white Americans have always cared so much about these things America is supposed to stand for, why this belated sense of urgency? Why did not Franklin Roosevelt, for instance, begin pressing for serious civil rights legislation nearly 40 years ago?" In the abstract, those who say this will be dead right. But the sad truth is that any national problem that is highly controversial, very difficult, yet possible to shove under the rug, invariably ends by getting shoved under the rug with extreme firmness. While the race problem in America was mainly a rural Southern problem, it could still be shoved under the rug. But in the last two decades and more, our race problem has more and more become a Northern urban problem, as well as a more and more urban problem even in the South, where the major cities show the same pattern of demographic change already traced above. In this new guise, the race problem cannot any longer be shoved under the rug. Justice must be done at last, or we must expect a gradual decline toward the sort of country that will choose a new President Verwoerd. Those are, literally, the choices before us. For my own part, I am confident that justice can and will be done, at no matter what cost to the budget and the taxpayer, if only we can manage to look at the problem in common-sense terms.

8

Robert Schwartz, Thomas Pettigrew, and Marshall Smith

FAKE PANACEAS FOR GHETTO EDUCATION: A REPLY TO JOSEPH ALSOP

From Robert Schwartz, Thomas Pettigrew, and Marshall Smith, "Fake Panaceas for Ghetto Education," *The New Republic*, September 23, 1967, pp. 16–19. Reprinted by permission of the publisher.

America has educationally failed fourteen generations of Negro Americans, and has paid a high price for this failure. Currently, the nation is failing to educate the fifteenth generation, and the price in human tragedy promises to be even greater. *The New Republic* readers recently (July 22) received the benefit of Joseph Alsop's thinking on this subject. Stripped of its rhetoric, Alsop's argument reduces to six central propositions:

(1) Negro children are not being adequately educated in America's schools.

(2) Effective action must be initiated at once to correct this situation.

(3) Ending *de facto* segregation is a "virtuous incantation" which cannot be a solution for many reasons. First, desegregation is not going to happen, "at any rate for a long time to come." Second, major federal studies which suggest the efficacy of interracial education in a variety of settings are either "extremely deficient" as in the case of the US Office of Education's monumental "Coleman Report," or "shocking," as in the case of the US Commission on Civil Rights' report on *Racial Isolation in the Public Schools.* Third, when Negroes are "unprepared" for desegregation, school quality goes "to Hell in a hack." Consequently, "unprepared desegregation" drives white parents to the suburbs, creates more school segregation, and causes our central cities to become increasingly Negro.

(4) "Brilliant Negro achievements is [*sic*] the answer." Only when Negro American achievements, as in athletics and the army, are conspicuous can white Americans accept desegregation.

(5) And brilliant Negro achievements will come only with quality ghetto education. Racially separate schools can do the job if only educators would take the newspaperman's advice and follow "a series of steps of the most ABC simplicity." These steps are demonstrated by the "complete victory" of New York City's "More Effective Schools" (MES) program.

(6) As to costs, only "a monster" would deny funds to such a reasonably reliable "cancer cure" as MES.

Few would contest Alsop's first two propositions: a majority of Negro children *are* being cheated out of their American birthright to a full public education; and massive corrective action *is* desperately required. But from this point on he loses the thread.

The desegregation of the nation's public schools is indeed a slow process as long as the necessary structural changes, such as metropolitan consolidation, are not achieved. Although Alsop pays lip service to interracial education as "the ideal solution," his article resists these structural changes by obscuring them. For example, he asserts educational consolidation in metropolitan Washington would require a constitutional amendment. This is absurd, for effective consolidation by no means necessitates a single metropolitan school district as initial efforts in Boston, Hartford, and Rochester demonstrate. Admittedly, metropolitan consolidation is politically difficult to achieve, but the federal government could encourage it in education as it has effectively done in other realms through multi-district funding incentives. In any event, Alsop worries that any pursuit of desegregation will deter his version of "the practical solution." Instead, we worry that Alsop is supplying the self-fulfilling rationale for racially segregated schools "for years to come."

No studies are definitive, nor do the Coleman and Civil Rights Commission reports claim to be final. But no fair-minded observer can pass off the second largest study of American education as "extremely deficient" without a full explanation. Nor could such an observer attack the Commission monograph with libelous charges without detailed elaboration. Apparently, Alsop is peeved that the MES program was not included in the report on *Racial Isolation in the Public Schools.* Had he the courtesy to call down the street to the Commission staff, he would have learned the reasons: the first long-term evaluation of MES appeared too late for inclusion in the Commission report; and, as we shall note below, neither the mode of operation nor the test data of MES are basically different from compensatory programs which are described in the study.

Most serious of all is Alsop's implication that the report of the United States Commission on Civil Rights is racist, that it maintains if you "put Negro with Negro, you get stupidity." If Alsop eventually reads the report, he will encounter the following rejoinder from Commissioner Frankie M. Freeman:

> The question is not whether in theory or in the abstract Negro schools can be as good as white schools. In a society free from prejudice in which Negroes were full and equal participants, the answer would clearly be 'Yes.' But we are forced, rather, to ask the harder question, whether in our present society, where Negroes are a minority which has been discriminated against, Negro children can prepare themselves to participate effectively in society if they grow up and go to school in isolation from the majority group. We must also ask whether we can cure the disease of prejudice and prepare all children for life in a multiracial world if white children grow up and go to school in isolation from Negroes.

Alsop would also discover the Commission finding that white children in mixed, predominantly white schools perform as well as those in all-white schools. He will learn, too, that only about one in 25 white suburbanites gives racial problems in central city schools as his reason for moving. Our largest cities are becoming increasingly Negro not because whites move to the suburbs at rates similar to those of other industrial nations, but because Negroes are not free to move with them.

Fortunately, neither Washington nor New York are prototypes of American cities. Urban areas with smaller ghettos can often desegregate without suburban cooperation—as Providence, Berkeley, White Plains, and Evanston illustrate. Cities with large ghettos, of course, pose the major difficulties. But metropolitan and public-private cooperation could do the job. Negroes comprise approximately the same percentage of metropolitan areas as they do in the entire nation—roughly 11 percent. And the six cities Alsop compares with Washington all have large Roman Catholic school systems that currently absorb large percentages of their school-aged whites. "The ideal solution" of desegregation *can* be accomplished but not by abandoning the goal and cursing reports which demonstrate its necessity.

Alsop's "brilliant Negro achievement" theory is an insult to the millions of Negro Americans who *have* achieved. Many achieving Negroes have painfully learned, however, that racial discrimination is still a part of their American experience. And this recipe for improved race relations blithely consigns yet another generation to ghetto schools while the brilliant achievers "inspire the next generation." As daily headlines make clear, America's racial problems will not wait that long. Desegregation is not something Negroes "earn" but is their right. Furthermore, Alsop's own examples of American institutions with remarkably reduced racial discrimination—"the hard-bitten army and harder-bitten professional sports teams"—forcefully demonstrate the efficacy of desegregation.

Alsop's belief in the possibility of quality segregated education seems to rest almost entirely on his impression of the achievements of New York City's More Effective Schools, an experimental program which was initiated in ten elementary schools in 1964–65 and expanded to eleven more in 1965–66. The idea originated with the city's teachers union, the United Federation of Teachers, and the UFT has made the further expansion of MES one of the key items in its current negotiations with the Board of Education. In Alsop's opinion the MES program, by starting in early childhood, providing small classes, employing backup teachers, and offering "all the obvious extras," has achieved a breakthrough: it is "literally the first to produce clear test results showing that ghetto children can be given a fully adequate education in ghetto schools."

The independent evaluations performed by New York's Center for Urban Education corroborate Alsop's favorable description of the climate and morale in the More Effective Schools. While the Center's most recent evaluation is careful to point out that there is considerable variation in quality among the 21 schools, most of the Center's observers agreed they would willingly send their children to the particular schools they visited. Given the apathy and despair that typically characterize ghetto schools, the optimism, sense of commitment and parental support that seem to prevail at most of the program's schools are in themselves significant achievements.

But what kind of academic success have these schools had? In Alsop's view, the test scores indicate "all [MES] children have shown a very great average improvement, and those children who have begun in pre-kindergarten and continued on from there are actually performing, on average, *at grade level or above.*" (Italics his.) What exactly is Alsop asserting? What does it mean to say that *all* children have shown a very great *average* improvement? How is this improvement to be defined, and what data does he have to support this high-sounding claim? His second assertion at least has the virtue of clarity: it should be quite easy to ascertain whether the children who enrolled in MES pre-kindergartens in 1964 are now performing at grade level. But since no citywide tests are administered until the second grade, it cannot possibly be supported or refuted.

The youngest MES children for whom we have three years of test scores are those who have just completed the fourth grade. When these children were first tested in October 1964, their median reading score was only .3 of a year below the city norm. At the end of the first year the gap had widened, but the hope was expressed in the Board of Education's preliminary evaluation that after another year or two of MES the gap would be closed. The sad fact is, however, that the April 1967 fourth grade scores reveal that in only two of the More Effective Schools is the average child reading at grade level. On further inquiry, one discovers that these two "above-average" schools are not ghetto schools at all, but are 70 percent white schools located in a predominantly middle-class section of the Bronx!

Stated flatly, the reading scores show that from the fourth grade on, no majority non-white school in the MES program is reading at grade level. Moreover, when we compare the slope of reading retardation in More Effective Schools with that in control schools (so designated by the Board of Education on the basis of comparable ethnic composition), we find little difference. At each grade level both sets of schools fall further and further behind the city and national norms. The second grade classes at the control schools are on average four months behind city norms, whereas the fifth grade classes are a year and four months behind. The MES second grade classes are one month behind the norm, while their fifth grade classes are a year and a month behind. Alsop is free to hail these scores as representing "a complete victory over that terrible educational lag that is the curse of America's Negro minority." He may well wish to publish them in "Mao-style Big Character posters," but we hope we may be pardoned for not joining in the celebration. It gives us no pleasure to have to state that the MES reading scores simply provide additional evidence to support one of the basic findings of the Civil

Rights Commission Report: compensatory programs in predominantly non-white schools have so far had little sustained success in raising the achievement levels of their students.

False Expectations

The saddest consequence of Alsop's headlong foray into the educational arena is that by creating false expectations he may have done irreparable damage to a program that is worth encouraging. Anyone who has worked in schools knows that there are no instant miracles. For a program as ambitious as the More Effective Schools, a three-year trial period simply isn't sufficient. At the very least, the program should be continued until the first pre-kindergarten classes have completed their eight years. Unless MES is continued, we will never know whether it could have made a difference for those children caught early enough.

As the evidence now stands, however, the verdict is at best a mixed one. Here are the concluding sentences from the summary of the Center For Urban Education's most recent MES evaluation, conducted by Dr. David Fox of City University:

> In short, this evaluation suggests that the basic program introduced under the label 'MES' has had a favorable impact on the adults in these schools, in terms of their observed behavior, their views of the programs, and the general climate of the school. But it has not had a comparable impact on the observed behavior, perception, or achievement of the children who attended.

Interestingly, Alsop talked with Dr. Fox and his colleagues before going out to spend two hours at two schools, so he cannot plead ignorance of their conclusions. We quote from a report of the Alsop visit written by Joseph Krevisky, chairman of the Center's Field Research and Evaluation Committee, and published in *The Center Forum*, July 5th:

> All consultants stressed the very tentative nature of our findings, and the great difficulty of generalizing about the success of this program or about the broader implications that MES is a possible solution to the crucial problems of education of Negro and Puerto Rican children.
> ... In general, these cautions made very little dent on Mr. Alsop, who disagreed with almost all the comments made and was irritated by some of them. He said at that point it was futile to discuss such points any more as *nobody would change his mind.*

There is also the little matter of money. Alsop disposes of desegregation as impractical, but does not explain how practical it will be to get the nation to "invest until it hurts cruelly." MES costs $1,263 per child, $700 more than in regular primary schools in the New York system. It also requires 30 percent more schoolrooms and roughly twice the staff members of regular elementary schools in the city. And since MES has so far obtained only modest test score increments at best, these costs are gross underestimates for achieving Alsop's goal of average performance at grade level. The newspaperman is advocating a national educational program which, if possible at all, would cost well in excess of ten billion dollars annually. We salute Alsop's resolute refusal to choose between guns and butter, but the question remains: will even the richest country on earth simultaneously support the Vietnam war and a national MES program?

The MES requirement of 30 percent more schoolrooms raises yet another difficulty. So far in New York, only schools with underutilized facilities have taken part. But nationally the program would require many new schools; and Alsop would have them built deep within the ghetto. This would institutionalize racial segregation and seal Negro children in the ghetto for generations. Instead, new school construction must take the form of large complexes, such as campus parks, which draw upon wide attendance areas, guarantee quality education, and maximize desegregation.

Why Interracial Schooling?

But to dwell on costs and construction would be to allow ourselves to be deflected from the fundamental sources of our disagreement with Alsop. Let us suppose that his facts are right, that we do have evidence that by spending $1,263 per child we could raise the reading scores of ghetto children to the level of those of suburban children. This would indeed signify equality of educational opportunity, and it would be a distinct improvement over what we now have. But would this fulfill the primary aims of a public school system in a multiracial society? Reduced to its simplest terms, our belief is that interracial contact is an essential component of quality education, that schools which are isolated by virtue of race, social class, or religion deprive their students of adequate preparation for a diverse society and world.

We don't want to fall into the trap of seeming to assert that integrated education is by definition good education; obviously, the mere presence of whites and Negroes in the same classroom is no guarantee of anything. But when we compare the findings of the Coleman and Civil Rights Commission reports with those of such compensatory programs as the More Effective Schools, we must conclude that the evidence suggests that minority group students perform better in integrated than in isolated settings.

Are the reasons for this so hard to discern? To quote again from the Krevisky report of Alsop's visit to the MES schools:

> The teachers stressed that neither MES nor other programs have yet succeeded in overcoming the sense of hopelessness in the commu-

nity, and the powerful barriers to incentives posed by discrimination in housing and jobs. . . .

Unless we are willing to change the fundamental realities of ghetto life in America, aren't we deceiving ourselves to think that any amount of money can buy quality segregated education?

Let there be no misunderstanding. We believe MES and other dedicated remedial programs are necessary efforts at this desperate juncture in American race relations. But they constitute neither a national model nor a permanent solution. At best, they buy time until racial desegregation becomes a widespread fact of American public schools. Full desegregation must be the goal, and all efforts, including MES, must point toward it. Indeed, MES was originally conceived in this spirit, as the May 1964 program description made clear on its first page. And Alsop encountered on his hurried visit the same position from MES teachers:

> . . . the teachers, mostly experienced and mostly Negro, sharply disagreed with Alsop's line. They refused adamantly to accept the solution of quality segregated education and questioned him insistently on what he was doing to educate white people to accept Negroes trying to break out of the 'ghetto'. They sharply challenged a statement he made that education was the only key to integration—by elevating the abilities of the Negro people, and leading to their acceptance by the white community. (*The Center Forum, July 5.*)

We agree with Mr. Alsop that "it is always wicked to hold out false hopes and offer fake panaceas to those in desperate need of hope and help." But even the best funded and most dedicated "compensatory" *ghetto* program is just such a "false hope" and "fake panacea" if it is advanced as a "complete victory."

9

Men of good will who are content to sit on their hands silently hoping that nothing will rock the boat are seemingly unaware that the use of their oars might stay the floundering craft; these men are not leaders, nor are they followers.

JAMES SILVER
Mississippi: The Closed Society

S. L. Halleck, M.D.

HYPOTHESES OF STUDENT UNREST

From S. L. Halleck, "Hypotheses of Student Unrest," *Phi Delta Kappan*, September, 1968, pp. 2–9. Reprinted by permission of the publisher.

Students can no longer be taken for granted. It does not matter that a great majority of students remain largely content, conservative, and apathetic. A determined minority of restless college students has forced us to examine and sometimes change institutions, rules, and values which were once considered inviolate.

The most significant aspects of student unrest can be described as follows:

1. Some students reject the political and economic status quo and are making vigorous attempts to change the structure of our society. These are the student activists.

2. Some students reject the values of their society as well as the values of their own past and are developing a style of life which is contradictory to the Western ethics of hard work, self-denial, success, and responsibility. These students sometimes participate in efforts to change the society, but for the most part they are withdrawn and passive. They can be described as alienated.

3. Both activist and alienated students tend to come from affluent middle- or upper-class homes. They are sensitive and perceptive individuals. They are also highly intelligent.

4. Both activist and alienated students have difficulty in relating to the adult generation. They are articulate, irreverent, humorless, and relentless in their contempt for what they view as adult hypocrisy. Such youth are highly peer-oriented. They turn to one another rather than their parents when shaping their belief systems or when seeking emotional support.

5. Alienated students and, to a lesser extent, activist students find it difficult to sustain goal-directed activity. Their capacity to organize for any kind of action is limited. They often fail at work or school. Even their political efforts seem highly disorganized.

6. Alienated students live at the edge of despair. Although they seem at times to be enjoying life, there is always a sense of foreboding about them. Often they become depressed and suicidal. Activist students are more emotionally stable but are also prone to deep feelings of hopelessness and self-pity.

There is no dearth of explanations of the above phenomena. Some explanations seem to be based on opinions which support the prejudices of differing political viewpoints. Others are more scientific and are presented with analytic objectivity. No hypothesis thus far advanced can be considered a sufficient explanation of student unrest. At best, each is only a partial explanation which sheds only a small light upon highly complex phenomena.

Certain propositions often made about students are not hypotheses but are value judgments. The unsupported statement that the behavior of our restless youth represents a healthy and sensible response to the corruptions of our world is exhortative rather than explanatory. Such a position is embraced by those who are discontent with the status quo and wish to emphasize and exploit student restlessness as a phenomenon that justifies their own grievances. Similarly, unsupported statements that students are more emotionally disturbed than they had used to be have no explanatory value. Implying that students act as they do because they are mentally ill serves to demean their behavior by casting doubts upon the validity of the messages which that behavior is designed to communicate.

A more interesting proposition concerning student unrest is that it is neither new nor exceptional. Precedents can be cited which suggest that there were times in our history when students were even more restless than they are now. Periods of unrest do seem to run in cycles, and it is conceivable that we happen to be in an active phase of a predictable cycle. This proposition is reassuring to those who look forward to a quiet future. Its weakness, however, is that it assumes that those forces which make for cyclical behavior will remain relatively constant. My own opinion is that the world is changing so rapidly that using historical precedents to predict future behavior is a risky business. We can deplore student unrest or we can welcome it, but we cannot ignore it or simply wait for it to go away.

I. *The Critical Hypotheses*—Those who are critical of student activism and alienation are most likely to seek its causes in factors which they believe have created a moral weakness in our youth. They believe students are restless because they lack discipline, values, or purpose. These deficiencies are believed to originate within the disturbed family, particularly that family which has been influenced by affluence, liberal thinking, and modern psychological notions of child rearing. While these hypotheses may also appeal to those who are sympathetic toward students, they are primarily critical in the sense that they imply that something is wrong with those students who protest or withdraw.

The Permissiveness Hypothesis—Perhaps the commonest explanation of student unrest is that it is the result of too much permissiveness in rearing children. The proponents of this view argue that some parents have, through painstaking efforts to avoid creating neuroses in their children, abdicated their responsibility to teach and discipline their children. In so doing they have reared a generation of spoiled, greedy youth who are unable to tolerate the slightest frustration without showing an angry or infantile response.

Although the permissiveness hypothesis has been used in the most crude manner to berate and deplore the behavior of youth, it cannot be lightly dismissed. There is considerable evidence that activist and alienated students are members of well-educated families, deeply committed to liberal doctrines. In such homes children are given unusual freedom to criticize, debate, and question. Restless students also have frequently attended primary and secondary schools dedicated to the ideal of progressive education, schools which in their efforts to maximize freedom and creativity seek to minimize discipline and frustration.

It can, of course, be argued that children raised in permissive homes will be better citizens than those raised in stricter homes. Restless students do seem to be more open to ideas, more involved with social issues, and more flexible than their peers. The critics, however, can point to other characteristics of restless students which seem to be related to their permissive upbringing, and which are not so healthy. The response of such students to discipline, for example, is in no useful sense adaptive. Arbitrary regulations enrage them. Even rational forms of discipline, such as the need to master basic concepts before moving on to more abstract ideas, bother them. Restless students also react inappropriately when their demands are not immediately accepted. They are prone at such moments to protest violently, to give up and withdraw, or to wrap themselves in a cloak of despair. Much of their abrasiveness and much of their ineffectiveness can be explained by their uncompromising demands for immediate gratification. This inability to tolerate frustration or delay must be considered a weakness or defect.

The Non-Responsibility Hypothesis—Many who are concerned about the dangers of permissiveness also believe that our culture has been "psychologized" to an extent where youth become unwilling to assume responsibility for their own behavior. The expansion of the social and psychological sciences has confronted the public with elaborate deterministic explanations of behavior. When a behavior is totally explained, there is a tendency for people to act as though they are no longer responsible for that behavior. They confuse the theoretical issue of scientific determinism with the society's practical needs to have its citizens remain accountable for their own actions.

When the sociologist documents the impact of poverty and discrimination upon Negro youth, he is conducting a logical and scientific exercise. The subjects of his research, however, are tempted to utilize his findings to support an individual and collective feeling of responsibility. The Nego adolescent who participates in a riot, for example, might say, "How could I do otherwise? I am moved by forces over which I have no control." Psychological explanations are also utilized to avoid accountability. It is becoming more common to hear criminals say, "I should not be held responsible for what I have done because I am neurotic or mentally ill."

Psychiatry, particularly Freudian psychiatry, has been maligned as a critical agent in producing a climate of non-responsibility. While there is nothing in the theoretical doctrines of psychoanalysis which favors abdicating personal responsibility, it does seem that the psychiatrist's ability to expand and legitimize the mental illness role has had an impact on the manner in which people view the question of responsibility. Behavior once considered bad is now considered sick. Sickness implies that one cannot help himself or that one is not responsible for his actions. The proponents of the nonresponsibility hypothesis would argue that by expanding the sick role to include forms of behavior that were once considered in terms of good or bad, the healing professions have helped to create a social climate in which more people manage to avoid accountability for their actions. Youth growing up in such a society are tempted to behave in a pleasure-seeking, antisocial, and irresponsible manner. Many feel that this is exactly what restless students are doing.

The evidence that activist and alienated youth are deeply influenced by a climate of irresponsibility is inconclusive. Some activist students are often impressively willing to hold themselves accountable for their actions. On the other hand, most alienated students are not. They tend to seek medical or psychiatric excuses from their obligations at the first sign of stress. They also have a discouraging tendency to break laws and to insist that their own personal needs and problems are such that they should not be held accountable for these actions. It is almost as if they say, "Because the world is so bad and because it has treated me so badly, I cannot be blamed for my actions. There is no point in holding me accountable for things which I cannot help doing anyway."

The Affluence Hypothesis—A third hypothesis which appeals to critics of student unrest is based on the alleged hazards of growing up in an affluent society. It is sometimes argued that affluence which is unearned, and which is unaccompanied by a tradition of service and commitment, creates a sense of restlessness, boredom, and meaninglessness in our youth. The child raised in an affluent society has difficulty finding useful goals. He does not learn to use work or creativity as a means of mastering some aspect of the world. He, therefore, according to this argument, is trapped in a neverending search for new diversions and new freedoms which sooner or later begin to feel sterile and ungratifying.

It does seem likely that man is less likely to be troubled if he is distracted by some monumental task which dominates his life goals. In a relatively poor society, the very need for survival creates a structured and seemingly purposeful life. In an affluent society, man has the time and freedom to contemplate the meaning of his existence. Many restless students do come from affluent homes and many have decided that their lives are devoid of meaning. Sometimes it seems that their provocative behavior is designed primarily to invent new struggles and even imaginary hardships which will free them from their lethargy and help them atone for their guilt over "having it so good."

The affluence hypothesis has certain undertones of criticism directed towards the parents of restless students. Affluence, after all, does not always produce protest or indolence. Traditionally, many of our most useful public servants have been products of wealthy homes. The critics of student unrest would reserve their harshest barbs for those newly affluent parents who have themselves become so caught up in materialistic, pleasure-seeking life that they have failed to meet their responsibility of teaching children the kinds of values which would lend meaning to a young person's existence.

The Family-Pathology Hypothesis—A number of explanations of student unrest focus upon the disturbed family. According to these hypotheses, activist and alienated students behave as they do because they are responding to an unresolved conflict within the family unit. It is usually suggested that the restless student has been subjected to too much pressure by his parents or is "acting out" a need of his parents. A more general approach to the problem focuses upon a family structure in which the father is a weak or shadowy figure. This approach emphasizes the breakdown in authority of the paternal figure, the confusion of sexual roles in our society, and the break with tradition which such confusion produces.

The evidence for the existence of a high degree of pathology in the families of restless students is inconclusive. Sociological studies of students and their families do not support any family-pathology hypothesis. In fact, such studies suggest that activist students, at least, come from rather stable families.

Psychiatrists, on the other hand, find some evidence of serious familial conflict in most of the families of restless students they treat. It must be emphasized, however, that the psychiatrist deals with only a small proportion of such students.

If family disorganization is an important cause of student unrest, the manner in which it exerts its influence must be complex and subtle. Sociological techniques are simply too superficial to get at the complexities of the problem. The findings of psychiatrists are based on depth explorations which may be valid for some families but which cannot be generalized. Neither sociologists nor psychiatrists can provide valid answers. The most we can say is that some aspects of student restlessness may be directly related to family pathology. Certainly, it is conceivable that in today's highly charged social climate, even minimal family disturbances may be translated into highly provocative behavior.

II. *Sympathetic Hypotheses*—The next group of hypotheses put the student in a favorable light. They view him as a victim of man-made circumstances and maintain that student unrest is a legitimate and rational effort to change these circumstances. The student is viewed as either a helpless victim of a world he never created or as a hero seeking to cleanse the world of the evils of previous generations. To be useful, these hypotheses must not simply define what is wrong with the world but must suggest how various factors have made students more capable of perceiving and acting upon the injustices and irrationalities of our world.

The Two-Armed-Camps Hypothesis—This generation of students has grown in an age when the world has been divided into two large camps which compete with each other ideologically, politically, and sometimes militarily. Since the Russians launched their first satellite, the competition has also been educational. Students today are trained in a school system which emphasizes the competitive acquisition of knowledge as a source of power and stability. By the time they leave high school they are better educated than any previous generation of students, but they are also more overworked.

All of this emphasis on education and competition is not easily sustained after the student arrives at the university. By this time he is at least partially "burned out." The personal benefits of intensive studying and searching for a profitable career begin to appear less attractive in an affluent world and particularly in a world which seems to be making it increasingly difficult for a young person to become an integral part of the economic system. As the student comes to view objectively the implications of our competitiveness with communism as a never-ending phenomenon, he also begins to question the social value of his efforts. Even if he maintains enthusiasm for academic work through the undergraduate years, by the time the student reaches graduate school he increasingly asks himself whether the competitive search for knowledge is worth it. At this point he begins to view our competition with the Communist world (and sometimes competitiveness itself) as a form of mass paranoia, and he views the university as an agent of a government which contributes towards the perpetuation of the paranoid system. He reacts by protest or withdrawal.

The War-in-Vietnam Hypothesis—Although student unrest began long before the war in Vietnam ever escalated to massive proportions, there can be little doubt that in the past few years this conflict has been the major factor influencing the behavior of students. The war is particularly unpopular on our campuses. A large proportion of students, perhaps the majority, see it as a misguided effort. A significant minority see it as wholly immoral. Much of the restless behavior of students can be directly related to their efforts to do something to stop the war or to their sense of total frustration when they feel powerless to stop it.

The draft and the inequities engendered by the "S" deferment also contribute to unrest. The major issue here is fear. The average male student is plagued with fears that he will fail in school, will be drafted, and will run the risks of being killed in a conflict he may not consider vital to our interests. A second issue is guilt. The university student knows that he is spared from military service only because he is richer or smarter than someone else. While he may believe that the war is immoral, he also knows that his privileged status is immoral. When he accepts the 2S status he suffers guilt. Much of the activism on our campuses is a means of atoning for that guilt. Much of the alienation on our campuses is a means of denying the relevance of the society that created such guilt.

Students also feel some shame in not participating in those aspects of military service that might make them feel more masculine. It is rare for anyone even in peacetime to embrace military service eagerly, and a normal late-adolescent has justifiable concern with interrupting his career to face the harshness of life in the service. The unpopularity of this war gives the student a cogent reason for avoiding military service, but it does not resolve his nagging fears that he is somehow or other being cowardly or less masculine by being treated specially.

It is also true that the anti-war climate on our campuses makes the student progressively more disinclined to serve in this war the longer he remains on campus. Education breeds a dislike of violence. Furthermore, whatever romantic thoughts a young man may have about the war at the age of 18 are somewhat attenuated with a year or two of maturation. Students spend many hours arguing about the war, the draft, and means of avoiding the draft. This preoccupation creates a highly tense situation in which the student feels supported only by his peer groups. He begins to relate to subcultures which become progressively more separated from the rest of the nation and particularly from the adult generation.

The Deterioration-in-the-Quality-of-Life Hypothesis—There are many who believe that student unrest is an appropriate response to the deterioration of the quality of life in America. Overpopulation which results in crowds, traffic jams, and businesses run on the basis of mass production has taken much of the joy out of life in our towns and cities. Personal care or service is hard to find in any shop, restaurant, or hotel. People begin to feel faceless and insignificant.

Students, it can be argued, are among the first to sense the painful anonymity associated with bigness. This is a particularly serious problem on overcrowded campuses where students are generally isolated from their teachers and other adults. A sense of student-faculty intimacy or a sense of scholarly community are sorely lacking on most of our large campuses. Students find it difficult to develop a sense of identification or loyalty towards a university that they perceive as monolithic and impersonal. In their complaints that they are treated like numbers or IBM cards they strike a poignant note for all of us.

Overcrowding is only a relative thing and would not be so destructive if it were not for the manner in which we have incredibly neglected the planning and development of town and country. Our cities grow with no respect for the land. Beauty and wilderness are easy prey for the builder and contractor. Clean air and clear streams are almost a thing of the past. An adolescent who grows up in a world in which we must sit back and watch beauty fade and pollution gain comes to despair of the future.

One way of looking at student unrest is as a massive reaction to the destruction of that kind of world and way of life which their forebears enjoyed but which will be denied to them. It is not uncommon to hear a student say to an adult, "In your world life had some hope and meaning, but in the world you have left me these qualities are gone."

The Political-Hopelessness Hypothesis—Many individuals see our mass society as immutable. It has been argued that our society is so complex, our systems of checks and balances so intricate, and our interplay of pressure groups so self-equalizing that really effective change is no longer possible. Our business-oriented economy has so indoctrinated us in the role of credit-bound consumers that we are all beholden to a way of life which may not be in our best interests. An increasing number of radical students are convinced that the forces of government, industry, and education are totally interdependent and allied to one another for the purpose of warding off any reasonable attempts to change the society. They believe that a system of life has developed in our country which simply absorbs legal efforts to change our society, even protest, in a manner which ultimately preserves the status quo.

Guided by the philosophy of Herbert Marcuse, many students are convinced that constructive change within our society is not possible by working through the system. They do not have any sort of vision as to what will replace the old order, but they are convinced that our society is fundamentally irrational and must be destroyed. They do not reject illegal acts or even violence as agents of destruction.

The Civil-Rights Hypothesis—The civil rights movement not only increased youth's awareness of an historical injustice which made it difficult for them to be proud of this country, but also served as a training ground for future radicals. The new campus protest began at Berkeley when students demanded the right to work freely on their own campuses on behalf of oppressed Negroes. Many campus radicals shaped their images of "the Establishment" and of unreasonable authority on the basis of their early work in the civil rights movement. Students throughout the country have developed an amazing empathy and identification with Negroes. Their commitment to the Negro cause has taught them the psychological meaning of oppression and has encouraged them to seek out and attack sources of oppression in their own lives.

III. *Neutral Hypotheses*—Some explanations of student unrest focus upon impersonal processes. The causes of unrest, according to these hypotheses, are not to be found in the actions or philosophies of other men, but are believed to reside in changes in our highly complex society which seem to create the need for new modes of psychological adaptation.

The Technology Hypothesis—Man has always lived with hope, particularly with the hope that his efforts in the present will be rewarded with gratification in the future. A certain degree of predictability in the future enables one to make commitments to goals and to other people. To the extent that we live in a society in which past, present, and future lose their interrelatedness, the power of hope to shape man's behavior is diminished. New means of adapting to the world must then be found and the manner in which people relate to one another must be profoundly altered.

Postwar America has been characterized by a massive and continuous growth of technology. Our society is one in which the conditions of everyday life are constantly changing. Moreover, the rate at which technology changes our lives is itself increasing. No one can predict what life will be like in 20 years, 10 years, or even five years. Today's knowledge, today's work skills, and today's values may be totally irrelevant to tomorrow's world. Kenneth Kenniston has described the manner in which some youth, who, when exposed to an ever-increasing rate of technological growth, come to perceive that the values of the past will be totally inappropriate for the world in which they will be adults. Moreover, they feel powerless to anticipate or direct the future. In this environment hope no longer sustains. It is adaptive to be cool, and to learn to live in the present.

What are the advantages and disadvantages of living in the present? The advantages are more or less obvious. One is more flexible, and superficially at least more comfortable. It is not necessary to delay gratification, nor need one allow himself to be tortured by the mistakes of the past nor be deluded by unrealistic hopes for the future. The disadvantages of life in the present are more subtle, yet more powerful. To live in the present one must narrow his commitments. He must travel lightly and be ready for anything. More intimate relationships are unlikely, since they cannot be sustained by reference to past experience or to promises of a better future. Passion and romantic longing must be avoided because they may breed pain or impair one's flexibility. In short, if carried to extremes, life in the present is a selfish life which is incompatible with the growth of that intimacy and passion which man has always found to be essential to a fulfilled life.

Distrust of the future and a determination to live in the present seem to be characteristic of both activist and alienated students. The student activist seeks immediate change and has difficulty in developing the patience or optimism for long-term planning. The alienated student adopts the philosophy of the hippie. Believing that the only certainty in life is change, or uncertainty itself, he adapts by "doing his own thing" and behaves as though he is responsible only to himself.

The Media Hypothesis—There are several hypotheses that attempt to relate the growth of new media, particularly television, to the troubling behavior of students. It can be argued, for example, that simply by being available to publicize the activities of protesters and hippies the media exaggerate the importance of these groups. The television camera forces all of us to take seriously forms of behavior that might have been dismissed lightly in earlier decades. Conceivably the medium may be creating a "climate of expectation" in which youth are subtly seduced into dissenting roles which may not represent their actual interests.

It is also true that many television commercials, radio ads, and most modern music are directed towards the youth market. The self-consciousness of youth is thereby heightened. Young people are made more aware of their potentialities and sometimes develop an exaggerated sense of their own power.

Another attempt to relate changing media to student unrest has been implied in the writings of Marshall McLuhan. McLuhan believes that electronic media are bringing us all closer together in a more truly communal and shared society than ever existed. Our youth who have grown up with the new media are ready for such a society. Elders who are committed to sustain the institutions of the past are not. Much of youthful rebellion can then be visualized as an effort to make older people see that the world has changed and that many of the values of the past are now irrelevant.

While McLuhan's hypothesis has some attractiveness, it does not seem as plausible as those which focus upon the psychological impact of the content of various media. Fredric Weotham believes that the massive degree of violence which young people see on television makes them more violent and less responsible. Vance Packard has argued that chronic exposure to the values implied in TV commercials could create a generation of unrealistic, demanding, and present-oriented youth.

I would like to propose my own hypothesis of student unrest based on the manner in which the media influence the character structure of youth by prematurely confronting them with the harsh truths and realities of life, as follows:

As an animal whose growth and development requires him to be dependent upon others for a long period of time, man learns to rely on others for an optimal amount of structure and order in his life. It is obvious that authority is not always benevolent or just, and yet it is true that no man can be at ease if he does not commit a part of himself to some authority, whether it be his church, his family, his government, or an ideology. Nor can one come to develop a firm sense of who he is without making such commitments. It is at least partly through experiencing limitations which are imposed by others, by respecting others, and by emulating those who are respected that one finds his own identity. The process by which one comes to terms with authority is not always deliberate or rational. Sometimes even benevolent authority relies on faith, mystique, or untruth to retain its control.

This is especially relevant to the situation of young people. The most well-meaning parents must on occasion deceive their children because they know that children would find many of the hard and cynical facts of life to be unbearable. Until recently it was possible for young people to begin to experience the world as adults know it only after they had reached adolescence. Most of the time the adolescent absorbed this new knowledge gradually and painlessly. Even when he did feel that his parents had been hypocritical or had deceived him, his awareness of their dishonesty came so gradually that his resentment and rebelliousness were restrained. Today it is different. One of the significant developments in postwar America has been the influence of mass-communication media (particularly television) which are capable of disseminating information to all age groups immediately.

Even before adolescence, television acquaints youth with the cynical facts of life at a time when such truths may be indigestible. Other media communicate knowledge so quickly now that there is little opportunity for anyone to live comfortably with myth or self-delusion. Beliefs which were once casually accepted are vigorously scrutinized. The belief that there is equality for all Americans can hardly be sustained when one has a front-row seat from which he can observe the Negro's unsuccessful struggle to maintain a decent life in this country. Blind faith in the veracity of national leaders is quickly lost when one can watch the proceedings of an organization such as the United Nations in his own living room. I have no doubt that diplomats have always lied to one another, but what is new about this world is that children can now watch them lie in living color.

The hypocrisies of the older generations have always been with us. What is new today is that it is ridiculously easy to expose them. The effect on our youth of premature emergence of truth has been to create a deep skepticism as to the validity of authority. Neither the family, the church, the law, nor any institution demands this decline in respect for authority, but in my opinion it is best understood in terms of the psychological impact of our new media.

The Reliance-on-Scientism Hypothesis—Today's restless young people have grown up in a world which has not been dominated by religious faith but which has sought many of the answers to the questions of life in science. Many of us believe that science can provide the answers to life. We ask that the speculations and opinions of the social sciences contain the same hard truths as more rigorous findings in the physical and biological sciences. In my work with students, I am often impressed to find how easily they believe or once believed in the perfectability of man. Hostility is not seen as an innate quality of man but rather as a response to frustration. The teachings of the social psychologist that aggression is a learned phenomenon have gained prominence over Freud's more ominous warnings that aggression is innate.

This generation of students seems to have grown up with the belief that original sin in the religious sense of Thanatos in the psychoanalytic sense does not exist. (Much of this belief has been reinforced by the mode of their existence. Many are affluent and have grown up in suburban communities where, except for what they see on television, they are shielded from the tragedies of life. The realities of their own lives convince them that whatever calamities are imposed upon others are not inevitable.) Statements such as, "Life is a vale of tears" or "The masses of men lead lives of quiet desperation" seem absurd to them. In their adherence to scientific rationality they also cannot accept guilt. They are convinced that in a perfectable world man should be joyful and guiltless.

When a person raised with such beliefs encounters the harsh realities of life, he has little to fall back upon. If he perceives his own aggressive tendencies, he is frightened by them and attempts to deny them. He may project his anger upon those whom he feels are frustrating him or he may simply deny that such anger exists. When he perceives the evil of others he is mortified. In his conviction that there are rational solutions to any problem, he cannot help but be intolerant of the irrationalities of those who prevent progress. In his belief that life and especially the sexual aspects of life can be enjoyed without guilt, he becomes highly disturbed when he discovers that he cannot escape his past and that a certain amount of guilt is inevitable. He even becomes plagued with additional guilt over the realization that he is guilty.

The restless student is one who has taken the message of science, rationality, and perfection literally. He is more open to action and change than were earlier generations of students. At the same time, however, he is not equipped to understand or deal with the depth of that irrationality in man which resists change and which leads man to seek his own destruction. Too often such a student finds it necessary to construct "devil" theories of history in which the existence of evil is attributed to only a few who block the progress of the many. He has sacrificed the comfort and patience which comes with the idea of accepting "original" sin.

Hopefully, this review has been more than an exercise in cataloguing. By emphasizing the diversity of explanations of student unrest, I have attempted to demonstrate the intellectual futility of searching for simple explanations of a highly complex phenomenon. As citizens we may wish either to support or attack the causes which restless students have dramatized. But as scholars concerned with educating and understanding and helping students we need a more objective approach. We must recognize that there is some truth to the most critical as well as the most sympathetic hypotheses.

Some of the hypotheses suggest guidelines for action. The critical hypotheses remind us that youth are not always as wise or powerful as we might suspect. Like adults, their actions are as much determined by personal weaknesses and selfishness as by sensitivity or idealism. While youths certainly do not need more paternalism and coddling, they still need our understanding and guidance. They can still learn much from adults who are committed to the pursuit of ideals in a climate of tolerance, compassion, and responsibility. The critical hypotheses need not be used only to berate students. If their validity is appreciated they can be helpful in freeing adults from that unreasonable guilt which impairs an honest confrontation with the issues which students have raised.

The sympathetic hypotheses emphasize the unusual degree of stress this generation of students has experienced. These hypotheses which

invoke the war, overpopulation, and pollution as sources of stress forcefully remind us that student unrest is often an appropriate response to
what sometimes seems to be a hopelessly troubled world. Other hypotheses raise many questions for those entrusted with the management of
our universities. Does the emphasis on education as a means rather than
an end have any meaning in an affluent society? Should youths be encouraged to remain in a passive role as students throughout the first
third of their lives? Are there means of bringing young people into important roles in the power structure of our universities and our social
system before they reach the age of 25 or 30? Is the 2S classification anything more than a bribe which weakens the moral position of dissenting
students and creates havoc upon our campuses? Should it be abolished?
To what extent can we continue to depersonalize and enlarge our campuses without creating a generation of alienated youth who feel no sense
of identity, no sense that they have a voice in what is done to them, and
no sense of commitment to anything but their own interests?

It is my belief that the neutral hypotheses are the most intriguing and
the most powerful valid explanations of student unrest. At the same time,
they are the most difficult to live with optimistically. If progress itself, in
the form of technology, science, or new media, is the most severe stress
in the lives of our young people, then we are faced with a seemingly
impossible task, namely, how to control progress and change rather than
allowing these forces to control us.

10

Having gone through some turbulent stages,
I state a conviction that's flat:
A youngster's most difficult age is
Whichever he's presently at!
                                    UNKNOWN

Bruno Bettelheim
CHILDREN MUST LEARN TO FEAR

I consider it not at all startling that we encounter violence today
on our campuses and on our streets. We are engaged in a process of re-

From Bruno Bettelheim, "Children Must Learn to Fear," *New York Times Magazine*,
April 13, 1969, pp. 125 ff. © 1969 by The New York Times Co. Reprinted by permission of
the author and publisher.

moving both inner and outer controls, and as long as this process is not reversed, ours will become a time of more violence still.

Violence is the most primitive path to an objective. The temper tantrum, so typical of the young child, shows how the destructive outburst comes long before the ability to master inner drives and the external world.

Almost any birthday party shows how normal this is. The birthday child will tear off the wrappings to get at his presents. And if the box he is ripping away at should have been part of the game, so much the worse for the game. Desire begets violence and violence may destroy the object desired.

Still, today's riots do not originate with small children, but with adolescents for the most part. It is a problem that calls for the most sensitive planning in earliest childhood, long before police action becomes necessary. To understand why pressures erupt in adolescence on a growing scale nowadays, and why controls seem to grow weaker, we must recognize that adolescent revolt is not a stage of development that follows automatically from our natural makeup. What makes for adolescent revolt is the fact that our society keeps the next generation dependent too long.

Years ago, when schooling ended for the vast majority at 14 or 15, and thereafter one became self-supporting, got married and had children, there was no need for adolescent revolt. Because while puberty is a biological word, adolescence as we know it with its identity crises is not. All children grow up and become pubertal, but by no means do all become adolescents. To be adolescent means that one has reached and even passed the age of puberty, is at the very height of one's physical development—healthier, stronger, even handsomer than one has been, or will be, for the rest of one's life—but must nevertheless postpone full adulthood till long beyond what any other period in history has considered reasonable. What preparation do we give youngsters for such a prolonged waiting, or for controlling their anger or violent impatience with the waiting?

Let me start with the obvious which is often neglected when we think about violence. Even Seneca knew in the first century that the best cure for anger begins with delay. Thus, to avoid violence, one must have learned first how to delay.

Our modern infatuation with speed is a very real handicap. Our new yardstick of time, even in human affairs, tends to be the machine, not the living cell. Our image of time no longer rests on the slow growth of trees, nor on the nine months it still takes before a baby is ready to be born. In today's affluent society, satisfactions are so immediate that children are less likely to have learned about delay as a natural dimension.

Before bottle feeding, the infant had to learn to accept delay once he had drained his mother of milk. Now, almost from birth, things are instantly *here*. Baby's bottle is ready in the refrigerator; food comes pre-cooked. Little wonder that youth expects instant solutions—even to problems that have plagued man for generations.

Photographs can be developed in an instant, the human fetus cannot. The same goes for inner controls. There are timetables in human development that can only be hurried (or delayed) at a painful and deadening cost. We can now do many things at our own time, but we have not learned yet what is the right time to do them.

Until recently this slow inner growth was supported by early parental teachings, later by the schools, and then by society at large. Call it the teaching of a middle-class morality, if you will; in psychoanalysis we call it the "reality principle," which holds that if we want to direct our own fate, we must learn to let go of present pleasures at times for greater ones in the future. And frankly, unless we have learned how to wait, then the business of learning (most of which is hard work) cannot go on because there is always some learning that gives no immediate pleasure. If this is true for school learning, it is doubly so for the learning of self-control.

So in the final analysis, whether or not violence occurs will depend on whether the individual has learned to brook delay, and whether better solutions are available and known. Violence is the behavior of the person who cannot wait and cannot visualize alternative solutions to his problem. For the mature adult, this search for alternatives is a rational process. But I am here less concerned with violence in adults than in how (and if) children learn delay and then control. My contention is that for self-control to develop, children must have learned to fear something before they enter society, which for children means school. If it is not the once crippling fear of damnation, then in our more enlightened days it is at least the fear of losing parental love (or later, by proxy, the teacher's) and eventually the fear of losing self-respect.

To fear the loss of self-respect, however, one must first have acquired it. Self-respect (and what it demands of us) is merely what has taken the place of an earlier respect for the parent who protects us from physical and emotional pain. If there has been no such protection, there is no fear of losing this reliable source of satisfaction, and hence no respect for him and his commands. And without having established this early respect, no self-respect can replace it, nor any fear of the loss of self-respect.

I dwell on fear because of a common misunderstanding of Freud: the vague feeling among parents and educators that children should never be made to feel frightened at breaking a moral command. Not only are our children ill-prepared to brook delay, they have also been confronted with a morality from which we have done our best to remove the basic motivation. We want to remove fear from the life of the child and at the same time we want him to restrain his tendencies toward violence as if we had not removed fear. Children's earliest controls of violence rest on fear and are largely irrational; they come from the moral commands of adults. On the basis of fear, not of rational judgment, they tell the child what he "must do" and "must not do." Only later does the mature ego apply reason to these commands and slowly subject them to a critical judgment. Only as maturity grows can we slowly free ourselves of fear.

What was wrong with old-fashioned, authoritarian education was not that it was based on fear. That is what was right with it. What was wrong was that it disregarded the need to modify the fear in a continuous process so that irrational anxiety would steadily give way to more rational motivation. Today, many parents are unwilling to face their children's displeasure when they impose controls. And they are also unwilling to invite the child to embark on the troublesome search for alternatives whenever frustration occurs. To such parents, modern psychology seems a way out. Certainly psychoanalysis suggests that we should not suppress our inner rages but should face them. But we were expected to face them only in thought, only when we had reached the age of reason, and only in the safely structured treatment situation. This has been understood by large numbers of the educated middle classes to mean that rage should always be expressed—and not just in thought. Thus, many children have no fear of lashing out and do not learn how to acquire control of their rages in childhood. Later, when adolescent pressures flood them with rage, they are helpless to control the rage or to restrict it to thought only. What Freud taught about the crippling effects of an over-repression of emotions due to excessive fear (that was where the shoe pinched in his day) has been wrongly extended to mean it is all right to discharge emotions in action without control of the discharge by thought.

Education also shows a parallel influence of psychoanalysis. We see it most typically in the tendency to applaud almost any disorganized thing the child does, because it reveals something. Or by viewing what he does as "creative," even when it is just an instinctual expression—such as smearing with paint or an outpouring in words of some formless inner pressures.

Now there is nothing wrong with the child's being able to mess and smear with paint or to voice aloud his chaotic feelings. At the right time and in the right place, it may be very good for him to enjoy the chance to let go, to be uncontrolled. It becomes damaging if the educator, who should know better, fools himself and the child into believing that if something has meaning as id expression, it is therefore ego correct (contains a meaningful message to others), which is not true.

It is very much the task of education to see that the sphere of the ego should grow. But to do that, the teacher must know clearly what is ego correct and what is not. We stunt the child's growth if we call id expressions creative, instead of being satisfied to recognize their possible value (that they may offer temporary relief to the child and deeper insight to the teacher into what is going on in the child). A dream may reveal what goes on in the unconscious. But dreaming is hardly an act of creation, nor will it advance intellectual growth.

Even when later scribbling or drawing becomes more expressive, it remains solipsistic. It becomes meaningful to the child and possibly valuable to others only if through a slow process of education; through observing and appreciating the efforts of others; through criticism, self-criticism, and the use of appropriate standards his mere self-expression is transformed into a meaningful message.

Life would still be simple, though different, if middle-class parents consistently encouraged their children to act on their instinctual tendencies. But where the old way of expression was at least all of a piece, the modern way is one of contradictions. Some instinctual tendencies are still repressed as before, while others are directed toward discharge without intervening thought and rational control. This makes no sense at all and is the source of the youngsters' insistence that our society does not make any sense. Even worse, the decisions on what to repress and what to discharge are based not on the interests of the child, but on the convenience of adults. And this is where the fatal error lies and what most enrages youth.

Let me use a minor example of what grates on many middle-class children every day. They are told they have a room of their own. But then they have to keep what has been called their possession just the way their parents see fit. And the same goes for toys: "It's your toy, but you must share it with others." Now it is possible to live without ownership, but it is more pleasant to have it. What is devastating is to be given to and then deprived in endless repetition. Some parents tell their children: "Since this is your room, you must take care of it," an utter perversion of the meaning of ownership leading to total rage and distrust. The same open lie and inner contradiction taints the unconscious of instinctual experience.

On the surface, it looks as if parents were indulging their children when they pick them up each time they cried. Actually they indulged the children only where it suited themselves, as if to say, "I indulge you now, but for that I'll expect you to be the brightest kid in school. Didn't I let you hang onto your bottle? Now go and be a whiz at school."

The same holds for toilet training. Yesterday's parents made up their minds when it was time for their child to be toilet trained and saw that it happened in a couple of weeks. There was nothing tentative about it, no if's or but's. Things were not easy for the child, but in two weeks the whole thing was over.

Modern parents let the child decide if he wants to toilet train or not. They say, "Do what you want, but by golly, it's time you did it." They say, "Oh, it's all right to make in your pants," but then they are disgusted. So the child must now live with parents' disgust for six months or a year.

And the message he gets is the following: "My parents are nice parents, but I'm a disgusting person." And this we call "permissive" training.

Even in families where I found a genuine desire to provide instinctual pleasure for children, it was expected that the children would therefore achieve intellectually even faster and at a much higher level. That is, instinctual pleasure was not given so the child could enjoy his own body and with it the world, but as a bribe held out to make the child a better feeder of parental narcissism.

I have known mothers of extreme campus activists who, when the children were infants, fed them goodies against inner resistance because that is what good mothers were supposed to do. And soon even the child's pleasure evaporated as he realized he was being indulged to make the mother feel good about herself. I think of them as being "permissive if it kills me." Good reason then, for such youngsters to make a farce of permissiveness by asking for everything, with no sense of obligation to give in return.

When I see some of these wayout students, unwashed and unkempt—though, of course, nothing I say here is true of all of them—I cannot help thinking: "There goes another youngster who, as an infant, was practically scrubbed out of existence by his parents in the name of loving care."

Their dress or hairdo demonstrates how they rebel against parents who told them they could dress as they liked, provided their appearance pleased the parents' narcissism and not the child's convenience. Yet in a strange contradiction—and I talk of the inner contradictions that tear the extremist apart and mark all his outer behavior, his hatred of self and society, of all adults over 30—he only seems to go contrary to his parents wishes or teachings. On the surface he seems to do the opposite; and he firmly believes that in his manner of dress he defies his parents, but, deep down, he merely copies their behavior. He mistreats and neglects the legitimate needs of his body just as much as his parents did, only this time not by total scrubbing, but by total neglect. It is the having been pushed out of infancy and childhood toward higher maturity in one area, while indulged or overstimulated in others, that tears them to pieces later on.

How natural it is that, as they strive for independence from their parents, some youngsters drop out while others resent the faculty, those parental figures once removed. And that the faculty is resented for some of the reasons I mention, may be inferred from the angry charges made by students that professors care more for their research than for teaching.

My thesis, then, is that more than anything else it is the emotional contradictions, if not the outright emotional lies, in which both extremists and dropouts are raised by their educated, upper middle-class parents, that convinces them that ours is a society that deserves to be destroyed.

We know that each society can raise the new generation in its own way. If a society does not taboo sex, children will grow up in relative sex freedom. But so far, history has shown that such a society cannot create culture or civilization; it remains primitive. Without sex repression, there is no prolonged span of intellectual learning. And the same goes for fear. Without fear, there is no inner control over instinctual tendencies.

Because Freud has shown the evil effects of too much fear, too much Victorian repression, because he concentrates on what most plagued the middle classes then, our own middle classes (to paraphrase Goethe) learned carefully how their master coughed and spat in order to totally disregard what he taught. Freud certainly knew that without strong inner controls, preferably conscious ones, man would sink back into barbarism. If he stressed it less, it was because the dominant pathology in his day came of too much, not too little, control. But with both teachings available, many middle-class families chose to follow Freud where it suited their convenience, and were as demanding of conformity as the worst Victorian parent where it did not. In either case, they evaded their adult responsibility.

THE POLITICAL DIMENSION: CONTROL OF EDUCATION

In recent years the politics of American education has been experiencing dramatic changes. Even though the legal framework for the control of education has always been found at the state level, there has been a general acceptance of extreme localism pervading the government of education. Needless to say, such is no longer the case. The federal government has become deeply entrenched in educational politics. This participation in education appears to be permanent. Since 1960, federal government support for public education has increased from 4.4 percent to more than 8 percent of the total revenues for public elementary and secondary schools. The nation has witnessed the passage by Congress of numerous pieces of educational legislation during the past few years. Most important of these new laws is the Elementary and Secondary Education Act of 1965. By attempting to equalize educational opportunity, this legislation, which approaches general federal aid, benefits almost all school districts to some degree. With this increasing intervention of the federal government in school policy making, with a broadening of the influence of the states in education, and with the new emphasis on decentralization in the big cities, students of educational politics have turned their attention to a search for the most meaningful relationship among the local, state, and federal levels of government.

Since the time that Thomas Eliot first identified the schools as political entities, the local-state-federal relationship has been in continual transition. This state of flux has been due mainly to the changing federal role in education and to the failure on the part of most state legislatures to comprehend the needs of disadvantaged children in the large cities. Several of the articles on the following pages have been chosen to illustrate the changing role of the federal government while others describe the creative thought being given to the challenge presented by the needs of urban education.

The purpose of this dimension is to stimulate thinking regarding the control of American education, that is, the influencing of public decision making relating to the allocation of limited resources for education. It is probably best to approach this task free of the traditional constraints acquired through experience with the educational system of the recent past. Some of these traditional constraints involve fundamental values. Indeed, the concept of local control of education referred to above might even have been considered a basic tenet of our democracy. If, as most of the following readings imply, there is to be developed a more effective allocation of resources for education, then many of the nation's basic educational values will undergo careful scrutiny in the near future.

The selections in this dimension have been chosen because they shed light on the future of the local-state-federal relationship in education. They raise significant questions and provoke further thought regarding the control of American education.

1

Neither the prevailing consensus, the creed, nor even the political system itself are immutable products of democratic ideas, beliefs, and institutions from the past. For better or for worse, they are always open, in some measure, to alteration through those complex processes of symbiosis and change that constitute the relations of leaders and citizens in a pluralistic democracy.

ROBERT A. DAHL

Peter Schrag
WHO CONTROLS EDUCATION?

Of all the big stories in American education, perhaps the biggest concerns the changes in power, influence, and structure that are reshaping the academic landscape. Americans are accustomed to relatively simple distinctions between public and private institutions, between religious and secular colleges, between local and national control. Not long ago we could draw uncomplicated organization charts culminating in a school committee or a board of trustees and say with some assurance that it was here, at the top, that the ultimate decisions were made.

But the events of the past decade have changed all that. The increasing secularization of the major Catholic colleges, the impact of federal programs, the militancy of the teacher's unions and the civil rights organizations, and our growing appetite for research exemplify developments that are blurring the lines so thoroughly that no one can say with any cer-

From Peter Schrag, "Who Controls Education?" *Saturday Review*, March 18, 1967, p. 60. Copyright Saturday Review, Inc. 1967. Reprinted by permission of the author and publisher.

tainty where the ultimate power lies or who controls a particular institution or set of institutions. To be sure, many schools and colleges remain relatively autonomous, and their administrators maintain—or feel they maintain—considerable freedom of movement in making decisions. But among the major institutions and organizations, be they the public schools of Chicago or the University of California, the options have become increasingly complex and circumscribed—so circumscribed, indeed, that one school superintendent recently pointed out that he controlled a bare 5 per cent of the budget of his system; the rest was politically beyond his reach.

Clark Kerr, who was himself a victim of the uncertainties of power, described part of the situation in *The Uses of the University*, where he defined the function of the multiversity president as that of mediator between conflicting pressures and responsibilities. But Kerr's problem, dramatic as it was, only reflects some even more pervasive tensions and changes in American education. It is not simply that influence is shifting from local to national institutions, from the school board to the desegregation machinery of Title VI of the Civil Rights Act, or from the states to the federal government; the changes involve, rather, an increasingly complicated set of demands associated with innumerable new organizations, interest groups, and social commitments.

The growing interest of Americans in education manifests itself not only in a willingness to pay higher school taxes or to establish community colleges, but also in the form of new institutional devices, mergers, and programs, and in tough organizations pressing their demands on trustees and school committees that are supposedly free to implement their decisions. The list of such organizations is virtually endless: the American Federation of Teachers, the various civil rights groups, the Office of Education, the Office of Economic Opportunity, the Department of Labor, the military, the various legislatures, and the vast and still growing research establishment supported by the National Science Foundation, the National Institutes of Health, the Atomic Energy Commission, and the American Cancer Society—not to mention the dubious and apparently ubiquitous presence of the CIA.

Clearly, legislative restrictions, alumni pressure, and periodic elections always checked the executives of educational power, but never have the checks been as complex or numerous as they are now. As a consequence, the modern university and the modern school system bear a growing resemblance to a corporation responsible not only to stockholders, but to labor unions, regulatory agencies (the Interstate Commerce Commission or the Securities and Exchange Commission), and the general considerations of public relations. All these responsibilities affect the decisions and the freedom of the organization. As described by A. A. Berle, Jr., in *Power Without Property:*

The power system emerging in response to public wants is at long last governed by public consensus. In creating, maintaining, and expending that consensus all of us have a part. It is a sort of continuing election in which there are no non-voters.

Increasingly, as an educational institution is beset by conflicting and countervailing concentrations of power, its own characteristics and structure begin to change. Is the Massachusetts Institute of Technology, where 75 per cent of the budget comes from the federal government, really a private institution? Could its trustees choose to close down all those research projects? Could they suddenly decide to convert MIT into a liberal arts college, or into a home for wayward girls? Similarly, could Ronald Reagan, all by himself, really "ruin" Berkeley? Who "owns" or controls the quasi-independent research organizations that operate on major university campuses? How does one influence the policies and research expenditures of the National Science Foundation, the National Institutes of Health, or the Atomic Energy Commission?

American education is increasingly becoming, not a network of distinctly private or distinctly public institutions, but a mélange of hybrid organizations supported—and, in a sense, controlled—by a combination of public and private individuals and agencies, federal, industrial, and philanthropic. As new demands have arisen, and as new organizations have grown to articulate them, new institutional devices have been developed: a regional busing program for deprived children supported by federal and foundation funds and directed by a board representing a variety of constituencies but not responsible to any single one; a research organization within a university, but sustained entirely by federal money and responsible to no one except the government accountants; a semi-independent demonstration program within a public school system wholly supported by federal funds; a corporation formed by public and private universities to seek funds for collaborative ventures. When the corporations that have recently entered the learning field (General Learning, IBM, Raytheon, Xerox) become active in the market, the distinctions will be blurred even further. It is difficult even now to determine where the National Aeronautics and Space Administration ends and the corporate aerospace industry begins; chances are that, in some sectors of education, that pattern will become increasingly prevalent.

The development of these new structures and relationships demands a drastic overhaul of our classic notions of institutional independence and our belief in the "nonpolitical" nature of education. The criticisms of federal influence are already vehement. Yet it is not only the federal presence that is altering the traditional relationships. The new demands, and the organizations growing from them, reflect the simple fact that we are now all involved. The development and financing of educational programs adequate to the complexities of the modern world seem to require organizational relations of equal complexity. If we want the education, we are going to have to confront the uncertainties and ambiguity that make it possible.

2

The politics of education is complex and everchanging. At various times and places it can appear to be an asset or a liability. But it is real. Only through understanding and making proper use of politics can education be improved.

WENDELL H. PIERCE

Thomas H. Eliot

TOWARD AN UNDERSTANDING OF PUBLIC SCHOOL POLITICS

Mounting concern over the aims and achievements of American public schools emphasizes the need for continuing analysis of how the schools are run and who runs them. The general theory is simple enough: schools are objects of local control, the people of a local school district exercise that control through an elected school board, and the board appoints a superintendent to act as the chief executive of the district. There are variations from this pattern—in some places school boards are appointed rather than elected, in others the school system is formally a part of the city government, and in a few districts other officials, such as a business manager or building superintendent, share the top executive authority—but it is by far the most common arrangement among the nation's approximately 50,000 school districts.

I

The formal structure is based on state constitutions and statutes, and the latter have tended to confirm the historical development of education in the nineteenth century, especially in one respect: the district system of organization. The desirability of *local* control of the public

From Thomas H. Eliot, "Toward an Understanding of Public School Politics," *American Political Science Review*, December, 1959, pp. 1032–1042, 1046–1051. Reprinted by permission of the author and publisher.

schools is an article of faith among most trained educators and many other Americans, including President Eisenhower. Laymen assume that local control means control by the people of the district, usually through elected representatives. Professional educators, however, are less clear about this. Their books and journals are rife with intimations that the people and even the school board members should keep their hands off the schools. Even James B. Conant's "report," after echoing the typical recommendation that school boards should confine themselves to "policy" as distinguished from "administration," says that they should refrain from interfering with curricular development. But where is educational "policy" made, if not in the development of the curriculum? Doubtless Conant's remark was an inadvertent slip, for his book as a whole deals primarily with the curriculum and is addressed to "interested citizens," a category which surely includes more than educators; but many educators are insistent in urging, in effect, that the schools are the special province of the professionals, the voters being a necessary evil who must be reckoned with because they provide the money. In this view, the school board's primary functions, aside from directing the district's business affairs, are to hire and support a competent professional as superintendent, defend the schools against public criticism, and persuade the people to open their pocketbooks.

This seems like turning representative government upside down. It also reflects a somewhat specialized concept of democratic theory, not unlike that expounded by Walter Lippmann—namely, that the experts should initiate policy and carry it out, with the people's representatives properly confined to the negative function of checking any gross abuse of power. Lippmann was referring primarily to foreign policy, and could argue plausibly that the control of foreign policy—Locke's "federative power"—was a matter for special treatment in an otherwise self-governing society. It seems questionable whether the considerations favoring executive (or expert) direction of foreign policy are equally applicable to the control of school districts. Nevertheless, there are observable reasons for the desire to limit the role of the school boards and the people who elect them. The chief one is the professionalization of public school education.

The professionals consist of three groups. Numerically the largest, and politically today the least significant, are the school teachers. A hundred years ago, school teaching, in contrast to university teaching, law, medicine, and the ministry, was a vocation rather than a profession. A prime purpose of the National Education Association, originated in 1857, was to raise it to a professional status. By a kind of bootstrap operation, this was largely achieved, though it took eighty years to do it. The early normal schools, essentially vocational training institutes, were supplemented by colleges and graduate schools of education; and states were moved to pass certification laws prescribing educational qualifications

for teachers. The second professional group is composed of the pedagogues' pedagogues—the faculties of teachers colleges and university
departments of education. Their professional status was ready-made, but
as the justification of their existence depended largely on the professionalization of school teaching itself, they naturally took a leading part in
that process. They also were foremost in creating the third group, the
professional school administrators. School administration, as a profession, is a latecomer, but in terms of understanding the politics of the public schools it is perhaps the most important of all. School administration
is a decidedly hierarchical and disciplined business and the top administrator, the local school superintendent, holds the key position in each
school district. Indeed, there seems to be professional agreement that
the most significant duty of the people's representatives on the local
school board is the selection of the superintendent.

The thoroughly defensible assumption that school teaching and school
administration are the specialized tasks of persons with professional
training and status leads inevitably to a professional distrust of lay interference. This distrust has been accentuated by the frequency with which
lay demands have conflicted with the convictions of the educators, seeming to them to be destructive of the very purposes of education. Even
well meant lay suggestions that more emphasis should be placed on the
"three r's" have caused flutterings of alarm, for too often such criticisms
have been the softening-up forerunners of assaults on the freedom of the
teachers and so on the whole professional concept. Such assaults have
caused one writer to describe the politics of public education as "ideological politics," otherwise a comparative rarity on the American scene.

But are we permitted to speak of the "politics" of education? To many
educators the word seems abhorrent: not even the admonitions of George
S. Counts can overcome their aversion to it. Again, this is understandable. Whole school systems have been blighted by the intrusion of certain aspects of politics, especially the use of patronage in appointments
and contracts in apparent disregard of the need to give children the best
possible education. Yet because school districts are governmental units
and the voters have ultimate responsibility, school board members and
school superintendents are engaged in political activity whether they
like it or not. The standard professional terminology for this—a semantic
triumph—is "community relations"; a successful superintendent, particularly, must be skilled in community relations. Why not say frankly
that he must be a good politician.

Surely it is high time to stop being frightened by a word. Politics includes the making of governmental decisions, and the effort or struggle
to gain or keep the power to make those decisions. Public schools are
part of government. They are political entities. They are a fit subject for
study by political scientists.

Yet neither educators nor political scientists have frequently engaged in the examination of public education from this angle. Educators have shied away not only from the word "politics" but from political scientists as well. (The terminology of social scientists who deal with "power structures" and "communications" they find more acceptable.) Their suspicion of political science stems in part from the writings of some public administration professors who have occasionally urged that school systems, being part of local government, should be merged with multipurpose local units—namely cities and towns—thus losing their "independent" status; and at the state level, that a department of education, like other departments, should be headed by an appointee of the governor rather than a quasi-independent board. These proposals are in direct conflict with the passionate convictions of professional educators, and so have given political science a bad name in the teaching profession.

As for the political scientists, the running of the public schools—except for national defense the most extensive and expensive governmental activity in this country—has seldom seemed worth more than a chapter or two in a text on state and local government. There are honorable exceptions, but they are very few indeed. The taboo has worked both ways, almost as if by tacit agreement: if politics has been anathema to educators, the governing of the public schools has seemed inconsequential to political scientists.

The taboo should be exorcised, for the future of public education, at every level of government, is not only a political issue but an increasingly crucial one. It requires analysis not only in terms of political institutions (almost the only point of contact, and friction, between educators and political scientists in the past) but in terms of voting behavior, ideological predispositions, the clash of interests, decision-making, and the impact of individuals and organizations on nation-wide trends in educational policy. Of these only the first two have been examined at all extensively (and then usually by social scientists whose primary concern is not politics), and even those have not been the source of any noticeable amount of published material. If all the significant political factors are revealed, the people can more rationally and effectively control the governmental process. Such, at least, must be the faith of the political scientist who, devoted to the search for truth, believes that "what can be" is no less the truth than "what is."

II

The most significant subjects for decision by whoever runs the public schools concern the curriculum, the facilities, the units and organization of government, and personnel; and partly shaping them all is the omnipresent issue of finance.

Since World War II a war of words over the *curriculum* has been waged at white heat. Because their professionalism seems to lack full public acceptance and because any attack may make it harder to raise the money needed for good schooling, educators tend to object vehemently to most lay criticism. The laity, of course, embraces most of us, including school board members and university professors (of everything but Education), so the inference might seem to be that no one but a professional educator has any business criticizing the methods or ideas of professional educators. This was a typical answer to the vigorous attack on the curriculum mounted by Arthur E. Bestor, professor of history at the University of Illinois. However, by stepping carefully even an outsider may win a hearing. Constructive suggestions so phrased as to avoid sensitive toes, especially if preceded by well-publicized and protracted study, are treated with respect: witness the generally deferential reception of the report of James B. Conant, who is just as much a "layman" as Bestor. Any citizen who wants to influence the conduct of the schools might be well advised to follow Conant's example. And the person seeking to portray the political process in relation to education must also resist the temptation to be drawn into the controversy over "progressive education," "life adjustment," whether Johnny can read and if not why not, and the curriculum generally. His task is not to say what should be in the curriculum, but how, by whom, and through whose influence that decision is or might be made.

It is hard to read professional pronouncements on this subject without concluding that in professional eyes, the curriculum is essentially the school superintendent's business. To be sure, a committee of the American Association of School Administrators, in a report addressed to school board members, did say that the school board had "general responsibility" for the curriculum. The emphasis, however, seemed to be on the word "general," as was indicated by the committee's statement that "Curriculum planning and development is a highly technical task which requires special training. . . . Board members do not have and cannot be expected to have the technical competence to pass on the work of expert teachers in this field. . . . Nor can the board pass upon specific textbooks." Conant likewise assumes that "the school board will leave the development of the curriculum to the administrative officers and the teaching staff but will be kept informed of all developments." Even this, however, leaves some doubt about the school board's role, or lack of it. Is curriculum "development" something different from educational "policy," and if so, what is the line that separates them?

A school board member, impressively instructed to stick to policy and allow others to develop the curriculum, might well ask this question. But he might also ask why, if the curriculum is of great importance in educating children, he and his colleagues on the board should not take the responsibility for developing it? They are the people's representatives, elected to run the schools. Professional educators may say that they should not run the schools, but the law says that they must. (The law, of course, was made by some more laymen, called legislators.) Of course a strong argument can be made that usually the curriculum stands a better chance of improvement if it is "developed" by knowledgeable experts. But one may also suggest that experts can occasionally be wrong. Even Conant tacitly admits this, in his assumption that the school board will be "kept informed" and, also, that its members will "reserve (and exercise) the right" to question the superintendent and high school principal. One can imagine school board members, reading this, who will snort: "Reserve the right? We have no right to *refrain* from questioning our employees; we're to govern the school district and not to have some one else do it. There has been too much delegation of authority by elected officials lately. The people elected *us* to run things and we're going to run them."

Although recent controversies give the impression that the professionals have made the curriculum "progressive" (whatever that may mean) and want the school boards to keep hands off, there are indications that in many districts the shoe is on the other foot. Through conviction, or perhaps through ignorance and indifference, school boards have often adhered to curricula which the superintendents consider sadly out of date. Neal Gross quotes as typical of a sizeable minority view among Massachusetts superintendents the following complaints: "The selectmen and the town finance committee take the attitude, 'What was good enough for me ought to be good enough for them (the children).' And so do some of my school committee members. How can you run a modern educational program with . . . a classical curriculum when 80% of the kids don't go on to college?" And again: "My committee is primarily interested in keeping costs down. They don't want to discuss or even consider the need to revise the curriculum." The burden is on those who want change: if the Bestors feel frustrated by the insistence on professional domination of curriculum-making, the professionals feel blocked by lay conservatism or apathy.

The question of whether board or superintendent should dominate is important, but nowhere near as significant as what the curriculum contains. The question is reminiscent of the excitement about balancing the Federal budget before World War II. Many people in the 1930s were convinced that to save the country expenditures must be drastically cut— which meant, of course, the reduction or elimination of the relief programs that gave work and wages to millions of otherwise unemployed men and women. Came the war in Europe, and by 1940 many of these same economizers, fervently pro-British and anti-Hitler, enthusiastically favored vast increases in Federal expenditures for defense and aid to Britain. Whether the budget should be balanced was less crucial than what the money was spent for. In the same way, while a certain form of board-superintendent division of authority may, like budget-balancing, seem generally sound, the real question is what kind of school it produces. The basic problem, therefore, is not one of "school administration"; it is the political issue of what is to be taught or read in our schools. We may wish to leave this decision to the experts; we may wish to make it ourselves. This issue is decided chiefly at the local level, and to a lesser extent in the state capitols by legislatures and state education departments. For the last forty years it has also been affected by national legislation granting federal aid for vocational education.

The decisions concerning *facilities*—chiefly school buildings—are made very largely in the districts, with a comparatively high degree of popular participation. The people get engaged in school-building politics more than in any other phase of public school politics, for two reasons. First, a building program requires a major capital outlay, and in nearly all states the bond issues which such capital outlays necessitate are by law subject to popular approval. Second, buildings being tangible and the distance a child must walk or ride to school being measurable, most people feel more qualified to have opinions about the need, nature and location of the schoolhouse than about what goes on inside it.

Closely allied with the location and adequacy of buildings is the issue of *district organization*. Like the former, it is profoundly affected by finance: the Conant report, for instance, calls for reorganization of districts to eliminate small high schools because a really good small high school is, Conant believes, prohibitively expensive. On the other hand, the problems of location cause Alvin Eurich of the Fund for the Advancement of Education to criticize this recommendation: in sparsely populated areas, a large high school would be too far from many children's homes. The decisions on district size are sometimes made directly by state legislatures, or by state departments of education, but more often by the voters in the districts affected. The local voters' capacity to consolidate districts is, however, profoundly affected by the kind of statutes enacted by the legislature. The internal organization of a district—its system of government, whether its board shall be elected or appointed, its budgetary connection with the municipality—is ordinarily decided at the state level, though some states permit a certain amount of local option.

Personnel decisions include one which, in most districts, is made directly by the people—the election of school board members. Here is politics at its plainest, despite the non-partisan ballot that prevails in the majority of such elections, yet few efforts have been made to analyze the nature of school board campaigns and patterns of voting behavior therein. The educators and such useful publicists for education as the National Citizens Council for Better Schools rightly emphasize the importance of choosing "good" school boards, but their hortatory efforts are seldom buttressed by information as to what factors actually decide school board elections. The next significant personnel decision is the selection of a superintendent by the school board. He is often the key figure (as the professionals wish him to be) on the local educational scene. Indeed, his selection or retention sometimes is the central issue in school board elections; the voters thus occasionally affect the choice directly, and their potential ability to do so influences board action. Also for local decision is the matter of appointment, retention, and promotion of the teachers. Here direct, official popular intervention via the ballot box is rare indeed, although it has happened, and although occasionally a school board election has revolved around the retention of a school principal or teacher rather than a superintendent. In the main the decisions, formally made by the board, are based on the superintendent's recommendations. Chiefly on the superintendent, therefore, beat the informal pressures for appointment, transfer, or removal of a teacher, often in an emotional context arising naturally out of the complex psychology of the teacher-parent relationship.

While these personnel decisions are made locally, in most districts they are constrained by state legislation, particularly laws prescribing minimum qualifications of superintendents, principals, and teachers, and governing the conditions of promotion and discharge. At the state capitols, more than anywhere else, the educators have fought and largely won their fight for professional status. Tenure laws are, in the main, protections against "politics," but a tenure system may enhance status as well as security. More important, as a recognition of professionalism, are the certification statutes. To be sure, state occupational licensing laws hardly confer professional status, in the traditional sense, on every occupation licensed, such as those of elevator operator or hairdresser. In the case of teachers, however, they have been accompanied—indeed, have often been preceded—by state provisions for substantial formal training. This gives an additional justification for the claim of professionalism, especially as certification requirements, which obviously influence teachers' college programs, may also be to some extent geared to the courses offered by the teachers' colleges. The establishment of teachers colleges, furthermore, has created an institutional pressure center which some critics claim has a dominant effect on state and local curriculum decisions and on the selection of superintendents.

Schools cannot be built, equipped, or staffed without money. The problems of *financing* are inherent in virtually all the issues just discussed. Indeed, they are so omnipresent and so grim that if we were required to give one general explanation of the behavior of professional educators, we might frame it in terms of a ceaseless search for funds. Here may well be the basic reason why educators react so emotionally to criticism: any adverse criticism may make it harder to raise money. When school board members are instructed to go out and "support the schools" in the community, it is not because the superintendents and teachers are thin-skinned or prefer praise to criticism. It is because schools, good or bad, cost money, which must be provided by vote of the people or of their elected representatives on the school board, in the city or county government, and in the state legislature. At each level, the issue of school finance is a focal point of several obvious and broad conflicts of interest. The desire for low taxes clashes with the wish for good schools, in a struggle which is waged not only in the community by organized groups but within the mind of the thoughtful householder. A conflict between the owners of real property, on the one hand, and retailers and consumers on the other becomes increasingly important as proposals are made to shift the growing burden from the real property tax to the sales tax. The interests of those who live in wealthy districts with low taxes and good schools clash with the need to provide good schooling in less fortunate districts, through consolidation or equalization formulae. The local taxpayer wants relief which can be provided by state or federal aid, yet fears such aid because it might open the door to state or federal control: he who pays the piper calls the tune. The professionals are apparently less fearful of dictation from distant seats of power, perhaps because what they really distrust is dictation from any lay source, including the local citizenry: the people should pay for the schools but the professional educators should run them.

III

Although political power is centered in groups and individuals, its effectiveness and use are shaped by institutions. The institutional pattern of public education may seem firmly fixed, firmly enough, certainly, so that any proposal, to have a chance of success, must appear to conform to it. The pattern, of course, is one of local control through the democratic process. Yet, as we have seen, questions can and should be raised as to the actual extent and nature of local democratic control. If the image is inconsistent with the reality, we should know it, and change one or the other.

The basic public objective is to have American school children taught what they should be taught by able and dedicated teachers. As to what they should be taught, the broad conflict seems to be chiefly between most of the professional educators and some articulate laymen. General public knowledge about school curricula is hardly less than general public interest in the subject—both are small. But the launching of the first sputnik did stir the people—including educators—more than had the books of Lynd and Bestor, Keats and Smith. A typical professional response was to start teaching algebra in the eighth grade—as an "answer to the Russians" and, more realistically, as a defensive move against possible public criticism. The question remained as to what affirmative role, if any, the layman should play in curriculum development.

The pressures for changes in the curriculum seem to have come from three sources. First is the professional viewpoint itself, shaped largely in teacher-training institutions and often reflecting or adapting the ideas of individuals of almost prophetic stature, such as John Dewey. Second is the need for money causing modifications of the program designed to anticipate public demand—a minimum obeisance to the sovereign people. Third is the activity of organized lay groups. At the local level, the "citizens' committee" usually lacks any real power base and hence is stalemated by the disciplined ranks of the professionals if it tries to engage in curricular reform. Other lay groups, however, such as industrial associations, unions, and patriotic organizations often seek to influence the content of the curriculum; if they have electoral strength in the community, they may be hard to resist. At the state level they may have an easier time, for the legislators are not professional educators. In the legislature, the educators' professional associations constitute pressure groups competing with the lay organizations, in the familiar fashion of American politics. Perhaps the very fact that the legislature constitutes a battleground which educators cannot dominate is a basic reason for the professional insistence on local control. By making local control a virtual article of faith to which all good Americans, including state legislators, should subscribe, the educators have gained an advantage at every capitol. They can always argue politely and persuasively that regardless of the possible merit of any legislative proposal to require the teaching of particular subjects, discretion must be left to each school district. Compulsory uniformity would be a departure from the American way.

As for the quality of the teachers, it may be true, as Bestor and others have implied, that the kind of training prescribed as a prerequisite to entry into the profession discourages able men and women from becoming school teachers. It is a reasonable hypothesis, too, that the vested interests of the teacher-training institutions impose overwhelming obstacles to any radical reform, for the laymen who would like to substitute subject-matter scholarship for courses in pedagogy have two or maybe three strikes against them before they begin. They lack political power, they lack the experts' status, and they can find no short and simple answer to the question: "As teaching is a profession, why shouldn't prospective teachers be taught how to teach?" If the reform of teacher-training must precede the recruitment of an adequate number of new and highly competent teachers, it must be sparked by the profession itself—or so, at least, the political realities seem to suggest.

The profession by itself cannot, however, gain the other objective which must be reached if first-class teaching is to be the rule: it cannot raise the money needed to hire and retain excellent teachers. Good salaries, by themselves, do not produce good teachers, as Eurich has emphasized, but bad salaries certainly are a factor in driving able teachers into more remunerative pursuits and in keeping potentially fine prospects out of the schools. Here, and also in the matter of school buildings, the educators have taken the lead and have sought to stimulate organized lay support. Their professionalism does not greatly enhance their persuasiveness, for salary scales and classrooms are not occult mysteries. In fighting for financial support, therefore, their influence must stem less from their specialized knowledge than from their dedicated concern or their political power.

As a working hypothesis concerning the political system of public education, the following summary might be useful in facilitating analysis and putting the emphasis on the significant spots: As to what should be taught, generally the professionals are dominant, and this may be altogether necessary and proper. Their financial dependence on public approval makes them somewhat responsive to reasonable public demands, tactfully presented, although their very professionalism forces them to resist proposals of which they disapprove and causes them to react adversely to most lay criticism. Professional influence is usually preponderant in local districts where the school superintendent is, or can be, the leader of the school system. It is much weaker in the state legislatures, but even there it is aided by the tradition of local diversity and the easy access afforded by the presence of professionals in official state positions—the heads of teachers colleges and state departments of education. As to who should teach, the profession has generally sought state protection against pressures for local personal and partisan patronage. This protection, as a by-product, has solidified the position of the teachers college where most prospective teachers must be trained and which increasingly influence boards of education in the selection of superintendents. As for the acquisition of sufficient funds to build and run adequate schools, the decision-making authority rests partly in the school boards, partly in the local electorates, and partly in the state legislatures. To these lay groups the profession comes as supplicant, its demands competing with other demands (for highways, hospitals, etc.) and meeting the inevitable resistance of the taxpayer. If there are to be good schools, the competition must be largely won and the resistance broken down. To achieve these ends at the local level, the professionals seek to stimulate public interest in education, at the risk of lay interference with the schools. Their achievement at the state level depends more on the effectiveness of the professionals operating as pressure groups, with lay support which is less likely to involve lay dictation in curricular and personnel matters. At the federal level they have not yet been achieved. Unsuccessful drives for federal financial aid have been sparked by the largest professional pressure group and have been balked by a combination of three factors: the peripheral but highly charged issues of religion and race, the pocketbook interests of taxpayers in relatively wealthy states, and the traditional fear of central dictation. Perhaps only the passage of time can overcome the first of these obstacles, though acute public awareness of a national need for better schools might be enough. Such awareness is obviously needed to overcome the second. The third is not likely to be overcome without a more thorough, comprehensive analysis of its validity or unsoundness than has yet been forthcoming.

The fact that the professionals, who have the greatest power stake in local control, are the people least afraid of federal aid may be an indication of the needlessness of any fear of federal control. But it may also indicate something more basic. Is it conceivable that national financial aid and its concurrent possibility of national standards is acceptable to a national professional organization because that organization itself believes in or recognizes the existence of national standards? Perhaps we have been tending for a long time toward a greater degree of national educational uniformity than the old theory of local discretionary control implies. The professionalization of the school superintendency surely pushes us in that direction. The superintendent, like a city manager, moves from district to district. His methods may alter to conform to the local mores, but his basic educational philosophy remains the same. And, by all appearances, one modern superintendent's educational philosophy is likely to be much like another's, for more and more of them qualify for the position through studies at teachers colleges of largely similar outlook. The profession is certainly not intellectually monolithic, as the debates and disagreements in journals and conventions show; but it may well be growing more unified in its devotion to agreed-upon professional standards and goals.

If this is so, what is the future for the "diversity" which justifies unimpaired local control? If local control in the most fundamental matters —curriculum and teaching—is largely in professional hands, are there even now fewer significant differences between districts than was formerly the case? Granted that state requirements differ, that local interests may differentiate programs in rural districts from those in urban districts, and that the curricula and teaching in particular schools or districts take account of the varying backgrounds and objectives of the student population; still, the classifications are broad. In thousands of districts the educational needs are similar. Conant may disclaim any intention to provide a blueprint, but his recommendations are not intended as the basis for a single district's experimentation: they are aimed at innumerable American high schools. And, significantly, the professional reaction to the Conant report has included little, if any, objection to the basic curricular uniformity which it implies. Perhaps, then, at least within broad urban-rural or socio-economic categories, local diversity is or will soon be significant only with respect to those matters where professional domination is weakest: school buildings (including site selection), transportation of pupils, and finance. Decisions as to the last, assuming any real public desire for improved schooling, will continue gradually to move out of local hands and into the state legislatures.

Certainly the extent and nature of inter-district diversity in basic educational processes need prompt analysis. If, indeed, they are minimal, then the lay proponents of complete local control must be prepared to defend their position in terms of their convenience and their pocketbooks rather than their concern for educational content.

3

It is the business of everyone interested in education to insist upon the school as the primary and most effective instrument of social progress and reform in order that society may be awakened to realize what the school stands for, and aroused to the necessity of endowing the educator with sufficient equipment properly to perform his task.

JOHN DEWEY

Nicholas A. Masters
THE POLITICS OF PUBLIC EDUCATION

One of the most potent political instruments in the American setting is the educational enterprise. Although we have found it symbolically useful to regard schools as apart from politics, there is no escaping the fact that our schools are the agencies that "propagate the historical lore of the people, the myths, the beliefs and the faiths and thereby aid in the process of political indoctrination." In the modern industrial state the schools are the apparatus through which social stratification is either preserved or overcome. It has been an integral part of the American dream to use public education as the means for upward social and economic mobility for those disadvantaged by social background or birth.

The Role of Free, Public Education
in the American Political System

Stated differently, the United States was the first nation to establish free, public education. The theoretical justification for such a

From Nicholas Masters, "The Politics of Public Education," *Perspectives on Educational Administration and the Behavioral Sciences* (Eugene, Ore.: Center for the Advanced Study of Educational Administration, University of Oregon, 1965), pp. 111–119. Reprinted by permission of the Center.

pioneer effort was explicitly political. The Jeffersonian vision of a political and social order that would not bury its talents under the rigidities of a class structure was essential to the egalitarian doctrine which has become so much a part of our political thinking. To be sure, the ideal has never been fully attained. Despite the creation of public supported institutions of higher learning, particularly in the Midwestern, Southern, and Western regions of the nation, the costs of higher education have barred many from going beyond high school. And, of more critical and fundamental importance, our educational system has been allowed to develop and flourish at all levels and in all regions without any cognizance of the special problems of the Negro. It is not news to point out that in some parts of the nation the Negro is still deliberately excluded from the opportunities our educational system provides. (I am at this juncture setting aside entirely the attendant problem of lack of motivation as a bar to higher education for the sons and daughters of parents of low status.)

Education—A Factor in Preserving the Political, Social and Economic Order. The schools, of course, can only be used as avenues for upward social and economic success if they indoctrinate the children with the basic values of our political society. *To move upward and operate within a social and economic system requires acceptance of that system and loyalty to it.* It was no accident that compulsory universal education coincided with our pattern of industrialization. Educational programs were designed not only to staff the manpower needs of the industrial complex, but also to pump in fresh blood at managerial levels that were committed to the system as it was evolving. The economic leaders of earlier generations were not, I am sure, motivated entirely by the Jeffersonian ideals. They had a *vested interest* in seeing to it that we had a more highly skilled and educated population. Education, much to the chagrin of many liberal arts professors, is still linked with our industrial, technological, and military needs. And to this has been added a new dimension, the threat of a competitive external political system. In brief, education is an instrument for developing and preserving our political, social, and economic order.

It is obvious that any social institution that performs such a significant role is not going to be allowed to roam freely within the political structure. Groups and individuals which possess the resources of power and influence exert, or will exert when they feel the occasion demands, tremendous efforts to shape and mold the system to their way of thinking and to tailor the curriculum to meet their special technological and scientific needs.

The importance of the schools in the power system is glaringly visible in regimes of a revolutionary character. Textbooks are rewritten or burned, teachers are brought into line or dismissed. In such a system the revolutionary leaders are inevitably elevated into paragons. Deposed leaders are either condemned or erased from the pages of history. In our educational system, however, the influence of those dominant in the political system is a bit more subtle, mainly because we adhere to the myth that our educational enterprise is a free and independent one. Business, labor, religious, patriotic and sundry other groups all attempt, in one way or another, to make their influence felt but only certain groups allow their concern to lead them into *direct intervention* in school administration matters. Needless to say, it disturbs a number of people that a few groups, usually "patriotic" in character, demand to review textbooks or demand procedures that will assure a certain type of political orthodoxy or the transmission of the values of the American culture as they see it. Episodic acts of direct intervention are not the usual pattern, however, in which educational practices are affected. Less formal and direct pressures are involved. These pressures, I think, are worthy of some further comment.

School authorities are guided by what I shall call the *biases* in the social and economic system, as indeed are most other public and private officials. Schools, like other social institutions, operate within a framework of values, myths, established procedures, and rules of the game. I call these biases, and they are usually mobilized in a particular direction. America is a society characterized by wide consensus on many fundamental political principles. It takes little systematically planned effort or extensive intervention to see that these values are preserved and reinforced within an educational system. For example, no secondary school principal would allow his social studies teacher to condemn or severely criticize the concept of private property. The biases in favor of private property are much too firmly embedded to permit an extreme expression of a defiant view.

Labor unions, despite their recent rise in respectability and status, still find it more difficult to get their viewpoints objectively presented in our schools than do business groups. School systems throughout the nation sanction and encourage junior achievement groups which indirectly have a pro-business orientation. This is not to suggest that such activities are necessarily anti-labor, but I know of no comparable school endeavor designed to develop labor leadership.

The fact that our educational system is controlled by lay authorities, the majority of whom are property owners or professional people, people who have an interest in perpetuating our present political system, means that they are not going to encourage or allow school authorities to embark on an ideological crusade to bring about a sweeping new society which would be organized along entirely different lines. In brief, patterns of power, despite their occasional fluctuation and variations, are able to restrict the content of the educational program while perpetuating the myth of the non-political nature of education. *This means that the myth itself is politically functional.*

Education in the Political Arena. It really doesn't take very much imagination or understanding, then, to see that schools are important political instruments, that they play a vital function in social mobility, political socialization, and preservation of the political system. But aside from these broad considerations, schools enter the political struggle in other ways and become intensely involved in the competition for money and other tangible benefits necessary for their operation.

Before I get into specifics, however, I think I should discuss the concept of politics I am using. It has long been customary to say that politics is a dirty word. There is much truth in this view. Politics is a hard and cruel business. It is cruel because it involves conflict or competition and in any competitive struggle not everyone can emerge victorious. To lose when the stakes are high, whether it be in poker, business, love or war, is never easy. A school principal, for example, who appeals to lay boards for a salary increase for his staff may well be placing his job in jeopardy. The ability of a professional group to represent effectively the interest of its members inevitably determines its or its leaders' longevity. The extent to which a professor concerns himself with research has an indelible impact on his career. Yet research funds and facilities are not unlimited. He must compete to secure them. As long as resources are scarce or not unlimited, politics will enter into all phases of man's life. Education is no exception.

To be sure, the ordinary conception of "politics" is that it involves some forms of favoritism or corruption. When someone says that politics was involved in this or that decision he usually means that a particular group received a favor to which it was not entitled. If the favor is outside the limits of the law, corruption is obviously involved; on the other hand, if all legal requirements are met, then the charge is simply "dirty politics." Certainly within the context that I shall use the term, politics involves the promotions of one's interest and the *use* of whatever resources are at one's disposal to protect that interest. Such activity may or may not involve corruption or favoritism.

Resources of Influence. Before proceeding with the examples, I should comment on what I mean by resources of power or influence. Resources are those objects tangible and intangible which are in demand and in short supply. Examples would be money and credit, votes, jobs, information, and status and prestige. Control of the dispensation of these items or commodities is what constitutes a power base. For example, the United Auto Workers in Detroit has extensive influence on many out-state Democratic organizations, including those in cities where there is no union membership. Query: What resources of influence can the UAW in Detroit bring to bear upon outstate organizations? The answer lies in the UAW's selective allocation of workmen's compensation cases involving union members to prominent outstate attorneys. Obviously such allocations are meant to be functional for the UAW's political purposes.

Educators abhor the idea that favoritism or corruption could ever be involved in any of their policies, deliberations or activities. Education must always be above the various confines of the interest of a particular group. Education must be in the "public interest" and the public is discussed as if it were an organized entity. But such is merely the language or symbolism used. Everyone who has ever been involved knows that decisions are not made in a public interest vacuum. The symbols serve *mainly to ornament the prose rather than to enlighten one about objective reality.* Yet, as I have said earlier, we continue to discuss educational decision-making in largely symbolic terms.

The purpose of this paper is to present a limited amount of evidence in order that the statements we make about our educational system will more closely fit the observable realities.

In seeking to unravel the puzzle of the place of politics in our educational system, I shall rely largely on the unstructured interviews I have had with hundreds of state educational, legislative, and administrative leaders. I assure you, however, that I do not intend to engage in muckraking or to magnify the importance of any particular political practice. My aim is to identify those who seek to influence the content of educational policy and the type and nature of the resources they utilize.

Educational Interests and Resources of Influence

Despite the rather extensive literature on the functions and activities of both organized and unorganized interests in our society, precise information about their political influence is often lacking. This is particularly true with regard to the activities of various interests in education. There are a number of difficulties that stand in the way of systematic analysis. First, we are unaccustomed to the idea that educational interests are engaged in political activity. Second, all group leaderships, and *educational leaders are no exception,* have a vital interest in concealing information. That is, they do not want all of their activities exposed to the public. And third, generalizations applicable to some groups miss the mark entirely when applied to others. But whatever the group or interest involved, whether it be large or small, well-heeled or desperately poor, each must use whatever resources it has at its disposal to affect the outcome.

The Junior College Movement. Let us examine, for example, the junior college movement in the United States. Almost every state has embarked on a program to expand the opportunities for higher education through the chartering of so-called junior colleges. These colleges, it is alleged, serve a dual function. First, they provide vocational training for those not qualified to go any further. And second, they serve as a feeder to institutions of higher learning, weeding out those who do not qualify.

These purposes, however, are often ignored by politically ambitious groups, particularly when there is no state-wide planning machinery.

Pressure mounts from all types of sources to transform a two-year college into a four-year institution and if this is accomplished, to transform a four-year institution into one offering a graduate program. These pressures take many forms. Heavy contributors to legislative candidates may "put the heat on" a local legislator in order to get him to push for expansion of the junior college. Obviously they perceive such expansion as beneficial to their financial interests. The institution itself becomes an entity capable of wielding pressure. Its spokesmen have status in the community and thus help to mobilize public opinion. Often overlooked is that educational institutions are large consumers and thus have some leverage over those who supply them. It should come as no shock that these levers are often used by a junior college president or dean to force suppliers to pressure the legislature to promote the college's interest.

The junior college movement has provided the field for another type of political battle. Should the teachers in community colleges be certified under existing state requirements in the same way as elementary and secondary teachers, or are the teachers in junior colleges to be treated the same as professors and not required to meet any certification requirements at all? Involved here is the often bitter struggle between liberal arts professors and educationists. Also involved is the opportunity for the state affiliates of the NEA to expand their membership and thus expand their opportunities to influence public policy. This cursory examination of junior college issues should suggest some of the ways in which education and politics merge.

Selection of School Board Members. Another "issue," if I may call it that, which affects every locale and every state is the selection of school board members. In Michigan, for example, the nominations of both parties for members of the State Board of Education are used to: a) provide an opportunity for a politically ambitious young man or woman to run on a state-wide ticket, and b) satisfy the wishes and desires of the state's main educational interests, particularly the Michigan Education Association and the Michigan Federation of Teachers. If this state, however, were ever to move toward the state-wide adoption of textbooks, then I suspect the politics of these nominations would be more along the lines found in the California system. In that state, certain textbook companies contribute substantial sums of money to the campaign coffers or the party coffers of those whom they feel will best represent their interests. I think I can safely say at this point that the importance of campaign finance and the extent to which money can buy influence within the educational system is badly overlooked and misunderstood.

In Chicago, New York, St. Louis, and Detroit the selection or election of the board members follows a pattern in which the influence of certain clearly identifiable interests are apparent. Negro groups, capable of marshalling tremendous financial resources as well as having deliverable votes, demand and get a representation on the board. It would be unthinkable for Wayne County Democrats to ignore the wishes of Negro groups on such a crucial matter.

The protection of certain interests through the appointment or election of supporters of that interest does not stop at the board level. In New York, it is customary to have a Jew, a Catholic, and a Protestant as assistant superintendents. When Negro groups complained of lack of representation at this level, a Negro Catholic was appointed, but only after a bitter fight within the board during which the Catholic members led the opposition.

The Church-State Issue. Another significant battle concerns the extent to which, or whether at all, church-related schools ought to be aided with public funds. Here the competition for scarce resources takes on a new dimension, dividing the educational community itself along religious lines. The First Amendment to the U.S. Constitution provides that "Congress shall make no law respecting an establishment of religion, or prohibiting the free exercise thereof." The U.S. Supreme Court has interpreted the so called "establishment clause" as stating a principle applicable to Federal and State government: government may not act to burden the free exercise of religion, and it may not act to benefit religion. Moreover, many states have similar constitutional or statutory provisions. Significantly, however, none of the church-state cases that has reached the Supreme Court has dealt *directly* with the constitutionality of a government's allocating money to a church-related institution for the purpose of aiding education, where the main purpose of the institution is considered to be education and not religion. Thus the battle over a proper interpretation of the First Amendment in this regard still rages at the Federal level, and within those states where the State Supreme Court has not dealt with such a case directly and declared public support of parochial schools to be violative of the state constitution. The National Education Association and various of its state affiliates have been in the forefront of the battle, exerting every effort to block the appropriation of public revenue to private schools.

As the positions of the antagonists have rigidified, the church-state issue has become (for the time being) non-negotiable at the elementary and secondary level, and the exacerbation of Protestant-Catholic animosities within Congress have divided the proponents of Federal-aid-to-education proposals so that Congress is immobile in this area.

The Federal Aid Issue. The Federal-aid-to-education issue involves yet another set of political conflicts at the state and local level. First is the basic question of *whether* Federal aid is desirable. Although the NEA and its affiliates continually represent the professional educators as being in favor of Federal aid, laymen who exercise formal control as school board members or informal influence as prestigious members of the community often oppose Federal aid. A host of liberal-conservative perspectives is involved here, mostly in terms of the scope of Federal activity and the locus of decision-making. Aside from the ideological question of whether the Federal government ought to widen its scope of activities to include direct aid to education, there is a more important question of *power* involved. Local influentials want the important decisions to be made at the local level where they exert control. Thus the ghost of "Federal Control" becomes real to them, and they oppose any increase in Washington's role *vis-à-vis* that of Centerville. On the other hand, those who stand to benefit economically from increased public expenditures prefer to broaden the scope of effective decision-making to the Federal level where they have more relative influence.

Additionally, the Federal-aid-to-education issue engenders controversy over the intended machinery of administering the proposed program. Groups compete to be named in the bill as potential representatives on any special state authority that might be created to administer a Federal aid program.

Competition Between Educational Levels. A related political battle concerns the competition between higher education and the public schools over the allocation of scarce resources. At the national level one need only point to the role of the NEA in defeating the college aid bill of 1962, and the consequent refusal the next year on the part of college-aid advocates in the House of Representatives even to consider a proposal for aid to elementary and secondary schools. At the state level there not only exists a similar dichotomy, but within some states, such as Wisconsin, the teachers' colleges and the University, under separate and autonomous boards of regents, compete for their respective allocations of the higher education share of public funds.

The Effectiveness of Educational Interest Groups. No sophisticated analyst supposes that the participants involved in the conflicts outlined above merely sit back and wait for public largesse because of the symbolic position they occupy in American society. Rather, these groups and individuals are involved directly in making claims on government. They are engaged in politics. They serve a function for the political system through their articulation of policy demands and their provision of political support for the demands.

Whether the educational interests are particularly effective in the political arena is altogether another question, but it is interesting to examine the NEA in this regard. In terms of the general status of its members (professionals), the legitimacy of the organization and the societal function it promotes (education), and the access its legislative division enjoys to governmental decision-makers, the NEA possesses the prerequisites of effectiveness as enunciated by most students of group theory. Yet, after 30 years' effort, the organization has been unable to secure passage of a direct Federal-aid-to-education bill!

What are the factors that tend to weaken the NEA as a political force? *First* is its regional character. The NEA is essentially a Western, Midwestern and Southern organization—that is, a rural, middle class organization in a rapidly industrializing, urbanizing society. In the larger cities the NEA must compete with teachers' unions, and often the union is the stronger of the two. *Second* is the membership character of the association. Classroom teachers are primarily young women, most of whom eventually leave the profession altogether, or severely limit their interest and participation after they become married and begin to rear families. This turnover of membership is a debilitating factor from the standpoint of maintaining a cohesive, active membership base as a political resource with which to reward friends and punish enemies.

The purpose of this article has been to demonstrate that schools at all levels are important instruments through which the social and economic values of a political system are transmitted, and to show that the schools also are identifiable political entities capable of wielding resources of their own. An attempt has been made to focus on some of the more outstanding educational issues to show that no matter how exercised school authorities may become over the charge, education is very much a part of politics.

4

The control and operation of education in America must remain the responsibility of State and local governments and private institutions. This tradition assures our educational system of the freedom, the diversity and the vitality necessary to serve our free society fully. But the Congress has long recognized the responsibility of the nation as a whole—that additional resources, meaningful encouragement and vigorous leadership must be added to the total effort by the Federal Government if we are to meet the task before us.

JOHN F. KENNEDY, 1962

LuVern L. Cunningham
FEDERAL INTERVENTION IN EDUCATION

In February, 1965, Peter F. Drucker, writing in *Harper's*, described some of the more prominent themes emerging in American life.

From LuVern Cunningham, "Federal Intervention in Education" and "Federal Role in Education Arouses Growing Concern Among School Officials," a two-part series of articles, *American School Board Journal*, April, 1966, pp. 7, 8, 51, and May, 1966, pp. 7, 63, 64. Reprinted by permission of the publisher.

Drucker identified, for example, an emergent center of power, wrapped up in the current crop of young people now in high schools and colleges throughout the country; he emphasized their predilections toward independence and their unwillingness to accept easily the political philosophies of our contemporary Democrat and Republican parties. Drucker was in a sense serving notice on the generation now controlling American life: "shape up or ship out."

Drucker went on to outline what in his judgment will become, in the immediate years ahead, the two parallel foci of domestic politics—the metropolis and the school. There will be a sustained set of enrollment increases with the obvious consequences of dramatic increases in the costs of education. And it will be impossible to avoid large-scale federal support for education; furthermore, it is sheer hypocrisy to pretend that federal control of education is possible without a considerable measure of national control. Indeed, he implied that some national control was desirable.

School-Centered Society

Our society will be school-centered; at least one third of the American people will be in school all of the time contrasted with one fourth who are there now. Total school expenditures will exceed our present defense budget by a substantial amount, and at the same time the structure of American education, its purposes, values, content, and direction, will become issues in which more and more people will become involved openly and emotionally. Drucker labels this new circumstance "the knowledge state." "Education is bound to become the focus of political life and political conflicts," a statement with which more and more school officials will not disagree.

So far, in Drucker's view, we have not even begun to think through national policies on education, let alone national commitment to educational values and purposes. "All we have so far—and it is a great deal—is a national commitment to education in quantity, and for everyone."

Education Contains Debate

The history of American education contains a fascinating chronicle of the debate surrounding the federal government and education. The issues which we explore in this article are not new; thus I doubt that we will enter any perspectives on the register that have not been recorded before.

The *Chicago Tribune* on September 17, 1881, carried an editorial entitled "The Sinking Fund and National Education"; it was an eloquent appeal for the federal government to provide a standing appropriation of $50 million annually in the aid of national education. The *Tribune's* plea was based on an increasing national affluence; funds were to be transferred to the schools from the sinking fund used to bolster public credit. The monies would have been distributed on a per capita basis. Later on in the same year the *Tribune* proposed a national whiskey tax, the revenue to be distributed for the support of the schools.

Even earlier in 1881, the *Tribune* supported federal aid to local schools and pressed for the close supervision of federal funds on the grounds that schools in the South were guilty of using textbooks that were filled with "treasonable nonsense." It is significant to note that the press in Chicago 80 years ago cited, regularly, deplorable educational circumstances in the South as justification for large-scale federal entry into the support of public education.

Perspectives on Federal Participation

The 1880's was the period when polarizations of perspectives on federal participation occurred. Cremin has observed that the debates over the several Blair bills, introduced in the 1880's, served to crystallize opinion and that there was more interest on the question then than any time up to the immediate post-World War II period. Henry W. Blair (Rep. N. H.) proposed his bill "to aid in the establishment and temporary support of common schools" five times during the 1880's.

Although there were some differences in the several bills introduced by Blair, in general they called for the following conditions in order for states to qualify for federal money:

1. Maintenance of a common school system for all of its children of school age;
2. A willingness to supply school statistics and information to the Secretary of the Interior;
3. A curriculum to include "the art of reading, writing, and speaking the English language, arithmetic, geography, history of the United States, and such other branches of useful knowledge as may be taught under local laws";
4. The provision that no funds received under the act be spent on school rental or construction, and that funds be used only for common, nonsectarian schools;
5. States and territories would have to match through local initiative the amounts of federal grants;
6. Portions of federal money might be expended for teacher training.

Briefly, the farm, labor, and business interest groups tended to favor the legislation; the Catholics opposed it; the education profession, as usual, was sharply divided. The Republicans, in general, supported the Blair bills; the Democrats lined up against them.

Summarized views

Gordon Lee summarized the views on the Blair bills in a dissertation completed at Columbia in 1949. The supporting arguments ran as follows:

1. A literate electorate, hence an adequate, effective school system throughout the nation is essential to the maintenance of democratic government.

2. Federal aid to education is unquestionably constitutional.

3. There is ample historical precedent for federal aid to education.

4. The legislation is the logical consequence of the winning of the Civil War and the enfranchisement of the Negroes.

5. Although the greater part of the bill's benefits accrue to the South, it is designed to meet the educational needs of the whole nation.

6. The bill is designed so that initial financial requirements on the states (matching federal grants) are small, and rise gradually as the life of the bill progresses.

7. Any bill of this nature would necessitate the imposition of certain requirements by the federal government on the states.

8. The bill involves only a temporary commitment of the federal government.

9. Public opinion definitely supports the bill, and Congress must respond to it.

The opposing contentions were:

1. Legislation of this sort will undermine the foundation of the government by causing the states to be dependent on the federal government.

2. No constitutional authority exists for legislating on the matter of education.

3. The historic precedents of land grants for education do not hold in this case.

4. Federal participation in education will inevitably introduce party politics into the schools.

5. The need for federal aid to education is nonexistent. The South is slowly but surely developing the ability to meet its own educational needs.

6. Unless states receiving federal money match these grants from the beginning, local initiative will be destroyed.

7. The proposal imposes too many conditions on the recipient states.

8. The idea of this measure as a temporary one is unrealistic. There will be tremendous pressure for its continuance.

9. The public has not expressed itself in favor of this measure sufficiently to warrant its adoption.

The abbreviated historical overview is my way of opening up the contemporary role of the federal government in education to examination. Like Robert Taft, I draw a distinction between the federal government "interfering" to regulate the people of the states, to take over the business of state and local governments and extending its power that way, and the federal government assisting the states. To quote Taft:

> Because of the way wealth is distributed in the United States I think we have a responsibility to see if we cannot eliminate hardship, poverty, and inequality of opportunity, to the best of our ability. I do not believe we are able to do it without a Federal aid system.

The roots of the Great Society's adventure into public education run deep; the Great Society programs manifest both Democrat and Republican chromosomes. Likewise the misgivings about the federal government and education are of long standing and reflect genuine anxieties that must be acknowledged and in my judgment dealt with. The federal government is here to stay in education and our task as local officials is essentially that of sustaining the Taft distinction—the federal government role is that of servant, not of master.

Interventions in the 1930's

I am impressed with the similarity between our behavior in 1966 with the apparent behavior of public school administrators 30 years ago. Most of us have forgotten the large number of federal laws containing provisions for public schools which were enacted in response to depression-induced conditions in the early and mid 1930's. During that period there were nine agencies of the relief and recovery programs of the federal government which were of importance to the public schools. They were the National Recovery Administration, the Agricultural Adjustment Administration, the Emergency Conservation Work Corps, later designated the Civilian Conservation Corps, the Civil Works Administration, the National Planning Board, the Public Works Administration, the Federal Emergency Relief Administration, and the National Emergency Councils. Among these the most prominent were the Federal Emergency Relief Administration, the Public Works Administration, and the Civil Works Administration.

Improved Social Life

The features in these programs included putting unemployed teachers to work in specially designed adult-education activities, providing leadership for "mental employment" and diversion for adults as well as children who were victims of unemployment, keeping rural school districts open, teaching reading and writing of English to adult illiterates in big cities, providing vocational training for unemployed adults, especially those who had been displaced through technological advances, rehabilitating farm families as well as urban dwellers who had been uprooted because of unemployment or migration away from submarginal land, aiding college students, and assisting nursery schools. Other legislation provided assistance on school building construction projects, as well as help with maintenance problems.

William Claude Reavis, professor of school administration at the University of Chicago at that time, summarized the impact of these several laws on the schools of Illinois in 1935. His analysis was thus:

1. The administrative experience of the school superintendent has been greatly enriched through the new problems which have been presented to them by the efforts of the federal government to promote recovery and to improve the conditions of social life. Some of the innovations which have been introduced into the schools might not have come by the process of evolution for many years. Local school systems now have federally supported nursery schools, general adult education projects, vocational rehabilitation and adjustment work, and classes for illiterates. The issue which confronts the local superintendent as the educational leader in his community is whether these activities shall be properly integrated with the local school program or allowed to grow sporadically in semi-educational isolation.

2. The federal government has shown its disinclination to usurp or to infringe on the local control of schools. If through diffidence or the abdication of responsibilities, the city school superintendents of Illinois compel the federal government to provide supervision and direction of the federally sponsored projects which the local superintendent should have provided, the censure for the complications which may arise must be borne by the local superintendents. The situation as it now exists calls for cooperation and tactful leadership in every urban community in the state . . . too many superintendents have yielded to other leadership in taking advantage of the opportunities provided through the federal projects.

3. . . . some city superintendents in Illinois have a defensive mental set toward educational change. The projects undertaken through federal aid in the local communities should be vitalized through the guiding leadership of the local superintendents. For a superintendent to permit traditional practices to prevail when new practices are required in meeting the federally sponsored projects in school communities reveals a weakness in professional leadership which cannot be condoned. The time is opportune for a shift to the

offensive in public school administration, and federal participation affords both the occasion and the challenge.

Obviously there are some sharp parallels in Reavis' analysis to our current situation. Reavis was calling vigorously for local school men to help draw and keep clear the master-servant distinction. Given Drucker's forecast, a growing realization that education is vital to the national interests, and because the states and local governments are finding themselves incapable of fulfilling their responsibilities for education in many instances, I suspect our alternatives are limited. Thus we must seek ways of making our complex system of government work for us. Indeed in President Johnson's message on January 12, there was language sufficient to cover this point plus a plan of action. Johnson recommended:

> To examine our Federal system—the relation between city, state, nation, and citizens—we need a commission of the most distinguished scholars and men of public affairs. I will ask them to move on to develop a creative federalism to best use the wonderful diversity of our institutions and people to solve the problems, fulfill the dreams of the American people.

Many of our critical reactions, as school people, to present efforts of the federal government are essentially negative responses to initiatory behaviors coming from the office of the President. We have not known a strong chief executive committed to education before, and now that we have him, we are finding it hard to cope with. In the past, we have looked to Congress and directed our lobbying energies toward senators and members of the House. We have not experienced, as a profession, the problems of relating to an executive branch that has strengthened education as a principal national objective. I suspect that our frustrations are matched by those of many congressmen who also have found it difficult to influence the executive branch of government.

Unable to Adjust

The best way I can describe our behaviors as administrators is that we are unable to make the adjustment from "initiators" to "responders." For decades professional educators have been pushing, fighting, clawing, clearing the way toward what was defined as an educational Hallelujah land. Now we are being pulled, or tugged along to better education, and our intuitive response is to set our feet, dig in our heels, and defy those "bad buys" from Washington. It has been interesting to note how quickly the lines were drawn in the Chicago dispute over Title I funds. The language was indicative; the "feds" were in town and everybody knew it. The attitude of the "fans in the stands" was "Why can't they just leave us our money and get out of town?" And "Why should we have to sign the receipt?"

We have under way, at the University of Chicago, a doctoral dissertation on the subject of "Political Action and National Policy Formation in Education." The purpose of the study is to trace the evolution of Public Law 89–10 and especially the role of President Johnson in its formulation and passage. All of us are familiar with the fate of dozens of federal-aid bills, some similar to 89–10. Past attempts have been replete with conflict among the many interest groups concerned. No consensus in support of a specific program had ever been achieved among the groups favoring some type of federal aid. Conflicts have revolved around such issues as race, religion, federal control, equalization, construction, and salaries. No individual or group was able to resolve these conflicts and thus create an effective alliance among the forces in favor of federal aid. Presidential support of federal aid bills has never been of sufficient intensity to give the necessary impetus to such proposals.

Aid Bill Enacted

Yet, suddenly, in early 1965 the nation witnessed the proposal, passage, and enactment of a substantial federal-aid bill. The entire sequence of events—from proposal through congressional study, debate, and passage, to presidential signing—required a period of 90 days. In view of all the negative factors noted previously—both governmental and nongovernmental—how was such a major piece of legislation successfully escorted through "the hazardous and labyrinthine" passages of the legislative process?

Kearney, the student doing the dissertation referred to above, believes that the President very skillfully structured events to ensure success with his educational legislative proposals. Let me quote from Kearney's research prospectus:

> Perhaps one strategy of President Johnson which contributed substantially to the enactment of the Elementary and Secondary Education Act of 1965 was the formation of the President's Task Force on Education. The Task Force was convened before the election with very little fanfare. Apparently the membership was never widely circulated, if announced publicly at all. John Gardner, then of the Carnegie Foundation and presently Secretary of the Department of Health, Education and Welfare, headed the group. Membership included: James E. Allen, Jr., Commissioner of Education, Albany, New York; Hadley W. Donovan, Editor, Time Magazine; Harold B. Gores, President, Educational Facilities Laboratory; Clark Kerr, President, University of California; Edwin H. Land, President, Polaroid Corporation; Sidney P. Marland, Superintendent of Schools, Pittsburgh, Pennsylvania; David Riesman, Professor, Harvard University; Father Paul C. Reinert, President, St. Louis University; Raymond R. Tucker, Mayor, St. Louis, Missouri; Ralph

W. Tyler, Director, Center for Advanced Study in the Behavioral Sciences, Stanford, California; Stephen J. Wright, President, Fisk University; Jerrold R. Zacharias, Professor, Massachusetts Institute of Technology; and *ex officio* member, Francis Keppel, U.S. Commissioner of Education.

President's Role

Tom Wicker described Lyndon Johnson's role in the passage of 89–10 in a *New York Times* story in April of last year; his observations support Kearney's perspectives. Wicker wrote:

> The fundamental reason for Congressional accomplishments so far is the big majority President Johnson carried into office with him in his landslide victory in the 1964 election.
>
> Still the speed of action so far and the total prospects for the year owe a good deal also to the effective strategy of the President and his legislative leaders, particularly their timing.
>
> Seizing on the momentum of his election, Mr. Johnson laid out his program and started sending bills and messages almost three weeks before his inauguration. He kept the pressure on with a constant flood of messages and proposals. . . .
>
> Mr. Johnson also deliberately set his priorities to get the medical and education controversies out of the way early. He and his leaders adapted their tactics, in each case, to take account of differing situations.
>
> The education bill, for instance, was developed entirely at the White House, with the general agreement of both Roman Catholic and Protestant leaders, education groups and important members of Congress. Then it was rammed through both Houses without change, on Mr. Johnson's insistence.
>
> The President also paid careful attention to personal lobbying . . . and in general has heightened the Congressional sense of rapport with the Executive.

Little more needs to be said if we reflect on the composition of the Task Force. The principal difference between our circumstances in 1966 and those described by Reavis in 1935 is the magnitude of the interventions and the power of the office of the President vis-à-vis the educational community. There is no doubt that President Johnson wants action, indeed specific kinds of action, and soon. There is no doubt either that he will have his way, even at great cost to the traditional way of doing things, unless the educational community can come up with a strategy for blending its influence into and through the new national power structure for education.

The Elusive Concept of "Control"

Recently I made a limited examination of the role of the federal government relative to a single need—that of in-service training of professionals in education. The scope and variety of federally sponsored in-service programs adds up to an impressive set of opportunities for professional improvements. It is difficult to conclude that there are overt, or even veiled attempts on the part of the federal government to dictate, or take over, or even weaken local school government through these programs. On the contrary, the important features in all of these acts seem to me to be options, not demands; they are occasions for local districts to capitalize on resources not available to them until now. In brief, I could find no evidence in these programs of the loss of local control.

We have prided ourselves in local school government and local school control, although some critics of school government in the United States believe that we make a fetish out of this notion and that it has worked to our disadvantage. I believe firmly in local school boards and local school districts; I think that the genius of American education can be attributed directly to the input of intelligence and wisdom from hundreds of thousands of citizens serving on local boards for more than a hundred years. I would not for a minute entertain the notion of moving away from this system of school organization and control.

Influences Cited

Contemporary critics of educational government have argued that local school boards are not making significant decisions about our schools anymore. These decisions, they maintain, are being made outside of the schools by foundations, professional organizations, state legislatures, and the big, bad federal government. They believe that local school boards are placed in the position of deciding only whether or not to become involved in, or the endorsement of, programs which originate outside of the local district. The evidence is clear that a host of "national influences" have been affecting our schools in recent years—but outside influences have always been bearing down on local school boards, and they always will.

What we do as local school officials is a curious blend of acting, and being acted upon. Local school decision-making does not go forward within isolated, autonomous decision bodies; it never has and it never will. But this does not reduce the significance of local school decision-making. We exist in a very political world; when we are visited by delegations of local patrons, our behavior is affected. When we are urged to apply for funds available under Title I of the Elementary and Secondary Education Act by special-interest groups, our behavior is affected. When we adopt a set of curriculum materials, textbook series, or what have you, our decisions are based on information that we have available to us from publishers, from other administrators, from whatever sources we can locate. There is an ebb and flow of influence occurring in all group decision contexts. It is not strange then to expect that federal programs will influence local policy; it is likewise reasonable to expect local school actions to influence federal programs.

In terms of local school districts and local administrators in our relationships with other units of government, I think that it is imperative that we be actors, rather than be acted upon—that we initiate, rather than respond; that we maintain a constant press upon state and federal governments for efficient and equitable administration of federal-financed educational programs. This is the essence of local responsibility.

Control is an extremely difficult thing to be explicit about. When we say that we are losing local control, I suspect we are saying that we are permitting ourselves to be influenced. Actually it is difficult to know who is controlling whom as we view the problems of administering current legislation. I am fairly confident that the "feds" vis ting Chicago in the enforcement of Title VI of the 1964 Civil Rights Act are not at all clear on this point. Most of us will agree that to challenge Superintendent Ben Willis is not a choice one would make if he had other alternatives.

We are in a trying period at the present time—it is difficult for those who must administer federal programs at the federal, state, and local levels. It is partially a case of too much too soon. At the same time, it is a case of men of goodwill and good intent being called upon to set in motion large-scale machinery, for which there is little precedent, scarce manpower, and, in terms of what has been demonstrated thus far, inept leadership. There will continue to be actions on the part of officials at all three levels of government which will appear to be arbitrary, even capricious, but much of this is to be expected. It is a part of the shake-down period in any large, new enterprise.

Summation and Recommendations

To say that there is growing concern about the role of the federal government in education is to understate the case. There appears to be a ground swell of disquiet. The continuing controversy over the withholding of funds from the Chicago public schools is just one example of an upsetting interaction between an agency of the federal branch of government, a state department of education, and a local system of schools (albeit the third largest public school system in the nation). It is but one of many that has occurred recently, involving chiefly the administration of Title VI of the Civil Rights Act of 1964. From the perspective of the local school administrator and school board member it appears that the federal government has flexed its muscles and violated the sacred language of the preambles to all federal-aid bills which stipulate, at considerable length, the non-control features in the laws. It appears that the

U.S. Office of Education and its series of "able young Commissioners" has trespassed upon the sacred preserve of state and local responsibility for education. (Note please that I have used the word "appears to have" since I doubt that we have been privy to all of the facts, from our positions as rather distant observers.)

As a further example of current concern about the role of the federal government in education one might cite the plans for the creation of interstate compacts, designed to tie together states that could, among other things, stand between the federal government and the state and local school systems. The five autumn conferences sponsored by the National School Boards Association in Chicago, New York, Atlanta, Denver, and San Francisco were addressed to "The Challenge Facing Lay Control of Education." As described in *Schoolboards,* these conferences were to focus on the increasing number of federal public education programs and the resulting pressures on local and state education agencies administering these programs. The conferences were to have provided opportunities for reformulating and redefining local responsibilities; identifying existing weaknesses in local and state machinery, and developing the kind of action which would remedy present inadequacies.

The anxieties evidenced by the National School Boards Association are shared to some extent by state and national associations of school administrators. The modest role played in last summer's White House Conference on Education by the National School Boards Association and the National Education Association gave pause to large numbers of traditional leaders of American education. Obviously there have been some substantial shifts in the leadership of public education, not only in terms of an emerging sharing of functions, but also in terms of the people who are calling the shots and establishing long-range directions for our schools.

As described earlier, we have witnessed the emergence of the executive office of the President as the center for educational policy midway in the decade of the 1960's. The long-time champions of broader participation on the part of the federal government in the financing of education cannot but have stood by in awe as they witnessed the passage of Public Law 89–10.

Sharing Responsibilities

Campbell and Sroufe have constructed a rationale for refining a more meaningful local-state-federal partnership among the three levels of government. Essential components of their proposal are the presence of (1) the sharing of responsibility for support of education; (2) strength in each of the three partners; (3) creative exercise of plenary power on the part of the state; (4) delegation of school operation to local districts; and (5) reservation of federal participation to the identification and support of national educational needs through state and local units.

Such a partnership, in my judgment, is not only defensible, but it is achievable. It is our responsibility as local school officials to work in that direction. As I see the particulars of our response to current federal interventions they are these:

1. We acknowledge the well-established precedent for large-scale participation in educational affairs on the part of the federal government;
2. We avoid assiduously the role of responder rather than initiator of educational policy;
3. We keep a sustained press on state and federal government administrators to insure efficient and equitable administration of the law;
4. We share freely with our congressmen our reactions to contemporary federal policy and keep them informed about state and local needs;
5. We capitalize thoroughly on present options for educational improvement available under federal auspices;
6. We continue to initiate local programs with local resources, and avoid the establishment of a dependency psychology;
7. We work toward the perfection of a viable local-state-national partnership, protecting always against the defilement of rights, privileges, and obligations of any one of the partners;
8. We exhibit maturity in our performance of the local partner role, since that role is by far the most pervasive in its impact and relevant to the perpetuation of local responsibility in American life.

5

The Federal Government has stepped up its participation and has an increasing impact everywhere in the field of education so that one of the questions that confronts [the states] is whether we shall continue to be led by these trends or take steps to lead and thus shape them ourselves. . . . We can and must play a more forceful role, most of us governors think, in determining the direction and content of educational change. . . . Though education is changing, we must not accept a reduced role for the states in developing educational policy.

RICHARD J. HUGHES

James B. Conant

THE ROLE OF THE STATES IN EDUCATION: THE FEDERAL GOVERNMENT A JUNIOR PARTNER

There has been a good deal of talk in recent years about the need for a national educational policy. As I have studied public education in this country at all levels, I have become more and more convinced that the phase "a national educational policy" is misleading. To be sure, a nation which has a centralized government does have a national educational policy. France is an example. So too is Sweden. Laws passed by the national Swedish parliament have recently transformed the whole structure of the educational system. But in a nation in which the basic governmental structure is in part Federal—as in the United States or Switzerland or the Federal Republic of Germany—one can hardly speak with meaning about a national educational policy. Each of the separate States in the United States has a more or less definite policy. And one could say that the summation of these policies plus certain Federal enactments and decisions constituted something approaching a vague nationwide policy.

Some people are quick to point out that in the last few years the Federal Government and the Federal judiciary have come to play an increasingly greater role. This is true. But the structure of our educational system is such that the Federal Government by itself cannot formulate and implement a national policy. Why? Because the power to establish and regulate elementary and secondary schools has so long rested with each State. So too it has the power to charter and establish colleges, universities and teacher training institutions.

The U.S. Commissioner of Education, Francis Keppel, said, and I quote:

> "In the long run nothing that we in education can do, whether in Washington or anywhere else, can be more important than strengthening the capacity of our States to respond to the educatonal needs of our time * * *. In education we look to the States to respond to the educational needs of our time * * *. In education we look to the States not merely as a matter of law or precedent, but as a matter of practical soundness and necessity. In this Nation of 50 States with vast and independent enterprises for education, the Federal Gov-

From James B. Conant, "The Role of the States in Education: The Federal Government a Junior Partner," *Vital Speeches of the Day*, September, 1965, pp. 686–688. Reprinted by permission of the publisher.

ernment can help as a partner, but only as a partner * * * and a somewhat junior partner at that."

I can do no better, this morning, than to take as my theme the Commissioner's words "the Federal Government as a junior partner" and add my own words—a partner in shaping a new and better nationwide educational policy.

Now we must all recognize the fact that in the last few years the resources and power of this junior partner have increased rapidly and enormously. There can be no doubt about it. The Congress of the United States and the electorate from which it derives its power have decided to make education throughout the Nation a matter of top priority. I see no signs that this trend will change. Quite the contrary. Right now the wise expenditure of Federal funds in the various States presents a set of complex administrative problems.

In any enterprise, public or private, spending money to implement a policy is difficult. But if the policy is not clear the wise expenditure of money becomes so confused as to be almost hopeless. And it is my contention that we have not as yet developed a clear nationwide educational policy adequate to meet the demands of the American public in the 1960's. Furthermore, we have no political machinery to enable the States to work together with each other and with the authorities in Washington to develop a 1960 model of a nationwide policy.

To be sure, the Council of Chief State School Officers has performed and continues to perform a most useful function. But in each State, with a few exceptions, the chief State school officer is concerned primarily with public elementary and secondary schools. And it is in regard to education beyond the high school that we find the greatest diversity among the States and the greatest uncertainty in many States as to what to do in the next few years.

In more than one State the question is being asked, How shall we expand public educational facilities for grades 13 and 14? Should we follow the California pattern with many 2-year community colleges, closely linked with both 4-year and multipurpose State colleges and a State university? Or shall we follow the lead of Indiana by establishing 2-year branches of the State university throughout the State? There is no study in depth of the experience of the different States in this vital matter. There is no way in which a State now considering the subject can obtain reliable and complete information from other States which have had many years of experience. Not that I yearn for the day when the pattern of post-high-school education would be the same in all the States. Not at all. Diversity we shall have and ought to have. But we ought to have, I believe, a mechanism by which each State knows exactly what the other States have done in each educational area and the arguments pro and con for any changes which are being considered. We ought to have a way by which the States could rapidly exchange information and plans in all educational matters from the kindergarten to the graduate schools of a university.

Interstate cooperation in the area of higher education in recent years has become possible through interstate regional compacts and agreements. I am sure you are all well aware of the existence of the Southern Regional Education Board, the Western Interstate Commission for Higher Education, and the New England Board of Higher Education. These arrangements have proved their worth. But they are by themselves not sufficient to develop a nationwide coherent policy for higher education and, as far as I am aware, there has been no attempt to extend the area of competence to include education up to and through the 12th grade. Yet, today the line between high school and college is very fuzzy. The continued expansion of 2-year colleges and the introduction of college work into 12th grade in many schools (the advanced placement program) underlines this point. Why not extend the idea of regional pacts both in terms of the area of education to be covered and also in terms of number of States to be included? In short, why not establish by interstate compact or agreement an interstate commission for planning a nationwide educational policy?

In a book published last fall entitled "Shaping Educational Policy," I answered this question in the affirmative. I suggested that the States enter into a compact or agreement to establish a commission which would be a planning commission with no administrative authority and thus differ from some of the regional boards. The prime purpose would be to study problems at all levels of education in such a way as to help the States plan together and with the Federal authorities.

This suggestion has been discussed by many groups and many individuals in the last 8 months. I am now convinced that the key person in each State to get the idea moving and keep it moving is the Governor. Here I only want to say that in any scheme in which the Governors take the lead, the Governor in each State is certain to call on the person or persons in his State who are responsible for higher education on the one hand and for the public elementary and secondary schools on the other.

Let me take a few moments of your time to spell out in detail how I think such an interstate planning commission might work. A vital part of my proposal is the creation of working parties appointed by the interstate commission and reporting to it. While the members of the interstate commission would be primarily laymen, the working parties would certainly include many educators and, in some cases, perhaps be composed exclusively of professors, researchers, teachers, and school and college administrators.

First of all the interstate commission would have to agree on certain basic principles to guide the activities of all the working parties. These principles would include a statement of the ends of education in preparing youth to function as responsible members of a free society, a statement that each State was committed to free schooling through 12 grades for all children, the right of parents to send children to private schools, the responsibility of the State for providing public educational opportunities beyond the high school, the support of a State university for advanced scholarly work and research and the guarantee of academic freedom for the teachers in the university.

The declaration of some such set of premises by a interstate commission would be the first step in shaping an educational nationwide policy. If each State legislature would pass a resolution accepting such a declaration, we would for the first time as a nation be officially committed to certain basic principles of educational policy. We now assume these principles to be valid, but in fact they have never been promulgated by representative assemblies and could not be promulgated by the Congress.

The working parties would be so chosen by the commission as to represent a variety of views. Unanimous reports would not be expected. The right of dissent would be guaranteed to each member. The reports would be reviewed by the commission and perhaps return to the working parties for fuller comment. In this way the diversity of State traditions and the differences State-by-State as to the nature of the problems would be reflected in the final report.

To each of these parties would be assigned a particular task. Let me give you a few examples of the kind of task which might thus be carried out by a working party. First, there is a question of obtaining a thorough study of the needs of the Nation on a State-by-State basis for people trained for the various vocations. I think it is generally agreed that we do not have yet anything like adequate information. The assistant commissioner of education emphasized this fact at a meeting I attended in Pittsburgh last winter. A second matter which might well be considered by a working party would be the dropout problem, again on a State-by-State basis, and here by the dropout problem I mean something far more than the dropout from high school. I mean to include the loss of talent between the high school and graduation from a college or university. A document published by the National Science Foundation some years ago brought out some alarming statistics which have not yet been fully appreciated by the American public. I have referred to these in my book, "The Education of American Teachers," and would merely like to repeat here what I have written in that book. According to estimates in a study by the National Science Foundation, it would appear that of the 30 percent most able students in the high schools of the country only 38 percent graduated from college (45 percent of men, and 31 percent of women), and even of the top 10 percent in terms of ability only about half complete college work. These data were obtained for the Nation as a whole by a sampling procedure. What we need are much more accurate data on a State-by-State basis, for the differences State-by-State must be considerable. Such data could be obtained by a working party established by the interstate commission.

To name another example—with the vast sums of money being spent on research and training research people I think it is time we had a look on a nationwide basis at the standards for the Ph.D. degree. There are only 219 institutions awarding this degree. One suspects the standards in some of these are low. We need a study of the whole problem of the doctorate. I think only at this high level would it be practical to consider the matter of degree standards. For the lower degrees the task is too great and the institutional standards too diverse. Before it is too late, however, we should see if we cannot develop a nationwide policy for the Ph.D. degree awarded by our universities. I do not propose that the interstate planning commission would attempt to enforce any standards. It would have no such power. What I envisage is a report finally agreed to by the commission and transmitted to each of the States. It would then be up to the States to take appropriate action by State authorities to accept or reject these standards and, if accepted, to enforce them.

Still another subject that requires attention by an interstate commission is one I have already referred to, I mean the provision of public education for the first two post-high-school years. Indeed, there is a special urgency in the demand for a thorough study of this problem. For many States are right now making far-reaching decisions. And I do not see how new funds—State or Federal—can be spent effectively in this area without much more careful planning and planning based on information as to what is contemplated in all the States.

Consider for a moment high school education. The widely comprehensive high school which enrolls all youth in a given area is an American invention. To my mind it is an essential element in our democratic society. I am certain it will continue in spite of some critics. But I am equally certain many comprehensive high schools need improvement—improvement in what is offered to those going on to a 4-year college and improvement in what is offered to the others. There has been a revolution in the high school curricula in the last 10 years. But no one can say how widespread has been the acceptance of the new physics, the new chemistry, the new biologies and the new approach to the study of foreign languages. We need to know what has happened in each State and the difficulties, if any, which have been met in introducing the new ideas.

More than one well-informed person believes the time has come for a national survey of the present status and future prospects of educational television and the use of other audio-visual aids to learning. This is a complex and thorny subject. What group could tackle it better than a working party appointed by an interstate planning commission?

A considerable fraction of our youth in some States is deprived of an adequate preparation for university work leading to a career in medicine or science or engineering. The deprivation arises from the fact that the only accessible high schools are very small. Such schools cannot afford to provide adequate instruction for able students in mathematics, science, and foreign languages. The cure is district consolidation and the establishment of good-sized schools with the students brought by bus. Here each State has full responsibility for the satisfactory or unsatisfactory situation which exists. The shape and size of school districts is a legal responsibility of the legislature. Progress has been made in the last 10 years in a number of States. But no document exists which shows the present situation in each State and reports on what measures have succeeded in promoting district consolidation and which have failed. Here is a task for a working party to which I would assign high priority.

There are many topics that I could have added to the list of possible subjects for study by the working parties of an interstate planning commission. You may well ask why the tasks which I have mentioned could not be as well performed by some committee appointed in Washington. My answer would be that I do not believe a report of a working party whose authority comes from the Federal Government either on the executive or congressional level would have the acceptance by Governors and State legislators as would the report of a working committee appointed by an interstate commission which would be, in the last analysis, composed of representatives of the States. Furthermore, a committee reporting to Washington unlike an interstate commission would not open the way to interstate communication and planning.

The legislature in each State has the last say in the question of money for education and in chartering colleges and universities. A legislature can, unless properly guided, pass legislation which is a detriment to the progress of American education. A legislature to my mind would be likely to listen with care to the views of a working committee whose report had been carefully analyzed and discussed by an interstate commission, particularly a report that dealt with State-by-State differences. Indeed it is the existence of these State-by-State differences of which I think you are all aware, which has persuaded me to make my radical suggestion, as a hope of making progress in developing a nationwide educational policy.

I am sure I do not have to tell you that I am not making an old-fashioned plea on the basis of States rights. This is a nation operating under a Constitution created by all the people; we are not merely a federation of 50 States. This question was settled 100 years ago on the battlefields of the Civil War. But unless we were to amend the Constitution the separate States have and will continue to have the responsibility of developing State systems of education. They will differ one from another in important points. It is important that there be a mechanism for the interchange of information and for informing the general public, the Congress and executive officers of the Federal Government of what the facts are in many a crucial situation.

Educational policy in the different States has been determined in the past by the more or less haphazard interaction of (1) the leaders of public school teachers, administrators and professors of education, (2) State educational authorities, (3) a multitude of State colleges and universities, (4) private colleges and universities, and (5) the variety of agencies of the Federal Government, through which vast sums of money have flowed to individual institutions and the States. Such a jumble of the decisions of influential private and public bodies does not correspond, it seems to me, to the urgent needs of the present day.

The whole free world is passing through a period of educational change, one could almost say educational revolution. I have already referred to what has happened in Sweden. Reform is in the air in France, Great Britain, Italy, and free Germany. Statesmen are coming to realize the truth of what some economists have been saying; namely, that there is a close parallel between national prosperity and the extent and level of education. The conclusion seems clear. No modern highly industrialized nation can afford not to improve its schools and widen the base of educational opportunity. Do not the same considerations apply to each of our 50 States?

I have referred more than once to the increased role of the junior partner—the Federal Government. This increased role in itself would demand interstate cooperation and better intrastate planning. Let no one think this issue can be bypassed. Either the States individually and collectively must plan or Washington will be forced to endeavor to determine detailed policy in many areas where the partnership of which Commissioner Keppel spoke should prevail. I hold no brief for what the Federal Government should do on the basis of any ideology about government. My case for an interstate commission is based on what Commissioner Keppel called "practical soundness and necessity." I am convinced Washington alone cannot do the job that must be done. The consequence of failure of the States to act together and together with the Federal authorities will be confusion doubly compounded. The vast increase in Federal funds for education, which I heartily welcome, is all too likely to result in a tangled mess that no one can straighten out unless the States take new and energetic action. And they can only plan together if they can obtain and share information. In short, without some such device as an interstate planning commission, I do not see how a nationwide educational policy can be shaped and made effective. The times challenge educators and statesmen alike. What will be the response from the States?

6

*Each level of government, by its very nature, has
different educational objectives. While at times some
of these objectives overlap, the differences are the
strength of the educational structure of this nation.
They represent the checks and balances necessary to
protect our educational and social interests and, simultaneously, the rich diversity necessary for creative
and imaginative approaches to the crucial education
issues of our time.*

WENDELL PIERCE

Roald F. Campbell and Donald H. Layton
THRUST AND COUNTERTHRUST IN EDUCATIONAL POLICY MAKING

Since World War II there have been some notable shifts in policy
making for American schools—the augmented roles of the federal government, the major foundations, and big business organizations. The
interrelationships among these agencies and organizations create a great
national impact on state and local government of education.

A recent study of the impact of federal legislation on state departments of education found that in one large state department 16 of its 26
divisions were devoting all or part of their attention to federally related
programs, and 64 of the 135 professional personnel in that department
were involved in federally related work. About one-fourth of its budget
was made available through the various titles of the Elementary and
Secondary Education Act of 1965.

The study also revealed the major impact of Title V on state education
departments. Designed specifically "to assist states in strengthening the
leadership resources of their state educational agencies, and to assist
those agencies in the establishment and improvement of programs to
identify and meet the educational needs of states," Title V has through
its grants permitted substantial growth in the size of professional staffs,
provided marked increases in operating budgets, and allowed departments to undertake new programs and expand existing programs.

The findings suggest that much of the new money went to reinforce
traditional programs and employ additional personnel. However, the
new legislation has made state departments even more dependent on

From Roald Campbell and Donald Layton, "Thrust and Counterthrust in Educational
Policy Making," *The Education Digest*, April, 1968, pp. 4–7. (Condensed from an article
originally appearing in *Phi Delta Kappan*, February, 1968.) Reprinted by permission of the
authors and publisher.

federal funds. This is an interesting dilemma. On one hand, many spokesmen for state and local control of education lament the expanding role of the federal government and other national influences. On the other hand, there is a ready acceptance of federal money even though it makes state departments more dependent on the federal government.

Most state departments of education, instead of interacting with federal agencies or even with local school districts as equals in a major enterprise, appear to be simply responding to forces about them. State departments engage chiefly in regulatory activities as required by their respective state legislatures. Responses to the federal legislation have been of the same general nature. More and more, the agendas of most state departments are being set by the federal government.

While many recent programs require state department participation, others have ignored or bypassed state departments. Contributing to this condition are the inadequacy of many state departments; the physical, financial, social, and educational plight of our cities which has required them to deal increasingly with the Congress and federal agencies; and the utilization of general government more than educational government to deal with educational problems. (Mayors, for instance, are more adept with congressmen than are most school superintendents.)

In the light of these circumstances, we can understand why such programs as Head Start are independent of state departments. An interesting case is found in Title III, ESEA, which gave state departments the right to review proposals for supplementary educational centers, but no veto power. For two years this has been a sore point with many state departments, and in the recent extension of Title III states have been given increased jurisdiction. In one sense, such action represents exactly the kind of activity we think state departments should be about—an influence in helping shape legislation instead of merely responding to it. In another sense, however, we question that many state departments are staffed at present with people who can exercise adequate judgment about the merits of many local proposals.

Another national impact on state departments comes as they receive federal money to help improve themselves and are confronted at the same time with new competing organizations financed entirely or largely with federal money. The first of these are the regional educational laboratories authorized by ESEA Title IV, new competitors in the field of disseminating knowledge designed to improve practices in the schools. Is it possible that regional laboratories, with no legal constraints such as those affecting state departments, will preempt the field and leave only regulatory functions for the state departments?

Another new organization requiring accommodation on the part of the state education department is the business firm devoted to education. Much of the recent legislation makes funds for educational purposes available to private firms, and these may become the educational consultants to schools and colleges. When this happens, the state department may find its alleged function performed by still another competitor in the field.

The new considerations posed by the regional laboratories, the entree of business into education, and increased federal aid to local school districts can be conceived in terms of conflict between state and federal government, or conceived within the context of interdependence. Recent federal legislation permits school districts to do things they could not or did not do before.

It is well to note, however, that the funds which make these programs possible represent categorical, not general, aid. If federal funds represent program elements that a district wishes to support, little outside control is felt. However, if a district finds itself being urged to support certain programs more generously than seems warranted to local board members, much outside control is felt.

In some instances local school districts are asked to implement programs which reflect national positions, even though such programs may not enjoy general support in the community. Thus the national forces— federal money often supported by officials of foundations and educational firms—provide new opportunities to boards of education, but they also place new demands on local boards.

Legislation has also affected the relationship of the superintendent vis-à-vis the board of education. Prerogatives ordinarily thought to belong to the board have been shifted to the superintendent and his staff. With the complexity of new federal programs, a tremendous burden would be placed on board members if they were required to consider in detail the merits of particular programs.

When citizens cannot get redress from the district board, they can now turn to federal agencies and ask them to apply pressure locally. Interrelationships, both horizontal and vertical, are illustrated by this practice. A local board of education serves its local constituency within a state and national context, while most groups within the local constituency have state or national ties. Numerous networks affect the local governance of education.

Counterthrust

The thrust toward increased national influence has also produced a counterthrust—a resurgence of state and local influence. Perhaps the best example is the Education Commission of the States. Through its establishment and activities we can sense both the aspirations and frustrations of policy makers at the state level.

Two years ago, during the Commission's earliest months, emphasis was on sponsorship of a series of educational studies. However, pressures soon began to turn the Commission toward becoming a public forum on federal-state relations in education. In May 1967, the theme of the Commission meeting in Denver, "Power-Play for Control of Education," reflected the new emphasis of the organization. Also at a September meeting, Gov. Calvin Rampton of Utah, steering committee chairman, urged that the Commission draft legislation which could be submitted to Congress on behalf of the states.

Clearly, the Commission was entering a new phase in 1967, shifting its focus away from research studies and seeking to find out how it ought to respond to the national government. The new thrust toward power-play politics—still largely at the verbal level—does raise questions. How appropriate is it for the Commission to become educational lobbyist in Washington for the states? Is there a "states" point of view on most educational legislation?

A study of the Compact for Education, which created the Commission, reveals that the Commission has questionable legal bases for a direct confrontation with Congress and other federal bodies. Its enumerated powers pertain almost exclusively to its relationships with its member states. These powers are advisory in nature. The Commission is empowered to neither set nor enforce policy. If it moves too quickly to implement lobbying activities in Washington, the action could be divisive.

It is important also to recall that this interstate body is essentially a confederation; states can adhere to or withdraw from the Compact with comparative ease. The Commission's existence depends on not offending its member states. If the states could agree on which educational questions were most important and what procedures were needed, the Commission might be in a position to argue partisan positions in Washington. But the states have diverse needs and priorities.

Perhaps the states approach consensus only on procedural questions, one of which may be the desirability of block grants rather than categorical aid. This may well be the first position the Commission will promote before Congress.

Both the thrust toward increased national influence in education and the counterthrust toward more state-local direction have more meaning if viewed within the context of a social system. The social system we speak of is not an organized one, but it may be conceptualized as existing in the larger society and it is as broad as the nation itself. The subsystems frequently have difficulty articulating with each other, but there is much interdependence. At all levels of government, agencies operate within the constraints set by the total social milieu. There is give and take, push and pull, conflict and cooperation. There are ways for resolving problems of national moment and those of local concern. But to be effective the system demands our understanding, our participation, and our willingness to consider alternative ways of achieving our ends. We think the national thrust is here to stay; we also think that states, subdivisions of states and combinations of states as illustrated in the Compact exercise some surveillance over that thrust.

7

The time is past when society as a whole, parents as individuals, and interested groups outside the school were willing to leave the control of education wholly to the public education system—to watch children vanish into the school in the morning and emerge from it in the afternoon, without being able to affect what goes on behind the school doors.

JAMES S. COLEMAN

George R. La Noue

POLITICAL QUESTIONS IN THE NEXT DECADE OF URBAN EDUCATION

Even a cursory glance at the current writing on the state of urban education makes it clear that the first question to ask is whether public schools will survive the next decade in the great cities. Public education is permanently established, it would seem, in the suburbs across the country and in almost all of the small and medium-sized cities except where integration problems are most severe. But will a public school system, as we have known it, continue to predominate in the large eastern and northern cities?

Washington is the prime example of a public school system that may be beyond repair. Neither expenditures, which have been about average for large cities, nor administrative devices designed to favor the remaining white middle class have succeeded. So much of the white population has fled to the suburbs or enrolled their children in private or parochial schools that the Washington public schools, which were 55% white before the Supreme Court's desegregation decision in 1954, are now only 10% white, and the city itself has a Negro majority. Fifty percent of the children in the Washington public schools now come from families beneath the poverty line ($3000). Educational achievement (50% drop-out rate) and staff morale are so bad that middle-class Negroes are now deserting the system or demanding class-segregated schools.

Washington, of course, has not been a typical American city either in its population trends or in its relationship of government to schools. Last year, however, Negroes comprised 40% of the school population in half of the 36 largest American cities, and demographers predict that these trends toward a non-white population will continue. Furthermore,

From George La Noue, "Political Questions in the Next Decade of Urban Education," *Teachers College Record*, March, 1968, pp. 517–528. Reprinted by permission of the author and publisher.

although no other school system has had to deal directly with a Congressional Committee for its appropriations and powers, there are other cities where the city administration has been as aloof and/or negative. In short, then, the question is not whether Washington has been typical in the past, but whether it is the prototype of the future. Can a public enterprise survive if it has lost the support of the white middle class, is losing support among middle-class Negroes, and is viewed with deep distrust by lower classes of both races?

Public Education's Future. Some clues as to public education's future might be found in examining the collapse of another urban public enterprise—the public hospital. Recently, the magazine section of the *New York Times* featured an article titled "The City Should Get Out of the Hospital Business." The author, a private hospital administrator, argued that public control and quality medicine were inherently incompatible and that all municipal hospitals should be turned over to voluntary groups. This proposal has attracted considerable support, and private hospitals are already politically powerful enough in New York so that their representatives are able to battle the Lindsay administration for designation as coordinators and recipients of federal funds. The predicament of the public hospitals seems to be characterized by three elements: (1) unresponsive and chaotic administration, (2) an operational policy focused on providing the cheapest medicine for the poorest people and a consequent inability to compete for a middle-class clientele and the best of staff and facilities, and (3) federal financial policies in the form of construction grants (Hill-Burton Act) that aided private hospitals relatively more than public hospitals and the Medicare program which grants funds to individuals who then purchase private medicine. Will this pattern characterize public education in the next decade?

Not surprisingly, public education's dilemma has caused many to question traditional assumptions about financing and administering education; and suggestions for restructuring public school politics or even setting up alternatives to public education are made with increasing frequency. There seem to be at least six live options or models for urban education in the future. Discussing the most private alternatives first, they are:

1. A tax-supported tuition or voucher system paid to individual parents who would then be able to purchase education from many competing schools in the market place.
2. A system of direct grants to private schools in publicly-determined categories.
   Either the tuition grant or direct grant system can be conceived of as complementary to or replacing the existing system of public support of public schools.
3. Contracts issued by public agencies to corporations, universities and other groups who would manage "public" schools.

4. Public schools managed by local parent groups. Both the contract and parent-managed schools would be legally public if they were tax-supported and open to all children in the neighborhood.
5. Public schools managed by a school board composed of various publicly-appointed representatives of community groups.
6. Public schools managed by a school board directly elected by the whole community.

On a public-private continuum these models might be represented as follows:

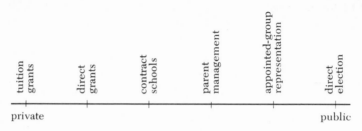

Against the Monopoly. The first three alternatives draw support from an unusual coalition of individuals as ideologically diverse as Professor Milton Friedman, Barry Goldwater's favorite economist, and Christopher Jencks, the education editor of the *New Republic*, and groups as different as the Chamber of Commerce, the Catholic Church, Black Power militants, and White Citizens Councils. One common argument made, though for many different reasons, is the need to create competition in education and to destroy the "public school monopoly." Jencks stated frankly in an article titled "Is the Public School Obsolete?":

> Either tuition grants or management contracts to private organizations would, of course, "destroy the public school system as we know it." When one thinks of the remarkable past achievements of public education in America, this may seem a foolish step. But we must not allow the memory of past achievements to blind us to present failures. Nor should we allow the rhetoric of public school men to obscure the issue. It is natural for public servants to complain about private competition. But if the terms of the competition are reasonable, there is every reason to suppose that it is healthy. Without it, both public and private enterprises have a way of ossifying. And if, as some fear, the public schools could not survive in open competition with private ones, then perhaps they *should* not survive.

Jencks and the others who have made this argument have, it seems to me, greatly oversimplified the need for and the effects of competition at the elementary and secondary level. In the first place, competition already exists. Except in the South, private schools enroll between 15% and 35% of all students in almost every large city. In addition, city public school systems compete against suburban public school systems; and the public schools within the city compete for appropriations, teachers, special projects, administrative status and in extracurricular activities. If decentralization takes place, competition will increase and students may have several different public choices.

Secondly, neither public schools nor private schools operate according to the classical free market pattern, so the assumption that public schools will automatically respond to private competition by becoming more responsive to their clientele and more efficient is quite doubtful. Neither public school nor private school managements are paid on the basis of their ability to expand their system's share of the student market. Indeed, the attractiveness of private education rests on its power to limit its student body on intellectual, socio-economic, religious or racial lines; and no public school can legally compete in that way. Since private schools want only the "best" students, their ability to skim off the "cream" may cause public schools to suffer from too much rather than too little competition.

As Peter Schrag has pointed out:

> The problem in Boston and in other cities is that escape [from public schools] is too easy, that the anger, the frustration, the civic fury that should and would manifest themselves are dampened by partial expedients and by the simple solution of a parochial school, a private school, or a move across city lines.

When large numbers of the most middle-class and most ambitious parents enroll their children in private schools, it makes it impossible for public schools to integrate racially; to maintain opportunities for lower-class children to learn from their middle-class peers, which is a key factor in achievement (Coleman report); or to find community support for educational reform. In other words, the existence of a readily available private school alternative may create a vicious circle: the more white, middle-class students leave the public schools, the poorer the image and quality of the schools become; the poorer the schools become, the more middle-class non-whites and lower-class whites leave. In the end, public schools are left with a clientele composed almost entirely of lower-class non-whites, as has happened in Washington and also in the municipal hospital systems of several cities. Reform becomes impossible.

As long as the image and reality of urban public schools remain as bad as they are, however, the demand for public subsidy of private alternatives will continue. What is the likelihood of success in the next decade?

Tuition and Direct Grants. The tuition grant alternative provides potentially the most funds with the least public control. Conservative groups like Citizens for Educational Freedom and the White Citizens Council have suggested tuition grants in the belief that this financial pattern does not create enough state involvement in private schools to provide an excuse for public regulation of discriminatory admission practices or curriculum indoctrination. Their legal assumption may be wrong, however, since tuition grant plans have been struck down by federal courts in Virginia and Louisiana on the grounds that they were attempts to avoid desegregation and by a state court in Vermont on the grounds that the plan aided parochial schools.

The legal problems in a system of direct grants to private schools are even greater, since the state involvement is clearer, since almost all state constitutions bar direct aid to parochial schools, and since all federal programs require non-discriminatory policies. Furthermore, the Elementary and Secondary School Act has established the precedent of allowing programs for private school children only if they are publicly administered. Although in practice this principle is sometimes ignored or circumvented, its existence is a formidable legal and political barrier to the development of the true private school alternative.

While it might be theoretically possible to design a tuition grant or direct grant program that would not assist racially-segregated or church-controlled schools, such a plan would have little political support. One of the basic problems with the private school alternative is that 90% of all private school enrollment is in Catholic parochial schools with only 5% in schools belonging to other churches and another 5% in non-sectarian schools. As the recent overwhelming rejection of the proposed New York State Constitution (which would for the first time have permitted aid to parochial schools) suggests, enrollment patterns in existing private-schools do not provide a broad enough political basis to greatly alter the existing public school monopoly of public funds. Furthermore, the Catholic Church, particularly, is having second thoughts about expanding its school system. To cite one example, the Marist order, which operates thirty-four schools in the United States, has announced that it is going to phase out the parochial school approach in favor of after-school ecumenical centers. This approach and shared-time arrangements seem more likely methods of providing religious education in the future than comprehensive parochial schools. Internal staffing problems, theological controversies, and a generally conservative outlook that seems out-of-touch with cultural trends make it unlikely that the parochial school-oriented churches will be able to maintain their growth rates or expand their school systems. If this is true, even a sizable increase in non-sectarian-college prep-type schools will not be enough to provide a traditional private-school substitute for public education in the next decade.

The Approach Contract. This situation has led some writers to suggest that a better and quicker method of creating competitive alternatives is to permit public agencies to contract with corporations, universities and other groups to manage schools. Although the management of these schools would be private, they would remain public schools since the public agency would be able to terminate the contract at any time and since the schools would not be permitted to discriminate or indoctrinate.

Some Job Corps centers have been managed in this pattern with mixed results. Antioch College is operating the Adams-Morgan district in Washington on a three-year contract, and several such relationships are contemplated in New York.

It seems unlikely that there will be a wholesale turning over of public schools to private management. For one thing, there will be tremendous political opposition among administrators, teachers, and established school groups. To offset this opposition there would have to be strong parental support. Ghetto parents, however, are already suspicious of corporations and universities and would prefer to run the schools themselves. Secondly, although corporations and universities might be willing to volunteer their services on a short-term altruistic basis, in the long run we would have to create profit and research-training opportunities so substantial as to undermine the utility of the schools for mass education. Hospitals affiliated with universities are wonderful places if you have an exotic disease, but they have never been very interested in providing day-to-day care for ordinary patients.

Although contracts for whole public school systems will be rare, there will be more private participation in public education than previously. As mentioned, shared time or dual enrollment arrangements will increase. New acceptance of educational research will bring in the universities and the tremendous innovations in educational technology will mean an expanded corporate role. Schools teach more than skills, however, and great care will have to be exercised to see that the corporate influence does not reduce education to the transmission of testable skills in the most efficient and profitable manner. Nevertheless, it is certainly conceivable that school systems will increasingly contract out food preparation, driver training, clinical services, and turn over curriculum development to universities or educational laboratories. If Berlitz has the methods and the personnel to teach basic language skills, why not permit them to do so, and let the teaching of literature and culture remain in school hands? This mix might allow the schools to utilize business efficiency while retaining control over areas of learning that require consideration of humane values and academic freedom.

Trends in Public School Politics. If, then, it seems likely that there will not be any massive replacement of public schools with private schools or private management, what trends in public school politics are likely? Cities without serious racial problems may expect to continue the status quo of elected or appointed boards made up of businessmen and professionals, but elsewhere the movement for parental or community controlled schools will be formidable. As Edgar Z. Friedenberg has predicted:

> Improvement in the urban schools will come when—and only when —the residents whose children attend those schools demand and get enough political power either to destroy and replace the present

school bureaucracy or to impress upon it that they can no longer be patronized. In practice, both processes will occur simultaneously; as black power grows in the city, the most rigid of the teachers and administrators will flounce off into retirement—but others will adapt like the white civil servants who decided to stay on in Kenya and who continued their careers quite cheerfully, once they admitted that the natives were capable of governing, not only themselves, but *them.* It is, as school personnel often say, only a matter of making it perfectly clear who is in charge, and what kind of conduct will be tolerated.

The tie-in of parental control to black power ideology is unfortunately a mixed blessing. Although there is much potential good in the black power concept: the development of personal pride, the resurrection of Negro history and culture, and the creation of effective economic and political power for ghetto residents, there is also an element of strident racial aggrandizement that cannot fail to harm the educational process. In those areas of New York City where ghetto parents have been given an increased role in school affairs, white staff members have been made to feel unwelcome. In the Ocean Hill-Brownsville area, for example, 17 of 18 assistant principals (all white) and most of the teachers have asked for transfers. Although there is a genuine need for more Negro staff and although, as Jonathan Kozol has so eloquently pointed out, many white teachers are by training or temperament incapable of reaching ghetto children, parents must not be allowed to create a racist purge in the schools. Surely the experience of all Negro southern schools and an 80% Negro staff in Washington indicate that racial identity alone is not enough to create a good learning situation for Negro youth. Ghetto schools need all the talent they can get.

Even without the black power issue, participation of large numbers of lower-class parents in the making of school policy will create problems. The fact that too many decision-makers make any decision impossible will be further complicated by lower-class political participation styles, which James Q. Wilson describes as "private-regarding" rather than "community-oriented" and suspicious of all leadership and parliamentary procedures. This makes communication extremely difficult even when school authorities have the best intentions. Furthermore, despite the need that professionals see to develop new approaches and new materials to make learning more relevant for deprived youngsters, their parents often reason that what is good enough for the suburbs is good enough for them and resist experimentation and any hint of a permissive approach.

Sharing Control. One solution may be to insist that parents share control of the schools with other parts of the community. After all, even in suburbs participation in school board and bond elections is open to all citizens. The Bundy decentralization proposal for New York City suggests local school boards made up of six members elected by the parents and five members appointed by the mayor from various community groups. This will insure parental access to the school yet provide some broader perspective. At any rate, this is the kind of pragmatic evolution of checks and balances that historically has characterized American government.

Several other trends in urban education including decentralization, metropolitanization, the community school concept, community-teacher tension, social indicators and program budgeting and, most important, the new role of mayors should be discussed.

Until very recently, the basic policy in school districting was consolidation so that in the last ten years more than 20,000 school districts disappeared in the name of efficiency and economy. Now we are discovering that districts or even particular schools of a certain size develop bureaucratic hardening of the arteries and become inflexible and impersonal. Hopefully research in this decade may be able to specify optimum sizes considering human as well as economic variables, but right now we have no such data. Even if thirty districts were created in New York, as Bundy proposes, they would still have 40,000 students each; and this may still be too many.

Decentralization proponents are often a strange coalition of white liberal intellectuals, white neighborhood school groups, and black militants. Ranged against them, if New York proves typical, will be administrators and teachers with promotion and tenure policies to protect and established school groups who want to preserve their political status.

Decentralization, where it occurs, will have many consequences. One is that it may facilitate the development of true metropolitan school systems. Suburban schools may be more willing to enter into cooperative agreement with a particular city district or join a limited purpose metropolitan federation when all the districts are about the same size. Cities may want to explore a system of exchanges based on the considerable adult educational resources in the city and on the suburb's secondary school advantages. One can imagine commuter rail and bus lines bringing adults into the city for business and education at 8 a.m. and returning with city youngsters bound for suburban educational centers. The transportation process would be reversed in the evening. A metropolitan system may also prove necessary if some of the suggestions in *Hobson v. Hansen* about equalizing educational resources should ever be legally enforced.

Broadening School Functions. Another consequence of decentralization and community participation will be a broadening of school functions. U.S. Office of Education projections show that the greatest expansion in school enrollment in the next decade will be in what is now considered pre-school and adult education. This new clientele will join the existing clientele to demand that the community's most valuable facility be open to more people for more hours. Particularly in poorer neighborhoods of the city, the twenty-four-hour-a-day, seven-day-a-week community school concept will be widely implemented.

We can also expect an increase in teacher-community tensions. Despite growing NEA militancy, if present trends continue in the next decade, most urban teachers will be organized by the AFT. A period of salary and working condition conflicts can then be expected, but disputes over professional status and seniority will also grow. The concept of tenure is already under attack by ghetto parents who see it as a device to protect unsympathetic and incompetent teachers. Tenure for teachers has had a different basis than ordinary civil service protection, since teachers, unlike civil servants, expect to make institutional policy as well as to carry it out. The traditional rationale for tenure—academic freedom—will, however, be undermined by the large number of para-professionals and corporate employees the schools will require to meet their expanded functions. While one may grant that senior faculty in a high school history or sociology department may need the same protection as their colleagues in the university, what about the school employee who teaches driver training or plays creatively with three-year-olds or programs teaching machines?

Another threat to the security of teachers and administrators will be the development and utilization of program budgeting and new concepts of social indicators. It will be increasingly possible to measure the efficiency of one teacher, one educational approach, or one school system against another in terms the public can understand. Since educational achievement is almost always measured in relative terms and since not everyone can be above the median, the development of the new measuring devices will put additional pressure on schoolmen to perform.

All of the above factors: increased parental participation, decentralization, metropolitanization, the community school concept, community-teacher conflicts and new forms of educational statistics, will contribute to the paramount trend in the politics of education in the next decade— the emergence of the mayor as the chief arbiter and policy-maker for education.

The original separation of public school management from city government was often a middle-class Protestant reformer strategy to keep education from falling into the hands of ethnic-dominated machine governments, which they regarded as corrupt and inefficient. Machine leaders, whose constituency largely preferred parochial schools anyway, found this an easy concession to make to the reformers. All of this history is now irrelevant to urban politics in most places, and few mayors are going to be able to hide behind the myth of keeping politics out of education. With expanded pre-school and adult education and the decline of parochial schools, public education will have a bigger constituency than ever before. New Negro voting blocs in the city will insist that mayors be responsible for public education. Increasingly, it is clear that education cannot be treated separately from problems of housing, welfare and unemployment. Any political leader who wants to save or even to improve his city is going to have to make public education a priority matter.

Changing School and City Politics. The mayor's intervention in school politics will mean a decline in relative power for school bureaucracies and the groups that have controlled school boards, but these groups have proven that they can no longer manage public education by themselves. Isolated from the sources of political influence in the city, the public school establishment has not had the strength to protect the public interest in financing, integration, or relations with private schools. As the number of participants grows through decentralization and as pressure group tactics become more sophisticated and more disruptive, the vulnerability of public education will increase without a radical injection of political energy.

Indeed, decentralization will absolutely require more leadership from the mayor and other political officials if the educational system is not to fly apart. These are not necessarily inconsistent trends, however, if the mayor confines his decision-making to the fundamental fiscal and interest-group issues and permits neighborhood groups to decide local personnel, curriculum and school culture policies. Central school boards may be preserved to advise on and, in some cities, to give consent to the mayor's decisions. The old autonomous central school bureaucracies will be replaced by an educational agency in the mayor's cabinet which gathers facts and implements, not creates, basic policy. The ultimate responsibility will be the mayor's, and he and his party will have to confront the voters at election time to defend the condition of the schools. Education is the city's most important task and its largest operation in personnel and expenditures. The issues in elections should reflect that fact.

The changes in school politics will also create changes in city politics. As the educational level of the electorate goes up and the educational responsibility of the mayor becomes clearer, a new breed of candidates will emerge; and the office of the mayor will be restructured. Communities may not be willing to entrust their school systems to the same kind of men they chose when police, fire, sanitation, etc., seemed to be the mayor's chief duties.

To some, this prognosis may have seemed overly pessimistic. This is, in my judgment, the wrong implication (though the problems obviously will be great). In the next decade, public schools will develop a broader clientele, increased functions, and a system of government that is both more sensitive to local interests and closer to the mayor, the center of power in the city. If these political changes lead to a breakthrough in learning for ghetto children, then public education will have met its greatest challenge and its future will be bright indeed.

8

The city schools are at the crossroads of three revolutions—in civil rights, in technology, and in the style of urban life itself. All three are making fantastic demands upon education and all three must be accommodated through an awkward political process that has never been efficient even in the best of circumstances.

PETER SCHRAG
Village School Downtown

Robert H. Salisbury
SCHOOLS AND POLITICS IN THE BIG CITY

After decades of silence, both social scientists and educators are at last explicitly examining and re-examining all the options regarding the relationship between the political system and the schools. Descriptive analysis has greatly enriched our understanding of how alternative structures operate. A full menu of recipes for changing the structures has been developed and here and there implemented. And while we are far from realizing closure on our uncertainties, the art of social engineering with respect to school-community relations is finally getting an underpinning of evidence and systematic analysis.

Broadly, there seem to be three themes running through this new wave of literature. One is primarily descriptive: How are educational decisions made, and what variables are relevant for explaining alternative outcomes? A second theme merges this descriptive task with a special concern: What accounts for variations in the money available to the schools, and implicitly, how might more money be made available? The third theme is a bit different. It raises a more complex question, and answers depend not only upon careful descriptive analysis but also upon performance criteria that are very difficult to work out: How may the school system do a more effective job in the total context of community life?

From Robert H. Salisbury, "Schools and Politics in the Big City," *Harvard Educational Review*, 37, Summer, 1967, pp. 408–424. Copyright © 1967 by President and Fellows of Harvard College. Reprinted by permission of the publisher.

It is apparent that the "context of community life" is a concept fraught with snares and difficulties. I propose to look at it mainly with reference to the problems of the core city; there, it encompasses major facets of the problems of race, of poverty, of physical decay and renewal, of perennial fiscal trauma, indeed most of those troubles we label "urban problems" in contemporary American society. The issue I wish to ruminate about here is whether one type of political system-school system relationship might be more effective than another in attacking these dilemmas of urban life. Specifically, I propose to consider the thesis that direct polit-ical-system control of the schools (historically anathema to educators) might have significant virtues in making the schools more effective in-struments of social change and development.

We know that many big-city school systems operate with substantial formal autonomy. They are not run by the political or administrative leaders of the city, but are insulated from those leaders and the interests they represent. In part this autonomy is a consequence of various formal features of local government which give to the schools the authority to run their affairs with little or no reference to the demands of other city officials. Perhaps in larger part, however, the insulation of the schools may be a function of the ideology, propagated by schoolmen but widely shared by the larger public, that schools should be free from "politics," i.e., the influence of non-school officials. Insofar as this view is shared, it has made formal independence a less relevant variable, and most of what evidence we have suggests that the formal structure of school-city rela-tions does not matter very much: the schools are largely autonomous anyway.

It has been argued that autonomy for the schools means that profes-sional educators would be free to carry out educational policies which they, as professionals, deem most effective without the intrusion of con-flicting and educationally deleterious demands from nonprofessionals. But autonomy and insulation may also result in other things. Auton-omous schools may be unresponsive to important groups in the commu-nity whose interests are not effectively served by the dominant values of professional schoolmen. Autonomy may mean a fragmenting of efforts aimed at solving community problems because of inadequate coordina-tion and planning. And autonomy may also bring vulnerability as well as insulation. If the schools are separated from the rest of the community's political system, they may be more easily exposed to the protests or de-mands of groups which are disaffected from that system, unable to work their will within its often labyrinthine structures, but able to organize direct popular support. And if they attempt direct protest action, they can make life most difficult for schoolmen who are unable to retreat into posi-tions of mutual support among city officials with many programs and agencies and client groups. Unable to trade off one group against another, the schools may be and often are the targets of protests which may well have its roots in other facets of the city's life, but are directed against the schools precisely because they are autonomous and vulnerable.

The argument that the costs of "political control" far exceed the costs of autonomy needs re-examination. I have been struck by the frequent reference in that argument to the allegedly baleful effects of Big Bill Thompson's 1927 campaign for election as mayor of Chicago in which he concentrated much of his flamboyant oratory on the issue of control of the public schools. Big Bill promised to sack the superintendent who was, said Thompson, a lackey of King George and the British. Educators have ever since been agreed that a mayoral campaign subjecting the schools to this kind of educationally irrelevant attack was ample evidence of the need for protection from big city politics. Thompson's rhetoric was, of course, so blatantly demagogic that he makes an easy object lesson, but behind the rhetoric the issue has other features which make its moral much less clear.

In a most interesting book, called *School and Society in Chicago*, George S. Counts examined the 1927 election soon after it happened. Counts' assessment is one of considerable ambivalence. On the one hand, he has no sympathy for Thompson's tactics of catering to his anti-British constituents by threatening to "punch King George in the snoot." Yet Thompson, in denouncing Superintendent McAndrew, was exploiting a very real conflict within the schools which had already engaged major socio-economic sectors in the community.

William McAndrew had come to Chicago in 1924 in the wake of a series of political scandals and convictions affecting members of the school board. McAndrew was looked to as a reformer who would use his office more vigorously than had his predecessors. Particularly, he was expected, apparently by all the most interested parties, to establish the superintendency as the center from which the schools would thereafter be run. Professional educational criteria were to prevail. No more politics!

McAndrew interpreted this mandate to mean that *he* would select the criteria; the classroom teachers would not. He believed that *professional* educators should embrace teachers and administrators in the same organizational units, so he effectively discouraged the previously vigorous teachers councils in the Chicago schools. Chicago had a strong and long-standing set of teacher organizations including units of the American Federation of Teachers, and McAndrews' unsympathetic view of their status led to abiding tension. Counts reports that the teachers' groups provided effective support for Thompson's election.

In addition, McAndrew had alienated organized labor in general. Not only had he rejected the propriety of the teachers' unions. He had introduced the junior high school. Chicago labor spokesmen construed this to be a step toward separate vocational training for working-class children. They viewed the junior high as an early breakaway from an equalitarian curriculum and this, they feared, was aimed at producing a docile, cheap labor force. Finally, McAndrew was a champion of the platoon system, or, as it was generally referred to, the Gary Plan. He favored the alleged efficiencies of the Plan and justified them quite frankly in a business-oriented way. Moreover, he actively and often consulted with representatives of the Chicago Association of Commerce; never with spokesmen of labor.

The result was a fairly considerable class conflict over McAndrew and his policies, both inside the school system and in the community. William Hale Thompson exploited these tensions and, in a way, helped resolve them. At least, after Thompson won, McAndrew was fired.

The important morals of this story seem to me to be the following: First, McAndrew provoked a severe conflict among the schoolmen themselves. The alleged intrusion of "politics" into the schools was really more the widening of a breach that already existed. Breaches among the schoolmen have been rather exceptional, from McAndrew's time until very nearly the present. Educators have proclaimed their fundamental unity of purpose and interest; and to a remarkable degree, they have lived up to it. But as teachers' unions grow strong and make demands and, occasionally, strike, and as community-wide controversies develop over the location, programs, and financing of the schools, the myths and practices which lead educators to maintain a united front in facing the outside, nonprofessional, world cannot survive. And, if there are conflicts, they will be exploited. The only question is, "By whom?"

The second lesson of the Chicago case of 1927 relates to the ultimate problem-solving machinery. McAndrew and the schools became a central issue in a partisan political race. Was this an appropriate mechanism for resolving a virtual class conflict involving the largest category of public expenditure? If it was not, then what is the regular political process for? Why are educational issues not properly determined in this arena? Why not indeed, except, perhaps, that Big Bill made the final determination. This dramatic fact has been enough to cinch the argument whenever some hardy soul could be found to play devil's advocate.

Later in this paper I shall explore further the two features I have drawn from the Chicago case; the political significance of unity among the schoolmen, and the possible consequences of determining school questions within the regular political processes of the community. Before I do, however, I would like to consider further what seems to me an important element of the context of school politics, in Chicago and every other city, then and now. This is what I shall call *the myth of the unitary community*.

George Counts concludes his analysis of the McAndrew affair by calling for "the frank recognition of the pluralistic quality of the modern city. Such recognition would involve the extension of a direct voice in the control of education to the more powerful interests and the more significant points of view." The recommendation troubled Counts. He believed that it would really only "regularize practices already in existence," since these groups were already actively engaged in the struggle for influence over the schools. Still Counts recognized that he was making a "radical" proposal. It went directly counter to an historic perspective which has long pervaded the thinking of educators: namely, that the city is a unity for purposes of the school program. That is, regardless of ethnic, racial, religious, economic, or political differences and group conflicts in other arenas of urban life, education need not, and should not if it could, recognize or legitimize those differences. Education is a process that must not be differentiated according to section or class. Learning is the same phenomenon, or should be, in every neighborhood. Physical facilities and personnel should be allocated without regard to whatever group conflicts might exist in the community.

Schools have not always been run this way in reality. In the nineteenth century, some concessions were made to such prominent ethnic groups as the Germans by providing special classes in the German language; but in St. Louis, these were discontinued in 1888, or just about the time that ethnic heterogeneity really blossomed in the city. In recent years, a good many departures from the norm can be observed. In many cities, ethnic representation on the school board has been accepted as a hostage to the times, though the tendency is generally to deplore the necessity of special group recognition. Representatives of labor, of Negroes, and of Catholics hold big-city board memberships today and their constituents would complain if they did not. But the prevailing doctrines have not altered as much as the practice, I suspect, and the perspective which denies the legitimacy of group conflicts over school policy is certainly still widely held.

Surely an important element of this view of the city was the egalitarian democracy espoused by a large portion of professional education's intellectuals. The common school, later the high school, and now the community college have been urged and supported as mechanisms for equalizing the life chances of everyone in the community. To introduce programs for one group that were not available to another, or to build different kinds of school buildings for different neighborhoods, would cultivate group and class differences in the twig-bending stage which would lead to deeper socio-economic cleavages in the adult community. Most people, it seemed, never considered the possibility that the havenot groups might receive *more* and *better* education than the middle class.

It looked like the poor could only get short-changed in a system of differentiated education and a caste system would result. This was the position not only of educators but probably of most actively concerned lay citizens too. It was an operative theory to guide education policy, and it was linked to a view of the community beyond the school system. For a consensual, integrated, organic community was and is an abiding standard for many American intellectuals. A proper city should manifest no deep-seated social or economic cleavages. Groups and classes with opposing interests are considered dangerous to the continued tranquillity of the polity. When they exist, as they increasingly did in the industrial city of turn-of-the-century America, it becomes necessary to adopt programs, such as universal education, and institutions, such as nonpartisan local government or at-large elections, that overcome the threatening heterogeneity.

But burgeoning immigration, the rise of the urban political machine, the emergence of corporate economic interests, and the enormous increases in scale of the urban community were parallel and closely connected phenomena of the 1880–1910 era. The metropolis which emerged threatened to erupt in group conflicts that would engulf the schools unless defenses could be found. The unitary-community perspective, more or less accurate as description a generation before and still serviceable for many smaller communities outside the metropolis, from that time on has been primarily a myth for the big city.

Still, it is a useful myth, and its uses were and are many. First, it served as a sharp contrast to the "political" world. Urban politics in the muckraker era was plainly a politics of group conflict and accommodation. The boss was a broker of social and economic tensions, and part of his brokerage fee to the community was the heightening of group consciousness. Ethnic identity for many Europeans was first achieved through the processes of American ward politics. Irish, Italian, or Czech nationalisms, for example, were much promoted in the cities of this era, as candidates and parties sought ways to secure the loyalties of the urban electorate.

With the political arena patently corrupt and marked by the conflicts of a myriad of "special" interests, the unitary-community perspective of education could justify the institutional separation of the schools from the rest of the political community. Independence from "politics" would keep out the selfish aims and corrupt tactics of the politician.

Independent school systems were not new of course. Institutional separation had always been a prevailing pattern. But in the larger cities, until the end of the nineteenth century, the structure of the independent school systems had been highly political. Many school boards were chosen by wards. Some were selected by the city council, some by direct and frequent election. Ward representation was not originally viewed as a way of representing diverse group interests in the city as much as it was a means of keeping the board in close touch with the electorate. It resulted, however, in highly "politicized" school boards, sensitive to neighborhood pressures, particularly in the area of school-building. The ward system promoted log-rolling among sections of the city over many components of the school program. Neighborhoods sometimes traded off advantages, thereby probably facilitating rapid construction in many cities. Wards might also block one another, however, and thus retard the whole system.

The development of the professional educator to fill the newly created position of superintendent of schools inaugurated a different approach to education in which lay control would operate in increasing tension with the professional expert. With ward representation, this tension might well have been unbearable, at least to the professional educator. But parallel to the rise of the superintendency came the elimination of the ward system, and at-large election systems were rapidly adopted for the selection of school-board members.

The unitary myth was and is of great use in justifying an at-large school board. If the community is an organic whole with a single public interest in education, the board member should be protected against local, "selfish," interests by giving him a city-wide constituency. Moreover, since there are no legitimate "special" group interests in education, any responsible citizen can serve on the board, and there is no reason to give particular groups in the community a seat. To give a seat to labor, for example, would be wrong because it would constitute recognition of a special-group perspective on educational policy. Indeed, in a unitary community, there is really no such thing as representation on the school board, since there are no interests to represent. If, as George Counts and others found, urban school-board members were drawn predominantly from middle class, WASP, business-oriented strata of the community, it was a fact without significance in a unitary community. In a recent study of school desegregation in eight northern cities, Robert Crain found that business and professional persons who serve on the school board, do so as individuals, not as class or elite spokesmen, and that such "nonrepresentative" individuals have been more acquiescent to integration than Board members elected by party or ethnic constituencies.

The myth has thus been important in underwriting equalitarian educational programs, in separating the school systems from the main political process of the city, and in validating middle-class control of the schools. In addition, it was a useful adjunct to the emergence of professional expertise in education and school administration. Expertise rested on the assumption that valid ways and means to run the schools existed and were independent of the particular interests and values of particular groups. A good school system is good for everyone, not just a portion of the community. Experts, those people with professional training in the field, are qualified by their specialized training to tell good from bad, and laymen, if they are sensible, should defer to this expertise. If the unitary assumption is undermined, however, then no one, however well trained, can identify or administer a "good" school system. One may then ask only, "Good for whom? For which groups?"

Apart from a social scientist's perverse interest in exploring the myths we live by, is there any point to this discussion of the unitary-community myth? I believe the answer is "Emphatically, yes!" When educators treat the community as a unitary phenomenon, they are less able to offer programs and facilities which are differentiated to serve the diverse needs and values of particular subgroups in the city. It is an indictment of educational political theory that head-start projects for the urban poor only began on a large scale in 1965. Not that schoolmen did not often recognize the differential needs of slum children and sometimes tailor programs to fit those special needs. Rather, they had to do it in an inarticulate, often *sub rosa*, fashion since such programs went counter to the main stream of schoolmen's thinking. And so the programs were generally ineffective in meeting a problem of such magnitude.

The unitary-community idea was not simply for the guidance of educators. As we have seen, it helped protect the independence of the schools from the community's political processes. Or did it? Raymond E. Callahan has argued that the independent urban schoolmen were, in the period from about 1910 to 1930, extremely vulnerable; not, perhaps, to partisan political pressure, but to the dominant socio-economic interests of the community. In this period, business was pretty generally dominant, and Callahan attributes the rise of the "cult of efficiency" in educational administration to the desire of vulnerable schoolmen to please the influential businessmen. In a way, Counts's story of Chicago confirms this point; during the relatively "nonpolitical" period when McAndrew was exercising full authority, the Association of Commerce occupied a very influential place while labor was excluded from school affairs. The "intrusion of politics" under Thompson meant the return of the teachers and other nonbusiness interests to active and influential positions.

Independent schools, operating according to the myth of the unitary community, were and are rather feeble instruments for seeking public support, and this weakness is one key to the business domination Callahan has described. School-tax rates and bond issues and, in some states, the annual school budget, may require specific voter approval in a referendum. How are the schoolmen to persuade the electorate to say yes? They have relatively little of what in urban politics is sometimes called "clout." They have no network of support from groups and interests for whom the educators have done favors in the past and who now can be asked to reciprocate. They may sometimes get the teachers and the parents and the children to ring doorbells, but such efforts are often ineffectual compared to the canvassing a strong party organization might do. Since approval of a school referendum invariably costs the taxpayers money immediately—there is no intervening lapse of time as there is between the election of a candidate to a city office and the possible future increase in taxes—a sizable negative vote may normally be assumed. Where is the positive vote coming from? Educators have gone on the assumption, quite probably correct, that the benevolent patronage of the business leadership was necessary if they were to have a chance of referendum success.

Today, in the big city, the structure of the situation has not changed.

Only the interests which effectively make demands upon the schools have changed. Negroes, the poor, middle-class intellectuals, and teachers have partially, perhaps largely, displaced the businessmen. The unitary-community myth is still used as a defense of the schools. In order to persuade predominantly Catholic, lower-middle-class voters of Irish or Polish descent to support higher taxes for public schools, it is very important to emphasize the undivided benefits which all residents receive from an undifferentiated educational program. The difficulty is that today the pitch is no longer believed. It is evident, for example, that Negroes do not buy the myth that the community is unitary. They know better. Moreover, even though a school board with a unitary-community perspective may permit integration, Negroes demand a differentiated school program with compensatory facilities to help them fight prejudice and poverty, to help them reach a high enough level so that equal educational programs will no longer leave them behind. Meanwhile, those ethnic groups whom Wilson and Banfield have shown to be comparatively unwilling to vote for public expenditures for *any* purpose are especially unenthusiastic about putting high-cost programs into Negro slum schools. Unions are anxious about job competition from the products of improved vocational programs. And although property taxes for schools may be only a minor problem for large corporate business, they are often severe in their effect on smaller business and on small householders. The latter groups, especially, are potential city dropouts; that is, they may move to suburbia if taxes go up, and the result may be to depreciate further the city's tax base while its educational needs increase. The unitary-community myth no longer serves to quiet the demonstrations or to pass the tax increase. It has largely outlived its usefulness. Yet it is still frequently articulated by schoolmen and lay supporters of the schools, perhaps because, as the inveterate gambler said in explaining his continued patronage of the crooked card game, "It's the only one in town."

There is another dimension in which unity has been emphasized with respect to schools. Educators have tried very hard to achieve and maintain consensus among all those engaged in the educational enterprise. Unity is a prerequisite to a reputation for expertise, and it thus adds to the bargaining power of schoolmen as they seek public support. Unity inside the school helps justify independence from "politics." In the Chicago case of 1927 and again today, in Chicago and elsewhere, the vulnerability of the schools to group pressures from the community depends heavily on the extent to which the board, the superintendent and his administrative associates, and the teaching staff remain as professional allies rather than splitting into conflicting camps.

The consensus among school interests is equally sought after at the state level, and as my colleagues and I have suggested in our study of state politics and the schools, a number of devices have been developed to help achieve and preserve unity, even at some cost in terms of goal achievements—dollar volume of state aid, or teacher tenure law protection, for example. The point I wish to make here, however, is that unity among schoolmen is frequently a considerable handicap for big-city school interests, particularly in their efforts to get increased state aid.

Let me illustrate my point with a discussion that leans heavily on experience in Missouri. There, a moderately malapportioned legislature for many years exhibited great fiscal prudence. They spend more than they used to, but the state still ranks much lower in comparison to other states in expenditures than in income. Education is no exception, but, thanks largely to the skillful efforts of the Missouri State Teachers Association, both district consolidation and equalization grants under a foundation program have steadily improved the financial condition of most *rural* schools. But these programs are of much less benefit to schools in the large cities.

St. Louis and Kansas City schools receive state aid, to be sure, but on a somewhat different basis from other districts. State aid is legally less assured in the large cities, and it gets a smaller portion of the job done. The city of today has high-cost educational needs as compared to noncity areas. The core-city wealth, which is effectively taxable by local action, is comparatively less great than it used to be. State-aid programs which aim at providing minimum per-pupil expenditure do not solve big-city needs, and the states have not been receptive to extra demands of urban educators any more than they have responded to other urban interests.

When the city-school interests go to the state capital to press their special claims, they carry with them the norms of their professional colleagues everywhere, the norms of unity. All educators are united in favor of education, one and indivisible, to be provided equally for all. Yet this same delegation comes to ask special treatment from the state, either in the form of additional state money or additional authority to act for themselves. Moreover, the statewide education interests normally take no stand on the requests of the city-school interests. The statewide groups are interested in equalization, not special programs for the cities. They might even oppose urban-oriented school legislation since it would either compete for monies desired for equalization or, at the least, serve the needs of "the city," a symbol which noncity school leaders look on with suspicion. And these school leaders occupy the state department of education and dominate the state teachers association. From the point of view of the city schools, the best thing, and the usual thing, is to have the state groups stay out.

The urban school forces, assuming they have at least the neutrality of the state educational groups, confront another unity norm when they arrive at the state capital. This is the unwritten rule of the state legislature for dealing with all "local" issues, and the school needs of a city like St. Louis are treated within the same system of legislative practice as a proposed salary increase for the sheriff. They are all local issues. The rule provides that the legislators will approve a request from a local community provided that the state representatives from that community are substantially united in their support of the request.

One might suppose that, since the school groups all strive for internal unity, the legislators' prerequisite would be easy to fulfill. Such is not the case, and much of the reason lies in the separation of the schools from the political system of the city. The problem lies in the relationship, or rather the lack thereof, between the spokesmen for the schools and the city delegation in the legislature. City legislators are not interested in the schools. They avoid service on education committees, take little part in debate on school issues, and generally are thought by other legislators who are concerned about state school policy to contribute very little. Urban legislators are likely indeed to be profoundly uninterested in the concerns of *any* groups which successfully keep themselves apart from the political system of the city. They, after all, are products of that system and their points of reference are mainly contained within it. The school representatives cannot eschew politics and still make meaningful contact with the legislature.

Although most state legislators would be merely indifferent to the schools' plea for state help, some may actively, though covertly, oppose the requests. In the St. Louis case, a number of influential city legislators identify themselves with the "state" as a fiscal entity apart from the "city," and resist increased state expenditures of any kind for the city. Others may reflect a Catholic constituency and say, for instance, that unless money is provided for transportation to parochial schools they will oppose extra funds for public education in the city. Still others have been known to be engaged in various kinds of alliances, for instance with school-building and maintenance crews, and hope to gain benefits for their allies by helping to block the school board's requests in the legislature. Most of the city-based legislative opposition will be behind the scenes. In a roll call vote it would seldom show up. Nevertheless it may effectively block passage of the program.

The key to the problem is in the fact that the schoolmen have no way to reach the pivotal legislators where it counts. There is no network of mutual obligation and support connecting the two groupings. The school board can cash no influence checks in payment for past or future favors done for legislators. There are a few favors the school can do for a highly political legislator, but every element in professional education training and ideology contributes to the refusal to think in these terms. Parenthetically, it might be noted here that lay board members seem to get more righteously indignant than professional superintendents at the suggestion that they do a little trading if they want their program passed. Political naiveté, especially at the level of articulated ideology, helps reinforce the incapacity of urban school interests (though not necessarily in rural areas where schoolmen are often highly skilled in the arts of "forks of the creek" politics) to get what they want from the state. Not only the congenital opposition of educators to these elemental political tactics, but the widespread misconception of the source of their opposition further confounds them. Newspapers and other "spectator elites" such as academics have assumed that it was the rural interests that were doing in the urban claims. The inability to understand that urban legislators were often unresponsive, not only regarding school problems but on many other desires of some city-based interests, has led to invalid inferences about what to do next. One of these has been simply to reassert the evils of politics and the importance of insulating the schools against their bitter breath. The second is to await with confidence the coming of reapportionment. "Give us an urban majority and our urban programs will pass," is the assumption underlying this optimism. But an urban state legislative majority may still not care much about the schools; and, without more political savvy than they have displayed in the past, the spokesmen for city school interests will continue to get unsatisfactory treatment.

There is, obviously, the now genuinely optimistic prospect of federal funding, especially rich for urban schools serving slum populations. I shall not explore this dimension in detail, but I want to note an important point: urban interests have for years done much better at the federal level than in the state capitol. The reasons are complex and not very well understood, but among them is the strong, warm, and skillfully administered relationship between city political leaders and federal officials. Federal officials in all the relevant branches and agencies have come to be responsive to political leaders and politically skillful administrators in the cities. Mayors, urban-renewal directors, and local poverty-program administrators are especially skilled, individually and through their national associations, at bringing their points of view to the sympathetic attention of Washington. The newspaper accounts of the federal treatment of the Chicago schools in 1965 suggest to me that, as Mayor Daley salvaged Superintendent Willis's federal school money from the fire, so the help of political leaders in other cities may be necessary to maintain satisfactory relationships with this newly opened source of major financial assistance to big-city schools. Indeed, the requirement, which Washington officials seem to be taking seriously, that poverty programs and the new educational programs be closely coordinated may, in turn, force the schools into closer relationship with many other agencies of city government and thus, inevitably, into the mainstream of urban politics.

Earlier I raised the question of the significance of deciding the McAndrew affair within a partisan electoral process. Let us return to that dimension of our general problem. I have suggested that autonomy and isolation have serious disadvantages for urban schools. What is to be said on the other side? What would it be like if the schools were a more integral part of the urban political system; if, for example, they were made a regular line department of the city government with a director appointed by the mayor to serve at his pleasure? How would such a process work? What would be the substantive effects on educational policy and on the city generally?

To examine this issue directly, we need to be clear about how city political systems actually function. No single formulation will do justice to the complexities of the question but at least three points seem especially pertinent. First, political scientists generally have found that in large cities, and some of the smaller ones too, influence is rather widely dispersed, specialized, and exercised in a discontinuous fashion. That is, one person or group will be active and influential on one set of issues while quite a different array dominates the next set. This tendency is perhaps accentuated when a specialized set of issues, such as education, is determined within a specialized institutional framework. But the institutional framework is primarily reinforcing, not by itself determining. A second, related, finding of political scientists' examinations of the urban community is that great pressure is generally exercised in questions of substantive policy program (though not so much on elections or top level personnel appointments or tax rates) by the program's professional and administrative experts. In urban renewal or public health and hospitals, to take two examples from regular city government, the professional personnel run the programs about as completely as schoolmen run the schools; perhaps, more so.

A third finding is rather different from the first two, however. In many cities, though by no means in all of them, a critical and continuing role of substantial import is played by the mayor. He is the chief organizer of the dominant coalition of interests and the chief broker among them. He is the chief negotiator in balancing not only the disparate and often conflicting groups in the city but also in representing city needs to state and especially to federal agencies. More than that the mayor is the single most important problem-solver. He is committed, out of sheer re-election necessity if for no other reason, to rebuilding the slums, attracting new business, renovating downtown, implementing equal rights and opportunity and, as federal money is at last making it possible, improving the life chances of the urban poor. Not all mayors face the same circumstances, of course. Some are weak in formal authority to control even their governmental environment; many are lacking in the fiscal and human resources to get the necessary leverage on the social and economic environment. Nevertheless, there is a substantial similarity in the orientation and role of big-city mayors, and this convergence has been especially pronounced during the past decade. In style or substance, mayors of today have little in common with Big Bill Thompson. Actually, mayors might not relish taking more direct responsibility for the schools. Why should they take on another large problem area when they too can fall back on the argument that the schools should be nonpolitical? If they were to accept a more active role, it might be because they really want to resolve the complicated difficulties of urban life, and solutions *must* include effective use of the schools.

These three generalizations are all relevant to my question but in somewhat different ways. They suggest that if the schools were integrated with the urban governmental system, the educators would continue to make most of the technical and administrative decisions but the mayor and his coalition of community support would play a major role in giving over-all program and fiscal direction. The schools would compete more directly than now with other city programs for available money. Their programs might be more differentiated among different segments of the community, as the mayor tried at once to solve problems and ease tensions and to please the major elements of the coalition that elected him. Their top administrative personnel might be more vulnerable to the vicissitudes of electoral fortune, though mayors might be only slightly more effective in breaking through the defenses of the educators' bureaucracy to choose (or fire) their own men than are independent school boards now. Educators might find themselves and their programs more often subordinated to other agencies and programs than is presently the case, but this subordination might be more a difference in perception than reality; an independent school system already must compete for money and support, but in an indirect and segmented manner. It is not clear that mayor-directed schools would be more generously financed from the local community but neither is it inevitable that they would be poorer.

In my judgment, the principal difference between the existing arrangements for the government of urban public education and this hypothetical control by the mayor would be in the schools' relationship with the increasingly pluralistic and tension-filled community. An independent school system asks for community support directly, unprotected by any of the confusions of mandate that attend the election of political officials. The schools are naked against community pressures except as their unitary-community ideology and whatever rational citizen demand there may be for their services may shield them. I have argued, and so do the protest demonstrations and the negative votes in referenda, that these are not sufficient protection if the urban schools are to perform the extraordinarily difficult, high cost, tasks of educating the urban poor. It is not coincidence, I think, that recently the schools have been so often the target of the alienated and disaffected elements of society. Whether protesting against *de facto* segregation, double taxation of Catholics, or alleged Communist infiltration, the pickets know that the schools are vulnerable to direct assault. No other programs or interests get in the way. No other issues or loyalties intrude.

But the processes involved in electing a mayor and a council, especially on a partisan ticket, but also in a large, heterogeneous city with nonpartisan government, do mute these kinds of pressures. Mandates *are* vague; constraints on the specific policy choices which the officials will subsequently make are loose. And the protection afforded to the professionals is considerable. They may administer their programs while someone else takes the heat, and diffuses it.

There is evidence that in the controversies over fluoridation those communities in which the voters decided the question in a referendum were often in the process racked by deep social conflict. In those cities where a mayor played a strong role, on the other hand, fluoridating the city water supply by administrative order, there was little untoward excitement. The schools have far more substantive impact on urban life than fluoridation, of course; the latter seems to be mainly symbolic. But educational issues are laden with affect, and they may come more and more to resemble fluoridation as a focus for the manifold discontents of the city. The broader political process might help to protect the schools against becoming the urban community's battlefield.

In all that I have said thus far, my principal points appear to be as follows: (1) more direct and effective political (mayoral) control of the schools will be difficult to engineer because of the resistance of schoolmen, regardless of formal governmental structure, to "nonprofessional" direction; and (2) big-city school interests might get a more receptive hearing in state and national capitals and be partially screened from local direct action protests if they merge their interests more fully with the over-all city administration. But would this type of result lead to more effective education? This, in my judgment, is precisely the *wrong* question. In the urban center, there is no education which is separate from the issues of race, poverty, housing, crime, and the other human problems of the metropolis. The issue we need to face is whether greater mayoral control would lead to changes in school policy (e.g., better coordination and cooperation with urban renewal, recreation, and poverty programs) which would make the educational program more effective in solving the larger complex of community problems. In a simpler era, one could argue that Big Bill Thompson may well have done just this in Chicago. And, forty years later, one might well feel that, in the same city, Mayor Daley might have achieved more effective integration than Superintendent Willis seemed disposed to provide had the mayor chosen to violate the educators' code of independence and exert more direct control of the situation.

At the same time, there should be no mistake about the fact that greater administrative integration of schools with city would, in many cases, mean subordination of the schools to the city government. Moreover, such subordination might often mean that the schools were being used as instruments to achieve policy goals which extended well beyond more narrowly defined educational objectives. To some extent, of course, this is happening anyway, and indeed it has always been so. But the issue of political control forces us to be explicit about the question of how the many goals we wish to achieve in the city can best be approached. If it turned out that education was not at the head of the list, educators would be compelled to acknowledge that fact in a situation where they had to bargain for their share of the local resources against the direct competition of other programs as well as against the fiscal prudence of the electorate.

Direct competition for local money; subordination of educators to other public officials with other interests and programs; the self-conscious use of the schools as instruments to fight poverty, improve housing conditions, or fight city-suburb separation: these have been virtually unthinkable heresies to devoted schoolmen. Yet, are they much more than an explicit statement of steps and tendencies already being taken or implicit in present practices? I think not; we are already moving this way, to some extent we always have been doing so, and the real question to be faced is: How might we do these things better? A greater measure of local political leadership in education and coordination of the schools with other portions of the community might well contribute to this end.

9

It is strange to see with what feverish ardour the Americans pursue their own welfare, and to watch the vague dread that constantly torments them lest they should not have chosen the shortest path which may lead to it.

DE TOCQUEVILLE
Democracy in America

Ronald Moskowitz
EDUCATION AND POLITICS IN BOOMTOWN

Houston is Boomtown U.S.A., the youthful upstart of America's cities. In the 130 years since its birth, it has mushroomed in its free-wheeling Texas way to become the country's sixth-largest city, with a greater-metropolitan area population of more than 1,500,000. Every year 40,000 new residents settle in Houston, drawn by the promise of good jobs, available housing, a reasonable cost-of-living index, and good schools. Houston is the center of the nation's oil and petrochemical industries, one of the world's largest ports and rail centers, and the home of the National Aeronautics and Space Administration. It is also one of the richest and most dynamic cities in America.

The city's skyline changes radically each year as new office, hotel, and apartment skyscrapers fill up the downtown core area and spread, like the city itself, in all directions. Mammoth freeways dissect this urban sprawl; someone suddenly transplanted there might easily believe he was in Los Angeles. Unhampered by any natural geographical impediments, Houston has expanded from an incorporated area of nine square miles in 1837 to 447 square miles today. Unrestricted by any zoning laws, new construction has soared. So have land prices. Building sites that were selling for $3,000 an acre less than twenty years ago are now going for as much as $120,000 an acre. The taxes on this land have risen with the prices, and the political battles over what politicians will spend all of this money for—and how—have resulted in some of the most hotly contested local elections in the country.

None has been more heated than the political battles for control of the Houston Independent School District. The seven-member Board of Education controls the district's budget, which for years has been larger than the city's. This year it exceeds $150 million, one-third of which is going to retire bonds that add an average of three new classrooms to the system each school day.

Houston, therefore, is probably the only large city in America where residents are more familiar with school board candidates and the issues they have raised than with their city councilmen or supervisors. It is probably the only large city in America where politics plays such an overt role in the operation of the public schools. Surprisingly, though, the Houston Independent School District has proved that a big-city school system can be good despite a city's preoccupation with power politics.

For more than a quarter of a century, a rigidly formed two-party system in Houston has vied for control of the board at every election. They call themselves liberals and conservatives. The labels used to fit. During all but two years of the 1940s and 1950s, the conservatives maintained at least a four-member majority, and the issues which kept them in power became the most controversial policies of the board.

The district board accepted no federal aid, not even for its under-financed free-lunch program, which was wrung out of local charities each year because "federal aid means federal control." It integrated none of its schools or faculties because "race-mixing is a plot from Washington." It would not even allow any of its teachers time off or travel expenses to attend National Education Association meetings because of that organization's policy advocating federal aid to education. The board even controlled the curriculum. Textbooks calling the United Nations a hope for world peace were banned, or—worse—rewritten to reflect the board majority's prejudices. During that time, the curriculum required two years of Texas history and one year of American history, but allowed world history to be an optional high school elective.

"We don't want our children exposed to this one-worldism too early," explained former board member and chief censor Birdie Maughmer, who later resigned after she shot her policeman husband.

The liberals, meanwhile, campaigning on such unemotional issues as better-qualified teachers, smaller classes, higher salaries, and quality education were seldom able to capture more than two of the seven seats.

Houston residents came to know the issues and the board members better than citizens in almost any other large city because of a long-standing board policy to televise its meetings—a policy discontinued two years ago because the liberal minority started looking too good, and because local citizens seeking attention used the meetings to get free air-time. The University of Houston operated the first education channel in the nation, and one of its first regular programs in 1955 was the Board of Education meetings, which soon became known as the Monday night fights. At times, they drew larger audiences than some of the network situation comedies—the dialogue was better. Once, for instance, Mrs. Lois Cullen, who is still on the board, suggested building all swimming pools outdoors under the trees, which could be used instead of diving boards. Another money-saving device was suggested by her former conservative colleague Mrs. Dallas Dyer. She asked that only beans and rice and tortillas be served in the free lunch program in Mexican-American schools.

But the dialogue wasn't all humorous. The conservatives made a point of using their air time to scare the viewers with their ideas of what horrible things could happen to their children if the liberals got in power and desegregated the schools. The irony was that, during 1955 and 1956, the only two years the liberals were in control—after the U.S. Supreme Court decision declaring segregated schools unconstitutional—they didn't have the political fortitude to integrate anything other than the school directory. And the conservatives resegregated that when they regained a majority in 1957.

While the newspapers and citizens were busy debating these various hot emotional issues, teachers and administrators did their best to keep the schools going. And the conservative majority—the board members who promulgated the stifling academic atmosphere—quietly reaped the rewards of their majority position.

Mrs. Dyer, a disgruntled teacher who quit to run for the board because she couldn't get assigned to the school in which she wanted to teach, went from a $6,000-a-year teacher to a member of the insurance underwriter's "Million-Dollar Round Table" in five years by selling more than $1,000,000 worth of insurance. Whether or not much of it was sold to teachers and administrators who wanted to get ahead, as the liberals charged, the fact remains that she used her board position—and the accompanying publicity—as an entrée to contacts she otherwise never would have made. She got her job from a fellow conservative board member who was an executive of the parent company which owns the insurance company.

Other majority members made sure that their friends and supporters were given much of the work in the school district's gigantic building program. They also made sure that promotions were handed out to those teachers and administrators who mouthed their controversial philosophies and supported them at election time. Still other friends, or relatives of friends, were raised to key positions in the district's administration in return for going along with favors expected by the board members who put them there.

Although such questionable practices still go on, the labels really don't fit anymore. Despite the fact that the conservatives have been in power for the last eleven years, the policies of the district have changed drastically. The district now accepts federal aid—all it can get. "The federal government is going to control education whether we accept their aid or not," one conservative member explains. It lets its teachers attend any professional meetings they wish. Textbooks are no longer censored or rewritten. The suggestions of the liberal board members for improvements in the educational program are no longer ignored. They are often heeded, even though the conservatives are apt to table them the first time they are mentioned, then bring them up a meeting or two later as though they thought of the ideas themselves.

The conservatives, cognizant of the great influx of new, more moderate residents into the city, simply aren't that conservative anymore—except at election time. Even then they have found that the sole issue of segregation, though really a moot question, is enough to get them re-elected. In the last election campaign, they finally defeated the liberals' chief spokesman for nearly a decade—Mrs. Charles E. White, a Negro—by charging without any evidence that, if re-elected, she would bus children out of their neighborhoods, take teachers' cumulative sick leave to pay for the busing, hire a Negro superintendent, and rotate teachers so everyone would serve some time in a Negro school. But although the conservatives have shifted their political position more toward the mainstream, they are still using their political power to reward their friends and supporters. Former Board President Robert Y. Eckels says he does not see anything wrong with the board taking a hand in such matters. Said Mr. Eckels, an insurance man who was recently charged with handing out his business cards at a school faculty meeting:

"I am, quite naturally, all things being equal, going to do what I can to see that those I know and have confidence in get the work, and I don't see anything wrong with it. Those friends that I have confidence in will get the air conditioning work. Sure, the superintendent's executive committee is supposed to recommend architects, but you and I both know that I go down [to the administration building] and say, 'Horace, I have a friend of mine who's an architect and I want you to look him over.'"

Eckels referred to Horace Elrod, the deputy superintendent in charge of administration and the building program. Mr Elrod is also the cousin of H. L. Mills, for thirty years the school district's business manager and the sparkplug of the conservatives until he was forced to resign in 1959 amid a scandal involving his office. Woodrow Watts, deputy superintendent for high schools, is Elrod's brother-in-law. Such blatant nepotism is one of the chief arguments the liberals use against the conservative majority, charging that it produces mediocre top administrators whose chief function is to pay homage to the board majority.

Glenn Fletcher has been superintendent since John W. McFarland, bedridden with an ulcer and a cataract, resigned two years ago in disgust. In the board election last fall, Mr. Fletcher campaigned actively for the board majority, both among school personnel and the general public.

Despite the generally poor leadership now available at the top of the school district's organization chart, Houston operates one of the most successful big-city school systems in the nation. The district seems to prove that the quality of big-city school programs can be high, even in cases where policy is often set for political rather than for educational reasons. This is due chiefly to the strong second-level administrators, who have ridden out the political storms by just doing their jobs well, and by the dedication of individual teachers in their classrooms, which are, for the most part, insulated from the politics.

But a great deal of the district's success also stems from the nature of the area's population. Like the city, the district is huge and sprawling. Its 314 square miles encompass not only most of the city limits but suburban areas such as Bellaire, West University Place, and Southside. As in most other big cities, Houston's white middle class is leaving the city's core for the suburbs, but most of the better—and even the best—residential areas in the Houston area are within the city limits or within the district's boundaries. The wealthy Memorial Drive and River Oaks areas, plus upper-middle-class Meyerland, Sharpstown, and Tanglewood, are but a few examples of the leading residential subdivisions within the district's boundaries. Therefore, the rich, lily-white, high-quality schools which usually surround other big cities in separate suburban school districts are part of Houston's district. The taxes of these richer parents help raise the entire tax base. But, more important, their better-qualified students help raise the average quality of the entire district.

This probably explains why results from standardized testing in the district in the spring of 1967 show that Houston's pupils are, on the average, achieving better than other pupils in Texas and the Southwest and better than pupils in most big cities throughout the nation. Third graders, for instance, scored in the seventy-sixth percentile when compared with other big-city pupils on the Iowa Test of Basic Skills. Results of the ninth-grade standardized test showed that the performance of Houston's students was higher than the national median in all areas except background in the natural sciences. They scored in the eightieth percentile in correctness and appropriateness of expression, ability to do quantitative thinking, ability to interpret reading materials in the social studies, and ability to interpret reading material in the natural sciences. The overall average put Houston students in the sixty-fifth percentile.

But other objective measurements of the district's quality show that academic achievement is scattered. Although there are twenty-one senior high schools, the seventy-four Houston semifinalists in the National Merit Scholarship Test given in the spring of 1967 all came from only nine of those schools. And more than half of the seventy-four—forty-eight—came from only three: Bellaire, Lamar, and Lee. No Negro high schools or students were included. It is obvious, therefore, that while the overall quality of the district may be high, the individual quality of the schools in Houston is only as good as the social and economic backgrounds of the residents around them. Individual schools range from excellent, like those in the wealthier southwest area, to poor; and many of the ghetto schools are poor. Even these, however, are not as bad as slum schools in many of the older, less wealthy cities.

Fact Sheet on Houston Schools

Total School District Population		1,230,000
Enrollment (1966–67)		240,797
Teachers and supervisors		10,500
Schools: Elementary	168	
Junior High	35	
Senior High	21	
Total Schools		224
Budget		$150,958,638
Sources: Property tax	61.67 per cent	
State	37.12 per cent	
Federal and other	1.21 per cent	

Government: Seven school board members elected for four-year terms. Elected in two groups—one of three persons, one of four persons—in odd-numbered years on the third Saturday in November. Three elected in 1967; four to be elected in 1969.

When the board was conducting its lengthy fight against integration in the courts, it rushed to put up as many new school plants in Negro neighborhoods as possible to prove to the courts that Negroes had schools that were as good as the whites'. In the Negro schools, however, the polish of the teaching has not matched the sheen of the new buildings. Furthermore, segregated black schools have been, until this year, staffed by Negro teachers usually trained in other inadequate Negro schools and colleges, thus perpetuating a cycle of poor instruction. But even this is changing.

Standards at Negro colleges and universities have been raised. Negro teachers are now coming from the University of Texas and other formerly all-white state colleges. The two segregated teacher organizations in Houston have been amalgamated and integrated into one. In-service training of all teachers has been increased. White teachers are now working in many formerly all-Negro schools. And now that the district accepts federal funds, a $3,216,800 program to strengthen the educational program in the slum schools has been inaugurated. Called "Focus on Achievement," it is designed to concentrate on smaller classes, more flexible grouping, more individualized instruction, and uses thirty-six instructional specialists to aid classroom teachers. The district has also, entirely at its own expense, begun the "Talent Preservation Program," aimed at keeping students, particularly those at the 80 IQ level, from dropping out.

Negroes also are better off in Houston than elsewhere because they make up only one-third of the total school population and live in several scattered areas rather than in one or two concentrated ghettos. Now that integration has been forced on the district by the federal courts, it has a better chance of succeeding in Houston, even under a modified neighborhood school pattern, since many of the neighborhoods could be—for school purposes—well integrated. But the board has refused to bus children or to change boundary lines to promote integration, so it is moving slowly despite a series of court orders and prodding from the Justice Department in Washington. A recent report shows that, after nine years of integration, the district this winter has fewer than 13,000 Negroes in formerly all-white schools and fewer than 150 whites in formerly all-Negro schools. Most of the Negro schools are still all black. And many of the white schools still have no Negroes.

Despite this, there has been only one short-lived boycott and little organized criticism of the board's inaction by the Negro community. Many liberals explain that Negroes had felt well represented on the board until Mrs. White was defeated. But now the only Negro left on the board is Asberry Butler, an attorney who is not considered as liberal or as articulate as Mrs. White. Furthermore, Mr. Butler has been discredited by the conservative majority, which hired private detectives and revealed that he had been convicted on two felony charges—subornation of perjury and felony theft—in cases involving insurance companies. Butler has received probated sentences on both, but is appealing them. One liberal spokesman expressed fear that with Butler as the only Negro spokesman on the board, the Negro community would no longer feel well represented and the city could expect trouble. But the Negroes may just be waiting to see what relief they can get from the federal government.

One integration suit is still pending in federal court, and the Justice Department is now in a position to threaten to take away the nearly $5,000,000 in federal funds the district is receiving unless more progress is made. The suit contends that the placement of more new schools in racially segregated neighborhoods will perpetuate segregation; it asks the school district to consider integration when planning new schools. The school district won the first round in the court battle, and by the time the Fifth Circuit Court of Appeals acts, all of the schools in the current $53,000,000 building program will probably be completed.

Joe Kelly Butler, president of the board, said that moving slowly on integration "has been our greatest strength. . . . We have come through all of these trying times with the very strong confidence of the people. You can't bus Negro kids into white schools without busing white kids into their schools. And you just can't rub the faces of your main investors in the school system in the dirt." But despite the slowness with which integration is proceeding, Butler is able to boast with good reason that "this school district has come a long ways in the last eight years since I came on the board."

The district's 10,000 teachers last year were given a 25 per cent raise. And public support for the school system has never been higher. Last year the citizens, after defeating two previous bond issues, voted to raise their taxes a total of $15,000,000 for educational improvement—including the salary raise. And, in the same election, while other school districts across the country were defeating bond issues for badly needed classrooms, Houston voters balloted 3 to 1 in favor of spending $46,000,000 to air condition every one of the 168 elementary, thirty-six junior high, and twenty-one senior high schools in the district.

Optimism has never been greater among the teaching staff, and the recent pay raise and the thought of teaching in air-conditioned comfort instead of Houston's almost intolerable humidity are not the only reasons. The staff and most of the schools' patrons are pleased that the district, which for years has operated like a collection of country schools, has started acting like the giant of public education that it is.

This change can be attributed almost entirely to Butler, a wealthy, independent oil man who has shown he cares more about the public-service aspects of his board position than handing out favors to friends. It was Butler who in 1957, at the request of the conservatives, authored the district's first integration plan. It called for stepping in a grade at a time, beginning with kindergarten. The conservative board majority refused to implement his plan, but two years later a federal court ordered that an almost identical plan be started. This fact lent credence to Butler's claim when he was elected to the board in 1959 that he was neither conservative nor liberal but a moderate. Since his election, however, he has almost always voted with the conservative majority. But, as most of the old-line conservatives have left the board, Butler has gradually moderated the newcomers and has emerged as the power behind the throne. It is under his leadership that the district has made its greatest gains.

At his suggestion, the district made its first long-range study of its needs in all areas. The study, which used some of the top professional consultants in the nation, projected needs to 1985 and showed that Houston was near the bottom in teacher salaries, per-pupil expenditures, and other vital fiscal measurements of the district's activity. The five-volume study, coupled with an imaginative public relations campaign, was credited with getting the voters, in May 1967, to approve an increase in the assessment of property by changing the ratio for determining taxable valuation from 40 to 53 per cent. This, together with additional state aid, enabled the district to raise the starting salary of teachers from $4,590 to $5,616 a year. Even this big raise still leaves Houston behind the nation's thirteen other major cities in starting pay—and behind Dallas and Fort Worth and five small, surrounding districts. But it did bring salaries to about the national average of large school districts—just where the long-range report indicated it should be at this time. The increased funds will also allow the district to raise per-pupil expenditures from $369.98 last school year to an estimated $461 for the current year, which would rank it among the upper 25 per cent of major districts.

The report has done more than bring badly needed finances to the district. It has spurred a variety of changes which board members hope will make possible a continuing program for improvement in all phases of the district's operations. More than fifty pilot projects in curriculum and instruction have been initiated, and administrators are looking for even more desirable innovations. Last year a specific study was launched to explore the entire curriculum with a view toward improving the mechanics and communications necessary to good curriculum development. The board has voted to affiliate with the Gulf Region Educational Television Affiliates for the use of in-service educational television. It has also voted to participate in an education service center sponsored by the Texas Education Agency, through which it can get large quantities of materials and advice on recent educational developments.

But the district, under Butler's leadership has made its greatest gains in educational and curriculum areas. It has expanded its special-education program to 254 classes involving some 2,547 pupils. This amounts, Butler says, to almost half the special-education classes in the entire state. It has nearly 9,000 of its brightest and most gifted students in an advanced-standing "major works" program. When a new administration building is completed, computers will be used not only to streamline the business office procedures but to relieve the teaching staff of some of its clerical work as well. And Butler is now talking about using the machines in the instructional program.

He is also talking about improving the counseling system by adding more and better-qualified counselors, and overhauling the curriculum so that more innovative methods can be utilized in almost every subject area. He is also planning in his mind an advanced technical high school to help make up for one of the system's most serious defects: its shoddy vocational technical offerings. A complete overhaul of vocational-technical education is sure to come soon. Several major companies have announced rejection of Houston as an expansion site because of an insufficiently trained manpower supply, and some have pointed to the school system's inadequate vocational program as the reason.

Butler notes with pride that Houston, without any state aid, has for years operated a free kindergarten program. His attention has now been turned to the obvious need for junior colleges and free instruction past the high school level. He predicts that a junior college district yet to be officially formed to serve the Houston area will have more than 40,000 pupils enrolled five years from now.

One of the greatest improvements in the district has been made through the cooperation of the liberal and conservative members. Several months ago, Mrs. Gertrude Barnstone, a stunning woman who is easily the most articulate liberal on the board, noted that libraries, especially in elementary schools, were woefully inadequate and asked that the matter be corrected. It was referred to a committee of which she is a member. At a subsequent meeting, the "bipartisan" committee recommended that, over a five-year period, library acquisitions be increased to a ratio of ten books per child, and that more space be allotted in new schools for libraries. The motion passed unanimously.

The liberals, the conservatives, and even Superintendent Fletcher agree that more of this type of cooperation between the two factions is the district's greatest need at this time. "Our greatest weakness," says Butler, "is that the Board of Education, historically, has been unable to have an effective dialogue on the problems of the district. If we were able to get across to the other side, or the other side to us, I think everyone would find that there are not nearly as many differences of opinion as some now think exist."

"Our greatest problem is school politics," agrees Fletcher, who participates in them with fervor.

It is doubtful whether Butler's call for a truce in the war between the liberals and the conservatives is a legitimate peace feeler. Even if it is legitimate, it is even more doubtful that the liberals would be willing to negotiate a peace. The conservatives' politics have been too dirty, and there is too much bitterness. They have made up lies to defeat opponents such as Mrs. White. They have hired private detectives to look for skeletons liberal candidates might be hiding in their closets to the point where it is difficult to find a well qualified person who will oppose them.

In the last election, for instance, Dr. George Oser, a physicist, forced Mrs. Cullen into a runoff on the primary ballot. When it looked as if he might win in the general election, the county tax assessor disclosed that Dr. Oser had registered late as a voter. While Oser and his attorneys were in Austin appealing the technicality, the conservative board majority had the board's attorney simply remove Oser's name from the ballot, and the court informally ruled that the question was then moot because the election was already in progress. Oser recently filed suit asking for an injunction to keep Mrs. Cullen from serving on the board and to call a new election for her seat.

This is the kind of power politics which is as much a part of Houston's school system as classrooms and teachers. Houston is a young city with fewer problems than most of its older, poorer sister cities. But it is growing up—and it is almost certain that in the years ahead it will start inheriting many of their kinds of problems. There will be, for instance, more unskilled Negroes moving in and more skilled whites leaving the district. If this, the chief problem of other big cities, and other major problems become political issues instead of the mutual problems of both factions, Houston could have real trouble.

THE LEGAL DIMENSION

School decision making is affected by numerous forces which interact in society. Some of these forces are derived from our social and political systems and are related directly to cultural traditions and customs. Other forces influencing school decision making are economic, religious, or scientific in nature. In this section, the effect of the law as a force which influences education will be examined.

Law can be thought of generally as a social institution composed of an organized pattern of rules and regulations that are intended to perpetuate the existing social order. In the process of directing social and cultural change, law permeates every aspect of our lives, including education.

Since education is primarily a state function, it is governed by state legislatures and administered through local school boards. The federal courts also play an important role in educational decision making. They can act directly, however, only in cases where an individual's liberty or civil rights are in question. But, despite this limitation, the federal courts have affected educational decision making in such areas as the relationship between church and state, the status of racial segregation in the public schools, and, recently, the matter of contractual relations with teachers.

In this section the emphasis is mainly focused on the action of the Supreme Court and the lower federal courts in the area of racial segregation. Following Reutter's general overview of the components of school law, Kaplan traces the significant decisions which led to the historic Brown case. It was in the Brown case that the court decided that the separate but equal doctrine had no place in public education. Thus the legal stage was set for the eventual elimination of school desegregation in the South. It was not until the early 1960's that a federal court demanded the desegregation of a northern school system. The description of the Gary litigation illustrates the reasoning behind what amounted to a temporary setback in the elimination of de facto segregation in northern schools. *Hobsen* v. *Hansen*, on the other hand, shows the determination on the part of a northern judge to correct the ills suffered by one of our large cities by altering school policies. In succeeding articles, both Hansen and Bickel are sharply critical of the *Hobsen* v. *Hansen* decision.

The final two articles in this dimension are included because it is hoped that they will stimulate thought about other aspects of school law. The La Noue article documents the continued difficulty encountered as the public schools try to remain neutral in religious matters. Implicit in the Brooks article are the seeds of future legal questions affecting educational decision making.

1

There is a legal ingredient in almost every educational decision—whether it involves punishing a pupil, requiring a pupil to take a course, operating a school cafeteria ... expending school funds ... or reciting the Lord's Prayer in school. In some situations the legal ingredient is the crucial factor; in others it is relatively insignificant.

E. EDMUND REUTTER

E. Edmund Reutter

OVERVIEW OF LEGAL FRAMEWORK FOR THE PUBLIC SCHOOLS

"Today, education is perhaps the most important function of state and local governments. Compulsory school attendance laws and the great expenditures for education both demonstrate our recognition of the importance of education to our democratic society. It is required in the performance of our most basic public responsibilities, even service in the armed forces. It is the very foundation of good citizenship. Today it is a principal instrument in awakening the child to cultural values, in preparing him for later professional training, and in helping him to adjust normally to his environment. In these days, it is doubtful that any child may reasonably be expected to succeed in life if he is denied the opportunity of an education." Thus in 1954 spoke the Supreme Court of the United States.

In the United States, differing from almost every other country of the world, the national government has no direct control or authority in the field of public education. Since education is not mentioned in the federal Constitution, under the Tenth Amendment it becomes one of the powers

From E. Edmund Reutter, "Overview of Legal Framework for the Public Schools," *Schools and the Law* (Dobbs Ferry, N. Y.: Oceana Publications, 1964), pp. 7–10, 105–107. Copyright © 1964 by Oceana Publications, Inc. Reprinted by permission of the publisher.

reserved to the states. The states have established local school districts with boards of education to operate the schools.

The concept of a free public school for all the children, however, was not very well developed when the United States became a nation. Early court decisions influenced a recognition of the legal purpose of the public school as the development of a citizenry capable of participating effectively in self-government. As public education evolved, it became from a legal point of view as much a duty of children to submit to instruction as a right that they had. The right of the government is limited, however, to requiring that children study certain subjects; it cannot demand that all children attend a public school. This is one of many situations involving education in which the rights of the state come into conflict with the rights of individuals, in this instance, parents. The federal Constitution, as interpreted by the Supreme Court, gives to parents the right to select where and how their children are to be educated so long as minimum essentials within the prerogative of the state to establish are observed.

Each state has established a public school system unique in some respects from those in other states. Yet, despite great diversity, often in important items, the similarities among the states on fundamental concepts are striking. The variations are more often those of form, rather than of substance, and more commonly of degree, rather than of basic approach. It is obvious from legal study that the states have tremendously influenced one another, and although each has gone its own way, rare is the situation in a state which has no counterpart in other states. Exceptions exist to every attempted generalization; yet frequently "the exceptions tend to prove the rule."

There are specific aspects of the law affecting public schools. By "the law" is meant all of the rules recognized by the courts. Some of the law is written and available in codified form, for example, state statutes and school board regulations. Most of the law, however, is not available in a precisely organized pattern. The latter is the so-called "common law," found in the court opinions through the years as judges have resolved controversies and recorded their reasoning. It is this phase of the law that frequently gives operational meaning to written regulations and that comes into play when written rules do not exist on a point.

There is a legislative hierarchy applying to the public schools. No act of a body lower in the system can be inconsistent with higher authority properly exercised. The federal Constitution heads the list, followed by federal statutes, state constitution, state statutes, regulations of the state-level educational agency, and regulations of local-level school authorities.

Also, there is a clear-cut organization of courts to interpret the law and decide legal issues. Most cases involving public education are handled in state courts, although some of those involving the federal Constitution appear in federal courts. Appellate courts exist to consider appeals from decisions of lower courts. The Supreme Court of the United States is becoming increasingly involved in educational matters as more and more litigants claim violations of the First, Fifth, and Fourteenth Amendments.

On the basis of concrete cases decided by courts through the years it is possible to find a degree of guidance as to what the law on an unadjudicated point is likely to be. Predictions are fraught with peril but, as with most things, there are levels of skill based on study and intelligence.

No other function of government has been separated legally from the main stream as has public education. Although generally true on the state level, it is most pronounced on the local level. Public education, almost universally throughout the country, is kept closer to the control of the people than other aspects of government. In about nine of ten school districts in the land the board of education is directly elected by the voters. The common situation is for local voters to elect two governing boards—one for general local government and one for the public schools.

Local boards of education enjoy wide discretionary powers. The states have not, however, relinquished their legal responsibility for education to local units. Local members of school boards are considered to be state, rather than local, officials. School buildings in legal contemplation are state property. Some states have accentuated the uniqueness of the public education function by establishing local school districts with boundaries distinct from municipal divisions. But even where boundaries are the same, school boards to differing extents are independent of control by officers of general government.

Public schools are public in the several senses of being open to all the children, of being financed by public funds, and of being subject to public control of policies. Citizens as individuals and as groups can influence educational policy in ways other than election of board members. Meetings of boards of education generally are open to the public. Regardless, the transactions are of public business, and the records are open to the public. Also, frequently citizens have a direct voice in determining expenditures.

The right of a parent to control the education of his child is deeply engrained in the common law. Judicial precedent dictates that legislation which changes the common law is to be narrowly construed. Parents' rights must yield only where their exercise impairs the general welfare.

From the perspective of the law, perhaps the point at which the individual citizen can exercise most influence is through what is known as a taxpayer's suit. This type of legal action arises when a taxpayer sues on the ground that an action is beyond the power of the body involved or that it represents an abuse of discretion in that a recognized power is being unreasonably or arbitrarily exercised. The element of spending public money generally is present, although in many instances the alleged improper expenditure is somewhat remote from the main issue.

Two of the most common suits broadly affecting educational matters are those where the intent is to require a governmental body or official to carry out a function that is alleged to be a duty, and those where it is sought to halt or to prevent some action that is alleged to be unauthorized by law. The complaint of one taxpayer is sufficient to activate the courts to examine a situation and to enunciate the law on the point. The fact that the overwhelming majority of affected people may approve a challenged action has no effect on its legality. Neither does the fact that a practice has been unquestioned legally over a long period of years.

2

... in the field of public education the doctrine of "separate but equal" has no place. Separate educational facilities are inherently unequal.
                    Brown v. Board of Education

John Kaplan
PLESSY AND ITS PROGENY

In any examination of the Supreme Court's treatment of segregation in education, the fountainhead case must be *Plessy v. Ferguson,* decided in 1896. Plessy brought an action to forestall his criminal prosecution for violation of a Louisiana statute requiring Negro and white passengers to ride in equal but separate railway cars. Plessy, who had attempted to ride in the car reserved for whites, alleged that he was not a Negro, being of seven-eighths Caucasian blood and, further, charged that in any event the statute requiring this racial segregation was unconstitutional. The Supreme Court found it necessary only to consider the latter question and upheld the segregation statute against constitutional challenge. The impact of the *Plessy* case would not have been so great had the Court confined its decision to segregation on railway cars which, after all, affects only a relatively small percentage of the population for

From John Kaplan, "Plessy and Its Progeny," from "Segregation Litigation and the Schools," Part II: "The General Northern Problem," *Northwestern University Law Review,* May–June, 1963, pp. 157–167. Reprinted by permission of the author and publisher.

relatively short periods of time. The opinion of the Court, however, was much broader than required by the facts of the case before it, and relied in great part upon the authority of previous state court decisions allowing segregation of white and colored races in the schools. For this reason the Court's reasoning was taken as a blanket declaration that in all areas, so long as facilities were equal, state-imposed segregation was inoffensive to the Constitution.

In approving the separate but equal doctrine, the Court had to meet two basic arguments. First, Plessy's attorney contended that if segregation on the basis of race were permitted, other types of segregation would have to be allowed, such as of those "whose hair is of a certain color, or who are aliens, or who belong to certain nationalities," and that it would be permissible to enact "laws requiring colored people to walk on one side of the street and white people upon the other, upon the theory that one side of the street is as good as the other." The Court, however, stated:

> The reply to this is that every exercise of the police power must be reasonable and extends only to such laws as are indicated in good faith for the promotion of the public good, and not for the annoyance or oppression of a particular class.

This facet of the Court's reasoning would seem much more appropriate to overturning the statute than to upholding it. While an examination of the Louisiana statute alone might not show any "oppresson of a particular class," the historical context of the statute makes its basic motivation and effect crystal clear. The segregation statutes enacted by the various Southern states were part of a concerted plan to remove the newly freed slaves from the political, social, and economic life of the South. For instance, in 1896, the year *Plessy* was decided, 130,334 Negro voters were registered in Louisiana. Eight years later, this number had been cut almost a hundredfold to 1,342. Similar effects were accomplished in other Southern states. Moreover, political rights were not the only ones affected by this movement. Statutes such as that of South Carolina which prohibited employers from allowing white and Negro workers to work together in the same room or to use the same entrances or toilets made it uneconomical for employers to hire Negro workers, other than as floor scrubbers who, by an exception to this segregation edict, were allowed to associate with white men in the factory. So long as the Court, as it did in *Plessy*, viewed the segregation issue as a simple, enforced separation between two equal groups, it could find no oppression. The fact was, however, that the white race in the South was dominant in terms of economic and political power. It would seem that the attempt by the state government to use its authority to accomplish the isolation of the Negro from this power would be oppressive enough.

Plessy's next argument, that both the motive of those exacting segregation statutes and the effect of such acts was to disadvantage the Negro psychologically, was answered by the Court:

> We consider the underlying fallacy of the plaintiff's argument to consist in the assumption that enforced separation of the two races stamps the colored race with a badge of inferiority. If this be so, it is not by reason of anything found in the Act, but solely because the colored race choose to put that construction upon it.

Again, although it may be difficult to imply any assertion of inferiority in the bland requirement that separate railway cars be provided for the two races, the contention assumes a different light when the context of segregation is considered. Many Southern states have held that a white person can recover damages for the humiliation of being forced to sit next to a Negro in a common carrier. Moreover, the Court's assertion that segregation did not in any way imply inferiority of the Negro is somewhat inaccurate as applied to jurisdictions which regard the imputation of Negro blood to a white man as so serious a charge that recovery may be allowed without any proof of damages.

Lastly, the Court buttressed its reasoning by asserting that segregation was not an evil since legislative and constitutional provisions, in any event, could not achieve equality for the Negro. "If the two races are to meet upon terms of social equality, it must be the result of natural affinities, a mutual appreciation of each other's merits and a voluntary consent of individuals."

This argument might be perfectly appropriate to a situation where the state by statute had attempted forcibly to mix the races, but here exactly the opposite situation was at issue. Here the state was attempting to prevent just the individual contact which the Supreme Court asserted was essential to equality.

The *Plessy v. Ferguson* decision may be explained, if not defended, by noting that it was decided relatively near the beginning of the drive to exclude the Negro from participation in the life of the Southern states. Since this drive reached full momentum only after the turn of the century, the Supreme Court may very well have not appreciated how completely state law would disadvantage the Negro. Viewed in this manner, the decision was wrong when it was handed down, although perhaps only a Court especially sensitive to the political mood of the South might have realized this at that time.

With the benefit of hindsight, the doctrine of *Plessy v. Ferguson* might be counted wrong on another, more pragmatic, ground. It is fair to say that, at least as applied to public education, the separate but equal doctrine in practice had turned out to be a failure. The Negro schools, which were undeniably separate, were generally by no means equal in their most obvious physical characteristics, let alone in more subtle matters such as their quality of education. For instance, in 1950, some 54 years after *Plessy v. Ferguson*, Mississippi, which had almost equal numbers of white and Negro students, had half again as many teachers in the white schools. Moreover, the widespread belief that from the 1940's on, the Southern states had moved with great energy and rapidity to ease the obvious inequalities in its schools, seems to be refuted by statistics. For instance, in 1952, 56 years after *Plessy*, rather than spending more on the Negro student to close the gap previously created between him and the white student, Mississippi's current educational expenditure per Negro pupil was 30 per cent of that per white pupil; South Carolina's was 60 per cent; Arkansas', 66 per cent; and Georgia's, 68 per cent. Roughly similar figures could be given for the capital expenditures on Negro and white schools. With only two exceptions, Southern states, rather than attempting to make up the deficiency in quality of buildings between white and Negro schools, were still spending more per pupil on the white schools. Georgia was spending 53 per cent as much per pupil on Negro school construction as on white school construction; Alabama, 60 per cent; South Carolina, 46 per cent. Generally, the same type of disparity was noticeable in the salaries paid teachers, the number of books purchased for school libraries, and almost every other characteristic investigated.

The reported lower court cases highlighted the flouting of *Plessy v. Ferguson* more graphically than could mere statistics. In a not atypical case in 1949, over 50 years after *Plessy*, the district court found that the city of DeWitt, Arkansas, provided a Negro elementary school which differed from the white one in that it had no indoor drinking fountain, an outdoor open pit instead of indoor toilet facilities, and furniture which the court characterized as "outmoded and in bad repair." In addition, the term in the Negro school was one month shorter than that in the white school. As if this inequality were not great enough, the community had embarked upon the construction of a new white elementary school which the court characterized as "luxurious." This additional white elementary school was being built at a cost of $140,000, as contrasted with the Negro school's value of $6,000. Nor was the discrepancy in the elementary schools the only one faced by the Negro students; while the DeWitt High School had an A rating, the Negro high school, some distance away, had a rating of only C. In this situation, however, the court decided that the admission of Negro children to the white schools was "not necessary for the protection of the constitutional rights of the plaintiffs."

The separate but equal doctrine was a failure not only because it was so openly and widely flouted, but because it was impossible to administer rationally. While equality of one railway car with another was susceptible of reasonably accurate measurement, equality of schools was not. For instance, how was a court to balance the fact that a Negro high school was in a newer building against the fact that it was a forty minute bus ride away for Negro students who lived within easy walking distance of a white high school? How could a court balance the availability of fine courses in woodworking in the Negro schools with the absence of a course in trigonometry there? As one district court judge stated,

> [The separate but equal doctrine] present[s] problems which are more than judicial and which involve elements of public finance, school administration, politics, and sociology. . . . The federal courts are not school boards; they are not prepared to take over the administration of the public schools of the several states.

The treatment of *Plessy* over the years in the Supreme Court shows a gradually growing awareness of its inadequacy. The first case applying the *Plessy* doctrine to education, and the high-water mark of the doctrine itself, was *Cummings v. Board of Education*, decided just three years after *Plessy*. There the Supreme Court was faced with a situation in which a Georgia county maintained a high school for white children but none for Negroes on the ground that it could not afford to maintain both.

The Court, in an opinion by Justice Harlan, who had dissented vigorously in *Plessy*, admitted that the benefits and burdens of public taxation must be shared by all citizens without discrimination against any class on account of their race. It went on to hold, however, that since the county had discontinued its operation of the Negro high school only temporarily and because of economic pressures, it had not violated the constitutional rights of the Negro students who were without any school. The Court therefore refused to enjoin expenditures on the white high school until Negroes could have equal rights.

The next case involving segregation in education came before the Court nine years later. There, in the case of *Berea College v. Kentucky*, the Court upheld the validity of a statute which provided that no educational institution could teach both white and Negro students at the same time. The Court's opinion did not even cite *Plessy v. Ferguson*, but rather proceeded on an entirely different ground—that the state had an absolute authority to control the corporations which it had chartered and hence could require them to segregate. The Court, however, did recognize that if the state attempted to prevent an individual, as distinguished from a corporation, from teaching white and Negro students together, "Such a [segregation] statute may conflict with the Federal Constitution in denying to individuals powers which they may rightfully exercise." . . . No reported case appears to have raised this question, however.

The first real indication of any weakening in the *Plessy* philosophy came 21 years after *Plessy* in *Buchanan v. Warley*, where the Court was confronted with a zoning ordinance which in effect segregated an entire city by race. Although the Court stated that *Plessy* was controlling insofar as segregation in education and transportation were concerned, it refused to carry the doctrine into the field of housing. It is difficult to determine the precise reasoning of the Court since the notions of civil rights for Negroes and property rights to dispose of land seem inextricably interwined in the opinion. *Buchanan*, however, did reject a rationale which, although unexpressed in the *Plessy* opinion, had been one of the primary justifications for all types of segregation. The Court stated:

> It is urged that this proposed segregation will promote the public peace by preventing race conflicts. Desirable as this is, and important as is the preservation of the public peace, this aim cannot be accomplished by laws or ordinances which deny rights created or protected by the federal Constitution.

Buchanan v. Warley is significant for yet another reason. It has been suggested that the case rests on the historical idea that each piece of land is unique and therefore it makes no sense to talk about equality of land within the separate but equal doctrine. If this is so, one might argue that no great insight into the educational process is required to see that a school and its student body are at least as unique as a piece of land.

Ten years later, in *Gong Lum v. Rice*, the Supreme Court was faced with its first case involving actual segregation in public education. There, however, the validity of the *Plessy* doctrine was conceded by the plaintiff, who was Chinese. He merely insisted that children of Chinese descent were properly placed in the white, as distinct from the colored, schools. The Court held that the state had the power, under the *Plessy* decision and cases cited therein, to classify Chinese in the same category as Negroes. In its opinion, however, the Court not only pointed up the fact that the validity of the *Plessy* doctrine had been conceded, but seemed gratuitously to cast a certain doubt upon it. The opinion by Chief Justice Taft stated that had it not been so often previously approved, the *Plessy* doctrine would call for "very full argument and consideration," and ruled against the plaintiff, "assuming the cases [such as *Plessy*] to be rightly decided. . . ."

It was not until 1938, in *Missouri ex rel. Gaines v. Canada*, that the Supreme Court struck down a state statute providing for segregation in education. Missouri maintained a law school for whites only and no equal, or even unequal, one for Negroes. Rather it offered to pay the tuition of any Missouri Negro at a law school in an adjacent state. In an opinion by Chief Justice Hughes, the Court rejected the state's contention that by paying tuition at equal law schools it had complied with the *Plessy* doctrine. Although Chief Justice Hughes seemed to base his decision entirely on the principle that a state was not providing equal education by requiring resort to another state's facilities, he did advert to the possibility that "equality" under the separate but equal doctrine might mean more than simple parity in physical facilities.

Twelve years after the *Gaines* case, in 1950, the Supreme Court was given an opportunity actually to analyze the ingredients of equality under the *Plessy* doctrine. The Court in two companion opinions, both written by Chief Justice Vinson, examined not only the intangible values associated with a particular school, but also considered the educational process itself. In *Sweatt v. Painter* the Court went beyond the mere physical facilities to find Texas' Negro law school inferior to Texas Law School in "those qualities which are incapable of objective measurement." These included the position and influence of the alumni, standing in the community, traditions and prestige. Moreover, for the first time in this context, the Court overtly recognized that in the United States the two races were not on an equal footing. It stated that the segregation deprived the Negro of educational contact with the dominant racial groups, which comprised 85 per cent of the population of the state and included most of the lawyers, jurors, judges, and other officials with whom a lawyer inevitably deals. On the same day that *Sweatt v. Painter* was decided, the Supreme Court handed down *McLaurin v. Oklahoma State Regents*, involving a closely related issue. There, Oklahoma, while admitting the Negro petitioner to its graduate school, had insisted that he conform to certain regulations:

> Thus he was required to sit apart at a designated desk in an anteroom adjoining the classroom; to sit at a designated desk on the mezzanine floor of the library, but not to use the desks in the regular reading room; and to sit at a designated table and to eat at a different time from the other students in the school cafeteria.

The Court held that these restrictions "impair and inhibit his ability to study, to engage in discussions, and exchange views with other students and, in general, to learn his profession." Chief Justice Vinson's opinion then struck another blow at the separate but equal doctrine and the rationale of *Plessy* by stating:

> There is a vast difference—a Constitutional difference—between restrictions imposed by the state which prohibit the intellectual commingling of students, and the refusal of individuals to commingle where the state presents no such bar.

Accordingly, when the Brown case and four other cases challenging state-imposed segregation in public grade and high schools finally reached the Supreme Court in 1952, the question was not so much whether the *Plessy* doctrine would be overruled as how it would be overruled. The Brown case itself requires careful study. For this reason, it is presented in its entirety elsewhere in this chapter.

3

*Our Constitution is color blind, and neither knows
nor tolerates classes among citizens.*
       JUSTICE JOHN MARSHALL HARLAN

BROWN ET AL. v. BOARD OF EDUCATION OF TOPEKA ET AL.

Opinion of the Court

MR. CHIEF JUSTICE WARREN delivered the opinion of the Court.

These cases come to us from the States of Kansas, South Carolina, Virginia, and Delaware. They are premised on different facts and different local conditions, but a common legal question justifies their consideration together in this consolidated opinion.

In each of the cases, minors of the Negro race, through their legal representatives, seek the aid of the courts in obtaining admission to the public schools of their community on a nonsegregated basis. In each instance, they had been denied admission to schools attended by white children under laws requiring or permitting segregation according to race. This segregation was alleged to deprive the plaintiffs of the equal protection of the laws under the Fourteenth Amendment. In each of the cases other than the Delaware case, a three-judge federal district court denied relief to the plaintiffs on the so-called "separate but equal" doctrine announced by this Court in *Plessy* v. *Ferguson*, 163 U.S. 537. Under that doctrine, equality of treatment is accorded when the races are provided substantially equal facilities, even though these facilities be separate. In the Delaware case, the Supreme Court of Delaware adhered to that doctrine, but ordered that the plaintiffs be admitted to the white schools because of their superiority to the Negro schools.

The plaintiffs contend that segregated public schools are not "equal" and cannot be made "equal," and that hence they are deprived of the equal protection of the laws. Because of the obvious importance of the question presented, the Court took jurisdiction. Argument was heard in the 1952 Term, and reargument was heard this Term on certain questions propounded by the Court.

Reargument was largely devoted to the circumstances surrounding the adoption of the Fourteenth Amendment in 1868. It covered exhaustively consideration of the Amendment in Congress, ratification by the states,

United States Supreme Court, 347 U.S. 483, 1954.

then existing practices in racial segregation, and the views of proponents and opponents of the Amendment. This discussion and our own investigation convince us that, although these sources cast some light, it is not enough to resolve the problem with which we are faced. At best, they are inconclusive. The most avid proponents of the post-War Amendments undoubtedly intended them to remove all legal distinctions among "all persons born or naturalized in the United States." Their opponents, just as certainly, were antagonistic to both the letter and the spirit of the Amendments and wished them to have the most limited effect. What others in Congress and the state legislatures had in mind cannot be determined with any degree of certainty.

An additional reason for the inconclusive nature of the Amendment's history, with respect to segregated schools, is the status of public education at that time. In the South, the movement toward free common schools, supported by general taxation, had not yet taken hold. Education of white children was largely in the hands of private groups. Education of Negroes was almost nonexistent, and practically all of the race were illiterate. In fact, any education of Negroes was forbidden by law in some states. Today, in contrast, many Negroes have achieved outstanding success in the arts and sciences as well as in the business and professional world. It is true that public school education at the time of the Amendment had advanced further in the North, but the effect of the Amendment on Northern States was generally ignored in the congressional debates. Even in the North, the conditions of public education did not approximate those existing today. The curriculum was usually rudimentary; ungraded schools were common in rural areas; the school term was but three months a year in many states; and compulsory school attendance was virtually unknown. As a consequence, it is not surprising that there should be so little in the history of the Fourteenth Amendment relating to its intended effect on public education.

In the first cases in this Court construing the Fourteenth Amendment, decided shortly after its adoption, the Court interpreted it as proscribing all state-imposed discriminations against the Negro race. The doctrine of "separate but equal" did not make its appearance in this Court until 1896 in the case of *Plessy* v. *Ferguson, supra,* involving not education but transportation. American courts have since labored with the doctrine for over half a century. In this Court, there have been six cases involving the "separate but equal" doctrine in the field of public education. In *Cumming* v. *County Board of Education,* 175 U. S. 528, and *Gong Lum* v. *Rice,* 275 U. S. 78, the validity of the doctrine itself was not challenged. In more recent cases, all on the graduate school level, inequality was found in that specific benefits enjoyed by white students were denied to Negro students of the same educational qualifications. *Missouri ex rel. Gaines* v. *Canada,* 305 U. S. 337; *Sipuel* v. *Oklahoma,* 332 U. S. 631; *Sweatt* v. *Painter,* 339 U. S. 629; *McLaurin* v. *Oklahoma State Regents,*

339 U. S. 637. In none of these cases was it necessary to re-examine the doctrine to grant relief to the Negro plaintiff. And in *Sweatt* v. *Painter, supra,* the Court expressly reserved decision on the question whether *Plessy* v. *Ferguson* should be held inapplicable to public education.

In the instant cases, that question is directly presented. Here, unlike *Sweatt* v. *Painter,* there are findings below that the Negro and white schools involved have been equalized, or are being equalized, with respect to buildings, curricula, qualifications and salaries of teachers, and other "tangible" factors. Our decision, therefore, cannot turn on merely a comparison of these tangible factors in the Negro and white schools involved in each of the cases. We must look instead to the effect of segregation itself on public education.

In approaching this problem, we cannot turn the clock back to 1868 when the Amendment was adopted, or even to 1896 when *Plessy* v. *Ferguson* was written. We must consider public education in the light of its full development and its present place in American life throughout the Nation. Only in this way can it be determined if segregation in public schools deprives these plaintiffs of the equal protection of the laws.

Today, education is perhaps the most important function of state and local governments. Compulsory school attendance laws and the great expenditures for education both demonstrate our recognition of the importance of education to our democratic society. It is required in the performance of our most basic public responsibilities, even service in the armed forces. It is the very foundation of good citizenship. Today it is a principal instrument in awakening the child to cultural values, in preparing him for later professional training, and in helping him to adjust normally to his environment. In these days, it is doubtful that any child may reasonably be expected to succeed in life if he is denied the opportunity of an education. Such an opportunity, where the state has undertaken to provide it, is a right which must be made available to all on equal terms.

We come then to the question presented: Does segregation of children in public schools solely on the basis of race, even though the physical facilities and other "tangible" factors may be equal, deprive the children of the minority group of equal educational opportunities? We believe that it does.

In *Sweatt* v. *Painter, supra,* in finding that a segregated law school for Negroes could not provide them equal educational opportunities, this Court relied in large part on "those qualities which are incapable of objective measurement but which make for greatness in a law school." In *McLaurin* v. *Oklahoma State Regents, supra,* the Court, in requiring that a Negro admitted to a white graduate school be treated like all other students, again resorted to intangible considerations: ". . . his ability to study, to engage in discussions and exchange views with other students, and, in general, to learn his profession." Such considerations apply with added force to children in grade and high schools. To separate them from others of similar age and qualifications solely because of their race generates a feeling of inferiority as to their status in the community that may affect their hearts and minds in a way unlikely ever to be undone. The effect of this separation on their educational opportunities was well stated by a finding in the Kansas case by a court which nevertheless felt compelled to rule against the Negro plaintiffs:

> "Segregation of white and colored children in public schools has a detrimental effect upon the colored children. The impact is greater when it has the sanction of the law; for the policy of separating the races is usually interpreted as denoting the inferiority of the negro group. A sense of inferiority affects the motivation of a child to learn. Segregation with the sanction of law, therefore, has a tendency to [retard] the educational and mental development of negro children and to deprive them of some of the benefits they would receive in a racial[ly] integrated school system."

Whatever may have been the extent of psychological knowledge at the time of *Plessy* v. *Ferguson*, this finding is amply supported by modern authority. Any language in *Plessy* v. *Ferguson* contrary to this finding is rejected.

We conclude that in the field of public education the doctrine of "separate but equal" has no place. Separate educational facilities are inherently unequal. Therefore, we hold that the plaintiffs and others similarly situated for whom the actions have been brought are, by reason of the segregation complained of, deprived of the equal protection of the laws guaranteed by the Fourteenth Amendment. This disposition makes unnecessary any discussion whether such segregation also violates the Due Process Clause of the Fourteenth Amendment.

Because these are class actions, because of the wide applicability of this decision, and because of the great variety of local conditions, the formulation of decrees in these cases presents problems of considerable complexity. On reargument, the consideration of appropriate relief was necessarily subordinated to the primary question—the constitutionality of segregation in public education. We have now announced that such segregation is a denial of the equal protection of the laws. In order that we may have the full assistance of the parties in formulating decrees, the cases will be restored to the docket, and the parties are requested to present further argument on Questions 4 and 5 previously propounded by the Court for the reargument this Term. The Attorney General of the United States is again invited to participate. The Attorneys General of the states requiring or permitting segregation in public education will also be permitted to appear as *amici curiae* upon request to do so by September 15, 1954, and submission of briefs by October 1, 1954.

It is so ordered.

4

*. . . I have seen nothing in the many cases dealing with
the segregation problem which leads me to believe
that the law requires that a school system developed
on the neighborhood school plan, honestly and con-
scientiously constructed with no intention or purpose
to segregate the races, must be destroyed or abandoned
because the resulting effect is to have a racial imbalance in certain schools where the district is populated
almost entirely by Negroes or whites. . . . There are
many expressions to the contrary, and these expressions lead me to believe that racial balance in our public schools is not constitutionally mandated.*
                    DISTRICT JUDGE GEORGE N. BEAMER

John Kaplan
SEGREGATION LITIGATION AND THE SCHOOLS

In the *New Rochelle* case the court had found it unnecessary to
decide the basic complaint of the Negro plaintiffs—that mere de facto
segregation involved a violation of constitutional right. The facts revealed at the trial allowed the court to base its decision on the narrower
proposition that the deliberate attempt to segregate or contain Negroes
in given schools by discriminatory drawing of attendance zone boundaries, site selection and the like, was unconstitutional. Though the
proposition of law enunciated in the *New Rochelle* case was undoubtedly correct, it does not give a great deal of guidance on the more basic
issue. Although many Negro leaders have asserted that, in almost all
cities, gerrymandering, or racially motivated zoning, has been the rule
rather than the exception, this is extremely difficult and expensive to
establish. Moreover, it involves a number of factual findings as to purpose which the Negro leaderhip would prefer not to leave in the hands
of the inferior courts—even the federal courts. Accordingly, Negro
leaders throughout the United States sought a legal theory which could,
as a matter of law, eliminate the difficulties of proof that could plague
plantiffs attempting to capitalize on the *New Rochelle* theory. In a sense,
it might be said that they were looking for a doctrine that would obviate
the need to prove deliberate purpose, very much as *Brown v. Board of*

From John Kaplan, "Description of the Gary Case" from "Segregation Litigation and the
Schools," Part II: "The General Northern Problem," *Northwestern University Law Review*, May–June, 1963, pp. 176–188. Reprinted by permission of the author and publisher.

Education had rendered unnecessary an expensive case-by-case attack upon school boards violating the separate but equal doctrine. If it could be established that a school board's purpose or its deliberate policy of segregation was as irrelevant as the tangible inequality of segregated schools, this could be accomplished. Thus, any action taken by a school board regardless of its purpose or other effects which caused in the main a separation of the races would be constitutionally as improper as the maintenance of a dual system of schools or as the gerrymandering of the zones of a single school district.

Although many cases presenting this theory have been brought to the federal courts, only a few, such as *Bell v. School City of Gary*, have reached judgment on the merits. Gary, Indiana's second largest city, presents an almost classic example of de facto segregation. Although the city is roughly "T" shaped, the vast majority of its Negro citizens live in a rectangular strip along the bottom third of the crossbar. Geographical school zoning in the city of Gary results, to a startling degree, in the division of Gary's schools into primarily Negro and primarily white schools. Seventeen of the city's 40 public schools, attended by 97 per cent of Gary's Negro students, had Negro enrollments of 75 per cent or more. In addition, of the 23,000 Negro school children in Gary, 16,000 went to schools that were 99 per cent Negro and a further 3,000 attended schools that were more than 95 per cent Negro.

The Gary plaintiffs in their complaint relied on three basic grounds for relief. First, they attempted to invoke the *New Rochelle* rationale by charging that the School Board was deliberately attempting to foster racial segregation by:

> assigning plaintiffs, and members of the class they represent, to racially segregated schools, in creating arbitrary attendance zones, in controlling transfers from school to school and in controlling assignment from elementary to secondary schools within the school system, in seeking to use a newly erected school and to enlarge presently segregated schools to further extend existing patterns of racial segregation. . . .

Secondly, they charged that the defendant School Board was "furnishing Negro minor plaintiffs assigned to segregated schools with unequal facilities in all respects, including, but not limited to, overcrowded and larger classes, and unequal recreational facilities. . . ." Finally they raised the basic issue, alleging that the School Board, by using the neighborhood school policy, had deprived the Negro plaintiffs of their constitutional right to attend racially balanced schools, and that "the defendants . . . have a constitutional duty to provide and maintain a racially integrated school system. . . ." The first two grounds for relief, being primarily factual grounds, are beyond the scope of this article, though it should be noted that, while the legal basis of the first ground is clear if the underlying factual allegations are proven, the second ground is not so simple.

The concern here, however, is solely with the last ground for relief. It is this ground which not only extends beyond Gary, Indiana, but is of vital importance in desegregation litigation all over the North and South. We must note at the outset that the plaintiffs were attempting to convince the court that de facto segregation in the schools—the racial imbalance which results when otherwise fair school districting is superimposed upon privately segregated housing patterns—is just as unconstitutional as districting based solely on race. Their argument did not concern itself with what a school board might *permissibly* do to further integration in its schools but rather with what a school board *must* do. The plaintiffs did not argue that deliberate effort toward racial integration is the better and the fairer course but rather that it is the only course open under the Constitution.

The plaintiffs in *Gary* admitted that this precise issue had not yet been decided by the Supreme Court. They argued, however:

> It is . . . manifest that attendance zone regulations and community concepts of education cannot take priority over . . . the end that all children may be afforded their fundamental rights to equal educational opportunities. . . .
>
> [S]egregated education is unequal within the meaning of the federal Constitution. That the segregation which ensues does not result directly from the imposition of state law can hardly be decisive.

This argument is a very broad one. If the School Board must guarantee each child an integrated education, it must take active account of race and bend positive efforts toward accomplishing that goal.

Before discussing the arguments put forth by plaintiffs in the Gary litigation, it would be well to point out that we are not concerned with whether school boards are permitted to take affirmative steps toward racial integration or even whether they should take such steps. The question here is whether the United States Constitution requires them to do so. Moreover, the plaintiffs in *Gary* did not assert that integration would be required merely of a board which had gerrymandered school zones passively by refusing for racial reasons to step in and modify a districting which they would have otherwise changed. Nor did they simply contend that the existence of an all-Negro school raises a presumption that some kind of racially motivated zoning has taken place. Although both of these propositions appear to have judicial support and in many situations would be the practical equivalent of the plaintiffs' argument, the plaintiffs went further. They argued that regardless of the purity of a school board's motives, and regardless of the burden placed upon it to show lack of racial motivation, a constitutional violation is inherent in de facto segregation. School boards must therefore actively attempt to remedy an all-Negro school even if its existence is clearly due purely to geographical zoning arrived at without any improper motivation. Essentially this contention is based on three propositions.

1.) The Supreme Court held in the *Brown* case that separate Negro schools are harmful to Negro children and therefore unconstitutional.

2.) An all-Negro school, regardless of how it is created, is just as unequal and harmful to its Negro children as those schools which are segregated by force of law.

3.) Therefore a school administration which maintains a de facto segregated school is acting unconstitutionally and must provide integrated schooling for its students.

The last of the three propositions raises the greatest number of problems. It asserts that because the same harm is visited upon Negro children by districting on purely geographical lines as would be visited by racial segregation under force of law, the geographical districting must therefore be unconstitutional. In a sense, this is reasoning from the converse of the *Brown* and post-*Brown* cases. Merely because racial classification without harm is unconstitutional does not mean that harm without racial classification is equally impermissible. Law provides us with many examples where a party may suffer identical harm under two different circumstances and have a legal right to redress under one and not the other. In simple tort law, a pedestrian hit by an automobile will be harmed just as much when the driver has had an unexpected heart attack as he will where the driver has not watched the road. Yet in the latter case, the law would afford relief and in the former, none. Similarly, a franchised retailer may be injured by the abrupt termination of his franchise just as much if the franchise is terminated completely arbitrarily as if it is terminated as a consequence of an unlawful merger or an attempt to fix prices. Nonetheless, he will receive relief from the courts in the last two cases and not in the first. This principle applies equally to racial problems. Although a literacy test, fairly administered in a given area, might result in the exclusion of Negroes from the political processes to the same extent as would a white primary or a grandfather clause, no constitutional authority has indicated that a literacy test would be invalid for this reason alone. In other words, merely looking at the harm created by an action is by no means sufficient; we must look at the action itself, and decide whether that action violates constitutional guarantees.

Admittedly, certain lower court cases have implied that it is the effect of state action in this area which is itself determinative. Thus in *Meredith v. Fair* the Court of Appeals for the Fifth Circuit asserted that it had, in a previous opinion, struck down a requirement that an applicant to the University of Mississippi present a certificate from two alumni or two citizens of the state because "the burden falls more heavily on the Negroes than on whites." A reading of the earlier opinion striking down this requirement, however, shows that the quoted language must be considered in the light of two facts. First, the obvious motive and purpose of the state legislature in enacting the requirement was to make it more difficult for Negroes to apply for admission. The court noted that the requirement was initially passed as part of the state's massive resistance plan. Secondly, the very fact that the alumni requirement did bear more heavily on the Negro was directly due to the previous wrong of the state—the refusal of Mississippi to admit Negroes to the university since its original founding. Certainly where the state's obvious motive is to "bear more heavily on the Negro than whites" or where a previous state wrong has been built upon to result in disadvantage to a racial group, the state action violates the Constitution. The mere differential effect on most Negroes or most whites, while it may be relevant, is not enough. If it were, we could decide the validity of a law merely by taking a census of those whom it affected. Thus the immigration laws fall more heavily on Americans of Chinese descent than on most other groups; the anti-polygamy laws bear, or at least bore, more heavily on Mormons than on those of other religions; and in all probability the antitrust laws bear more heavily on whites than on Negroes. Obviously the fact that members of certain groups may be injured more by a law than members of other groups is not sufficient in itself to hold that law a violation of the equal protection clause. Deciding whether a state action violates constitutional guarantees is not a mechanical process but a subtle one involving many different factors, including, among others, the weight to be given to the differing interests entitled to consideration, the difficulty of formulating standards, the type of remedy available, the importance of uniformity throughout the nation, and the degree of deference to be accorded to state decisions and to the judgments reached by the political processes.

Of course a differential effect on two groups entitled *a priori* to equal treatment is relevant. Thus in a nonracial area, in *Griffin v. Illinois* a rule requiring purchase of a transcript before an appeal in a criminal case could be taken, bore more heavily upon the poor than on the rich and was held to be unconstitutional. In that case, although there was no opinion which a majority of the Court could agree upon, the result reflected the exceptionally high duty placed on the state in administering its criminal procedures. Moreover, it was not the mere differential application to rich and poor that the Court found offensive; it was the fact that the poor litigant was effectively barred from any review at all. This application of the rule, the Court felt, was so harsh that it violated the equal protection clause.

In this situation we must ask whether in a city such as Gary, which has a predominantly Negro residential area, the geographical districting based upon place of residence, in the absence of any improper motivation, is so unreasonable a classification as to offend the equal protection clause.

Although it should certainly not be regarded as binding more than ten years later, it is interesting to note that Thurgood Marshall in the first argument of the segregation cases conceded away this very point.

> Mr. Justice Frankfurter: You mean that, if we reverse, it will not entitle every mother to have her child go to a nonsegregated school?
> Mr. Marshall: No, sir.
> Mr. Justice Frankfurter: What will it do?
> Mr. Marshall: The school board, I assume, would find some other method of distributing the children by drawing district lines.

To examine this question afresh we may begin by pointing out that geographical districting is a traditional, although concededly not a universal, method of distributing students among schools. On the surface it appears no less arbitrary than any other method one can conceive of, and has many advantages of convenience to justify it.

First of all, it allows the school to serve as a neighborhood center and an area where children may play after hours and yet be close to their homes. Secondly, proximity to the homes of the students is an added safety factor, since it is well known that railroads and large highways do take a certain toll of children crossing them on their way to school. Lastly, although the distance from home to school may not be so important in areas of the country which are blessed with an equable and pleasant climate throughout the school year, in most Northern areas minimization of walking distance to school is an important consideration. For instance, in Gary last year the temperature dropped on several occasions to under 10 degrees below zero and often fell below zero. Moreover, on many occasions two feet of snow lay on the sidewalks and in the streets. Where this type of climate prevails, it is hard to say that a method of distributing children among schools which minimizes their exposure to the elements is so arbitrary and unreasonable as to offend the Constitution.

It is true that the problems of dangerous crossings and exposure to the elements would be greatly reduced where the school authorities provided transportation for their students. On the other hand, although a strong argument may be made for such a program in many communities, it is hard to argue that a failure to bus children to and from school can be so unreasonable as to violate constitutional commands. Although a constitutional violation cannot be excused by the fact that to correct it would cost money, where the ultimate question may depend on the reasonableness of one choice over another, financial considerations need not be ignored. The existence of constitutional violations often turns upon practical considerations, and as between adopting a plan which required students to walk or provide their own transportation, and bussing these children, there are powerful financial reasons to reject the latter. Where communities are already having difficulty meeting the financial requirements of teachers' salaries and school construction, requiring them to incur expenses for bussing might siphon funds from much more valuable educational projects. Furthermore, even aside from its cost, bussing presents many practical difficulties, such as the method of selecting which children are to be bussed, the difficulty of parent contact with a receiving school which is some distance from the home, tardiness or absence from school when the school bus is missed (if no alternative transportation exists), reduced participation in after-school programs, the need for teacher supervision on the bus, and the problem of dealing with illness during school. This is not to say that residence is the only reasonable way to assign children among schools. It may very well be that other methods, such as open enrollment or even drawing artificial districts so as to maximize integration, may be preferable. Each of these methods, while reasonable in many areas, has obvious disadvantages. Open enrollment is not only extremely difficult to administer in any large city but by permitting white children to "escape" from integrated situations may actually increase racial imbalance in the schools. For this reason it has been opposed in many areas by the NAACP. Similarly, drawing of district lines to secure integration may be practical in some fringe areas but toward the center of any large Negro area it is obviously useless. Moreover where geographically irrational district lines are drawn to secure integration, the increased racial balance may be purchased at the price of causing children to travel unreasonably long distances or cross dangerous streets. True, in some situations each of the aforementioned means may be preferable and all are reasonable. The Constitution, however, does not dictate that a specific choice in classification be made among many reasonable alternatives, and so long as the method adopted is not a disguised racial classification or for some other reason completely arbitrary and irrational, the Constitution would not appear to be violated.

Some might deny this and assert that the cause of racial integration is entitled to a "preferred position" in the hierarchy of constitutional values. In such a case it might be argued that the standard is not whether the school authorities have fairly chosen among reasonable alternatives, but whether a reasonable alternative existed which would result in more integration than the school board zoning plan. One commentator in fact has so argued, relying primarily on some of the substantive due process cases which are now completely in disrepute and a number of cases involving the freedom of expression guaranteed by the first amendment. It is hard, however, to argue that the cause of mixing Negro and white children, taken as it must be from the vague words of the equal protection clause, deserves the same standing as the right of free expression which not only is founded in the explicit wording of the first amendment, but also is at the very basis of any free society which attempts to keep within itself the power for beneficial change. Integration may be an important value of our society but it is hard to argue that it is more fundamental than the right of the state to provide for the health, safety, and education of its children.

At least as applied to geographical zoning, this view also appears to comport with the intention of the framers of the fourteenth amendment. It is one thing to argue, as did the plaintiffs in the *Brown* case, that the framers meant to abolish deliberate racial segregation in public education. This involves a difficult historical question, at least in part because, in the main, those areas which had developed public school systems when the amendment was adopted did not practice segregation and vice versa. It is much more difficult to argue that there was any intent to prevent geographical zoning when that was the most common method of assigning children to schools where public education existed.

An examination of problems associated with acceptance of the plaintiffs' contentions sheds light on certain other difficulties inherent in their arguments. Since acceptance of their contentions would require a school board to eliminate de facto segregated schools, we would have to define what we mean by this type of segregated school. We might do as some have done and define a segregated Negro school as one which is known within its community as a Negro school. The difficulties of proof in this matter, however, might be extreme. Even putting aside the question of who in the community must know a school is "Negro," there are other problems. While there is no doubt that a school populated exclusively by Negroes might be known in all communities as a Negro school, a 75 per cent or 60 per cent Negro school might be a "Negro" school in some communities and not in others. It would be a strange proposition to assert that the Constitution would then place a duty on the one school administration and not on the other. The second method of classification would be to define a school by the percentage of Negroes in it. This involves even greater difficulties. First, at least in a few close cases, one might encounter a problem which has caused a great deal of litigation in the South—just who is and who is not a Negro. Where a state cannot draw such distinctions at all, this problem does not come up; but if we attempt to place a positive duty on a state, we must define with some rigor exactly who is the beneficiary of this duty. Even putting this problem aside and assuming the Constitution provides us with some unambiguous and easily applicable definition of a Negro, we are still put in the position of asserting that the Constitution requires action to alleviate a racial unbalance in a school with a given percentage of Negroes and not in one having a percentage only slightly lower. Not only is this not, in general, the stuff of which constitutions are made, but it even seems to be outside the normal function and competence of the judiciary.

Not only would the acceptance of the plaintiffs' contention force the courts into drawing fine lines, but it would involve their fashioning completely arbitrary standards. The plaintiffs in Gary, through their expert witness, argued that a school in a given community was "segregated" if its percentage of Negroes was more than one-third above or more than one-third below the percentage of Negroes in the community at large. The Urban League, however, defines a segregated school as one which is over 60 per cent Negro. Although each of these definitions may in some pragmatic way have a value, it is hard to imagine that a court might say that one or the other was incorporated into the United States Constitution under the general purposes and framework of the fourteenth amendment. One might ask with reference to the plaintiffs' definition, "Why not 40 per cent above or below the community's percentage of Negroes?" With respect to the Urban League's definition, one might question, "Why not 65 or 70 per cent Negro?" We might also ask, "Does this definition of segregation apply only to the school or to each class within it? In an integrated school where middle class white children are integrated with lower class Negroes, does this definition bar the use of ability grouping?" It should be noted that these questions are not the pettifogging demands to draw the line where the line will never be susceptible of exact definition. If that were the only problem, the court might hold as a matter of law that a school was "segregated" if it was all Negro and turn the question over to the jury in all other cases. Here the arbitrary and mechanical quality of the lines advocated tends to show two things: first, that in this area, even though the question can be expressed in precise terms, no such lines can be drawn; and second, that such an arbitrary standard does not comport with the general intention and broad language of the fourteenth amendment.

It is true that this part of the problem can be obviated by simply substituting a rule of reason for consideration of artificial absolutes. Such a rule would assert that de facto segregation need not be abolished by school authorities in all cases, but merely that, where the school board had a choice among methods of districting, it must give due weight to integration as a goal. This rule has a certain appeal. Integration of disparate groups is not only an ideal in democratic society, but also is a help in reducing prejudice and bigotry. The Constitution, therefore, would be violated by a school board which—concededly without racial motivation —had nonetheless, without a sufficient reason, drawn a district line in a way which did not maximize racial integration. This is in many ways similar to the preferred position argument and would fail for many of the same reasons. Where the school board has reached a result which is not arbitrary or irrational and which does not involve a racial classification either overt or covert, then it is hard to fashion a reasoning which a court might use to require more. The example usually given of this rule in practice involves the school board which has drawn an east-west line between two school zones, resulting in one Negro and one white school, where an equally practicable line could be drawn in a north-south direction and result in two integrated schools.

Granting that consideration of integration might be a good rule for school boards to follow, it is questionable whether the courts could or should enforce it under the Constitution. Real cases invariably turn out to be a great deal more complex than the usual example illustrating the requirement that school boards must work for integration. In the example, the School Board has drawn an east-west line dividing part of the district into two school zones, one Negro, one white, while a north-south line would differ only in causing two integrated schools. If this were so, it might support a finding that the Board had indeed considered race in an attempt to segregate and this would dispose of the case. In practice, however, things are never that neat and an attempt to require consideration of integration would involve the courts in a whole range of difficulties similar to those the courts encountered in evaluating whether schools were equal within the separate but equal doctrine. How can the courts weigh the value of a 30 per cent increase in integration against a requirement that students cross a dangerous traffic artery or walk five extra blocks? How could the courts weigh the achievement of integration through bussing children against the greater cost and a somewhat larger class size? Not only could the courts not decide these questions themselves, but they are ill-equipped to insist that school boards give due weight to integration. School boards would always be able to come into court and say, "We did give the question of integration some weight, but we felt that under the circumstances of the case it was outweighed by the practical advantages of the neighborhood school policy." In the absence of any clear standards, such a defense would be hard to overcome. The Gary trial itself provided dramatic proof of this point. The plaintiffs' expert, Dr. Wolff, had prepared as one of the plaintiffs' exhibits a school plan for Gary wherein changes in districting, different utilization of buildings, and new construction could vastly increase the degree of racial integration in the schools. Selected questions from the cross-examination by Mr. Gavit, the attorney for the School Board, in addition to showing the enormous disadvantages under which a non-resident expert labors, make very clear the great variety of possible arguments school boards can rely on to support their own methods of school organization.

> Mr. Gavit: Did your studies take you far enough in either, or any of your three or four days that you say you were around Gary or in your map reading elsewhere, that you learned how many railroads cross Gary from east to west?
> Dr. Wolff: I don't know.
> Mr. Gavit: Do you learn this much, that there isn't a single railroad in Gary that runs from north to south?
> Dr. Wolff: I don't know.
>
> Mr. Gavit: Assuming that the river, the Little Calumet River crosses Gary from east to west, or west to east, . . . how many streets along

the [river, the] north boundary of the Lew Wallace School area, cross that river?
Dr. Wolff: I don't know.

Mr. Gavit: Now, did your investigation go far enough to find how many streets are open from the south side of the present Vohr attendance district across both Wabash and the Pennsylvania main lines to get over into Beckman School area, the Beckman district?
Dr. Wolff: No.

Mr. Gavit: Don't you know that along the southern boundary of the present Vohr attendance district, running for at least 15 blocks, there is only one street open across those tracks?
Dr. Wolff: Maybe.

Mr. Gavit: Under the present feeder pattern that you told us about yesterday, by which children go from Jefferson to Vohr, do they have to cross any railroad tracks from the Jefferson area to get into the Vohr School site?
Dr. Wolff: I don't think so; I don't know.
Mr. Gavit: Well, in fact, they don't, under your proposal that the children from Jefferson go to Froebel instead of to Vohr—under that feeder pattern, would they have to cross any railroad tracks?
Dr. Wolff: Yes.

Mr. Gavit: Do you know what, if any, north or south streets within the Jefferson School District area are open to cross the railroad to get into the Froebel area?
Dr. Wolff: No.

Mr. Gavit: First of all, take the change from eight to four high schools, how much would it cost?
Dr. Wolff: It would not cost very much.
Mr. Gavit: How much would it cost?
Dr. Wolff: I don't know, but it is not important, the amount is unimportant.

Mr. Gavit: Did you do any investigating as to the availability of sites for these three new high schools?
Dr. Wolff: Yes.

Mr. Gavit: Did you find out who owns the land that you might want to use for that?
Dr. Wolff: The City has an opportunity to get the land, whoever owns it.

Mr. Gavit: Do you know whether it is part of the land owned by Indiana University?
Dr. Wolff: No, I don't know.

Mr. Gavit: Do you know that U.S. 12 is one of the most heavily traveled arterial automobile highways in the United States?
Dr. Wolff: Yes.
Mr. Gavit: Would those children have to cross U.S. 12?
Dr. Wolff: Maybe.

Mr. Gavit: Do you know how much bonding power the City of Gary has?
Dr. Wolff: I don't know, indeed, I don't

Mr. Gavit: Do you know what our present tax rate is for school funds?
Dr. Wolff: No.

Mr. Gavit: Do you know what tax rate would be required to accomplish your Exhibit 24 plan?
Dr. Wolff: I do not know what tax rate is necessary to develop the school system which I suggested.

In view of the enormous variety of local conditions which might influence a school board to adopt one system of school organization instead of another, perhaps the best that we can expect from the courts in this area is to ensure that the political bodies remain neutral as far as race is concerned. It is difficult to find in the Constitution support for any greater duty.

In addition, unless the Negro is claiming a place as the special ward of the Constitution (a status which admittedly has some historical support) it is hard to frame a reason why the same rights should not be extended to other ethnic groups—Mexican Americans, Italian Americans, Jews, and Orientals.

True, the history of the Negro over the past three hundred years has been such as to exert a moral claim on Americans beyond that of any other group with the possible exception of the American Indian. On the other hand it is also probably true that there exist groups of Negroes who, for one reason or another, have not suffered the deprivations visited upon their race as a whole and that in fact in some areas there exist groups of whites who would benefit by integration just as much as certain groups of Negroes. Nor can it be argued that the harm caused to Negroes by imbalance in their schools is completely different from that which may be visited on all other groups. Putting aside the Puerto Rican and the Mexican American whose claim might be quite similar to that of the Negro, there is respectable authority for the proposition that in many large cities the Polish or the Italian American is being harmed, and isolated from the main stream of American culture, by the fact that they live and go to school in overwhelmingly Polish or Italian areas. Similarly, although the harm visited on the Jew may be of a different type, recent attacks on the "ghetto mentality" have asserted that the Jew, perhaps in more subtle ways, has been harmed by failure to be more thoroughly integrated in American culture. Nor can these other groups be distinguished by the assertion that only the Negro is required by residential discrimination to live in compact areas. First of all, it is hard to see the relevance of this fact on the question of the duty of the state to provide equal education for its children. Secondly, we do not actually know how great an effect residential discrimination has on Negro residential patterns. No careful study has shown how much of the Negro ghetto is due to other factors such as the inability of many Negroes to afford other accommodations and the possibly greater feeling of security that comes of living among one's friends who are generally of one's own race. It is possible, indeed probable, that residential discrimination is primarily responsible for the fact that many middle class Negroes live in Negro ghettos and that such discrimination has not caused the persistence of most Polish, Italian and Jewish areas. However, it is hard to assume more without careful inquiry.

Moreover, those arguments which would put a duty on the board to work for integration seem to operate regardless of the consent of those to be integrated. Thus, so long as plaintiffs could be found to bring the action, a board might have the duty of attempting to integrate by transporting a whole group even though the majority of its members who lived in the same area did not want integration at this price. This is not the argument of the segregationist who argues that the majority of Negroes actually prefer their segregated schools. In such a case it is not difficult to hold that the Negro, no more than the white person, has no right to pick and choose the races of people with whom he will go to school. On the other hand the administration of any constitutional rule involving a duty to integrate would be made that much more difficult by the fact that the integration involved might be done over the objections of at least a substantial number of the victims of de facto segregation.

Nor does there appear to be any reason why the plaintiff's principle would apply only to ethnic groups. If, as would appear obvious, the state could not force children of manual laborers or those whose families earn less than $5,000 to go to a separate set of schools, one could argue that school boards have a constitutional duty to prevent the same separation from occuring through geographical zoning. The very complexity of balancing the large number of constitutional commands in a heterogeneous population would seem to be a powerful argument against adoption of the plaintiff's argument.

The duty, which the Gary plaintiffs would place upon school authorities, of eliminating de facto segregation is also open to attack on an entirely different ground. It proves too much. We must remember that the fourteenth amendment acts upon school boards in a given community only because they are creatures of the state. Since a school district is a subsidiary governmental body of a state, just as a municipality or county, the state may change its boundaries at will. It is therefore hard to see, if the plaintiff's contentions were accepted, how we might constitutionally take account of boundaries between separate school districts while disregarding their attendance zone districts for individual schools. Certainly it would appear that any duty of the state to prevent the existence of a de facto segregated school could not be hindered by the state's own administrative units. Thus Negro students in the large city, and especially those who live near its borders, would be given a constitutional right to attend schools in the suburbs. It is true that many arguments may be made for just this type of legislative policy, but it is fair to say that almost no one would contend today that this would be constitutionally required. The financial and administrative structure of school systems is almost universally predicated upon the existence of school districts as separate taxing and governmental agencies. It is difficult to assert that one district's boundaries must be ignored to ease a situation existing in another district without the fault of either.

Probably the most serious drawback to the plaintiff's argument is that their interpretation of the Constitution would require governmental authorities to re-enter the field of racial classification. This is exactly what the plaintiffs' attorneys urged the Supreme Court to prohibit in the *Brown* case, and for good reason. Although today a court might rule that the state is required to consider race in a benign way, tomorrow this might well prove a precedent for a much less happy result. Moreover, even today it is not easy to decide whether a given racial classification is benign. A perfect example of this difficulty is found in the justification many school administrators have given for a concentration of Negro teachers in the overwhelmingly Negro schools. They often defend this type of segregation on the grounds that it is a benign consideration of race since sociological studies show that Negro teachers provide an image with which Negro students may more easily identify; that the more Negro students see teachers of their own race, the clearer it becomes to those students that they too can achieve respectable occupations and middle class life in general; that Negro teachers, identifying with their students and having racial pride, work harder to make a success of their classes than would white teachers who lack the common background which the Negroes possess. Our knowledge of the subtle effects of racial classification on children, both white and Negro, is so limited today that in many areas an equally plausible case might be made for their being either helpful or harmful. The very difficulty of making such determinations, especially in the context of litigations which may not even bring to bear our limited knowledge on the subject, would seem to militate strongly against any attempts by the courts to require states to consider race in a benign manner.

5

... [*We can*] *predict hopefully that the moral and constitutional soundness of the Supreme Court position will continue to gain support until at last there will be complete attainment of the goal of integration in public schools throughout the United States.*
ROBERT B MCKAY

Hobson v. *Hansen*

Summary

[1] In Bolling v. Sharpe, 347 U.S. 497, 74 S.Ct. 693, 98 L.Ed. 884 (1954), the Supreme Court held that the District of Columbia's racially segregated public school system violated the due process clause of the Fifth Amendment. The present litigation, brought in behalf of Negro as well as poor children generally in the District's public schools, tests the current compliance of those schools with the principles announced in *Bolling*, its companion case Brown v. Board of Education of Topeka, 347 U.S. 483, 74 S.Ct. 686, 98 L.Ed. 873 (1954), and their progeny. The basic question presented is whether the defendants, the Superintendent of Schools and the members of the Board of Education, in the operation of the public school system here, unconstitutionally deprive the District's Negro and poor public school children of their right to equal educational opportunity with the District's white and more affluent public school children. This court concludes that they do.

In support of this conclusion the court makes the following principal findings of fact:

1. Racially and socially homogeneous schools damage the minds and spirit of all children who attend them—the Negro, the white, the poor and the affluent—and block the attainment of the broader goals of democratic education, whether the segregation occurs by law or by fact.

2. The scholastic achievement of the disadvantaged child, Negro and white, is strongly related to the racial and socio-economic composition of the student body of his school. A racially and socially integrated school environment increases the scholastic achievement of the disadvantaged child of whatever race.

3. The Board of Education, which is the statutory head of the public schools in the District, is appointed pursuant to a quota system which,

U.S. Federal Court 269, Federal Supplement 401, 1967.

until 1962, for over half a century had limited the Negro membership of the nine-man Board to three. Since 1962 the Negro quota on the Board has been four, one less than a majority. The city of Washington, which is the District of Columbia, presently has a population over 60% Negro and a public school population over 90% Negro.

4. Adherence to the neighborhood school policy by the School Board effectively segregates the Negro and the poor children from the white and the more affluent children in most of the District's public schools. This neighborhood school policy is relaxed by the Board through the use of optional zones for the purpose of allowing white children, usually affluent white children, "trapped" in a Negro school district, to "escape" to a "white" or more nearly white school, thus making the economic and racial segregation of the public school children more complete than it would otherwise be under a strict neighborhood school assignment plan.

5. The teachers and principals in the public schools are assigned so that generally the race of the faculty is the same as the race of the children. Thus most of the schools can be identified as "Negro" or "white," not only by reference to the predominant race of the children attending, but by the predominant race of the faculty as well. The heaviest concentration of Negro faculty, usually 100%, is in the Negro ghetto schools.

6. The median annual per pupil expenditure ($292) in the predominantly (85–100%) Negro elementary schools in the District of Columbia has been a flat $100 below the median annual per pupil expenditure for its predominantly (85–100%) white schools ($392).

7. Generally the "white" schools are underpopulated while the "Negro" schools generally are overcrowded. Moreover, all of the white elementary schools have kindergartens. Some Negro schools are without kindergartens entirely while other Negro schools operate kindergartens in shifts or consecutive sessions. In addition to being overcrowded and short on kindergarten space, the school buildings in the Negro slums are ancient and run down. Only recently, through the use of impact aid and other federal funds, have the Negro slum schools had sufficient textbooks for the children's use.

8. As they proceed through the Washington school system, the reading scores primarily of the Negro and poor children, but not the white and middle class, fall increasingly behind the national norm. By senior high school the discrepancy reaches several grades.

9. The track system as used in the District's public schools is a form of ability grouping in which students are divided in separate, self-contained curricula or tracks ranging from "Basic" for the slow student to "Honors" for the gifted.

10. The aptitude tests used to assign children to the various tracks are standarized primarily on white middle class children. Since these tests do not relate to the Negro and disadvantaged child, track assignment

based on such tests relegates Negro and disadvantaged children to the lower tracks from which, because of the reduced curricula and the absence of adequate remedial and compensatory education, as well as continued inappropriate testing, the chance of escape is remote.

11. Education in the lower tracks is geared to what Dr. Hansen, the creator of the track system, calls the "blue collar" student. Thus such children, so stigmatized by inappropriate aptitude testing procedures, are denied equal opportunity to obtain the white collar education available to the white and more affluent children.

Other incidental, but highly indicative, findings are as follows: a. The June 1964—December 1965 study by the Office of the Surgeon General, Army, shows that 55.3% of the 18-year-olds from the District of Columbia failed the Armed Services mental test, a higher percentage than any of the 50 states. b. The average per pupil expenditure in the District's public schools is only slightly below the national average. The 1964–65 Bureau of the Census Report on Governmental Finances shows, however, that the District of Columbia spends less per capita on education generally than all states except Arkansas and Tennessee. c. The same report shows that the District of Columbia spends more per capita on police protection than all states without exception. In fact, the District of Columbia spends more than double any state other than Nevada, New York, New Jersey and California. The inferences, including those bearing on the relationship of the quality of education to crime, which arise from these findings are obvious. Indeed, the National Crime Commission's Task Force Report: Juvenile Delinquency and Youth Crime indicates that the very deficiencies in the District's public school system noted by the record in this case—prejudging, through inappropriate testing, the learning abilities of the disadvantaged child as inferior to the white middle class child; placing the child in lower tracks for reduced education based on such tests, thus implementing the self-fulfilling prophecy phenomenon inherent in such misjudgments; placing inferior teachers in slum schools; continuing racial and economic segregation of pupils; providing textbooks unrelated to the lives of disadvantaged children; inadequate remedial programs for offsetting initial psychological and social difficulties of the disadvantaged child—all have contributed to the increase in crime, particularly juvenile crime.

In sum, all of the evidence in this case tends to show that the Washington school system is a monument to the cynicism of the power structure which governs the voteless capital of the greatest country on earth.

Remedy

To correct the racial and economic discrimination found in the operation of the District of Columbia public school system, the court has issued a decree attached to its opinion ordering: 1. An injunction against racial and economic discrimination in the public school system here.

2. Abolition of the track system. 3. Abolition of the optional zones. 4. Transportation for volunteering children in overcrowded school districts east of Rock Creek Park to underpopulated schools west of the Park. 5. The defendants, by October 2, 1967, to file for approval by the court a plan for pupil assignment eliminating the racial and economic discrimination found to exist in the operation of the Washington public school system. 6. Substantial integration of the faculty of each school beginning with the school year 1967–68. 7. The defendants, by October 2, 1967, to file for approval by the court a teacher assignment plan fully integrating the faculty of each school.

IV. The Track System*

The District of Columbia school system employs a form of ability grouping commonly known as the track system, by which students at the elementary and secondary level are placed in tracks or curriculum levels according to the school's assessment of each student's ability to learn. Plaintiffs have alleged that the track system—either by intent or by effect—unconstitutionally discriminates against the Negro and the poor. In support of this claim they—and the defendants in meeting it—have introduced a massive array of testimonial and documentary evidence. The court will first turn its attention to the beginnings of the track system before moving on to a discussion of the evidence concerning the present-day operation of ability grouping in the District.

A. *Origin.*

The track system was approved for introduction into the Washington school system by the Board of Education in 1956, just two years after the desegregation decision in Bolling v. Sharpe. As Superintendent Hansen has conceded, "to describe the origin of the four-track system without reference to desegregation in the District of Columbia Public Schools would be to by-pass one of the most significant causes of its being. Desegregation was a precipitant of the four-track development in the District's high schools * * *." Plaintiffs, citing this concession and certain observable segregatory effects of the track system, have claimed that the principal motivation behind the system was and is to resegregate the races in violation of the *Bolling* decision. Defendants have denied this, arguing that the track system is and always has been a legitimate pedagogical method of providing maximum educational opportunity for children of widely ranging ability levels; and that any racial effect is but an innocent and unavoidable coincidence of ability grouping.

There is evidence which on its face supports defendants' claim that racial considerations were irrelevant to the decision to adopt the track

---

* The question of ability grouping is but one of a number of issues in *Hobson* v. *Hansen*. It was selected arbitrarily to illustrate the legal arguments.

system. Yet, as in certain other administrative decisions where defendants have purported to act without regard to race, the taint of segregation hangs heavy over their actions. Although Dr. Hansen has maintained that the origins of the four-track curriculum "clearly precede the event of desegregation," there is no escaping the fact that the track system was specifically a response to problems created by the sudden commingling of numerous educationally retarded Negro students with the better educated white students.

On May 17, 1954, the day Bolling v. Sharpe was handed down, there were 44,897 white students (43%) and 59,963 Negro students (57%) in the District schools. By the following September 73% of the schools were—in varying degree—racially mixed. Until that time no one was aware of the overall achievement level of the Negro students because achievement scores had not been reported on a city-wide basis in the old Division II (Negro) schools. However, soon after integration Dr. Hansen, then Assistant Superintendent in charge of senior high schools, began to receive "reports of very serious retardation in achievement in the basic skills * *" The results of a reading and arithmetic achievement test taken by tenth grade students early in 1955 and for the first time reported on a city-wide basis confirmed the reports: (1) Both reading and arithmetic scores ranged from second to beyond twelfth grade; (2) nearly 25% of the students were at or below sixth grade level in reading, and 44% were at or below sixth grade level in arithmetic. The low achievers were predominantly from the Division II schools. It was the discovery of this large number of academically retarded Negro children in the school system that led to the institution of the track system.

Given these unhappy consequences of "separate but equal" education, Superintendent Hansen cannot be faulted for moving in 1955 to treat the casualties of *de jure* segregation. The court is persuaded that Dr. Hansen personally was then and is now motivated by a desire to respond—according to his own philosophy—to an educational crisis in the District school system. On the other hand, the court cannot ignore the fact that until 1954 the District schools were by direction of law operated on a segregated basis. It cannot ignore the fact that of all the possible forms of ability grouping, the one that won acceptance in the District was the one that—with the exception of completely separate schools— involves the greatest amount of physical separation by grouping students in wholly distinct, homogeneous curriculum levels. It cannot ignore that the immediate and known effect of this separation would be to insulate the more academically developed white student from his less fortunate black schoolmate, thus minimizing the impact of integration; nor can the court ignore the fact that this same cushioning effect remains evident even today. Therefore, although the track system cannot be dismissed as nothing more than a subterfuge by which defendants are attempting to avoid the mandate of Bolling v. Sharpe, neither can it be said that the evidence shows racial considerations to be absolutely irrelevant to its adoption and absolutely irrelevant in its continued administration. To this extent the track system is tainted.

[9, 10] The court does not, however, rest its decision on a finding of intended racial discrimination. Apart from such intentional aspects, the effects of the track system must be held to be a violation of plaintiffs' constitutional rights. (*See* Opinion of Law.) As the evidence in this case makes painfully clear, ability grouping as presently practiced in the District of Columbia school system is a denial of equal educational opportunity to the poor and a majority of the Negroes attending school in the nation's capital, a denial that contravenes not only the guarantees of the Fifth Amendment but also the fundamental premise of the track system itself. What follows, then, is a discussion of that evidence—an examination of the track system: in theory and in reality.

B. *Track Theory.*

Basic to an understanding of the conflict between the parties in this lawsuit is an appreciation of the theory that motivates the track system as it operates in the District school system. The most comprehensive statement of that theory can be found in Dr. Hansen's book, FOUR TRACK CURRICULUM FOR TODAY'S HIGH SCHOOLS, published in 1964. Although Dr. Hansen disclaims full responsibility for creating the track system, a reading of his book leaves no doubt that it was his firm guiding hand that shaped that system in its essential characteristics. Thus, as principal architect of the track system and as Superintendent of Schools, Dr. Hansen presumably can be looked to as the authoritative spokesman on the subject.

Purpose and philosophy. Dr. Hansen believes that the comprehensive high school (and the school system generally) must be systematically organized and structured to provide differing levels of education for students with widely differing levels of academic ability. This is the purpose of the track system. In expressing the track system's philosophy Dr. Hansen has said, "Every pupil in the school system must have the maximum opportunity for self-development and this can best be brought about by adjusting curriculum offerings to different levels of need and ability as the pupil moves through the stages of education and growth in our schools." (Ex. 9, C–16: *How We Are Meeting Individual Differences.*) And he has identified as the two objectives on which the track system is founded: "(1) The realization of the doctrine of equality of education and (2) The attainment of quality education."

Student types. Within the student body Dr. Hansen sees generally four types of students: the intellectually gifted, the above-average, the average, and the retarded. He assumes that each of these types of students has a maximum level of academic capability and, most importantly, that that level of ability can be accurately ascertained. The duty of the school is to identify these students and provide a curriculum commensurate with their respective abilities. Dr. Hansen contends that the traditional school curriculum—including the usual two-level method of ability grouping—does a disservice to those at either end of the ability spectrum.

The gifted student is not challenged, so that he becomes bored, lazy, and perhaps performs far below his academic potential; his intellectual talents are a wasted resource. The remedy lies in discovering the gifted student, placing him with others of his own kind, thereby stimulating him through this select association as well as a rigorous, demanding curriculum to develop his intellectual talent. Indeed, "the academically capable student should be required as a public necessity to take the academically challenging honors curriculum."

On the other hand, continues Dr. Hansen, the retarded or "stupid" student typically has been forced to struggle through a curriculum he cannot possibly master and only imperfectly comprehends. Typically he is slow to learn and soon falls behind in class; he repeatedly fails, sometimes repeating a grade again and again; he becomes isolated, frustrated, depressed, and—if he does not drop out before graduation—graduates with a virtually useless education. Here the remedy is seen as separating out the retarded student, directing him into a special curriculum geared to his limited abilities and designed to give him a useful "basic" education—one which makes no pretense of equalling traditionally taught curricula.

In short, Hansen views the traditional school curriculum as doing too little for some students and expecting too much of others. As for the latter type, whom Dr. Hansen characterizes as "the blue-collar student," going to school—a "white-collar occupation"—can be an artificial experience.

> "Twelve years of white-collar experience is unrealistic preparation for the young man or woman who will suddenly make the change into work clothes for jobs in kitchens, stockrooms, street maintenance or building construction.

>   ❖   ❖   ❖   ❖   ❖   ❖   ❖

> "One reason [for education's failure to meet the needs of the blue-collar student] * * * is that it is at best an environment artificially created for the education of the young. From the beginning of his career in school, the child enjoys the comforts of a protected and unrealistic environment. Most of the Nation's classrooms are insulated from reality. To many students what happens in the classroom has little connection with what happens outside the classroom.

> "Another reason * * * is that the school environment excludes most of the sterner discipline of the work-a-day world. * * *"

Tracking. In order to tailor the educational process to the level appropriate to each student, Dr. Hansen adopted the track system. Each track is intended to be a separate and self-contained curriculum, with the educational content ranging from the very basic to the very advanced according to the track level. In the elementary and junior high schools three levels are used: Basic or Special Academic (retarded students), General (average and above-average), and Honors (gifted). In the senior high school a fourth level is added: the Regular Track, a college-preparatory track intended to accommodate the above-average student.

The significant feature of the track system in this regard is its emphasis on the ability of the student. A student's course of instruction depends upon what the school system decides he is capable of handling. "It took a while for everybody on the [working] committee to understand that *ability was to be the primary key to the placement in a curriculum sequence, and that this factor, not the subject-matter emphasis, was one of the unique characteristics of the four-track system.*"

Flexibility. Dr. Hansen, while assuming that some students can be educated to their maximum potential in one of the four curricula, also anticipates that not all students will neatly or permanently fit into a track. Thus a second important assumption underlying the track system is that tracking will be a flexible process. Flexibility encompasses two things: First, although a student today may demonstrate an ability level which calls, for example, for placement in the General Track, a constant and continuing effort must be made to assure that he is at his true ability level. This calls for instruction directed toward correcting any remediable educational problems which account for the student's present poor performance; and it calls for close analysis and counselling to determine whether these remediable deficiencies exist and when they have been sufficiently corrected. When the latter is determined, the student is to be upgraded to the next higher track. Second, even though a student may not be in a position to make an across-the-board move from one track to another, his ability level may be such that he needs to take courses in two track levels on a subject-by-subject basis. This process, known as cross-tracking, is critical: it is the mechanism the system relies upon to assure that students whose ability levels vary according to particular subjects are not thwarted in developing their strong areas because their weak areas result in their being placed in a lower curriculum level. It also serves as a way of selectively raising the intensity of instruction on a subject-matter basis as a part of the process of gradually upgrading a student.

Fundamental assumptions. To summarize, the track system's approach is twofold. The separate curriculum levels are for some the maximum education their abilities permit them to achieve. For others, a track is supposed to be a temporary assignment during which a student's special problems are identified and remedied in whatever way possible.

The express assumptions of this approach are three: *First*, a child's maximum educational potential can and will be accurately ascertained. *Second*, tracking will enhance the prospects for correcting a child's remediable educational deficiencies. *Third*, tracking must be flexible so as to provide an individually tailored education for students who cannot be pigeon-holed in a single curriculum.

C.   *The Tracks.*

1. *Honors.*

Purpose. The Honors Track is for the gifted student, its purpose being to provide him with an enriched, accelerated curriculum and to stimulate scholarship by placing him with similarly gifted students.

Criteria. Elementary school children are eligible for Honors classes upon "recommendation by the principal and teacher, based upon the pupil's school record and physical maturity with achievement at least one year beyond national norms in reading and arithmetic * * *."

At the junior high school level the student is judged in terms of the following: "1. Scholastic ability; 2. History and good study habits; 3. Emotional and physical stability; 4. Achievement-test scores above grade level in English and mathematics; 5. Interest in being in the Honors Track; 6. Approval of parents and principal."

For senior high school the criteria are as follows:

> "The student is admitted to this curriculum only on his own election and only if he is eligible. Eligibility for the honors curriculum requires the following: (a) demonstrated ability to do difficult academic work as shown by previous academic record; (b) ability to read two or more grades above grade level; (c) achievement test scores in the upper quartile in standardized tests in language and mathematics; (d) mental ability indicated to be in the upper quartile; (e) emotional and physical stamina for difficult work; (f) demonstrated enthusiasm for honors placement; and (g) the written approval of parents or guardians.
>
> "If a student shows a general aptitude for honors placement, he may be programmed in the curriculum even if he is deficient in up to two of the foregoing prerequisites."

Structure. Honors classes do not begin until the fourth grade. At that time an eligible student may be placed in a separate Honors class at his own school, if there are enough other eligible students to warrant setting aside classroom space and assigning a teacher. If there are not, apparently an Honors group might be organized within the regular classroom although this would seem to be contrary to the concept of having wholly separate curricula. More commonly, the student has to transfer to the nearest school having an Honors class to obtain such instruction.

Curriculum. In elementary school the Honors curriculum is an accelerated and enriched version of the standard curriculum. The same is generally true for the junior high school; in addition, some senior high school subjects are offered to ninth graders.

In senior high school the content of the various curriculum levels is significantly different, as are graduation requirements. To graduate from the senior high school Honors Track the student must complete 18 Carnegie units, 16 of which are required and 1½ elective. The required subject areas are English (4 units), mathematics (Algebra I and II, and plane geometry; 3 units), foreign language (4 units), social studies (ancient-medieval history, U. S. history, and U. S. government; 2½ units), and science (biology, chemistry and physics; 3 units). There is a wide selection of electives, including many advanced academic subjects.

2. *Regular.*

Purpose. This is a college preparatory track, found only at the senior high school level. It "provides the hard-core of academic offerings normally required for college entrance." According to Dr. Hansen, it merely continues the advanced curriculum found in all high schools having a two-level curriculum sequence (*i. e.*, college preparatory and terminal) although he suggests embodying it in a track level tends to enhance its prestige and effectiveness in stimulating scholarship.

Criteria. To qualify for the Regular Track the student must have:

"° ° ° (a) demonstrated ability to do academic work successfully as indicated by the student's scholastic record; (b) ability to read at grade level or above; (c) achievement scores in standardized tests at or above grade level in language and mathematics; (d) mental ability at or above high normal; (e) physical and emotional stamina to undertake a demanding program of studies; (f) interest in doing college preparatory work; and (g) written approval of parents or guardians."

Another version of these requirements includes the statement that the student must have "generally, high normal IQ, or above ° ° °."

Curriculum. Sixteen Carnegie units must be completed to graduate from the Regular Track. Of these, 10½ are in these required subjects: English (4 units), foreign language (2 units), mathematics (algebra, geometry; 2 units), science (biology, chemistry or physics; 1 unit), and social studies (U. S. history, U. S. government; 1½ units). As in the case of the Honors curriculum, offered electives include a number of advanced academic subjects.

3. *General.*

Purpose. At the elementary and junior high school levels the General curriculum serves the bulk of the students, excepting only those considered bright enough for Honors or slow enough for Special Academic.

At the senior high school level, however, the nature of the General Track becomes more specific. It is expressly a curriculum "designed to serve students of normal intelligence levels who plan to go to work immediately upon graduation."

Curriculum. For elementary and junior high schools the General curriculum is simply a normal primary or secondary program. However, given the fairly broad range of ability levels in the General Track, there is subgrouping of students so as to narrow the range of differences; thus there may be a slow General group and a fast General group.

In senior high school, in keeping with its terminal nature, the pure General curriculum is vocationally oriented. Students who desire a college preparatory curriculum must, for the most part, elect courses from the Regular Track, but may do so only if qualified for the more advanced instruction. Sixteen Carnegie units are required for graduation, 7½ of them in these required subjects: English (4 units), mathematics (general mathematics, business arithmetic, or—if qualified—algebra; 1 unit), science (descriptive biology; 1 unit), social studies (U. S. history, U. S. government; 1½ units).

4. *Special Academic (Basic).*

Purpose. The Special Academic Track is for those students who have been variously described as "slow learners," "retarded," "academically retarded," "retarded slow learners," or "stupid." Its purposes are to provide a useful education for students whose limited abilities prevent them from successfully participating in the normal curriculum; and to give remedial instruction in the basic subjects—especially reading and arithmetic—to those students who can eventually qualify for upgrading to the General curriculum.

Criteria. In general, the criteria for Special Academic Track placement are inability to keep up with the normal curriculum, emotionally disturbed behavior, an IQ of 75 or below, and substandard performance on achievement tests.

In junior high "in order to be transferred from Basic to General Track, *in general* the student must be functioning at no more than 2 years below grade level in reading and arithmetic. * * * In cases where the pupil does not meet this standard BUT there is evidence of diligence, recent growth, and good study habits in the fundamental skills, the student may be given trial placement in the General Track."

In senior high school Special Academic placement is recommended when

> "(a) a student is functioning three or more years below grade level as shown by achievement tests (at sixth grade or below in reading and mathematics in the ninth grade); (b) his preceding academic record shows him to be unable to cope at a minimum level with tra-

ditional content in language and mathematics; (c) his teachers believe him to be in need of placement in the basic track; (d) his mental retardation is indicated by an I.Q. index of 75 or below."

Dr. Hansen has said that "academic retardation in this curriculum is severe, particularly in reading."

School policy used to be that students identified as belonging in the Special Academic Track were mandatorily required to enroll in that curriculum. "Admission to the upper three curricula should be selective. The student who is ineligible because of low achievement should not be admitted to the traditional high school program." This policy, followed in elementary and junior high schools as well as in the high schools, was amended in the fall of 1965 to require parental consent for Special Academic placement. Most parents, however, acquiesce in the school's recommendation.

Structure. Elementary school children may be placed in the Special Academic Track as early as the first grade, although most wind up there after an attempt at the normal first and perhaps second grade curriculum. Some schools place all Special Academic children in one class, so that youngsters ranging from first to sixth grade age levels may be taught in the same classroom; actually, the age spread may be even greater since Special Academic students who do not progress academically to a point where they can be promoted into the junior high school level remain in elementary school until they pass their thirteenth birthday. Other schools divide the track into two groups, the primary Special Academic (grade levels one through three) and the intermediate Special Academic (grade levels four through six), thus reducing the age spread.

At least at the elementary school level, Special Academic classes are ungraded. A child's grade level equivalent is ascertained from his scores on standardized or informal achievement tests. Whereas the child in the General curriculum can usually be expected to progress at the rate of one grade level per year, the Special Academic student typically will progress at a much slower rate. For those who continue to learn at this slower rate, the Special Academic Track will be a permanent assignment until such time as the child passes his thirteenth birthday and is moved on into the junior high school Special Academic Track. It is not clear whether classes are ungraded in the secondary schools.

A major distinction of the Special Academic Track is that classes are to be kept relatively small, the usual pupil-teacher ratio being about 18 or 20 to one. This is to enable more individualized attention than is possible in a larger class.

Dr. Hansen has indicated that teachers in the Special Academic Track need to be specially prepared to deal with the special problems that characterize slow learners. The great majority of those teaching in the Special Academic Track, however, either have had no formal training in special education or have had very little. About half of the teachers are nontenure, or temporary.

Curriculum. The Special Academic curriculum at the elementary and junior high school level can be characterized as a highly simplified, slower-paced version of the standard curriculum. The concepts taught are simpler; the vocabulary is easier, the words being less complex and fewer in number; instructional materials may be simplified versions of materials used in the normal classroom, the effort being made to keep pace with the child's age-level interests while at the same time reducing subject content to his grade-level ability. There is an emphasis on "basic" subjects—reading, English, and arithmetic.

At the senior high school level, in addition to carrying forward the simplified course content, the curriculum focuses on preparing the student for a variety of low-skill vocations. Graduation requirements in the Special Academic Track are 16 Carnegie units, 9½ in these required subjects: English (4 units), mathematics (arithmetic; 2 units), science (basic science; 1 unit), social studies (social studies, U. S. history, and U. S. government; 2½ units), business education (basic business; 1 unit). The elective courses are in such areas as home economics, shop (all at the low-skills level), or business-related functions (typing, filing, office machine operation, etc.).

5. *Junior Primary.*

The Junior Primary is an ability-grouped class intermediate between kindergarten and first grade. Its purpose is to bring children up to a level of readiness for normal first grade instruction, the usual problem being inadequate preparation in reading-readiness skills. Some students in Junior Primary have not had kindergarten training (many Negro children do not attend kindergarten because of lack of space; other children simply are not enrolled by parents); others are slow learners who have not fully developed in kindergarten.

A decision as to whether a child requires Junior Primary placement is based on his score on a standard aptitude test and the teacher's judgment. For those students who have not had kindergarten, however, the test score would have to be the controlling factor since the child would not have had any prior contact with the school and thus would not be known to a teacher.

Of those who go into Junior Primary, some advance directly into the second grade, but most go into regular first grade after spending a year or less in the special class. And for some children Junior Primary is simply preliminary to placement in the Special Academic Track.

In these five junior high schools, the only ones with a significant biracial enrollment, the per cent of white students in the Special Academic Track was consistently lower than the per cent of whites in the total

TABLE A

ELEMENTARY SCHOOLS

School Year	Basic Track No.	%	General Track No.	%	Regular Track No.	%	Honors Track No.	%	Total
1962–1963	2,839	3.3	69,908	95.0			1,269	1.7	74,016
1963–1964	2,876	3.8	Unknown°				Unknown		75,807
1964–1965	2,984	3.9	72,971	94.6			1,196	1.5	77,151
1965–1966	2,495	3.1	75,762	95.1			1,382	1.8	79,639
1966–1967	1,919	2.4	Unknown				Unknown		81,513

JUNIOR HIGH SCHOOLS

	Basic Track No.	%	General Track No.	%	Regular Track No.	%	Honors Track No.	%	Total
1959–1960	2,569	11.9	18,068	83.3			1,045	4.8	21,682
1960–1961	3,124	13.0	19,455	81.1			1,419	5.9	23,998
1961–1962	3,457	13.1	21,356	80.9			1,570	6.0	26,383
1962–1963	4,218	15.0	22,215	78.9			1,722	6.1	28,155
1963–1964	4,499	15.5	22,758	78.3			1,793	6.2	29,050
1964–1965	4,209	14.4	23,253	79.5			1,799	6.1	29,261
1965–1966	2,767	9.5	24,181	84.9			1,585	5.6	28,533
1966–1967	2,193	6.9	Unknown				Unknown		29,182

SENIOR HIGH SCHOOLS

	Basic Track No.	%	General Track No.	%	Regular Track No.	%	Honors Track No.	%	Total
1958–1959	3.026	22.6	5,575	41.7	3,884	29.0	892	6.7	13,377
1959–1960	2,904	22.0	5,594	42.4	3,795	28.8	900	6.8	13,193
1960–1961	2,321	18.3	5,572	44.1	3,780	29.9	969	7.7	12,642
1961–1962	2,074	16.1	5,692	44.2	4,002	31.1	1,106	8.6	12,874
1962–1963	1,799	12.6	6,455	45.3	4,856	34.0	1,155	8.1	14,265
1963–1964	1,760	10.8	7,812	48.0	5,628	34.6	1,075	6.6	16,275
1964–1965	1,629	9.0	8,941	49.6	6,426	35.6	1,035	5.8	18,031
1965–1966	1,451	7.9	9,355	50.5	6,710	36.2	1,007	5.4	18,523
1966–1967	Unknown		Unknown		Unknown		Unknown		18,858

° Data not available.

school population (*compare* Col. 1 *with* Col. 4); in all cases a higher proportion of the Negro students in these schools were in the lowest track than were the white students (*compare* Col. 5 *with* Col. 6).

Clearly, then, race cannot be considered irrelevant in the operation of the track system. Even if the effects of tracking are not racially motivated, the Negro student nonetheless is affected.

Effects of the distribution pattern.

The data just reviewed reveal the two important effects of the track system. First, tracking tends to separate students from one another according to socioeconomic and racial status, albeit in the name of ability grouping. Second, the students attending the lower income predominantly Negro schools—a majority of District school children—typically are confined to the educational limits of the Special Academic or General Track.

a. *Class separation.* The track system is by definition a separative device, ostensibly according to students' ability levels. However, the practical effect of such a system is also to group students largely according to their socio-economic status and, to a lesser but observable degree, to their racial status. Two examples will suffice to prove the point.

(1) *Western High School.* Western is a high school serving the neighborhood with the second highest income level ($8,649). However, the 1965 enrollments in the Special Academic and Regular Tracks did not conform to the general rule linking income with track placement—three schools (Coolidge, Roosevelt, McKinley) of lower income levels than Western having fewer students in the Special Academic Track, and two of those (Coolidge, McKinley) having more in the Regular Track.

Defendants suggest as a reason for this deviation an influx of transfer students, implicit in which is the further suggestion that these were lower income students who would tend to gravitate to the lower tracks. Evidence shows that in 1965, 405 out-of-boundary students were enrolled in Western, representing 31% of the student body. A breakdown of Western's enrollment by median income level as of May 1966 showed the following: 29.7% of the students were from income levels below $5,000; 34.2% were from the $5,000–$6,999 level; 10.7% were from the $7,000–$8,999 level; and 25.4% were from levels $9,000 and above.

Accepting defendants' explanation as correct serves to strengthen the economic-correlation finding. But more significantly, it proves the segregatory effect of tracking. Thus the indigenous upper class, predominantly white, Western student body is cushioned from the full impact of a substantial influx of lower class outsiders. And given the predominance of the Negro in that class, there is a high probability that the cushioning effect is racially as well as economically related.

(2) Confirmation of the cushioning effect from a racial standpoint is found in the data where it was shown that Negro students in the "integrated" schools go into the Special Academic Track in greater proportion than their white classmates. Although whites and Negroes certainly are not wholly segregated in these schools as a consequence of this, there can be no disputing that the greater the number of Negro students placed in the lower tracks, the less will be the impact of the Negro enrollment on the upper track levels. In short, there is substantial evidence that tracking tends to thin out the number of Negroes in the higher curriculum levels, thus redistributing the racial balance in integrated schools —increasing the proportion of Negroes to whites in the lower tracks and decreasing that proportion in the upper tracks.

*   *   *   *   *   *

The reason for the track system's separative effect (and concomitant cushioning effect as well) inheres largely in the placement methods used in the District, pupils being programmed on the strength of their performances in class and on standardized aptitude tests, both of which criteria are heavily—and, as it turns out, unfairly—weighted against the disadvantaged student. Moreover, as will be seen shortly, once a student is separated it tends to be both permanent and complete at least insofar as classroom contacts are concerned.

b. *Availability of Honors programs.* As observed earlier, because of the socio-economic and racial correlations the poorer Negro students for the most part receive the limited offerings of the General and Special Academic Tracks. But more than that, there is a total absence of any Honors programs at a substantial number of schools—almost all of them having predominantly Negro enrollments.

Defendants' explanation for this absence—at least with respect to the elementary schools—is that there are not enough students with the apparent aptitude for advanced work enrolled in the individual schools to warrant organizing an Honors program. For those students who do show Honors potential, the usual option given them is to transfer—at their own expense—to the closest school offering an Honors course. As a practical matter, the burden is such that many parents are forced to leave their children in their neighborhood school and the gifted Negro student stays in the General Track. Presumably these children are at some disadvantage when they move on to junior high school and begin to compete with the more fortunate students—black or white—whose schools were able to provide them with the advanced course work.

At the senior high school level, the virtually all-Negro, low income Dunbar High School has gone without an Honors Track for at least the last seven years. Apparently out of the approximately 1,500 students enrolled at Dunbar each year not enough bright students have been found to justify an Honors program. There is no evidence as to whether Honors-capable students in the Dunbar zone are allowed to transfer to a school offering such a program; presumably they would be, if they could afford the time and expense of going beyond neighborhood boundaries. On the other hand, for those students not qualified for full-scale enrollment in the Honors Track but capable of and interested in selected Honors-level courses, transfer is apparently not an option. This means, of course, that the maximum education open to a Dunbar student is the standard Regular Track course of instruction; there can be no supplementing of that program with an occasional Honors course.

Both this circumstance and the broader problem of requiring transfers to obtain the best education point up a distinct inflexibility in the track system. Being committed to organizing a whole curriculum rather than individual courses at a given time in a given subject, the capital investment required in the form of potential student enrollment is much higher. Thus, while programs are to be individualized for the student there must first be enough individuals for the program. This is a distinct disadvantage for the fast developing student enrolled in a school where the student body, because of impoverished circumstances, is unable to furnish an adequate supply of candidates for a full-scale Honors program.

E. *Flexibility in Pupil Programming.*

The importance of flexibility to the proper operation of the track system has been adverted to earlier in this opinion. No better statement of this principle can be found than in the words of Dr. Hansen:

> "When the four-track system was put into operation in 1956, the intent was not to make pigeon-holes into which pupils would be permanently sorted like mail of different classes. The expectation was, rather, that a student's election of a curriculum sequence, or his assignment to one, would restrict his choice of subjects to a pattern of interrelated disciplines. The coordinated curriculum plan was developed to provide for flexibility when the interests of the pupils demanded it. Can a more restrictive and less individualistic curriculum plan coexist with a reasonable degree of flexibility in pupil programming?
>
> "Experience has shown that flexibility can be and is a salient feature of the four-track plan. This outcome is not automatic. It must be insisted upon by the central administrative office as it works to set up standard practices against the natural gravitational pull toward separateness in secondary school administration. High school administrators tend toward individuality in management, resist pressures from the central administrative office, and make their schools self-contained and self-governing principalities.
>
> "The flexibility described here is of two kinds: (1) the transfer from one track to another as conditions warrant and (2) crosstracking, that is, the election of courses by eligible students outside their own track placement."

Plaintiffs, of course, have taken issue with Dr. Hansen's conclusion that "experience has shown that flexibility can be and is a salient feature * * *" of the track system. They are joined in this view by none other than the President of the School Board, Dr. Haynes, who has stated in testimony before this court that the track system puts District School children in a "straitjacket." Defendants have been content to resist the charges of inflexibility by relying on a somewhat sparse statistical showing of the amount of movement between tracks—upgrading and crosstracking—that actually takes place.

These data speak for themselves: flexibility in pupil programming in the District of Columbia school system is an unkept promise.

1. *Movement Between Tracks: Upgrading.*

The pattern observed with respect to upgrading from the Special Academic Track is repeated in all track levels. Movement between tracks borders on the nonexistent.

In the period from September 1963 through June 1964 the total number of junior high school students upgraded was 262, or less than one per cent of the student body; and of those upgraded, almost all were Special Academic students going to the General Track. Only 30 students out of all those enrolled in General Track in the 25 junior high schools existing at that time were able to qualify for the Honors curriculum during that period. Moreover, for every student upgraded another student was downgraded to a lower track. The tendency for downgrading to counterbalance upgrading is generally consistent throughout the primary and secondary schools.

At the senior high school level intertrack movement assumes even greater significance because of the dichotomy in subject matter emphasis between the two lower tracks and the upper or college preparatory tracks. Here again the pattern is one of rigidity.

Thus in the 1963–64 school year, where the figures show the highest amount of intertrack movement, almost 92% of the senior high students did not leave their assigned track. Moreover, 44% of the students who did move, moved downward.

What is most important, however, is the miniscule amount of movement from the lower tracks to the college preparatory tracks. Of the approximately 7,800 General Track students, only 404—about 5%—moved up a level, none going into the Honors curriculum. Although five Special Academic students were able to jump ahead two levels to the Regular Track, the number not moving at all remains by far predominant. In sum, then, of all the students in the two lower tracks—constituting almost 60% of the student body—only 4.8% advanced to the college preparatory curriculum. And at the same time, it should be noted, 320 students—or 4.8%—from the Regular or Honors Track fell back to the lower tracks.

Viewed as a whole, the evidence of overall movement between tracks conclusively demonstrates the defendants' failure to translate into practice one of the most critical tenets of the track system:

> "Pupil placement in a curriculum must never be static or unchangeable. Otherwise, the four-track system will degenerate into a four-rut system."

The tragedy has occurred.

2. *Movement Between Tracks: Cross-Tracking.*

As noted above, cross-tracking is track terminology for electing courses above or below an assigned curriculum level. (Tr. 329,2647; Ex.B-11, p. 188.) The purpose of cross-tracking is to assure flexibility in meeting individual students' needs, allowing students who cannot qualify for—or who do not require or desire—full-time assignment to a higher or lower track (upgrading or downgrading) to take one or more courses at an advanced or simplified level.

In practice cross-tracking of the sort described is confined to the senior high level, there being structural reasons why elementary and junior high pupils do not really "cross-track." And even at the senior high school level cross-tracking proves to be the exception, not the rule.

VI. The Track System

Plaintiffs' attack on the track system, Superintendent Hansen's special form of ability grouping, touches yet another phase of the District's administration of the public schools, here the concern being specifically the kind of educational opportunities existing within the classroom. The evidence amassed by both parties with regard to the track system has been reviewed in detail in Part IV of the Findings, where the court has already had occasion to note the critical infirmities of that system. The sum result of those infirmities, when tested by the principles of equal protection and due process, is to deprive the poor and a majority of the Negro students in the District of Columbia of their constitutional right to equal educational opportunities.

At the outset it should be made clear that what is at issue here is not whether defendants are entitled to provide different kinds of students with different kinds of education. Although the equal protection clause is, of course, concerned with classifications which result in disparity of treatment, not all classifications resulting in disparity are unconstitutional. If classification is reasonably related to the purposes of the governmental activity involved and is rationally carried out, the fact that persons are thereby treated differently does not necessarily offend.

Ability grouping is by definition a classification intended to discriminate among students, the basis of that discrimination being a student's capacity to learn. Different kinds of educational opportunities are thus made available to students of differing abilities. Whatever may be said of the concept of ability grouping in general, it has been assumed here that such grouping can be reasonably related to the purposes of public education. Plaintiffs have eschewed taking any position to the contrary. Rather the substance of plaintiffs' complaint is that in practice, if not by design, the track system—as administered in the District of Columbia public schools—has become a system of discrimination founded on socio-economic and racial status rather than ability, resulting in the under-education of many District students.

As the court's findings have shown, the track system is undeniably an extreme form of ability grouping. Students are early in elementary school sorted into homogeneous groups or tracks (and often into subgroups within a track), thereby being physically separated into different classrooms. Not only is there homogeneity, in terms of supposed levels of ability—the intended result—but as a practical matter there is a distinct sameness in terms of socio-economic status as well. More importantly, each track offers a substantially different kind of education, both in pace of learning and in scope of subject matter. At the bottom there is the slow-paced, basic (and eventually almost purely low-skill vocational) Special Academic Track; at the top is the intense and challenging Honors program for the gifted student. For a student locked into one of the lower tracks, physical separation from those in other tracks is of course complete insofar as classroom relationships are concerned; and the limits on his academic progress, and ultimately the kind of life work he can hope to attain after graduation, are set by the orientation of the lower curricula. Thus those in the lower tracks are, for the most part, molded for various levels of vocational assignments; those in the upper tracks, on the other hand, are given the opportunity to prepare for the higher ranking jobs and, most significantly, for college.

In theory, since tracking is supposed to be kept flexible, relatively few students should actually ever be locked into a single track or curriculum. Yet, in violation of one of its principal tenets, the track system is not flexible at all. Not only are assignments permanent for 90% or more of the students but the vast majority do not even take courses outside their own curriculum. Moreover, another significant failure to implement track theory—and in major part responsible for the inflexibility just noted—is the lack of adequate remedial and compensatory education programs for the students assigned to or left in the lower tracks because of cultural handicaps. Although one of the express reasons for placing such students in these tracks is to facilitate remediation, little is being done to accomplish the task. Consequently, the lower track student, rather than obtaining an enriched educational experience, gets what is essentially a limited or watered-down curriculum.

These are, then, the significant features of the track system: separation of students into rigid curricula, which entails both physical segregation and a disparity of educational opportunity; and, for those consigned to the lower tracks, opportunities decidedly inferior to those available in the higher tracks.

A precipitating cause of the constitutional inquiry in this case is the fact that those who are being consigned to the lower tracks are the poor and the Negroes, whereas the upper tracks are the provinces of the more affluent and the whites. Defendants have not, and indeed could not have, denied that the pattern of grouping correlates remarkably with a student's status, although defendants would have it that the equation is to be stated in terms of income, not race. However, as discussed elsewhere, to focus solely on economics is to oversimplify the matter in the District of Columbia where so many of the poor are in fact the Negroes. And even if race could be ruled out, which it cannot, defendants surely "can no more discriminate on account of poverty than on account of religion, race, or color." Griffin v. People of State of Illinois, 351 U.S. 12,

17, 76 S.Ct. 585, 590, 100 L.Ed. 891 (1951). As noted before, the law has a special concern for minority groups for whom the judicial branch of government is often the only hope for redressing their legitimate grievances; and a court will not treat lightly a showing that educational opportunities are being allocated according to a pattern that has unmistakable signs of invidious discrimination. Defendants, therefore, have a weighty burden of explaining why the poor and the Negro should be those who populate the lower ranks of the track system.

Since by definition the basis of the track system is to classify students according to their ability to learn, the only explanation defendants can legitimately give for the pattern of classification found in the District schools is that it does reflect students' abilities. If the discriminations being made are founded on anything other than that, then the whole premise of tracking collapses and with it any justification for relegating certain students to curricula designed for those of limited abilities. While government may classify persons and thereby effect disparities in treatment, those included within or excluded from the respective classes should be those for whom the inclusion or exclusion is appropriate; otherwise the classification risks becoming wholly irrational and thus unconstitutionally discriminatory. It is in this regard that the track system is fatally defective, because for many students placement is based on traits other than those on which the classification purports to be based.

The evidence shows that the method by which track assignments are made depends essentially on standardized aptitude tests which, although given on a system-wide basis, are completely inappropriate for use with a large segment of the student body. Because these tests are standardized primarily on and are relevant to a white middle class group of students, they produce inaccurate and misleading test scores when given to lower class and Negro students. As a result, rather than being classified according to ability to learn, these students are in reality being classified according to their socio-economic or racial status, or—more precisely —according to environmental and psychological factors which have nothing to do with innate ability.

Compounding and reinforcing the inaccuracies inherent in test measurements are a host of circumstances which further obscure the true abilities of the poor and the Negro. For example, teachers acting under false assumptions because of low test scores will treat the disadvantaged student in such a way as to make him conform to their low expectations; this acting out process—the self-fulfilling prophecy—makes it appear that the false assumptions were correct, and the student's real talent is wasted. Moreover, almost cynically, many Negro students are either denied or have limited access to the very kinds of programs the track system makes a virtual necessity: kindergartens; Honors programs for the fast-developing Negro student; and remedial and compensatory education programs that will bring the disadvantaged student back into the mainstream of education. Lacking these facilities, the student continues hampered by his cultural handicaps and continues to appear to be of lower ability than he really is. Finally, the track system as an institution cannot escape blame for the error in placements, for it is tracking that places such an emphasis on defining ability, elevating its importance to the point where the whole of a student's education and future are made to turn on his facility in demonstrating his qualifications for the higher levels of opportunity. Aside from the fact that this makes the consequences of misjudgments so much the worse, it also tends to alienate the disadvantaged student who feels unequal to the task of competing in an ethnocentric school system dominated by white middle class values; and alienated students inevitably do not reveal their true abilities—either in school or on tests.

All of these circumstances, and more, destroy the rationality of the class structure that characterizes the track system. Rather than reflecting classifications according to ability, track assignments are for many students placements based on status. Being, therefore, in violation of its own premise, the track system amounts to an unlawful discrimination against those students whose educational opportunities are being limited on the erroneous assumption that they are capable of accepting no more.

Remedy

As to the remedy with respect to the track system, the track system simply must be abolished. In practice, if not in concept, it discriminates against the disadvantaged child, particularly the Negro. Designed in 1955 as a means of protecting the school system against the ill effects of integrating with white children the Negro victims of *de jure* separate but unequal education, it has survived to stigmatize the disadvantaged child of whatever race relegated to its lower tracks—from which tracks the possibility of switching upward, because of the absence of compensatory education, is remote.

Even in concept the track system is undemocratic and discriminatory. Its creator admits it is designed to prepare some children for white-collar, and other children for blue-collar, jobs. Considering the tests used to determine which children should receive the blue-collar special, and which the white, the danger of children completing their education wearing the wrong collar is far too great for this democracy to tolerate. Moreover, any system of ability grouping which, through failure to include and implement the concept of compensatory education for the disadvantaged child or otherwise, fails in fact to bring the great majority of children into the mainstream of public education, denies the children excluded equal educational opportunity and thus encounters the constitutional bar.

6

...The Constitution does not put at the disposal of judges the resources to prevent, abolish, or even alleviate poverty, juvenile delinquency, slum housing, or rotten schools.

ALEXANDER M. BICKEL

U. S. News and World Report

DANGER FACING NATION'S SCHOOLS?
(AN INTERVIEW WITH DR. CARL HANSEN)

Q. Dr. Hansen, you have had 13 years of experience with integration in Washington schools. Out of that experience, what is the major conclusion that you have drawn?

A. I think the main conclusion is that integration is a possibility if we forget about race in relation to it. What we have to deal with, I think, is people—people having different degrees of development and capacity to improve themselves. And I think we should get off the racist binge that we've gotten into the last few years.

Q. What has stimulated this "racist binge," as you call it—the Government?

A. It seems to me that Government is involved to some extent in apparently encouraging—particularly through the antipoverty activities—a response that is based pretty much on economic status and race. So, in this respect, the Federal Government may be quite heavily responsible for what is going on.

A possible outcome in this situation, I think, is class warfare—class in terms of money, status, economics—the idea that I've got more money than you, therefore I should share some of it—and race.

The most unwholesome part of the current racist emphasis is that it discourages the process of integration.

Q. What is integration?

A. In my judgment, integration is simply defined as the capacity of people to be together without being conscious of race—the appreciation of each other regardless of race or economic status or religion.

Q. Are Washington schools integrated?

A. I would maintain they are, in that no child is ever denied a place or any activity because of race or creed or any other external condition. The children are all subject to the same rules and regulations in respect

From "Danger Facing Nation's Schools?" (an interview with Dr. Carl Hansen), *U. S. News and World Report*, July 24, 1967, pp. 40–46, 48. Copyright 1967 by U. S. News and World Report, Inc. Reprinted by permission of the publisher.

to where they attend school. And there is actually some degree of bi-racial membership in most of our schools. As many as 85 per cent of Washington children attend schools in which there are some children of the other race.

Now, of course, in some cases there may be only three or four white children in a school that's otherwise Negro. The integration factor there is not very strong if you think of integration as requiring some kind of arbitrary balance—for example, 50 per cent white and 50 per cent Negro.

Q. What do you think of this idea of seeking an arbitrary racial balance?

A. In my judgment, this is a ridiculous concept. And it's foolhardy, too, because you can never achieve it. You can't by edict declare that "you white folks are going to have to send your children to this school and you Negro parents are going to have to send your children to that school to get a racial balance."

Q. What do you see as wrong in this idea of moving children around for racial balance?

A. The basic flaw in this particular practice—I was about to call it phi-losophy, but I don't think it justifies that kind of term—is that the soci-ologist or whoever it is who conjures up such grandiose schemes is exploiting the children to accomplish what the adults are not willing to accomplish themselves.

In so-called ghetto areas, for example, parents often say, "Don't move us; move the children."

Q. In city after city, you find complaints about schools, and demands being made for changes in schools. Why is this?

A. The public schools are being made scapegoats, not only in Wash-ington, but in New York, Chicago, Kansas City, Detroit, Cleveland. You can't escape the very clear evidence that the social and economic prob-lems of the poor in the larger cities are being transferred to the systems of public education in those cities.

Schools are being asked to do what they cannot do.

Schools cannot remake a family, except, perhaps, by affecting the next generation. It's almost impossible for any sociologist, really, to recon-struct a family that has deteriorated.

Now, I have another belief which I can't really document, but which I think is fundamental and important:

It seems to me there is very clear evidence that the concerted attack upon public education around the country may be motivated by the de-sire of people in high political office in Washington to set the pattern from which they would like to have education cut throughout the country.

Q. Do you mean their aim is for federal control over the local schools?

A. I think it is very clearly that—to break down regional or local con-trol, to take the schools out of the hands of the people and centralize their management on a national scale.

Q. Who are the people who want to do this?

A. There are people who sit in the offices of the Office of Economic Opportunity and in the Office of Education who believe that they have a kind of omniscience—that they can see and do what ought to be done for the good of the whole country. They have said that to me, in conferences at the Office of Economic Opportunity where I protested certain requirements which intruded upon the rights of boards of education to make appointments and to conduct the operation of the Head Start program.

These men—well-intentioned, I am sure—say to me: "We can't be sure that boards of education will do these things right." So in the quiet of their offices they make patterns for education around the country.

The intention may be good, but I think the objective is tremendously dangerous to the very essence of our freedom, which is that schools be decentralized and locally operated.

Q. These people sitting in their quiet offices who, you say, are planning these things—what kind of people are they?

A. In my contacts with people from the Office of Education and HEW [Department of Health, Education and Welfare] I am impressed by the—let me put it in the most pleasant term—by the innovative aspect of their approach to education. For them, the old ways won't do. Just simply to have a teacher to teach youngsters to read in a direct manner—that's not acceptable.

They want change. These men are brought into these offices because they've got some kind of reputations for being innovators, for being imaginative. Put that label on any school man, and he can go any place he wants in the Office of Education.

In addition to that, it seems to me that we are seeing the social activists rising to dominance. Some of my severest critics here in Washington are social activists who are employed by HEW.

Q. What are social activists?

A. These are people, in my judgment, who first seem to make it their business to create disturbance—not physical violence, but disturbance; to be constantly critical of the establishment, the school system; to be involved in all kinds of group activities in stimulating very small numbers of parents to participate in the social revolution.

Now, I don't know what the people propose to do in terms of social revolution, but they seem to be bent on accomplishing change without, sometimes, being too much concerned about what that change is going to be.

Q. Is it only from appointed officials that these attacks on our educational system come?

A. Antagonisms sometimes come from very prominent Senators—whom I won't name—who give me the impression that their attitude toward free public education in the American style is so negative that they never miss a chance to deride it, to speak of it as a failure.

Abuse of Education—

Q. What could be the end result of all this?

A. There is no one party in power nationally that can now use the schools to perpetuate itself in power. So you ask: Why this attack on public education?

I think there's a definite motive to disturb confidence in public education and in boards of education so that there can be an accumulation of controls in Washington. This may be a kind of benign despotism to start with, but I think ultimately it could be misused for such purposes as Hitler used education in Germany. You may remember that the first thing he did was to take over education of the young. Mussolini did this [in Italy]. The Russians have done it. The totalitarians perpetuate themselves in control through the use of the education of the child.

I have anxiety about this. It seems to me that these things ought to be thought about.

Q. Is federal money being used to break down local control over education?

A. Of course. The money from the poverty program—I'm talking here about Operation Head Start—has to be spent in accordance with guidelines laid down by the Economic Opportunity office.

There is some flexibility in the Office of Education funds right now because I think that office is running a little bit scared at this time—they're frightened. But there are guidelines set down there, too—and I'm not talking here about desegregation.

I think schools ought to be completely desegregated in terms of *de jure* segregation [segregation by law or official policy]. But, even in this case, it seems to me that the guidelines for local people to follow are being set down by people who are a long way from the battlefield.

Rules such as U. S. Judge J. Skelly Wright has set down for the schools of the District of Columbia [on June 19] are actually a demonstration of judicial control over education.

Q. What do you think is going to be the effect of Judge Wright's ruling on the Washington schools?

A. The immediate effect is going to be inconsequential, because most of the things he ordered were already in the process of being done.

Judge Wright ordered abandonment of the track system of assigning pupils to courses of study according to their learning abilities. The school board obviously was going to abandon the track system anyway. Judge Wright did not have to tell them to do it.

The judge ordered busing of children from Negro neighborhoods into schools of the Northwest part of the city [a predominantly white area]. The board is already busing children into Northwest schools to relieve overcrowding.

The judge ordered the elimination of optional zones [in which pupils have a choice of schools to attend]. The board already had received proposals to eliminate the optional zones—not because we regarded them as racist in nature, but just because we don't need them now.

So, in terms of the court's decrees, the board was on the way to enacting them. But the long-term effect of the Wright decision is the hazard— the effect of every school-board decision being checked by the court, of the school board having to go to Judge Wright to get clearance on major policy questions allegedly involving desegregation. This is the hazard.

Whether the board can function effectively this way in the long run is a question. You don't know how many years this court control might last. It may last as long as Judge Wright is on the bench here, because there is no apparent end to this control.

So, in my judgment, it is inevitable that the Washington schools will suffer uncertainty and chaos. I'm sure the principals must be wondering what is going to happen this autumn. They must be wondering how to organize.

Q. Do you think that one effect of all this might be an increase in the movement of white children out of the Washington public schools?

A. It is already accelerated. The private schools are being swamped by applications. There's a panic in those areas of the city affected, particularly in the Northwest sections—also among teachers who wonder what is going to happen to them.

Q. Are teachers thinking of quitting?

A. Yes—because, you see, under the judge's order to get more integration of faculties there may be an arbitrary transfer of many teachers. In a predominantly white school such as Eaton, for example, they may take 50 per cent of the white teachers out of that school and say to them, arbitrarily, "You go to this school or that school" which has mostly Negro pupils. And there would be the moving of a similar number of Negro teachers into mostly white schools.

This is the most unbelievable employment practice I could imagine.

Whether teachers will quit or not—well, some cannot afford to quit, because they have too much at stake in retirement benefits. But many will quit. Those who can retire will retire. Some are doing it now.

So, by this measure, it's going to be quite a different school system, even in September, than it was in June.

Q. Is all this going to make integration even more difficult in schools that are already 91 per cent Negro?

A. It destroys any possibility of integration, obviously.

Violence Among Students—

Q. Enrollment records show that there are 31,317 fewer white pupils in Washington public schools now than there were 13 years ago, when the schools were first desegregated. What is the reason? Why are so many white families leaving Washington?

A. The main reason is that a school is the children in it, more than anything else. This is a concept that is hard to make clear.

Woodrow Wilson High in Washington is a great school because it has fine, middle-class, intelligent, concerned, well-motivated youngsters in it.

Now, the tendency of a parent is to regard this as a good context for the education of his child. This is not necessarily snobbishness or racism. It is a feeling that, first of all, the child will be fairly safe. He's not likely to be beaten or robbed—that sort of thing.

Q. Do such things go on in some Washington schools?

A. There is a great deal of that, yes. Not in the classrooms, actually. They are generally under good order. It is when children leave the classrooms that they get into these troubles—occasionally in the hallways or the playgrounds, but generally while going to and from school. Groups of children will waylay an individual child on the route to school. One of the Southwest schools had four or five incidents of that within a week's time.

Q. What causes this lawless behavior?

A. It tends to become a way of life, where even survival requires the capacity to fight back. I've had reports that mothers who go off to work tell their children to "hit back, fight back." Sometimes these children carry small weapons in order to protect themselves. It's a defensive kind of thing.

Then, apparently, when people live in great congested units, such as in public-housing units, feuds develop. Children are fighting battles in the halls, going into each other's apartments and committing acts of vandalism. They become hostile toward each other.

This is not a racial thing, you see. It's a condition of intense hostility, bitterness and anger which permeates the relationships of many children, particularly in congested housing—real slum dwellings, where there is nothing but anger surrounding them.

Q. How can you isolate pupils from this element?

A. Parents whose children are not capable of survival in this kind of situation want them in a school setting where they will be challenged mentally—not by the threat of physical violence. They want schools where they will be stimulated by others who are anxious to work and make good, by children who are motivated. They want schools where their children will not be held back by other children whose parents have not inspired them to perform.

Both Negroes and whites want that kind of school—and not solely the affluent or middle class, but also often the poor Negro and the poor white. A great majority of the poor want a school that is orderly and safe for children and where they will have a chance to learn.

Q. If Washington schools deteriorate, what is going to be the effect on the Negro middle class? Are they going to be squeezed out of the Washington schools, too?

A. They're already leaving as fast as they can—for the same reasons that the white middle class is leaving.

Q. If both white and Negro middle-class people are going to be fleeing these schools in even greater numbers, are we going to wind up here in Washington with schools attended exclusively by lawless elements, leaving the schools a "blackboard jungle"?

A. I want to avoid any impression that the schools are blackboard jungles. If you visit schools you'll find the classes are in good order. Occasionally you may find a teacher having some trouble with the pupils. But the school itself is not a dangerous environment.

What is dangerous is that so many of the children are unmotivated, with poor attitudes toward work or learning, so that middle-class Negroes and middle-class whites who want a more stimulating environment for their children spend every effort to get their children into private schools or go out into the suburbs of Maryland or Virginia.

Differences of Ability—

Q. Are there important differences of ability among children?

A. I suspect that even going back to the very earliest history this has been recognized as a fact.

There have always been generals and there have always been privates. Some people are capable of developing constitutions. Others are best able to build dams or repair machines. Ability differentials are taken for granted. We have very bright Negro children; we have very bright white children. We have very slow Negro children; we have very slow white children.

Let me give you an illustration: A white mother came to me about a year ago and said:

"I'm grateful to you for the track system. I'll tell you why. I have a very bright child, and this youngster is in the honors curriculum. I have a very slow child, and he is in the basic curriculum. The track system is supplying the needs of my entire family."

She was saying, in effect, what everyone knows: that the differential can occur within a family, by nature, by accident. There can be a child who needs special attention in terms of his limited intellectual capacity, and another child who needs special attention because he is very bright.

So the existence of differential in ability is extremely important in education.

Q. Is your so-called track system an attempt to deal with these differences?

A. Yes.

Q. Has it worked?

A. I think it has, but few now in control of schools seem to believe me.

Q. What is the track system? How does it work?

A. Actually, it's a very simple system based upon one primary principle, which is that every youngster needs to be taught strongly in the fundamental skills, whether he is intellectually gifted or whether he is intellectually handicapped.

In a class, you have to reduce the range of differences so the teacher can teach a narrower target—teach the child who has a handicap in reading some of the simplest reading techniques, but teach the child who can read 750 words a minute not just how to read but how to improve the quality of his thinking in terms of getting the meaning out of what he reads. This is the difference.

So we have four tracks—four sequences of study:

There is a program for children with severe retardation which we call the basic program. It stresses the basic skills.

The regular, or general program—where really the bulk of the children are—offers the usual variety of school subjects, but again the stress is on the academics, or fundamentals, which I think every child must have if he's going to be competent as a citizen.

For children who are planning to go on to college, there is the college-preparatory program.

Then there's the honors curriculum. If the child is gifted, willing to work, we offer him especially challenging courses, such as three years of mathematics—the top-quality math, not the easy stuff—four years of a foreign language, and so on.

Q. Can a child move from one track to another?

A. Of course. Many do. About 7 or 8 per cent a year made a significant improvement and moved up from the basic to the regular curriculum.

Q. Then why have some Negroes charged that the track system was used to freeze segregation?

A. That charge is one of the patently demagogic elements in the attack charging resegregation on the basis of race. In a school system which is 91 per cent Negro, how can you do that? What we were actually doing was to try to find means by which to improve the quality of learning.

Q. Why do Negroes say this system is unfair to Negroes?

A. We want to make this clear: It is chiefly the civil-rights leaders who say this. I think, actually, if the rank and file of the Negro parents really knew what the track system is, they would vote to keep it. But now the track system has been so belabored—it's made a scapegoat for every problem a child has—that I think the track system is useless in Washington.

Q. Is the criticism based on the idea that more Negroes than whites are in the basic track?

A. The contention has been that a principal would predetermine what a youngster was capable of doing by placing him in a certain slot—like mail. But this is not how it operates. There is a continuous guidance program. We have more guidance than ever before, more testing, more evaluation of pupils—and we are learning more about how to teach slow learners than ever before. Incidentally, there are special problems in learning how to teach gifted youngsters.

I would say that all of this is going to go by the board when the track system is eliminated.

Q. Is there some other form of grouping that might work and be accepted?

A. There probably will still be some form of ability grouping, but I'm not able to imagine what it will be. I'm going to have to leave that to the bright minds that are now guiding the board of education. I don't know what they are going to propose.

There are those, apparently, who dream of putting children together completely heterogeneously.

Q. Isn't there some form of ability grouping in nearly every American school?

A. Even within the elementary schools there is ability grouping. I think that people who believe that it is possible to avoid knowledge of the level at which school work is being done by dropping titles are naïve.

Encouraging Mediocrity—

Q. What is likely to be the effect of eliminating the track system?

A. The sad part about the loss of the honors curriculum is that this system identifies and stimulates high-level scholarship. I used the word "honors" deliberately when I introduced the program in 1955. Education had gone through a period when scholarship was rather unfashionable. The bright child was afraid to be too smart. Scholarship was not honored. The "honors" system put the spotlight on scholarship—gave it distinction. I think it's been a good thing, because our honors students have performed very well on the basis of every standardized test given them.

Now all of this is to be submerged in mediocrity, where a bright child doesn't dare to be too bright, and where a slow youngster is pacified into believing that he's doing well.

When we took over the integrated schools in 1955, I found chemistry classes in the high schools that were offering no more than the simplest general science. The subject was called chemistry, and everybody was happy. But the pupils were living in a fool's paradise. As soon as they knocked on a college door, they were disillusioned.

So here is the dilemma: I don't believe that you can, in the long run, safely submerge the importance of scholarship. And I am sure you cannot submerge in anonymity the hazard of retardation. If you do, you let the children slip by and get a high-school diploma unchallenged by the fact that they really have not moved along, educationally.

Q. Why is it that some children just can't be brought up to advanced levels in school?

A. You're asking me a question that gets to the problem of nature, and how nature makes people.

Genetically, there are always people who have intellectual limitations. This is not a racial thing. We are talking here about a group of people—perhaps no more than 10 per cent of the total school population—who never actually are going to be able to do abstract mathematics, for example. I have taught youngsters like this. I have taught slow high-school students who were wholly unable, for example, to get the concept of agreement between subject and verb. The only way you could teach them would be to say, repetitively, "You were," not "You was"; and "They are," not "They is."

There's a point of view that asks: "Why can't you develop all youngsters into the genius class? Why can't you get them all ready for college?"

The answer is that you can't. This is simply the way things are. So the schools must develop a program which is geared to the way children actually learn.

Q. Is this a problem of home environment?

A. Some of this may be environmental. But we have tried to separate the child who has a cultural, environmental handicap from the child who has apparently a genetic, intellectual handicap. The child who has the environmental handicap can respond to more abstract instruction, and he is placed in the regular programs but given special assistance and special enrichment courses.

Q. What happens if you try to teach these slow learners in the same classes with fast learners?

A. The teacher has to make a choice. If she gives the kind of attention to the slow learner that he needs to make progress, then she's going to neglect the faster learner.

In this kind of heterogeneous class, what the teacher really does is teach the middle group—the average. She believes "the bright child will learn anyway"—and the very slow, she can't do much with—just lets them drag along.

Some people dream that if the slow child sits beside the bright one that some kind of osmosis will take place and he will become able to learn.

Q. What about the idea that Negroes will do better in school if they sit beside white pupils?

A. I think that is racist nonsense. It presupposes that the Negro is by nature inferior to the white man.

The so-called Coleman report [on a federally financed survey of educational opportunity] has been cited by the Office of Education as justifying the conclusion that a Negro child in a middle-class white school does better than a Negro child in a Negro school. The report does not justify such a conclusion at all. There is not sufficient evidence to do that.

Q. Then you don't think that just mixing the races in the classroom is the answer to Negroes' educational problems—

A. No, not arbitrary mixing. The color of children's skin should not be a factor in deciding what children go to school together.

Real Need: Better Schools—

Q. Would it be more effective to pour more money and more teaching skills into the schools as they are, rather than trying to change the complexion of the schools?

A. This is exactly the only solution—improving the quality of schools in the poverty areas.

This is something we have been trying to do for the last 20 years in Washington. And we have succeeded to some extent, despite the common assumption that every school in downtown Washington is a rotten school. We have been putting in more teachers, giving children greater opportunities than they have ever had before. The idea that a child is being isolated in so-called ghetto schools is stupid.

Q. Where did Judge Wright get the idea he expressed in his decision —that Negro children and children in the low economic group have been discriminated against in terms of educational expenditures in Washington?

A. He misused statistics. Let me explain this:

We have a very limited number of schools in the far Northwest section of Washington where the pupil-teacher ratio is low because the enrollment is small. These are small schools.

Q. Are these predominantly white schools?

A. Yes. But some of the so-called white schools actually have a majority of Negroes, because the Negroes have come in on the open-school basis. For example, one small school with a $600-per-capita expenditure is predominantly Negro.

The point is that the cost of operating a building and supplying the principalship direction, the administrative cost, is measured against the number of pupils.

Apparently the judge took a half dozen of the small schools of the type that I have mentioned that were predominantly white and computed the per capita expenditure in those schools. Then he computed the per capita expenditure in other schools, larger schools, that are predominantly Negro. And he found a differential of, I think, $100 in per capita spending.

Now, statistically, this sounds overwhelming, and editorial writers have said: "Look, you are discriminating against Negro children in favor of whites."

But these few schools are statistically insignificant in relation to the total 85,000 youngsters in our elementary schools. And there is a really more accurate measure of school resources. That is: What are you doing for the schools in terms of adjunct services?

Most of the schools in the so-called poverty areas are receiving additional administrative aid in terms of assistant principals, counselors, librarians, and so forth. They get special reading instruction, other free services, and food—free lunches—none of which is computed in the per capita cost.

So we see here statistical analysis being misused to form a conclusion which is utterly unsound. The judge failed to point out that there are certain schools in Negro sections where the per capita costs exceed anything in any school in the most affluent section of the city. He also failed to point out that Woodrow Wilson, a high school in our most affluent area, is receiving less in terms of dollars and services than many high schools which are predominantly Negro.

Q. Does it cost more to educate children from poor, predominantly Negro areas than it does to educate children from more-affluent white neighborhoods?

A. There has to be what everybody calls compensatory education. A youngster with a handicap has to receive more attention. I'd like to point out that this is not a new concept in American education. For example, it is always more expensive to educate a blind child or a physically handicapped child.

The same, I think, can be said of the child who is handicapped by a lack of proper food and clothing, or by a poorly structured home, or by situations in which he has not been properly developed or stimulated or motivated.

We have argued and worked—in Congress and every other source—for more money for the children with these special needs.

Generosity of Congress—

Q. Congress appropriates the money for Washington schools. Has Congress been responsive to your pleas?

A. Extremely responsive. The average annual increase for operating costs for the past five years was three times higher than for the five years before I became superintendent. In terms of construction, the capital outlay in the last three years has been about 18 million dollars. In the three years before I became superintendent the average was about 3 million dollars. You would think that people who were really working for the Negro and the poor would say: "This kind of support is pretty good. Let's be careful we don't lose it."

Q. What about the charge that Southern Congressmen are holding the purse strings and cutting down on the D. C. school budget?

A. This is a name-calling device which demeans the civil-rights movement and the people who use it. I reject the concept that the Southerner is automatically opposed to good education. It is pretty clear that the Congress has given an extraordinary amount of concentration and energy on improvement of education in Washington.

Q. How do Washington expenditures for schools compare with those in other major cities?

A. We are next to New York in per capita expenditure. We are above all the other major cities. This year the estimated expenditure per capita here will be $750. In 1957–58 it was something over $300. Spending has more than doubled.

Q. One of the things that Judge Wright questioned in his decision was the system of neighborhood schools. He suggested that, as presently administered at least, they result in harm to Negro children that cannot constitutionally be fully justified. Do you think neighborhood schools should be broken up to get more racial integration?

A. They should not be broken up, because a neighborhood school is the best educational device yet developed, just from the educational point of view. To break them up in order to get integration is a will-o'-the-wisp operation.

When you put Negro children in a forced mixture with white children whose parents are fearful, don't want them there, those parents are going to move their children out—even if they have to build private schools of their own to do it. Enforced integration of this kind does not work.

If Schools Get Too Big—

Q. What about the idea of such integrational devices as educational parks, making them community centers?

A. You are talking about contradictory terms. I am strongly in favor of the community-centered school, and we have moved in this direction, with five of them partially organized. I have talked for 10 years about the 7-to-11 type of school—open at 7 in the morning until 11 at night. That is a community-centered school, where the community actually can come in and use it.

An educational park is the exact opposite. When you put a lot of children—as many as 15,000 of them—in a big school cluster, you separate them from their community. I'm utterly opposed to this.

Q. Another idea suggested by Judge Wright was that D. C. school officials explore the possibility of co-operation with the suburbs—a sort of merger of city and suburban schools to bring together Negroes from the city and whites from the suburbs. Would this really help?

A. I doubt that it would. We might get better racial statistics out of it. Instead of a school system 91 per cent Negro, it might be 50 per cent Negro and would look better on paper.

But I'm beginning to think that bigness is not a virtue, that it is a good thing to have smaller jurisdictions running their own schools. And I certainly cannot conceive of a totalitarian system of artificially moving children around by race, forgetting everything else that should be considered.

Q. In the light of recent federal court decisions, do you see the time coming when such changes might be forced upon the schools of this country?

A. Unless there is a reawakening of public responsibility with respect to what is going on. The inertia is terrific.

Even my desire to appeal this ruling of Judge Wright's is causing me great anxiety. Should I or shouldn't I appeal? With my announced retirement as superintendent, will I be accepted as an appellant? Many people have said they would like to appeal, but don't quite know how to do it.

Many people in all walks of life think that Judge Wright's decision is a disgrace to the bench, but they don't know what to do about it.

So unless there is some way that people can express their attitudes on these problems, it is very possible that courts will be running public schools around the country.

Q. One nationally known Negro leader said recently that the idea of improving schools is gaining priority among Negroes over integrating schools. Do you see any evidence of that trend of thinking?

A. Yes. There seems to be a definite trend in the direction of building quality schools where the children are. I see a great deal of evidence of that here in Washington.

For example, I have had an association with a group of Negro ministers who have been visiting with me periodically. These are ministers of local churches—not the civil-rights type of minister, such as you often find in Washington. They are completely opposed to busing for racial mixing. They want the type of school where children will be taught in a disciplined, structured way. They don't want this innovation nonsense, as they call it. They just want the children to be taught. And I believe they speak the mind of the bulk of Negro parents in saying: "Teach our children where they are, and teach them in the basic style."

Q. Yet this idea seems to be rejected by many Negroes—

A. You are listening to the voices of a few who have maneuvered themselves into control. They represent an extremely limited number of people.

Q. How did they get in control?

A. Through manipulation and behind-the-scenes activity. There is no question about it. I think other cities have not seen the change in the quality of their boards of education that has occurred here in the last two years.

Acts of Intimidation—

Q. Where do the average Negroes fit into this picture?

A. The good Negro, like the good white, is being tryannized by fear. We have an atmosphere of intimidation in Washington such that the Negro who believes in holding to a line of strong, structured education is afraid to speak up.

I have received letters—anonymous letters from purportedly Negro teachers—who say that they are very sorry to see me and my methods leave the school system, but are afraid to say anything about it.

There is a level of intimidation now among some members of our own school board that is almost unbelievable.

I know of a principal who has been called late at night and castigated for an alleged error in administration.

Q. Called by whom?

A. By a member of the board of education.

I have seen letters written by an individual member of the board to principals and other school staff in which the school-staff members were severely taken to task for some action of which that board member disapproved.

At a recent board meeting, I am told that one of the new board members said to members of the school staff—highly respected educators:

"When we want you to talk, we will call on you. All you are to do is to carry out our orders."

Q. What kinds of organizations are involved in this intimidation?

A. Well, the only Negro rights group—and I'm not sure that it deserves this kind name—is the so-called ACT group headed by a man named Julius Hobson, who has a coterie of extraordinary personalities around him—many of them white. [Mr. Hobson brought the suit that produced Judge Wright's ruling.] For example, after a Negro board member voted for my reappointment, members of this group approached him in a threatening manner and called him an "Uncle Tom." Recently a Negro minister who spoke in my behalf before the board was surrounded and followed, with the group booing and yelling epithets at him.

Now this is a small group. But rational people are being silenced by a very small group of people.

Q. If their numbers are so small, why aren't they the ones who are being hooted down?

A. Because there is nobody there to hoot them down. It is coming to the point where the only people who come to board of education meetings are those in this little group of activists.

Q. Why is there so much question about the possibility of appealing Judge Wright's ruling?

A. The board of education has ordered me not to appeal. It said in effect, "If you appeal you will have to leave our employ—we will fire you." So I have submitted my resignation, which the board seemed happy to receive.

Q. Why are you so anxious to appeal the Wright ruling?

A. Because it is my deepest conviction that there are basic issues involved which should be tested in the highest court in the land. I have put my job on the line to back this conviction.

Q. What are the issues you think should be tested?

A. First, there is the court's challenge to the authority of the local board of education to run the local schools. For example, the order to abandon the track system is an invasion of the board's authority to decide how to organize the teaching system.

Judge Wright has now become, in fact, the board of education and the superintendent of schools. And I believe that the principle involved here is so deep that it has to be tested out—whether our local board has to run to Judge Wright with hat in hand with every proposal it is considering.

Unless this trend is checked, local management of schools is out.

Q. Do you mean that judges will become the rulers of the schools in this country?

A. Yes, by this means. I am sure the Wright decision will be a landmark decision for other court decisions.

I also want a higher court to check on Judge Wright's misuse of facts and the misconclusions he has drawn.

Then there is the question of *de facto* segregation. Without explicitly saying *de facto* segregation is unconstitutional, the decision so treats the question as to require the board of education to come to Judge Wright with plans for increasing racial integration.

The question of whether there is such a thing as unconstitutional segregation by economic class is also left vaguely handled in the decision. But the question is there. This could be the most far-reaching kind of determination that one could imagine. Will children have to be moved around for an economic mix as well as a racial mix?

These are questions of fundamental importance that one judge should not be allowed to settle alone.

Overlooking the Student—

Q. Dr. Hansen, in this country we are spending more money than ever on education. Do you think we are getting better education for our money?

A. I don't think we are now, because we are not getting adjusted to using the additional resources. I think Washington schools are a case in point. We have tripled our supervisory and administrative staff and our adjunct-service groups because we have the money to do it now. But we have robbed the classrooms of our best teachers. This has been a loss, though I think a temporary loss.

But what we are suffering from is a de-emphasis on the importance of the individual in the learning process.

We have lost sight of this very simple fact: When all is said and done, it is the learner himself who must do the learning, must supply the energy. You cannot supply that motivation by external social change.

7

That the responsibility of those who exercise power in a democratic government is not to reflect inflamed public feeling but to help form its understanding, is especially true when they are confronted with a problem like a racially discriminating public school system. This is the lesson to be drawn from the heartening experience in ending enforced racial segregation in the public schools in cities with Negro populations of large proportions.
JUSTICE FELIX FRANKFURTER

Alexander M. Bickel
SKELLY WRIGHT'S SWEEPING DECISION

In a long, passionate opinion in the case of *Hobson* v. *Hansen,* Judge J. Skelly Wright of the US Court of Appeals for the District of Columbia, sitting by assignment as a District Judge, has roundly indicted the Washington school system and its superintendent, Dr. Carl F. Hansen, declaring the former, and quite possibly also the latter, unconstitutional. The opinion is a jeremiad and as such commands respect. The inner city of Washington, with its slums, its poverty, its juvenile crime and its schools, is a disgrace. Against this, Judge Wright cries out, from the heart. But Judge Wright is a judicial officer administering the Constitution, and the Constitution does not put at the disposal of judges the resources to prevent, abolish, or even alleviate poverty, juvenile delinquency, slum housing, or rotten schools.

The Constitution forbids segregation enforced by law and requires federal judges to remove its vestiges. This involves no making of educational policy, and certainly no effort to rearrange a deteriorating social and economic environment. It involves removing the coercive force of the state as a cause of segregation, and then neutralizing its lingering effects. But with very few exceptions, federal judges other than Judge Wright have felt unable to tackle situations of massive *de facto* segregation in major urban centers. They have failed to act, because, as Judge Wright unwittingly demonstrates, they have no well-developed body of principles to fall back on in reforming such educational institutions as the neighborhood schools. They enter, in the area of *de facto* segregation, territory that is unfamiliar to them, in which they are not entitled to have special confidence in whatever answers they may evolve, for these

From Alexander M. Bickel, "Skelly Wright's Sweeping Decision," *New Republic,* July 8, 1967, pp. 11–12. © Harrison-Blaine of New Jersey, Inc. Reprinted by permission of the publisher.

are likely to reflect no more than their own personal preference or orders of priority. There was, in contrast, a good bit of history and principle to fall back on in deciding that legal segregation, coerced by the state, was unconstitutional. Judges have failed to act also because, even if they knew some answers, they would still lack the resources—the money, the personnel, the machinery—to put them into effect. This is not a question of being obeyed. Law always runs the risk of being disobeyed, as *Brown v. Board of Education* often was. That case, however, was a "stop" order. When courts undertake to issue a "go" order, as Skelly Wright has done, they need resources which are not at their disposal.

Judge Wright's indictment of the superintendent and the school administration is rife with imputations of bad faith, but in the end it comes to rest on a charge of complacency only, not on a charge of intentional segregation. He condemns as unconstitutional the track system, optional school zones, teacher assignment practices, and in some measure the entire neighborhood school policy, but he does not quite come to hold that these features of the Washington school system were instituted or maintained in order to perpetuate segregation in the schools.

It seems quite clear to Judge Wright that the optional zones, for example, operate to allow white children in a relatively integrated neighborhood to escape from a predominantly Negro school into an integrated, but substantially white school. And yet it is far from clear that if the optional feature of the zones were removed, the result might not be more segregation than at present, either because rigid neighborhood lines would have that effect, or because more whites would simply flee. Moreover, the option is available not only to whites but to Negroes, and is availed of in some measure by both. Despite his imputations of bad faith, Judge Wright fails to prove his case concerning the optional zones.

One of the purposes of the track system of ability grouping is the remedial one of helping the slow and disadvantaged student. Another is to permit the quick to advance at their own pace. Judge Wright makes a persuasive case against the system as it operates in Washington. It is too rigid, it tends to validate its own predictions, which in turn are made on the basis of tests that yield much less certain a measure of true ability than is often supposed; and it does not fulfill its remedial purpose, because it is not supported by sufficient remedial resources. No doubt it could be improved and perhaps it should be abandoned. The difficulty comes in declaring a well-intentioned—and debatable—educational policy unconstitutional, either because one deems it wrong, or maladministered, or, for whatever reasons, a failure. If this is the function of the Constitution and of our judges, they have their work cut out for them.

Another portion of Judge Wright's opinion deals with supposed inequalities in facilities and quality of instruction between predominantly Negro schools in the District and the few predominantly white ones.

Here there is no doctrinal difficulty. Whatever the intention behind them, demonstrable inequalities in treatment at the hands of government that run along racial lines are unconstitutional. They were well before *Brown* v. *Board of Education.* The prior constitutional doctrine commanded equality in separation. The Constitution now forbids separation, but it has not abandoned the goal of equality. So the issue is a factual one. As to physical facilities, the evidence seems to be neither here nor there. Negroes are vastly in the majority in the Washington school system, and in consequence they occupy some of the oldest and some of the newest buildings. But Judge Wright makes out a persuasive case concerning the distribution of teachers in the District.

The predominantly white schools have apparently had more than their share of experienced, tenured teachers. Whether this is a real advantage may be questionable, and the school administrators in Washington apparently do question it. But since experience is a criterion of competence in most professions, it is not easy to see why it should be discarded in the teaching profession. At any rate, the decisive consideration is that the Washington school system has not discarded it, but has simply tolerated a smaller proportion of experienced teachers in Negro schools.

Judge Wright is also persuaded that there is a substantial disparity in per capita expenditures per pupil among white and Negro schools, with greater expenditures, of course, in the white schools. To the extent that the disparity is real, it seems to be a function of the greater proportion of tenured—and hence higher salaried—teachers in the predominantly white schools. So it scarcely proves anything additional to that.

Finally, though faculties and other school personnel are integrated in Washington, Judge Wright finds that white teachers tend to be assigned to white schools and Negro teachers to Negro schools. It is natural that in a school system with over 90 percent Negro pupils there should be a great majority of Negro teachers; and so there is—some 78 percent. Given these two large percentages, it is a mathematical certainty that there will be great concentrations of Negro teachers in predominantly Negro schools. And many Negroes feel—they made that clear in the dispute about School 201 in Harlem—that Negro pupils *should* have Negro teachers, who should displace as authoritative figures the white teachers who predominated in the past. Be that as it may, the preferences of white teachers for white middle-class schools do seem in some measure to have been informally respected by the Washington school administrators.

Declaring De Facto Segregation Unconstitutional

Judge Wright deals with these matters by forbidding the track system outright, and ordering abolition of the optional zones. As to teachers, he orders the Board to present a plan for teacher assignment which will fully integrate the faculty of each school. Since many of the white schools in the Northwest section are underpopulated, he orders the school administration to provide busing to the Northwest schools for such children in overcrowded, predominantly Negro schools, as volunteer for it.

But all this is, relatively speaking, less important detail. The main and most innovating thrust of Judge Wright's opinion is the proposition, which he adopts more squarely than any court has yet done, that *de facto* segregation as such is unconstitutional. And what does he propose to do about that? "Because of the 10-to-1 ratio of Negro to white children in the public schools of Washington," Judge Wright says, "and because the neighborhood policy is accepted and is in general use throughout the United States, the court is not barring its use here at this time." However he requires the school system to prepare and present to him a plan "to alleviate pupil segregation," and to "consider the advisability" of educational parks, school pairings, "and other approaches toward maximum effective integration." But what kind of maximum effective integration can there be in a school system in which Negroes constitute over 90 percent of the school population, and in which they may well ultimately constitute even more? In tacit recognition of this unanswerable question, Judge Wright adds that he will require efforts at compensatory education, to provide equal opportunities even in predominantly Negro schools. But how is Judge Wright going to see that effective methods of compensatory education are invented, how is he going to produce the trained personnel to apply them, and how, even if he could guarantee success, is he going to see to the financing of these efforts?

Here, then, is the heart of the matter. Judge Wright's remedy for conditions that he found to be unconstitutional is still in an early stage of development, but it is reasonably clear that he, no more than anyone else, has a remedy or can put one into effect. What then is the use of such judgments? What is the use of a hortatory constitutional pronouncement urging Washington, D.C., to solve its social and economic problems? Judge Wright's opinion might have been a document issued by some group of civic leaders, or some foundation or research organization, and whatever disagreement one might have had with this or that aspect of it, one would have welcomed its attention to the school problem. But the Constitution and the judges who guard it have a well-defined role to play, which no one else can play. They are to address themselves to those features of the society with which law can deal by defining rights, obligations and goals. No charitable organization and no study group can do that job, can invoke the power of government to those ends. It is no service to any worthy cause to saddle legal institutions with functions they cannot discharge, and to issue in the name of the law promises the courts cannot redeem.

8

Believing . . . that religion is a matter which lies solely between man and his God; that he owes account to none other for his faith or his worship; that the legislative powers of the government reach actions only, and not opinions, I contemplate with sovereign reverence that act of the whole American people which declared that their Legislature should "make no law respecting an establishment of religion, or prohibiting the free exercise thereof," thus building a wall of separation between Church and State.

THOMAS JEFFERSON

George R. LaNoue

THE CONDITIONS OF PUBLIC SCHOOL NEUTRALITY

Toward the end of the Supreme Court's opinion in *Abington School District v. Schempp*, Justice Clark took special note of one of the most common arguments against the removal of prayer and Bible reading from the public schools:

> It is insisted that, unless these religious exercises are permitted, a "religion of secularism" is established in the schools. We agree, of course, that the State may not establish a "religion of secularism" in the sense of affirmatively opposing or showing hostility to religion, thus "preferring those who believe in no religion over those who do believe." *Zorach v. Clauson* supra, at 314. We do not agree, however, that this decision in any sense has that effect. . . . [Prayer and Bible reading] are religious exercises, required by the States in violation of the command of the First Amendment that the Government maintain strict neutrality, neither aiding nor opposing religion.

Two of the concurring opinions in *Abington* also utilize the concept of neutrality between religion and irreligion as the decisive principle, but they warn of the difficulty in applying the concept. Justice Goldberg, joined by Justice Harlan, wrote:

> It is said, and I agree, that the attitude of the state toward religion must be one of neutrality. But untutored devotion to the concept of

From George R. LaNoue, "The Conditions of Public School Neutrality," in Theodore R. Sizer, ed., *Religion and Public Education* (Boston: Houghton Mifflin Co., 1967), pp. 22–36. Reprinted by permission of the publisher and the author.

neutrality can lead to invocation or approval of results which partake not simply of that noninterference and noninvolvement with the religious which the Constitution commands, but of a brooding and pervasive devotion to the secular and a passive, or even active, hostility to the religious. Such results are not only not compelled by the Constitution, but, it seems to me, are prohibited by it.

Justice Brennan, in his seventy-six page concurring opinion, added,

Inevitably, insistence upon neutrality, vital as it surely is for untrammelled religious liberty, may appear to border upon religious hostility. But in the long view the independence of both church and state in their respective spheres will be better served by close adherence to the neutrality principle. If the choice is often difficult, the difficulty is endemic to issues implicating the religious guarantees of the First Amendment. Freedom of religion will be seriously jeopardized if we admit exceptions for no better reason than the difficulty of delineating hostility from neutrality in the closest cases.

The Court's affirmation in *Abington* of the constitutional requirement that the public schools be religiously neutral was hardly a novel position. In 1943 the Court accepted the concept of neutrality when it considered the issue of compulsory flag salutes, a secular ritual with religious overtones for some. Justice Jackson, speaking for the Court in *West Virginia State Board of Education v. Barnette*, insisted:

Free public education, if faithful to the ideal of secular instruction and political neutrality, will not be the partisan or enemy of any class, creed, party or faction. If it is to impose any ideological discipline, however, each party or denomination must seek to control or, failing that, to weaken the influence of the educational system.

Later in Jackson's opinion the neutrality concept was reiterated in a famous passage, the relevance of which to American life is as great today as it was in 1943:

If there is any fixed star in our constitutional constellation, it is that no official, high or petty, can prescribe what shall be orthodox in politics, nationalism, religion, or other matters of opinion, or force citizens to confess by word or act their faith therein.

Four years later Justice Jackson again took up the theme of public school neutrality but this time coupled with some tantalizing questions. In *Everson v. Board of Education* he noted in passing,

[The public school] is organized on the premise that secular education can be isolated from all religious teaching so that the school can inculcate all needed temporal knowledge and also maintain a strict and lofty neutrality as to religion. The assumption is that after the individual has been instructed in worldly wisdom, he will be better fitted to choose his religion. Whether such a disjunction is possible, and if possible whether it is wise, are questions I need not try to answer.

Since Jackson was dissenting on entirely different points in *Everson*, he probably did not have to answer his own questions. But the questions will not go away. They are woven into the two great church-state questions of our time: religion in the public schools and tax aid for parochial schools. Can public educational policy be truly neutral toward religion?

The Challenge to Public School Neutrality

In 1961 the National Catholic Welfare Conference (NCWC) prepared a lengthy legal brief in rebuttal to the Department of Health, Education and Welfare's (HEW) "Memorandum on the Impact of the First Amendment to the Constitution upon Federal Aid to Education." The HEW memorandum, written largely by Attorney General Robert Kennedy's staff in the Justice Department, predictably agreed with President John Kennedy that general aid to parochial schools was unconstitutional, while the NCWC brief not very surprisingly reached the opposite conclusion. What is significant here is that one of the NCWC's principal arguments for public support of parochial schools was that public schools were not really neutral. The brief notes that

> . . . an "orthodoxy" is expressed—inescapably so—even in a curriculum from which religious "orthodoxies" are absent. . . . there is little guarantee that the public schools can, in actuality, maintain a completely non-"value"-inculcating program. Since life itself, humanity, history, and the social sciences are all involved in the daily life of any educational institution, "values" inevitably creep in.

Furthermore, public educators have often claimed a deep concern for moral and spiritual values, although, as the Educational Policies Commission of the National Education Association and the American Association of School Administrators has stated, "as public institutions, the public schools of this nation must be non-denominational. The public schools can have no part in securing acceptance of any one of the numerous systems of belief regarding a supernatural power and the relation of mankind thereto." The NCWC brief points out, however, that withdrawing the public schools from promotion of "any one of the numerous systems of belief regarding a supernatural power" hardly solves the problem. Citing Leo Pfeffer (doubtless tongue in cheek) and *Torcaso v. Watkins* as evidence, the brief notes that modern legal theory accepts the fact that there are religions or substitutes for religion that are non-supernatural—secular humanism, for example. Consequently, the NCWC brief concludes that, if no constitutionally valid line can be drawn between supporting supernatural religions and non-supernatural religions and that if all schools teach values, the only solution is to provide public support for all schools.

Recently the challenge to public school neutrality has been motivated by opposition to the Supreme Court's decision banning public school prayer and Bible-reading. The coalition that has been formed to amend the First Amendment in order to reintroduce these rituals into the schools includes such unlikely theological bedfellows as Bishop James A. Pike and Bishop Fulton J. Sheen, but the movement has been mainly generated by pressure from right-wing Protestantism. The fundamentalists (of whatever denomination) argue that the Court decisions took God out of the schools. They intend to put Him back in. They want neither public schools nor a government that is neutral toward religion. Citing as evidence a long list of public documents from the Declaration of Independence to the revised pledge of allegiance, the fundamentalists are determined to restore their version of the nation's religious heritage through constitutional amendment. They will not be satisfied until both the government and its schools are committed to, at the very least, Judeo-Christian theism. Public school neutrality toward religion, even if possible, is as abhorrent to the fundamentalist as personal religious indifferentism.

Whether the challenge to public school religious neutrality has come from those with financial or theological axes to grind or from those genuinely concerned for academic freedom and cultural pluralism, their contentions must be taken seriously. Until some system can be worked out that defines and guarantees such neutrality, proposals to strengthen the role of religion in the public schools will be educationally and constitutionally unstable and the public schools themselves subject to continued attack.

The Legal Concept of Religious Neutrality

Philosophers may doubt that any position is really neutral, for there are value judgments in every commitment. The concept of legal neutrality, however, is simple and easier to define, since it must prove practicable when implemented in the daily affairs of the state. Legal neutrality is not value-free, nor does it require that the state's policy be balanced precisely at the midpoint of the claims of all the contending interest groups. Either of those requirements would be impossible to fulfill in the real world of political life. Legal neutrality toward religion is, instead, a state policy of refraining from weighting the scales of religious choice by refusing to commit the state's prestige or resources to either help or hinder religion. To use the classic phrase, neutrality requires that the state not intervene in the marketplace of ideas on behalf of any of the forces of religion or irreligion contending there. Since the public school is the central marketplace of ideas in our democracy, particular care must be taken to see that the scales of religious choice are not weighted in the classroom.

The basis of the legal concept of religious neutrality is, of course, the First Amendment of the federal Constitution ("Congress shall make no law respecting an establishment of religion, or prohibiting the free exercise thereof") and also Article VI ("no religious Test shall ever be required as a Qualification to any Office or public Trust under the United States"). It is important to note that philosophically neither provision is neutral or value-free. Doubtless in 1789 these constitutional principles were more acceptable to religious dissenters and non-believers than they were to the established Congregationalists in Massachusetts or to the Anglicans in Virginia. Nevertheless, non-discrimination, non-establishment, and religious liberty are neutral principles since they forbid the state from coercing belief or disbelief. The process of interpreting these principles is a continuous one, however. The Supreme Court's ruling that Bible-reading and prayer violate the neutrality of the public schools by no means exhausts the question of what full religious neutrality requires.

The Implementation of Legal Neutrality

The Prohibition of Religious Discrimination in Personnel Policy. The Constitution initiates its policy of religious neutrality in Article VI with a prohibition against religious discrimination in the hiring of public personnel, and that is the point at which public school neutrality must begin. Any school that attempts to screen out candidates on the basis of their particular religious affiliations or beliefs would obviously not be neutral. Attempts to enforce sectarian codes of morality or discrimination against those who voluntarily follow such codes would also be unneutral. They would, in Justice Jackson's words, permit a public official (in this case a petty one) to prescribe what is orthodox in religion.

There is an alternative approach to religious neutrality. One might try to strike a religious balance by seeking out candidates who represent the various religious traditions. This is often the pattern followed in staffing departments of religion in state universities. A less satisfactory example is the New York City Board of Education, whose membership has traditionally and rigidly been three Protestants, three Catholics, and three Jews. This pattern has often been reflected in top administrative positions in the public school system and is reinforced by the three religious associations for school personnel.

Whatever the merits of attempting to represent the various religious traditions in university departments of religion, this approach has some obvious disadvantages for public schools. In the first place, when the religious balance concept is utilized, promotion within the system often requires continued acceptability to the religious leadership in the community. It can lead to a conflict of interest when public school officials must defend the school's academic freedom or conduct negotiations with parochial school officials about participation in public programs. More important, the religious balance concept tends to discriminate against non-believers, for they belong to a less definable and less organized group. Furthermore, since talented personnel is scarce in almost every educational field, the introduction of a restrictive religious factor in hiring impedes educational progress.

In short, the only educationally and constitutionally sound policy for the public schools to follow is to bar all questions about religious affiliation, practice, or belief from the hiring process. In general, state policy does forbid formal questions of this kind although informal probing still occurs illegally in some parts of the country. Where such inquiry does occur, it is most often directed toward ferreting out religious skeptics rather than the religiously orthodox.

Even though all the evidence on public school personnel policies is to the contrary, there are still those who claim that the public schools are citadels of godlessness or secular humanism. This caricature is sometimes supported by a few selected quotations on religion from John Dewey or William Torrey Harris, as though their credos were somehow binding on all public school personnel; but any sociological examination of the almost 27,000 public school districts in this country would quickly dispel this notion. To be sure, there are those (some influential) in the system who support Dewey in matters of religion, but there are many more who look to Buddha, Moses, or Christ for their principles. Actually public school teachers tend to be theistic, just as the general American public tends to be theistic. If one were to compare the various professions, public school teachers would probably turn out to be among the most theologically orthodox. Their religious backgrounds will reflect regional variations, of course. One would expect to find more Catholics teaching in Massachusetts than in Mississippi and more atheists in New York than in New Hampshire. Overall, however, the public schools' staffs are educated in various types of institutions, secular and religious, and hold as many different theological viewpoints as there are in America.

In addition to distorting the reality of the religious attitudes in the public schools, the creators of the caricature have failed to distinguish between the legal neutrality of the public school system as a system and the personal values of the people who staff it. A public school staffed by people who are mainly secular humanists does not necessarily create an "establishment of secularism" any more than a school staffed by people who happen to be Christians creates an "establishment of religion." Legal establishment requires some *systematic state action* to benefit or hinder religion. A discriminatory hiring policy would be that kind of state action, but if there is no discrimination, the personal views of public officials are not a criterion of establishment.

A personnel system based on merit rather than on religious affiliation is a major condition for legal neutrality. In most cases, if teachers are then left free to teach, and students to learn, the school will be legally neutral. At some points, however, the school must make official policy on the treatment of religion, and these points will require careful consideration if neutrality is to be preserved.

The Prohibition of a "Religion of Secularism". In the passages cited earlier, Justice Jackson, for one, seemed to equate a secular education with a religiously neutral education. Such an equation without further examination begs the question. "Secular," of course, is a word with many meanings; and it bears different, even antithetical, connotations. Although in works like Harvey Cox's *The Secular City* the concept carries with it no threat to true religion, nevertheless, "secularism" or "secularist" commonly refers to a rejection of religion. Even if the term "secular" is confined to meaning not touching on or dealing with religion, a secular education may still not meet the constitutional test of neutrality. In other words, must a public school accept some responsibility for providing opportunities for religious education (however defined) if the school is to be fully neutral?

In *Abington*, after Justice Clark ruled out any establishment of a "religion of secularism" in the public schools, he suggested,

> In addition, it might well be said that one's education is not complete without a study of comparative religion or the history of religion and its relationship to the advancement of civilization. It certainly may be said that the Bible is worthy of study for its literary and historic qualities. Nothing we have said here indicates that such study of the Bible or of religion, when presented objectively as part of a secular program of education, may not be effected consistent with the First Amendment.

There are two important aspects of Clark's statement. First, the treatment of religion the Justice suggests is objective and empirical (comparative religion, history of religion) rather than doctrinal and normative. Since the *McCollum* decision, the objective-empirical approach seems to be constitutionally required when religion is taught *in* the public schools. Second, the role of "objective" religion in the public schools is considered an educational problem—"one's education is not complete"—rather than a constitutional problem. The Court's language regarding the inclusion of "objective" religion is permissive, but are there instances in which constitutional neutrality requires that the public school accede to demands for opportunities for religious education?

Approaches to Religious Education. Several solutions to the problem of religious education and the public schools are currently being widely discussed. There is the "objective" approach, by which religion is taught as a part of other subjects or as a separate subject in the public schools, and the "sectarian" approach, by which religion is taught through released-time or shared-time arrangements by the churches themselves. The public schools' constitutional obligation, if any, for each of these methods of religious education requires separate consideration. All answers in this area must be regarded as highly tentative, based as they are on only fragments of judicial pronouncements.

The objective approach. Of all the approaches to the teaching of religion, the one probably receiving the most support among educators is that the religious aspects of history, literature, art, music, drama, etc., ought to receive fair (academically justified) attention in the teaching of those subjects. The educational merit in this approach is obvious, but is such an arrangement also constitutionally required? Suppose the program of a particular public school were challenged on the grounds that it purposely and systematically excluded information about religion from its curriculum. The Anti-Defamation League and the NAACP have made similar kinds of charges regarding the treatment of minority groups in certain public school textbooks. If the allegations about the omission of either religious or racial information were true, would this school practice violate the equal protection clause of the Fourteenth Amendment or (in the case of religion) the establishment clause of the First Amendment? If purposeful exclusion of information were proved, it would seem to be evidence that the public schools had illegally become, in Justice Jackson's words, "a partisan or enemy of [a] class, creed, party or faction" and that there ought to be some judicial remedy.

The courts would, of course, be very reluctant to enter into the matter of curriculum design or textbook selection. Nevertheless, after two decades of church-state cases, integration cases, and academic freedom cases, it is apparent that the Supreme Court is, in Edward S. Corwin's phrase, functionally a national school board. Although the courts would properly place a heavy burden of proof on allegations of discriminatory exclusion of racial or religious information, this kind of issue is within the courts' responsibility to preserve a neutral school. Finally, it should be said that, although neutrality may require proper consideration of religion throughout the curriculum, there is no constitutional protection from academic analysis or criticism of religion.

Some would contend, however, that teaching about religion through other subjects is not enough. There are no more intellectual grounds, they would argue, for teaching religion as a part of history or literature than vice versa. Consequently, they insist that comparative religion or some other form of objective teaching about religion should take its place as a separate subject alongside the other disciplines in public schools. This contention has a certain logic, but it has met with resistance from public educators. Assuming it were possible to design a satisfactory comparative religion course, the enormous shortage of qualified teachers in this field remains a serious problem. To begin programs in religion without trained teachers would be to open the schools to the possibility of overt religious proselytizing. Furthermore, in most public schools, initiating a program in religion would mean hiring one or perhaps two new teachers. These teachers would be in such a sensitive position that their personal beliefs might become the subject of intense community interest. Generally the teacher and the course would have to reflect the religious attitudes of the dominant segment of the public school's constituency to a much greater degree than when religion is integrated throughout the curriculum. One can imagine a Jew or an agnostic teaching about religion in public school literature or history classes in most parts of the country, but it seems unlikely that persons of those persuasions would be hired to teach public school comparative religion classes, no matter how competent they were. Regardless of who taught the course, friendly examination of non-Western religions or rigorous scrutiny of local "established" sects would be discouraged. In short, the very visibility of the courses creates so many problems that relatively few courses in comparative religion can be found in the public schools. There are a growing number of "Biblical literature" courses, particularly in the Midwest, but they are often neither comparative nor objective. They are, instead, a defensive response of cultural Protestantism to the Court decisions barring prayer and Bible-reading.

Assuming that an objective course in religion could be designed and, avoiding questions about the proper procedure for instituting it, do parents and students have a constitutional right to demand such a course in the public school curriculum? Such a contention seems extremely dubious to me. If the right exists, it would have to rest on the free exercise clause of the First Amendment. I can find no language or inference in the Supreme Court's opinions to support this right, nor can I logically construct a case for it. There seems to be no more of a religious *right* to a course in comparative religion than to one in comparative government or comparative literature. The existence of such a course appears to me to be primarily a matter of educational rather than of constitutional considerations.

The sectarian approach. In general, the public seems to concur in the administrators' lack of enthusiasm for comparative religion courses. What most of the parents interested in religious education really want is to have their children trained in the traditional faith of their fathers. This "sectarian" approach cannot, of course, take place legally within the public schools; but the schools may cooperate with either released time (students primarily enrolled in public schools who take their religious instruction in religious schools) or shared time (students primarily enrolled in parochial schools who take some courses in the public schools). Both programs can create formidable administrative problems, but, on the plus side, they turn over the sticky issues of how religion should be taught and who should teach it to the religious groups themselves. Although the responses have been mixed, requests for released time and shared time have sometimes met resistance by public school authorities. When this happens, can a parent constitutionally demand such an arrangement?

Two court cases provide some insight, though they are far from conclusive. The state of Oregon has had for many years a law which states: "Any child attending the public school, on application of his guardian or either of his parents, may be excused from such school for a period or periods not exceeding 120 minutes in any week to attend weekday schools giving religious instruction in religion." The critical words are "may be excused." When the superintendent of School District 24 refused a parental request, the case went all the way to the Oregon Supreme Court. *Dilger v. School District 24* is not a classic document of religious liberty; the Court split four to three, and the majority opinion is timidly written. The justices appeared to be more concerned with Oregon's traditions of statutory construction than with questions of conscience. Nevertheless, the majority decided that "may be excused" had to be interpreted "must be excused." The Court found that school officials could determine the time of the release, but that giving them discretion over an individual's right to be released for religious instruction would be "illegal." No interpretation of the Oregon State Constitution or of the First Amendment was made, nor were any precedents on discretionary power involving religion cited, so the case provides little help regarding the overall problem.

The shared-time case is even more obscure. The eastern public high school developed generally from college preparatory academies. Training in manual and vocational arts was added later, usually in separate departments or schools, but under public auspices. The Pennsylvania law of 1911 governing such training stated that "no pupil shall be refused admission to the courses in these special schools or departments by reason of the fact that his elementary education is being, or has been received in a school other than a public school." Despite the statute, when a seventh-grade pupil from a parochial school applied to a manual training program in one of the Altoona public schools, he was refused on the grounds that such admission would illegally aid the parochial school. The student's guardian then sought a writ of mandamus from a state district court and was successful. After pointing out that the parochial school would receive no public funds from the arrangement, the district court declared:

> It must be borne in mind that the entire common school system in Pennyslvania was created and devised for the elevation of our citizenship as a whole. It is often termed a public or free school system, thereby meaning it is supported by the public, and to be open

to all of lawful age who will avail themselves of its advantage, subject only to necessary regulations and limitations essential to its efficiency.

On appeal, the state Supreme Court affirmed the district court's ruling but confined itself to a narrow, statutory interpretation without utilizing the dicta or the logic of the lower court opinion.

Since the Pennsylvania case, there have been various administrative rulings in several states on the question of whether shared time illegally aids parochial schools, but no court has faced that issue or the question of whether a request for shared-time attendance must be honored if the program is legal in a particular state. Assuming that the constitutionality of shared time will be upheld on a national level and in most states (as I assume), is there a constitutional right to such an arrangement?

I believe the answer to the question of a constitutional right is the same for both released time and shared time. If some legal programs exist in a state on the basis of a permissive state statute or unchallenged custom, then public officials may not arbitrarily deny a request to participate in them in the parts of the state where they exist or *to initiate them in other parts of the state.* Public school officials should be permitted a reasonable amount of time and flexibility in working out the arrangements, but they should not be given unregulated discretion over an educational opportunity that involves an act of conscience. To arbitrarily give such an opportunity to some in a state but not to others might violate the equal protection clause. If, however, there is no provision or practice in a state for released time or shared time, then there seems to be only a moral, not a constitutional, mandate on state legislatures to permit such arrangements.

In *Zorach v. Clauson,* Justice Douglas, speaking for the Court, suggested that

> When the state encourages religious instruction or cooperates with religious authorities by adjusting the schedule of public events to sectarian needs, it follows the best of our traditions. For it then respects the religious nature of our people and accommodates the public service to their spiritual needs.

The Justice, however, did not indicate that the free exercise clause requires the creation of released-time programs. If such a right exists, it would probably be sustained on an equal-protection-clause argument in a case involving a permissive statute like Oregon's.

A public school's formal arrangements for the teaching of religion can certainly affect its legal neutrality. It has been suggested here that fair treatment of the religious aspects of other subjects may be constitutionally required while separate courses in religion are optional. Although provision for released time or shared time is not in itself constitutionally mandatory for every state, once it exists the state must extend equal protection of the law to every child wishing to participate. Furthermore, if such an arrangement "follows the best of our traditions" because it "respects the religious nature of our people," then the tone of neutrality in the public schools would be enhanced by provisions for this kind of opportunity.

Other Issues Bearing on Religious Neutrality. In addition to the formal arrangements for religious education in or out of the public school, there are some other issues that will affect the quality of religious neutrality in every school. For example, what should be the school policy on the teacher's freedom to respond to questions about religious truth? Public school students are a captive audience and teachers should not be permitted to proselytize, but the First Amendment does not bar either an honest question or an answer. There are, of course, professional considerations regarding the maturity of students and explanation of opposing points of view, but within these canons of good teaching (applicable to any subject) religious questions may be discussed vigorously and faculty opinions stated. If the teachers are chosen on a non-discriminatory basis, the pattern of their responses, if given freely, will meet the legal test of religious neutrality.

Another question that has troubled many communities is whether baccalaureate services and the celebration of Christmas should be permitted in the public schools. The nature of baccalaureate ceremonies varies among communities, but, in general, the baccalaureate is the religious counterpart to graduation and, as such, should not continue as a school-organized or school-sanctioned event. There is no reason, however, why baccalaureate services cannot be held in local churches separately or, if local conditions permit, cooperatively, with attendance by school officials if they wish.

Christmas and the celebration of other primarily religious holidays present a more complex problem. The failure of the public schools to recognize that in December, for one reason or another, Christmas is being celebrated may lead to a certain artificiality in education at that time of the year. Still, it is quite clear that public schools may not participate in the religious aspects of the holiday without violating the establishment clause. On the other hand, for the Christian the true meaning of Christmas is profoundly religious and any public school emphasis or promotion of the secular aspects of the holiday is, if not actually hostile to religion, at least degrading to the occasion. Therefore, the conditions of neutrality are probably best met when the public school avoids involvement in religious holidays except to the extent of permitting students and teachers released time for their personal celebrations.

Public School Neutrality as a Compromise

One may object to the considerations outlined here on the grounds that, despite its pretensions to neutrality, the public school system would, nevertheless, still be more acceptable to religious liberals and agnostics than to religious fundamentalists and militant atheists. The same argument, however, could be made against the First Amendment itself. It was not satisfactory to all groups in 1789, and it is not today. A government that remains uncommitted for or against religion and refuses to coerce religious belief or disbelief is still a comparative rarity even in the modern world. When put to the test, not all Americans believe in such a government; and they, of course, have the right to amend the Constitution. Those who would change our constitutional policy have rightly concluded that the decisive struggle is for control of the public schools and of public educational funds.

For these reasons, the religiously neutral public school system must be preserved. Whether the challenge comes from fundamentalists, who want "cultural Protestantism" taught in the schools, or from militant atheists, who want every trace of the role of religion in our culture excised from the schools, the attack must be resisted. Both sides would substitute indoctrination for education. Nor can we afford to accept the idea that the public schools are inherently godless or secularistic and that consequently the only fair solution is to publicly finance separate religious schools. Acceptance of such a theory would not only undermine the public school system but radically alter our traditional standards of justice. Educationally, the theory would have the ugly consequence of providing a rationale for overt religious hostility in public schools. Legally, it would be comparable to a decision in race relations to give up attempting to provide equal treatment for Negroes and to concede that the Black Muslims were right all along by financing a separate "black state." Finally, financing separate private schools would hardly be neutral since 95 per cent of them are religious schools and 90 per cent of them belong to one church.

The neutral public school is a compromise. It provides perfect satisfaction for neither the believer nor the non-believer. Alternatives to the public school should be permitted, and the public schools themselves should be as flexible as is constitutionally possible in providing opportunities for religious studies. If the public school is a compromise, so is the First Amendment; and that fundamental compromise requires that public educational policy (schools and funds) remain neutral toward religion.

Public school neutrality is not an easy ideal to achieve. After exhausting administrative alternatives, litigation may be necessary. Should a public school discriminate against religion, the same judicial remedy exists as was available when the public school attempted to promote religious rituals. The claim that the public school cannot be legally neutral must be rejected. If the public schools cannot be neutral, the government itself cannot be neutral, and our 176-year-old experiment in religious liberty will have become a hollow pretense.

9

*The danger in ingenious hardware is that it distracts
attention from education. What good is a wonderful
machine if you don't know what to put on it?*
                                        SOL LINOWITZ

John Brooks
XEROX/XEROX/XEROX/XEROX

A major problem of xerography is the overwhelming temptation
it offers to violate the copyright laws. Almost all large public and college
libraries—and many high-school libraries as well—are now equipped
with copying machines, and teachers and students in need of a few
copies of a group of poems from a published book, a certain short story
from an anthology, or a certain article from a scholarly journal have developed the habit of simply plucking it from the library's shelves, taking
it to the library's reproduction department, and having the required
number of Xerox copies made. The effect, of course, is to deprive the
author and the publisher of income. There are no legal records of such
infringements of copyright, since publishers and authors almost never
sue educators, if only because they don't know that the infringements
have occurred; furthermore, the educators themselves often have no idea
that they have done anything illegal. The likelihood that many copy-
rights have already been infringed unknowingly through xerography
became indirectly apparent a couple of years ago when a committee of
educators sent a circular to teachers from coast to coast informing them
explicitly what rights to reproduce copyrighted material they did and
did not have, and the almost instant sequel was a marked rise in the
number of requests from educators to publishers for permissions. And
there is more concrete evidence of the way things have been going; for
example, in 1965 a staff member of the library school of the University of
New Mexico publicly advocated that libraries spend ninety per cent of
their budgets on staff, telephones, copying, telefacsimiles, and the like,
and only ten per cent—a sort of tithe—on books and journals.

To a certain extent, libraries attempt to police copying on their own.
The photographic service of the New York Public Library's main branch,
which fills some fifteen hundred requests a week for copies of library

From John Brooks, *Business Adventures* (New York: Weybright and Talley, 1969).
"Xerox Xerox Xerox Xerox" appeared originally in *The New Yorker*, 1967, pp. 46 ff. Reprinted by permission of Weybright and Talley, Inc.

matter, informs patrons that "copyrighted material will not be reproduced beyond 'fair use'"—that is, the amount and kind of reproduction,
generally confined to brief excerpts, that have been established by legal
precedent as not constituting infringement. The library goes on, "The
applicant assumes all responsibility for any question that may arise in
the making of the copy and in the use made thereof." In the first part of
its statement the library seems to assume the responsibility and in the
second part to renounce it, and this ambivalence may reflect an uneasi-
ness widely felt among users of library copiers. Outside library walls,
there often does not seem to be even this degree of scruple. Business
people who are otherwise meticulous in their observance of the law
seem to regard copyright infringement about as seriously as they regard
jaywalking. A writer I've heard about was invited not long ago to a seminar of high-level and high-minded industrial leaders and was startled to
find that a chapter from his most recent book had been copied and distributed to the participants, to serve as a basis for discussion. When the
writer protested, the businessmen were taken aback, and even injured;
they had thought the writer would be pleased by their attention to his
work, but the flattery, after all, was of the sort shown by a thief who com-
mends a lady's jewelry by making off with it.

In the opinion of some commentators, what has happened so far is only
the first phase of a kind of revolution in graphics. "Xerography is bringing a reign of terror into the world of publishing, because it means that
every reader can become both author and publisher," the Canadian sage
Marshall McLuhan wrote in the spring, 1966, issue of the *American
Scholar*. "Authorship and readership alike can become production-
oriented under xerography. . . . Xerography is electricity invading the
world of typography, and it means a total revolution in this old sphere."
Even allowing for McLuhan's erratic ebullience ("I change my opinions
daily," he has confessed), he seems to have got his teeth into something
here. Various magazine articles have predicted nothing less than the dis-
appearance of the book as it now exists, and pictured the library of the
future as a sort of monster computer capable of storing and retrieving the
contents of books electronically and xerographically. The "books" in
such a library would be tiny chips of computer film—"editions of one."
Everyone agrees that such a library is still some time away. (But not so
far away as to preclude a wary reaction from at least one forehanded publisher. Beginning late last year, the long-familiar "all rights reserved"
rigmarole on the copyright page of all books published by Harcourt,
Brace & World was altered to read, a bit spookily, "All rights reserved.
No part of this publication may be reproduced or transmitted in any
form or by any means, electronic or mechanical, including photocopy,
recording, or any information storage and retrieval system . . .") One of
the nearest approaches to it today is the Xerox subsidiary University
Microfilms, which can, and does, enlarge its microfilms of out-of-print

books and print them as attractive and highly legible paperback volumes, at a cost to the customer of four cents a page; in cases where the book is covered by copyright, the firm pays a royalty to the author on each copy produced. But the time when almost anyone can make his own copy of a published book at lower than the market price is not some years away; it is now. All that the amateur publisher needs is access to a Xerox machine and a small offset printing press. One of the lesser but still important attributes of xerography is its ability to make master copies for use on off-set presses, and make them much more cheaply and quickly than was previously possible. According to Irwin Karp, counsel to the Authors League of America, an edition of fifty copies of any printed book can be handsomely "published" (minus the binding) by this combination of technologies in a matter of minutes at a cost of about eight-tenths of a cent per page, and less than that if the edition is larger. A teacher wishing to distribute to a class of fifty students the contents of a sixty-four-page book of poetry selling for three dollars and seventy-five cents could do so, if he was disposed to ignore the copyright laws, at a cost of slightly over fifty cents per copy.

The danger in the new technology, authors and publishers have contended, is that in doing away with the book it may do away with them, and thus with writing itself. Herbert S. Bailey, Jr., director of Princeton University Press, wrote recently in the *Saturday Review* of a scholar friend of his who has cancelled all his subscriptions to scholarly journals; instead, he now scans their tables of contents at his public library and makes copies of the articles that interest him. Bailey commented, "If all scholars followed [this] practice, there would be no scholarly journals." During the past couple of years, Congress has been considering a revision of the copyright laws—the first since 1909. At the hearings, a committee representing the National Education Association and a clutch of other education groups has argued firmly and persuasively that if education is to keep up with our national growth, the present copyright law and the fair-use doctrine should be liberalized for scholastic purposes. The authors and publishers, not surprisingly, have opposed such liberalization, insisting that any extension of existing rights would tend to deprive them of their livelihoods to some degree now, and to a far greater degree in the uncharted xerographic future. A bill that was approved recently by the House Judiciary Committee, is now being considered by a Senate subcommittee, and is expected to come to a vote in both houses during 1967 seems to represent a victory for them, since it explicitly sets forth the fair-use doctrine and contains no educational-copying exemption. McLuhan, for one, is convinced that all efforts to preserve the old forms of author protection represent backward thinking and are doomed to failure (or, anyway, he was convinced the day he wrote his *American Scholar* article). "There is no possible protection from technology except by technology," he wrote. "When you create a new environment with one phase of technology, you have to create an anti-environment with the next." But authors are seldom good at technology, and probably do not flourish in anti-environments.

In dealing with this Pandora's box that Xerox products have opened, the company seems to have measured up tolerably well to its lofty ideals as set forth by Wilson. Although it has a commercial interest in encouraging—or, at least, not *dis*couraging—more and more copying of just about anything that can be read, it makes more than a token effort to inform the users of its machines of their legal responsibilities; for example, each new machine that is shipped out is accompanied by a cardboard poster giving a long list of things that may not be copied, among them paper money, government bonds, postage stamps, passports, and "copyrighted material of any manner or kind without permission of the copyright owner." (How many of these posters end up in wastebaskets is another matter.) Moreover, caught in the middle between the contending factions in the fight over revision of copyright law, it has resisted the temptation to stand piously aside while raking in the profits, and has shown an exemplary sense of social responsibility—at least from the point of view of the authors and publishers. The copying industry in general, by contrast, has tended either to remain neutral or to lean to the educators' side. At a 1963 symposium on copyright revision, an industry spokesman went as far as to argue that machine copying by a scholar is merely a convenient extension of hand copying, which has traditionally been accepted as legitimate. But not Xerox. Instead, in September, 1965, Wilson wrote to the House Judiciary Committee flatly opposing any kind of special copying exemption in any new law. Of course, in evaluating this seemingly quixotic stand one ought to remember that Xerox is a publishing firm as well as a copying-machine firm; indeed, what with American Education Publications and University Microfilms, it is one of the largest publishing firms in the country. Conventional publishers, I gathered from my researches, sometimes find it a bit bewildering to be confronted by this futuristic giant not merely as an alien threat to their familiar world but as an energetic colleague and competitor within it.

THE TECHNICAL DIMENSION

Perhaps the title of this volume which embraces the words criticism, conflict, and change is most appropriate to introduce a section on technology in education. The post-Sputnik era in American schools was characterized by a hardware revolution. The passage of legislation enabling schools to install and equip language laboratories, for example, helped spark a continuing interest in technology. But interest was often followed by discontent. The teaching machines were not durable; their programs were often inept. Our technical competence had exceeded our talent for effective implementation.

Of significance, however, was an opportunity for educators to perform the one task which had eluded them for decades—individualizing instruction. Regardless of group size, technology could now provide tailor-made programs simultaneously with the bright and less bright proceeding at various rates with materials of varying difficulty. With learners attending their "machines" the teachers were released to execute more "professional" tasks, and the learners seemed to respond to the new devices. Television was often more interesting; listening stations were quieter; light boards were clearer.

Despite technical opulence, the dissonance increased. Critics talked of dehumanizing education. Teachers, they claimed, were becoming automatons. The machine was replacing the teacher. It hasn't, and it won't. Industry has become more attentive to classroom needs. The equipment has become more sophisticated, more durable, less costly, and more appropriate for learning environments. Videotaping capabilities, for example, are no longer beyond reasonable implementation. Increased business involvement in the new educational industry has also not been without conflict. Fear of a business "take-over" prevailed as corporate giants merged with publishing houses and marketed multimedia and systems approaches. Some educators apparently found the industrial profit motive somehow inconsistent with educational motives. The corporate involvement in the education market, however, has been beneficial. Computer-aided instruction, for example, will be economically feasible because of increasing competition for the educational investment.

The articles in this section are representative of the best writing in this area. Several authors raise provocative and persisting questions. The editors have attempted to present a sampling of current trends described by the trendsetters themselves. Einstein once wrote, "imagination is more important than knowledge." The technology described here is rapidly bridging the gap between imagination and knowledge.

1

Modern man is not convinced that he is sick. He strides about the globe in scientific splendor, matter in one hand, energy in the other, proclaiming his conquest of the elements. But once back from the campaign, he hasn't the faintest idea of what to do with all his technological plunder.

VAN CLEVE MORRIS

Jerome Bruner

THE NEW EDUCATIONAL TECHNOLOGY

The pages of this section attest to the ferment that characterizes American education today. More than ever before, we are concerned with the nature of the educational process, with the goals of education, with the impact of change—and, besides, with the techniques and devices that can be used in improving the educational enterprise. There has been much inventiveness. New curricula have been devised in the sciences and mathematics, and new efforts at curriculum construction are under way in the social studies and humanities and in the study of languages and literature. Film, the book, the laboratory, the "teaching machine"—all have come under close scrutiny in the effort to hasten and deepen the learning process. Indeed, to the outside observer it must seem as if we were preparing to embark upon a permanent revolution in education. And I think we are entering just such a period.

What characterizes this period is a change both in the conception of the educational enterprise and in our view of the learning process. With respect to the enterprise—or the educational Establishment—there is a quickened recognition that the educational profession must be far broader in scope than previously conceived. It is symbolized by the presence of Nobel laureates in physics devoting their talents and energies to the devising of school curricula in science. The underlying conception is that those who know a subject most deeply know best the great and simple structuring ideas in terms of which instruction must proceed. But the matter goes further than that. It also encompasses the application of the policy sciences to education. There has begun to dawn a recognition that "educational" administration and "educational" economics and "educational" architecture are not special fields, but parts of the more

From Jerome Bruner, "The New Educational Technology," *The American Behavioral Scientist*, Vol. VI, No. 3, November, 1962, pp. 5–8. Reprinted by permission of the publisher, Sage Publications, Inc.

general fields from which they derive. The *ad hoc* administrative, economic, and architectural ideas that have been the currency of educational practice are being re-examined today in the light of the general principles that inform administrative theory, economics, and architecture. And we are asking whether an enterprise that spends less than one tenth of one per cent of its resources on research and development—as is the case in American public education—can indeed carry out this task with any effectiveness. One cannot help but compare this outlay with practices in such new industries as electronics and chemicals where the expenditure for research and development is as high as 20 per cent. Education, in short, is being brought into the mainstream of national life—both intellectually and from the point of view of the forming of policy.

The revolution in our view of the educational process itself is, I think, premised upon several new and startling conceptions. At least they are new in their application and they are certainly startling when put bluntly. One of them has to do with our conception of the child and his intellectual processes. Consider the working hypothesis that *any subject matter can be taught to anybody at any age in some form that is honest.* The question of "when to teach what" must, then, be premised upon some more discerning criterion than "readiness." As I observe the various efforts to construct curricula, I sense that this is indeed the prevailing doctrine. But interestingly enough, it is not a point of view that denies the striking differences between the mind of the child, of the adolescent, and of the adult. Rather, it is a recognition of the fact that, with sufficient effort and imagination, any topic can be rendered into an honest form that is appropriate to the level of comprehension of students at any age.

It is worth looking in some detail at what this implies. I shall postpone for a moment the question of how "true" the hypothesis is. For there are certain matters that must be made clear before we can understand how one would go about "proving" such a proposition. Consider first a famous theorem of Turing that is central to the theory of computation—the theory of "thinking machines," if you will. In simple form, it states that any problem that can be solved can be solved by simpler steps than those now employed. For the theory of computation, this implies that there are steps simple enough to be carried out by even a digital computer: steps as simple as "make a mark in a certain place," "move the mark next to another mark," "erase the mark," etc. Thanks to high speed devices that can swiftly run off a large number of these simple operations in a manner prescribed by its program, the machine is able to solve stunningly difficult problems in very short order—and if the program is interesting, to do so with a certain amount of originality. To be sure, the theorem applies only to well-formed problems amenable to a unique solution (although this includes approximation tasks based on the use of iterative operations).

Let me propose that Turing's theorem has a profound relevance for all problem solving—whether the work of human problem solvers or artificial ones. It implies that any complex problem can be restated in a manner such that it can be brought within reach of any solver, even though he has only a limited repertory of operations that he can bring to bear on the problem. The inventive task is to find the translation of the problem that is appropriate to the powers of the person being asked to master it.

The layman—and popular magazines—always appear to be astonished that eight-year-olds can be taught quadratic functions, or that first graders can be introduced with intellectual profit to set theory, or that the conservative laws in physics can be made clear to the ten-year-old. The achievement is not astonishing. What is astonishing is that the adult should believe that quadratic functions are obscure—a kind of arbitrary game played with equations in the form of $X^2 + 6X + 9 = (X + 3)^2 = X (X + 6) + 9$. He is projecting his own confusion, produced by bad teaching, on the child who has not yet been confused. To avoid such confusion, one begins teaching with some simple embodiment of the idea of the quadratic within the reach of even a young child—such as the geometrical or "ordinary" square. The properties of geometric squares are made clear by giving the child, first, a way of constructing them and then, a way of describing their constituting elements. In time, the language he has learned for dealing with geometrical squares is extended to other forms of the quadratic or mathematical square—such as the balance beam. And gradually a mathematician is formed. The object is not to produce mathematical geniuses, but simply to make mathematicians who think and talk mathematics and enjoy its beauty rather than merely cranking out rote computation.

II

It seems to me that the present approach to the conduct of education calls for a fundamental reformation of the sciences supporting education. Perhaps it is best if I illustrate by reference to the field I know best—psychology. It has been argued in the past that a psychology of learning is central to any doctrine of education. A psychology of learning elucidates how the child learns and, besides, indicates what kind of past experience leads the child to be receptive to learning. I think that any close observer of the educational scene would admit that over the past forty years there has been little direct influence of *learning* theory on the actual conduct of education. Learning theory, a descriptive discipline, has described how learning occurs in certain circumscribed situations that have been studied because they related to theoretical issues within the theory of learning. The theoretical issues in question have had little to do with the concerns of the educator. They reflected, in the main, debates that centered around conceptions of the nervous system or conceptions about the growth of personality. Typical of the former category were such matters as the continuity or discontinuity of the acquisition of responses, the status of reinforcement as "confirmation" or "reward," whether the fundamental element in learning was a stimulus-response connection or some more superordinate structure, and so on. Typical of the latter concern, personality growth, was the study of the role of early anxiety as a factor in character structure or whether drive level had an effect upon the acquisition of a response or only upon its performance. These are lively issues and fundamental ones, but they are not directly to the educational point.

For they are all descriptive, all concerned with what happens when learning occurs. The psychology of learning has only been tangentially concerned, until very recently, with the optimal means of *causing learning to occur*. Very little of learning theory is given over to the designing of optimum orders of encounter for the learning of materials. In most theories of learning, it is assumed that encounter with what is to be learned is random. Indeed, we even utilize techniques of experimentation in the study of learning that randomize the order of presentation, and then use materials to be learned that have a minimum of structure or of structurability.

Such research, and it can easily be justified, does not preclude another kind of research, research that poses the question: how can material of a certain kind be so presented and so sequenced that it will be most readily and most transferably learned? The results of such research would provide a basis for a *theory of instruction* that is complementary to a *theory of learning*. There is every reason to believe that a theory of instruction would both broaden and enrich theories of learning. Not until we have developed a theory of instruction will we be able to test propositions about the best way of teaching something. It is just such a theory that is required for "proving" ideas about curriculum.

Without a theory of instruction, we are likely to accept uncritically some particular *description* of learning as a *prescription* for optimal learning. A case in point is the idea that, in programed instruction, "small steps and immediate reinforcement after each step" is the best practice. What is a small step? How should one choose a path up which the small steps lead? In short, what is the program of programed learning? The evidence on optimum program sequences is virtually nil.

A theory of instruction would probably have three aspects. The first would be concerned with the optimum experiences that predispose the learner to learn. The second would deal with the kinds of structures in terms of which information or knowledge is optimally organized by a learner. The third would inquire into the sequences of encounter with materials to be learned that would be optimal. It is quite plain that there is much work of a highly general nature that can be done in each of these areas. It is also clear that there is much *specialized* work that would also be required in order to translate a theory of instruction into a particular curriculum—whether Roman civilization or finite mathematics. But what seems most promising to me is that the eventual contact of a particular curriculum effort and learning theory would be better assured by the existence of a mediating theory of instruction.

Is there a comparable point to be made about the other sciences that contribute to educational theory and practice? I think there is, and the issue is quite parallel. The point is well illustrated by anthropology. Anthropologists, adept at describing the internal coherence and interdependence of the elements of a culture, have given us a theory of social change that, in effect, warns that change in one major feature of a culture will produce widespread, perhaps chaotic effects in the rest of the culture. The theory of culture has rarely addressed itself to determining how in fact cultures can be and are changed with minimal disruption or maximum predictiveness. It is a pity—and a predictable one—that anthropologists are absent from the council table when the issues of *how* to regulate socio-economic development in backward areas is up for discussion. But again, one senses a change and today there is the beginning of theories of economic and social development that are geared to the prescriptive task of regulating the educational development of newly emerging states.

III

Changes in educational practice have more often reflected the conceptual *atmosphere* of the behavioral sciences than they have been based upon the conceptual propositions available in these sciences. The "history of the school chair" reflects the "style" of prevailing theories of learning more than the actual content of such theories. When the Thorndikean model of association learning was at its height, chairs were ordered in rows, fastened to the floor. The student was tacitly regarded as a recipient of materials to be associated or otherwise stored away. Dewey's instrumentalism led schoolmen to unfasten the chairs from the floor, to group them according to the projects at hand. The child-centered school produced a circle of seated children surrounding the teacher. The new emphasis on phenomenology and the experience of the child— particularly his "social perception"—led to the semicircular arrangement. Perhaps our emphasis upon the structuring of information, the arrangement of optimum sequences for learning, and the rest, reflects a new concern with the efficient use of information in a period of exploding knowledge. In the pages of this section there are accounts of how information retrieval can be used more effectively in libraries (more the expression of a hope than the statement of a theory or practice), there are accounts of how to organize groups to change the teaching of English (again, more in the spirit of aspiration than of plan), and there are statements on how testing may be improved so that more searching criteria of achievement can be established. It is important, in view of the notable gap that has existed in the past between "reflecting the conception" and actually using the concepts, to sound a note of caution. There is a long effort ahead. Present ideas about automatic information retrieval, still primitive when matched against our knowledge of the subtle requirements of human memory organization, may leave us rather dreamily satisfied. And, indeed, a few libraries of a specialized kind may be recoded for retrieval by some such system as "key-words-in-context." But the brute fact of the matter is that we have not yet come to grips with the basic theoretical issues involved in matching machine systems to human memory needs. So too in the teaching of written English. There are interesting contending conceptions of grammar—finite state theories, transformational theories, and phrase-structure theories. A vast amount of empirical and theoretical work will be required before we can understand the implications of linguistic theories for the teaching of language.

A smattering of rule-of-thumb linguistics in our texts on grammar is no more explicit a recognition of the problem of how to teach English than is the decision to unbolt the chairs from the floor a recognition of the implications of an instrumentalist theory of learning. We are indeed on the edge of a great period of revolution. But it would be a great pity if our zeal were too easily assuaged by partial victories. We do well to recall that most revolutions have been lost precisely because they did not go far enough.

2

The reasonable man adapts himself to the world; the unreasonable one persists in trying to adapt the world to himself. Therefore all progress depends on the unreasonable man.
                    GEORGE BERNARD SHAW

Peter Drucker
EDUCATION IN THE NEW TECHNOLOGY

As far as the average citizen is concerned, automation's greatest impact will not be on production technologies and will not be on employment. The greatest impact of automation will be on our intellectual

From Peter Drucker, "Education in the New Technology," *Think Magazine*, Vol. 28, June 1962, pp. 2–5. Copyright 1962 by International Business Machines Corp. Reprinted by permission of International Business Machines Corp. and the author.

and cultural life. Automation, after all, is first and foremost an idea. It is
an idea which organizes other ideas, and its impact on ideas accounts
for the far-reaching implications.

What might the impact be? Indeed, as soon as we ask the question we
see very great changes—and changes that are already in full swing and
are no longer speculation regarding the future. As in any change proceeding from a new insight of man, there are opportunities and challenges.

A society in which automation has become a governing concept of
production and distribution is, of necessity, an "educated society." It is
a society in which knowledge rather than man's animal energy is the
central resource. It is a society which puts to work the one specific
quality in which the human being excels—for man is neither a particularly strong animal nor endowed with oustanding manual dexterity. In
the highly advanced industrial countries, the largest employee group is
already the people who are supposed to work with knowledge rather
than with their hands. In this country, the groups which the census calls
"Managerial, Technical and Professional" became the largest employee
group during the last decade—rapidly overtaking the semi-skilled machine operator, that characteristic employee of the mass production age
based on the assembly line. In other industrialized countries the same
process is under way. And these groups, the knowledge workers, are the
only employee groups which are growing very rapidly.

For the first time in human history this has made possible a society
in which everyone with the intellectual capacity to acquire knowledge
can be given an advanced education. In the past, where physical brawn
or manual skill alone were productive, the number of people to whom a
society could afford to give an education, was severely limited. For
earlier society (including the society in which the men now 50 grew up)
did not consider knowledge an economic resource, let alone the central
capital of the economy.

Even the richest economy before our time could afford only a very
small number of people who did not contribute directly to economic
production through working with their hands. Today, increasingly, we
worry about not having enough educated people. We can, increasingly,
not afford to leave anyone uneducated who has the capacity to become a
knowledge worker.

The immediate result has been a complete change in opportunities
available to the individual. Historically, occupations, even in the freest
society, were basically hereditary. In the Indian caste system this
reached the extreme where the son of the weaver could only become a
weaver, the son of the goldsmith or the merchant only a goldsmith or a
merchant. But much more flexible societies—including 19th century
Europe and even 19th century United States—differed less from the
complete rigidity of the Indian caste system than they differ from the

complete freedom of opportunities of the new educated society. This or that son of a weaver might acquire another craft, might even become a professional man. But the majority was by and large confined to staying within the craftsman class.

Only 30-odd years ago, when I myself was a student, one of my friends in England wanted to become a mathematician. He had done mathematical work of unusual distinction in college—though he was not of genius rank. The entire family—a professional, highly educated family of reasonable affluence—converged on him to dissuade him from so asinine an idea. "How could one make a living as a mathematician?" they all asked. Perhaps, in the case of an unusually gifted man, a fellowship at a college might be available. But otherwise there was no future for a mathematician except as a badly paid wretch of a schoolmaster. The only ways in which an "educated man" could make a living were the "old professions": the law, the church, the army, medicine and the civil service. And the point of this story is that the family was right—as recently as 1930. Today, needless to say, one does not have to worry about job opportunities for a mathematician.

The same applies to other areas of knowledge. There are few today for which there is not constant and increasing demand in industry, in government, in the universities. This gives our young people an abundance of choice unprecedented in human history. And if freedom is defined as "ability to choose," then the advent of the educated society, based on the ideas that underlie automation, is one of the biggest steps towards freedom in the history of the race.

This also changes the structure of society itself. Our books, our newspapers, our political speeches still assume that in an industrial society there are two groups: a very small group of "bosses" and a huge, undifferentiated group of "workers." This, of course, is the basic picture of society on which Marx built his entire theory—but he only accepted what to anyone in the 19th century (or at any earlier time) was obvious, God-given and apparently unalterable. Today, however, the most important as well as the largest group—let alone the most rapidly growing one—are neither bosses nor workers, but "knowledge employees": the accountant and the public health doctor, the sales manager and the chemical engineer, the industrial psychologist and the operations researcher. None of these is a boss in the old sense; they are all employed. And few of them expect to become top management, or even want to move into such a position. Yet they are also clearly not workers.

Our very largest employee group is indeed the group that transmits the knowledge on which our modern educated society is based: teachers. They are already the largest employee group in the American economy —and the one that will have to grow the fastest. Teachers rather than workers on the automobile assembly line are the representative employees of an educated society. They are clearly not bosses; but they are equally clearly not proletarians. They belong to the new, the third big group, the typical and dominant group of an educated society: middle-class, educated, employed and yet independent—if only because in knowledge they possess a "property" of much greater value to the productive process and of greater impact on society than land, gold mines or factory buildings.

But there are no opportunities that do not create their own challenges.

To avail ourselves of the opportunities of the educated society will require great changes in schools and education. What we will have to teach is, above all, ability to learn new things after one has left school. And yet we also clearly need people who have greater and more systematic knowledge in the various disciplines.

A generation hence, we may, for example, have no engineering schools as such and no medical schools as such. We may find out that technology, that is, the application of systematic knowledge to work, is a common and universal concept which has to be understood by the man who applies knowledge to inanimate matter just the same way as by the man who applies knowledge to the living body. We might, therefore, well have schools of technology. And yet, obviously, both the engineer and the doctor need increasingly specialized knowledge in their own fields.

Perhaps we face the greatest challenge to traditional education in respect to skills. It used to be that a man who acquired a specific skill as a boy had learned what he needed to be able to do for the rest of his life. A skilled man was a man who had learned a traditional craft. Today, increasingly, craft skills as such become meaningless. In organizing the economic job as a "process" based on automation, that is, on the systematic flow of information and material, skills that never were together become one at a given place of work. And skills that formed a cohesive whole, let us say that of the electrician, become parceled out among a great many pieces of work in a great many different places. Worse still, skills that were apparently eternal only yesterday, may overnight become obsolete—and new skills, not yet visible, may become required overnight.

We have already seen such radical obsolescence of skills. The flight engineering craft, for instance, had a life of 15 years—from the coming in of the multi-engine propeller plane to its replacement by the jet plane. Similarly, some traditional skills of the printing craft may become obsolete as we replace the mechanical transfer of ink with reproduction through heat, chemical reaction or electronic image. Great skills will be needed for these new processes, but not the traditional printing skills.

We may need, therefore, a change in the very idea of "skill." Instead of being what one has learned, skill will have to become the capacity to learn, that is, to apply ideas regarding work to new tasks. We speak today of an I.Q., an intelligence quotient, and mean thereby the ability of a man to apply knowledge to new situations. We may have to develop something like an S.Q., a skill quotient that measures the ability of a man to transfer experience from one kind of material and one set of tools to new materials and new tools.

An even bigger challenge may well be that of the uneducated minority. There is today a great deal of concern over the dropout, the child who does not finish high school. Twenty years hence, the child who has not gone to college will increasingly be such a dropout problem. For, in an educated society the jobs to be done do not only tend to call for people with higher education; the opportunities tend to be restricted to people who can produce the formal evidence of higher education: the college degree, if not an advanced degree.

The uneducated will be both a minority and underprivileged. And an underprivileged minority is worse off than an underprivileged majority. It lacks the votes to change its position.

Here, therefore, may be a major social problem. I should not be surprised to see, a generation hence, strong agitation against the denial of opportunities to those without the academic ability for higher education. After all, scholastic ability is as much an accident of birth as race or color of skin and, in a democratic society, as questionable a ground for a denial of opportunities. It may not be too fanciful to imagine, in another generation, agitation to forbid asking for educational information on the employment application as it is now forbidden, in some states, to ask for race or age.

Making higher education general and the prerequisite for access to opportunities would also tend to create what our society has always rejected: an intellectual elite.

The employment manager who insists on a college degree, the university that demands a Ph.D., or the civil service commission that prescribes a higher education—everyone who makes access to opportunity or to advancement dependent upon evidence of formal education— subordinates man and society to the analytical, the intellectual faculty, and makes intellectual ability the governor of human affairs.

But man is not an intellectual, analytical being only, not even in his higher, human faculties. He is perceptual and spiritual in addition to being conceptual. Indeed, the highest achievements of man are not conceptual achievements—the achievements of saint and statesman, artist, poet or entrepreneur. Even the achievements of the truly great scientists are as much based on perceptual as on conceptual ability. They are works of art rather than essays in logic, visions of the unknown rather than technical process (which always presupposes that one already knows).

A society which puts intellectual ability into the driver's seat would be a poor and lopsided society. It might also be a sterile society.

At least this was the fate of the one society that based itself on higher education and proven intellectual ability as the dominant qualifications for leadership: the China of the Mandarins. This destroyed the creative ability of the Chinese within a few centuries. From being origi-

nal and creative inventors (we owe, after all, gun powder, printing and papermaking, among many other inventions, to the genius of the early Chinese technologists) China became completely unproductive technologically, completely frozen in its tools and techniques. The very great art of China—and few peoples have equaled the painting, poetry and ceramics of Sung-period China—became equally sterile.

To take full advantage of the tremendous advance in potential and capacity, in opportunites and knowledge, which the ideas underlying data automation make possible, we therefore need balance. We need balance in the education of the individual, balance which stresses and rewards perceptual if not also spiritual qualities and achievements. We need balance also in society, balance which stresses the aesthetic and spiritual contributions as much as it stresses the analytical ones. This is not something the designer of computers has to worry about. Nor is it a problem for the user of the computer. It is a problem, however, for every citizen and for every member of our society.

The vistas, while wide, are admittedly highly speculative. But the opportunities are great enough to warrant keen interest in these new concepts and techniques on the part of the educator, the writer, the statesman, the student of society and culture. And the problems, too, are likely to be great enough to warrant concern on the part of the scientist, the logician, the engineer, the economist.

The fundamental insights that underline automation are insights of great power, of great beauty of structure, rhythm and architecture. They enable us to do great new things socially and culturally as well as technically and economically. They therefore call for great responsibility and true understanding in their application and use.

3

The very first casualty of the present-day school system may well be the whole business of teacher-led instruction as we now know it.
MARSHALL MCLUHAN AND GEORGE B. LEONARD

Francis Keppel
THE BUSINESS INTEREST IN EDUCATION

A picture seems to be forming in the mind of the American educator: Knocking at the door of the little red schoolhouse is the giant

From Francis Keppel, "The Business Interest in Education," *Phi Delta Kappan*, January, 1967, pp. 187–190. Reprinted by permission of the author and publisher.

fist of American business—big business: International Business Machines, Xerox, General Learning Corporation (the affiliate of General Electric and Time, Inc.), Radio Corporation of America, Raytheon, merchants of hardware, makers of electronic computers, of copying machines that can make a million sheets of paper look exactly like the original, and above all, makers of money. On the other side of the door is the classroom teacher, facing something unknown and frightening, and protecting children huddled in a corner. In a seeming competition for the mind of the school child, America's tycoons appear pitted against a lonely, underequipped, underpaid classroom teacher. It is a modern picture of Goliath and David, and it is the result far more of fear than fact.

Yet the fear is a fact, and must be faced. All of us in education need a calm and rational idea of what the entry of "big" business into education means and what it does not mean; what capabilities business now has for helping education and what it does not have; what capabilities it hopes to develop and those it has no expectation of trying to develop.

In order to understand the so-called confrontation with Goliath, let us examine the situation of David as a teacher in a one-room schoolhouse whose employers are a school board consisting of a farmer, a lawyer, and a housewife. Although this is obviously far from a typical picture of an American school, it may be a useful picture because it represents in ultimate simplicity the basic American idea of locally controlled, citizen-operated education. And it is a good idea. For all the criticism leveled against the idea of control by local school districts, no system of education has operated so successfully and democratically in the history of mankind. And no one should underestimate the power of the local board today.

Our classroom teacher David is harassed by the responsibility of too many children, all making demands from different directions. (In the country school, David's children may be of different grades. His colleague in an urban school is hardly better off; while his pupils may be all of the same grade, they are stimulated by dissimilar experiences, spurred by disparate curiosities, and they learn at different rates.) David is charged with an almost Godlike task of nurturing the minds of these children toward lives as independent, knowledgeable, ambitious, productive adults. What tools does he have? Indeed, like David of the myth, hardly more than a slingshot. His school board has equipped him with a room, a blackboard, and a few textbooks; now and then a movie, a trip to a museum, a peek through a microscope. With so little, David has succeeded in accomplishing so much. Give him more—a more up-to-date textbook, new scientific aids to learning, a new movie projector, an extra microscope—and it is reasonable to think that he would do even better. For the truth is that David's greatest classroom asset is himself—his warmth, his genuine interest in children, and his ingenuity in somehow managing time for giving individual care to so many.

But what might happen to this all-important personal touch if a computer is rolled in? What can David, backed by his country school board, do against the combined might of America's largest corporations who have declared their intention of moving into the schoolhouse, as some believe, to erase the blackboard and take over the teaching?

By oversimplifying this picture, I am by no means trying to draw a ludicrous one. The fear is real and understandable. As my friend and competitor, Lyle M. Spencer, president of IBM's Science Research Associates, has observed, "There are those who fear that new educational systems involving technology such as computers, video communication systems, and facsimile printing systems will destroy the diversity of our education. Such concern is natural. It is healthy. It is unfounded."

To understand why such concern is unfounded, we have to turn our picture around and see the same schoolhouse situation from the view of modern industry.

Needless to say, one of the things that attracted the eye of industry was the sheer dollar-size of the present and potential national school expenditure. Average expenditure per year per student has risen steadily since the war, and it is not unreasonable to assume that the figure in the $300 range in the mid-1950's will double in the mid-1970's. This possibility is not made less attractive by the recent addition of more than a billion dollars a year of federal aid, an annual figure that can also be expected to grow. True, this newly added amount is hardly more than a small percent of the total local expenditure for public schools. But it is a particularly interesting percent. For one thing, unlike the funds invested by states and local school districts, the new money is not necessarily claimed by commitments to teacher salaries, bonded debts for school buildings, or even by old ways of buying textbooks and filmstrips. On the contrary, a chief purpose of the money is to encourage innovation, new ways of useful educational investment. A billion dollars looking for a good, new way to be spent does not ordinarily turn the American businessman into a shrinking violet. Nor should it, for industry has talent and production facilities and distribution systems that can contribute to the cause of education.

But what good, new ways for spending this money are there? Education, which in a sense is America's largest industry, lacks the sound research and the knowledge of the results of its own experience and tested ideas on how to meet the demands that will confront it in the almost immediate future. It is unequipped with such research because until very recently no one has been charged with a large-scale undertaking of it. The federal government has now entered the field, but it can only provide the funds and leadership. Education itself will have to provide the ideas and programs, and it will need help in their development. This is where the "new" industry will play its part, as a member of the team and not as its director. The fist pounding at the schoolhouse door is the wrong picture. The clasped hands of fellowship would be more appropriate.

Americans live in an era when research and development are greatly esteemed in industry, in technology, in medicine—in almost every major enterprise but education, where research has long been undervalued and underfinanced. A few American industries spend up to 10 percent of their gross revenues on research and development.

But where did the nation stand in regard to public schools, an enterprise which stood at the base of research for knowledge and the development of human talent? In an enterprise costing over $40 billion a year at all levels, the nation spent less than one-half of one percent of its educational funds on research to improve the educational process itself.

This figure—one-half of one percent—was not a figure from the distant past but an improvement on the recent past. It included the new research funds voted by the "Education Congress" in 1965. But it did not include the promise of new private investment, much of which will probably fall in the category of "development" rather than pure "research," if those words are given an academic definition.

In the middle 1960's, for the first time, supplies of private capital have become potentially available for the development of new ways of developing scientific aids to learning and for making them widely available to a decentralized educational system. One observer of the scene, Dean Theodore Sizer of Harvard, regards the development as comparable in importance to the expanding role of the federal government in education.

But what new contribution can private corporations make in research and development that educators have not already discovered on their own, or will discover as a result of research now being undertaken? My own guess is that industry's contribution will be far less in the area of creating new ideas or reshaping the content of the curriculum, and far more in making such contributions widely available. The decisions on what should be taught and to whom will rest where they belong, in the hands of the educators and scholars supervised by boards of education and trustees or others representing the public interest. Industry's role is not to set objectives for American education. It is to help to meet those objectives.

The innovations of recent years, supported by foundations as well as government, have shown that change is possible. Yet these innovations, although many seem promising, have not yet produced substantial alterations in the educational picture. This may be because projects have been separately conceived, while major change can be brought about only if many projects are organized together with the goal of developing new systems of education. New curricula influence the preparation of teachers; scientific aids to learning are inextricably related to to the organization of schools. The scattered bits of innovation have to be drawn together, organized by a philosophy, tested and revised by

research, and implemented by methods that lend themselves to reproduction. This is a task for which the research community in education,
and the educational community itself, has not been prepared by habit
or experience, and for which it needs all the help it can get. Business
and technology can provide some of that help, but can not do more than
help. The public and the educational community realize that there is
need for change. The question is not whether to change, but how.

What has industry traditionally done in the face of a demonstrated
need, a market ready and able to buy needed goods, and the demand
for new offerings? By tradition, American industry sets about to create
them. It is a further tradition of industry to develop competing products
to vie against each other on various levels of performance and price to
satisfy various levels of demand in the market. This process leads not
only to sales and profits, but to great diversity of choice and great differences in the ways of serving the public. It also describes a basic factor
in the relation of industry and education: The latter chooses from the
products of the former. If the products do not meet the need, they will
not be purchased. Industry must then seek ways to find out what educators need and want (not always an easy task, incidentally), or else go out
of business. There seems little doubt that needs and wants exist.

As American industry viewed this need, it was natural to think in
familiar terms. Some companies were makers of machines. A few who
knew nothing but how to make machines were hasty in rushing newfangled wares to market, without adequate analysis of what the educator
really needed or wanted. They sold "teaching machines" before anyone
really knew what the machines could or should teach. And for every
sophisticated machine that a manufacturer was impatient to sell, there
were some unsophisticated buyers impatient to purchase whatever was
new, flashy, and prestigious. As Harold Howe II, the Commissioner of
Education, has aptly put it, "Like the drug for which there is as yet no
disease, we now have some machines that can talk but have nothing to
say."

By now, it is generally understood that any "teaching machine" is
simply a piece of equipment. It has no more inherent value than a blackboard or a piece of chalk. What gives it force is the written program that
goes *into* the machine and the use to which it is put. Therefore, much
speculation about teaching machines would be more relevant if it were
speculation about "programmed instruction" and the learning process
itself. If by programmed instruction we mean a way to bring the student
into the development of an idea step by step, giving him a way to check
his own progress, then we come closer to the basic need of helping to
make a student realize his successes and errors as soon as he makes them
—not days later when the quizzes are returned.

This example is worth our attention in considering the topic of the
relation of business, technology, and education. The idea of programmed

instruction was not invented by makers of machines but by psychologists and educators. The contribution of a manufacturer to programmed instruction has to be like the contribution of an editor and publisher to a good manuscript of a textbook. He is an agent of transmittal. If he goes beyond his role, he risks failure. The lesson to be learned is that the new offerings of business and technology to the educator have to be developed with the needs of education as a basis, and the cooperation of education as the means.

Creating a better connection between educational content and the equipment that makes it available to learner and teacher can contribute to the improvement of educational methods. It seems obvious that one can hardly move ahead without the other. Neither the authors of instruction nor the makers of machines know precisely in what direction they should move. This is why the nation has recently seen a pooling of interests in the form of corporate mergers between manufacturers of electronics and publishers of the printed word. Understandably, the large number of dollars involved in these mergers have caught public and professional attention, even though they are small compared to the national budget for the schools and colleges. What has received less attention is in reality more important: that these mergers are an attempt to merge talent and professional skill for the support of education, talents that before operated largely in isolation from each other. They include the talents of the editor and publisher, the systems analyst and the engineer, the market analyst and the distributor—all of these as teams to serve the teacher and the school. It is this effort to pool a variety of skills to work on a common task that will prove more significant than the pooling of dollars.

Yet the ultimate test will rest with whether the services and products that result from these combinations actually serve education's needs and wants. This depends, it seems to me, even more on the educators than it does on industry. The objectives to be met, the organization of schools and colleges to meet these objectives, the content of the curriculum, all rest with the educational institutions. If there is to be effective action, the world of education will have to put these new resources to work. This implies both a desire for change and a willingness to work together.

There is evidence that a new educational technology is being created in response to a need for change already described by educators. As Lois Edinger, a classroom teacher and recent president of the National Education Association, has pointed out, the purpose of the new technology is not to supplant the classroom teacher. "The purpose," she says, "is to supplement the efforts of the teacher and change the traditional role of the teacher. I rather think the term 'classroom teacher' will soon be a misnomer, if it is not already so, for the teacher will no longer be confined to a classroom. The pattern is changing in many places, and we shall soon find ourselves speaking of teachers and educators in many roles and as teaching in learning centers. No longer will we think of the classroom in its traditional box shape. Indeed, we may soon call the *teacher* a manager of learning resources in an instructional resources center."

In casting its eye about this new marketplace, industry views some immense problems of distribution. These very problems, it seems clear, are also David's greatest protection against Goliath. The idea of American industry "taking over" American education (even if it wanted to, which of course it does not) is ludicrous. In fact, the men of these new industries have already learned the first lessson from Commissioner Howe, who recently pointed out, "My guess is that the businessman will find the education field difficult to attack in an organized way, because decision making is so highly dispersed. The education system of the United States is not a system at all. It is a non-system. And being such, decisions about what to spend and what to spend it on are not centralized decisions at all. The public schools are managed by some 25,000 operating school boards. Their domains range in size from more than one million pupils down to a dozen. Each board prizes its autonomy and has to be dealt with individually. To compound the difficulty, decision making within any school system may be obscure or diffuse. For example, each system has its own peculiar ways of handling purchase orders— they could be signed by the teacher, the principal, the business manager, the superintendent, the school board, the purchasing agent, or even the mayor."

As long as there is competition among the makers of new educational devices, and as long as this is reinforced by vast decentralization of decision making as to what devices shall be brought into the schoolhouse, there can hardly be a national conformity in the education process foisted upon schools by industry. If such a national conformity has not been accomplished by the publishers of textbooks in the past, it is hardly threatened by makers of machines in the future. The educational messages transmitted by new devices—and supervised by teachers—will be designed by educators, researched and tested under the supervision of educators, selected and bought by educators. Let me borrow again from the wisdom of Lyle Spencer.

"If technology is to limit the alternatives in education, then it must do it either on the basis of economy or quality. But to conclude that the schools will actually buy a learning system because it is cheaper is to accept a position inconsistent with current buying habits. . . . Any time that educators make economy the basis for selecting educational materials, our schools will be in serious trouble—for economy leads to conformity and, as my electronic friends might say, delimits choice. Educators will reject such a pattern.

"This leaves quality. Might it not be possible for one giant corporation to produce a program so sound that all other publishers would be squeezed out of the classroom?

"None of us, even in his most wildly optimistic moments, feels capable of producing an instructional system so superior that it finds acceptance by the vast majority of educational institutions. There are simply too many significant differences of opinion about what an instructional system should do and what its educational content should be to allow this."

It must be evident from these considerations that the real problem of the relation of education and the "new" industry is not whether the American pattern of educational policy and practice will be shifted from present hands to the hands of industry, but rather whether the "new" industry can adapt its offerings to the needs of education and whether education can develop ways of defining those needs and providing the ways for developing and testing the new offerings. As one who has spent his professional life in education, I have become a strong believer in the constant need of bringing fresh points of view and new skills to solving education's problems. The "new" industry offers such a possibility.

But I have also learned through sometimes bitter experience that the pooling of talents and energies is far easier said than done. New vocabularies have to be learned. New techniques have to be developed. Faith in the good intentions of the collaborators has to be built up. All of this takes time and patience. The "new" industry has to accept, as I believe it has already, that this is a business where quick profits are not necessarily good policy; that long development time, in close collaboration with educators and schools, is essential; and that pluralism is "the name of the game." Education will in turn need to be willing to use talents and points of view that are not easy to assimilate, and will have to state its needs and wants both more precisely and perhaps in different language. It will have to bear major responsibility for deciding, through ever more sophisticated purchasing techniques, what to choose from industry's new offerings. Both groups have much to learn, and the only safe assumption is that the road to effective collaboration is long and probably rocky. But one point is already clear: It is not a picture of David and Goliath. It is a picture of a team at work on a common task.

4

Let schoolmasters puzzle their brain
With grammar, and nonsense, and learning;
Good liquor, I stoutly maintain,
Gives genius a better discerning.
        OLIVER GOLDSMITH

Don Fabun

TOM SWIFT AND HIS ELECTRONIC WHATYAMACALLIT

Some 200 years ago a strange contraption was described by Gulliver in his account of his travels. He found it at the Grand Academy of Lagado, and it was called a Frame. This "contrivance" (for so he described it) filled a very large room, and was composed of square bits of wood connected by slender wires. On the faces of each piece of wood were pasted scraps of paper on which were written "all the Words of their Language in their several Moods, Tenses, and Declensions, but without any Order." Forty iron cranks were attached to it, and when they were turned the wooden bits moved, changing the disposition of the words.

Supervised by the Professor who invented it, forty students attended the Frame six hours a day, turning cranks and stopping whenever three or four words fell in a sequence that made sense. These were recorded and the cranking proceeded. When enough volumes of these "broken Sentences" had been collected, the Professor, said Gulliver, "intended to piece them together and out of these Rich Materials to give the World a complete Body of all Arts and Sciences."

Today's computers may use a similar basic operating principle, but when it comes to technical sophistication and ultimate usefulness, they have a few more things going for them than their mythical progenitor at Lagado. We're even more realistic about their capabilities, for no one but the most starry-eyed programer would share for a moment Gulliver's contention that by using such a device, "the most ignorant Person at a reasonable Charge and with a little bodily Labour, may write Books in Philosophy, Politicks, Law, Mathematicks and Theology, without the least Assistance from Genius or Study."

The potential of computers in education lies somewhere between this rather magical talent and the ability to correct a student who thinks that $1 + 1 = 3$. The significance of this potential will not be found in the in-

From Don Fabun, "Tom Swift and His Electronic Whatyamacallit," *Kaiser Aluminum News*, Vol. 25, No. 1, 1967, pp. 14–19. © 1967. Reprinted by permission of Kaiser Aluminum & Chemical Corp.

struction manuals that accompany this new electronic hardware into the school building.

At the most fundamental level the computer is, like the glass slides and the static-ridden phonograph records of 50 years ago, no more than a classroom tool, to be used as teachers, schools and school systems may desire. It is easy to forget this, and so we can already hear sporadic cries of protest from teachers and administrators who feel that they may soon be outmoded. A similar outcry was heard when textbooks first came into wide use in American schools during the 19th century. Under the flaps of our technological overcoats there always seem to lurk stubborn little stains of doubt, placed there by fears over something really new and not understood.

The computer may indeed, as at least one educator has suggested, herald the second great stage in the history of education (the first being after the introduction of movable type), but its role will remain ancillary to the cause itself. With regard to teaching it is less the seasoned professor than a promising new instructor who also grades papers and keeps records.

Rather than putting teachers and educational institutions on the sidelines to watch, the computer offers a challenge for new approaches to teaching that can be met only through the most far-sighted and creative relationship between man and machine. As C. Jackson Grayson, Jr., of Tulane University, has observed: "In the future, I predict, education and technology will be much like love and marriage: 'You can't have one without the other.' In this era of radical change, educational technology, man and machine, are locked together in man's life struggle to survive."

In fact, computers offer the realization of something that has been lost to man, for the most part, since the building of the first schoolhouse. The "sitting on a log" method of individualized instruction, with each student able to pursue knowledge in his own way and at his own pace under a single teacher is once again a possibility. Computers can store, evaluate, and act on huge amounts of information, in the form of both subject matter and data about the student. They can tailor the pace and thoroughness of what is being imparted according to each student's needs and abilities, and can simultaneously provide the teacher and researcher with what is literally a "running commentary" on each student's progress. With this information the curriculum is constantly re-evaluated in relation to each student's own talents, ability and interests. Presentation of the subject matter can be kept at the most challenging and stimulating levels. This fact in itself can make the gaining of knowledge its own reward, and may result in eliminating grades as an incentive for education.

"Perhaps the most important single advantage of adding a computer to the arsenal of educational technology is the responsiveness the system offers to the student," says Don D. Bushnell in the *Saturday Review* (July 23, 1966). According to his responses, each student can daily move up and down to levels of greater or lesser difficulty. Class grade levels therefore become meaningless, because the system is the very antithesis of traditional methods that place a student on one track with others his age for an entire school year. It appears that we have never really known enough anyway about individual achievement or ability to justify our customary "single track" approach.

The student-computer "interface" is a remote console, or terminal, connected to a central information-storing computer that is able to tailor individualized instruction to at least 30 students or classrooms simultaneously. In most programs the student is asked questions by his electronic instructor with a pre-recorded voice over a set of earphones, or by words or pictures shown on a display screen. He may then respond by using a typewriter keyboard or a "light pen," with which he indicates answers, or his own questions, by writing directly on the display screen. The speed and correctness of his responses, of course, determine his progress. Sometimes the computer may have to explain or demonstrate, by word and picture, something the student has not understood before proceeding to additional material.

The teacher's role becomes that of a troubleshooter, able to devote more time to helping students who are encountering difficulty or need personal attention for other problems. The teacher is also freed of nearly all the record-keeping and other administrative work (including grading) that is so time-consuming. More time is available for individual attention to the student's needs, and for preparing good additional material.

In the immediate future, of course, "computer-assisted instruction" (for so it is called) will play only a supplementary role in teaching and will compose comparatively little of the daily student schedule. But the proportion will certainly change. Eventually computers may perform as much as 30% of the more routine classroom instruction. At Brentwood Elementary School in California, computers have for the first time been assigned the responsibility of teaching a complete segment of the curriculum to first graders. The children, nevertheless, spend relatively little time each week sitting at each of the school's 18 computer consoles. This is largely a pilot project, however, due to lead to further involvement of computer systems in more schools, with greater portions of classroom time devoted to computer-directed curriculums.

Computer-assisted instruction can be categorized into three distinct areas of use. The first two, drill and practice systems and tutorial systems, are aimed at removing from the teacher the methodical and time-consuming, though necessary, tasks of rehearsing students in certain skills and in teaching these skills initially. Based on what has been called "programed directivity," these systems guide students along predetermined learning paths at their own pace.

Drill and practice systems can administer practice exercises in such subjects as math, grammar and spelling to develop the student's proficiency in these fields. Tutorial systems, which are more difficult to program, can actually teach subjects such as foreign languages, logic, science, mathematics and even basic reading in the first place. In tutorial systems the computer's principal job is to assess the validity of inferences made by each student. Any valid inference based on material already presented is accepted—a far more realistic approach than the strict "right way, wrong way" criteria used in most textbooks.

By far the most promising use of computer-assisted instruction is what has been called the dialogue system. Although not perfected as yet, such a system would establish a basis for genuine challenge, response and discussion with each student. Little in the way of a predetermined teaching pattern would be programed into such a system—a concept that has been termed "programed docility."

But programing problems for such a system are unique. To be able to answer a freely constructed interpretive question from a student, for instance, the computer must first be able to understand what is being asked, and then must have the "savvy" to relate the question to information in its memory banks.

As in the case of the computer that translated "Out of sight, out of mind" into what amounted to "Invisible idiot" in another language, it is easy to envision the hopeless confusion that could arise if questions of an interpretive nature are badly misunderstood, or not understood at all, by a classroom computer. In addition, unreliable information returned by the computer could over a period of time have disastrous effects on students and be very hard to remedy.

The secondary problem, of giving the computer enough basic data to draw on in answering various questions, appears to be largely a matter ot time. Researchers at the University of California at Berkeley, for example, are amassing an inventory of questions asked by students in various subjects, so that computers can be prepared for them in the future. The law of averages would indicate that over a long enough period most of the possible questions can be foretold and included in dialogue programs.

There seems little doubt that dialogue systems offer the most exciting and far-reaching prospects of any form of computer-assisted instruction in the future. Though experts differ on whether or not true dialogue systems will ever be built, it appears likely that they will. If so, the first real breach of the practical and psychological barriers between man and machine, student and electronic instructor, may finally occur. Dialogue systems may even prove to be the talisman of a new, unfragmented approach to subject matter mentioned in a previous section. With the ability to interrelate facts, theories and ideas from many disciplines, knowledge would be offered to the student as a unified whole by the computer, rather than as a sequence of fragmented bits and pieces.

No matter how talented they may become, however, computers can hardly be described as a panacea for education. It is a little like the development of the automobile to replace the horse and buggy—we may be able to get there faster, but do we yet know just where it is we want to go?

The mere transference of much of the classroom workload from teachers to electronic devices signals little more than an efficiency achievement unless the more fundamental questions are answered.... Just what do we want to accomplish with computers in education, and how do we want to go about it?

We go about it, as far as computers are concerned, through programing. What we program a computer to do and how to do it is based upon the techniques at hand, and in education, these techniques are limited by curriculums that are old and barely adequate any longer. In order to match the fullest promise of computer-assisted instruction, we may have to set about the task of bringing these techniques up to date. This could well provide the impetus for the sort of thorough curriculum reassessment and revision we suggest elsewhere on these pages. Simulated models of untried curriculum approaches can even be tested as are programs in other fields, by running them through the computers to determine how effective they may be in classroom situations.

Perhaps our technology itself suggests a new approach. It offers, rather than a generally accepted new curriculum standard, the very absence of one in favor of a means for letting each student establish his own. Patrick Suppes, writing in the *Saturday Review* (July 23, 1966), has stated: "Contrary to the expectations of many, the computer may make classroom teaching more, rather than less, an individual affair. And in doing so it will facilitate learning at a speed and depth of understanding that now seem impossible to achieve."

In such a climate the very basis of traditional education theory may well be questioned. Since it is the most central nature of computers in education to develop individual cognitive styles through highly personalized computer instruction, we may soon have to face the very real question of how far we want to allow this individualized development to go. Will we want to preserve some uniformity of education as we do now, or will we develop a new philosophy that permits each person to learn what he likes under a system that caters to accentuating individual differences in ability and interest? The problem, if there is one, distills itself in the question: How much diversity do we want to have?

Our society has a notable record for efficiency, achieved with the emphasis not on producing the finest product, but on producing at the lowest cost. In terms of human minds, one would hope that such a value scale is not applied. Marshall McLuhan and George B. Leonard, writing in *Look* magazine (Feb. 21, 1967), have stated: "When automated electronic production reaches full potential, it will be just about as cheap to turn out a million differing objects as a million exact duplicates. The only limits on production and consumption will be the human imagination." Applied to the uses made of computers in education, this would appear to be a prophetic observation.

The ancient learning machine at the Grand Academy of Lagado has traveled a long and bumpy road to enter today's classrooms, spewing its broken sentences along the way. Now that it is here, what will be the price tag in simple equipment cost to put it into general use as a regular instructor? On the elementary school level, which is the natural starting point, it would today take nearly $2 billion to install the necessary systems in this country's one million classrooms alone. The cost of computer terminals is expected to drop by half within a reasonable span of time, however, so overall cost could fall to $1 billion. In the next decade, it is expected that this country will spend $500 billion on education, or 5 percent of our Gross National Product. By this standard, the $1 billion expenditure for computer equipment seems a wise and thrifty one, for besides their value as instructors that grade, evaluate and keep complete records on each student, computers can also aid schools by helping to counsel students according to their past course programs, arrange complicated class schedules, maintain payroll and all accounting records, serve as a library of ready data, and even predict which students will have difficulty in specific areas.

Robert Theobald has said: "It is the task of education to make the impossible appear relevant." Computers seem to hold the promise of just such a feat.

5

Like the drug for which there is as yet no disease, we now have some machines that can talk but have nothing to say.

                                        HAROLD HOWE, II

Patrick Suppes
THE COMPUTER AND EXCELLENCE

Probably no one doubts the proposition that children are capable of learning more than they actually do in school. Probably no one doubts, either, that the structure of courses and the curriculum can be improved.

From Patrick Suppes, "The Computer and Excellence," *Saturday Review*, January 14, 1967, pp. 46, 48, 50 (a special issue produced in cooperation with the Committee for Economic Development). Reprinted by permission of the *Saturday Review*.

The hard problem is to become clear about how we can reorganize our schools and the curriculum in order to provide our children an opportunity to learn more. Perhaps the most important point to emphasize about this search for improvement is that we should not anticipate that it will come to an end.

The problem of adjusting the pace of curriculum in any subject area to the background knowledge and motivation of students is a deep and complicated one. I don't pretend to be able to offer a general solution. But some of our experiences at Stanford in elementary-school mathematics, I think, represent a feasible approach to the problem.

Let me begin with two examples from my own experience. The first concerns the teaching of geometrical constructions in the first grade. Starting in 1958, Newton Hawley and I taught a first-grade class daily, two weeks at a time, in the special subject of geometry. We tried to go through as many of the constructions in Book 1 of Euclid's *Elements* as we could. The students we were teaching were bright and able, but we were working with an entire class, not with some specially selected subgroup. Rather than try to summarize what we did, I will quote from my diary entry for May 2, 1958:

> The entire session was spent on review of the things we have done during the past two weeks. The main part of the review was to elicit from the students a list of the eight constructions we have considered which are, namely,
> 1) draw a circle with given radius;
> 2) draw a circle with given center and one point on the circle;
> 3) construct an equilateral triangle with given base;
> 4) find the midpoint of a line segment;
> 5) draw an acute angle;
> 6) draw an obtuse angle;
> 7) bisect a given angle;
> 8) given three line segments, construct a triangle.
> We then had some discussion of which of these eight constructions was the most difficult. We took a vote and the class results were: No. 8 was the hardest, and No. 4 followed. The students enjoyed this procedure of voting on the most difficult very much.

Almost ten years later, talk about these constructions in the primary grades is not as surprising as it was then. But at the time there was scarcely an elementary school in the country in which such matters were being taught.

The second example concerns the teaching of mathematical logic to bright fifth and sixth graders. We have done this for ten years, with the important practical result that we have found that the elements of logic, as ordinarily taught in introductory college courses, can be mastered without great difficulty by able elementary-school students. Indeed, in the summer of 1964 we even taught a substantial body of material to some very bright children who were about to enter the second grade. These examples suggest that if we can train teachers and provide the appropriate circumstances, it is a relatively simple matter to teach a good deal more of mathematics and also of other subjects to the abler students in our schools.

There are at least two major obstacles to this straightforward approach. One is a complicated matter of policy, illustrated by the remark of a mother of one of the students I was teaching several years ago: "I don't see any reason for teaching so much mathematics to our children. What they need is a great deal more poetry." Practical decisions must be made about the amount of time devoted to poetry and the amount of time devoted to mathematics, or to social studies, or to English, but it is absolutely essential for all of us to realize that as yet we have scarcely the beginnings of a serious, rational method for making these relative determinations.

A kind of feudal-fiefdom concept dominates the organization of curriculum. Each subject area is allocated a certain percentage of time; for example, elementary-school mathematics ordinarily amounts to about 15 to 16 per cent of the curriculum. It is relatively easy within this 15 or 16 per cent to discuss the advantages and disadvantages of increasing the amount of geometry or giving some exposure to logic. It is quite another thing to discuss whether or not another 1 per cent should be added to the mathematics portion of the curriculum at the expense of literature, elementary science, or social studies, or whether the mathematics curriculum should be reduced in order to provide more time for poetry and belles-lettres. I can't begin here to discuss the complexities of the issues. We are far from having a clear approach to them, let alone a way to resolve them.

The second difficulty results from one of the best substantiated facts in psychology and education: the existence of significant individual differences in learning ability. In 1963 at Stanford we began an accelerated program in mathematics with a group of bright children selected from the first grades in four culturally advantaged schools. Their IQ range is from 122 to 160, with a mean of about 137. Strikingly large individual differences exist even within this relatively homogeneous group of children.

During the first year, for example, the fastest student did 400 per cent more work than the slowest student, as measured by the number of problems completed, which is indicative of the relative speed with which they progressed through the curriculum. To take a slightly different measure for comparison, during the second grade the top four students in the group did about 170 per cent more work than the bottom four students, again as measured by the number of problems completed during the year. We are just completing the analysis of the data for their third-grade work, and the results appear to be comparable to the second grade, although the difference between the top four students and the bottom four students is greater. These differences in learning rate, it is important to emphasize, were not well correlated with IQ, but are due to factors we cannot at present identify.

Examples of significant individual differences in learning ability, even among relatively homogeneous students, are in no sense restricted to mathematics. In experiments with Stanford undergraduates over several years on various aspects of learning Russian, we have been struck by the highly significant differences in ability to learn a second language. In a controlled experiment on the learning of a spoken vocabulary of 300 Russian words, the difference in learning rate, as measured by the number of items successfully mastered in ten sessions, was more than 300 per cent between the slowest and the fastest student in the group. In this case we did not have IQ measures, but we may assume that all the students were highly motivated since they volunteered for the experiment. The data on the slowest and fastest student were not unusual; the other students in the experiment spread out between the two bounds in a relatively uniform fashion.

What can we do to accelerate learning in the schools, especially in a way that is sensitive to the large individual differences in learning rate? Previously, I have discussed in these pages the proposal that for the foreseeable future computer-assisted instruction provides the only practical and economically feasible solution to these problems [see "Plug-In Instruction," SR, July 23, 1966]. Here I would like to describe further how content is handled in computer-assisted instruction—the character of the curriculum and, in particular, the impact of individualization.

Research showing the desirability of regular drill-and-practice in basic mathematical skills, particularly those in arithmetic, goes back for over forty years and is well documented in the literature on mathematics education. Clearly, the computer can offer a regular and standardized program on an individualized basis in this area. During the academic year 1965–66 we wrote and tested such a program of individualized instruction. We divided curriculum for each of the grades three to six into concept blocks and each of these concept blocks was presented for between four and ten days. All students began each concept block at the middle level of difficulty. On subsequent days they moved up or down, depending upon their performance levels. Drills on five different levels of difficulty were available. The student found his own level of difficulty, which could vary over the course of the concept block, depending upon his performance. A very considerable advantage of such an approach is that students are not put in tracks at the beginning of the school year and thereby fixed once and for all at the level at which they should work. We know far too little about evaluation of ability and achievement to make such decisions on a permanent basis.

Consider what would be required of a classroom teacher to conduct such a program of individualized review and practice in arithmetic. At the beginning or end of each day, she would need to assign each student to a level of difficulty based upon his past performance. Upon completion of the exercise she would have to grade and evaluate the student almost immediately to avoid a lag in assignment to the next level.

During the current academic year we are striving for a still deeper level of individualization. In addition to the five levels of difficulty on a concept block, approximately 30 per cent of the work is devoted to review of past concept blocks. We keep a running score of the student's work for the entire year and continually review his weakest areas of competence. The same five levels of difficulty are used in the review of the concept block on which the student's past performance was the worst. For example, if the student exited from a concept block with a score corresponding to a level-two performance, he enters review work on this block at the same level. The student is branched upward or downward in levels of difficulty, depending upon his daily performance. With a score of 80 per cent or better he branches upward, unless he is already at the top level; with a score running between 60 and 79 per cent, he remains at the same level; and with a score below 59 per cent, he is branched downward.

The preliminary evidence from 1965–66 is that such a program leads to specific improvements in performance on arithmetic-achievement tests as compared to the performance of control groups. This is no surprise. It only confirms research, running back many years, that regular exercises to provide practice on basic skills and concepts will improve long-term performance in arithmetic. The computer provides a standardized and regular way of doing this on an individual basis, tailored to the needs of each student. In principle, such a program could be put into practice by a teacher. But in fact, the elementary-school teacher already has too many responsibilities in too many areas to provide such a daily individualized program.

A common criticism of programed instruction is that the answers required of students are too simple and too stereotyped, and that not enough individual freedom and diversity is permitted. These criticisms do not necessarily apply to properly organized computer-assisted instruction, as shown by the subject of logic, which we have been teaching at computer consoles for several years.

We initially give children work with "sentential inferences" of the following sort: *If John is here, then Mary is at school. If John is here, where is Mary?* We move on to examples in simple mathematical contexts of the rules of inference that most readers have encountered in secondary-school geometry. We want to provide an environment in which they may make conceptual progress as rapidly as possible. We want to avoid giving the children restricted multiple choices; on the other hand, we do not want to ask them to write out constructed answers, which is tedious for children, particularly at the elementary-school age level. In such a case, we can simply ask the child to input the rule of inference he wishes to apply to the given premises or to the given lines in the proof. Usually, the child needs only three or four characters on the keyboard of the console, which in almost all circumstances is like a standard typewriter keyboard. We use two letters to abbreviate the rule, and in most cases, the rule applies to two previous lines of premises or proof.

In the example about John and Mary given above, the student would use what we call the IF rule. He would input on the keyboard, "IF 1 2," which indicates that the IF rule is to be applied to the lines 1 and 2. The program then would automatically type out the result of applying this rule to those two lines. This is a very simple example. Actually, the student has a large number of opportunities for different types of responses, even essentially different proofs, as he learns an ever larger body of rules of inference and is exposed to larger bodies of laws and facts to be used as premises in inference.

During the current academic year elementary algebra also is being included in this program. We are recording all the different proofs that students give in order to collect objective data on how much genuine diversity students exhibit in coming to grips with a subject—a question that has been of continual concern in discussions of new mathematics and social science curricula. (One of the most positive aspects of computer-assisted instruction is the possibility of gathering complex objective data on student reactions to a given curriculum.)

The presentation of special topics to able students, the provision for selected topics in smaller rural schools, and patient and intensive work with some of the very slow students—all can be handled by computer-assisted instruction, and at present there is no feasible alternative method in sight. Soon, for example, it will be possible to offer an essentially self-contained computer-assisted instruction course in elementary Russian in many high schools throughout the country, without supervisory personnel who are trained in Russian or themselves are prepared to teach Russian. Soon it also will be practical to offer a calculus course in rural high schools by use of computer-assisted terminals connected by telephone lines to a central computer located several hundred miles away.

Today, to equip every elementary-school classroom with a console connected by telephone lines to a computer located at the school district office or some nearby central point would cost approximately $2,000 per terminal, but mass production probably could reduce the cost to not more than $1,000 per terminal, including the cost of curriculum development and preparation. There are approximately 1,000,000 elementary-school classrooms in the country. Thus over a ten-year period the total investment to install a minimum of one terminal per classroom would be approximately $1 billion. This is a great deal of money, but during this same ten-year period the country will spend approximately $500 billion on education, and this $500 billion dollars will itself represent only approximately 5 per cent of the gross national product.

We are all aware of how rapid the spread of television has been in the twenty years from 1946 to 1966. It would be foolish to predict that the spread of computer-assisted instruction will follow the same rapid course, but it is fair to forecast that in the next ten years the impact of computer-assisted instruction will be felt in a very large number of school systems in this country. The technology alone is not important. What is important is that by the use of computers we can realize the goals of individualized instruction that have been discussed in American education since the beginning of this century. And we can take another significant step toward realizing the full learning potential of our children.

6

Contrary to the expectations of many, the computer may make classroom teaching more, rather than less, an individual affair. And in doing so it will facilitate learning at a speed and depth of understanding that now seem impossible to achieve.

PATRICK SUPPES

Richard S. Barrett
THE COMPUTER MENTALITY

With the introduction of computers into education, there has come to sudden prominence a system of beliefs that may best be called "the computer mentality." It is found most often in the computer programmer, although members of other professions occasionally become fascinated by the magical box and adopt the way of thought that springs up around it.

There are two major sources of the computer mentality. The first is natural selection. Computer programming is an exacting profession, one

From Richard S. Barrett of Case and Company, Inc., "The Computer Mentality," *Phi Delta Kappan*, April, 1963, pp. 430–433. Reprinted by permission of the author and publisher.

that appeals to those who possess the capacity for meticulous attention to detail and a willingness to adapt to the rigid means of communication dictated by the computer. They are fascinated by its complex gadgetry and language. The second is environmental. Once involved with the computer, the computer mentality comes gradually to accept the idea that the whole world can be understood in the same terms as the computer. The computer mentality looks for and finds the pervasiveness of mathematics, the rule of logic and order, and a simplicity and predictability in the most complex psychological and social processes.

Here are some of its distinguishing beliefs:

1. *Everybody is fascinated by the computer.* To prove this point, the computer mentality cites evidence, much of which is drawn from studies of bright children in a university lab school, members of a mathematics club who volunteer to learn how to use the computer, and neophyte computer programmers who are learning their trade. Also cited is the common impression that visiting firemen enjoy the computer room where they can see the tape reels whirl, lights flash, typewriters type (seemingly of their own volition), and listen to equipment which is programmed to play "She'll Be Comin' 'Round the Mountain." Children, with an apparently innate love of gadgets, enjoy the demonstration in which they type messages to the computer and the computer types back.

Short demonstrations may be fascinating, but even for the high school dropout education is likely to run nearly 200 days a year for almost 10 years. For some of us it goes to 16 to 20 years. If the student operates the computer for about a half-hour a day, he can easily spend 1,500 hours working with it from kindergarten through college. Strange as it may seem to the computer mentality, there may be people who will find that exposure too much. Even more strange, there are people who go through life with no particular interest in the computer. The soul of the poet, the used car salesman, the mountain climber, and the Trappist monk may well find the computer and the way it teaches to be objectionable.

Even those who are sympathetic to the computer can be frustrated by it. Flaws in the original programming or simple mistakes by the student in typing the material to be entered into the machine can force him to repeat steps he already knows and can do perfectly. Despite the awesome speed at which the computer can process data, there can be substantial delays when a number of students are being served simultaneously by one computer, however large its capacity. The frustrations caused by the machine are neither trivial nor transient. Computers have suffered physical violence from dissatisfied users.

2. *Tell 'em once and you've told 'em.* No one has to tell the computer the same thing twice. Barring breakdowns, once an instruction is satisfactorily entered, it will be followed repeatedly and without fail. People, on the other hand, rarely absorb anything complex on one trial, requiring a variety of approaches, explanations, applications, and elab-

orations before they get the point. As soon as the material is learned, the student begins to forget it, and he requires review to make it stick in his mind.

The computer mentality sometimes recognizes the need for redundancy in exposition, but there is a tendency to introduce complex and specialized terms for use by the layman, describing them once and thereafter using them as if they were perfectly clear and completely understood. The greater problem is in review. In those cases where the student types his material on a standard typewriter keyboard and the computer types its responses, he can take a copy of his printout with him for later review. By the time the end of the term arrives, however, he may find it difficult to interpret the cryptic comments that he and the computer have made to each other. Reconstructing the exercise may be more trouble than it's worth. He is in even worse shape when the material is presented to him and his responses are made ephemerally on a television screen. Not only is the material unavailable for review later in the year, it is even destroyed during the course of the lesson so that he cannot go back to see what he did or to find his mistakes.

3. *Telling the student that he got the right answer is informative and rewarding.* To the computer mentality, it is obvious that if someone got the right answer, he must know the subject; and if he is told he got the right answer, he knows that he knows the subject, and he feels good. Students, as well as those who study the behavior of students, know that people can go mechanically through a step-by-step routine and get the right answer without understanding what they are doing. The alert student who has just been told that he has successfully solved a problem given to him by the computer may well wonder whether he could apply the information in a different context.

Computer programs vary widely in the ways in which they inform the student that he is right. Some simply acknowledge correct responses with a symbol, such as a plus sign, or a letter "R" for "right." Others spell out "good," or may even be more effusive in their praise. The student who has stumbled through many blind alleys or has been deliberately giving some wrong answers to see what the computer will do, can be counted on to look with a little cynicism on such feeble attempts to reward him. Besides, many people do not need to be rewarded every few seconds for their proper behavior, and they find the constant repetition of "good" or "well done" to be a bore, especially when they know they have not done particularly well.

4. *The computer is responsive.* To the computer mentality, a teacher with a class of 30 students cannot be responsive because there is so little time for individual interaction; but the computer, since it is used on an individual basis with each student, is truly responsive. If we take the first definition in Webster's International Dictionary, second edition, of *responsive* as being characteristic of something "that responds; an-

swers; replies," the computer programmer mentality is indeed correct. The machine does respond, answer, and reply to the student. A little further reading in the same dictionary yields another definition, "ready or inclined to respond, or react; as a *responsive* child; always *responsive* to affection; his eloquence stirred a *responsive* chord in his listeners." That sounds more like a good teacher, even one with 30 students, than it does like a computer.

5. *The computer will individualize instruction.* Conceptually, the model for individualizing instruction is clear. The students at the beginning of instruction are given a long, thorough diagnostic test. Each student's performance is analyzed to determine the kind of instruction he needs to achieve the goals of the unit of instruction. The appropriate prescription is made for him to read materials, solve problems, watch films or video tapes, or get private tutoring or some other form of instruction. At various points throughout the sequence his progress is assessed, and a new prescription is given if necessary.

All of this sounds very neat and elegant, but there remains one unsolved problem—the nature of the tests that should be given and the kinds of prescriptions that are appropriate. Aside from the pervasive fact that smart people learn faster than dull people, we do not yet have a firm basis for diagnosing skills and making a prescription. The answer to this problem comes from the development of tests that meaningfully assess the student's achievement, and the adoption of techniques for making prescriptions that are better than the common-sense assignments of a reasonably capable teacher. Further research must be made into the allied processes of teaching and learning. Once the basic information is at hand, the computer may or may not be a useful and economic tool.

6. *Science is data.* According to the computer-programmer mentality, simulation of the laboratory, particularly in physics and chemistry, will teach the student in a way that is impossible today, because the computer can simulate experiments that cannot be conducted in a typical laboratory of the school or college. The plan is that the student will be able to set up experimental conditions, and the computer, having been programmed in advance by someone who knows the mathematical principles involved, will give him the data that he would have read from his instruments in real life. Experiments that are dangerous, expensive, or impractical can be simulated in a way that gives the student an experience beyond that he would have by reading about the experiment or observing it on film. He could, for example, learn about the laws of ballistics by firing simulated guns with varying angles of elevation and muzzle velocity, or he could study physical phenomena in the inaccessible regions of outer space.

When the objection is raised about the unreality of it all, the computer mentality concedes that there must be enough laboratory work to give the student some real practice. Or, rather patronizingly, the point is made that once he has washed a few test tubes, looked through a few microscopes, and weighed a few samples on laboratory balances he has had enough hands-on experience. What he really needs, the computer mentality argues, is data.

This emphasis on data can lead to the false impression that numbers are the stuff of science, when actually science is a complex and disorderly process, beginning with some knowledge of the phenomenon being studied, from which hunches and, later, formal hypotheses may be derived. These are tested, the blind alleys are abandoned, and the more promising leads followed. New hunches and hypotheses develop, and are tested, until a meaningful conclusion can be reached. During this process the alert mind must be opened to accept and understand the unexpected and to capitalize on the happy accidents that occur.

Of course, much of the scientist's effort is directed to developing data collection procedures, particularly when he is exploring near the fringes of his science. But he does not blindly rely on the numbers that come out, since he knows they are no better than the techniques by which they have been collected. He can obtain some index of the reliability of his information by analyzing the numbers themselves, but the more important criteria are that the data collection procedures are relevant to his problem, that they do not leave out important information whose absence will distort his results. Viewed in this context, the actual numbers that appear on the machine take on limited significance.

7. *Computation serves no useful purpose in education.* The computer, it is further argued, can be used not only to generate the simulated data, but also to perform the calculations that are necessary to develop an understanding of the physical laws involved. More intricate problems requiring too much calculation for what they are worth could then be handled as broadening the scope of the student's learning.

Computation is tedious, and extended computations can kill the motivation of the student. Indeed, before the modern computers, many investigations were not undertaken because the results were seen as not being worth the computational labor involved.

Nevertheless, letting the computer do all the computation leaves something out of the learning process. There once was a psychologist who had only hand-operated calculators in his laboratory, explaining that the physical action of literally cranking numbers into the machines gave his students a feel for the data that they would not otherwise have. Perhaps this was a rationalization for his inability to get a more modern calculator, but most people have found that by doing problems, whether the course is arithmetic, physics, or statistics, they have learned something they did not get simply by reading the material or watching the teacher work out problems on the blackboard. We learn, to some extent, with our fingertips. Being handed the answers to all our mathematical problems by the infallible computer may breed a generation of students with basic deficiencies in understanding the data that they are dealing with.

Let us agree that there is some virtue to the proposition that, after the student has done enough calculations to get what psychologists in their technical jargon call a gut-level understanding of what his computations mean, there is still need for him to have access to computed results from raw data. Is the computer necessary? Can we not give him tables showing the data as if he collected it in an experiment and the correctly calculated results? Tables are much cheaper than computers. If tables won't work, can they use slide rules, calculators, or more limited but cheaper computers that are already available?

8. *The world is at its foundations mathematical.* The computer mentality, preoccupied as it is with numbers, tends to build instructional systems that emphasize the numerical aspects of the subject, and to deemphasize its qualitative feature. Much of physics, astronomy, and chemistry is best understood mathematically; but particularly insofar as the nonspecialist is concerned—and this includes the vast majority of those who never learn about these subjects—many of the most fascinating issues need not be presented mathematically. The political and moral issues that evolve from man's mastery of nuclear fusion, the questions of whether the universe started all at once with a big bang or is continually being created, and the economic and medical issues that stem from the widespread use of insecticides, can all be dealt with by intelligent citizens without the intimate knowledge of the data and the calculations essential for the specialists.

9. *Computers will bring about a revolution in education.* It is easy to understand how the computer mentality can expect a rapid revolution in education, because the computer has brought about such a great and dramatic revolution in handling information. In a scant 25 years, operations that were timed in thousandths of a second are now timed in billionths of a second. Slow-acting electromechanical relays gave way to vacuum tubes, which in turn were replaced by transistors that are now being supplanted by minute printed circuits. One might say that the physiology of computers has gone through several evolutionary cycles, changing in form, structure, function, size, and capability. In the same 25 years, the physiology of the student who is to learn on this computer has changed little, if at all. He carries on his shoulders his own portable computer, miniaturized beyond the dreams of the computer engineer, endowed with a remarkable memory and retrieval system, but slow in processing information, and subject to lapses in memory to inattention, and to distraction. This is the equipment that the educator has to work on, and he cannot redesign it.

During the millions of years during which man has been evolving, he has always been concerned with teaching his young. He has told them directly what he knows, and he has tried to help them to discover it on their own; he has rewarded and punished; he has given instruction in concentrated doses and he has spread it out; he has applied the simplest forms of Pavlovian conditioning and the most intricate, complex learning theories; he has offered intrinsic and extrinsic motivation; he has wheedled, threatened, stimulated, and diverted; he has, in fact, tried just about everything he could think of. Certainly, he will develop new techniques that will be successful, but one can hardly say that there is a wide open field for the development of radically different and successful techniques.

There will be significant progress in education, but changes will take time. If, by exerting the massive efforts now being undertaken with government support, we are able to improve the effectiveness of education by 3 percent per year for 25 years, it will then be more than twice as effective as it is today. This would be a revolution indeed, and to expect a single electronic tool to have the revolutionary impact predicted by the more enthusiastic supporters of the computer is to invite disappointment with more modest but truly significant improvements.

10. *Computer-assisted instruction is economical.* Computers have won their place in business because they save clerical time and provide information that is too expensive to collect in any other way. A saving of 10 percent in the salary of the office force can be balanced directly against the cost of the computer, and the competitive advantage of better information can be estimated even when it cannot be directly calculated. The situation is different in the schools because students aren't paid, and it is difficult to estimate the value of what they learn from the computer that they would not learn in more conventional instruction. Emphasizing the savings that might accrue by displacing instructional staff is obviously a poor selling point among teachers.

Making an economic study of the computer in education is virtually impossible because no realistic figures are available. Wild estimates that it will cost 25¢ per hour for each student are not backed up by a sober analysis of the rental cost of the computer and the terminal at which the student works, the cost of tie-lines that must be leased to connect the schools with centrally located equipment, the number of student hours that can be realistically scheduled in the school year, the extent to which costs can be defrayed by using the computer for other purposes during off-hours, and the share of the cost to be charged for developing equipment and materials. However, it is safe to say that it will be a long time before computer-assisted instruction can be profitably sold at $1.50 per student hour, a rate at which the school could hire one teacher for every four or five students and give them close personal attention.

11. *Computer-assisted instruction will be so good that it will be accepted on the basis of its merit.* Truth will prevail, but truth prevails only when it has won a long struggle to overcome the *status quo*. Let us

look briefly at some of the things that have to be accomplished before the computer will take its rightful place in education.

Students will have to take time away from other activities to learn how to use the computer. The school operates on two budgets. In addition to the financial budget there is a time budget of the student, already burdened; in fact, there are many voices saying that we are demanding too much of our students and that we should reduce the load imposed on them. Somewhere in this time budget the school must find time to train students to use the computer, even though they may never see a computer again after they leave the school. No one yet knows how long it will take to train the typical student to use the computer with the same level of ease that the engineer uses his slide rule, but indications are that it is substantial.

Teachers will need to be trained to use the computer. Some of them must be trained to teach the students to use it, and all of them must be able to deal with malfunction and to recognize the need for maintenance. Not only that, they must learn how to teach with the computer at their elbow. The well-programmed computer is going to be more up to date and more knowledgeable than many teachers, who must either update their education or run the risk of looking foolish. Certainly all reasonable people are in favor of teachers having a broad and up-to-date store of knowledge, but not all teachers are reasonable and some of them will resist.

Teachers must learn to turn over much of their rights, duties, and responsibilities to an inanimate object over which they have little control and toward which at least some of them will have considerable hostility. It will take a long process of education and motivation to make sure that teachers accept the contributions that the computer can make.

With all its problems, the computer has tremendous potential for improving education. With careful study of the learning process, development of methods of instruction that have not been thought of yet because the unique capabilities of the computer have not been available, and long-term planning of the introduction of the computer into the classroom, it can become one of the most progressive forces in education. For this program I would like to add one assumption of my own:

The use of the computer in education is too serious a business to be left to the computer mentality.

7

*The argument that programed instruction will re-
place the teacher is a kind of sensational and unin-
formed journalism which is unworthy of attention.
Along with textbooks, teaching films and slides,
instructional television, workbooks, chalkboards, and
many other such things, programed instruction is one
of an arsenal of teaching devices at the command of
the teacher to help him do his job better.*
WILBUR SCHRAMM

Wilbur Schramm
WHAT IS PROGRAMED INSTRUCTION?

The thesis of this report is that programed instruction is, in the best sense of the word, a truly revolutionary device; but it is revolutionary, not so much in itself, as in its ability to interact with certain other developments in education. This interaction has the potential of freeing schools and men from old bondage and outworn theories and practices. But the potential is, so far, largely unrealized.

I am going to try to make clear what I mean, by talking about programed instruction as it is today, then about some of the currents in education which are boiling up around it, and finally about what it might be tomorrow, in connection with which I shall make some suggestions as to how a desirable rate and pattern of development might be encouraged.

But first let us be sure that there is no misunderstanding of what we mean when we speak of "programed instruction."

By programed instruction I mean the kind of learning experience in which a "program" takes the place of a tutor for the student, and leads him through a set of specified behaviors designed and sequenced to make it more probable that he will behave in a given desired way in the future—in other words, that he will learn what the program is designed to teach him. Sometimes the program is housed in a "teaching machine" or in a "programed textbook." If so, the machine or the book is little more than a case to hold the program. The *program* is the important thing about programed instruction. It is usually a series of items, questions, or statements to each of which, in order, the student is asked to make a response. His response may be to fill in a word left blank, to answer a question, to select one of a series of multiple-choice answers, to indicate agreement or disagreement, or to solve a problem and record the answer.

From Wilbur Schramm, "What Is Programed Instruction?" *Programed Instruction Today and Tomorrow* (New York: Fund for the Advancement of Education, 1962), pp. 1–4.
Reprinted by permission of the Fund for the Advancement of Education.

As soon as he has responded to the item, he is permitted to see the correct response so that he can tell immediately whether his response has been the right one. But the items are so skillfully written and the steps are so small between them that the student practices mostly correct responses, rather than errors, and the sequence of items is skillfully arranged to take the student from responses he already knows, through new responses he is able to make because of the other responses he knows, to the final responses, the new knowledge, it is intended that he should command.

> *To sum up, then, these are essential elements of programed instruction:*
> (a) *an ordered sequence of stimulus items,*
> (b) *to each of which a student responds in some specified way,*
> (c) *his responses being reinforced by immediate knowledge of results,*
> (d) *so that he moves by small steps,*
> (e) *therefore making few errors and practicing mostly correct responses,*
> (f) *from what he knows, by a process of successively closer approximation, toward what he is supposed to learn from the program.*

We have described a Skinnerian type of program. About 19 out of 20 programs being made today are Skinnerian programs. There are other types, however. One of them is the Crowder type, represented in the Tutortexts which are in the form of scrambled books. Crowder's programs use the response as a test of whether the student has grasped an essential point of a passage of text, and provide for frequent errors by explaining why an erroneous response is wrong. There are also some training devices which are essentially programs, but not precisely of a Skinnerian type. Pressey's punchboards, employed usually as review tests, are also a type of program. All these devices, like Skinnerian programs, depend for their effect on some type of psychological conditioning, although whether it is Skinner's operant conditioning. Pavlovian or classical conditioning, or Guthrie's contiguity learning, or some combination, depends on the program and is to some extent a matter of disputed interpretation.

However, there are two other characteristics of the making of programs which are very important in the total effect. Before a program can be designed, it is necessary to specify very clearly the desired end products—the responses the student is supposed to be able to make when he has completed the program, the skills and understandings to be learned. This requires a fresh look and often some hard thinking about the necessary content of teaching, an experience which is highly salutary and frequently results in long-overdue revision of courses and requirements. Secondly, when a program is being made it is necessary to test it. This is ordinarily done by trying it on one student, revising it to take care of the difficulties encountered in his learning experience, trying it on another student, revising it again, and so on until it has been tested on eight or ten individual students, at which time it is usually tested on larger groups. Experienced programers feel that by the time eight or ten individual tests and revisions have been completed, the program is capable of teaching 98 per cent of all the students who approximate the school and ability level of the students so far tested. This process is a very important one because (a) it focuses attention on the individual learning process ·in a way that group teaching seldom does, and (b) it virtually guarantees that a program so made will "work." About a program so made, one feels a confidence that few textbooks can command.

It is obvious that what happens in programed instruction might well happen at a skillfully planned and organized tutorial session, in which the tutor leads the student along, question by question, toward given learning goals. A teacher is an ideal "teaching machine;" and excellent teaching, if it requires active responses by the student, employs strategy and tactics which we should call a "program." In a sense, teacher training and preparation for classroom teaching is "programing" the teacher, although much teaching—for example, lecture teaching which minimizes active response from the student—does not make use of the methods of programed instruction. But no one contends that a very skillful teacher could not do whatever a program can do, at least as well as the program can do it—except in one respect: the teacher can tutor only one student at a time.

8

The word has come down from the Dean,
That with the aid of the Teaching Machine,
King Oedipus Rex,
Could have learned about sex,
Without ever touching the Queen.

William E. Hoth

FROM SKINNER TO CROWDER TO CHANCE: A PRIMER ON TEACHING MACHINES

Teaching machines, feared, jeered and not widely understood, stand ready in the on-deck circle about to come to bat with team teachers,

From William E. Hoth, "From Skinner to Crowder to Chance: A Primer on Teaching Machines," *English Journal*, September, 1961, pp. 398–401. Reprinted by permission of the National Council of Teachers of English and the author.

accordion-partitioned gyms, language labs, driver training fleets, congenial administrators, and air-conditioned school buses as members of the home team in the secondary school ball game. Their use is basic to the Trump plan and their "programmed" materials fill a full day in the Diederich plan. Their debut causes a dean of English teachers to compose a delightful parody. Quite clearly all of us in the profession need to get acquainted with them. Let's begin our lesson.

First, to be very sure, these electronic devices are not yet *teaching* machines. Better to call them *training, tutoring,* or to be more flattering to their proponents, *learning* machines. For machines they are, capable of controlling what is presented, how much, when, for how long, and how often but incapable of performing any act which their "programmer" has not anticipated, and completely insensitive to the quizzical look of an eager but confused mind. Given these limitations, what makes these contrivances different enough from a phonograph, or a motion picture or slide projector, to justify the special label; why not just refer to them as a new audio-visual device? Let's look at a definition:

> ".... teaching machines [are] devices which (1) present a unit of verbal or symbolic information visually, usually in question form; (2) provide the student with some means of responding to each unit; and (3) inform the student as to the correctness of each response."

The distinctive feature seems to be the presentation of information to the learner in predetermined increments. As the learner masters each of these increments, he moves or is moved on to the next unit. These increments and the sequence in which they are presented make up the *program*, a term without which you cannot talk about teaching machines for long. If these automated lectures had been developed by classroom teachers, then something like *text* or *learning materials* might have been used for *program*; and *planning* for *programming*; and *teacher-author* for *programmer*. For *programmers* are writers whose programming consists of organizing information into sequential increments according to the rationale of the particular machine with which they are working.

Rationales

For beginning students, it's fair to say there are two major rationales. The first is identified primarily with Skinner. In his work, Skinner underscores the necessity of small bits of information which are readily acquired by the learner. Written so that it is very hard not to get the right answers to questions, Skinner material (or *programming*, remember) leads the learner through a series of successes and this insistence on immediate reward is fundamental to the rationale.

Quite the contrary is the rationale of Crowder. In his Auto Tutor, the information is accompanied by multiple-choice questions. Here the learner is confronted with four choices, three of which are wrong. If the learner chooses correctly, he gets the next increment of information and the next set of choices. If he chooses incorrectly, the machine presents review material characteristically by taking the learner through a more simplified series of steps leading up to the question he originally missed. In a device called a "scrambled book," the method works like this, for example: the learner is given some information and then confronted with a multiple choice question. If he chooses A (an incorrect response), he is directed to read page 28; if B (also wrong), p. 19; if C (right), the next page; if D (wrong), p. 81. On page 28, 19, and 81 are presented explanatory information, clarification of terms, simplified breakdowns of complex elements in the question, etc. The trick in this method is to predict the kind and source of error and then "teach" to it. Programming in a Crowder program is always dependent on *branching* or rerouting the learner.

Now it is apparent that the rate at which any learner moves along is completely dependent on the individual; or in more technical terms, both Skinner and Crowder programs are self-pacing. Each step confronts the learner only as he responds to the one preceding. The informed student moves through both types of programming quickly. The slower student pursues detours in Crowder programs and is led hesitantly along in Skinner programs. In both, while the program put into the machine can be standardized (the same for all students), the way in which it becomes "learned" is more individualized than in many classroom practices today.

The Pros and Cons

That is just one argument of machine enthusiasts. Further, they point to the release of teachers from routine question-and-answer sessions, from drill, from routine testing, and from some kinds of lecturing and other schemes for presenting information. They stress that students do not have to be graded on responses to programmed materials. Tests can be conducted quite separately so that the machines are simply for "learning," and cheating becomes impossible. Any student who paces himself through the program falsely doesn't do well on the test, it is alleged.

In fairness to enthusiasts it should be pointed out that educators who favor machines see them as real helpers whose widespread use will enable good teachers to impart spiritual and moral values through better teaching and the guidance made possible by the time gained in release from routine tasks. Some, too, are almost poetic in their talk of the dialogue between machines and students.

Detractors, to date, come from many camps. Some are generally suspicious of machinery in the classroom. Others fear a lock-step curriculum that shows little regard for the individualized nature of growth and development. They sense an emphasis on mastering facts and concepts without accompanying insight, the illumination without which the learning of any content is a hollow reward. Some critics are afraid that teachers who now rely exclusively on workbooks, true-false tests, teacher asks-student answers, and other mechanical methods will be armed with a superior weapon to abuse young minds. A real controversy abides.

What of English? To date there have been efforts to program English materials along Skinner lines. Blumenthal, for example, uses small step-by-step methods to take the learner through fairly traditional textbook information about usage and what most of us had grown accustomed to calling grammar, before we heard of descriptive linguistics. To illustrate his plan, Diederich has prepared some mimeographed material that leads a student through the disciplined reading of a lyric poem. In an advanced curriculum course in English Education at Wayne State University in winter, 1960, two young teachers developed a program for introducing students to elementary concepts in the study of poetry. In Denver, programming on the mechanics of writing is being tested this year.

In fact it is in this realm of inexpensively reproduced materials, prepared according to the rationale of the machine psychologists, that teachers are most likely to encounter the "modern" point of view initially. The machines can be expensive and school administrators may be reluctant to install rows of them (although as language lab experience shows, Federal matching funds work wonders). Yet it is relatively simple to allow a class to pace themselves individually through a printed program. The task for the profession is (1) to supervise the preparation of materials so that the best of what is known about any body of content (literature, language, composition, etc.) gets written in, (2) be informed on details of rationale so as to advise school administrators intelligently, (3) create curriculum designs that capitalize on the released time to provide better face-to-face contacts between teachers as mentors and students as inquirers.

So the keystone combination may be from Skinner to Crowder to an informed profession that knows a truth of modern life. Automatic wash machines do not "free" a housewife. They allow and almost compel her to maintain a cleaner supply of clothes. Language labs do not "release" a modern language teacher for rest nor personal pleasure. They make it more difficult for him to apologize for students who cannot speak a word after a year's study and they compel him to find a substitute for routines which the machine has usurped.

Among us English teachers are many, and some in high places, who suspect the machine because it is not a book. They should not fear. For the machines present an exciting challenge. At last, good teachers can demonstrate their unique skills and their specific usefulness. In the not too distant future we may hear no longer of the wonderful senior English teacher whose students remember how sternly she drilled them on diagramming and mechanics. If the machines take over that which can be learned mechanically, what a fine chance for the really competent English teacher to contribute what is distinctly human.

9

We should avoid gadgets which fix the attention without engaging the mind.

JEROME BRUNER

R. J. Heathorn
LEARN WITH BOOK

A new aid to rapid—almost magical—learning has made its appearance. Indications are that if it catches on, all the electronic gadgets will be so much junk. The new device is known as Built-in Orderly Organized Knowledge. The makers generally call it by its initials, BOOK.

Many advantages are claimed over the old-style learning and teaching aids on which most people are brought up nowadays. It has no wires, no electric circuits to break down. No connection is needed to an electricity power point. It is made entirely without mechanical parts to go wrong or need replacement.

Anyone can use BOOK, even children, and it fits comfortably into the hands. It can be conveniently used sitting in an armchair by the fire.

How does this revolutionary, unbelievably easy invention work? Basically BOOK consists only of a large number of paper sheets. These may run to hundreds where BOOK covers a lengthy program of information. Each sheet bears a number in sequence, so that the sheets cannot be used in the wrong order. To make it even easier for the user to keep the sheets in the proper order they are held firmly in place by a special locking device called a "binding."

Each sheet of paper presents the user with an information sequence in the form of symbols, which he absorbs optically for automatic registration on the brain. When one sheet has been assimilated a flick of the finger turns it over and further information is found on the other side. By using both sides of each sheet in this way a great economy is effected, thus reducing both the size and cost of BOOK. No buttons need to be

From R. J. Heathorn, "Learn with BOOK," *Harper's Magazine*, April, 1963, Vol. 226, No. 1355, p. 52. © *Punch*, London. Reprinted by permission of the Ben Roth Agency, Inc.

pressed to move from one sheet to another, to open or close BOOK, or to start it working.

BOOK may be taken up at any time and used by merely opening it. Instantly it is ready for use. Nothing has to be connected up or switched on. The user may turn at will to any sheet, going backwards or forwards as he pleases. A sheet is provided near the beginning as a location finder for any required information sequence.

A small accessory, available at trifling extra cost, is the BOOKmark. This enables the user to pick up his program where he left off on the previous learning session. BOOKmark is versatile and may be used in any BOOK.

The initial cost varies with the size and subject matter. Already a vast range of BOOKS is available, covering every conceivable subject and adjusted to different levels of aptitude. One BOOK, small enough to be held in the hands, may contain an entire learning schedule. Once purchased, BOOK requires no further cost; no batteries or wires are needed, since the motive power, thanks to the ingenious device patented by the makers, is supplied by the brain of the user.

BOOKs may be stored on handy shelves and for ease of reference the program schedule is normally indicated on the back of the binding.

Altogether the Built-in Orderly Organized Knowledge seems to have great advantages with no drawbacks. We predict a big future for it.

10

The major advances in civilization are processes that
all but wreck the societies in which they occur.
ALFRED NORTH WHITEHEAD

John M. Culkin

A SCHOOLMAN'S GUIDE
TO MARSHALL McLUHAN

Education, a seven-year-old assures me, is "how kids learn stuff." Few definitions are as satisfying. It includes all that is essential— a who, a what, and a process. It excludes all the people, places, and things which are only sometimes involved in learning. The economy and

From John M. Culkin, S.J., "A Schoolman's Guide to Marshall McLuhan," *Saturday Review*, March 18, 1967, pp. 51–53, 70–72. Reprinted by permission of the author and publisher.

accuracy of the definition, however, are more useful in locating the problem than in solving it. We know little enough about *kids*, less about *learning*, and considerably more than we would like to know about *stuff*.

In addition, the whole process of formal schooling is now wrapped inside an environment of speeded-up technological change which is constantly influencing kids and learning and stuff. The jet-speed of this technological revolution, especially in the area of communications, has left us with more reactions to it than reflections about it. Meanwhile back at the school, the student, whose psyche is being programed for tempo, information, and relevance by his electronic environment, is still being processed in classrooms operating on the postulates of another day. The cold war existing between these two worlds is upsetting for both the student and the schools. One thing is certain: It is hardly a time for educators to plan with nostalgia, timidity, or old formulas. Enter Marshall McLuhan.

He enters from the North, from the University of Toronto where he teaches English and is director of the Center for Culture and Technology. He enters with the reputation as "the oracle of the electric age" and as "the most provocative and controversial writer of this generation." More importantly for the schools, he enters as a man with fresh eyes, with new ways of looking at old problems. He is a man who gets his ideas first and judges them later. Most of these ideas are summed up in his book, *Understanding Media*. His critics tried him for not delivering these insights in their most lucid and practical form. It isn't always cricket, however, to ask the same man to crush the grapes and serve the wine. Not all of McLu is nu or tru, but then again neither is *all* of anybody else. This article is an attempt to select and order those elements of McLuhanism which are most relevant to the schools and to provide the schoolman with some new ways of thinking about the schools.

McLuhan's promise is modest enough: "All I have to offer is an enterprise of investigation into a world that's quite unusual and quite unlike any previous world and for which no models of perception will serve." This unexplored world happens to be the present. McLuhan feels that very few men look at the present with a present eye, that they tend to miss the present by translating it into the past, seeing it through a rear-view mirror. The unnoticed fact of our present is the electronic environment created by the new communications media. It is as pervasive as the air we breathe (and some would add that it is just as polluted), yet its full import eludes the judgments of commonsense or content-oriented perception. The environments set up by different media are not just containers for people; they are processes which shape people. Such influence is deterministic only if ignored. There is no inevitability as long as there is a willingness to contemplate what is happening.

Theorists can keep reality at arm's length for long periods of time. Teachers and administrators can't. They are closeted with reality all day long. In many instances they are co-prisoners with electronic-age students in the old pencil box cell. And it is the best teachers and the best students who are in the most trouble because they are challenging the system constantly. It is the system which has to come under scrutiny. Teachers and students can say, in the words of the Late Late Show, "Baby, this thing is bigger than both of us." It won't be ameliorated by a few dashes of good will or a little more hard work. It is a question of understanding these new kids and these new media and of getting the schools to deal with the new electronic environment. It's not easy. And the defenders of the old may prove to be the ones least able to defend and preserve the values of the old.

For some people, analysis of these newer technologies automatically implies approbation of them. Their world is so full of *shoulds* that it is hard to squeeze in an *is*. McLuhan suggests a more positive line of exploration:

> At the moment, it is important that we understand cause and process. The aim is to develop an awareness about print and the newer technologies of communication so that we can orchestrate them, minimize their mutual frustrations and clashes, and get the best out of each in the educational process. The present conflict leads to elimination of the motive to learn and to diminution of interest in all previous achievement: It leads to loss of the sense of relevance. Without an understanding of media grammars, we cannot hope to achieve a contemporary awareness of the world in which we live.

We have been told that it is the property of true genius to disturb all settled ideas. McLuhan is disturbing in both his medium and his message. His ideas challenge the normal way in which people perceive reality. They can create a very deep and personal threat since they touch on everything in a person's experience. They are just as threatening to the establishment whose way of life is predicated on the postulates he is questioning. The establishment has no history of organizing parades to greet its disturbers.

His medium is perhaps more disturbing than his message. From his earliest work he has described his enterprise as "explorations in communication." The word he uses most frequently today is "probe." His books demand a high degree of involvement from the reader. They are poetic and intuitive rather than logical and analytic. Structurally, his unit is the sentence. Most of them are topic sentences—which are left undeveloped. The style is oral and breathless and frequently obscure. It's a different kind of medium.

"The medium is the message," announced McLuhan a dozen years ago in a cryptic and uncompromising aphorism whose meaning is still being explored. The title of his latest book, an illustrated popular paperback treatment of his theories, playfully proclaims that *The Medium Is the Massage*—a title calculated to drive typesetters and critics to hashish and beyond. The original dictum can be looked at in four ways, the third of which includes a message of importance.

The first meaning would be better communicated orally—"The *medium* is the message." The *medium* is the thing to study. The *medium* is the thing you're missing. Everybody's hooked on content; pay attention to form, structure, framework, *medium*. The play's the thing. The medium's the thing. McLuhan makes the truth stand on its head to attract attention. Why the medium is worthy of attention derives from its other three meanings.

Meaning number two stresses the relation of the medium to the content. The form of communication not only alters the content, but each form also has preferences for certain kinds of messages. Content always exists in some form and is, therefore, to some degree governed by the dynamics of that form. If you don't know the medium, you don't know the message. The insight is neatly summed up by Dr. Edmund Carpenter: "English is a mass medium. All languages are mass media. The new mass media—film, radio, TV—are new languages, their grammars as yet unknown. Each codifies reality differently; each conceals a unique metaphysics. Linguists tell us it's possible to say anything in any language if you use enough words or images, but there's rarely time; the natural course is for a culture to exploit its media biases. . . ."

It is always content-in-form which is mediated. In this sense, the medium is co-message. The third meaning for the M-M formula emphasizes the relation of the medium to the individual psyche. The medium alters the perceptual habits of its users. Independent of the content, the medium itself gets through. Pre-literate, literate, and post-literate cultures see the world through different-colored glasses. In the process of delivering content the medium also works over the sensorium of the consumer. To get this subtle insight across, McLuhan punned on message and came up with massage. The switch is intended to draw attention to the fact that a medium is not something neutral—it does something to people. It takes hold of them, it jostles them, it bumps them around, it massages them. It opens and closes windows in their sensorium. Proof? Look out the window at the TV generation. They are rediscovering texture, movement, color, and sound as they retribalize the race. TV is a real grabber; it really massages those lazy, unused senses.

The fourth meaning underscores the relation of the medium to society. Whitehead said, "The major advances in civilization are processes that all but wreck the societies in which they occur." The media massage the society as well as the individual. The results pass unnoticed for long periods of time because people tend to view the new as just a little bit more of the old. Whitehead again: "The greatest invention of the nineteenth century was the invention of the method of invention. A new method entered into life. In order to understand our epoch, we can neglect all details of change, such as railways, telegraphs, radios, spinning machines, synthetic dyes. We must concentrate on the method in itself: That is the real novelty which has broken up the foundations of the old civilization." Understanding the medium or process involved is the key to control.

The media shape both content and consumer and do so practically undetected. We recall the story of the Russian worker whose wheelbarrow was searched every day as he left the factory grounds. He was, of course, stealing wheelbarrows. When your medium is your message and they're only investigating content, you can get away with a lot of things —like wheelbarrows, for instance. It's not the picture but the frame. Not the contents but the box. The blank page is not neutral; nor is the classroom.

McLuhan's writings abound with aphorisms, insights, for-instances, and irrelevancies which float loosely around recurring themes. They provide the raw materials of a do-it-yourself kit for tidier types who prefer to do their exploring with clearer charts. What follows is one man's McLuhan served up in barbarously brief form. Five postulates, spanning nearly 4,000 years, will serve as the fingers in this endeavor to grasp McLuhan:

1) 1967 B.C.—*All the senses get into the act.* A conveniently symmetrical year for a thesis which is partially cyclic. It gets us back to man before the Phoenician alphabet. We know from our contemporary ancestors in the jungles of New Guinea and the wastes of the Arctic that preliterate man lives in an all-at-once sense world. The reality which bombards him from all directions is picked up with the omni-directional antennae of sight, hearing, touch, smell, and taste. Films such as *The Hunters* and *Nanook of the North* depict primitive men tracking game with an across-the-board sensitivity which mystifies Western, literate man. We mystify them too. And it is this cross-mystification which makes inter-cultural abrasions so worthwhile.

Most people presume that their way of perceiving the world is *the* way of perceiving the world. If they hang around with people like themselves, their mode of perception may never be challenged. It is at the poles (literally and figuratively) that the violent contrasts illumine our own unarticulated perceptual prejudices. Toward the North Pole, for example, live Eskimos. A typical Eskimo family consists of a father, a mother, two children, and an anthropologist. When the anthropologist goes into the igloo to study Eskimos, he learns a lot about himself. Eskimos see pictures and maps equally well from all angles. They can draw equally well on top of a table or underneath it. They have phenomenal memories. They travel without visual bearings in their white-on-white world and can sketch cartographically accurate maps of shifting shorelines. They have forty or fifty words for what we call "snow." They live in a world without linearity, a world of acoustic space. They are Eskimos. Their natural way of perceiving the world is different from our natural way of perceiving the world.

Each culture develops its own balance of the senses in response to the demands of its environment. The most generalized formulation of the theory would maintain that the individual's modes of cognition and perception are influenced by the culture he is in, the language he speaks, and the media to which he is exposed. Each culture, as it were, provides its constituents with a custom-made set of goggles. The differences in perception are a question of degree. Some cultures are close enough to each other in perceptual patterns so that the differences pass unnoticed. Other cultural groups, such as the Eskimo and the American teen-ager, are far enough away from us to provide esthetic distance.

2) *Art imitates life.* In *The Silent Language* Edward T. Hall offers the thesis that all art and technology is an extension of some physical or psychic element of man. Today man has developed extensions for practically everything he used to do with his body: stone axe for hand, wheel for foot, glasses for eyes, radio for voice and ears. Money is a way of storing energy. This externalizing of individual, specialized functions is now, by definition, at its most advanced stage. Through the electronic media of telegraph, telephone, radio, and television, man has now equipped his world with a nervous system similar to the one within his own body. President Kennedy is shot and the world instantaneously reels from the impact of the bullets. Space and time dissolve under electronic conditions. Current concern for the United Nations, the Common Market, ecumenism, reflects this organic thrust toward the new convergence and unity which is "blowing in the wind." Now in the electric age, our extended faculties and senses constitute a single instantaneous and coexistent field of experience. It's all-at-once. It's shared-by-all. McLuhan calls the world "a global village."

3) *Life imitates art.* We shape our tools and thereafter they shape us. These extensions of our senses begin to interact with our senses. These media become a massage. The new change in the environment creates a new balance among the senses. No sense operates in isolation. The full sensorium seeks fulfillment in almost every sense experience. And since there is a limited quantum of energy available for any sensory experience, the sense-ratio will differ for different media.

The nature of the sensory effect will be determined by the medium used. McLuhan divides the media according to the quality or definition of their physical signal. The content is not relevant in this kind of analysis. The same picture from the same camera can appear as a glossy photograph or as a newspaper wirephoto. The photograph is well-defined, of excellent pictorial quality, hi-fi within its own medium. McLuhan calls this kind of medium "hot." The newspaper photo is grainy, made up of little dots, low definition. McLuhan calls this kind of medium "cool." Film is hot; television is cool. Radio is hot; telephone is cool. The cool medium or person invites participation and involvement. It leaves room for the response of the consumer. A lecture is hot; all the work is done. A seminar is cool; it gets everyone into the game. Whether all the conections are causal may be debated, but it's interesting that the kids of the cool TV generation want to be so involved and so much a part of what's happening.

4) *We shaped the alphabet and it shaped us.* In keeping with the McLuhan postulate that the "medium is the message," a literate culture should be more than mildly eager to know what books do to people. Everyone is familiar enough with all the enrichment to living mediated through fine books to allow us to pass on to the subtler effects which might be attributed to the print medium, independent of the content involved. Whether one uses the medium to say that *God is dead* or that *God is love* (--- -- ----), the structure of the medium itself remains unchanged. Nine little black marks with no intrinsic meaning of their own are strung along a line with spaces left after the third and fifth marks. It is this stripping away of meaning which allows us to X-ray the form itself.

As an example, while lecturing to a large audience in a modern hotel in Chicago, a distinguished professor is bitten in the leg by a cobra. The whole experience takes three seconds. He is affected through the touch of the reptile, the gasp of the crowd, the swimming sights before his eyes. His memory, imagination, and emotions come into emergency action. A lot of things happen in three seconds. Two weeks later he is fully recovered and wants to write up the experience in a letter to a colleague. To communicate this experience through print means that it must first be broken down into parts and then mediated, eyedropper fashion, one thing at a time, in an abstract, linear, fragmented, sequential way. That is the essential structure of print. And once a culture uses such a medium for a few centuries, it begins to perceive the world in a one-thing-at-a-time, abstract, linear, fragmented, sequential way. And it shapes its organizations and schools according to the same premises. The form of print has become the form of thought. The medium has become the message.

For centuries now, according to McLuhan, the straight line has been the hidden metaphor of literate man. It was unconsciously but inexorably used as the measure of things. It went unnoticed, unquestioned. It was presumed as natural and universal. It is neither. Like everything else it is good for the things it is good for. To say that it is not everything is not to say that it is nothing. The electronic media have broken the monopoly of print; they have altered our sensory profiles by heightening our awareness of aural, tactile, and kinetic values.

5) 1967 A.D.—*All the senses want to get into the act.* Print repressed most sense-life in favor of the visual. The end of print's monopoly also marks the end of a visual monopoly. As the early warning system of art and popular culture indicates, all the senses want to get into the act. Some of the excesses in the current excursions into aural, oral, tactile, and kinetic experience may in fact be directly responsive to the sensory deprivation of the print culture. Nature abhors a vacuum. No one glories in the sight of kids totally out of control in reaction to the Beatles. Some say, "What are the Beatles doing to these kids?" Others say, "What have we done to these kids?" All the data isn't in on what it means to be a balanced human being.

Kids are what the game is all about. Given an honest game with enough equipment to go around, it is the mental, emotional, and volitional capacity of the student which most determines the outcome. The whole complicated system of formal education is in business to get through to kids, to motivate kids, to help kids learn stuff. Schools are not in business to label kids, to grade them for the job market or to babysit. They are there to communicate with them.

Communication is a funny business. There isn't as much of it going on as most people think. Many feel that it consists in saying things in the presence of others. Not so. It consists not in saying things but in having things heard. Beautiful English speeches delivered to monolingual Arabs are not beautiful speeches. You have to speak the language of the audience—of the *whom* in the "who-says-what-to-whom" communications diagram. Sometimes the language is lexical (Chinese, Japanese, Portuguese), sometimes it is regional or personal (125th Street-ese, Holden Caulfield-ese, anybody-ese). It has little to do with words and much to do with understanding the audience. The word for good communication is "Whom-ese"—the language of the audience, of the "whom."

All good communicators use Whom-ese. The best writers, film-makers, advertising men, lovers, preachers, and teachers all have the knack for thinking about the hopes, fears, and capacity of the other person and of being able to translate their communication into terms which are *relevant* for that person. Whitehead called "inert ideas" the bane of education. Relevance, however, is one of those subjective words. It doesn't pertain to the object in itself but to the object as perceived by someone. The school may decide that history is *important for* the student, but the role of the teacher is to make history *relevant to* the student.

If *what* has to be tailored to the *whom*, the teacher has to be constantly engaged in audience research. It's not a question of keeping up with the latest slang or of selling out to the current mores of the kids. Neither of these tactics helps either learning or kids. But it is a question of knowing what values are strong in their world, of understanding the obstacles to communication, of sensing their style of life. Communication doesn't have to end there, but it can start nowhere else. If they are tuned in to FM and you are broadcasting on AM, there's no communication. Communication forces you to pay a lot of attention to other people.

McLuhan has been paying a great deal of attention to modern kids. Of necessity they live in the present since they have no theories to diffract or reflect what is happening. They are also the first generation to be born into a world in which there was always television. McLuhan finds them a great deal different from their counterparts at the turn of the century when the electric age was just getting up steam.

A lot of things have happened since 1900 and most of them plug into walls. Today's six-year-old has already learned a lot of stuff by the time he shows up for the first day of school. Soon after his umbilical cord was cut he was planted in front of a TV set "to keep him quiet." He liked it enough there to stay for some 3,000 to 4,000 hours before he started the first grade. By the time he graduates from high school he has clocked 15,000 hours of TV time and 10,800 hours of school time. He lives in a world which bombards him from all sides with information from radios, films, telephones, magazines, recordings, and people. He learns more things from the windows of cars, trains, and even planes. Through travel and communications he has experienced the war in Vietnam, the wide world of sports, the civil rights movement, the death of a President, thousands of commercials, a walk in space, a thousand innocuous shows, and, one may hope, plenty of Captain Kangaroo.

This is all merely descriptive, an effort to lay out what *is*, not what should be. Today's student can hardly be described by any of the old educational analogies comparing him to an empty bucket or a blank page. He comes to the information machine called school and he is already brimming over with information. As he grows his standards for relevance are determined more by what he receives outside the school than what he receives inside. A recent Canadian film tells the story of a bright, articulate middle class teen-ager who leaves school because there's "no reason to stay." He daydreams about Vietnam while his teacher drones on about the four reasons for the spread of Christianity and the five points such information is worth on the exam. Only the need for a diploma was holding him in school; learning wasn't, and he left. He decided the union ticket wasn't worth the gaff. He left. Some call him a dropout. Some call him a pushout.

The kids have one foot on the dock and one foot on the ferryboat. Living in two centuries makes for that kind of tension. The gap between the classroom and the outside world and the gap between the generations is wider than it has ever been. Those tedious people who quote Socrates on the conduct of the young are trying vainly to reassure themselves that this is just the perennial problem of communication between generations. 'Tain't so. "Today's child is growing up absurd, because he lives in two worlds, and neither of them inclines him to grow up." Says McLuhan in *The Medium Is the Massage.* "Growing up—that is our new work, and it is *total.* Mere instruction will not suffice."

Learning is something that people do for themselves. People, places, and things can facilitate or impede learning; they can't make it happen without some cooperation from the learner. The learner these days comes to school with a vast reservoir of vicarious experiences and loosely related facts; he wants to use all his senses in his learning as an active agent in the process of discovery; he knows that all the answers aren't in. The new learner is the result of the new media, says McLuhan. And a new learner calls for a new kind of learning.

Leo Irrera said, "If God had anticipated the eventual structure of the school system, surely he would have shaped man differently." Kids are being tailored to fit the Procrustean forms of schedules, classrooms, memorizing, testing, etc., which are frequently relics from an obsolete approach to learning. It is the total environment which contains the philosophy of education, not the title page in the school catalogue. And it is the total environment which is invincible because it is invisible to most people. They tend to move things around within the old boxes or to build new and cleaner boxes. They should be asking whether or not there should be a box in the first place.

The new learner, who is the product of the all-at-once electronic environment, often feels out of it in a linear, one-thing-at-a-time school environment. The total environment is now the great teacher; the student has competence models against which to measure the effectiveness of his teachers. Nuclear students in linear schools make for some tense times in education. Students with well developed interests in science, the arts and humanities, or current events need assistance to suit their pace, not that of the state syllabus. The straight line theory of development and the uniformity of performance which it so frequently encourages just don't fit many needs of the new learner. Interestingly, the one thing which most of the current educational innovations share is their break with linear or print-oriented patterns: team teaching, nongraded schools, audio-lingual language training, multi-media learning situations, seminars, student research at all levels of education, individualized learning, and the whole shift of responsibility for learning from the teacher to the student. Needless to say, these are not as widespread as they should be, nor were they brought about through any conscious attention to the premises put forward by McLuhan. Like the print-oriented and linear mentality they now modify, these premises were plagiarized from the atmosphere. McLuhan's value is in the power he gives us to predict and control these changes.

There is too much stuff to learn today. McLuhan calls it an age of "information overload." And the information levels outside the classroom are now higher than those in the classroom. Schools used to have a virtual monopoly on information; now they are part-time competitors in the electronic informational surround. And all human knowledge is expanding at computer speed.

Every choice involves a rejection. If we can't do everything, what priorities will govern our educational policies? "The medium is the message" may not be bad for openers. We can no longer teach kids all about a subject; we can teach them what a subject is all about. We have to introduce them to the form, structure, gestalt, grammar, and process of the knowledge involved. What does a math man do when a math man does do math? This approach to the formal element of a discipline can provide a channel of communication between specialists. Its focus is not on content or detail but on the postulates, ground rules, frames of reference, and premises of each discipline. It stresses the modes of cognition and perception proper to each field. Most failures in communication are based on disagreement about items which are only corollaries of a larger thesis. It happens between disciplines, individuals, media, and cultures.

The arts play a new role in education because they are explorations in perception. Formerly conceived as a curricular luxury item, they now become a dynamic way of tuning up the sensorium and of providing fresh ways of looking at familiar things. When exploration and discovery become the themes, the old lines between art and science begin to fade. We have to guide students to becoming their own data processors to operate through pattern recognition. The media themselves serve as both aids to learning and as proper objects of study in this search for an all-media literacy. Current interest in film criticism will expand to include all art and communication forms.

And since the knowledge explosion has blown out the walls between subjects, there will be a continued move toward interdisciplinary swapping and understanding. Many of the categorical walls between things are artifacts left over from the packaging days of print. The specialist's life will be even lonelier as we move further from the Gutenberg era. The trends are all toward wholeness and convergence.

These things aren't true just because Marshall McLuhan says they are. They work. They explain problems in education that nobody else is laying a glove on. When presented clearly and with all the necessary examples and footnotes added, they have proven to be a liberating force for hundreds of teachers who were living through the tension of this cultural fission without realizing that the causes for the tension lay outside themselves. McLuhan's relevance for education demands the work of teams of simultaneous translators and researchers who can both shape and substantiate the insights which are scattered through his work. McLuhan didn't invent electricity or put kids in front of TV sets; he is merely trying to describe what's happening out there so that it can be dealt with intelligently. When someone warns you of an oncoming truck, it's frightfully impolite to accuse him of driving the thing. McLuhan can help kids to learn stuff better.

11

Technology will have an impact. We can wait for to-morrow, but our children cannot. Some of us are al-ready deeply involved. Our experimental classrooms already reflect tomorrow. Others will follow, some soon, some later. The change is inevitable.

                                    J. W. BECKER

James W. Becker
IT CAN'T REPLACE THE TEACHER—YET

It would be quite easy to offer some optimistic arguments about what education and the blending of technology will produce by, say, 1970 or 1980. One could start with the notion that computer-assisted instruction (properly and educationally initialed CAI) will replace teachers and solve most of our educational problems. That such a pursuit has become a popular pastime can be best demonstrated by reviewing some of the current professional literature. But—panaceas do not work. Yes, the new technology has discovered that education is big and a rapidly changing business; no, the impact of technology on education will not be as rapid as many people suppose.

Change in education is more apt to be evolutionary than revolutionary because:

—Technology is in competition with the role of the teacher.

—Education and technology promise more than they deliver today.

—The majority of existing educational institutions have been designed for stability of operation and not for rapid adaptation and change.

—The commitment in dollars required to accelerate the pace of change appears to be more than we are willing to pay.

From James W. Becker, "It Can't Replace the Teacher—Yet," *Phi Delta Kappan*, January, 1967, pp. 237–239. Reprinted by permission of *Phi Delta Kappan*.

For these reasons, most of the schools of 1970 through 1980 will still look much like they do today.

Competition with the Teacher

The prophets of the new technology in education promise a revolution in the teaching-learning process. The same marvels of efficiency and speed which automation has brought to industry and business operations can, they say, be translated into the educational enterprise. The computer, the teaching machine, the talking typewriter, video tape, closed-circuit television, and goodness knows what other marvels will finally bring the schools into the bright light of the mid-twentieth century. Perhaps they will, but my guess is that they will not do so until some way is found to deal realistically with a seemingly impenetrable element—two million teachers.

There has been some technology for a long time, and those of us with some long memory in education can remember when the prophets promised that radio would revolutionize the classroom. It did not. And the reason it did not is the same as the reason why movies and television have not.

What the prophet of the new technology has always missed, it seems, is that the teacher is a captive of an administrative and instructional strategy which depends upon him to enact the role of dispenser of information. He perceives himself to be, because in fact he is, the controller of the learning process and the primary input mechanism for each of the learners who sit before him. To such a teacher who has these well-founded perceptions of himself and who, more importantly internalizes the "rightness" of the role he performs, any machine can be, and usually is, a threat. Can the disembodied voice in the language lab speak French more fluently than he? Well, if it can, who needs it? Does the teaching machine have more patience than he? Who needs it? Can the computer assist instruction more tirelessly than he? Who needs so "human" a machine? Technology is a threat because technology is in conflict with the fondest perceptions of self and the most fiercely determined aspirations of the human teacher. The teacher brings warmth and understanding and love. He brings patience in the right amount and an accent that is good, if not perfect. He brings efficiency, which though not perfect is suffused with the warmth of the human relationship.

The teacher worries about the technology, and he should. The technology is in conflict with him, and all of the assurances of the neatly dressed, bright boys from IBM will not reassure him.

Education needs the technology, as it does anything that can make teachers function better and learners learn better. There is only one way out of the bind. As long as the teacher retains the primary role as dispenser of information, or, in fancier terms, as long as the instructional strategist maintains the teacher role as information giver, the technology must be a threat. Adaptation by the schools to the new technology will be slow. Some observers may argue that the new technology is so dramatic and effective that it will somehow override the reluctance of teachers to accept it. But this does not give adequate weight to the calculated "no-power" of a determined opposition.

The point is that a new instructional strategy has to be involved which, in Paul Mort's old phrase, makes "the teacher an observer and guide." If the teacher can become an organizer of a system for instruction, a diagnoser of learning problems, a prescriber of instructional remedies, a coordinator of educational "helps to the learner," then there is a chance that the teacher will become the most eager of receptors to the blandishments of the marketeers of the educational technology. Such is the hope and challenge.

More Promise Than Delivery

A case in point is the computer, an exciting but "threatening" new technology. Unlike any previous invention, the computer not only holds the promise for fulfilling the dream that each learner can receive individualized materials of instruction, but it also has the capability of becoming an observer and guide, as well as a dispenser of information.

One use of the computer, computer-assisted instruction, represents an excellent example of more promise than delivery. A realistic appraisal of CAI would tend to indicate the following:

—Computer-assisted instruction currently utilizes hardware that is a synthesis of the digital scientific computer, the data processing or business computer, the process control computer, and the communication control computer. At the present time the synthesis of these four approaches demands a software package which is greater than the sum of its four parts. To date this software capability has not been developed.

—The author languages necessary for writing instructional materials to be used in the computers are too inflexible. To date a flexible language has not been developed.

—Too few CAI experimental studies are under way. The half-dozen exciting studies currently being conducted are encountering many difficulties with both the hardware and the software. For example, the audio capability of CAI is still fraught with problems.

—The research dealing with learning theories and the behavior of the learner is quite primitive. Too little is known about the potential effects of CAI on the learner.

—The bulk of the instructional materials being used for CAI experiments are no better and often not as good as existing workbooks.

—Curriculum makers have not developed the ability to state learning in terms of specific behavior or outcomes.

—The technologists (including our large companies) have not provided much help in evolving a new systems approach to instruction in which the teacher is the manager of the system.

Existing Educational Institutions

The majority of our educational institutions have been structured for stability of operation and not for rapid adaptation and change. Typically, this has resulted in the classic time gap of 35 to 50 years between the invention and mass adoption of a new educational practice.

For more than 200 years our schools operated on the theory that a local school system ought to make its own curriculum. A leading educational argument for local home rule has always been that children differed in different places, and that local educational authorities could study local needs and prescribe what was best locally. In less than a decade the argument for stability of operation and local control has been seriously challenged by a number of intervening forces, some of which include: the reorganization of school districts, the federal government, the merger of publishing houses and electronic firms, the National Science Foundation, research and development centers, and the latest creation— a national network of 20 regional educational laboratories.

What the total and combined effects of the intervening forces will be is still untested. The National Science Foundation, one of the older of the new institutions, has had considerable experience in promoting an increase in the adoption of new educational ideas. Some NSF curricula, created by combinations of scholars and teachers, have been widely adopted. It must be remembered, however, that teachers have always been ready to buy new instructional aids which posed no threat to them —papers, magazines, exercise books, textbooks, and the like. Compare the above readiness to their reluctance to use the radio, television, video tape, programmed learning, and some of the more threatening media. No clear-cut answers are emerging.

The Money Commitment

Superintendents who operate the public schools are caught in the position of deciding what alternatives to select when they make decisions about the new education and technology. Should they develop a minimum educational program for all children? Should they begin "innovative" programs without being concerned about a minimal program? Or should they elect to follow a revolutionary process and change the whole structure of education? Any decision will cost money.

An inescapable truism is that it will take a heavy dollar commitment to accelerate the pace of change. The facts about money are:

—The tax rates in many communities are quite high. New state and federal funds must be found to increase the local base of funds.

—Superintendents are confronted with restrictive money from both state and federal sources. How does the superintendent operate programs started under these funds if funding is later withdrawn? What programs does he delete?

—Generally, salaries account for 75 percent of the total school budget. In some cities the figure is close to 90 percent. Where does the superintendent get the necessary money for massive program reform?

—The average instructional expenditure per pupil attending the average school in America is approximately 45 cents per hour. The average estimated cost of computer-assisted instruction per pupil per hour is $1.50. How will the initial difference in cost be met? How can the costs of education be reduced and still meet the challenge of providing individualized instruction?

These are but a few of the facts that superintendents face when planning for new programs.

The Challenge

Humanizing individuals is what education is about. For the first time man has the capacity of using technology to achieve this end. Within our grasp is the individualization of instruction for the learner, thus making it possible to achieve maximum opportunity for all of the learners in our schools. It can be done, and at a much faster rate, if teachers can be brought to see and accept the revolutionary aspects of a new and exciting role, if the gap between promise and delivery is closed, if existing institutions begin to cooperate with intervening forces, and if they are willing to commit more dollars to the cause.

Yes, technology will have an impact. We can wait for tomorrow but our children cannot. Some of us are already deeply involved. Our experimental classrooms already reflect tomorrow. Others will follow, some soon, some later. The change is inevitable.

THE OPERATIONAL DIMENSION

Across the nation within an infinite variety of field settings, educational change is being effected. This is the professional domain "where-the-action-is." Where once scholars pontificated upon the "cultural lag" within the educational arena they now proclaim the striking rapidity of change. This, then, is the hallmark of modern public education—this accelerated pace of change has been characteristic of schooling processes for over a decade. Noteworthy in the urban fringes, change, slower but perhaps more dramatic by contrast, is also being effected in urban cores and in rural settings. Multiethnic curricular materials, for example, are gradually replacing less representative selections in most cities.

The market place is also the scene of increasing teacher and, currently, student militancy. In the Hegelian sense where there is no conflict, there is no progress. And it does appear that learning environments and teaching conditions are improving. Perhaps militancy and its concomitant short-circuiting of bureaucratic niceties does enhance the pace of change. But as each new instant revolt is calmed, the persisting enigmas remain: How do we teach? How do we learn? Are there coincidental relationships? The search for solutions is relentless.

The elementary schools frequently provide seedbeds for tryouts in curricular reform, grouping techniques, and staffing patterns. These changes, often described as "innovative," frequently prompt similar modifications in secondary and, occasionally, in higher education programing. American schoolmen are busy people, often *too* busy. They frequently adopt or adapt the inventiveness of a neighbor because the strange politics of educational change insist that such behavior is somehow appropriate. Schoolmen are charged with being aggressively task oriented, too busy, as Edna Millay suggests, rushing "from mass to market and have not time to think." Perhaps many schoolmen are less inclined to act from the imagination to include and the courage to exclude. But not all such changes are desired; not all are defensible; and not all are destined for universality. Some trends seem vital and viable. The following selections are somewhat representative of changing operational climates within the nation's elementary and secondary schools. The prognosis for continuous change appears quite positive.

1

Every revolution was first a thought in one man's mind, and when the same thought occurs to another man, it is the key to that era. Every reform was once a private opinion, and when it shall be a private opinion once again, it will solve the problems of the age.

RALPH WALDO EMERSON

Dwight W. Allen

INNOVATIONS IN ELEMENTARY AND SECONDARY EDUCATION

If we were to have a national suggestion box labeled "elementary and secondary education," the chances are that it would be filled to overflowing. Some of the ideas finding their way into the box would be old proposals cast in a slightly new light. Others would be fresh and unique. Many would be trivial, some important. Some would support each other. Still others might be in conflict. The suggestion box symbolizes our dedication to innovation, a distinctly American characteristic for accepting new ideas from wherever they may come.

The Process of Innovation

Innovation in education is not a one-step process with a termination point. It is a continuous evolutionary process of identifying alternatives, examining and testing them, and making alternatives into new forms.

The range of alternatives to be considered for improving education is wider today than ever—"new" proposals abound. Of greater significance are the methods used for assessing their worth.

Three kinds of educational innovations may be identified:

1. *Those consisting of genuinely new ideas and approaches to existing problems.* A new perspective often presents new alternatives. Limitations are often no more than a lack of imagination. For example, it is assumed that students should be under constant supervision while they are at school; yet when school is dismissed they often are on their own for several hours, particularly as they reach high school age. New proposals for individual study suggest that students should be given the

From Dwight W. Allen, "Innovations in Elementary and Secondary Education," *Contemporary Issues in American Education* (U.S. Office of Education *Bulletin* 1966, No. 3). Reprinted by permission of the author.

opportunity to demonstrate their ability to accept increased responsibility as one of the major goals of learning.

2. *Those made up of new technologies which offer possibilities heretofore not feasible.* One example is the use of computers to give us new information on which to base more sophisticated decisions.

3. *Those arising from new needs and demands on the educational system* due to social change, merging scholarly insights, cultural invention, altered perspective on scientific and technological developments. No longer, for example, can we prepare students for jobs and responsibilities that are clearly understood, well defined, and stable. Nor can we assume that many people will spend all or most of their lifetimes in the same place.

Educationally innovative efforts today are too often isolated and fragmented. We need comprehensive frameworks within which they can be studied.

How can we examine the context of innovation? How can responsible educators and educational policy makers make valid decisions regarding individual innovations and systems of innovation? We must begin with the goals of education and examine proposed curriculum changes, new processes and alternative structures for the probable effects on these goals. The goals, themselves, must be subjected to scrutiny for they may have unintended results. For example, an increased emphasis on science and mathematics as a worthwhile educational goal may have unanticipated results in weakening the humanities curriculum unless the structure of education is changed to accommodate the new curriculum goals.

We will attempt to identify some of the elements in the uneasy balance of expedients that characterizes the current educational program. Not enough is known to propose solutions. Examining alternatives is therefore much more important. It is hoped that the following issues will provide a substantial basis for discussion.

New Goals

Significant new goals for elementary and secondary education are emerging in this decade. For example: higher education for a greater proportion of the population; occupational choices in the national as well as in the individual interest; and commitment to an international community.

In the past, the goals of education have too often been stated as pious hopes and in vague generalities. In the past, goals have been like New Year's resolutions. This is no longer adequate. We are beginning to learn that goals must be tied specifically and realistically to what students shall be expected to think, to feel, and to do.

National Curriculums

Should the curriculum be locally or nationally determined? This debate often blocks any innovation at either level. Some skills, for example, in reading, writing, arithmetic, and social studies have long been common to almost all school programs in the United States. Other aspects of the curriculum belong uniquely to a local situation. For example, a school district near a mountain wildlife refuge may conduct an open-air laboratory, using the unique local resources to study ecology, provide the stimulus for creative writing activities, or engage in the study of geological formations. To deny an individual school district the right to develop its unique aspect of the curriculum would be as foolish as to deny the nation the right to be served by those agencies which are alone powerful enough to cope with national problems. The argument should shift to one of which parts of the curriculum can better be developed on a national scale, and which at a state and local level.

For some subjects a properly devised national curriculum could provide a program flexible enough to meet the educational needs of a wide variety of students. Because of a concentration of effort, these national curricula can be more effective than most locally devised programs. Local programs lack resources to build the individualized programs they seek to provide. It is unrealistic to think that a group of teachers, however dedicated and competent, spurred on by curriculum consultants, can, at a series of meetings at four in the afternoon, devise a curriculum as powerful as a national effort on which specialists in learning theory, academicians, teachers, administrators, professors of educational methodology, and others, as well as the most competent teachers, are available to spend years of concentrated study.

Instructional Systems

In early times the teacher was the instructional system. With the invention of the motion picture projector, teachers, it was predicted, would be turned into little more than projector operators. These dire predictions of the obsolescence of the teacher, never realized, continue apace as new technologies roll off the assembly lines: programmed learning, video tape, and computer-based learning systems. Partisan enthusiasts (not necessarily those developing the technology) foretell the day when the teacher will be replaced by a machine. Any teacher who can be replaced by a machine should be.

The teacher does not perform a single function called "teaching," rather he is in turn: lecturer, counselor, evaluator, questioner, stimulator, encourager, coach, listener, arbitrator, friend, critic, interpreter, helper, and judge among others. No teacher can perform each of these functions equally well. Some may be better performed by the new technologies. The organization of learning as we now know it places undue emphasis on certain of these tasks at the expense of others. It is unlikely that each of these tasks should occupy the same time or that they are equally significant. Nevertheless, we are unable to agree on their relative importance or to determine the balance required for each student. The availability of machines only highlights the long present need for the development of more precise instructional systems. The problem is to render unto the machine those things which are the machine's, and to direct to the teacher those that are truly human.

Personnel Considerations

Education is the concern of the entire society; education is not confined to formal institutions. Personnel of quality are in short supply in all segments of society's endeavors. How important it is to use the competences of all to the best advantage.

Society recognizes that the home is where the child gets his initial education. It is from this base of initial family training that all formal education proceeds. New proposals for an earlier beginning point for formal education for some children underline the importance of this initial education.

This is but one way in which education becomes the direct responsibility of the community at large. This responsibility continues throughout the fabric of community life. Industries train their workers to perform specific tasks. Mass media seek to cultivate audiences both shaping and reflecting educational values. As our society becomes more complex, there is need for higher levels of education in both the formal and informal structures. There is also need for more coordination between formal and informal education. More precise definitions are needed. Parents need to know what schools are teaching, and schools need to know the assumptions they can make. As instructional systems become more comprehensive, general policy makers will have less ability to monitor the specific instructional procedures; new criteria for evaluation will need to be developed, and new bases for collaboration worked out.

The most competent teachers should be called upon to perform only responsibilities at the highest level. Tasks that can be performed with a lower level of training and competence should be assigned to other staff members. The tacit assumption has been made in the past that all teachers are interchangeable parts.

Once a concept of teacher specialization is introduced, a number of alternatives become available. The beginning teacher is not required to assume full professional responsibilities immediately upon completion of formal training. At present, the beginning teacher frequently gets the most difficult and complicated assignment and the most difficult students to teach. Teachers tend to promote themselves away from responsibilities for difficult teaching situations as they gain staff seniority. If levels of responsibility could be identified so that senior teachers would have genuinely different tasks to perform, this trend might be reversed.

Team teaching and cooperative teaching offer alternatives which create interesting challenges for senior teachers and provide for systematic assistance from less highly trained members of the instructional staff. We can no longer afford the meaningless luxury of having highly trained personnel performing tasks irrelevant to their training at the expense of having less competent personnel performing tasks requiring the highest level of skill.

The Sequence of Educational Offerings

Focusing attention on the individual progress of the child is important, yet organizing students by arbitrary grade level destroys many opportunities to deal with the unique combination of skills and accomplishments of any one individual. A non-graded approach overcomes much of this difficulty. No completely non-graded programs have yet been established at either elementary or secondary level, due partially at least to the difficulty in identifying concepts which must be taught sequentially as compared with those which are independent of other experiences.

Assumptions about sequence are not always valid. Physics is a 12th-grade course not because it depends upon 11th-grade science concepts, but only because 11th-grade mathematics is used in the problem sets which accompany physics. Some topics in physics obviously depend upon relatively advanced mathematical notions; most elementary topics do not. Geometry, traditionally a 10th-grade high school subject, has been successfully taught at various elementary levels. Questions of sequence are still relevant; just because you *can* offer a subject earlier or later in the curriculum sequence for any or all students does not mean you *should*. Some blurring of sequences has already taken place. Algebra is offered at an earlier age; reading is now commonly taught in the senior high school.

Sequence within subjects is inconsistent. Our goals almost always talk of "building and maintaining" skills in the various subjects. Yet, especially at the high school level, we often have a "stop-and-go" curriculum. In mathematics, for example, non-college students rarely study any mathematics after the ninth grade. There is no *educational* reason for this lapse; but present *organizational* alternatives demand that a subject be taught five hours per week or not at all. If curriculum sequences are be be more educationally valid, students must have the opportunity to study in each major curriculum area each year, though for substantially differing times and in differing arrangements, depending upon their interests and abilities.

Individual Student Attention

Individual attention diminishes through the elementary grades, reaches a low point during senior high school and college undergraduate years, and comes back to a level approximating the kindergarten degree of attention when a candidate reaches the final work for his doctorate. The assumptions which underlie this policy call for identification of the appropriate advisory relationship for teachers. These should be based upon educational considerations rather than organizational or administrative *de facto* relationships.

Time

In the early development of education in our country the assumption was appropriately made that *more* education was needed. Yet *more*, in and of itself, is an inadequate basis for making intelligent decisions regarding educational offerings.

New conceptions of time are challenging the long established assumptions which have permeated elementary and secondary education. We now tend to organize school programs into rather arbitrary segments such as the school year, semester, course, and period. Too often we begin with units of time and then turn our attention to what will be placed within those units. It is appropriate to ask whether any such arbitrary time units should be identified at all. We should also ask whether all content at all levels should be taught to all pupils within a rigid, hardened time framework. Time can be easily adjusted to purposes if we think of it as a variable resource instead of a preordained absolute.

Other time facets should also be considered. The optimum length for a school day and a school year needs analysis. Different standards of open and closed campuses and set school hours could be developed. Schools might be opened for longer periods of time, but students, depending upon their experience, might not be required to come and go at set times.

Flexible Scheduling

To avoid limits on the curriculum because of time restrictions, new organizational concepts are being tried. Flexible scheduling has received considerable attention. It allows for different combinations of teachers and students, provides for new dimensions in the development of individualized instruction, and encourages different levels of student responsibility in independent study. Greater variation in class size and period length is made possible. Instruction in large groups can be presented as appropriate; small groups of students can gather with a teacher for discussion; and individual students can practice or pursue ideas on their own with teachers available to help when needed. Length of class time, class size, sequence of studies, and the organization of instruction can differ for each subject and for each student. The impact of flexible scheduling has been primarily at the secondary level. Elementary schools are currently examining flexible scheduling alternatives: scheduling resource centers, instituting individual study time, and developing cooperative staff arrangements.

Self-Contained School Day

Our objective is to create a school day which provides a variety of learning experiences for pupils, contact with a wealth of ideas and materials, and a significant amount of personal encouragement from the teachers. By eliminating the assumption that homework is a necessary and desirable part of the educational system, thereby bringing individual work within the context of the school day, a closer monitoring of learning becomes possible. The discouragement of learning something wrong and having to relearn it can be avoided, and socioeconomic differences which make it more difficult for certain groups of students to accomplish homework become less important. Students are no longer left to their own resources to understand a hastily explained assignment. Teachers are no longer limited to assigning individual work that requires only those resources which can be counted upon to be available at home. Perhaps the establishment of resource centers for individual and independent study at school and the provision of time within the school day for their use will eliminate homework entirely as an obsolete educational notion.

Facilities

Facilities are an integral part of present innovations. Issues here are permanence, adaptability, and aesthetics. The goal is maximum adaptability of facilities with minimum financial outlay. Often a combination of highly specialized facilities will provide for more educational adaptability than will multi-use facilities. Facility limitations discourage innovation. Current innovations call for facilities for individual study, teacher offices, open laboratories, and sites for different kinds of student research. Planning is also necessary so that facilities may serve diverse community activities, summer school, adult education, and extended school days. Since programs will continue to change, we should plan facilities which will not freeze current programs in concrete and mortar.

Schools need to be planned which will accommodate new technologies. The role of programmed learning is not yet determined. In some instances, programmed learning has assumed the full burden of instruction in given course materials; in other instances it has been used to supplement teaching; and it has also been used as a remedial device. Similar experiments with computer-based learning will come soon.

Finance

The sources and amounts of financial support for the schools is not a concern for this panel. Of importance here is the expenditure of available resources. The emphasis has long been on annual "per pupil cost," how much money it costs to keep one pupil in school for one year. The description of a "learning unit cost" would be more educationally relevant. A "learning unit" would be defined in terms of *specific perfor-mance*. For example, "level one in reading" would include a specified level of performance in reading skills such as vocabulary recognition, reading speed, and comprehension. Research would indicate the finan-cial resources needed to obtain that level of performance for students of different ability levels and educational experience. This cost would vary with alternative technological devices and under different instruc-tional situations. Learning units would be independent of time. Some districts would elect to concentrate "level one in reading" into 15 months of instruction; other districts, perhaps with different circum-stances, might elect to take double that time for most students. The time would also differ widely for individual students within each situation. The advantage of thinking of "learning unit cost" rather than annual "per pupil cost" is that it focuses on the level of learning, not the main-tenance of children in school. Communities can make conscious deci-sions about the intensity of learning units they wish to support. This will provide a more direct basis for evaluation of needed financial equal-ization as a district can point to experience with student and community factors influencing comparative "learning unit cost."

Conclusions

Innovation in elementary and secondary education is not the property of any one group. School systems must have the freedom to innovate. State departments of education must develop legal and oper-ational structures which encourage alternatives. Legislative bodies must make funds available for research and experimentation. Com-munities must place more premium on exploration of new ideas and procedures. Teachers, administrators, educational innovators at all levels must be given the right to be wrong.

The following structure is suggested for discussion:

1. *Advanced research centers.* These centers would be analogous to the advanced research centers of a number of industrial complexes where study is not limited to the immediate practicability of ideas. Re-search staff would have a free run to investigate new ideas. Such re-search facilities need not be exclusively "laboratory oriented" but would include experimental schools providing real student and teacher populations available for the testing of innovations.

2. *Experimental application centers.* Innovative programs could be tested. Curriculum areas, school organization, staff use, time variables,

administrative structures and other wide-ranging studies would be appropriate for such experimental investigations. These activities would be supported as specific areas of inquiry, but without consideration of practical restraints or economic considerations. The difference between the experimental application laboratories and the advanced research laboratories would be that the advanced research laboratories would not limit their staff to particular areas of inquiry whereas the experimental application laboratories would have a specific focus.

3. *Developmental centers.* These groups would be responsible for taking procedures and programs from the experimental centers and making economic determinations of feasibility, considering the training of staff for their use, and developing models of implementation.

4. *Dissemination centers.* Dissemination facilities would systematically provide for familiarization and adoption of innovation on a widespread basis.

Our part in the course of educational innovation offers exciting possibilities for responsible action. The contribution of each citizen is necessary if we are to continue in a democratic environment where freedom to grow is a major value. We are a part of the changing times, and we must learn to live with it, to direct it, and to gain from it. America has pioneered frontiers in mass education that have contributed substantially to the growth and maturation of our democracy. The emphasis has been on the education of all the children of all the people. But even as the physical frontiers have pushed into new dimensions, our educational frontier must be raised to an ever higher base of quality in education. The search for quality will demand approaches, techniques and systems as different from the tools of mass education as the ether of space differs from the rails of iron that bound together a new Nation.

2

*Nongradedness takes it place among the other promis-
ing components of what I like to call "the innovative
package," team teaching, flexible space, and hierarchies of teaching personnel backed up by mechanical
and electronic instructional systems and devices.
This mosaic of mutually reinforcing concepts and
arrangements has demonstrated greater potential
potency for individualizing instruction than any
other design conceived so far.*

CALVIN GROSS

B. Frank Brown
THE GRADE DILEMMA

The most serious of the many problems confronting education
today is what to do about the grade. The dilemma is a formidable one.
The grade has become anthropologized, historized, psychologized, and
polarized into the process of learning. The graded organization is like
an ice tray guaranteed to freeze into rigidity everything that is put into
it. Iconoclasts have condemned it as "a cage for every age."

Origins of the Grading System

The idea of classifying students into grades on the basis of age,
with each grade aimed at a particular age level, is almost literally medieval. It was first conceived by John Sturum, who gave general currency
to this organizational plan by establishing the first graded school in
Strassburg, Germany, in 1537.

The derivation of the word "grade" underscores the antiquity of the
concept. When Sturum first began to group by age, he seated all of the
boys of the same age on a bench together. This bench, which had no
back, was called a "form." The bench, or form, nearest the teacher
contained the first grade, the next one the second grade, and so on. From
this beginning the word "form" later came to mean class or grade in
school. "Form" is still used to denote the division of classes in England
and in many private schools in the United States.

Credit, or discredit, for introducing Sturum's graded school plan to
the American school system must go to John Philbrick of Boston, who
worked out the details for initiating this innovation in America in 1847.
Under Philbrick's direction, the Quincy Grammar School of Boston

From B. Frank Brown, "The Grade Dilemma," *The Nongraded High School* (Englewood
Cliffs, N.J.: Prentice-Hall, 1963), pp. 27–30, 32–33, 37–40. © 1963 by Prentice-Hall, Inc.
Reprinted by permission of the publishers.

formally opened its doors in 1848, becoming the first completely graded school in the United States, with each grade directed at one age level. Much of the success of Philbrick's project was due to the warm and enthusiastic support given by Horace Mann, then Secretary of the State Board of Education for Massachusetts. Just prior to the opening of Philbrick's graded school, Mann had visited Europe and had been impressed with the idea of grouping children by age, which was the common practice in the schools of Prussia.

The Quincy School admitted its first pupils in 1848, and by 1870 American education, which had begun as a flexible enterprise, was lockstepped to the grade. As one observer put it, the schools had moved "from no system to nothing but system." A succinct description of America's first graded school was printed recently in a brochure of the Educational Facilities Laboratories of the Ford Foundation:

> In 1847 the epochal Quincy School was built in Boston. For a century to come it set the design of American schools. It sorted the children into grades, and every grade had its own private meeting place—a classroom—where a teacher and fifty-five children of about the same age sat together for a solid year. This schoolhouse consisted of twelve rooms, each the same as the next, four to a floor piled one atop the other for three floors.
>
> For a hundred years after 1847, the pattern of separate and equal boxes set by the Quincy School remained essentially unbroken.

The Quincy system of a grade for every age level served well in the epoch of rigid Prussian-type education. It was appropriate to the needs of nineteenth- and early twentieth-century America. It simply is not relevant to the conditions of missileology, the hydrogen bomb, and a moving frontier of knowledge.

The Antiquated Conventional Curriculum

The essence of the matter is that the conventional curriculum structure has been inherited from the past, even the remote past, and it corresponds far more closely to the needs and opportunities of former generations than to those of our own. In America we have the peculiar notion that a thing is good merely because we have been doing it a long time; but a school program several centuries old is woefully inappropriate.

In the years since the grade was introduced, the inadequacy of chronological-age education has grown increasingly apparent. The demand has steadily risen for more attention to intellectual needs than is possible in age grouping. This demand, which shows a far more enlightened attitude toward education, has encouraged the innovation of intellectual rather than chronological grouping.

The harsh inflexibility of the old graded school was fittingly described by one of its early critics as resembling "A Procrustean Bed." Procrustes, it will be remembered, was a legendary highwayman who tied his victims to an iron bed. If they did not fit the bed, he either stretched their legs or cut them off to adapt them to its length. This comparison is apt. The grade endeavors to restrain or stretch the intellect as the student surpasses or fails to measure up to its arbitrary standards.

The dilemma of the grade may be compared to the history of bridges in New England. When the early settlers began to conquer the wilderness, one of the first things they did was build bridges across the streams. Snow fell on these bridges and they often collapsed under the weight of deep snow. The settlers then put sloping roofs on their bridges to protect them from heavy loads of snow. Unfortunately, sleighs could not cross on the snowless boards of the covered bridges. The settlers reacted by employing men to shovel snow onto the bridges following a snowstorm. This practice continued through the years and one New England county recently discovered that it was paying a man twenty-five dollars to shovel snow onto a bridge which the snowplow came along and promptly cleared.

This is the same sort of obsolescence we have built into the curriculum with the grade. Schools are attempting to adapt curriculum innovations to an educational structure that is centuries old. The good people of New England have solved their covered bridge problem, but the grade remains an entrenched anachronism.

A New Plan Is Needed

A central theme in the exciting Rockefeller Report on education is the search for a new educational organization designed to meet the needs of talented and creative individuals. Questions raised by the Rockefeller study are highly pertinent to the problem of the grade as an organization for schools.

The relevant questions then become: What organizational patterns and practices may be devised that are least destructive of individual initiative and autonomy? How is it that with all the intricacy of social mechanism, a good many astonishingly free, flexible, creative, and independent individuals exist—some of them in the very heart of the great bureaucracies? How may we best prepare our young people to keep their individuality, initiative, creativity in a highly organized, intricately meshed society? How may we rescue talented individuals from the lowered aspirations, the boredom, and habits of mediocrity so often induced by life in a large and complex organization: How do we shatter the informal ceilings placed upon performance in an organizational setting in which order, harmony, and predictability seem to be given more emphasis than individual achievement?

When we arrive at questions of this import, we are no longer simply talking about the cultivation of talent. We are talking about some of the gravest issues in the future of our society. A continuing tension between the effectiveness of the group and the creativity of the individual may well be one of the most fateful struggles in our future.

The towering obstacle to the development of students as individuals is the lockstep of grade organization, for the grade places a formal ceiling on learning. It is a citadel of routine, requiring the individual to conform to a fixed pattern of learning. In brief, the grade is a bureaucracy for children. A classic example of this is the psychologically bloodied under-achiever. Problems in dealing with these youngsters raise significant questions: Could confinement to the grade be a primary reason why one-third of our youth never finish high school? The percentage of dropouts has not diminished over the years and the problems of youth are increasing. If the educational system is really good, then why doesn't the dropout rate decrease? The emphasis has been on keeping children in schools; it should shift to getting them out. I am not talking here about sending them to switchblades and the streets, but about moving them along *in school* at a better rate.

The allegation that graded education may be a major contributor to the dropout problem is not new. At the end of the nineteenth century, it was said of German students that one-third went to the devil, one-third broke down, and the remaining third went on to govern Europe. In America, one-third of the students continue to drop out of high school. This group is creating a vast social problem. Changing technology makes it imperative that schools deal more imaginatively and effectively with the potential dropout. There is a vast need to salvage his potential for leadership, creativity, and service.

The Schools and Change

Saddled with graded education, disconsolate school patrons, unhappy with the status quo, frequently pose the question: How can changes be brought about in the schools? This is a leading question and a difficult one to answer. The need to diffuse new ideas and innovative practices is great. To accomplish change in a traditionally oriented enterprise is a tremendously complex problem.

One of the difficulties is that a new instructional program is seldom invented in a local school system. The schools are not able to develop provocative new programs intramurally. This is because individuals who go into school administration must have an abiding love of the status quo. School administrators resist the idea of change in the schools with the same vigor that ministers of the gospel would oppose changing the Sabbath from Sunday to Wednesday.

Change Must Come

Despite these problems, the opportunity which nongraded education offers for a new emphasis upon individual learning is a very real one. We must hope that school administrators will be sufficiently bold and imaginative to meet the challenge of youngsters straining at the academic leash, that they will do a quality job of developing continuous learning in the high schools of tomorrow.

Organization is the keystone of the educational enterprise. The military division of Gaul into three parts for administrative purposes may have been an efficient organization; but the division of secondary education into three or four graded parts has seriously impeded the progress of all high school students. If we are to take the ceiling off learning, the graded school like Gaul, must become a part of ancient history.

3

The nongraded school is defensible only because the the graded school is indefensible.

William P. McLoughlin
THE PHANTOM NONGRADED SCHOOL

Few propositions for educational change have generated and sustained as much interest as the nongraded school. It is discussed at nearly every major educational conference, and symposiums on the nongraded school are increasing in popularity. Furthermore, the body of available literature is increasing rapidly; most leading professional journals have published several articles on this topic. Through these and other means, educators have learned more of the promises of the nongraded school than they have of its accomplishments.

This is understandable, for nongrading appears to be preached more than practiced and practiced more than appraised. In fact, few dependable estimates on the present status and anticipated growth of

From William P. McLoughlin, "The Phantom Nongraded School," *Phi Delta Kappan,* January, 1968, pp. 248–250. Reprinted by permission of *Phi Delta Kappan* and the author.

the nongraded school are currently available and sound studies on its accomplishments are even more difficult to come by. From what is available one would be hard put to determine just how many schools have nongraded their instructional programs and how many are seriously contemplating the change. If findings in these areas are obscure, the outcomes of the evaluations of existing nongraded programs are even less definitive.

The available estimates of the number of schools with nongraded programs fluctuates from 5.5 percent to 30 percent. These, it must be pointed out, are unqualified estimates; they do not consider the quality of the programs purporting to be nongraded. When this element is added, estimates of the number of schools with *truly* nongraded programs shrink considerably. Goodlad, in 1955, estimated that less than one percent of the schools in the country were nongraded and in 1961 he felt there were probably fewer than 125 schools to be found with *truly* nongraded programs.

If uncertainty marks present estimates of the number of schools operating nongraded programs, certainly forecasts for future growth are dubious. In 1958 the NEA reported 26.3 percent of the respondents to its survey saying they intended to nongrade their schools. Five years later, however, this estimate had dwindled to 3.2 percent. On the other hand, the USOE's pollings reverse this trend. Of schools queried in 1958, only 13.4 percent expected to become nongraded, but two years later this estimate doubled and 26.3 percent of the respondents reported considering nongrading their schools. With these conflicting findings it is difficult to know if the nongraded school is coming into its own or passing out of existence.

One thing seems clear from these surveys, however: nongrading is related to district size. Nearly all available surveys confirm this; the larger the district, the more likely it is to have one or more nongraded units. Here we should stress that this does not mean that nongrading is the principal organizational pattern in large school districts. It simply means a nongraded unit is operating in one or more of the district's several elementary schools.

Studies of the influence of nongrading on students are rare, too, and their composite findings somewhat bewildering. Thirty-three empirical studies of the influence of nongrading on student academic achievement have been identified. Not all of these, however, consider the same variables. About half of them assess the influence of nongrading on reading achievement, while 25 percent look at its influence on arithmetic performance. Only 11 percent of the studies question the impact nongrading has on the student's development in language arts. Nine percent report on the total achievement scores of children. The remaining studies are spread so thinly through the other curricular divisions that a detailed consideration of their findings is hardly profitable.

Judged by these studies, the academic development of children probably does not suffer from attending a nongraded school; there is some evidence, admittedly sketchy and tentative, to indicate it may be somewhat enhanced. One thing is certain; children from graded classes seldom do better on these measures than children from nongraded classes. More commonly, children from nongraded classes excell their contemporaries from graded classes.

For example, 15 studies considered the influence of nongrading on the general reading achievement of children. Seven of these report no significant difference between children from graded and nongraded classes. In other words, nothing is lost by having children attend nongraded classes. But only two studies found children from graded classes outscoring children from nongraded classes, while six studies found the general reading attainments of children from nongraded classes superior to that of children in graded classes.

Similar though less distinct outcomes are attained when the reading subskills of comprehension and vocabulary development are examined. Again, the principal finding of 14 studies is that there are no marked differences in the accomplishments of children in these areas regardless of the type of organization in which they learn to read. Furthermore, for every study showing greater gains for children from graded classes, there is an equal number of studies counterbalancing these findings.

The mirror image of this picture emerges when the arithmetic attainments of children from graded and nongraded classes are contrasted. Eleven studies considered the influence of nongrading on children's general arithmetic achievement, and their findings are inconclusive. Three report differences favoring children from nongraded classes, five found differences favoring children from graded classes, and three found no difference.

But when the arithmetic subskills of reasoning and knowledge of fundamentals are examined, different outcomes appear. Of the 12 published studies in these areas, one reports differences favoring children from graded classes but six report differences favoring children from nongraded classes. The remaining five show no real difference in the achievement of children in these areas, regardless of the type of class organization.

In language arts, too, there is scant evidence to demonstrate that organization influences achievement. Seven of the 10 studies in this area report no true differences in the language skills developed by children from graded and nongraded classes. One reports achievement test scores of children from graded classes as superior to those of children from nongraded classes, while two studies found the observed differences in the achievement of children from nongraded classes indeed significantly superior to that of controls in the graded classes. Apparently, nongraded classes are no more effective in developing language arts skills than are graded classes.

Total achievement test scores, too, seem remarkably immune to change because of changes in organizational pattern. Half of the eight studies using them to measure the efficacy of the nongraded school found no significant differences in the achievements of children from graded and nongraded classes. The remaining studies divide equally: Two reported differences favoring children from graded classes while two found differences favoring children from nongraded classes. So here, once again, the influence of nongrading on the academic development of children is indeterminate.

Better student achievement is not the only claim put forth for the nongraded school. Its advocates maintain, implicitly or explicitly, that superior student adjustment is attained in the nongraded school. Certainly student adjustment and personality development are crucial concerns of educators and, quite reasonably, they are interested in developing learning settings which foster this goal.

Unfortunately, studies assessing the influence of nongrading on student adjustment are even more rare than studies assessing its influence on their academic achievement. Moreover, the diversity of procedures utilized in these studies to measure adjustment lessens their cumulative value. Sociograms, adjustment inventories, anxiety scales, and even school attendance records have all been used as indices of pupil adjustment. But no matter how measured, there is scant evidence to support the contention that superior student adjustment is realized in nongraded schools. On the 32 separate indices of adjustment used in these studies, the overwhelming majority, 26, indicate that there is no significant difference in the adjustment of children from graded and nongraded classes. Only four of the measures (general adjustment, social adjustment, social maturity, and freedom from age stereotypes) showed differences favorable to children from nongraded classes, while the remaining two (social participation and freedom from defensiveness) were favorable to children from graded classes.

Research, then, finds little to impel or impede practitioners interested in nongrading. Under either organization children's adjustment and achievement appear to remain remarkably constant. For those to whom the nongraded school is a magnificent obsession, these findings must come as a numbing disappointment. Taken at face value, current research on the nongraded school seems to say that its contribution to the academic, social, and emotional development of children is marginal.

But should these findings be taken at face value? It might be naive to rest the fate of the nongraded school on past research. The validity of these studies should be rigorously tested, for they depend on one tacit but critical assumption: that the experimental schools, those purporting to be nongraded, are *truly* nongraded. If this assumption is not met and the experimental schools are not nongraded, then research has told us nothing about the efficacy of the nongraded school.

Too often, on close inspection, one finds that schools credited with operating nongraded programs are not nongraded at all. Homogeneous grouping and semi-departmentalization of instruction in reading and arithmetic are frequently passed off as nongraded programs. These techniques must be recognized for what they are. They are administrative expediencies developed to make the *graded* school work. They are not nongraded instructional programs.

If these are the "nongraded" programs represented in these studies, then researching their effectiveness is an exercise in futility, for the *experimental* schools are as graded as the control schools and no experimental treatment is being tested. Research has done nothing more than contrast the performances of children from graded schools called graded schools with the performance of children from graded schools called nongraded schools. Essentially, we have simply researched the age-old question: "What's in a name?"

The nongraded school is defensible only because the graded school is indefensible. Its justification flows from its efforts to correct the instructional errors of the graded school. It is reasonably unlikely that any amount of manipulation of the physical arrangements of schools will produce discernible differences in the academic or psycho-social development of children. Every grade label can be cleansed from every classroom door in the school without influencing the school's attainments with children as long as graded instructional practices prevail behind these doors.

Nongrading begins with significant alterations in instructional, not organizational, procedures. As long as schools seek practices designed to group away differences they are *not* nongraded. The nongraded school never held this as a goal, for it is impossible. Rather, nongrading says: "Accept children as they are, with all their differences, and teach to these differences. Don't try to eradicate them!" Until educators develop instructional programs that will meet this challenge they are not nongrading. They are simply masking their old egg-crate schools with a new facade.

4

Even in a palace it is possible to live well.
MARCUS AURELIUS

Fred T. Wilhelms
SCHOOL AS A WAY OF LIFE

There probably isn't a schoolman alive who doesn't enjoy prowling somebody else's schoolhouse. No matter how often one gets to do it, it never gets old, because every school creates a sensation all its own. One day recently as I was strolling through a building, waiting for a program to start, a sudden thought struck me: "This is a place where people *live!* The students live here several years, and some of the teachers and administrators may be here till they retire." Not a particularly novel thought, probably; but it nagged at me till I started asking myself, "Suppose we thought of a school as a place to live when we planned the building or laid out the program. What difference would it make?"

It must make a lot of difference, because some schools feel so much more livable than others do. And it isn't much a matter of the age or fanciness of the building, either. It seems to be more a question of whether people *care* enough to be ingenious. The newer buildings do have an edge, of course. We've been getting away from the dark-tunnel corridors flanked by noisy, steel-blue lockers and floored with brown linoleum. You can't say "blackboard" any more because the architects have been sneaking in some soft pastels. In many buildings a bit of fieldstone or rough brick here or there supplies a touch of texture. And one campus we know used 62 colors in place of institutional gray, at a trifling addition in cost. At least in the library, there may even be a carpet on the floor.

Still, even the new buildings average out more aseptic than homey. The endless walls of bare cinder block—or slick monotone! The *efficient* cafeterias that never dreamed of gracious eating! The rest rooms that were never for the weary! There are exceptions, but the common tone is still *institutional,* and the root of this evil is not money; it is lack of imagination or simply of the wish.

Special facilities do help, of course. Our mind goes back 25 years, to the old Western Hills High School in Cincinnati, where every stair landing or suitable nook framed a cluster of original paintings by some

From Fred T. Wilhelms, "School as a Way of Life," National Association of Secondary School Principals *Spotlight,* No. 77, March–April, 1967, pp. 1–4. Reprinted by permission of the author and NASSP.

local artist. We think of Tamilpais High School in California where, on good days, a barbecue pit is going and the students can buy the makings and broil their own hot dogs and hamburgers. We delight in facilities like the "L" Room at Lakewood High School in Ohio, with its soft music and its furniture indistinguishable from the lounge of the best student unions. Even some little touch, like an informal snack bar open all day, helps so much to create a lived-in feeling that we probably ought to finagle whatever we can into even the oldest building. The imaginative school, with murals in the dining room and a flow of music during the luncheon hour, achieves something basic over the one where the garbage can sits in the middle of the floor and invariably spills over before the last student has scraped his tray into it. With all the free energy we have available in our students, it shouldn't take much but a little thinking with them to beat that.

Time Is More Important Than Space

But physical facilities are not the main thing. Let's let *schedule* stand for a youngster's way of life. In the past few years, two groups have carried out "shadow studies," with each adult following one student through a day to see what his life was like. Each time the result has been a shock reaction so strong that there has been pressure to suppress publication of what they saw. As some teen-agers may still say, "Dullsville!"

A growing number of schools are deciding that the sit-and-listen routine of five classes a day five days a week is neither necessary nor effective. They believe they can get more vigorous learning if they cut the youngsters loose to do more on their own. Sometimes they drop class meetings to two or three or four a week, and they often vary the lengths of periods to suit the jobs to be done.

The minute a school drops the notion that students need to be everlastingly taught-at and supervised—the minute it makes its bet on independent work and self-control—some fascinating side effects appear. For one thing, space opens up. You don't need so many classrooms if you don't hold class all the time. So, even in an old building, there is a chance to "play with" some rooms creatively. One finds that he can have departmental learning resource rooms, if that is what he wants. And there is space and time for art activities or something of that sort. In Detroit, when they cut English classes back to fewer days per week, they developed free-reading rooms managed by para-professionals, with superior results.

More important, *time* opens up. Then a faculty has to make up its mind whether to police this free time just as closely as they do class time—or move to a looser system. Schools differ. Some permit a good deal of movement to various facilities, but keep it on a check-in-and-out "pass" system. Others go further and dispense with the passes. Some compromise and issue "gold passes" that permit the "trusties" to move freely, while others are checked more cautiously and study halls are provided for them. In any case, schools that have opened up time tend to offer their students a variety of places to go and work: the main library, departmental resource rooms, "open" laboratories and activity rooms, etc.

Now there is an added murmur in the air. A few schools are beginning to offer another option which is not a place "to go and work" at all, but rather a place where young people can sit around and chat with their friends—maybe even eat an ice-cream cone. They leave it to the student to decide how and when to get his work done, so long as he does it. Schoolmen in such places argue that this is the way we adults live. They tell you, sometimes a little defensively, that socializing is important in its own right. They do not blink at the fact that some students cause problems as they learn to use freedom constructively. But they argue that— whether in college or on a job—this is a learning young people must master sooner or later—and it had better be sooner. More fundamentally, they claim that the youngsters soon get more work done because they throw more enthusiasm into it.

Most of us are so used to controlled orderliness that such ideas may seem far out. And there *are* enough practical problems so that we had better feel our way along, to see what can be done in each situation. But, judging by the enthusiasm of those who have dared to loosen things up, it may be time to question boldly whether we really need all the institutional neatness we've assumed we do. When adolescents are relied upon, they generally come through better than the adults expected them to.

These are the reflections of one man, who wanders around in a lot of schoolhouses but never stays in one long enough to get so used to it that he thinks it has to be the way it is. He sees the best things that ingenuity and energy have produced here and there and then inevitably wonders whether they couldn't be adapted to fit elsewhere. He may be wrong, and he is practical enough to know that there is often some risk attached to daring ventures that break down old forms and habits. But he has come to feel that most schools need less "institutional" rigidity for both students and faculty. And he has a hunch that a good way to start is to take a thoughtful look at how people *live.* Marcus Aurelius said that, "Even in a palace it is possible to live well"—and it ought to be easier in a schoolhouse.

5

The school is an old, dark, brick, two-story contrap-
tion, a Norman fortress, built as if learning and virtue
need a stronghold, one defended by old-fashioned
weapons, a place of turrets and parapets, with narrow
slits in the bricks through which scholars with cross-
bows can peep out at an atomic world.
                                    JOHN HERSEY

Harold B. Gores
THE BIG CHANGE

Margaret Mead, whose observations of primitive peoples shed light on the habits of the over-developed, has said that in a simple society, where change is slow, the culture can be handed down economically from parent to child, father to son, mother to daughter. The whole bundle of social agreements—what's U, what's non-U, and what's taboo—can be transmitted within the family and tribe without the loss of hardly a speared fish.

But when life gets complicated by the accumulation of more facts and more non-facts, it becomes more economical, and therefore more neces-sary, to assign the transmission of the culture to special people called teachers. Parenthetically I point out that in the Western World this has been going on for quite awhile. Indeed, as recently as 300 A.D., Rabbi Raba came up with a formula for determining class size, a handy device that is even today just as much a part of a principal's professional kit as is how to turn on the public address system. The good Rabbi declared— and knowing old school administrators as I do, undoubtedly issued a bulletin to the effect—that whenever a class exceeded 25 an assistant should be employed, and at 40 it should be split.

Miss Mead goes on to say that when life gets very complicated, when cultural change is exceedingly rapid, having older people called teach-ers teaching younger people called pupils is too sluggish an arrange-ment. In periods of rapid change everybody must learn from everybody else; the young from the old to be sure; but also the old from the young. If I understand Miss Mead correctly, the following is an illustration of the new hazards of teaching.

A generation ago a competent sixth-grade teacher could answer about every question a sixth-grader was likely to ask. How many legs has a grasshopper? What's the capital of Montana? How far away is the moon?

From Harold B. Gores, "The Big Change," a speech, 1962. Reprinted by permission of the author.

Teachers had stored in their heads the encyclopedic facts of life and these were enough to get them through the day without loss of face from "not knowing the answer."

Today no teacher can be sure. There may be lurking in the back of the sixth-grade room an 11-year-old demon who's been watching television or reading the more solemn columns of the newspapers and is ready to pounce with the question, "Teacher, the Russians are going to use solid fuel to get to the moon. Why are we sticking to liquids?"

If the teacher is a normal, well adjusted, educated person, she won't have the slightest idea. She had better ask the kid what *he* thinks and remember what he says.

When the pace of cultural change is rapid, everybody must learn from everybody.

If the individual pupils are learning not alone from the tribe as in primitive times, or from their teachers as in the Judaic-Christian centuries, but from everybody as of now (including their shadows on a tube), what is the meaning for education?

First, let's look at the schoolhouse, the most public of public buildings, the public building more people care about, get angry over, and take up sides about. Look at them, if you can, as though you hadn't spent half of your life in one.

With few exceptions, a schoolhouse is a big box filled with equal-sized little boxes called classrooms. The classrooms are like our kitchens —hard, reflective, reverberative, utilitarian, indestructible, and antiseptic. Their motif is dictated by a municipal desire to frustrate any errant scholar who, unsheathing his jacknife, might try to carve his initials in this ceramic vault the taxpayers have provided for his childhood.

The very architecture sorts the children. It helps the administration to establish groups of uniform size—25 pupils if the community is rich, 35 if it is poor, and 50 if it doesn't care. In each box is placed a teacher who will be all things to all children all day all year. If it be a secondary school, bells will ring to signal the musical chair game that is played a half-dozen times a day as groups exchange boxes. This is known as secondary education.

The interior layout of schools has been this way ever since the Quincy School was built in Boston in 1847 thereby preserving an ice-cube tray arrangement. Incidentally, the Quincy School, well into its second century, was scheduled for abandonment because Boston, which was described as a cemetery with lights, found the Quincy School a detriment to the exciting rebirth of that city.

The new schools being built this year may be only at half-life in the year 2000, when this year's first-graders will be only middle-aged; when one-half of all the people alive on this "one inhabited star" will be Chinese and Russian; when Americans may comprise only 5% of the world's population; and when this nation may bear the same relation to the world's economy that Switzerland does today—a relatively small nation of inventive people who prosper through their inventiveness and industry.

The difficulty is that many boards of education regard the new school as the solution to a present problem; i.e., we have more children than we have seats, therefore a new school, or addition to the old, is needed to provide more seats. Yet a new school, if it is to make any real difference to America, is more than just more seats. The new school, or even the addition to the old, should help solve the problems of the predictable future. Building is not for the purpose of getting yourself out of trouble; it is as much to help keep succeeding generations out of trouble. Therefore, the board which today consents to buildings that are unchangeable, immutable, unresponsive to what the future will confront, is not only wasting present funds and setting a trap for future boards, but is also exhibiting a cultural arrogance that no swift-moving society can afford. The school board that sees itself as the end of the line rather than in the stream of change endangers us all.

It is not surprising therefore that the rearrangement of pupils and teachers is bringing about the rearrangement of school interiors. Literally, the schools are busting out of their boxes. Within a decade it is quite possible that the capacity of a school will not be measured by units called classrooms but by zones of space.

Changes are evident in schools I have seen, and in schools which are, as yet, only lines on paper. In general, these schools are moving toward what business and industry have already embraced—generalized space made special not by precise design, room by room, but made special by the nature of the portable equipment assigned to a particular section of the general space. After all, education is a fluid process, according to John Lyon Reid, eminent school architect, and, like all fluids, tends to take the shape of its container. What such a school can do for children is obvious. But what it can do toward reinvigorating a city is equally important. And it is not entirely inappropriate that a school for children could lead commercial construction toward more humane and esthetic expression.

The swing is away from standard groupism and toward the individual. As learning gradually takes precedence over teaching, and as the individual differences among teachers come to be recognized and capitalized upon, the chambered nautilus schoolhouse, whose interior is as unchangeable as though its partitions were made of calcium, gets in the way. This, then, is the big change.

6

If it were the national intention to empty our cities of parents and children, the city schoolhouse that is a masonry fortress afloat on a sea of blacktop, bounded by a hurricane wire fence with two basketball hoops, is the ideal instrument.

HAROLD B. GORES

William W. Caudill
HOUSING TOMORROW'S EDUCATIONAL PROGRAM

My subject is "Housing Tomorrow's Educational Program." If you ask me it's a pretty superficial title. The word "housing" connotes a covering like that cloth on Smithfield hams. And as Virginians know, it's not the covering that counts—it's the peanuts that do the job. A good school plant is more than an inert covering. It has insides like the ham, and it's the insides that count.

I shall stop this ham analogy before I get myself into trouble. A better comparison is that of the machine to the schoolhouse. And here again, it's not the housing that is important, it is the insides—the works. The schoolhouse is a machine for learning. It helps the teacher teach. And it is the biggest, the most important, and the most expensive teaching machine we have in education. We had better begin to think about the schoolhouse as a machine when we talk about tomorrow's educational program—if we are going to get our money's worth. So, if you don't mind, let me change the title of my speech from what you see on the program to "Designing the Cotton Pick'n Schoolhouse."

This may not be as factious as you think. When I was a kid growing up in Durant, Oklahoma, I did a little cotton pick'n—since we had no tobacco to harvest. I wasn't very good at picking cotton. I remember I picked only nineteen pounds in one day, and that included the big rock I tossed into the sack just before it was weighed. I know how hard it is to pick cotton, consequently I hold in high esteem the modern cotton picking machine. It is designed to do a specific job and it does it well. If you can get yourself a two-row picker, self-propelled, with a 70 H.P. engine, you can go right down two rows simultaneously about two miles an hour and gather about 1600 pounds of seed cotton in no time at all—and I picked all day to get nineteen pounds. It's a wonderful

From William W. Caudill, "Housing Tomorrow's Educational Program," *Summary of Conference on the Schools of the Future,* May, 1962 (Richmond, Va.: Virginia Education Association, 1962), pp. 39–42. Reprinted by permission of the Virginia Education Association and the author.

machine. I can tell you this about that cotton picking machine—it's not worth a darn for threshing wheat. You need another kind of machine. If you want to do a good job of threshing wheat, you should buy yourself a McCormick Combine No. 181 that will give you an eighteen foot cut. Its built-in 80 horses will cover an acre in six minutes. It's quite a machine, but it won't pick cotton.

Now what does all this have to do with schoolhouses? Quite a bit. A few months ago, our firm was commissioned to investigate the cost of *converting* (I use the word advisedly) an old high school building to facilitate a new program. This old ark in Connecticut didn't have a crack in it. No problem there. The only trouble was that this piece of machinery was designed to do one job; now it needed to be converted to do another. It's pretty tough trying to convert a machine designed to thresh wheat into a machine which will pick cotton—our task was no easier. A school plant designed to facilitate a highly departmentalized setup is not readily adapted for a "school within a school" program, superimposed with the Trump 40-20-40 program, as well as with the team teaching. But this is what they wanted to do in Connecticut.

We found that to convert this old machine to do a new job was very costly. By the time we gutted the insides, and brought the heating and lighting up to date, plus completely rearranging inside spaces and creating a few new ones, we could have bought a new school for a third more. Study the anatomy of a schoolhouse and you will find the covering, or housing, if you please, only runs about one-third of the total cost of the building. It's the educational "insides" (or educational machinery), and the light and air that go to make up comfort, that cost money.

If we want quality education, we shall need all the help we can get from the schoolhouse machine. We know now that a good schoolhouse can help the teacher teach; and the only time we get our money's worth is when it does, regardless of the square foot cost. Had school planners known thirty years ago what they know today, they could have saved tax payers millions. Had architects and educators known during the pre-war days what they knew right after World War II, they could have saved tax payers millions more. If we knew today what would happen in education ten years from now, our problems of housing tomorrow's educational program would be solved. We need to know what we want our machine to do. We must look ahead if we are to get our money's worth out of every square foot. Speaking of square foot, I wish to dispel the notion that the lower the square foot cost, the better the project. Low scores are good in golf, but not necessarily in business—nor in buying a cotton picking machine—nor in buying a teaching machine (the schoolhouse)—small or large.

The other day I had nothing else to do, so I ran a square foot cost analysis on a project in Houston—not ours, by the way. I followed the A.I.A. formula for a schoolhouse, and I gave the big overhang an equivalent of one-half the enclosed space. It was a big project. It ran around

$4,000,000. As a matter of fact, the cost per square foot was amazingly high. It ran $1,282.05 per square foot. Now, did the people who bought this unbearably high-cost thing get gypped? No! The people who bought it are well satisfied. They happen to run the Delta Airlines, and the project under study was the Convair 880. Despite the high square foot cost of this piece of equipment, it does the job well that it was designed to do—and it makes money doing it!

So the next time you think in terms of square foot cost, simultaneously think in terms of educational performance. Is this schoolhouse a good machine for learning? Only when it is, will we get our money's worth.

A two-row cotton picking machine costs about $18,000. That sounds exorbitant compared to the penny a pound they paid me, but it's money in the bank to the business-like farmer to have an efficient machine.

Now back to the cotton pick'n schoolhouse. If your topflight educators are going to use the tax payer's money wisely, we must devise ways to make the school plant serve as an efficient teaching machine; it has to work; it can't be just a mere housing for an educational program; it must facilitate the educating process; it must be more than a storehouse for children—an egg crate for egg-heads.

We had better think sharply and deeply and make sure our schoolhouse machines are designed to facilitate the programs which are best for our boys and girls. By designing efficient schoolhouses that will stay up-to-date, we can save the tax payers untold millions on the housing of tomorrow's educational program—by knowing how to specify the performance of these mammoth machines.

But how should these schoolhouse machines perform? Let me show you what is happening in education and you can decide for yourself.

The egg crate school has had it! And these people are not going to like it:

> Teachers, principals, and superintendents who like to teach their eggheads by the cartons—two dozen or so in a box.
>
> Architects who like to design schools to look like egg crates.
>
> State officials who check to make sure that the architects continue to make new schools look like egg crates.
>
> Lawmakers who want to legislate standard egg crates.
>
> School board members who insist on buying the obsolete machines for learning.

And who is breaking up these egg crates? Both educators and architects—particularly those who are convinced that the pupil can be developed into a self-actuating scholar; that it is more important to teach the individual than it is the class; that learning experiences need a variety of spaces and, consequently, the standard classroom box won't fill the bill; and that learning doesn't stop at the classroom threshold.

If the egg crate school is out, what will we have in the future? Today is part of the future. A few new schools are not egg crates. They are designed to help the teachers teach. They serve the individual. They facilitate the educational program, not get in the way of it. They provide the right kind of teaching spaces at the right time. We need more schoolhouses like these. What we need are lean, clean teaching machines. What kind of teaching spaces? Here are a few:

1. Adaptable loft spaces which allow instantaneous and simultaneous grouping of many types and sizes of learning situations.

2. A place for the individual to study—space which he can call his own—a "locker" in which to work.

3. A center for up-to-date news on world affairs—complete with TV, radio, and teletype.

4. A science barn where the motivated student, gifted or not, can "own" a nook for his creative endeavors.

5. Spaces that have functional atmospheres as well as functional equipment.

6. A subdivision of scientifically designed, semi-permanent spaces that can take care of a variant number of class sizes and learning experiences.

These are only a few, but they point out that the traditional egg crate school will no longer do the job. What we need are schoolhouses that are clean, lean machines.

7

The people shape their buildings; thereafter the buildings shape the people.
                    WINSTON CHURCHILL

John H. Fischer
THE SCHOOL PARK AS A POSSIBLE SOLUTION

In school districts where redistricting, pairing, open enrollment, and busing offer little hope of producing lasting integration and high quality school programs, the school park may well offer a satisfactory

From John H. Fischer, "The School Park," *Education Parks* (Washington, D.C.: U.S. Commission on Civil Rights, October, 1967), pp. 1–3. Reprinted by permission of the U.S. Commission on Civil Rights and the author.

solution. School parks (called also educational parks, plazas, or centers) have been proposed in a number of communities and are being planned in several. The schemes so far advanced fall into several categories. The simplest, which is appropriate for a small or medium-sized town, assembles on a single campus all the schools and all the students of an entire community. As a result the racial character of a particular neighborhood no longer determines the character of any one school. All the children of the community come to the central campus where they can be assigned to schools and classes according to whatever criteria will produce the greatest educational benefits. The School Board of East Orange, N.J., has recently announced a 15-year construction program to consolidate its school system of some 10,000 pupils in such an educational plaza.

Another variant of the park is a similarly comprehensive organization serving one section of a large city as the single park might serve an entire smaller town. Where this plan is adopted the capacity of the park must be so calculated that its attendance area will be sufficiently large and diversified to yield a racially balanced student body for the foreseeable future. Merely to assemble two or three elementary units, a junior high school and a senior high school would in many cities produce no more integration than constructing the same buildings on the customary separate sites.

Less comprehensive schemes can also be called school parks. One, applicable to smaller communities, would center all school facilities for a single level of education—e.g., all elementary schools, or middle schools, or high schools, on a single site. Single-level complexes serving less than a whole community are also possible in large cities. The 1964 Allen Report for New York City proposed middle school parks to enroll 15,000 pupils each and to be located where they would assure as many children as possible experience in well-integrated schools.

In its 1966 study of the Pittsburgh schools, the Harvard Graduate School of Education proposed that all high school programs be housed in five new education centers, each to be located where it will serve a racially balanced student body for the foreseeable future.

A fourth, and the most comprehensive, type of park would require a number of changes in school planning and administration. This is the metropolitan school park designed to meet the increasingly serious problems posed by the growing Negro population of the central cities and the almost wholly white suburbs that surround them. The proposal, briefly stated, is to ring the city with school parks that would enroll the full range of pupils from the kindergarten to the high school and possibly including a community college. Each park would be placed in a "neutral" area near the periphery of the city. Each attendance area would approximate a segment of the metropolitan circle with its apex at the center of the city and its base in the suburbs. Since many students would arrive by school bus or public carrier, each site would be adjacent to a main transport route.

The potentialities of school parks in general can be explored by projecting what might be done in such a metropolitan center. We can begin with certain assumptions about size and character. In order to encompass an attendance area large enough to assure for the long term an enrollment more than 50 percent white and still include a significant number of Negro students from the inner-city ghetto, the typical park, in most metropolitan areas, would require a total student body (kindergarten to Grade 12) of not less than 15,000. It would thus provide all the school facilities for a part of the metropolitan area with a total population of 80,000 to 120,000. The exact optimum size of a particular park might be as high as 30,000, depending upon the density of urban and suburban population, the prevalence of nonpublic schools, the pattern of industrial, business, and residential zoning, the character of the housing, and the availability of transport.

The site, ideally, would consist of 50 to 100 acres but a workable park could be designed on a much smaller area or, under suitable circumstances, deep within the central city by using high-rise structures. Within these buildings individual school units of varying sizes would be dispersed horizontally and vertically. On a more generous plot each unit could be housed separately, with suitable provision for communication through tunnels or covered passages.

The sheer size of the establishment would present obvious opportunities to economize through centralized functions and facilities, but the hazards of over-centralization are formidable. To proceed too quickly or too far down that path would be to sacrifice many of the park's most valuable opportunities for better education.

Because of its size the park would make possible degrees of specialization, concentration, and flexibility that are obtainable only at exorbitant cost in smaller schools. A center enrolling 16,000 students in a kindergarten-4-4-4 organization, with 1,000–1,300 pupils at each grade level, could efficiently support and staff not only a wide variety of programs for children at every ordinary level of ability, but also highly specialized offerings for those with unusual talents or handicaps.

Superior libraries could be maintained, with strong centralized and decentralized collections of books, tapes, discs, films, and a rich combination of services for every unit in the park.

Such an institution could operate its own closed circuit television system more effectively, and with lower cable costs than a community-wide system, and with greater attention to the individual teacher's requirements. A central bank of films and tapes could be available for transmission to any classroom, and the whole system controlled by a dialing mechanism that would enable every teacher to "order" at any time whatever item he wished his class to see. Other forms of information storage and retrieval could readily be provided for instruction, administration, or teacher education.

The pupil population would be large enough to justify full-time staffs of specialists and the necessary physical facilities to furnish medical, psychological, and counseling services at a level of quality that is now rarely possible. Food service could be provided through central kitchens, short distance delivery, and decentralized dining rooms for the separate schools.

The most important educational consequences of the park's unprecedented size would be the real opportunities it would offer for organizing teachers, auxiliary staff, and students. In the hypothetical K-4-4-4 park of 16,000, for example, there would be about 5,000 pupils each in the primary and middle school age groups, or enough at each level for 10 separate schools of 500 pupils.

Each primary or middle school of that size could be housed in its own building, or its own section of a larger structure with its own faculty of perhaps 25. Such a unit, directed by its own principal, with its own complement of master teachers, "regular" teachers, interns, assistants, and volunteers, would be the school "home" of each of its pupils for the 3, 4, or 5 years he would spend in it before moving on to the next level of the park. A permanent organization of children and adults of that size employing flexible grouping procedures would make possible working relationships far superior to those now found in most schools. Moreover, since a child whose family moved from one home to another within the large area served by the park would not be required to change schools, one of the principal present handicaps to effective learning in the city schools would be largely eliminated.

While not every school within the park could offer every specialized curriculum or service, such facilities could be provided in as many units as necessary and children assigned to them temporarily or permanently. Each child and each teacher would "belong" to his own unit but access to others would be readily possible at any time.

The presence on a single campus of all school levels and a wide range of administrative and auxiliary services would present the professional staff with opportunities for personal development and advancement which no single school now affords. The ease of communication, for example, among the guidance specialists or mathematics teachers would exceed anything now possible. It would become feasible to organize for each subject or professional specialty a department in which teachers in all parts of the park could hold memberships, in much the way that a university department includes professors from a number of colleges.

For the first time, a field unit could justify its own research and development branch, a thing not only unheard of but almost unimaginable in most schools today. With such help "in residence" the faculty of the park could participate in studies of teaching problems and conduct experiments that now are wholly impracticable for even the most competent teachers.

Much would depend, of course, on the imagination with which the park was organized and administered and how its policies were formed. Since the metropolitan park, by definition, would serve both a central city and one or more suburban districts, its very establishment would be impossible without new forms of intergovernmental cooperation. At least two local school boards would have to share authority, staffs, and funds. The State educational authority and perhaps the legislature would be required to sanction the scheme and might have to authorize it in advance. Public opinion and political interests would be deeply involved as would the industrial and real estate establishments of the sponsoring communities.

The planning of a metropolitan park would have to be viewed as a concern not merely of school people, parents, and legislative or executive officials. It would have to be approached from the outset as a fundamental problem in metropolitan planning. Its dependence on quantitative projections of population and housing data is obvious, but equally important is its relation to the character of the housing, occupancy policies, and ethnic concentrations. To build a park only to have it engulfed in a few years by an enlarged ghetto would be a sorry waste of both money and opportunity. No good purpose, educational or social, would be served by creating what might become a huge segregated school enclave. A school park can be undertaken responsibly only as part of a comprehensive metropolitan development plan. Where such planning is not feasible, the establishment of a metropolitan school park would be a questionable venture.

It may be reasonable in some circumstances to project a park within the limits of a single school district. Where the analysis of population trends and projected development justify a single district park, the intergovernmental problems disappear, but agreements within the municipal structure will still be important and may be quite difficult to negotiate. The need for comprehensive community planning to assure the future viability of the park is certainly no less necessary within the city than in the metropolitan area.

Once the park is authorized, the question of operating responsibility must be addressed. In a sense that no individual school or geographic subdivision possibly can, the school park permits decentralized policy development and administration. Because of the natural coherence of the park's components and their relative separation from the rest of the district—or districts—to which it is related, the park might very well be organized as a largely self-contained system. The argument for placing the park under a board with considerable autonomy is strong whether it is a metropolitan institution or a one-city enterprise. For the first time it could thus become possible for the citizens in a section of a large community to have a direct, effective voice in the affairs of a school serving their area. Such details as the size of the board, length of terms, and method of selection would best be determined in each case according to local needs, but with full readiness to devise new statutes in order to take maximum advantage of the new opportunity.

Citizen participation would have to occur at points other than the board, however. If the park is to be strongly related to its communities, and integrated in fact as well as in principle, parents and other citizens would have to be involved, formally and informally, in many of its activities. These might range from parent-teacher conferences to service on major curriculum advisory groups. They could include routine volunteer chores and service as special consultants or part-time teachers. The specific possibilities are unlimited but the tone of the relationships will critically affect the park's success.

Because of its size, diversity, and compactness the park will present possibilities—and problems—in internal organization and administration that have not been encountered before. If the management of these new institutions only replicates the forms, procedures, and errors of present school bureaucracies the battle for a fresh approach to universal education could be lost before it began. Plans can and should be designed to make the most productive use of the central resources of the park as a whole while at the same time taking maximum advantage of the diversity among its component units. Any community or metropolitan area contemplating a park would do well not only to select its administrative and supervisory staff with great care but to assemble it a semester or even a full year before students are admitted in order to plan the working arrangements.

Obtaining the necessary cooperation to build a metropolitan park will not be easy but the financial problems will be equally severe. A park accommodating 16,000 pupils can be expected to cost in the neighborhood of $50 million. The financial pressures on cities and suburban districts make it clear that Federal support on a very large scale will be required if school parks are to be built. But it is precisely the possibility of Federal funding that could provide the incentive to bring the suburbs and the central city together.

While categorical support through Federal funds will continue to be needed, effective leverage on the massive problems of urban education, including, particularly, integration, can be obtained only through broadly focused programs of general aid, with special attention given to new construction. Little can be done toward equalizing opportunities without a sizeable program of school building expansion and replacement. Such aid, moreover, must be available for both the neglected child and the relatively advantaged.

If much of this new assistance were expressly channeled into creating metropolitan parks, on a formula of 90 percent Federal and 10 percent

State and local funding, it would envision equalized, integrated schools of high quality in most cities within a period of 10 to 15 years.

Would such a program mean abandoning usable existing school buildings? Not at all, since most school districts desperately need more space for their present and predictable enrollment, to say nothing of the other uses that school systems and other government agencies could readily find for buildings that might be relinquished. The impending expansion of nursery school programs and adult education are only two of the more obvious alternate uses for in-city structures.

Is the school park an all-or-nothing question? Is it necessary to abandon all existing programs before the benefits of the park can be tested? Short of full commitment, there are steps that can be taken in the direction of establishing parks and to achieve some of their values. The "educational complex" put forward in the Allen Report for New York City is one such step. As described in that report, the complex is a group of two to five primary schools and one or two middle schools near enough to each other to form a cooperating cluster and serving sufficiently diversified neighborhoods to promote good biracial contact.

An educational complex should be administered by a *senior administrator*, who should be given authority and autonomy to develop a program which meets appropriate citywide standards but is also directly relevant to the needs of the locality. Primary schools within the complex should share among themselves facilities, faculties, and special staff, and should be coordinated to encourage frequent association among students and parents from the several units. Within the education complex teachers will be better able to help children from diverse ethnic backgrounds to become acquainted with one another. Parent-teacher and parent-school relations should be built on the bases of both the individual school and the complex. The children—and their parents—will thus gain the dual benefits of a school close to home and of membership in a larger, more diverse educational and social community. The concept of the educational complex arises in part from the view that the means of education and much of their control should be centered locally.

Although it may not be possible to desegregate all primary schools, ultimately most of them should be integrated educationally. This will aid the better preparation of students for life and study in the middle school; it will more nearly equalize resources; and it will give the staff in the primary schools new opportunities for innovation and originality in their work.

Experimental projects on a limited scale might also be set up between city and suburban districts to deal with common problems. The Hartford and Irondequoit projects transporting Negro students to suburban schools are examples of what can be done.

Additional efforts could include exchanging staff members; involving students, particularly at the secondary level, in joint curricular or extracurricular activities; setting up "miniature school parks" during the summer in schools on the city-suburban border; conducting work sessions in which board and staff members from metropolitan school systems examine population changes, common curriculum problems, and opportunities for joint action.

Establishing school parks would mean a substantial shift in educational policy. In addition, as has been pointed out, the metropolitan park would require concerted action among governmental units. New forms of State and Federal financial support and sharply increased appropriations would be essential. In some cases teacher certification procedures would have to be altered and administrative routines adapted to tasks never before attempted. New forms of school architecture would have to be devised and more extensive transportation services instituted. In brief, a number of quite sweeping reforms would have to be accomplished. Parents and other citizens, school leaders, public officials and legislators will be justified in asking for persuasive factual and logical support for such radical proposals.

The response must be that critically important educational, social, and economic needs of a large part of urban America are not being met by our present policies and practices and that there is no reason to think that they will be met by minor adjustments of the present arrangements. The evidence is irresistible that the consequences of racial segregation are so costly and so damaging to all our people that they should no longer be tolerated. Through bitter experience we are learning that the isolation of any race is demeaning when it is deliberate and that it is counterproductive in human and economic terms, no matter how it is caused or explained. The elimination of this debilitating and degrading aspect of American life must now be ranked among the most important and urgent goals of our society. The task cannot be done without concerted action among many forces and agencies. Participation by private agencies and by government at every level will be needed. But central to every other effort will be the influence and the power of the public schools. Those schools, which have served the nation so well in achieving other high purposes, can serve equally well in performing their part of this new undertaking—if the magnitude of the task is fully appreciated and action undertaken on a scale appropriate to a major national purpose.

The steps that have heretofore been taken to cope with segregation have been of no more than tactical dimensions. Most of them have been relatively minor adaptations and accommodations requiring minimal changes in the status quo. It should by now be clear that we cannot integrate our schools or assure all our children access to the best education unless we accept these twin goals as prime strategic objectives.

Responding to commitments of comparable significance at other stages in our history as a nation, we built tens of thousands of common schools; spanned the continent with a network of agricultural and mechanical colleges; devised systems of vocational education in every state; and, most recently, set in motion a spectacular expansion of scientific research and development.

Establishing rings of school parks about each of our segregated central cities would, to be sure, require decisions to invest large sums of money in these projects. The prior and more important commitment, however, must be to the purpose to which the money will be dedicated: effective equality of educational opportunity at a new high level for millions of our young people.

The school park is no panacea. In itself it will guarantee no more than a setting for new accomplishment. But the setting is essential. If we fail to provide it or to invent an equally promising alternative, we shall continue to deny a high proportion of our citizens the indispensable means to a decent and productive life.

8

August examples show that no limit can be set to the power of a teacher, but this is equally true in the other direction; no career can so nearly approach zero in its effects.

JACQUES BARZUN

E. Glenn Fennell
THE CHANGING STATUS OF TEACHERS

From its inception, American society has been characterized by change, sometimes gradual, at times fairly rapid; but seldom has change been as rapid as that which has occurred since the 1940s. In less than three decades we have seen a series of changes that have touched almost every element in our society, including education. Until very recently little attention was paid to these changes in education; but now the American people are beginning to realize what school people have known for a long time: in most communities education is the single biggest industry.

Society has undergone change, education has undergone change and with these has come a change in the status of the teacher. The term

From E. Glenn Fennell, "The Changing Status of Teachers," *Education Age*, May–June, 1968, pp. 6–7. Copyright 1968 by Visual Products Division, 3 M Company, St. Paul, Minnesota, and reprinted by permission of the 3 M Company and the author.

"schoolteacher" is as archaic today as the society that spawned it. It is not merely redundant; the mental image it generates no longer applies in 20th Century America.

"Schoolteacher" conjures up a prim, colorless, conservative maiden of some indeterminate years beyond the age of consent—Miss Dove, let us say—who devoted most of her waking hours to her pupils and her community, was a bastion of morality, idealistic, genteel, refined, devout, perhaps obsequious, certainly acquiescent, the product of a respectable middle-class family who diligently endeavored to pass on to succeeding generations a respectable middle-class code. Her ideals were high, her manner mild. She had taken refuge in one of the few occupations deemed acceptable by her society for respectable females and unprotestingly shouldered the responsibilities heaped upon her. She scarcely had a life of her own; hers was a life of service. In return she received a pittance benevolently bestowed on her by a penurious and patronizing employer.

Is this portrait too harsh? Just about a century ago a New York City principal whose name has been lost in the dusty pages of educational history posted these rules in his school:

> Teachers each day will fill lamps, clean chimneys and trim wicks.
>
> Each teacher will bring a bucket of water and a scuttle of coal for the day's session.
>
> Make your pens carefully. You may whittle nibs to the individual tastes of pupils.
>
> Men teachers may take one evening a week for courting or two evenings if they go to church regularly.
>
> After 10 hours in school, teachers should spend the remaining time reading the Bible or other good books.
>
> Teachers who marry or engage in other unseemly conduct will be dismissed.
>
> Every teacher should lay aside each pay day a goodly sum of his earnings for his benefit during his declining years so that he will not become a burden on society.
>
> Any teacher who smokes, uses liquor in any form, frequents pool or public halls or gets shaved in a barber shop will give good reason to suspect his worth, intentions, integrity and honesty.
>
> The teacher who performs his labors faithfully and without fault for five (5) years will be given an increase of 25 cents per week in his pay providing the Board of Education approves.

These rules reflect the nature of 19th Century society—and 19th Century schools. And Miss Dove, like every good teacher, past or present, endeavored to fulfill her school's basic role, which was to reflect, preserve, maintain, defend—and if possible improve—the society it served.

The role of the school has not changed in the 20th Century; the basic role of the teacher has not changed. But there are vast differences between Miss Dove and the teachers in our classrooms today. Miss Dove did not change, but her society did; and in her place today we have Mr. and Mrs. Hawk, products of that change.

Let's take a look at Mrs. Hawk. To begin with, she is a teacher from choice, not circumstance. She has had at least four years of college, compared with Miss Dove's one or two years of Normal School. In addition to her formal training she has the moral, physical and personal characteristics that, research has shown, are possessed by good teachers; the fact that these same qualities correlate highly with the attributes most men desire in a wife is attested to by the fact that she is "Mrs."

Miss Dove's contract stipulated that she would be dismissed immediately should she marry "or engage in other unseemly conduct." Mrs. Hawk's contract stipulates only that she notify her immediate superior not later than her fifth month of pregnancy and advise the chief school officer of the length of her maternity leave, should she choose to exercise this prerogative. Mrs. Hawk, in short, is much less a second-class citizen in the community than Miss Dove was. In fact, Mrs. Hawk may not even live in the community in which she teaches; Miss Dove was required to maintain residence as a condition of employment.

Mrs. Hawk may have a husband, children and live where she chooses. She also enjoys professional status. She commands, commensurate with her training and experience, the same salary male members of the faculty receive. She has a high degree of job protection, once she successfully completes her probationary period, against the whims and fancies of her Board of Education.

Mrs. Hawk, like Miss Dove, *can* be dismissed for incompetency or immoral conduct, but in fact neither is likely to occur. She may *be* incompetent but high birth rates for nearly 20 years coupled with increased longevity have produced a population imbalance: only about 40 percent of the total are in the work age bracket and the ancient law of supply and demand is much in evidence.

Mrs. Hawk's moral conduct must of course conform to those standards her community considers acceptable for professional people. And members of every profession have responsibilities other members of the community do not; but these responsibilities ought not to be—and today are less likely to be—discriminatory. Mrs. Hawk is less likely to be confronted by a double standard than Miss Dove was. Professionals have not lowered their ethical standards but communities have become more liberal; communities are less likely today to insist on *higher* standards for their professionals. Few communities today will raise their collective "plucked eyebrows" at Mrs. Hawk's. She will not be considered a fallen woman if she wears lipstick or stylish dresses, goes to a beauty parlor, dyes her hair or wears a wig.

These changes, in part superficial, are also in part manifestations of some basic changes in our society. Since World War II we have seen a gigantic population shift to suburbia. Traditional community roots have been severed. Studies have shown that suburbia is likely to be fairly homogeneous (most of its citizens are young marrieds, geographically and socially mobile and share a common desire for quality education for their children) but the population shift has badly battered the traditional social structure. Family background, source of wealth and residential location have little validity in the new communities; education and annual income are the basic criteria.

Moral values have shifted along with the population, from the absolute to the relative. This shift has been called a revolt against the hypocrisy of the Puritan ethic and the "establishment." It is also called "liberalism." And it is challenging many sacred cows.

There is still another factor, insofar as education is concerned. An increasing number of men have entered education and at the same time certification requirements have become more rigid: a fifth year of preparation coupled with an area of specialization is not now uncommon and may soon be standard. These men view themselves as college-trained professionals and heads of families and wish to attain what they feel to be appropriate community status. They may be forced to "moonlight" to provide an adequate income for their families, but they find this personally and professionally degrading.

It is out of these changes that Mr. and Mrs. Hawk have emerged. They are indeed a sign of conflict but this should not be surprising: society is in a state of flux. The old order changeth—and yet it does not. Miss Dove was a traditional teacher in a traditional world. The parents of suburbia seek teachers with attitudes, viewpoints and desires like their own—the Hawks. The Hawks are "militant" and this is viewed with apprehension by many both in and outside of education. And yet, behind the headlines, Mr. and Mrs. Hawks' goals are really not so different from Miss Dove's. Miss Dove, however, was willing to accept the concept of cultural lag. The Hawks are not: they are convinced this is a luxury no dynamic society can afford.

They are committed, too, to the proposition that increases in teachers' salaries are a means to an end. They are concerned that, without increases, their community will neither attract nor keep competent teachers—and their children, too, are students. They are committed to the proposition that education today requires expertise and no longer can remain solely the responsibility of laymen. They are convinced they have something to offer in the effort to provide quality education; their demands for "improved working conditions" might also be considered demands for "improved learning conditions."

In short, we have a paradox. Teachers as a group are conservative, but they now find themselves, in their efforts to prepare their pupils for present-day society, disturbing that same society. There is solidarity in their purpose ... but no general consensus on how best to proceed. Miss Dove, like McGuffey's Reader a dusty reminder now of days long past, deserves a "well done" for her duty and devotion in another era. And it may be well to extend to Mr. and Mrs. Hawk the wish that, when the time comes to replace them, they will have done as well.

9

I am not willing that this discussion should close without mention of the value of a true teacher. Give me a log hut, with only a simple bench, Mark Hopkins on one end and I on the other, and you may have all the buildings, apparatus, and libraries without him.
JAMES A. GARFIELD

Kevin Ryan

WHERE ARE WE GOING AND HOW CAN WE GET THERE?

We here today have the responsibility to shape the teaching profession. In twenty-five years American education will be in the hands of our students. There can be little doubt that our vision—or lack of vision—will have profound effects. It would seem useful, therefore, to project our thought to the future, to extend some of the current pioneer efforts to hypothetical fulfillment.

Prophecy is the occupation of wise men and fools. While I seriously doubt that this discussion of the schools and the profession in twenty-five years will qualify me for the first group, the wise men, I hope that it will not mean that I have cast my lot with the fools. I submit this potpourri of predictions and premonitions well aware of the vagaries of history. Much happens in twenty-five years. Who among us in the year 1943, as we listened at our radios to Fibber McGee's closet crashing in on him, would have foretold the coming of Petticoat Junction in living color? When we had Sophie Tucker with plunging neckline before the nation's eyes, who would have anticipated Twiggy in the mini? In 1943, when the Brooklyn Dodgers were the kings of Flatbush Avenue, who would have predicted that one day they would be playing in the smog

Kevin Ryan, "Where Are We Going and How Can We Get There?" An address, January 19, 1968. Reprinted by permission of the author and the National Education Association.

of Los Angeles? And who, twenty-five years ago, would have thought that the tinkerings of a few scientists in an abandoned squash court at the University of Chicago would thrust us into a new era, the Atomic Age? We can be certain, then, that by 1993, the world will have pulled a few surprises on us.

Before trying to read the fortune of the future, let us see what the tea leaves of the present tell us. What is the current mood of educators? For one thing, the old egg-carton school building, with its standardized classrooms and standardized teaching, is passing. With it is going the school day dominated by the bell, signaling the beginning and the end of neat slices of time—45- or 50-minute packages of knowledge to be uniformly consumed by all. We are being forced to abandon the belief that children learn best in classrooms of twenty-five or thirty pupils and in quiet libraries with quiet books. We are moving away from the idea that education is something that a teacher does to a student, something he impresses on a child, like Mr. Locke and his tabula rasa. We are rejecting the notion that all children, even within the same tract, should receive the same information and proceed at the same rate. Although there are still great counterpressures to the contrary, there is a growing disaffection with the principle of solving the problems of American education by programming the children with more and more information. We are becoming vividly aware that we are not providing equal educational opportunities to our minority groups and that we cannot survive as a free society without quickly and dramatically eradicating our present inequalities.

At the same time that we are rethinking the education of children, we are rejecting the idea that we can train teachers for today's classrooms using the same old mold and the same tired formula. We are doubting that our present organization of the profession is adequate. We are recognizing that our traditional job description for the classroom teacher is unrealistic and unworkable. We are leaving behind all these ideas and structures because we are discovering that even our more intense efforts of the last ten years are fundamentally bankrupt. We have been getting better and better at preparing children for a world which no longer exists.

Where Are We Going?

The School of 1993. What, then, will replace our assembly-line schools? What follows is an admittedly optimistic view of the 1993 schools. Although I make the predictions with great hesitation, I am firm in the belief that on some cold winter's night in 1993 these predictions will provide some diligent graduate student reviewing the history of TEPS with a good laugh.

Frankly, I have no idea what the schools of 1993 will look like from the outside or how the bricks and mortar will be arranged. Some may be

housed in huge skyscrapers. Some may be in educational parks, minia-
tures of our present college campuses. More intriguing, however, is
what they will look like on the inside. My guess is that there will be
much more open space. Students will move about quite freely. There
will be much less structuring of time than at present. Right now, regimentation is necessary because we are unable to truly involve students
in the essential task of the schools—learning. Once we are able to stimulate students and sustain involvement, regimentation will be dysfunctional and will pass away. The maintenance of the student's high interest
will be a major operating principle. The child's natural curiosity will be
king and carefully nurtured. The schools of 1993 will be imbued with
respect for human diversity and originality. The curriculum will finally
become a careful and rational order of learning experiences. Like regimentation, grades, too, will be dysfunctional and pass away. Our present
grading practices will be looked upon by future generations as we now
look upon dunce caps, or perhaps even thumb screws.

To foster deep involvement, much of the school will be devoted to
learning environments toward which the resource centers of our most
advanced schools are just beginning to move. Professionally produced
films and tapes on almost every subject will be available for individual
or collective viewing. Students will have at hand materials and equipment for all sorts of projects, whether it be recreating the life of the early
pilgrims in New England or recreating the life of the first residents on
the moon. Much of what students struggle to master now will be learned
through games. It does not seem too far-fetched to suggest that children
will learn languages through conversations with other children in distant
countries. A child may have a telstar pen pal in Paris and another in
Peiping and daily talk to each using his video phone. To counteract life
in the man-made environment that is concomitant with urbanization,
students will spend a good deal of time on field trips which occasionally
will be in quite distant and exotic places. Where better to get the total
impact of Greek culture than in Athens?

The student will do much of his exploring of the world in school,
however, at his computer-information-bank console. In terms of increased learning, computer-assisted instruction will be the real breakthrough. By 1993, the present computer consoles being used in the
Suppes-Atkinson project at Stanford will be museum pieces, viewed
with the same curious affection which we now have for the Model T
Ford.

Today, as I read about computer-assisted instruction (CAI) in the educational journals, I get the feeling that the teaching profession is being
handled rather gingerly, that the CAI people are employing a soft-sell
approach. One gets the impression that they are selling a new detergent.
CAI is represented as being a wonderful new formula that will take the
drudgery out of teaching and do the dirty work, such as basic instruction

and drilling in the skills of reading, spelling, and arithmetic. A truer analogy may be to a completely automated household that will leave the housewife with little to do except wonder about her fate. We are being sheltered from the great shock that the self-pacing, individually focused CAI units may be able to teach everything from the ABC's to metaphysics, from addition to the newest science, with greater efficiency and effectiveness than most fine teachers. I am talking here about CAI units that act as individual tutors, that contain all the knowledge and theory developed by mankind; computers that are programmed with all we know about learning theory and put it into practice, that are programmed with all the learning characteristics of each student and operate from up-to-date profiles of the skills and knowledge of each student. It is expected that these CAI units will be programmed not simply to teach skills and information but also the important intellectual processes. Given the assumption that these units will be continually pacing the student at his maximum level and thereby cutting out all needless repetition and relearning, it does not seem unreasonable that in two or three hours a day at his console the student will be learning three or four times what he is presently learning in school. In brief, we may have the educational ideal of the student at one end of the log, and instead of Mark Hopkins at the other end, we will have the IBM Mark 93.

Many of us are uneasy with the idea of children spending huge amounts of time interacting with computers. Some feel that the experience will be dehumanizing and that the educational process will become depersonalized. Although this is a very real possibility, I am sure that the same thoughts were stirred by the advent of the book. Too, we should keep in mind that much of what is at this moment going on in our classrooms is dehumanizing. Besides the legions of students who are bored with the content and pace of instruction, there are many who are being left behind and cast aside. For many, our traditional classrooms are prisons where students are fettered by frustration and ignorance. However, we still have ahead of us the important task of harnessing the computer. As John Goodlad of UCLA pointed out recently, it is our challenge to "find out how human beings and machines are to live together productively in tomorrow's learning-teaching environment."

A major benefit of the new efficiency that will come with computerized instruction is more time—time to develop the student's social, moral, and aesthetic dimensions. Students of all grade levels will have much more time to work and play together. It is hoped that the distinction between these two words, work and play, will be lost in the process. Although much of the student's day will be spent in a variety of different groups. all students will be involved continually in independent study. Right now, independent study is like international peace: everyone is for it, but no one can quite bring it off. Further, all students, not simply the athletically gifted, will have more training in how to use their bodies. In the present school curriculum there is little room for the dance, for singing, for artistic expression generally. In the school of the future, much of the day will be devoted to these oft overlooked but most humanizing activities.

The New Teacher. If we are to have a new school in 1993, we will need a new teacher. Of this one thing we can be sure. The role of the teacher as we now know it will be drastically changed. With the coming of movable type and the easily accessible book in the fifteenth century, the teacher no longer had a monopoly on knowledge. His role as total source of knowledge was severely altered. The technological revolution taking place in the schools will demand a change of role of an even greater magnitude. As the Year of the Non-Conference has vividly pointed out to us, the technological revolution and the change in the teacher's role are happening already in many schools with tremendous speed. In 1993, many of the present roles performed by teachers, such as information dispenser, drillmaster, disciplinarian, money changer, record keeper, and grader, will have vanished or will have been taken over by paraprofessionals.

What, then, will be the teacher's role? One possibility is that, whereas we once had teachers functioning as entire instructional systems, in the future the teacher will be the director of an instructional system. He will have at his disposal many instructional aids, such as simulators, program materials, video tapes, films, and computer-based learning systems. As director of a large system, the teacher will have to be a skilled diagnostician, aware of the abilities of the students and potential contributions of each component in his system. Since different students have different learning styles, the teacher's main task will be to apply the systems with intelligence and sensitivity. In doing this, he will be supported by many specialists and paraprofessionals who will be working directly with children. Bruce Joyce, in a recently issued Year of the Non-Conference publication, has developed this idea quite fully.

As the teacher assumes the role of director of an instructional system, he is going to need specialized help. At present, there seem to be three groups of specialists that will support the teacher, three additional role groups that will be added to the school.

The first group we will call inquiry specialists. These people will be highly, perhaps narrowly, trained to aid children in mastering specific inquiry skills. Examples of some of these are specialists in search skills and problem solving, specialists in group discussion, specialists in learning games and game theory. While many of these specialists may be linked to a particular discipline, many will cut across several disciplines, being essentially process specialists.

The second role group will be that of therapy specialists. I am not speaking here of what we presently refer to as the counselor, a professional charged with vocational and academic guidance. That role, too, may pass in the age of the computer. In 1993 we will know much more about mental health and human relations. The whole area will become much more important if we are to keep civilization from flying apart. Therapy specialists will work with the instructional staff to improve the social climate of the school. Their major task, however, will be to help individual children gain a greater insight and control over their own behavior.

The third group will be scholars and researchers, people who are working at the frontier of knowledge but who are also working in the schools at all levels. Right now there are relatively few people working on the edge of knowledge. In twenty-five years we can expect two things: a larger frontier of knowledge and many more people engaged in scholarly pursuits. These scholars-researchers-teachers will relate to schools in many different ways, depending on their own abilities and desires. Some will help guide independent study projects. Others will guide group projects which will often further their own research. Some will teach in settings that look very much like our present advanced doctoral seminars. Few, however, will spend more than ten or fifteen hours a week with students. The schools will share many of these scholars with industry and research centers.

All three of these role groups will share in the teacher's traditional role of model for children. However, in the school of the future, the professional staff—the process specialist, the therapist, and the scholar-researcher—will be chosen especially because they are examplars of man at his finest, man striving to know and to love.

How Do We Get There?

Right here I am going to retreat from these somewhat heady heights. Having heard the first section of this paper, many of you may not wish to go along for the ride. Now I would like to move into the second part, and here, too, I am sure that many will object to the mode of travel.

The Structure of the Profession. Few people are satisfied with the way we have structured the elementary and secondary segments of the teaching profession. What appears on the surface to be a neat, efficient, and egalitarian system reveals several severe internal problems. For one thing, there is no career line for the classroom teacher. Teaching is a one-step career. Excellence in the classroom is rewarded by promotion out of the classroom, away from children. One type of promotion in high schools is to department chairman. This means the gifted teacher teaches fewer students and gets to open the mail from the book companies. Also, he is expected to supervise other teachers, a job for which he is rarely trained and for which he may have no interest or aptitude. Another type of promotion is to become an administrator, which means he teaches no children. And, of course, there are those, many of the best, who promote themselves out of teaching completely.

Another problem is related to the job requirements. We give a freshly certified 21-year-old awesome responsibility for the learning of large numbers of children for an entire year. We expect him to be highly skilled in all aspects of teaching, from control of content to human relations, from motivation to evaluation. And then we expect him to spend the next forty years of his life carrying out essentially the same responsibilities. This seems to be an unrealistic demand on the beginner and a deadening prospect for the experienced teacher. Another problem in the way we structure the profession is that we make little room for individual differences. It is odd that we teachers, who are continually faced with individual differences, have no way of acknowledging them in our profession. The individuals who come into teaching bring with them different talents, different weaknesses, and different interests. Nevertheless, we insist that all teachers be all things to all children. Instead of tailoring the teaching assignment to an individual, we tend to force all teachers into the same, easily interchangeable molds.

At the inauguration of NEA Executive Secretary Sam Lambert last October, Harold Howe put several questions to the teaching profession, two of which bear directly on its structure. Howe asked, "How can we get the teaching profession to develop a hierarchy within its ranks? How can the profession be encouraged to adapt the best aspects of a system that obtains in colleges and universities, where the strongest teachers receive large responsibilities and larger rewards?" One answer to these questions and our present difficulties is a differentiated teaching staff. The differentiated teaching staff is based on the idea of human differences in intelligence and commitment and the observation that presently there are many roles assumed under "teacher." A differentiated staffing system replaces the system in which all teachers carry out the same responsibility for the same reward. Although many schools have made moves toward staff differentiation, I know of none that have such a daring plan as the one devised by the teachers and administrators of the Temple City, California, schools. The teaching staffs of the Temple City elementary and secondary schools are restructuring themselves into four different categories of teachers. To the four teacher categories are being added academic assistance, educational technicians, and various types of paraprofessionals. Each of the four teacher categories has a different job definition and salary scale and calls for different competencies. While all will be classroom teachers, much more in terms of time and effort and leadership will be demanded of some. People in higher categories will be responsible for long-range planning in curriculum and instruction. Some will have major responsibility for in-service programs. Others in lower categories will have more restricted requirements, frequently acting as team members. The range of competence and responsibility is reflected by the salary scale that starts at $6000 and reaches to $18,000.

The differentiated teaching staff would appear to have several advantages. First, it provides a career line within teaching and hopefully will keep the brightest and most able teachers in classrooms in front of children. It does not seem unjustifiable that the outstanding teachers in the school should receive salaries comparable to the top administrators. Second, the differentiated teaching staff is designed to make the best use of each teacher's talents, especially by providing more opportunity for specialization. For example, the teacher who is especially gifted at small group instruction will spend the major portion of his day in this activity. Also, he will be provided with free time to work with other teachers who are attempting to develop the skills involved in small group instruction. Third, such a staffing arrangement will allow for leadership within the teaching staff. Excellent teachers will have a wider channel for influence, both with students and with colleagues. Fourth, the development of a hierarchy among classroom teachers will undoubtedly lead to teachers having a greater share in decision making. Although this new demand for a greater voice in decision making is somewhat new, it seems regrettable that so often the demand is only in the areas of salary and benefits. The faculty of a school with a differentiated approach to its teaching staff will have a voice in policy making in all areas. Incidentally, at Temple City the teachers are structuring themselves into an academic senate similar to the university model.

We should bear in mind that the differentiated teaching staff is a new, untested idea. Although it appears promising, it will have to be applied in many different settings and studied carefully. We can, of course, be confident that it will not solve all our problems. However, it may solve many of our problems and lead toward greater professionalism in teaching.

The Preparation of Teachers. Another area to which we must give special attention if we are to get to our school of the future is the preparation of teachers. Few of us, whether involved in undergraduate or graduate programs, are satisfied with the current results. Certainly, we have no dearth of critics to keep us humble. It is quite possible that one major source of our trouble is that we have patterned teacher education on the wrong model. Much of what is done in America to train teachers fits what I call the exposure-immersion model. I am speaking here of the professional component, not the academic component. In order to prepare students for the active role of teacher, we expose them to a series of education courses. The teacher-to-be is the passive recipient of information about children and teaching. After passing the paper-and-pencil examinations which are supposed to indicate that he can do all the things covered by the courses, we then immerse him in the active role of teacher. All of a sudden, the student teacher or intern must stand before thirty or so children and translate all the passive preparation into skillful action.

Passive exposures and complete immersion! It is a minor miracle that so many can survive. One wonders how such a questionable preparation model ever got started. A possible explanation is that when teacher education was absorbed into colleges and universities some sixty or seventy years ago, it conformed to the prevailing patterns of these institutions. Except for student teaching, the preparation for teaching was treated like preparation in mathematics or English literature. Formal, and essentially passive, courses became the dominant mode. I am not suggesting that there is no place for formal course work in teacher education, rather that there is much more to be done. If we are truly to prepare our teachers-to-be for the complex, active role of teacher, there is a whole fabric of training experiences that must be woven. These experiences should be a bridge between foundations courses and student teaching.

Some of these training experiences and activities are as follows:

1. *Paraprofessional Services.* For example, the college student takes over hall monitoring or other supervisory duties for teachers. The main idea is to put the college student in contact with youngsters, but in a new relationship, one in which he has adult responsibilities.

2. *Resource to Students.* In this role the beginner is assigned to a library or to a study area simply to be a resource for students. With a little training, most college students could be quite helpful to lower school students, getting them started on library projects or helping them with certain study skills.

3. *Teacher Aide.* Here the beginner is assigned to a teacher or a team of teachers. He is put in a working relationship with experienced teachers and is given the opportunity to observe and study the teacher role he is planning to assume. Such exposure to teachers and education-on-the-hoof should provide experiences that enrich his education courses back on the campus.

4. *Teacher Simulation Exercises.* Here I am thinking of the simulation exercises developed by Donald Cruickshank of the University of Tennessee. Trainees learn about a hypothetical class and school. Then they attempt to solve common teaching problems in role-playing situations. In a safe, simulated situation they learn many of the complexities of the teacher role, for instance, how to cope with irate parents.

5. *Clinical Exercises.* These clinical exercises normally would take place in a school and can be quite varied in nature. For example, one such exercise might be having a trainee sit in on a class with the express purpose of identifying and closely observing an inattentive student. He

records the student's behavior, makes some guesses about his achievement and social adjustment, and after class checks his perceptions with the teacher. Later these experiences are discussed back on the campus.

6. *Tutoring.* Here the beginner works with one student for several weeks. His assignment is to identify the student's learning problems, plan and execute a program. Not only does the future teacher have close and prolonged contact with one student, but he also is forced to do some hard thinking about the learning process.

7. *Microteaching.* Microteaching is a practice setting for teaching. The trainee teaches brief lessons to a few students and then gets feedback from several sources: the students, a supervisor, and by watching video tapes of his performance. Usually in microteaching the trainee practices specific technical skills of teaching, such as controlling student participation or asking open-ended questions.

There is nothing new about this list of training activities and exercises. Although I know of no program that does not at least suggest to its students some of these activities, I know of no program that uses the full range of these activities. Finding time in the curriculum seems to be the big barrier. Each year the total undergraduate curriculum gets more crowded. Greater and greater demands on students are being made. At the present time it may be totally unrealistic to think that we can prepare a liberally educated individual and a highly skilled teacher in the normal four-year period. I am not necessarily advocating fifth-year programs. There are problems here, too. Rather, I am suggesting the adoption of five-year programs in which liberal arts study and professional education are integrated over the entire five years. This would give future teachers ample time to work in schools and go through the type of training activities mentioned above. At the end of his fifth year, the student would receive his baccalaureate degree, certification, and be well on his way toward an M.A. in education. Of course, the time could be shortened for those who choose to study during their summers. It seems clear, however, that the level of education and professional preparation demanded of the new teacher cannot be met in the traditional four-year sequence.

In-Service Training. Let us turn briefly to in-service training. Today the culture is changing with increasing rapidity. Knowledge is expanding and being defined daily. However, teachers, whose role is the transmission of the culture and the dissemination of knowledge, have the meagerest opportunity to keep pace. We hear a great deal of talk about the teacher as continuous learner, but little provision is made for this slogan to become a reality. It is little wonder that commentators like the mythical J. Abner Peddiwell of *Saber-Tooth Curriculum* fame and Marshall McLuhan, the newly discovered prophet of the age, have faulted the schools for being irrelevant to the world in which children must live. If we are to have relevant schools, surely we must find new ways to keep teachers from falling behind the advances in both their fields and pedagogy. We not only need new ideas, but we will have to commit to this effort much more time, money, and energy. On this score, education can learn a great deal from the military and industry. The armed forces are continually retraining their personnel, not only through combat exercises, but also through a vast network of schools. The major industries, too, are allocating large portions of their annual budgets to education. IBM is said to be presently devoting 30 percent of the time of its employees, from executives to technicians, to training and re-training.

Although there are numerous approaches to the teacher obsolescence problem, there are two we will consider briefly. One is external to the ongoing school and the other is internal. The first approach is to develop a wide variety of retraining programs away from the school. Given the present need for highly qualified teachers, it does not seem unreasonable that every four or five years teachers return to the universities or special centers for a semester or perhaps a full year of advanced work. Also, the summer institute programs should be expanded for many more teachers and for teachers of all subjects and grade levels. These opportunities should be opened up particularly to the career teacher who has made a definite commitment to classroom teaching. Teachers should be able to attend without having to make any more financial sacrifices. We can learn from the recent experience in Japan that has helped to revolutionize the teaching of science there. To keep teachers abreast of the developments in the teaching of science, the Japanese have formed local science education centers that draw teachers out of the schools and retrain them for periods from as short as one week to as long as a semester. Almost all of what is studied at these centers is immediately applicable when the teachers return to their classrooms.

The second approach to the in-service problem is internal to the school. Time for study and retraining should be built into the *daily school schedule*. This does not mean simply more free time or in-service courses tacked on at the end of a draining day of teaching. Time should be scheduled during the school day for teachers to come together and learn. The most logical people to lead these in-service courses would be those who have just returned from external training programs. These in-service experiences would be especially valuable for inexperienced teachers and those who have returned to teaching after raising a family.

Although the full spectrum of teacher education needs much greater financial support, particular consideration should be given to the experienced teacher. Certainly when we consider the tremendously high drop-out rate in the early years of teaching, it is easier to understand why such a small investment is made in preservice training. What is so difficult to comprehend is why we make such a paltry investment in the training of those who stay—the career teachers.

Change in Education

Most of what I have suggested with regard to where we are going and how we can get there hinges on our willingness to change. Also, it presupposes massive change in an endeavor that traditionally had been quite resistant to change. Frankly, I think that this is all over now. Change is the new reality. Change may well be the *only* constant in our lives. Recently, I read a report of a letter from an 80-year-old woman: "Dear Sir," she wrote, "Why do we have to go to the moon? Why can't we stay on this earth and watch television the way the Good Lord intended?" Last November, McGeorge Bundy, president of the Ford Foundation, took a very different tack and stated the issue quite clearly: "We are in a grave and deepening crisis in public education. The burden of proof is not on those who urge change. The burden of proof is on those who do not urge change." It is our job as educators to inform and direct this change.

Although the magnitude of change being suggested calls for financial expenditures the like of which we in education have never seen, we are gathering support. People in government, people in industry, and people on the street are realizing a simple fact: We cannot afford not to change the schools. The state, whose fundamental purpose is national survival, has realized that the human mind is our basic and most valuable national resource. It looks to the schools to develop the genius and supporting talent that will solve the frightening problems that confront us. Many Washington watchers are expecting the government to pump huge sums into education once we extricate ourselves from Southeast Asia.

Industry, too, has a vested interest in the schools. It looks to the schools to provide it with the scientists, managers, and technicians to support and expand the technological society. More recently, industry has found in the schools a vast, relatively untapped market for its goods. The mergers of the "software" and "hardware" industries like IBM, SRA, GE and Time, Inc., are a powerful indication that American industry is in the schools in a big way. For many members of the business community, the words of Calvin Coolidge in the twenties, "The business of America is business," have been updated to "The business of America is education."

The third force for change in the schools is what I have called the emerging will of the people. People are becoming increasingly aware of our potential for developing the good life. Not simply the rich life, but a qualitative improvement in the very character of life. We are slowly realizing that the new frontier is not outer space—our interest here is already wanting—but the human potential. If the civil rights struggle has taught us anything, it is that words like "quality education," "equal opportunity," and "the human potential" are not simply to be in the future the province of the few. The American school, which classically had been used for upward mobility, is now being viewed as instrumental in the attainment of a new good life that may well be within our grasp.

These three pressures for change in the schools—the state, business, and the emerging will of the people—are not equal. It would seem that right now we are moving faster toward a "meritocracy" that lavishly rewards those who advance the power of the state or business. However, there is something dangerous about educating people. They become dissatisfied with the merely adequate. They become critical of the imperfect. They develop new appetites. They seek new alternatives. My suspicion is that, the more we educate, the more people will demand the truly humanistic education in a truly human life.

THE TEACHER-EDUCATION DIMENSION

Teacher education is a significant aspect of higher education. The term is not universally considered synonymous with liberal education, but perhaps it should be. Today, nearly one-third of the nation's population is directly involved in the teaching-learning process; the portent of this process directly affects the remaining two-thirds. One easily remembers the power of the farm bloc in shaping American political history. Today, there are more teachers than farmers. Teacher power is a vitally new pressure source.

How are teachers trained and by whom? The dilemmas associated with teacher preparation seem ageless. Only a Socrates is exempted from criticism. Speaking in a heavy Greek accent, wearing old sheets and prone to poisoning in stress situations, he is excused from our current certification rites as an unqualified applicant. Emerging patterns in staff differentiation, however, are testing the traditional requirements to teach. Witness the deepening talent reservoir for the nation's schools. Teacher-aides, or paraprofessionals, artists, and scientists are tentatively assisting in the schooling process. In urban centers, especially, increasing citizen participation in all dimensions of education is evident.

The issues, historically, have been persistent. How can quality in preparation programs prevail when quantity demands a higher priority? Once learned, how are teaching skills renewed and refined? What kinds of interrelationships might schools and colleges jointly effect to improve schooling on all levels? One specific dilemma concerns the balance or blend of liberal arts content with offerings in professional education. Some institutions are embracing the "all-university approach" by committing total resources to the preparation of teachers. This endeavor can no longer be considered the exclusive domain of professional educators.

The teacher education dimension may be characterized as one of rising expectations. The problems are staggering but, as John W. Gardner writes, "We are all faced with a series of great opportunities—brilliantly disguised as insoluble problems." The dilemmas are not hopeless; those seeking solutions are not helpless. The following articles do not encompass all of the issues. Neither do they exhaust the dialogue for those selected. Included are examples of conflict and criticism within higher education relevant to the education of teachers. A few general concerns affecting higher education are also dissected. The selections represent a partial sampling.

444

1

The main problem is that the leaders of America—not only in Government, but in the universities, the churches, the big corporations, the newspapers and the television networks—are so overwhelmed by the problem of doing things that they have little time left to think about what they are doing. Operations dominate purposes. The practical men have taken over from the ideological men, and this has many advantages, but pragmatism may be misleading us.

JAMES RESTON

Robert M. Hutchins
THE ISSUES

A British scholar remarked recently that education was something like the Kingdom of God in former times. It is within us and amongst us, yet it somehow lies ahead. The elect possess it and hope to gather in those who are not yet saved. But what on earth it is has seldom been made clear.

Much the same may be said of the university in its global manifestation. It is generally agreed to be a Fine Thing, though a certain mysticism attaches to the reason why. In new or developing nations it appears to be a necessary symbol of national sovereignty and modernity. When asked why his country needed an army, a leader of the Third World replied, "Why does a civilized man wear a necktie?" He might have made the same answer if the question had been about his national university. There is something pathetic, moving, and characteristic about the following official statement of a foreign government: "The aims of higher education are inextricably bound up with national aims and development. . . . If Liberia is to hold a position of leadership in the modern world it must have highly trained personnel at all levels."

A gallop through the million and a half words on higher education published recently by UNESCO, covering everything from Pitcairn Island to mainland China, shows that the institution called the university is almost everywhere afflicted with difficulties associated with the birthrate and the desire of an increasing proportion of an increasing population to acquire whatever it is that attendance at and recognition by a university confers. Of the Western countries only Portugal reports that

From Robert M. Hutchins, "The Issues," in C. Kerr, R. Park, J. Barzun, E. Ashby, R. Hutchins, *et al.*, *The University in America* (Santa Barbara, Calif.: Center for the Study of Democratic Institutions, 1967), pp. 4–8. Reprinted by permission of the Center for the Study of Democratic Institutions.

"the number of university students graduating each year has not risen at a sufficient rate to meet the needs of the country."

Even Portugal is not free from other difficulties felt almost everywhere, those arising from the restlessness of students. I have made a partial list of the disorders sufficiently disturbing to reach the public prints between 1962 and 1965. It shows that in twenty-one countries students demonstrated, sometimes with guns, against conditions they found objectionable in their universities and that in twenty-nine they became at least equally riotous about the policy of their country or of some other. Without attempting to pass on the specific complaint alleged in any of these instances, and with due recognition of the practice in some countries of inciting students to riot for political purposes, we may yet acknowledge the possibility, in view of what we know about universities and about national policies, that in some cases the students may have been right.

When we pass beyond these phenomena, exponential growth and student disorders, any resemblance between the American university and the university anywhere else is purely coincidental. UNESCO has to print a glossary to make our educational system intelligible, in the most rudimentary sense, to the non-American reader. It covers two very large pages of very fine print. One of the words it vainly tries to define is "university."

There is practically no country in the world outside the Communist orbit that does not report to UNESCO that its universities are autonomous. Whether or not they are in fact autonomous is not now in issue. The point is that every country finds it necessary to claim they are. They appear to believe that autonomy is an essential, defining characteristic of the institution called a university. Unless it is autonomous, it is not a university. It must be autonomous, even if all its support comes from the state. The United States has only the most limited conception of autonomy in this sense. The meaning of autonomy elsewhere is that the faculties are in actual control, no matter what the extent of the nominal powers of ministers of education, legislatures, or boards of trustees may be.

In no country in the world is the university the cannibal it is in the United States. Every other nation assigns some tasks of education, training, and research to other institutions. Nowhere else is it automatically assumed that everything anybody wants by way of educational experience beyond the high school or anything anybody would like to see done by way of solving practical problems, collecting data, investigating the universe, or cleaning up the landscape may as a matter of course be a function of the university.

The responsibility of the professions for the preparation and induction of neophytes, the operation of training schools and research institutes outside the university, and a break of the greatest significance between secondary and higher education are the general rule in other countries and unknown or exceptional in the United States.

The last point deserves, perhaps, a word more. In the United States we do not believe that secondary education amounts to much, and we do not really care. Those who are graduated from high school may not have learned anything, but many of them will go on to college, where they will be accommodated by what have been called the six R's, remedial reading, remedial 'riting, and remedial 'rithmetic. The program of a Canadian undergraduate seems to us shockingly narrow and specialized—and it is perhaps too much so. But we cannot appraise it without recalling the difference between what is expected in a Canadian in contrast to an American high school and what is therefore regarded as the function of a Canadian in contrast to an American university.

These considerations suggest that whereas other countries have an idea of a university, however inadequate, vague, or even erroneous, we have none. The idea of an *omnium gatherum* cannot be taken seriously. An idea enables you to tell what is appropriate and what not, what is to be included and what left out. The idea shapes the constitution, the external and internal relationships, and the activities of the university. It holds the place together and defines and protects it. All we have to do to decide whether we have an idea of a university is to ask ourselves whether there is anything imaginable that would seem inappropriate in an American institution of higher learning.

I shall never forget—though I have often tried—the last meeting of the Big Ten presidents I attended, fifteen years ago. The President of the University of Michigan said, "Say, I want to ask you fellows, what are we going to do about embalming?" He went on to report that the embalmers in his state wanted to become a profession for the double purpose of limiting competition and raising their social standing. This they proposed to accomplish by establishing a school of embalming at the University of Michigan and requiring all practitioners to have a degree from the school before being permitted to embalm any resident of the state.

None of us could think of any reason why the embalmers of Michigan should not have their way. The only consolation offered the President of Michigan came for the President of the University of Minnesota, who assured him that the embalming program at that great university had not interfered with its smooth operation.

If the President of the University of Michigan could get no help from us, he could find none either in the works of our predecessors or contemporaries.

The platform on which Charles W. Eliot, Andrew D. White, David Starr Jordan, and Benjamin Ide Wheeler took their stand was that any subject, interest, or activity was as good as any other. Nothing was more important or more trivial than anything else.

In justice to these great and good men, I must add that their rhetoric may have seemed warranted at the time. They were trying to break open an ancient, narrow curriculum in order to let science in. But they did not foresee where their argument would lead. In his inaugural address in 1869 Mr. Eliot said, "It will be generations before the best American institutions will get enough growth to bear pruning."

But by 1905, Henry Seidel Canby of Yale wrote, a young instructor could look upon an American university, this unheard-of combination of sporting resort, beer garden, political convention, laboratory, and factory for research, with a mind as confused as a Spanish omelet. And Norman Foerster could report by 1931 that a student at the University of Nebraska could take courses in early Irish, creative thinking, American English, first aid, advanced clothing, ice cream and ices, third year Czechoslovakian, football, sewerage, and a man's problems in the modern home.

The most recent historian of the American university says the principle that any subject is as good as another led to a kind of armed truce among departments and specialists—live and let live became the slogan. "The university," he says, "went several different ways at once. It crystallized into a collection of divergent minds, usually ignoring each other, commonly talking past one another, and periodically enjoying the illusion of dialogue on 'safe' issues."

Even departments and schools now seem to be loose associations of professors who are seldom, to borrow a phrase from physics, in a solid state. They are here today and gone tomorrow, consulting, advising and conferring. The situation would have delighted Heraclitus: you cannot put your foot in the same university twice.

The historian I have quoted says that what holds the place together is bureaucracy—the standardized practices by which everybody has to live in order to live at all.

But standardized practices cannot hold anything together unless the object of the exercise is first understood and agreed upon. What *is* the object toward which the procedures of the American university are directed? I am reminded of a recent cartoon depicting a group of cavemen arranged in hierarchical order. The caption underneath is, "Now that we're organized, what the hell do we do?"

President Pusey of Harvard has a reply. To the question, is there a central dominating idea enlivening the American university today, he says, "The answer is, most certainly, yes. For such an idea is found in the devotion to learning which permeates the whole community and in recognition of learning's importance for a full manner of life. . . . Though scholars today often appear to pursue separate ways within universities —quite unaware of their colleague's existence . . . —still by and large they all are, and know they are, working in a common vineyard. They know it is not their specialties but 'learning' . . . that they have in common. The connecting link for all within the university remains learning thus understood, a compact of knowledge, effort, and hope."

A professor on the other side of the tracks, at Boston University, remained unimpressed by the arcane union in a common vineyard of workers unaware of one another, indiscriminately cultivating grapes and thistles, and unable, in fact, to tell one from the other. He spoke for many when he said, "I consider such statements . . . falsely reassuring and deeply misleading in masking the contemporary crisis in the American multiversity."

I gather the current answer to the grape-thistle question is that it is all much ado about very little. We have decided that all thistles are grapes, or that a few thistles won't damage the wine. At any rate, since there is more demand for thistles than grapes, the question is not interesting.

Mr. Pusey's vision of the vineyard cannot match, for sheer unrestrained lyricism, the metaphor of President Perkins of Cornell. He says, "The university and the other institutions of society—including the corporation, the farm, the cultural center, and the government agency—have now been joined together by a new kind of blood stream, made up of the ideas, the trained intelligence, and the manpower which provide the driving energy for our society. And the university is the great pumping heart that keeps this system fresh, invigorated, and in motion."

One is tempted to resort to one of General Eisenhower's more expressive utterances and say simply, "Golly!"

But such primitive sounds are unequal to the demands of an occasion like this, and we must press on to more elaborate formulations of awe and wonder. The objection to the great pumping heart is not merely that it is an example of the fallacy of misplaced physiological concreteness— one would have expected Mr. Perkins to refer to the brain. The fundamental objection is that it takes the society as given, with all its folly and pretentiousness, and asks the university to supply some of the facilities, most of the hands, a lot of the energy, and all of the ideas that will enable the society to achieve its mistaken goals.

This is really the old service station, refurbished, with plush lounges, fluorescent lights, and gaudier signs in bigger words. Whatever the society wants the university will do, provided it gets the money to pay for it. And it is not even what the society wants. It is what the most vocal pressure groups demand.

Some light on this subject comes from an unlikely source, the government of the United Arab Republic. Its official statement is, "It is not an accepted practice for universities to undertake supported research from private organizations or Government agencies. This has safeguarded the freedom of research and has made it possible for the teaching staff to devote more time to basic research."

The old service station rendered service of a kind; there is no doubt about that. And there is no doubt that the new one, with its far more lavish resources and equipment, will render more and perhaps better service of that kind. The only question is whether we lose something in the process. Perhaps we lose the university.

An institution is defined by its task. Its task is defined by asking what it alone can do, or what it can do better than any other institution. The functions of the service station can be carried out by training schools, junior colleges, research institutes, hospitals, commercial laboratories, experiment stations, or what you will. There are services offered by the Boy Scouts, the YMCA, public libraries, settlement houses, city planners, and professional athletic teams. But the greatest service, the service the country needs most, cannot be performed by a service station, no matter how modern its facilities or how elevated its advertising. What the country needs most the university, and only the university, could supply, and that is intellectual leadership. The university could fashion the mind of the age. Now it is the other way round. The demands of the age are fashioning the mind, if one may use the expression, of the university.

If it is to fashion the mind of the age and not be fashioned by it, the university must be a center of independent thought and criticism, an autonomous thinking community. If it could be that, it would automatically rid itself of its cannibalistic tendencies; it would have to disgorge a vast range of miscellaneous, irrelevant activities that it has swallowed. By disgorging the freshman and sophomore years and limiting its professors and students to those capable of independent thought it would get rid of many aspects of immaturity that now confuse it and its supporters. It would at the same time solve the ancient problem of teaching vs. research. Professors and students could be joined together in an endeavor in which teaching and research were indistinguishable.

To be an autonomous thinking community a university would have to be small. Lord James of Rusholme has lately proposed that universities should be limited to three thousand students, that they should be made up of small colleges, and that when an existing university was threatened by larger numbers, a new one should be built across the street. Something of this sort has happened in Toronto. A university of this size, organized on this plan, would be small enough to be a community and small enough to get along without an overwhelming bureaucracy.

When Karl Jaspers suggested something new in Europe, a technological faculty in the university, he did it for a most un-American reason. He explicitly did not do it because he was concerned that his country, or Europe, was falling behind in the production of engineers, or because he wanted to make the university the great pumping heart of the industrial system. He did it because he wanted to put technology in its place. He wanted to bring it within the circle of knowledge and not leave it to technicians. He wanted to subject other disciplines to interaction with it and it to interaction with other disciplines. His summary statement was: "The university must face the great problem of modern man: how out of technology there can arise that metaphysical foundation of a new way of life which technology has made possible." This dark Teutonic saying means that the university has the task of fashioning the mind of the technological age. This task cannot be performed by great pumping hearts. Perhaps it could be by centers of independent thought and criticism, by autonomous thinking communities.

The chairman of an Irish company, on hearing the results of operations for the year, said, "This is all right in practice. But how will it work out in theory?"

He had a point. He knew that unless the operations were intelligible they might not long be profitable.

On this principle one must marvel at the euphoric lyricism of Henry Steele Commager, who has announced that the American university is the greatest success in the history of the world without advancing any theory of its function except that it should continue to perform any tasks society assigns to it. Perhaps any theory of the American university is impossible. Clark Kerr in his brilliant book almost reaches this conclusion. But at the end he offers hope that the university may find that it needs a brain, and he seems optimistic that it will be able to discover one. The brain, if it can be found, might then decipher the idea of the enterprise.

The field upon which we enter with this Convocation has often produced lush crops of doubletalk. Almost every sentence is likely to begin with "Yes but—." A recent book by a Nigerian on Nigerian education, after beginning with the usual tribute to the global nature of learning and of the university ideal, ends by saying that in Nigeria even Shakespeare's Sonnets must be taught with a view to "the light they shed on contemporary African dilemmas." I could not figure out how this could be done until my friend Dr. Bronowski suggested the requirement could be met by working on the problem that has puzzled all the experts on the Sonnets, the problem of the Dark Lady.

It has been said that to be educated is not to have arrived at a destination; it is to travel with a different view. We shall not soon solve the problem of the American university. But we shall be educated about it. We shall travel with a different, and a clearer, view.

2

The modern university student lives in a state of constant frustration, like a man dying of thirst beside a lake, surrounded by men of learning with whom he has only fleeting contact and so hemmed in by academic requirements of an exacting but regurgitory kind that he has little opportunity to develop dialectically as an intellectual and social being.

WILLIAM R. TAYLOR

Paul Shepard
THE VIRTUES OF ANONYMITY

Among the numerous explanations for the rebellions of college students is that the system reduces them to ciphers, professors do not know them as persons, and machines are depriving them of individuality.

This complaint has become a convention. Large student bodies and large classes, mechanization of record-keeping, professors' preoccupation with their research, mass feeding, and housing seem to create a brave new world of personal nonentity.

As a convention it is readily exploited by viewers with alarm. Like most conventions it is a stereotype for a limited perspective. As a college teacher with experience in large and small institutions, I am convinced that numbers and machines are not the causes of student dissatisfaction, nor are they necessarily bad.

Most parents have no idea what they want a college to do for their children. Schools and children are so different from when they were young that they are wholly at sea when it comes to picking a school for Sarah or Johnny. They talk of academic excellence and well-rounded educations, but the truth is that they fear what Sarah will do when she is on her own.

Small colleges have exploited that anxiety for years. They deliberately created an image of the institutional family. The president is the daddy and the dean of students is the mommy. Teachers are friendly uncles or big brothers.

During the past two decades, some colleges have perpetuated that image to their sorrow. Most of them are internally divided about the extent to which they should be substitute moms and dads.

But the damage has been done. There is now a large generation of adults who remember, with misplaced though profound sentiment, the intimate atmosphere of their college classes and kindly old Professor Warmheart who took a personal interest in each of them.

Who are the students who want old Warmheart's attention today, and why? And why does he give it to them? My experience is that three out of ten students bring to him problems that are not even superficially academic. These problems old Warmheart has no business meddling in; they should be left to parents, professionals, or even friends of the students. Five out of ten are exploiting the opportunity for attention. They may keep the talk on Warmheart's special field of Mesozoic worms, but privately, and perhaps unconsciously, they are simply going through the motions of getting their money's worth. Two of the ten need his knowledge of worms, his scholarly advice, and the benefits of his experience.

And why is old Warmheart putting himself through all this? Surely he can distinguish the scholars from the neurotics and the ego-feeders after all these years?

He can. But he has his own problems and his own ego. If he has given up serious research or scholarship he has a big gap to fill. He is clever, articulate, and possibly self-deluded. The easiest, most deadly downhill road for the scholar is becoming a buddy to the students.

Fatuous and fatheaded Warmhearts, whose specialty is bull-slinging at an intimate level, are common though not limited to small colleges, which make a "thing" of small classes and individual attention.

As a teacher, I know that small classes are better than large classes— for certain subjects at certain times. But once a class enrolment exceeds seminar size—perhaps fifteen—it might as well be 1,500. As a student, I much prefer to hear a brilliant lecture in an auditorium than to participate in a windy discussion around a table. The place for small groups is in advanced courses and laboratories. My guess is that the proportion of these is as great as it ever was, in schools of all sizes.

What is missing in all the complaining about mass education is recognition of the virtues of anonymity. The Warmhearts, cosy social planning, and the familial aspects of academia add up merely to frippery. The opportunity to pursue the subject of Mesozoic worms to the limits of one's capacity, to stay up all night reading poetry, to experiment intellectually, socially, or sexually, have nothing to do with whether or not somebody is known to the institution and its functionaries as Sarah Tanner or as "74790."

What is so bad about being known in the registrar's office and the professor's book as "74790" instead of Sarah Tanner? We can readily imagine a stone-age student at good old Neolithic U. complaining that she was no longer confronted as an individual because she was represented by symbols spelling her father's occupation: Tailor, Shepherd or Tanner;

then, later, at Medieval Tech., the young Tanner girl, bitter at the depersonalization forced on her by the addition to her name of one of a limited number of biblical names.

Names composed of letters now have ten centuries of literary-astrological superstition behind them. Number symbols for people have no such mystique going for them.

There are, to be sure, real problems in mass education, such as educationist puffery, pockets of decaying scholarship, administrative inertia, the entrenchment of uncritical thinking, and standardized tools. There are a few professors who do not want to talk to students—sometimes for justifiable reasons. But most professors, in institutions of all kinds, are deeply conscientious and sympathetic. Students must learn that their offices are not perpetual openhouses. But I have never known a teacher who was vitally engaged with his subject to refuse to help a serious student—at a personal level.

Unless he has succumbed to fuddyduddyism, the teacher gets very sharp at recognizing fakers and seekers for parental surrogates. He knows that the student out to master a subject is too busy to waste time at pseudo-dialogue, in parading personal problems, or worrying about whether the college computer thinks of him in letters or numbers.

3

Education should try to lessen the obstacles, diminish the friction, invigorate the energy, and should train minds to react, not at haphazard, but by choice, on the lines of force that attract their world. What one knows is, in youth, of little moment; they know enough who know how to learn.

HENRY ADAMS

Harold Taylor
THE NEED FOR RADICAL REFORM

One of the astonishing facts about the otherwise unastonishing White House Conference on Education of 1965 was its neglect of the problem of teacher education. All the subject got was an almost unreadable paper that rehearsed once more the conventions of Mr. Conant's

From Harold Taylor, "The Need for Radical Reform," *Saturday Review*, November 20, 1965, pp. 75–76, 92–93. Copyright Saturday Review, Inc., 1965. Reprinted by permission of *Saturday Review* and the author.

thinking and ended with a curious summary of hypothetical issues, along with a two-hour panel discussion session that yielded some of the least surprising conclusions ever reported to the plenary session of any conference or to any occupant of the White House.

If one wishes to think of the conference itself as a reflection of the present situation in public rhetoric and private thinking about education in America, the place assigned to teach education at the conference was about what it is everywhere else. That is to say, it is put off to one side and dealt with perfunctorily, as if its major questions had all been answered by a call for more academic preparation, better practice-teaching, and a less inhibiting system of accreditation. The direct link between the education of teachers and the going concerns of every sector in American society from the poor and the deprived to the intellectually and financially well-to-do, the direct connection to the major political and social issues of contemporary world society, the direct responsibility for the quality and scope of America's cultural and moral life, have all been missed or ignored.

In short, the education of teachers has been separated from the major intellectual and social forces of contemporary history. It is conceived to be the acquisition of a skill, a skill in assembling authorized information, distributing it to children and young adults, and testing their ability to receive it and reassemble it.

In fact, it is nothing of the kind. The role of the teacher in any society lies at the heart of its intellectual and social life, and it is through the teacher that each generation comes to terms with its heritage, produces new knowledge, and learns to deal with change. Provided, that is, that the teacher has been well enough educated to act as the transforming element.

The education of teachers is at the nerve center of the whole educational system, and if it fails to function there, the system fails. When we talk about equality of opportunity for all American children we are really talking about an equal chance for every child to be taught by a teacher who understands him, takes his limitations and strengths into account, and has command over a body of knowledge relevant to his teaching and to his place in contemporary society. When we talk about educating the gifted, we are really talking about people who are gifted enough to teach the gifted. When we talk about educational failures and weaknesses we are really talking about failures and weaknesses in teachers and teaching, if teaching is defined as the means through which those who are taught are enabled to learn.

Why, in the face of these facts, which are at the very least self-evident, has the education of teachers never received the attention its massive importance demands?

Mainly, I think, because the public concept of education itself has been too narrow for the large dimension of the task to which it has been assigned. The task is to sustain the spiritual force of a democratic ethos and, at the same time, to create the conditions out of which the millions of children and adults of an expanding society can each make a contribution to the creation of great art, great discovery, great works, great science, and a great society. In a democracy, the welfare of the society rests on its educational system.

But the concept of education held in the public mind and reflected in the practices of the schools is that of a formal training in academic subjects leading toward the achievement of a favorable position in society. Higher education thus becomes a higher form of the same kind of training, leading to a higher position in society. Lower education, or vocational training, is for those whose abilities do not reach to the expert use of language and abstractions, or skill in the academic disciplines, and who will normally occupy a lower place in the society. Those who fit neither vocational nor academic education are left without anything. They drop out, it is said. In reality they are left out.

What is missing in the concept is the idea of education as a liberation of oneself into new levels of intellect and emotion, education as a means of achieving new capacities and insights, which can then become part of the stream of contributions made by the human race in the development of societies and civilizations. The concept contains no call to lend oneself to great enterprises, to become *useful* in the larger sense.

Consequently, the idea of teaching and of the education of teachers has been narrowly conceived to fit a narrow concept, and the teacher is less an intellectual or cultural leader than an agent of social service. He prepares himself, not to serve as an example of man thinking or of man bringing ideas into life, but as man transmitting a curriculum. It follows that his education as a teacher need consist of nothing more than a knowledge of the material in the curriculum which he has learned how to transmit to pupils by studying methods of transmittal and practicing them in a classroom with practice-children.

The education of teachers, or teacher-training, to use its name, is therefore of no great consequence in the public mind. The teacher is a person who is certified as a practitioner of cultural transmission. It is not necessary for his employment that he be a scholar with an intellectual life of his own, nor is it necessary that the people who administer the schools be scholars or even teachers. They are cultural entrepreneurs, responsible to the parents and the community for seeing to it that the cultural transmission occurs properly and that the children become qualified for entry into further education and entry into a congenial place in society.

We will never achieve the goals we seek in education until we alter these concepts and turn again to the truth about teaching, that it is a creative art, a healing art, that it demands for its true accomplishment the qualities of character and intellect that can be gained only by those who are moved to reach out toward them. The beginning point and the secret of the whole undertaking lies in the sense of fulfillment that comes to the one who is able to make an honest act of commitment to a vocation in the true sense of that word, the kind of commitment the poet, the dancer, the painter, the sculptor, the doctor makes when he decides that this is what he must do and what he must be. Once a commitment has been made, the image of oneself as a dancer, a doctor, a scientist, an architect, a teacher, begins to take effect as a goal toward which each separate effort day by day in preparation makes its own contribution. One sets out to become what has been imagined, and the discipline of becoming is then undergone willingly and gladly, in the way the violinist lends himself to the demands of his instrument. The problem with so much of undergraduate education, for the general student and for the teacher, is that it is not undertaken for a purpose; it is not infused with energy by an act of commitment to prepare oneself for carrying out a task of known significance.

It is the sense of commitment to a useful purpose that sustains the Peace Corps volunteer, both in his act of volunteering and his preparation for Peace Corps service. The volunteer is asked to give himself, in whatever his capacity, to the world's task of improving the lot of mankind. His two years of service are a contribution to the sum total of human welfare, and his self-assignment for low pay in difficult conditions is like that of the civil rights workers who leaves his career in college or elsewhere to teach and to work with the Negro in the South. To begin the reformation of teacher education it is necessary to return to the roots of the matter, in the restoration of teaching to its place among vocations.

Until now, we have never mounted a full national attack on the problem of educating teachers, using large resources in money and intellect, no matter what proclamations have been made about the crucial role of education in the national welfare. The universities have left it to the teachers' colleges, the teachers' colleges have now begun to model themselves on the universities and to seek the respectability of not being colleges for teachers. In doing so they have usually given up the idea of teaching as a vocation in favor of the idea of the teacher as a man who has met university requirements. Nor have we ever called upon American youth to take up teaching as a vocation in which all their talents can be used to the full in the cause of American society. We can no longer afford our negligence. The urgency of the present situation demands head-on action, on a large scale.

When I speak of the present situation, I begin with the proposition that the radical social changes of the postwar years have far outrun the ability of the educational system to keep up with them. It is of course true that there is always an organic connection between changes in society that force new demands upon education, which, in turn, by the character of its response, transforms the demands into a series of further changes within the society. If the demands are for more scientists and technologists, who are then produced by the educational system, the mere existence of an expanded body of scientific talent produces new possibilities for change within the society. Except in general terms, certain of the changes can neither be predicted nor controlled; the process of change has a life of its own and throws off events and phenomena that cannot be stopped and that simply must be dealt with.

Yet the function of education is to anticipate and to give direction to changes that are occurring day by day within world society and its local counterparts, not simply to confirm those changes. The circumstances of contemporary American society are now making extreme demands that the educational system is not ready to meet—demands for an education of quality for those who have until now been deprived of it, demands for the reconstruction of society from top to bottom in order to bring the fruits of an expanding economy in a post-industrial era to all American citizens. The dimensions of the reconstruction reach from establishment of equality in economic and social opportunity to the enrichment of the cultural and esthetic life of all citizens.

When we look for the sources of new ideas in education to meet these needs, we find them more often among the energetic and concerned activists of government, busy with new plans and new legislation, and among the activist college students, than we do in the ranks of the educators. In fact, few people outside government have come to understand the enormous power for educational and social change that lies in the new federal legislation. It is jammed with educational provisions, not merely in the clauses of the Elementary and Secondary School Act, but in the Community Action program of the Civil Rights Bill, the Economic Opportunity Act with its Job Training Centers, the Domestic Service Corps, VISTA, Head Start, the Peace Corps.

Although it has never been fully described, there is a social and educational philosophy implicit in the legislation that holds the seeds of a powerful new educational movement. The Anti-Poverty Program and the Peace Corps movement are a call to public service; the funds provided by the legislation are merely the catalyst for voluntary effort. A power for action through this legislation lies in the deep strain of voluntarism and individualism in American life out of which have come the thousands of voluntary organizations to deal with everything from protecting animals and children to directing American foreign policy. It also lies in the progressive tradition of social thinking that has its roots in Emerson, Horace Mann, John Dewey and others—the idea of participatory democracy, indigenous leadership, activism, pluralism, experimentalism, with the test of an idea to be found in the way it works in practice.

It is this power that must now be used in joining the forces of social change in a frontal attack on the problem of educating teachers. We have already seen the power at work in the student movement in civil rights through which dozens of new programs in education, both for teachers and for children, have emerged in the Freedom Schools established by students and in the adult education programs that they have organized as part of voter-registration projects. The students from the North, the West, and the Midwest who in these past three years have volunteered for service in the rural South and in the slums of big cities found themselves immediately faced with all the problems of education as soon as they joined the movement. In one sense the student movement became one vast program in teacher education, in which the student volunteers were forced to educate themselves, to invent their own teaching methods, write their own mimeographed texts, organize their own classes, create their own curricula, and motivate their students while surrounded by a hostile and potentially dangerous white community.

As they joined forces with the young Southern Negroes whose education had either been interrupted or had never begun, the white college students began to see ways in which college study, if it were made relevant to actual conditions within American and world society, could become an essential component in the development of political awareness and social action. Knowledge was seen as something necessary to the achievement of broad social goals. In some cases the students developed new work-study programs and proposals for their own education that were accepted by colleges and universities on their return there; in other cases they called upon faculty members in schools of education and universities for special help in teaching courses and seminars on the spot to the Southern students, Negro and white.

In a comparable way, the experience of the Peace Corps volunteer abroad could be classified as a program in teacher education through which he learns to use his wits to find the ways of being useful to the community he serves. He may not be teaching a school subject, although in many cases he is thrust into service as an English or science teacher whether he has been prepared for it or not, but whatever he does abroad is an aspect of the task of teachers—to help a community to help itself.

We have here the concept and the elements for a radical reform in the education of the American teacher. The reform starts with an exact reversal of the philosophy dominant in present programs. That is to say, rather than thinking of the number of courses, credits, and subjects necessary to certify a teacher, we set aside all formal requirements and start from the beginning with the question of what is to be done to enhance the personal and intellectual growth of the person who is learning to be a teacher.

One of the first things we would then do is invite all those students who have done volunteer service in the rural and urban slums to come into the schools of education and the universities to work out fresh and interesting programs of study and experience through which they could prepare to become members of the teaching profession. A general invitation would be made to all other interested youths to join in a national recruitment of teachers backed by state and federal scholarships.

For those interested in social science or literature or biology or sculpture, arrangements would be made for work in depth in the field of their concern, regardless of whether or not they intended to teach in it. Each student would be asked to work out a tentative study plan for his first two years, identifying the areas of study he proposes for his own education and the reasons he has chosen them. Each would be asked to suggest an appropriate program of field work for himself, either in a nonresident term or year devoted to the civil rights movements, VISTA, counseling, or elsewhere in government or private social welfare programs. Each would be asked to choose one of the creative arts in which to engage himself for a time, to suggest possibilities for foreign travel, work, and study of the kind developed through the Experiment in International Living.

Direct relations would be established between federal and state agencies responsible for various parts of the antipoverty program and social welfare legislation, to discover how students preparing to become teachers could work directly in the programs as part of their curriculum. Other arrangements would be made with the Peace Corps for a variety of programs similar to the five-year Peace Corps curriculum at Western Michigan University, which includes two years of overseas duty as part of the degree requirements. Direct arrangements would be made with slum schools in all the major cities for the placement of teams of student-teachers who would serve the teachers and children there as tutors, assistants, apprentices, and recreation leaders for three to six months at a time.

In other words, starting from a base in a concern for the total development of each teacher, the university or school of education would work with him to put together an individual program of experience and study that placed a major responsibility on the student himself for choice and decision about the content of his own education. His preparation might take four years or five, depending on the length of time that seemed appropriate for the various stretches of work and study. His experience in preparation would naturally include direct work with children in subjects that he had mastered at a respectable intellectual level.

But that kind of experience could start even before college, when the teacher-candidate was in high school, through tutoring assignments in nearby elementary schools after hours, or through experience in leading seminars, discussions, and tutorials in the high school, provided his talents had developed sufficiently in that direction. He would also be given the chance to teach his peers in his university classes as well as to share in the development of new courses in collaboration with the faculty, using materials from his own research and field work experience.

It would be an education in which everyone taught everyone else, since, in a reformed program of teacher education, the major part of the instruction would be through student-run seminars, tutorials, independent study, and discussion. How else could a teacher learn what it means to teach?

Students of foreign language and of foreign cultures would travel abroad for their field periods, and new international centers would be started on a number of campuses to which would be invited foreign students and foreign teachers in large numbers for the express purpose of joining in the teacher-preparation programs. Foreign and American students would work in teams, preparing, in the case of Latin American students for example, to work together for voluntary service in Latin America and in the United States, Soviet and Eastern European students could be invited to attend the international centers to act as teaching assistants in foreign languages and literature, and to prepare for volunteer service both here and at home.

The first step toward the larger support of teacher education has already been taken in legislation proposed for recruiting experienced teachers for work in deprived areas, for financing experimental projects in teacher education, and for financing the education of teachers through national and state fellowships. If the invitation from Congress and the President to experiment in teacher education were taken up by the colleges and universities, and a national program of reform of the present system were to begin through such experiments, a large-scale attack on the problem would then find its support in the power of the social changes now moving through the world of the poor and the deprived. The intention of the President and his Administration is very clear. The President aims to develop the pent-up resources of the American people through a continually expanding program of education, and what we have seen this last year is just a beginning. Educational expansion can go only as far as the teachers can take it.

What becomes of what has been so highly regarded as the major problem of the education of teachers, the problem of their certification? It slips back into its rightful place as a technical matter connected with record-keeping. There is no reason why students preparing to become teachers should not enjoy serious and sustained work in the history, psychology, and philosophy of education, and learn something about its methods by work-study programs and practice-teaching in Venezuela, Iran, Bakersfield, or Selma. There is no reason why responsible universities and colleges cannot bestow the correct number of credits on their students for work in these fields when it satisfies the requirements of honesty, integrity, intellectual achievement, and educational experience. There is no reason why we cannot begin again, with bigger conceptions than we have ever had in our history, the historical task of raising the level of democratic society by raising the level of its education.

4

Boswell:
"We talked of the education of children; and I asked
him what he thought was best to teach them first."
Johnson:
"Sir, it is no matter what you teach them first, any
more than what leg you shall put into your breeches
first. Sir, you may stand disputing which is best to
put in first, but in the meantime your breech is bare.
Sir, while you are considering which of two things
you should teach your child first, another boy has
learnt them both."

Paul Woodring

THE TWO TRADITIONS OF TEACHER EDUCATION IN THE UNITED STATES

Many of the conflicts and confusions found in teacher education today grow out of the fact that we have two distinct traditions of teacher education in the United States. The older tradition, which long controlled the education of secondary teachers, and which still controls the education of college teachers, provides the basis for what may be called the academic or liberal arts view of teacher education. The second tradition —which is newer although it now has a history of well over one hundred years—is that of the professional educator and is most evident in the normal schools and teachers colleges which have long provided a substantial number of elementary teachers and now prepare secondary teachers as well. The teacher education found in the university schools of education is an unsuccessful marriage of the two which has failed so far to synthesize the two philosophies. This failure may be seen in the sharp conflicts of view which may be found between professional educators and academic professors in many an American university.

These two divergent traditions have led to differing conceptions of the proper curriculum for teacher education, and the widespread emphasis given to these curricular differences has tended to obscure the fact that the underlying conflict is philosophical. The two traditions represent totally different concepts of the nature of man, of the learning process, and of the proper role and limitations of free public schools. Although both traditions stress the importance of the human individual, the older one holds that *formal* education is properly centered in the

From Paul Woodring, "The Two Traditions of Teacher Education in the United States," *New Directions in Teacher Education* (New York: The Fund for the Advancement of Education, 1957), pp. 17–26. Reprinted by permission of the Fund and the author.

world of knowledge and is concerned with the development of the mind. The newer traditions prefer to place the stress upon the "whole child." It places great emphasis upon the learning process and interprets this process in a way which extends it far beyond academic or intellectual learning. It is no accident that the newer tradition first gained its foothold in the elementary schools or that higher education has clung more firmly to the older tradition. The secondary schools have been caught between the two.

The early American secondary schools were, in large part, college preparatory institutions and it seemed natural that an academy which prepared students for Yale or Harvard should draw its faculty from among the graduates of those colleges. It was assumed that a sound liberal and academic education was also the best teacher education and that, in selecting teachers, scholarship should be the prime prerequisite. The major responsibility for learning was placed upon the student and, if he failed to learn, the fault was held to be his rather than the teacher's.

The public high schools, which developed during the second half of the nineteenth century, continued this tradition and an A.B. degree was accepted as satisfactory evidence of preparation for high school teaching. The high school teacher was expected to demonstrate competence in his subject, he was not expected to accept any large responsibility for the student's social adjustment or his recreation and rarely did he take an active part in planning the high school curriculum. If he taught his subject well, and lived within community mores, little more was expected of him. Professional training was rarely considered to be a necessary or even a desirable part of the high school teacher's preparation. This concept of the role and the training of the secondary teacher continued well into the present century and even today provides the basis for much of the criticism of the teacher education found in the teachers colleges.

As the academic content of schools and colleges became increasingly departmentalized during the nineteenth century, secondary teachers became more and more specialized. High school teachers, like the college professors who taught them, came to think of themselves less as teachers than as historians, classicists, scientists, or mathematicians. This was something new in the educational world, for the great philosopher-teachers from Socrates to Kant were never specialists in this sense.

Although the new tradition of the teacher as a subject specialist eventually reached down through the secondary school, it never reached into the elementary schools except possibly in the case of music teachers. Teachers for the elementary schools were of a different breed. Rarely, until recent decades, were they college graduates, and rarely were they expected to be scholars. Prior to the development of the normal schools in the second quarter of the nineteenth century, few elementary teachers had any specific instruction for their work and few had themselves progressed beyond the elementary school. Undoubtedly some were kindly and intelligent but others were the Ichabod Cranes—itinerant ne'er do-wells who taught because they could do nothing else or as a step toward a more remunerative and more respected profession. Far from being a profession, elementary teaching was a temporary job available to almost any literate person who would accept it and who could maintain some degree of order in the classroom.

The normal schools were developed for the specific purpose of improving elementary education by providing a new kind of teacher for the lower schools. Beginning in New England, about 1830, the normal-school movement spread across the country until by 1900 such institutions had come into a dominant position in elementary teacher education. Some were under private auspices while others were state or municipal institutions, and in the rural areas there were many county normal schools offering brief summer courses.

The normal-school movement was sponsored by devoted men and women and the devotion was to the improvement of elementary education for all. The movement was influenced by the writings of Rousseau, Herbart, Pestalozzi, and Froebel and later James and Dewey. The early normal schools accepted the prevailing emphasis on the three R's but added a new emphasis on the nature and needs of the child as a growing human being. If their view occasionally was sentimental, based perhaps upon a too-easy acceptance of Rousseau's doctrine of the inherent goodness of the child in his natural state, it also was consistent with the growing humanitarianism of the century. It gave the teacher a new responsibility for understanding the child and for providing motivation and interest in the learning process. There seems little doubt that the graduates of the normal schools brought about great improvement in elementary education.

The early normal schools were in no sense collegiate institutions and it was not intended that they should be. Students came directly from the elementary schools and returned as teachers after a period ranging from a few weeks to two years. Academic instruction was at best on the level of that provided in the academies with the addition of instruction in pedagogic skills and a review of the subjects taught in elementary schools.

It was the rapid development of the free public high school after 1870 that changed all this and resulted in the development of normal schools into degree granting teachers colleges. By 1900, high school graduates were available in sufficient numbers so that many normal schools could require a high school diploma for admission, and by 1920 many normal schools were offering four-year post-high-school courses terminating in a college degree. By the mid-1930's many normal schools had changed their names to teachers colleges or colleges of education and by 1950 many of the state institutions had dropped the words "teachers" or "of education" from their titles and had become general or liberal arts colleges, or, in some cases, universities.

The change has been by no means in name only. Liberal arts offerings have been greatly increased and the faculties have been strengthened by the addition of graduates of leading graduate schools. In Ohio, for example, where teachers colleges went out of existence more than twenty years ago, the institutions which once were normal schools, and then teachers colleges, at Bowling Green and Kent, are now large state universities with highly diversified offerings. To continue to call such institutions "teachers colleges" because of their historical origin is as meaningless as it would be to refer to the University of Pennsylvania as an academy because it was so designated by its founder.

As a result of these changes the term "teachers college" is fast becoming obsolete. A generation ago there were nearly three hundred such institutions supported by the states in addition to many city and county normal schools of less than collegiate status. Today the normal school has gone the way of the stagecoach and the number of state teachers colleges has dropped to a little over one hundred. The teachers college as an institution separate from universities and liberal arts colleges has disappeared in twenty-one of the forty-eight states although in all these states there are many colleges, both public and private, which prepare teachers along with their other responsibilities.

Most of the teachers colleges which remain are rapidly becoming general colleges in everything but name and many have plans to make requests of state legislatures for changes in their names, scope, and functions. It seems a safe guess that within twenty years, perhaps within ten years, the separate undergraduate teachers colleges will have gone the way of the dodo. The state college which replaces it is a generalized institution in which only a fraction of the students are preparing to become teachers.

One result of this change is that much of the recent criticism of teacher education has missed its proper mark. The critic who attacks teacher education in terms of the teachers college is likely, when he looks around him, to find he is attacking a ghost rather than a reality. The remaining teachers colleges are responsible for the education of only about 20 per cent of all new teachers entering our elementary and secondary schools. In contrast 32 per cent come from private liberal arts colleges and universities and 48 per cent from public liberal arts colleges and universities. It seems clear that if changes are to be made in teacher education we must give our attention to all the colleges that prepare teachers rather than to teachers colleges alone.

Even the remaining teachers colleges have increased their liberal arts offerings until today virtually every subject taught in any liberal arts college is available in some of the better teachers colleges and is taught by men and women with the same academic background as professors in universities and liberal arts colleges—teachers who hold Ph.D. degrees from universities and whose professional commitment is to an academic discipline rather than to education as a profession. The academic world seems to be unaware of the change for the charge is repeatedly made that teachers colleges teach nothing but "methods." It would be more accurate to say that the typical student graduating from a teachers college, if he is preparing for high school teaching, receives about three-fourths of a liberal arts course. If he is preparing for elementary teaching about one-half to two-thirds of his work is in the liberal arts. The *quality* of the liberal education varies from college to college, just as it does in colleges granting the A.B. degree.

It is true, however, that the teachers colleges, as a group, have continued to place a larger emphasis on professional courses than do liberal arts colleges which prepare teachers and this is particularly true of the programs for elementary teachers. The emphasis is not on methods alone, but is on educational psychology, educational principles, and educational philosophy. To refer to these professional courses as "methods" is misleading; the psychology of learning is no more a course in methods than is physiology as taught in a medical school and educational philosophy, if it lives up to its name, is the very antithesis of methodology. Yet the heavy emphasis on professional requirements, and on an extended period of practice teaching, amounting in some colleges to full time for an entire semester, has made it impossible for most teachers colleges to require a full sequence of courses in liberal education and a concentration in a major subject comparable to that usually required for an A.B. degree. One result has been that the graduate of a teachers college, who has greatest need for subject matter concentration on the graduate level, often finds the graduate school reluctant to admit him for a course leading to a master of arts degree in his chosen subject. If he wishes to take graduate work he is forced to take it in education. At the same time the student whose undergraduate work was in the liberal arts frequently is refused admission to a graduate program in education because of his lack of undergraduate professional courses. In each case the student gets more of what he least needs and has no opportunity to fill in the gaps in his preparation.

Many liberal arts colleges have, for many years, offered professional courses for teachers but they have offered them reluctantly and more with an eye to legal requirements for teacher certification than from any real conviction of the value of such courses. Rarely, prior to 1950, did they take the lead in the improvement of the professional part of the teacher's education.

During the first half of the present century, while many liberal arts colleges turned their backs on the problems of teacher education, legal requirements for certification were established in nearly all states. In general the trend was away from certification on the basis of examination and toward certification on the basis of completion of course requirement in colleges and universities. Because the total number of college years required for teaching, particularly for elementary teachers, has steadily increased, there has been increased opportunity for both professional *and* liberal education but the legal requirements have been much more specific about professional courses and have allowed the colleges more discretion in the field of liberal education. Many states specify certain courses which must be taken in professional fields so that the responsibility for curriculum making has, in part, been taken away from the colleges.

When the academic community awoke to what had happened it was loud in its denunciation of the certification laws and the professional educators responsible for them. In the new requirements some thought they saw a conspiracy on the part of professional educators to take the responsibility for teacher education away from the world of scholarship.

There was no conspiracy, of course, but it is quite true that the responsibility for teacher education had been allowed to slip out of the hands of the academic scholars. What happened was that while the liberal arts colleges were preoccuped with other things, while they ignored the problems of teacher education, a like-minded group of school administrators and other professional educators came to agreement among themselves on the necessity for professional preparation for teachers and transmitted their convictions into law. It was during this same period that the educators became imbued with a new philosophy of education, one far removed from the academic traditions of the liberal arts colleges.

Many liberal arts professors remained convinced that professional courses of any kind were inconsistent with the proper aims of the liberal arts college and that the presence of such courses in the curriculum would vitiate the liberal arts program. It was feared that the increasingly heavy load of professional requirements would make it impossible to prepare teachers with a sound liberal arts background and a number of colleges refused to offer any professional courses whatever. Professional educators, however, were adamant in their insistence that professional requirements could not be lowered and ought, indeed, to be raised still higher.

The conflict between the two points of view reached a climax in the early 1950's with the publication of numerous controversial books and magazine articles and a renewed public interest in the schools and their teachers. It was into this atmosphere of confusion, uncertainty, and acrimony that The Fund for the Advancement of Education was born and the work of the Fund in teacher education can be assessed only in terms of these problems, their history, and their consequences.

With encouragement and financial assistance from the Fund a number of liberal arts faculties have, in the past five years, explored the problems of teacher education. The faculties which have given careful atten tion to the problems have come, often reluctantly, to the conclusion that a certain amount of professional preparation is a necessary background for both elementary and secondary teachers, regardless of legal requirements for certification. Some have sought ways of providing this outside the regular four-year liberal arts curriculum, either through summer school courses or during a fifth year which includes an internship in the public schools with correlated professional seminars or classes. A few, after a thorough investigation of the entire problem of teacher preparation, have introduced reorganized professional courses into the undergraduate curriculum. As the findings from these projects are correlated and disseminated new patterns begin to emerge.

If we assume that teacher preparation must include *both* liberal and professional education and that these two must be brought into harmony with each other in some organized pattern, there would appear to be four ways of approaching the problem:

1. A fifth year of professional training and experience can be provided for liberal arts graduates.
2. Liberal arts colleges can be encouraged to incorporate essential professional training into their programs in ways in which will not vitiate the liberal arts program.
3. Universities can be encouraged to devise new programs which represent the best thinking of both academic and professional faculties.
4. Teachers colleges can be assisted in providing better liberal arts programs and in reorganizing their professional courses in such a way as to eliminate proliferation and duplication.

The fourth possibility has so far received little attention from The Fund for the Advancement of Education. Perhaps the reason is that the presidents of teachers colleges have shown too little indication of willingness to attack these problems vigorously and have submitted too few imaginative proposals for Fund assistance.

Much more attention has been given to programs of teacher education within liberal arts colleges and universities but the major emphasis, during the early years of the Fund's existence, has been upon fifth-year programs for liberal arts graduates. This emphasis has opened a new source of teacher supply and has provided for the schools many liberally educated teachers who without the new programs would have been lost to the profession.

The long-range solutions, however, must affect all institutions which educate teachers whether they be universities, teachers colleges, or colleges of liberal arts. We cannot ignore the fact that the greater numbers of our teachers always have come, not from the upper income groups where parents prefer to have their children enter the more remunerative professions, but from among the more intelligent boys and girls of the lower economic classes who look upon the teaching profession as an opportunity to be of service while moving upward from the unskilled and skilled labor groups. Such potential teachers are not found, in large numbers, among the graduates of the more socially selective private colleges. They must be found wherever they are and provided with opportunity for the best kind of teacher education we know how to give them.

Never has there been a greater need for research and experimentation in teacher education and teacher recruitment, but neither has there been a time when experimentation was so certain to lead to controversy. The conflict of views has been brought to the attention of the American people at a time when the teacher shortage is one of alarming magnitude and threatens, at the higher levels particularly, to become increasingly serious.

Programs for the improvement of teacher education must include an effort to synthesize the conflicting views and at the same time must look for new sources in teacher recruitment. Experimental attacks must be bold, imaginative, and philosophically oriented as well as adequately financed. Money alone is useless unless it is coupled with sound ideas.

5

Unless we in teacher education come to grips with what the teacher is and set about producing the environment in which the teacher can grow as a person —in all his uniqueness—little else that we do will have a substantial effect. The growth of the teacher as an individual human being is the central problem of teacher education. Our failure here is responsible for the failure of our schools to develop excitement in learning on the part of their pupils. In addition, even though this is our central problem it gets little attention in teacher education.

ERNEST O. MELBY

Sam P. Wiggins
TEACHERS COLLEGES:
EVOLUTION OR DEVOLUTION

Change and progress are not identical. Yet, some of us view a change with pride before we examine its nature and implications. Like-

From Sam P. Wiggins, "Teachers Colleges: Evolution or Devolution," *Battlefields in Teacher Education* (Nashville, Tenn.: George Peabody College for Teachers, 1964), pp. 63–74. Copyright 1964 George Peabody College for Teachers. Reprinted by permission of the publisher and author.

wise, pining for a return to the "good old days," as do those in the *status quo ante* group, is of the same magnitude in sophistry. Finally, the notion that "we have arrived"—an uncritical loyalty to the status quo—rounds out the trio of folly.

Rising out of such views, billows of smoke engulf the struggles of teachers colleges in American life. The struggle has been more intense than it is today, but the issue remains a live one. After the teachers college as an institution has been given a decent burial, there will continue to be skirmishes and guerilla warfare. A reconstruction period full of friction will bear the scars of this battle.

The Struggle Upward

The unorthodox thinking and action of Nicholas Murray Butler set the stage for the conflict. In 1886, feeling a growing demand for the professional education of teachers, he began offering Saturday morning lectures at Columbia College to test his conviction. The idea, which had been predicted to be futile, proved to be so successful that no auditorium at Columbia College could accommodate the teachers who wished to attend. From this beginning, inauspicious in planning but highly auspicious in actuality, emerged in 1887 the New York College for the Training of Teachers, and five years later, Teachers College.

There is no struggle until there is a threat to something one holds dear. The development of the normal schools, in the latter half of the nineteenth century, was looked on with only mild interest by the officials of colleges and universities. The early rise of the teachers colleges at the turn of the twentieth century did not occasion any immediate major threat or any struggle.

Emerging from the normal schools, the teachers college became the name of high repute. In 1908, the Department of Normal Schools of the National Education Association prepared a policy statement for the normal schools which became the platform for transformation of normal schools to teachers colleges. "Good as the word normal is," the policy announced, "it should be dropped from the name of these schools, and they should be called 'teachers colleges'." The resolution following this policy statement explained how the normal school might logically evolve its new, broad, and higher function of preparing teachers for secondary as well as elementary schools.

The parallel of the near extinct of the normal school and the present near extinction of the teachers college is interesting. During the period 1910 to 1930, the danger existed that the normal school would be "left stranded, high and dry on the banks of the broadening educational current." The big squeeze to prevent the new teachers colleges from developing made the battle a fierce one. The liberal arts colleges and state universities then began to feel the threat, and came to view these developments with concern. The "three musketeers" in preventing the teachers colleges from being crowded out were Homer Searley of Iowa; John Kirk of Missouri; and David Felmley of Illinois.

Both sides of the fray mustered up their most scholarly arguments in defense of their positions. Some of the real reasons for the contest, which would not have sounded so scholarly, were not included. The main arguments of the teachers college leaders were (1) the historical and legal position of the teachers college, (2) the inconsistency of separating the preparation of elementary and high school teachers, (3) the rejection of professional courses in education on the part of the liberal arts colleges and universities, and, finally, (4) the freedom to experiment within a professional outlook that was considered unique in the teachers colleges.

During the period up to 1940, the battle was uphill all the way for the teachers colleges, but, in the main, they won it. Between 1920 and 1940, *103* normal schools were converted to teachers colleges, most of them raising the level of education from two years of college to a basic four-year program.

The fight for recognition in higher education was long and slow. Various regional accrediting associations were grudging and condescending in their final acquiescence to consider a teachers college for accreditation. The Middle States Association of Colleges and Secondary Schools demurred in its accreditation of teachers colleges until 1936. The Southern Association took the step somewhat earlier. The North Central Association later. During the period between 1920 and 1940, The American Association of Teachers Colleges, which had banded together for improving the character and reputation of teacher education, opened its membership to other colleges which at least professed a strong interest in teacher education. In 1947, the organization became the American Association of Colleges for Teacher Education.

College administrators have customarily taken the position that liberal arts scholars have permitted whatever weaknesses there are in teacher education to develop by default. Others have taken a neutral position, arguing for conciliation but refusing to take sides in the efforts to conciliate. Former Chancellor L. A. Kimpton of the University of Chicago expressed the view that if the schools of education hold a monopoly on the training of secondary school teachers "it is only because no one else has paid any attention to them."

In his address before the American Council on Education in 1958, President Virgil Hatcher of the State University of Iowa explained the reason for the lack of sustained attention to teacher education by professors in other academic fields. He pointed out that the learned professors of the nineteenth century felt it beneath their dignity to prepare teachers for the common school. He said it would be a glorious prospect if we could expect all professors to concern themselves with a long-range program for the improvement of schools, but that their professional interest and professional advancement, by their own criteria, lead them into other pursuits. He predicted that within five years most, if not all, of the present critics among the group would "have returned to Beowulf or Chaucer or the political policies of Sir Robert Walpole, or the causes of the French Revolution, or the peaceful uses of atomic power." He expressed the view that high school teachers of English and social studies and science will again need to turn to the professional educationists "who are their only constant and true friends in time of need." The intervening years have proven him to be right, with the notable exception of Vice Admiral Rickover who refuses to go back to his atomic submarine. While these positions may be true as generalizations, they neglect an important minority group within the various disciplines where sustained interest in teacher education continues to prevail.

The struggle continues, but its form is different. A generation ago it was easier to blame the ills afflicting teacher education upon the teachers college. There were scores of them, and a large number of them shared a guilt in whatever sins were committed in the name of teacher education. The current situation, however, is one of teachers college obsolescence. During the period 1964–70, the picture is virtually certain to continue further in this direction.

King for a Day

The year 1939 was a significant historical date for American teacher education. It marked the end of a century of public teacher education, which had its humble origin in Lexington, Massachusetts. Here three young ladies on July 3, 1839, began attending the first state supported school for the exclusive purpose of preparing teachers. Cyrus W. Pierce, the principal of the school, was getting something started that resulted a century later in almost two hundred teachers colleges enrolling more than 100,000 students.

Some teachers colleges attempted to gain prestige by imitating those institutions which already had acquired it. Others, which had a more intrinsic sense of purpose, were led by educators who felt that teachers college degrees should be developed to the point that they would be recognized on their own merit. President Bruce R. Payne of George Peabody College for Teachers, for example, told his faculty he wanted, above all, a college that was "right for teachers." These educators were interested in the qualitative significance of programs more than in the accolades of scholarly respectability and reputation.

Despite many struggles within the states against the threat of the "educational colossus in the state university," the teachers college seemed firmly established in 1939. As Harper analyzed the situation at this peak point of the teachers college life, "the teachers colleges are just beginning to emerge from the paralyzing effects of the old classical, traditional, medieval liberal arts curriculum pattern."

A major point of contention in gaining the approval of accrediting institutions (notably that of the North Central Association of Colleges and Secondary Schools) had to do with that part of professional education which deals with practice or apprenticeship experiences. The less bookish the experience, the less respectability could be claimed for it. This is an ironic note of history in view of current criticisms of teachers colleges by Conant, Koerner, and others. The one remaining aspect which is generally recognized as being essential is the student teaching experience. The respectable bookish requirements of a generation ago are now rejected, and what was then the object of scorn remains as the sole subject of praise.

During its hey-day, the teachers college was undergoing many crucial tests. No greater test was given it than that of wisely selecting, from the oversupply of applicants, those students who were most likely to become teachers worthy of the educational programs available to them. The incurable desire for bigness in America may have proved to be the Achilles heel of the teachers college. There are many plausible, expedient reasons why they—especially the state supported colleges—could not be selective. Yet, we in retrospect, can but wonder how things might have been different. We pause as we reflect upon the statement of Charles Harper that there was no doubt as to the future greatness of the American teachers college, depending on the extent to which the faculties were inspired to give "their full energy and unhampered intelligence to the grave problem involved in preparing teachers capable of meeting the new day in education." The tragedy is that, all too often, the teachers colleges proved unequal to that challenge.

The TC Bugle Sounds "Retreat"

Soon after the teachers college in America reached its peak of influence and of national effectiveness, its descent from the throne was swift and of epidemic proportions. The whole story cannot be told simply, but main threads in it can be easily identified. Paul Woodring explained it in positive terms as a natural evolution which represents progress. He regards the teachers college as a "way station between the normal school and the next stage in the development of these institutions" because "the seeds of its own destruction were inherent within it."

The origin of the concept of "seeds of self-destruction" is of no particular significance in this context. These particular seeds refer to faculty members, brought into the teachers college from English, science, mathematics, or from other academic fields, whose commitments were not to the education of teachers but to their own academic interests. These people were lured into the teachers colleges, Woodring explains, but were not sympathetic to their purposes. Students who did not wish to be teachers were also enticed into these institutions, according to Woodring. They, too, were anxious to expand the function of the colleges beyond teacher preparation.

Both factors had a bearing on the situation, but other factors influenced it, too. During the period of considerable shortage of students, prior to World War II, teachers colleges and liberal arts colleges were competing for students to such an extent that liberal arts colleges began introducing teacher education curriculums and teachers colleges expanded their curriculums so that in their recruiting tactics they became colleges for everybody.

The phenomenon of "invasion," a sociological term generally employed with reference to housing areas within a city, appears to have had some bearing upon the rapid abandonment of the term "teachers." As a city grows naturally outward, some few "undesirable" families move into a "good" neighborhood. This creates a kind of irrational panic on the part of home owners. Whether the undesirable attributes are real or imagined has no bearing upon the fact. When invasion begins or when it is rumored to begin, it is like shouting "fire" in a crowded theatre— every person becomes his own enemy by creating or contributing to a panic situation. When a few teachers colleges, in their upward striving for prestige or for other reasons, dropped the name "teachers" to become state colleges and subsequently universities, a lot of other things happened, too. But, whatever the factors that prompted the initial development, the phenomenon of invasion was evident.

One could make a cogent argument, as Paul Woodring does, that a multipurpose institution has many advantages over one which claims only to educate teachers. If this were the only reason for the change, the development would assure a true evolution in teacher education. To the extent that factors springing from a lower actual dedication to teacher education are involved, teacher education is moving backward toward the normal school era and is calling it progress. Henry H. Hill, President Emeritus of George Peabody College for Teachers, may have stated the case prophetically when he said that if the successors to teachers colleges become mediocre and abandon their concern for teachers "another generation will have to start teachers colleges all over again."

In the twentieth century, a great deal of significance has been attached to names, one way or the other. The fact that regional accrediting associations would not consider for accreditation, for a time, any institution which bore the name teachers college is an illustration. From the standpoint of historical consistency, of course, the liberal arts college had to maintain that it had always been an institution for educating teachers and that professionalizing its curriculum was a minor event in the total structure of college life and thought.

The teachers college, however, in abandoning its singleness of purpose needed to review the name by which it lived. Two arguments supported change. One was a matter of semantics. Was it accurate to call an institution a teachers college if training teachers was only one of its multiple functions? The answer to that question is surely "no," from the standpoint of the linguistic purist.

The second argument was the more dominant one, but less respectable for free and open discussion. This dealt with the matter of expansion. The transition from a single purpose institution to a multipurpose one could be explained on the basis that it is good for future teachers to be educated along with other future professionals in law, in medicine, and in business and that it is good, also, to recognize the multipurpose nature of a college in the title of the institution. But the real reasons and the publicly stated reasons for change did not always square with each other.

During and since the 1950's, the teachers college in America has virtually gone out of business under that name. The change of name, however, has not frequently meant that the business was under new management. There has been a reorientation of administrative aspirations. The college must grow and flourish. The public state college was trying to be a little university, moving as it could toward one year or more of graduate offerings. The faculty supported the administration, partly for prestige reasons. Meanwhile, the small private institution became more generalized, regardless of how few students it was able to attract and serve. With the rapidly growing enrollment in higher education, we could mass-produce professors, just as Americans could mass-produce houses, automobiles, or washing machines.

What is in a name indeed! America is caught up in the magic of image-making and public posture. All the while we know that the important thing about an institution is the nature and quality of its educational program rather than what it calls itself. A great deal of high-quality teacher education is going on today in public and private colleges and in universities. Likewise, superior and inferior teacher education programs may be observed in institutions called teachers colleges. Whether an institution is public or private makes no difference, per se, as to the quality of its educational program.

Then why all the consternation about the name "Teachers College"? The teachers colleges have had their defenders and their attackers. Some educated people believe in their abolishment, the good with the poor. Others, with equally stout conviction, believe the remaining ones need to be maintained and strengthened for genuinely distinctive pioneering functions in teacher education.

For any teachers college today, the question of name is a crucial one. A teachers college which does not aspire above mediocrity of performance would be well advised to hide its program under the cloak of anonymity, abandoning the word "teachers" in its title. It will not be called upon to defend itself from critics if it will simply forego its prime public allegiance to teacher education. What happens inside its program —what it does for the liberal and professional education of men and women—then becomes relatively unimportant from the standpoint of its reputation. It is no longer so quickly vulnerable to attack.

If, however, a teachers college is enthusiastic in its efforts to develop a distinctive program for future and present teachers, that institution is announcing to the world its level of intention and is inviting friend and foe alike to study·its efforts, its process, and its products. Such a teachers college must be a substantial cut above the standards in colleges and universities at large and must meet the criticisms which will come from many quarters as it takes a valiant stand for a scholarly and functional approach to teacher education.

Teachers colleges which continue to use the name will either sink into oblivion as second or third rate institutions or they will establish a distinctive function and will fill a role of educational leadership in national terms. To perform the role of educational leadership will involve a great deal of care in the selection of students. It will involve a recasting of the educational program to provide a liberalizing education far different from the typical liberal arts sequence of courses. It will demand a functional professional program calculated to develop skills and insights far different from those found in conventional patterns of teacher preparation today.

The battle over the survival of the teachers college has nearly ended. In thirty-two of the fifty states, they no longer exist at all. In seven others, a solitary teachers college remains. In only ten states do we find two or more senior colleges carrying the word teachers in its name.

As the smoke clears and white flags are run up, we find ourselves moving into a true reconstruction period. In 1970, perhaps a half dozen truly reputable teachers colleges will remain, with an unprecedented opportunity for distinction available to them. The big problem that will then be created for the critics of teacher education will be to find new quarters for the continuing engagement in conflict between pforessional and academic education. Among the many useful purposes served by the teachers colleges in this century has been that of scape goat for the many ills of public education. With this symbol of guilt removed from the American scene, what will be excoriated in its place?

The outcome of the unprecedented ordeal in teacher education will depend upon the statesmanlike qualities of college professors, whether they be professors of elementary education or of Greek; and of public school officials, whether they be classroom teachers or superintendents of schools; and of private citizens, whether they be volume customers of public schools with many children of their own enrolled, or other citizens who are interested in the education of their neighbors' children.

The future of teachers colleges in America is of no grave consequence, but the future of teacher education continues to be of tremendous significance if our free society is to survive and prosper.

6

Concerned mother: Q. Isn't this toy rather complicated for a small child?
Sympathetic clerk: A. It's an educational toy, madam, it's designed to adjust the child to live in the world of today. No matter how he puts it together, it's wrong.

D. S. Greenberg

QUESTIONS AND ANSWERS WITH GRANT SWINGER

Q. Dr. Swinger, what is the Center for the Absorption of Federal Funds?

A. It is an organization, created by a consortium of several institutions, for the purpose of surveying preliminary steps toward a fresh look at some of the more vexing problems of research, education, and society.

Q. What are some examples of its work?

A. I'll be happy to tell you, but first I think it should be understood that the Center does not take any problem to the closure mode.

Q. The closure mode?

A. Yes, that is, we don't finalize any problems. We confine ourselves to pioneering in developing new approaches. We tend to be technique oriented.

Q. Specifically, what are some examples of the Center's work?

A. Well, the Center staff members have resolved the conflict between teaching and research.

Q. How?

A. By doing neither.

Q. I see. Then what do they do?

A. They confer, they comment on each other's past papers, they travel a good deal. There is no shortage of activity. In fact the pace is cruel. It is

From D. S. Greenberg, "Questions and Answers with Grant Swinger," *Science*, Vol. 151, March 11, 1966, p. 1201. Copyright 1966 by the American Association for the Advancement of Science. Reprinted by permission of the American Association for the Advancement of Science and the author.

just that our people don't want to get into the classic dilemma of having to choose between the classroom and the laboratory or library.

Q. What else does the Center do?

A. Well, it is doing some preliminary work toward the development of new programs, procedures, and goals for our member institutions.

Q. Such as?

A. We are investigating the establishment of a new undergraduate program to be known as Junior Year on Campus.

Q. I see.

A. In addition, we are looking into the possibility of new sources of support. For example, there is the Pan-American Chair.

Q. In Latin-American studies?

A. Oh, no, this is actually a chair on a Pan-American airplane. It would be set aside for traveling members of the Center and the associated institutions.

Q. Yes.

A. And we are also looking into the establishment of the first $1-million chair at any university.

Q. A million-dollar endowment?

A. No, a million-dollar salary, and that would be for 9 months. The resulting publicity and prestige for an institution with such a chair would be simply fantastic.

Q. The salary would cover only 9 months?

A. Yes, to provide opportunities for consulting and travel in the summer months. Furthermore, our preliminary investigations suggest that, to maximize the prestige, the recipient should have neither teaching nor research duties, and in fact should rarely, possibly never, be on campus.

Q. What are some of the other services performed by the Center?

A. Because many universities are experiencing difficulty in filling administrative positions, we have established a Rent-a-Dean service.

Q. Rent-a-Dean?

A. Yes, we will provide a dean for a flat daily charge, plus so much for each decision he renders. The advantage to the university, of course, is that it does not have to make a permanent commitment and may return the dean at any time, which, in effect, is what now goes on anyway with many major appointments.

Q. I see.

A. We also have an assortment of related services, such as Rent-a-Fellow, if an institution is unable to fill the fellowship that it has available.

Q. Are there other activities of the Center?

A. Yes, for example, we are devising new types of tests and examinations. The most promising development so far is one in which the student is furnished with, let's say, 25 footnotes, and is required to write a paper incorporating them in the given order.

Q. Are there other activities of the Center?

A. Yes, we are looking into the creation of a new academic title to reflect some of the realities of modern-day education and research. We have tentatively decided upon the title post-doctoral emeritus. Finally, we do a great deal of international consulting. For example, I will be leaving for Africa in the morning for a conference on Space, the Atom, Particle Physics, and the Emerging Tribe.

Q. How long will you stay?

A. Oh, it's just for the afternoon. I have to be in L.A. the next day for an international conference that will be attended by about 200 persons.

Q. On what subject?

A. As far as I know, a topic has not yet been selected.

Q. Dr. Swinger, this may be a delicate matter, but how can these activities be justified to the public authorities?

A. Oh, I think that an examination of the historical record shows that we are well over that hump. But the advice of our Committee on Research and Publications is that, if questions arise, they usually can be settled with a few brief references to hybrid corn, penicillin, atomic energy, and serendipity. Really not a problem.

Q. What future do you see for the Center?

A. Quite obviously it can only grow bigger. We have adopted the motto, "As Long As You're Up Get Me a Grant." I think we can only grow.

Q. Thank you, Dr. Swinger.

7

The more a professor knows, the more he knows what he does not know. In a properly conducted college, the faculty are simply the more mature students with a special responsibility for keeping the conversation going.

LYNN WHITE, JR.

Lindley J. Stiles

PUBLISH-OR-PERISH POLICIES IN PERSPECTIVE

The fervor with which recent criticisms of publish-or-perish policies in higher education have been brushed aside in some sections

From Lindley J. Stiles, "Publish-or-Perish Policies in Perspective," *The Journal of Teacher Education*, Vol. XVII, No. 4, Winter, 1966, pp. 464–467. Reprinted by permission of *The Journal of Teacher Education* and the author.

of academia reminds one of Hamlet's observation: "The lady doth protest too much, methinks." At the same time as the aptness of these policies is challenged, their existence is denied, and the use of publications as the exclusive mark of the scholar is defended.

Clearly, many of the defenders, both professors and administrators, would prefer this matter to be off limits for both their colleagues and the public. The vigor with which they move to the defense, to censor as heretics those who dare to raise questions about the reliability of the policy or its impact on overall institutional developments, suggests that the visible smoke does not come from imaginary fires. Further, the impression is conveyed that personnel policies in at least some institutions of higher learning will not stand public scrutiny.

What is well known to anyone associated with higher education, and what the general public needs to know, is that a policy of publish or perish—a constant threat to a balanced faculty in comprehensive universities—is currently being overemphasized in certain institutions of higher learning. The reasons behind such a trend need to be examined and the full implications understood. Furthermore, the public, which supports all higher education either through taxation, tuitions, or direct contributions, deserves to be heard.

Let it be said here that I intend no criticism of research, either basic or applied; nor do I downgrade publication as a useful and proper channel of communication for the scholar in any field. In fact, in the field of education, more and better research and publications are badly needed, and my own professional commitments and activities are heavily biased in this direction. Nor do I accept categorically the conclusion that emphasis on and support for research, both basic and applied, is detrimental to the interests of higher education; to argue, as a congressional committee recently did, that expansion of research in colleges and universities harms education is to ignore the broader picture. Without research, higher education is dead; with it, teaching need not be de-emphasized. My view is that the weakening of teaching, which the congressmen properly deplore, results from the erroneous practice in some institutions—and in certain fields of inquiry—of assuming a one-to-one relationship between effectiveness in research and excellence in teaching. I suggest that we do not deal with an either-or type of problem. The concern is for breadth and balance in personnel policies appropriate to the varieties of specialized professional talents needed today for teaching, research, and public service in complex and comprehensive institutions of higher learning.

It is my observation that the controlling establishment of scholars in some major universities takes a restricted view of the method by which insights and knowledge may and should be exchanged: they hold publication in technical books and professional journals to be the only approved technique. Out of this bias has come the practice in some institutions of assessing scholarship—and often all professional contributions—solely on the basis of a publication record. When such judgments are translated into faculty and administrative policy for tenure, promotions, and salary increments, the publish-or-perish mandate becomes not an oversimplification, as its adherents often claim, but a straitjacket of reality. As has been pointed out, under this doctrine he who does not publish, no matter how competent or promising his scholarship nor how effective his teaching and public service, does in a very real sense perish. Such a policy should indeed be labelled "publish or perish," and those who champion it should be held accountable for the results.

Such a narrow-gauge standard for judging scholarly inquiry, I submit, is in itself unscholarly and neither sound in theory nor supported by reliable research evidence. It is merely a dogma and not a proven way to evaluate a professor's contribution. The extension of logic beyond the bounds of its reach is easily identified in the number one argument used to support the publish-or-perish doctrine: By evaluating the quality and quantity of a faculty member's publications, an indirect but reasonably accurate assessment can be made of his teaching competence since good teaching goes hand-in-hand with scholarship. All would agree that good scholarship is essential to good teaching, but it does not follow that publication is the only and exclusive evidence of good scholarship. Nor has evidence yet been accumulated that the scholars who publish the most—or even the best—books and papers are the best teachers.

The publish-or-perish doctrine results from a contemporary stereotyping in terms of acceptability of the types of communication among scholars and between scholars and the public at large. All scholarship imposes an obligation to share insights and knowledge; consequently, dissemination is the obligation of the scholar. Publication is one useful means to fulfill this obligation; teaching is another, one that is older in tradition and has been proven indispensable to the preservation and extension of scholarship in all fields. Additional useful and effective ways to disseminate the results of scholarship include lectures, discussions, consultations, creation of art forms, production of structural designs, development of new programs, and the preparation of audio-visual and other types of learning resources.

The mass communication media—newspapers, popular journals, radio, and television—typically reach a greater audience and convey knowledge more effectively than do published scholarly reports in books or journals which reach only segments of the scholarly community and rarely come to general public attention. If the concern is for the extension of knowledge, the use of mass media—a procedure sometimes shunned and deplored by academic scholars—may well be the most effective means of dissemination. Consider, for example, the greatly multiplied influence of Dr. Harvey White, who pioneered the use of educational television as a means of disseminating recent scholarship on a nationwide basis. Very likely Dr. White will be remembered for his television teaching as much as for his publications; yet, had he been a young assistant professor bucking for tenure, his teaching via television might have been discounted as evidence of his intellectual and scholarly qualifications.

Overemphasis on publish-or-perish policies can have devastating effects on higher education. They can undermine the importance of teaching and reduce the quality of public service provided by an institution. Younger professors particularly, but some established scholars as well, respond to preferred incentives in much the same way as other human beings. They compete in what has been described as the marketplace of higher education for the usual types of rewards—financial gain, advancement, security, the approbation of associates, and of course, prestige. Whatever criteria an institution holds before its faculty as the steppingstones to such goals may be expected to guide the expenditure of professional time and energies. If publication is considered the *sine qua non* for advancement, everything else a professor might want or be expected to do stands a good chance of receiving low priority.

One of the most detrimental results of the publish-or-perish policy is the negation of efforts to evaluate the quality of teaching in colleges and universities. It must be admitted that most institutions have done little to examine the nature and characteristics of good teaching; the types of scholarship that contribute to effective teaching at different levels, undergraduate and graduate, and in various subject fields have received scant attention. Professional educationists must take some responsibility for this omission; we have been too busy preparing elementary and secondary school teachers and too isolated from interdisciplinary partnerships with our colleagues across the campus to be of help. Another fundamental reason for this neglect, I would suggest, is the erroneous assumption that good teaching will be reflected in scholarly publications. In effect, the exclusive concern with publication causes teaching to be neglected and turns the searchlight of assessment away from prevailing deficiencies.

A correlate responsibility of the college and university teacher which gets slighted when he is forced to publish in order to progress professionally is the informal assistance to and counseling of students. The growing gulf between faculty members and students, particularly in large universities, has had considerable attention recently, and a cause cited in almost all cases is the low priority given by professors to such services. Students, aware of their teachers' overloaded schedules, either hesitate to ask for help or do so apologetically.

There are similar, valid arguments regarding the detrimental effects of publish-or-perish policies on the public service of faculty members. The professor who helps to extend a state university for the benefit of the people and who concentrates on applying the results of his scholarship to help solve problems of the farms, the schools, and the cities will experience understandable confusion, frustration, and discouragement if denied merit increases in salary, tenure, or advancement because his method of disseminating knowledge fails to meet the publish-or-perish standard.

Higher education is undergoing multiple changes as it seeks to adapt to growing enrollments, increasing rates in expansion of knowledge, greater demands for scientific research, and the ever-present gap between resources and responsibilities. The publish-or-perish trend may well be but an overreaction to selected pressures which will tend, in due time, to correct itself. On the other hand, the possibility exists that some universities are on their way to becoming new types of research institutes in which both teaching (particularly for undergraduates) and public service will be permanently downgraded. If so, other institutions will have to assume these responsibilities, unless they, too, are caught up in the publish-or-perish dilemma.

The concern of scholar-teachers and of the public at large should be with examining evident trends and evaluating their overall impact on higher education. Conscious decisions need to be made about goals, emphases, and outcomes in terms of their usefulness to society. In my view, such examination should be a process of "sifting and winnowing by which alone truth is found" to ascertain the extent to which publish-or-perish policies now exist; to assess their overall impact, both positive and negative; and to find an answer to the vital question, Are there better criteria for assessing the various professional contributions which must be combined to create and maintain a high-quality institution of higher education?

8

Today the trumpeting outside is so strongly for action that cloistered learning has become almost something to be deprecated. This mood is now having a strong effect on universities.

NATHAN M. PUSEY

Noel Perrin
PUBLISH AND PERISH—1984

The chairman of the philosophy department was talking to a candidate for an instructorship. "One thing you must realize," he said,

From Noel Perrin, "Publish and Perish—1984," *The New Yorker*, December 4, 1965, pp. 205–214. © 1965 The New Yorker Magazine, Inc. Reprinted by permission of the publisher.

"is that we have a very strict publication policy." "I'm used to that," answered the candidate. "At Columbia, you're not allowed to print your first article for three years after you take your Ph.D., or your first book for seven years."

"Ours is stricter. To begin with, we say seven years for everything, even book reviews, and I'm told Columbia makes numerous exceptions. We make none."

The candidate looked mutinous. "What if you've written something that can't wait?" he asked. "Seven years is a long time."

"There are two answers. First, if your stuff really can't wait, or even if it can, you're perfectly free to publish it anonymously. You have to act in good faith, of course. If you go around showing people the galleys of your book, or if the Publication Committee even hears a rumor connecting you with an article, it will investigate and, if necessary, make the usual evaluation."

"That sounds like no fun at all," the candidate said. "What's the other answer?"

"That in a sense you do have the right to publish under your own name during the first seven years. It's just that if you do, the Publication Committee automatically makes an evaluation. And unless there's a two-thirds vote that what you've written is—I won't say of permanent value, because who knows what is—but a work of real and obvious merit, well, you've published and you perish."

"You certainly make Columbia look like a bunch of amateurs," the candidate said. "I almost wonder if the policy isn't too strict."

"Not a bit," said the chairman. "Look. In the first place, there's no stigma whatsoever to publication after the novitiate—indeed, we encourage it. In the second place, if a young man is writing because he has something to say, and not because he wants a promotion, being anonymous is no great hardship. But most important, in the twelve years since we and Yale started this, 72 learned journals have ceased publication. The survivors are half their old size and about three times their old quality. Not one new university press has been founded. Keeping up with one's field is becoming almost a pleasure."

"You make a good case," said the candidate. He hesitated. "If only there were some way to apply the same rules to college presidents."

"There is," said the chairman, laughing. "We do. A new president here in his first seven years is not allowed to publish any of his speeches, or give a single honorary degree. He can't receive any, either. Mr. Mansell has six years to go."